Y0-BUY-026

THE REDS

McClintock's cover illustration for 'Strife' is striking in its simplicity. A masculine figure of far more conventional proportions than usual struggles to hold back the forces that threaten to engulf him. (Source: J.N. Rawling collection, Noel Butlin Archives Centre, ANU N57/1994)

STUART MACINTYRE

JQ
4098
.C6
m33x
1998
West

ALLEN & UNWIN

Copyright © Stuart Macintyre 1998

All rights reserved. No part of this book may be reproduced
or transmitted in any form or by any means, electronic or
mechanical, including photocopying, recording or by any
information storage and retrieval system, without prior
permission in writing from the publisher.

First published in 1998
Allen & Unwin
9 Atchison Street, St Leonards 2065, Australia
Phone: (61 2) 9901 4088
Fax: (61 2) 9906 2218
E-mail: frontdesk@allen-unwin.com.au
Web: http://www.allen-unwin.com.au

National Library of Australia
Cataloguing-in-Publication entry:

Macintyre, Stuart, 1947– .
   The reds: the Communist Party of Australia from origins to
   illegality.

   Includes index.
   ISBN 1 86448 580 9.

   1. Communist Party of Australia—History. 2. Communism—
   Australia—History. I. Title.

335.430994

Set in 11/14 pt Janson Text by DOCUPRO, Sydney

Printed and bound by Ligare Pty Ltd, Sydney

10 9 8 7 6 5 4 3 2 1

Contents

Abbreviations

AA	Australian Archives
ABC	Australian Broadcasting Commission
ABS	Australasian Book Society
ACCL	Australian Council for Civil Liberties
ACTU	Australasian Congress of Trade Unions, later Australian Council of Trade Unions
ADB	*Australian Dictionary of Biography*
AGPS	Australian Government Publishing Service
ALP	Australian Labor Party
AMIEU	Australasian Meat Industry Employees' Union
ANU	Noel Butlin Archives of Business and Labour, Australian National University
ANUP	Australian National University Press
APCOL	Alternative Publishing Cooperative Limited
ARU	Australian Railways Union
ASP	Australian Socialist Party
ASSLH	Australian Society for the Study of Labour History
AWU	Australian Workers' Union
BHP	Broken Hill Proprietary Company
CC	Central Committee of the CPA
CEC	Central Executive Committee of the CPA
CI	Communist International Archives

CIB	Commonwealth Investigation Branch
Comintern	Communist International
CPA	Communist Party of Australia
CPD	*Commonwealth Parliamentary Debates*
CPGB	Communist Party of Great Britain
CPSU	Communist Party of the Soviet Union
CUP	Cambridge University Press
DC	District Committee of the CPA
ECCI	Executive Committee of the Communist International
FIA	Federated Ironworkers' Association
FOSU	Friends of the Soviet Union
ICWPA	International Class War Prisoners' Aid
Inprecorr	*International Press Correspondence*
IPC	International Peace Campaign
IWW	Industrial Workers of the World (Wobblies)
LAI	League Against Imperialism
MAWF	Movement Against War and Fascism
ML	Mitchell Library, State Library of New South Wales
MM	Minority Movement
MUP	Melbourne University Press
NLA	National Library of Australia
NSWUP	New South Wales University Press
OUP	Oxford University Press
PB	Political Bureau (Politbureau)
PPTU	Pan-Pacific Trade Union organisation
PWIU	Pastoral Workers' Industrial Union
RILU	Red International of Labor Unions
SLP	Socialist Labor Party
SLV	State Library of Victoria
SPA	Socialist Party of Australia
SRC	Spanish Relief Committee
SUA	Seamen's Union of Australia
THC	Trades Hall Council
TLC	Trades and Labor Council
UAP	United Australia Party
UFAF	United Front Against Fascism

UMA	University of Melbourne Archives
UQP	University of Queensland Press
UWAP	University of Western Australia Press
UWM	Unemployed Workers' Movement
VCAWF	Victorian Council Against War and Fascism
VSP	Victorian Socialist Party
WDC	Workers' Defence Corps
WEA	Workers' Educational Association
WIR	Workers' International Relief
WWF	Waterside Workers' Federation
YCL	Young Communist League

Acknowledgements

A work such as this relies heavily on the assistance of others. A large number of former communists and students of its history have helped me. Some have been extraordinarily generous with gifts and loans of material, information and suggestions; others might scarcely recall the reflections they shared but their interest and support greatly encouraged me. I thank Brian Aarons, Eric Aarons, Laurie Aarons, Mark Aarons, Bruce Anderson, Vic Bird, Audrey and Jack Blake, Barbara Boles, Bob Boughton, Verity Burgmann, Hazel and Joe Butorac, Rowan Cahill, Frank Cain, Annette Cameron, David Carter, Lloyd Churchward, Walter Clayton, Madge Cope, Pat Counihan, Barbara Curthoys, Joy Damousi, Phillip Deery, Miriam Dixson, David Dutton, Ross Edmonds, Maurice Edwards, Pat and Alex Elphinston, Carole Ferrier, Ross Fitzgerald, Charlie Fox, James Franklin, Eric Fry, Bob Gollan, Daphne Gollan, Patricia Graham, Norma Grieve, Gerry Harant, Evelyn Healy, Colin Holder, Karen Hunt, Jack Hutson, Amirah Inglis, Audrey Johnson, Monty Johnston, Stelios Korbetis, Bill Latter, Margaret Lindley, Peter Love, Wendy Lowenstein, Janet McCalman, John McKenzie, David McKnight, Robert McWilliams, Laurence Maher, Ken Mansell, Max Marginson, Philip Mendes, Kevin Morgan, Meaghan Morris, Jack Mundey, Angela O'Brien, Greg Pemberton, John Playford, Carolyn Rasmussen, Len Richardson, Margaret Sampson, Betty Searle,

John Sendy, Tom Sheridan, Carmel Shute, Chips Sowerwine, Jim Staples, Martin Sullivan, Bernie Taft, Pat Troy, Ann Turner, Edgar Waters, Al Watson, Anna Yeatman and Sandra Goldbloom Zurbo. Phillip Deery, Miriam Dixson and John Sendy have been particularly patient and perceptive commentators on drafts; Ann Turner kept up a constant and invaluable flow of information on early communist history, while Verity Burgmann has done her utmost to draw me out of the shadow of the Kremlin.

Others, now deceased, have shared their memories in correspondence, conversation and friendship, sometimes going back long before I embarked on this present work. They include Les Barnes, Noel Counihan, Hume Dow, Lloyd Edmonds, Denis Freney, Ralph Gibson, Bill Gollan, Jack Lindsay, George Matthews, Stephen Murray-Smith, Ted Roach, Alec Robertson, Edna Ryan, Ian Turner and Judah Waten.

I am obliged also to librarians and archivists who were generous with their time and expertise. These include Jim Andrighetti and Rosemary Bloch at the State Library of New South Wales; Mark Cranfield, Graeme Powell and Bill Tully at the National Library of Australia; Jock Murphy at the State Library of South Australia; Elizabeth Ho at the State Library of New South Wales; Clive Besson, Emma Jolley, Ewan Maidment and Michael Saclier of the Noel Butlin Archives at the Australian National University, and Cecily Close, Suzanne Fairbanks, Mark Richmond and Frank Strahan of the University of Melbourne Archives. The manuscript has benefited from suggestions made by John Iremonger and Mary Rennie, while Rebecca Kaiser has contributed her skills as senior editor. In my own Department of History at the University of Melbourne I owe particular gratitude to Lynne Wrout and Martine Walsh, who no doubt hope that the completion of this volume will mend my errant ways.

I commenced the project in concert with Andrew Wells of the University of Wollongong, who persuaded me to join him in response to an invitation from the trustees of the former Communist Party. Together we obtained a grant from the Australian Research Council, which enabled us to employ Beverley Symons as a research assistant for three years. That term scarcely does justice to her role: Beverley brought to our joint enterprise both an extensive experience in the Communist Party and superb research skills. She collated an enormous mass of material to which I have referred constantly throughout the writing of this book. Her bibliographical research resulted in the publication of *Communism in Australia, A Resource Bibliography*, which was published by the National Library in 1994, and is an indispensible guide for anyone working in the area. Concurrently she completed her own BA honours thesis on communism during the Second World War, and embarked on doctoral research on women's activity in the labour movement. Meanwhile Andrew Wells pursued our task enthusiastically, shared the fruits of his work and regularly discussed with me the lines of inquiry that developed from our mutual endeavours. While other duties prevented him from contributing to the writing of these pages, I thank him for his crucial role in their gestation. We hope to collaborate in a sequel to this volume that will complete the history.

As mentioned above, this work began in response to an invitation from the Search Foundation, the successor to the Communist Party and the custodian of its records. I should make it clear that the members of the Search Foundation placed no conditions on my work. They encouraged it, they made available all their records, they asked former members to cooperate, and they waited with remarkable patience. At the outset Andrew Wells and I agreed with the foundation that any differences that might arise in the use we made of the records would be referred to a reference group of distinguished scholars, Bob Gollan, Bernard Smith and Ann Curthoys. It proved unnecessary to call on them to perform this role. I thank them for agreeing to their supernumerary duties as well as the encouragement and assistance they provided me.

Over the past six years I have discussed the history with members of the Search Foundation, and provided them with drafts to obtain their response. It should go without saying that this is my work and not theirs. For that matter, there are other former communists, including some who parted company with the party before its final dissolution, who have tendered testimony and advice. For every former communist, there is a story to be told and, as often as not, someone eager to see it recorded; and I am sure that many will think my emphases and interpretation are awry. But at no point have I felt any pressure to tailor what I have written to individual or collective views of party members. I thank them for their forbearance.

As I do one particular former communist. My wife Martha joined the party with me a quarter-century ago, and our shared discovery of communist ideals was part of our courtship. It gave us warm friendships that still endure, loyalties and interests that persist. Our only serious quarrel arose over my enthusiasm for that most doctrinaire of communist theoreticians, Louis Althusser. Then, as now, she was wiser, and her continuing patience with the antisocial habits of a distracted author is not the least of my debts to her.

Introduction

The interest that led me to this subject began nearly 30 years ago when I was a postgraduate student. Like many of my generation, I was caught up in the radicalism of the 1960s. A whole range of campaigns and causes—anti-war protest, colonial liberation, removal of immigration restrictions, opposition to capital punishment, civil liberties, democratisation of the university—led me to communism. Both as a historian and a participant, I responded to the aura of communist tradition. For the best part of the 1970s, as the currents of twentieth-century history eddied and then turned, I joined with others who sought to empty the Stalinist cargo from the revolutionary vessel.

It was communist history that drew me into communism and now I return once more to that history, but in different circumstances. Communism is no more. It passed irrevocably with Gorbachev's *glasnost* and *perestroika*, the fall of the Berlin Wall, the overthrow of the people's democracies of Central and Eastern Europe, and then the collapse of the Union of Soviet Socialist Republics itself. The communist parties of the West have dissolved, the ageing followers of the lost cause in Russia and elsewhere fall back on nostalgic nationalism, the last regimes that still lay claim to the title are mere mockeries of what communism promised.

Communism collapsed under the weight of its failures. Its refusal of freedom created a barren tyranny. Its command economies were unable to adapt to changing circumstances of production and consumption; they became rife with inefficiency and corruption, until eventually they could not meet even basic expectations. As an official doctrine, communism ossified into lifeless ritual; as a system of government its monolithic one-party rule became a dead hand that snuffed out initiative and vitality. It fell not just because its critics swelled into an overwhelming opposition but also because its custodians finally lacked the will to defend it. It ended as much in inanition as in protest.

With its passing, communism has become almost unintelligible. I teach a course of contemporary history to first-year undergraduates, which takes as one its principal themes the competing doctrines of freedom that strove for supremacy in the postwar world. The one doctrine, freedom based on private property and liberal democracy, is represented by a passage from Friedrich von Hayek's *The Road to Serfdom* (1944). The other doctrine, freedom as liberation from capitalism and imperialism, is introduced with a passage from Joseph Stalin's speech to the Nineteenth Congress of the Communist Party of the Soviet Union (CPSU) in 1952. My students find von Hayek instantly familiar and Stalin so strange as to be almost incomprehensible. That Stalin commanded the greater popular following at the end of the Second World War and that postwar events initially seemed to bear out his boasts, strikes them as preposterous.

It is not just that Stalin employed a vocabulary that no longer possesses meaning to these young people: such words as 'capitalism' and 'bourgeoisie', 'vanguard party' and 'toiling masses' have no purchase in their experience. More than this, their understanding of communism is so shaped by the events of 1989 that its earlier success seems akin to a dark age. In this they are encouraged by the triumphal anti-communism that currently prevails both in academic writing and the popular media, a set of assertions about communism that allow it no other meaning than tyranny. The end of communism is now taken as its beginning. From the Russian Revolution to Reagan's Evil Empire, it was something hateful imposed by force and sustained only by fear. There is no indication that communism was also a popular phenomenon that people in all countries grasped as a spar of hope against other forms of oppression; that it gave meaning and purpose to idealists in a wide range of circumstances; and that it was not a simple divination of evil but a complex body of thought and action that altered over its life-course. It might have been expected that the extinction of communism as a historical phenomenon would allow some less Manichean evaluation of its consequences, and when the present body of anti-communists exhaust their exultations that re-evaluation is likely to occur.

It is unlikely, however, that it will so readily separate Stalinism from communism, as so many communists sought to do. Lenin, his predecessor and the founder of communism, warned from his sick-bed in the winter of 1922 to 1923 against Stalin's authoritarian ways. Khrushchev, Stalin's successor, denounced his crimes at a party congress in 1956. But Lenin had no solution to Stalin's arrogation of authority, much less an explanation of how such a man should have become party secretary, and Khrushchev was unable to undo his legacy. Stalin undoubtedly bears responsibility for millions of deaths by execution or starvation, but to attribute these atrocities to one man and his -ism is to pass over the clear symptoms in earlier communist practice and absolve a movement that hailed him as the architect of socialism and leader of the world revolution. Any history of communism must ask what made Stalin possible and why it was unable to find a lasting alternative to his methods.

Like all other sections of the Communist International, the Communist Party of Australia succumbed to Stalinism. After a first decade of improvised, enthusiastic and generally ineffective activity, it became an utterly faithful follower of the policies and practices laid down by the Soviet leader. That evolution is one of the concerns of this history, and an explanation of it presents some striking challenges. It was both voluntary and imposed. Communism in Australia was a commitment made freely, without the sanctions that Stalin exercised in his own country. Those who joined and accepted the remarkable regimen that membership entailed, a regimen without precedent in the political culture of the Australian labour movement, did so of their own choosing. It offered few material rewards and demanded great sacrifice. The reasons for making such a commitment form one of the themes of this history. Equally, Australian communism spilled repeatedly into unanticipated directions. A hierarchical form of organisation imposed over a far-flung membership of strong-minded followers could hardly avoid heresy and error. Just as dealings between Moscow and the Australian party leadership during the 1920s were marked by mutual misunderstanding, so the constituent sections of the party threw up their own interpretations of policy in the 1930s, as they sought to apply it to obstinately intractable local conditions.

Communism put down its deepest Australian roots in the organised working class. But communism was always something more than a union movement. Its revolutionary mission extended into a whole range of emancipatory projects: the abolition of sexual inequality, freedom for Aborigines and all other colonised peoples, the removal of the White Australia policy and full acceptance of national minorities were just some of them. It connected Australians to the outside world in new ways that broke with older colonial linkages and went beyond the normal reference points of the Anglophone diaspora. It engaged in a wide range of educational and cultural activities: party classes, workers' art, literature, music and theatre. These activities were at once oppositional and affirmative, exploring new modes of activity that would put knowledge and feeling at the service of the working class. Communism entered into the intellectual and cultural history of twentieth-century Australia as an alternative source of value.

How should its history be written? There is a large body of internally directed and homiletic literature that uses the past for inspiration and instruction. Such works typically distinguish truth from error by demonstrating the perfidy of reformists and revisionists, and extolling the heroic efforts of the faithful. In treating the fortunes of the communist movement itself, they establish a lineage of correct theory and practice that provides a warrant for future success. In later years, as Australian communism splintered into competing sects, their leaders put forward their own alternative accounts in order to lay claim to legitimacy. Conversely, Trotskyist histories of Australian communism explained its failure in departure from their exemplar's insights.[1]

Apart from their self-serving and partisan character, such histories exhibit a common tendency to treat the fortunes of communism as a reflex of appropriate endeavour. Victories confirm the wisdom of the party, defeats are attributed to factionalist deviation from the correct line by left adventurists or right opportunists. The historical process they record is highly schematic, the party treated as a responsive instrument, the flux and contingency of human frailty regarded as a mere epiphenomenon of impersonal class forces. Insofar as such communist history considers questions of motivation, it employs a model of heroic effort. The Australian communist who emerges from these accounts is resolute, capable, fearless, indefatigable, purged of all weakness and doubt. The party constructed this model comrade in instructions and reports, as well as in fiction and in graphic art; and veterans employed the same imagery when they recounted their experiences or memorialised others in such works as *Reminiscences of a Rebel, Of Storm and Struggle, Comrades Come Rally!* and *Solidarity Forever!* Such works evoke the world of the communist in a record of constant engagement, a celebration of commitments, beliefs and hopes set down in a form that leaves little room for doubts or uncertainty, let alone critical reflection on what went wrong.[2]

Not that Australian communists eschewed the lessons of the past. On the contrary, they were convinced historical determinists who enlisted Comrade History as one of their most valuable recruits, and they applied themselves to analysis of their own country's historical record through the lens of Marxist historical materialism as attentively as communists elsewhere sought to gauge their particular circumstances. Leading interwar communists such as Esmonde Higgins, James Rawling and Lloyd Ross pioneered research in Australian labour history. After the Second World War, when a new generation of communist academics established labour history as a scholarly discipline, Lloyd Churchward, Miriam Dixson, Bob Gollan, Ian Turner and others grounded the history of Australian communism in studies that traced the rise of an organised working class as a force for national progress. After them came other academics who built up a very considerable literature, consisting of books, articles and theses that treated various aspects of communist history, whether by region, period, occupation or sphere of activity. Sometimes critical and sometimes celebratory, such work is predominantly sympathetic and merges into the local and thematic histories produced from within the communist movement.

The dimensions of this literature are indicated by the bibliography prepared by Beverley Symons. It lists nearly 200 books wholly or partly concerned with Australian communism, more than 600 articles and a further 200 theses, the great majority produced in the past quarter-century.[3] The variety of subjects they traverse is striking, but more striking is the fact that there has been no general history of communism since Alastair Davidson's *The Communist Party of Australia: A Short History* appeared in 1969. That work was based on a doctoral thesis on the early history of the party submitted in 1965, and was assisted by the new party leadership of the 1960s in a spirit of critical reappraisal that accompanied the party's break from monolithic conformity. Its argument, that the party was making 'a stumbling, groping, limping move back to Australian traditions with the weight of past errors' on its shoulders, pleased neither the liberals nor the diehards.[4]

Davidson worked mostly from the published record. Many major archival sources have since become available but so far remain largely unused. The reasons for such neglect are partly to do with the changed interests of historians. Davidson's was a political history that concentrated on policy and its implementation. The more recent work listed by Symons has moved from political history to social and cultural concerns, emphasising history from below, lived experience, radical imagery and textual representation. This in turn registers a loss of confidence in politics, a growing realisation that the communist project had failed and a corresponding intention to connect certain forms of communist activity to the concerns of the new social movements and the circumstances of postmodernism. Hence we have studies of communist encouragement of early Aboriginal activism, communism as a precedent for community campaigns, communism as a mobiliser of women, communism in a multicultural mode, anti-communism as a discourse of surveillance. Such studies present a far richer appraisal of communism's presence and effects, if one that some of its legatees are loath to acknowledge, but these studies leave communism itself as an unexplained phenomenon.

The final decline of communism has produced another kind of writing that returns once again to the first person from the third, this time in a more intimate register. These are the memoirs of former communists looking back on a lost political cause. They write retrospectively in a familiar autobiographical mode that traces the journey from innocence to experience, a transition intensified in their case by the fact that they lost their faith before it was taken from them. For the writers of these memoirs rejected the authoritarian dogmas of Stalin in advance of the collapse of communism—as is suggested by the title of Oriel Gray's memoirs, *Exit Left*, and Dorothy Hewett's *Wild Card*. They therefore look back across a double rupture to their youthful enthusiasm, and seek both to affirm and to question the cause that illuminated their lives without the self-justificatory insistence of most political autobiography. For the most part they write in an informal, highly personal style that admits elements excluded from the older communist autobiographies, the very elements that communism denied—hence Daphne Gollan's memoirs of 'Cleopatra Sweatfigure', Bernice Morris's *Between the Lines* and Amirah Inglis's *The Hammer & Sickle and the Washing Up*. The opening up of subjectivity is a particular feature in the recorded testimony of communist women, as in *Taking the Revolution Home* or *Bread and Roses*, but it is also an important dimension of Bernard Smith's evocation of *The Boy Adeodatus* or Roger Milliss's intergenerational 'autobiographical novel', *Serpent's Tooth*. Such remembrance extends from drama, as in Dorothy Hewett's *Chapel Perilous*, into film in *Children of the Revolution*, and is frequently revisited in the lifestyle sections of newspapers, since many of these former communists remain active in public life. Irony and humour mitigate the loss, but all of these reflections share an elegiac poignancy. This genre of communist remembrance is far more noticeable in Australia than in Britain, the United States or elsewhere.[5]

The present work seeks to apply the insights of such remembrance to the early history of the party. It was conceived as an account of communism in Australia that would seek to narrate it, describe it, explain it to readers who know little or nothing of its forms. I wanted to show how it was that Australians became communists, what that meant, what they sought to do, how far they succeeded, as well as suggest the far-reaching consequences of their endeavour. In writing it I have combined a systematic account of the party's organisation, doctrine and practice with more descriptive passages of social and ethnographic detail. In relating the party's activities I have tried to capture the idiom of Australian communism and have paid particular attention to its local forms. I have dwelt on the experience of party members, and perhaps laid too much stress on their foibles and idiosyncrasies, in order to suggest the diversity of human qualities that lay behind the hard outer shell. I have tried to evoke the milieu of Australian communism and have at the same time tried to stand outside it and grasp it as a historical phenomenon.

Yet to write the history of communism is to be drawn into its arcane complexities. It was a form of politics more closely controlled than any other. The hierarchical form of organisation, the prescriptive language and authoritarian procedures present the historian with an official record of daunting opacity. From the end of the 1920s stenographers attended every party assembly of significance to record a verbatim transcript of proceedings. Meetings of the central committee alone, at which leading state officials and organisers of the various party auxiliaries reported on their work in sessions stretching over several days, yielded typed documents of hundreds of pages every few months. The purpose of these records was invigilation and their effect was to impose a verbal uniformity. A reader of these documents is thus confronted by an esoteric code in which every new turn in policy finds apparent acceptance, differences have to be gleaned from subtle shifts in emphasis, and actual results are hidden under an overburden of dutiful rhetoric. The overwhelming bulk of this material has not been used before, and there is no alternative but to work with it since it provides a far more detailed and systematic record of the Communist Party than earlier historians have possessed. I have tried to use it critically and not succumb to its clichéd formulations, its self-validating framework of reference, but any history of communism that enters fully into its subject matter cannot wholly escape its effects.[6]

Much the same holds for the equally voluminous record compiled against the Communist Party by government agencies. The Australian Archives holds thousands of files compiled by the Investigation Branch of the Commonwealth Attorney-General's Department, which had principal responsibility for official surveillance of communism in the 1920s and 1930s. Its agents provided reports on communist activity, copies of correspondence and even original versions of party documents. The accuracy of the documentation is generally high, the picture of Australian communism it provided is seriously deficient. Coming at a time of turmoil and disorder, the Australian intelligence service construed the formation of the Communist Party of Australia as a sinister plot. In digests and summaries it presented a pathology of cranks and rogues, utterly immoral and self-seeking, who exploited the gullibility of the labour movement. The Investigation Branch grossly exaggerated the dimensions of this movement to augment its own activities. It gathered much of its information for the purpose of criminal prosecution under laws designed to combat the communist menace. I have consulted a large number of intelligence files but by no means all of them. They provide corroborative and supplementary details of the movements, the actions and even the statements of individual members in reports that are always coloured by their own provenance and purpose.

Australian communism consumed an extraordinary quantity of paper. By the 1930s it sustained a national newspaper, published twice a week, four state newspapers, and a score of magazines and periodicals. Its presses issued a constant flow of books and pamphlets; its bookshops distributed as many more foreign publications; local branches and auxiliary units produced hundreds of their own roneoed bulletins. There never has been a political movement so committed to the printed word. Then there is the unpublished record of the party. The archives of the central committee are deposited in the Mitchell Library in more than 200 boxes, augmented by a subsequent deposit of material from the first two decades that was long thought to have been lost: it includes full proceedings of the national conferences and congresses, minutes of all the important subsidiary committees, correspondence and subject files. Similar archives of some state committees are held in state libraries, along with major collections assembled by individual members. In 1991 a microfilm copy of the relevant archives of the Communist International was deposited in the Mitchell Library. It consists of ten reels and reproduces many Australian party documents as well as records of the deliberations of the Communist International on Australia. To these party sources can be added the records of trade unions and other organisations in which Australian communists played a significant role, as well as those of rivals and opponent organisations, and the extensive personal papers of such assiduous anti-communists as John Latham and Robert Menzies, both deposited in the National Library. There are some very large collections assembled by historians of communism. That of James Rawling runs to 17 shelf-metres and nearly 2400 items. It is held in the Noel Butlin Archives at the Australian National University, along with substantial collections assembled by Ian Turner and John Playford.

Confronted by these dispersed mountains of print, typescript and holograph material, I have had to read selectively. I have studied all the national serials and consulted state newspapers and journals less comprehensively. I have used the national and Communist International archives in their entirety, and trawled through some of the state and personal ones. I have read the party's major monographs and pamphlets, and much of its ephemera. In making these choices, I was guided partly by leads offered in secondary studies and partly by the picture I assembled in the course of the research. My own emphases of treatment are by no means the only ones that might have been made, and many other thematic and case studies would be possible, but some selection is inevitable in a work that already tests the reader's patience. I have tried to bring out regional and local variations with consideration for the party's centres of gravity, and the strong concentration on the eastern seaboard at the expense of South Australia, Western Australia, Tasmania and the Northern Territory reflects the distribution of the party's strength in its first two decades.

Most of all, I have tried to make this a history of communism and communists as well as the Communist Party. Communism and anti-communism had a significance beyond the ambit of the party in interwar Australia. For a few dissidents, the Australian party betrayed the revolutionary cause, and I summarise their critique of it, but these dissidents were scarcely a significant presence until the Second World

War. For many conservatives, the spectre of international communism far outweighed the efforts of its local practitioners, and I have made some references to this anti-communist mentality. But any history of communism in these years is necessarily a history of the party.

Communism is no more, and some might feel that such a lengthy history of its first two decades in Australia is redundant. Others allow such history only if it condemns its subject. I make no apologies for treating the history of Australian communism as fully and as seriously as I have. It was a small outpost on the very margins of the Communist International, and even in the late 1930s had only a few thousand members; but it had a much larger following and influence. In the middle decades of this century it presented a palpable challenge to the existing forms of Australian national life. The foundations for its successes and failures were laid in the 1920s and 1930s when it gathered up a disparate range of enthusiasts and led them into new forms of activity against overwhelming odds and in conditions of utmost adversity. Such a history has a drama and a pathos that is worthy of remembrance.

Foundation

No one could agree as to just who did turn up. Those who were there remembered the spring sunshine that sparkled on Darling Harbour as they made their way through the waterside streets to their dingy meeting place. They recalled the ardour of the participants and the rancour of their disagreements. One who travelled up from Melbourne had keen memories of the incessant cough of his companion which had kept him from sleep the night before, as well as the prodigious Sydney cockroaches that swarmed over their hotel bedroom. But the men and women who gathered on this Saturday morning were too habituated to such assemblies to be able to distinguish the names and the faces at this meeting from those who had met before and would meet again.[1]

Some 60 invitations to participate in the creation of the Communist Party of Australia were issued:

> In an endeavour to bring about the unified action of all who stand for the emancipation of the working class by revolutionary action, we have decided to arrange a conference to be held on Saturday, 30th October, 1920, in the ASP Hall, Liverpool Street, City. We have much pleasure in inviting you to appoint a delegate to attend same.[2]

Twenty-six persons answered the call. Afterwards, as memories grew vague and the role of the founders took on a hallowed significance, lists circulated in an effort to fix precisely who they were.[3] The Investigation Branch of the Attorney-General's Department had followed the preparations keenly but its zeal so far outran its intelligence as to associate almost every dissident in Australia with the occasion.[4] Even the minutes secretary was deficient in historical foresight: he counted the heads but omitted to record the names of those present.

The invitations were issued in the name of the host organisation, the Australian Socialist Party, and six of its members were present. There was Arthur Reardon, ASP secretary. Originally from the English midlands, he worked at the Clyde Engineering Works as a skilled blacksmith in charge of the apprentices. Emphatic in opinion, a self-taught worker-intellectual with interests that ran from metallurgy to English literature, he was as definite and exacting in his socialist rectitude as he was in the practise of his craft. At his right hand on this Saturday, as always, was Ray Everitt, the theoretician of the party and editor of its weekly newspaper, the *International Socialist*. And making up the 'Holy Trinity' of the ASP was Arthur's wife Marcia, a forceful speaker and writer, who popularised that theory with homilies on the miseries of capitalism and the great happiness that was to come. Then there was Bob Brodney, a more recent recruit. Born Arthur Tennyson Brodzky in 1896, the son of a muckraking Melbourne journalist, he had moved with his family to San Francisco, London and New York before working his way back to Australia in 1918. Brodney had no sooner joined the ASP in 1919 than he began working as an organiser. Gifted, restless, lean and saturnine, the young newcomer had a precocious capacity to divine new possibilities where more habituated dogmatists saw only confirmation of their established convictions. His enthusiasm for this meeting overcame the caution of his comrades.[5]

The Australian Socialist Party was one of many points in a constantly shifting constellation of agitation, education and revolutionary rhetoric on the fringes of the labour movement. Such organisations formed and collapsed, merged and split around their diagnoses of the present discontents and their schemes for building on the ruins of capitalism a new social order that would replace oppression and exploitation with freedom and equality. With memberships of a few hundred at most, they sustained a demanding round of activities: production and sale of a weekly newspaper; study of socialist texts; open-air meetings; dances and socials, usually on Saturday evening; lectures and classes on Sunday. Much of their energy was spent in fierce polemics against the futility of reform, the perfidy of Labor politicians, the inadequacy of existing trade unions that only served to gild the chains of wage slavery, and above all, the errors of their socialist rivals. Since each group distinguished itself from the others by marking out its own version of socialist doctrine and socialist strategy, the promulgation of which was both its primary purpose and ultimate consolation, heresy hunting was endemic. Ritual exhortations to unity broke on the unyielding rock of doctrinal rectitude. As the ASP executive explained after a previous effort to bring the various socialist organisations together proved fruitless, 'The ASP stands for revolution. Nothing less. Revolutionists don't compromise.'[6]

That the ASP was prepared to host a unity conference in October 1920 suggested some relaxation of this obduracy. The recent experience of common resistance to wartime repression was one new factor predisposing the socialist sects to suspend their differences. For while the Australian left was uncompromising on points of dogma, gladiatorial in style and vilificatory in tone, it was also capable of closing ranks against an external threat. The recent Great War had strengthened that capacity. Just as the Australian government drew no distinction between the anti-war actions of socialists, syndicalists and feminists, all of whom it subjected to censorship, surveillance, prosecution, deportation and imprisonment, so the committees that formed to assist the victims were able to set aside doctrinal differences in the defence of political freedom. Even as they met, the participants were working for the release of jailed comrades.

The Great War of 1914–18—as it was known by contemporaries, who could not foresee the second round of hostilities to come within a quarter of a century—drew old adversaries into common causes. It also split the Labor Party, radicalised the unions and fostered a far greater international awareness in the Australian labour movement. More than this, the war strained the established world order to breaking point. None of the principal European combatants emerged from their prolonged ordeal without crippling losses.

Monarchies were overthrown, boundaries redrawn, colonial posses-sions reallocated, but neither the victors nor the vanquished re-established the structures of authority that had provided security and prosperity over the past century. Institutions, habits and values that once ordered society lost their force. A nationalist uprising in Ireland against the imperial overlord, put down with brutal excess during the Easter of 1916, presaged the new disorder: 'All changed, changed utterly: A terrible beauty is born'.

Above all, the war brought the Russian Revolution, an event that was at once specific in its causes and forms and universal in its impact. It is difficult now, in the aftermath of communism, to appreciate the enthusiasm with which onlookers responded to the news from Russia during 1917: the overthrow of the Tsar in March, the formation of 'soviets', or councils of workers, peasants and soldiers, to liberate the Russian people from a notoriously backward and despotic order, and then, in October, the Bolsheviks' use of the soviets to seize power from the national assembly, followed by Russia's unilateral withdrawal from the war. A series of aftershocks followed. There were shortlived communist republics in the former Austro–Hungarian empire, a failed uprising in Germany, further reverberations in Italy, France, Spain and beyond. New revolution-ary movements emerged in China, India, Latin America. If few of the tobacco workers who formed their own soviets in Cuba knew even where Russia was, their adoption of the term demonstrated the reach of the Russian Revolution.

Before 1917 Marxism had provided just one strand of theory that informed the strategy of socialists, who in turn were but one of a constellation of oppositional movements—anarchism, syndical-ism, populism, vitalism—that formed in response to the transition to capitalist modernity. After 1917 the methods of the Communist Party (the title adopted by the Bolsheviks after 1917) and the doctrines of communism (a term popularised by Marx and Engels in their *Communist Manifesto* of 1848) absorbed or displaced alter-native traditions of social protest. Communism lit a beacon that beckoned to the oppressed and subject peoples around the world. It called on them to rise up in order to replace capitalism and impe-rialism by force. It constituted a party of a new type, a disciplined army of human emancipation. It created a new model of historical progress, universal in application, dogmatic in its certainty, that put knowledge at the service of power. Millions would die for communism, millions would die by it, and the reckoning of its effects would preoccupy the generations who lived under it. As the ideals of the French Revolution shaped history after 1789, so the ideas of the Russian Revolution have shaped the twentieth century.[7]

The call by the Russian communists for the working class of all countries to follow their lead and make their own revolutions was answered by the ASP at the end of 1919, when it declared allegiance to the new Communist International.[8] Had that been all that was involved in the establishment of a communist party of Australia, it would hardly have been necessary to convene the gathering at the ASP hall ten months later. The additional socialists it gathered in were few enough—one from the small ASP branch in Brisbane, an official from the defunct Social Democratic League of New South Wales, a dissident branch of the rigidly impossibilist Socialist Labor Party, and some former members of the Victorian Socialist Party, which had recently rejected the Bolshevik model.

These were mere embellishments of a more ambitious alliance. For also present at the conference was the secretary of the New South Wales Labor Council, Jock Garden, along with a group of his lieutenants known as the 'Trades Hall Reds'. Despite their name, they represented the very trade union officialdom that socialists denounced, and John Smith Garden himself was an unlikely revolutionary. From Lossiemouth, on the north-east coast of Scotland, he had come to Australia as a preacher in 1904 and only gravitated to Labor politics during the war, after he was dismissed for fraudulent conversion from a job in the Defence Department. Garden brought to socialism the same fiery enthusiasm he had applied to his other schemes of redemption by faith and by works, and like that other celebrated 'Lossiemouth loon', Ramsay MacDonald, he could carry sympathisers away on flights of rhetoric; the sceptics he sought to reassure with a broad wink. From his base in the Sydney Trades Hall he threw in his lot with the scheme for One Big Union in order to unify and strengthen the industrial wing of the labour movement in a crusade to overthrow capitalism. Simultaneously he worked with Albert Willis, the coalminers' leader, to impose the same objectives on the Labor Party. Defeated at the 1919 state conference and expelled from the Labor Party, Garden and Willis had little success with their Industrial Socialist Labor Party. Courageous, generous, a born fixer and utterly shameless in his opportunism, Garden needed a new political base to continue the intense factional conflict that characterised the New South Wales labour movement; but if his intrigues threatened to enmesh the new Communist Party in some embarrassing alliances, he also offered invaluable institutional support. Among the Trades Hall Reds he brought with him were Jack Howie, the recent president of the Labor Council, Jack Kilburn of the Bricklayers, Arthur Rutherford of the Saddlers, Bob Webster of the Miscellaneous Workers and Chris Hook of the Municipal Workers.[9]

There was another unexpected face, that of Tom Glynn, still marked by the pallor of nearly four years in gaol. He was one of the twelve Sydney 'martyrs' of the Industrial Workers of the World convicted in 1916 of seditious conspiracy for their campaign of direct action against the war. More commonly known as the Wobblies, the Industrial Workers of the World had initiated the idea of One Big Union. Unlike Garden and the Trades Hall Reds, however, they scorned the constraints of trade union officialdom for organisation and action on the job in a heroic vision of participatory industrial democracy that knew no divisions of leader and led. And unlike the socialists, the Australian Wobblies, who took their lead from the Chicago-based IWW, were vehemently anti-political. Parliament was for the bosses. The workers should simply bypass it and create the structure of the new order within the shell of the old. In keeping with such an heroic project, the Wobblies were distinguished by their reckless effrontery as the guerillas of the class war in the years leading up to and into the Great War. They cultivated a style of reckless defiance of order and respectability, a style commonly described as 'bummery' after their iconoclastic boast, 'Hallelujah! I'm a bum!' In such effrontery no one exceeded Tom Glynn. An Irishman, who was a trooper in the Boer War and a Transvaal policeman after it, Glynn had plunged into industrial agitation in South Africa. As the secretary of the Sydney branch of the IWW and one of the most articulate strategists of its antiwar agitation, he was a prime target when the Australian government suppressed the organisation late in 1916. Released from prison in August 1920 by the new Labor government of New South Wales in response to a popular campaign, he quickly set about reviving the Wobbly cause. In September he contributed a foreword to the Communist International's appeal to the IWW in which he accepted that 'something more than the industrial weapon' was needed to combat the 'machinations of the capitalist class during the transition period towards a Communist social order'. Industrial unionism was still an urgent necessity, but so rapidly was capitalism approaching its collapse that the 'old idea' of building a new society within the shell of the old 'can no longer be maintained'.[10]

Two other celebrated rebels were there, Tom Walsh and Adela Pankhurst Walsh. He was the secretary of the Seamen's Union, an Irish rebel, who as 'Sinbad the Sailor' contributed broadsides to Wobbly publications. She was the daughter of the famous English suffragette, Emmeline Pankhurst, and younger sister of the equally formidable Christabel and Sylvia—the younger sister who came to Australia in 1914 in the hope that she might establish her own identity, only to play out her sisters' roles. Emmeline and Christabel turned to feminist patriotism in the war against the bestial Hun; Adela and Sylvia, who saw womanhood degraded by capitalism and militarism, turned instead to revolutionary internationalism. Like her mother before the war and Sylvia during it, Adela became a martyr to her cause. On the platform of the Women's Peace Army and later the Victorian Socialist Party, she courted notoriety. Imprisoned for antiwar activity, she averted deportation by her marriage, while on remand, to Walsh. She embraced imprisonment, only to write from Pentridge Prison to implore her husband, whom she had appointed as guardian of her political conscience, to let her come home: 'I am afraid I can't stand any more of it.' He was put away himself in the following year for organising a seamen's strike. Now reunited in Sydney, they took their infant daughter Sylvia to the foundation meeting of the Communist Party and Adela had to leave the hall when the baby started crying.[11]

The Walshes had resigned from the Victorian Socialist Party

when they shifted up to Sydney for Tom to take up his union position. Another leading member of the VSP, Carl Baker, was expelled for his part in the formation of the Communist Party. He was an optometrist and a rationalist, an American—he had abandoned his Christian names, Clarence Wilbur, along with his Christianity—with the gift of the gab who spruiked his cause on the Yarra Bank.[12] With him on the trip up from Melbourne was Guido Baracchi, the knight errant of Australian radicalism. The son of the Victorian government astronomer, educated at Melbourne Grammar and the University of Melbourne, he had spent some years in English socialist circles before he took up legal studies back in Melbourne in 1914. There his antiwar activities brought him a drenching in the university lake, expulsion from the university and a spell in Pentridge. A man of considerable wealth and emotional spontaneity, utterly without guile or worldly ambition, of luminous innocence and limitless self-centredness—his marital and romantic arrangements were in a constant muddle—he edited the Melbourne Wobbly paper, *Industrial Solidarity*, and was a founder of the Victorian Labor College.

His partner in that educational enterprise, Bill Earsman, differed from Baracchi in almost every respect. William Paisley Earsman was a canny Scot who outlayed his emotions as shrewdly as his bawbees. He had arrived in Melbourne in 1910, become active in his craft union—the Amalgamated Society of Engineers—and an executive member of the Victorian Socialist Party. A keen enthusiast for independent working-class education, despite his own erratic spelling and shaky syntax, with a sharp instinctive intelligence and a good conceit of himself, he persuaded some trade unions to support the formation of a labour college in 1917: Baracchi taught Marxist economics while Earsman took classes in industrial strategy with a strong syndicalist emphasis.[13] In 1919 he moved to Sydney, leaving his wife and family in Melbourne. With him went Christian Jollie Smith, a lawyer, daughter of a Presbyterian minister and close university friend of Baracchi—she had left the Commonwealth Solicitor's office under suspicion of having passed information about deportation proceedings to Adela Pankhurst Walsh's lawyer.[14] In Sydney they enlisted the support of Garden and the Trades Hall Reds for a New South Wales Labor College. Earsman was its secretary, Jollie Smith his assistant; she taught English literature and grammar, he offered his lessons in industrial strategy. The epigones of the socialist sects were scornful of this self-appointed dominie, with his two-tone shoes and Baden-Powell hat, his syndicalist sympathies and 'colossal ignorance' of the Marxist texts; but with trade union backing Earsman was difficult to ignore.[15]

He had another vital ally in Petr Simonov, the self-styled Soviet consul-general. Peter Simonoff, as his name was usually spelt, was among the substantial community of Russian exiles who had made their way to Australia via the Pacific in the early years of this century. There were Russian groups in both the ASP and the VSP, while their own Union of Russian Workers had branches in Brisbane, Sydney, Melbourne and elsewhere that spanned the spectrum of the left. When many of the notables left for home upon the fall of the Tsarist regime in March 1917, Simonoff assumed leadership. With the Bolshevik seizure of power at the end of the year, he moved to Melbourne to establish a consulate. That the Australian government refused it recognition and then gaoled him for six months for defying a prohibition on public appearances only augmented his prestige in radical circles. Impatient to establish an Australian communist party, he shifted his base of operations to Sydney and opened an impressive office in Rawson Place, by the Central Railway Station. Those who had known him when he was always down on his uppers found him suspiciously flush with funds: one compatriot remarked with astonishment that he now drank in saloon bars.[16] His self-importance grew also as he scouted the alternative socialist groups he might back. The ASP might seem to have best claims, given its declaration of adherence to the Communist International, but writing under the pseudonym P. Finn in August 1920, Simonoff declared it inflexible, too dogmatic, too remote from the masses. He had decided to support an alternative political enterprise whose broker was to be Earsman.[17]

Their scheme was hatched in secrecy, though rumours abounded at the time and some details emerged afterwards in unguarded boast and angry recrimination. The account that Earsman constructed for the Communist International in the following year invested the sequential steps with the precision of a meticulously planned clandestine operation.

In 1920 a small group of revolutionaries decided to establish the Communist Party of Australia, which they did as a secret organisation. We got to work among the trade unions and formed a number of groups, whose main object was the spreading of Communist principles and the white-anting of these unions. From time to time we issued leaflets to the workers advising and instructing them in their every-day struggles with the master class. Then we sent out a manifesto and programme in keeping with the principles of the Third Communist International, and a call to form a legal Communist Party.[18]

This melodramatic account was calculated to impress Earsman's Russian audience, and certainly confirmed the Australian Investigation Branch's conviction that there was a controlling intelligence behind the formation of the Communist Party, constituting 'the most silent, militant and dangerous' of malign infestations, one that 'plants its own members in places where they in turn become "germ cells", thus multiplying itself fission fashion—retaining its own virility while ever extending the sphere of its cankerous inoculation'.[19] Both versions suppress the improvisation, the blunders and sheer messiness of the process.

The first step was to establish communist groups in Melbourne, Brisbane and Sydney. Earsman's associates in the Melbourne labour college, Baracchi and the socialist bookseller Percy Laidler, launched a new journal, *Proletarian Review*, in June 1920 to publicise communist principles, while Carl Baker and the Russian activist John Maruschak tried and ultimately failed to win over the VSP. In Brisbane, where the Russian presence was stronger, the ASP branch declared itself a communist group in August 1920 with the publication of their journal, *Communist*. Meanwhile in Sydney, Earsman, Simonoff and Jollie Smith drew Jock Garden into their meetings as they prepared the manifesto and programme of the proposed party. At this point Reardon and Everitt of the ASP launched a pre-emptive strike. They obtained a copy of the draft manifesto and published it early in October with this introduction:

It was discovered blowing around the city, and the only clue as to its origin was 'The Central Executive of the Australian Communist Party'. After quoting the closing paragraph of the 'Communist Manifesto' by Marx and Engels, wherein it is stated that 'The Communists disdain to conceal their views and aims', the author, or authors, evidently took fright at their own audacity and ran for the hollow log, before giving their name and address to the printer.[20]

As Reardon and Everitt anticipated, this shrewd thrust drew the authors of the document into the open. Discussions opened that led almost immediately to the calling of the conference for 30 October. While the ASP issued the invitations, Garden and Earsman provided Reardon with the names and addresses of the bulk of the invitees. It was an uneasy arrangement since neither party trusted the other while each depended on mutual cooperation. As the most significant of the socialist groups, the ASP had the assets—most importantly, premises and a printing press—and the putative claim to be an affiliate of the Communist International. The others had the wider contacts, the intangible authority of the Soviet representative in Australia, and the initiative.

The conference passed without open breach, though the points of tension were readily apparent. Garden was elected to the chair, Earsman kept the minutes. Everitt moved that the conference accept the principles of the Communist International and pledge itself to establish 'a well disciplined centralised party'; a Trades Hall Red moved the amendment 'That this conference now form a Communist Party', and the amendment was carried. Or so the minutes recorded—Reardon's version was that the conference agreed to take immediate steps to form a communist party. Earsman defeated Reardon as secretary in the ballot for a provisional secretary; there were just three ASP members elected to a provisional executive of twelve. Brodney and Glynn wanted to thrash out the programme and principles there and then; Earsman and Garden prevailed with their suggestion that the task be entrusted to a drafting committee. The group charged with the task—Earsman, Jollie Smith, Tom Glynn, Bob Brodney, Ray Everitt—quickly adopted a slightly modified version of the documents the *International Socialist* had so recently derided.[21] On the Sunday evening they celebrated the successful formation of the new party with a rally in the Liverpool Street Hall, where Glynn, Baker, Baracchi and Reardon were the speakers. Glynn expressed his appreciation of the ASP's magnanimity: 'contrary to all expectations, the ASP had sunk everything in the interests of that unity for which they had called the conference'. Reardon thanked Glynn for his words of praise, noting 'it was altogether a new sensation to receive anything but bitter criticism'. The conference, he said, had met in 'a peculiar atmosphere. Many delegates had gathered, each with the idea that the ASP sought only to reinforce itself and to sail along with little more than perhaps a change of name.' Indeed they had, but most present had something more in mind.[22]

The manifesto and programme released in the following month suggests the nature of their enterprise. While appealing to the authority of the new Communist International, it still took as its starting point the evolutionary outlook of the old Socialist International. Capitalism was a system that had 'done great service to humanity', but had now outlived its usefulness and must give way. It had created the seeds of its own destruction in the augmentation of productive capacity, choking the owning class with wealth while denying the producing class the fruits of their labour. Meanwhile the capitalists controlled the state and used it to coerce or trick the workers into submission. Onto this familiar historical diagnosis and gloomy political prognosis the manifesto grafted the idea of the communist party as the educator, the organiser and the leader of the working class. The distinctive character of Lenin's conception of the party was barely glimpsed ('The Communist Party is essentially a fighting organisation and not a debating club'), though the need for a dictatorship of the proletariat 'for the complete annihilation of the bourgeoise as a class' was stated. Nor was there any consideration of the provenance of this device, or how it might be applied in Australia. The programme of the party invoked the Bolshevik method—

> Forming groups of its members in every mill, factory, workshop and field, so that it is always in a position to direct and control through its members every industrial dispute and disturbance of the workers, keeping always in mind the same end—social revolution—and trying to utilise every spontaneous action of the workers for that one end;

—without further thought as to how such direction and control might be achieved and exercised. Instead, the manifesto was concerned to strike a balance between those old bugbears of Australian socialism and syndicalism, the 'industrial question' and the 'political question'. On the industrial question, it conceded to the syndicalists the desirability of industrial over craft unions since 'up-to-date efficient industrial unions' would have greater revolutionary potential and assist in the future communist reconstruction. At the same time it insisted against the syndicalists that communists should participate in all existing unions and seek to win office within them. On the political question it called on communists to participate in parliamentary elections in order to demonstrate the bankruptcy of capitalist institutions to the 'toiling masses'. But in a concession to the anti-parliamentarians, it allowed membership to those holding contrary views 'providing that they submit to party discipline'.[23]

Such equivocations were hardly surprising. The success of the Bolsheviks was undoubtedly the catalyst for the formation of the new party. Its choice of name, declaration of allegiance and intent are quite clear. Australian radicals had always borrowed freely from other countries. The first wave of Australian socialism was discernibly British in its doctrine, language and temper, with a continental European leavening. In the first decade of the twentieth century, North America became the salient influence, both through De Leonite socialism and Wobbly doctrines. Now a third wave was building.

> Into old rhyme
> The new words come but shyly.
> Here's a brave man
> Who sings of commerce dryly.
>
> Swift-gliding cars
> Through town and country winging,
> Like cigarettes
> Are deemed unfit for singing.
>
> Into old rhyme
> New words come tripping slowly.
> Hail to the time
> When they possess it wholly.

The new words never did wholly possess the author of this poem, Lesbia Keogh, who wrote it in 1917 when she was the lover of Guido Baracchi and made a Wobbly of him. A friend of Christian Jollie Smith at the University of Melbourne, she moved to Sydney in 1918 and boarded with the wife of Tom Glynn. She bore the reputation of a 'Rebel Girl' who sought to combine women's freedom and class emancipation. Just three weeks after the foundation of the Communist Party she married Pat Harford, a Wobbly artist, and withdrew from politics. Following her death in early middle age, Baracchi would claim that she was a romantic revolutionary unsuited to a strictly disciplined organisation like the Communist Party.[24]

A range of experience and temperament can be seen in those who gathered in Sydney to form the Communist Party. Of the score who can be positively identified, a little more than half were Australian-born; the others hailed from England, Scotland, Ireland, the United States and one from Russia. Only three came from outside New South Wales for the occasion but at least half had lived for extensive periods in one or more of the other states. Most had only a few years of formal schooling, and the two with degrees were quite exceptional, but all of them, even the most rough-tongued, cultivated a particular style of intellectual self-improvement. Their work experience covered construction, bush labouring and skilled crafts. Christian Jollie Smith, a solicitor, and Carl Baker, the optometrist, were the only professionals, though a narrow majority held full-time organisational or agitational positions in 1920. Nearly all had had brushes with the law since 1914, and at least half a dozen had served time. They were young: Tom Walsh, born in 1871, was easily the oldest; Bob Brodney, at 24, probably the youngest. Most were still in their thirties. And they were largely masculine. Only three women are known to have been present: Christian Jollie Smith, Adela Pankhurst Walsh and Marcia Reardon, and all three had partners there as well.

The composite portrait that emerges is of a particular generational segment fired by 1917. They were restless, cosmopolitan, resourceful, impatient, tested in the crucible of combat and still keen for more. They were an insistently political assembly, defining themselves by word and gesture in vehement rejection of the existing order, and they practised a gladiatorial style whose highest form was the challenge to formal combat by debate, issued by the champion of one group to another. Yet the political culture they created and inhabited was by no means as narrowly oppositional as might be supposed. Russian musical evenings were a great drawcard at this time when the audience would thrill to the strains of 'The Peasants' Song', 'The Fairy Song' and 'The Revolutionary Fighting Song'.[25] Just as the Reardons performed theatrical readings for the members of the ASP, so Brodney lectured on classical music at the Trades Hall to the piano accompaniment of Jollie Smith.

Perhaps that type of artistic performance offers a clue to the gendered pattern of revolutionary politics. Within the socialist ranks there was a sexual division of labour. The men were the activists, speaking and practising a distinctively masculine language of virile defiance, and women who could engage in that arena earned an enhanced reputation as Amazons. Typically, however, the women were cast in a supportive, nurturing role, sustaining the socialist fellowship and prefiguring the higher life that was to be. When the ASP lost patience with the reformist VSP, it pronounced that it consisted of 'dear old ladies of both sexes'.[26] Among the industrialists this division was even more pronounced. The Trades Hall Reds organised their members on inner-city sites where men sweated and toiled, and they did their deals in the pubs around the Trades Hall. The Wobblies drew their strength from the bush workers, the isolated mining communities, the waterfront and transport industries, and the fraternity of unattached men constantly on the move.

Militant activism offered a particular kind of critique and affirmed a particular kind of alternative. It valorised a single-minded dedication to the cause unencumbered by sentimental ties. When it identified the evils of capitalism, inequality, poverty, exploitation and corruption, this activism returned insistently to capitalism's destructive effects on family life. Wage slavery was an affront to masculine capacity, and such palliative devices as arbitration emasculated the working man. The very first issue of the communist newspaper featured an article by Adela Pankhurst Walsh on 'Communism and Social Purity', which explained how capitalism degraded sexuality and forced women into prostitution.[27] This was a long-established theme in Australian socialism: in perhaps its formative text, *Workingman's Paradise* (1892), William Lane explained the impossibility of true marriage and healthy procreation until the serpent was expelled from the garden and the safety of the race secured.[28] But it assumed particular salience in wartime circumstances when the existing gender order was disturbed by the departure of the young men. The 'Red Plague' was the term commonly used to denote the consequent danger of venereal disease, and a congruence may be noted between this image of rampant infection and the language used by the Investigation Branch about communists. These communists were the men of military age who had not gone overseas to fight but stayed home to wage the class war. Male as well as female socialists advertised the insidious spread of venereal disease for which socialism and secure, companionate sexual partnership were the only reliable antidotes. Bill Thomas, one of the ASP representatives at the founding conference, was celebrated for his lantern-slide lectures on the subject.[29]

The Communist Party of Australia was formed on the ebb tide of labour unrest. Within a year the Communist International would declare that the period of revolutionary crisis was spent and a new phase of temporary capitalist stability had begun. Its signs were already apparent. The great general strike of 1917 had paralysed industry for three months, the maritime strike of 1919 tied up the ports for three months more; by 1920 only the Broken Hill miners were engaged in that form of industrial seige. Wartime hardships were easing as economic growth resumed. The strains that had split the Labor Party so recently had weakened, but not dislodged, its attachment to parliamentary reform. Above all, the iron heel of the militarised state had crushed the most dangerous rebels and with the return of the soldiers, whose blood sacrifice provided conservatives with a symbol of sacral nationalism, the country turned inwards, eschewing the exotic, the alien and the dissident. The period of capitalist stability was indeed temporary. Unemployment, deprivation, dissatisfaction did not disappear. Yet the Communist Party could no longer assume a ready response to its message of class war.

What was to be done?

For the whole of his adult life, Lenin, the leader of the Russian Bolsheviks and founder of the Communist International, was a professional revolutionary. Born Vladimir Ilyich Ulyanov in 1870, the son of a provincial official and himself a graduate in law from the prestigious St Petersburg University, he had first come to the attention of the authorities in 1887, when his elder brother was arrested and hanged for conspiracy to assassinate the Tsar. In the following year he discovered the writings of Karl Marx and joined the underground socialist movement; in 1895 he travelled to Germany, France and Switzerland to meet the followers of Marx who had recently come together to form a Socialist International; later in the same year he was arrested in St Petersburg (Leningrad), and subsequently exiled to Siberia. There he formulated the strategies and methods that would enable an illegal socialist party to flourish, and published them under the pen-name Lenin. From 1900 he lived successively in Brussels, Paris, London and Geneva, reading, writing, organising, intriguing. Through his ferocious polemics he gained leadership of the more militant faction of the Russian Social Democratic Labour Party, a confederation established in 1898. In 1903 these militants gained the upper hand and assumed the name of the Bolshevik or majority party. In 1905, when the Tsarist autocracy yielded to the groundswell of demands for a representative assembly,

Lenin returned to St Petersburg to organise the Soviet, or workers' council, which had sprouted during the national crisis and briefly contended for control over the elected Duma, or parliament. With the collapse of that popular insurrection, he escaped to Finland and then resumed the life an *émigré* conspirator in Switzerland, then France and finally in a province of the Austrian empire hard up against Russia. The outbreak of war in the summer of 1914 forced him back to neutral Switzerland. But that war, the Great War, eventually broke the Tsarist regime and took Lenin back to his native land.

While Lenin led the Bolsheviks to power in Russia, his gaze crossed national boundaries. He apprehended capitalism as a world system that connected an investor in Amsterdam to a plantation in Java, a textile manufacturer in Leeds to a sheep station in Victoria. The very concatenation of imperial rivalries that brought war in 1914 and revolution in 1917 demanded a global response. Thus communism, which became the generic term for the Bolshevik doctrine and practice he created, was at once a particular application of Marxist socialism to Russian circumstances and a universal application of that formulation to all countries. It was the outcome of a campaign Lenin had waged in the Socialist International, even when the Russian Social Democrats were a small and beleaguered contingent, trailing far behind their Western European counterparts in numbers, prospects and prestige. Widely read and deeply studious— one of his projects during the Siberian exile was to translate Sidney and Beatrice Webb's history of British trade unions—Lenin confronted the German, French and British socialists as a fanatic, utterly ruthless and single-minded in his revolutionary purpose. He followed developments in these and other countries keenly, construing press reports of foreign correspondents from around the world as despatches from the far-flung battlefields of a unified class war.

It was not until 1913 that Lenin registered his first impressions of the workers' movement in distant Australia. This was a brief commentary in a Bolshevik newspaper on the recent federal election that had resulted in the defeat of the Commonwealth Labor government formed in 1910, which had been the first in that country or in any other country to hold a parliamentary majority. For the ardent Lenin it was remarkable that a labour party should have enjoyed supremacy in a national legislature for three years without even threatening the capitalist system. He explained the paradox by clarifying the identity of the Australian Labor Party. It was not a socialist but a 'liberal-bourgeois party'. Historically, the term 'bourgeois' denoted one who enjoyed the freedoms of the city, but in socialist usage it referred to the class that derived its wealth and power from ownership of capital. How could a political movement so unmistakably plebeian in its composition as the early ALP be described as bourgeois? Lenin explained: 'In order to understand the real significance of parties one must examine, not their labels, but their class character and the historical conditions of each separate country.' Australia was a young British colony, Australian capitalism still formative and the workers mostly immigrants from England under the grip of liberal illusions formed while England still enjoyed economic supremacy. Hence those liberals in Europe and Russia who pointed to Australia to show that the class war was obsolete only deceived themselves. Once Australia matured as an independent capitalist state, the conditions and the consciousness of the workers would change and a socialist labour party would emerge.[1]

Lenin's brief review of Australian politics relied on sketchy press reports and contained numerous inaccuracies. His appraisal of Australian exceptionalism, on the other hand, took up well-developed issues in European socialist discussion. The rapid formation of the Labor Party at the turn of the century, its early electoral successes and speedy achievement of office—by 1914 there had been Labor governments in every one of the Australian states as well as the Commonwealth—the introduction of industrial legislation, a basic wage, welfare benefits and state enterprise, all seemed to confirm the antipodes as a 'workers' paradise'. From the end of the century investigators travelled from Britain, France, Germany and elsewhere to this 'social laboratory' of advanced democracy in order to discern the implications of its state experiments, in much the same way as visitors to Silicon Valley or the Asian Tiger economies have more recently divined the future.[2] Those who pinned their hopes on a democratic advance from capitalism to socialism saw Australia as blazing a trail that other countries might follow to escape the class war. For revolutionaries, however, Australia posed a challenge, and the gauntlet was taken up by another Bolshevik,

Fedor Andreevich Sergeyev. His substantial report on antipodean developments appeared in the St Petersburg journal *Proveschenie* (Enlightenment) three months after Lenin's, but he had been sending back reports from Australia since 1911, and Lenin might well have drawn upon them.

Sergeyev's life followed a similar path to that of the leader he served so faithfully. Born in 1883 in the Ukraine, he joined the Social Democrats in 1901 and was almost immediately gaoled. Upon release he travelled to Paris and met Lenin, led the Bolsheviks in Kharkov during the 1905 uprising, was arrested, gaoled, escaped, arrested again, exiled to Siberia and escaped to arrive in Australia in 1911. As Big Tom Sergeyeff he worked in railway construction, bricklaying, farm labouring and waterside lumping, joined the Brisbane branch of the Australian Socialist Party, established a Russian-language newspaper, took part in a free-speech campaign and served time in Boggo Road gaol. 'I cannot stand the sight of unorganised masses', he confessed. As soon as the news of the overthrow of the Tsar reached Australia, he returned to Russia and under the *nom de guerre* of Artem rose rapidly in the ranks of the Bolsheviks during the civil war, only to die in a train accident three years before Lenin's own premature death.[3]

'I am writing from a country which, due to a strange set of circumstances, is called "Australia, the Lucky Country".' Sergeyev's introductory sentence signalled two objects: to discredit the appellation and explain the circumstances that gave rise to it. As he acknowledged, the celebrants of Australian exceptionalism 'exclaim[ed] in rapture at the touching experience of class co-operation', rejoiced in the equality of women with men and celebrated the end of economic exploitation that seemed to render the doctrinaire programme of social democracy superfluous. His refutation worked from personal experience of a harsh penal system, restrictions on the press (he had been forced to deposit a bond before his paper could be published), limits on public meetings, fines for strikes, compulsory military training, exclusion of women from public life and prohibitive deposits demanded of workers who wished to stand for parliament. He found the explanation in the infancy of capitalism in Australia and the absence of an industrial proletariat. The Labor Party was not a workers' party but a party of the petty bourgeoisie and local manufacturers, and Sergeyev quoted from its platform to illustrate the nationalistic and racist principles it espoused. Even though the Labor Party was 'decisively supported by almost all trade unions', they neither controlled it nor determined its character. The Australian Socialist Party was 'sprouting up like mushrooms after a rain' but it 'would have to work very hard before it succeeds in rejuvenating the political life of Australia and making Australia even a remotely democratic country'.[4]

It is apparent from these early Bolshevik estimates that the prospects for a communist party of Australia were not encouraging. There was certainly a substantial socialist tradition. Socialists had played a vital role in the formation of the Labor Party in the 1890s, but Labor quickly subordinated socialist principles in the quest for electoral popularity. Its rapid achievement of office confronted Australian socialists with a dilemma that their European counterparts did not have to resolve until some time later: were they to accept the limits of parliamentary democracy in order to ameliorate capitalism or should they insist on nothing less than a complete reconstitution of politics, the economy and society? The great majority chose the first course, leaving the ASP, the Socialist Labor Party and the other such groups as isolated critics. Socialists had also been active in the recovery and spread of trade unionism after the disastrous defeats of the 1890s, but here again the advance of industrial organisation brought a painful choice: did the state recognition of unions through the system of compulsory industrial arbitration merely bind workers more fully into wage slavery or was it possible for them to combine in ways that would enable them to take control over their working lives? Most socialists accepted the institutional constraints of the system of industrial relations, leaving the Wobblies as vehement dissidents. To suggest that there was a division between the reformist and revolutionary wings of Australian socialism was to put a brave face on a more fundamental incapacity of Australian socialists of all varieties to align their principles and practice.

The distinction between reformist and revolutionary socialism emerged gradually out of a spectrum of schemes for human redemption formulated during the nineteenth century in response to the spread of capitalism. Socialists, utopian and scientific, ethical and philosophical, religious and rationalist, insurrectionary and gradualist, authoritarian and libertarian, took issue with capitalism for its violation of certain fundamental social values. Capitalism was a system that extended the market to every aspect of material life, treating even the most basic necessities—land, labour, food and shelter—as mere commodities, to be bought and sold for profit. It replaced custom and mutuality with an impersonal logic of calculation that set every person against all others. It deemed everyone free and equal to buy and sell, only to heap up vast inequalities of wealth and esteem. It linked the economic freedom of the market with representative forms of government, yet created agglomerations of power that nullified democracy. It justified the private ownership of property as the basis of personal autonomy, but allowed the few to command the labour of the many, and thereby produced a whole class of property-less workers or proletarians entirely dependent on the sale of their labour to another class that monopolised the means of production—the capitalists. It made exploitation the mechanism of the process of capital accumulation.

In the course of the nineteenth century, industrial capitalism expanded from its Western European cradle to transform the world. Its technologies of mass production replaced handicrafts. It drew men, women and children into giant factories that obliterated subsistence forms of household production and bound families to the tempo of the machine. Its steamships and railways shrank distance. Its weapons overcame resistance to territorial expansion. It settled great tracts of land and incorporated them into empires. Its methods of government and techniques of administration extended surveillance and control from coercion into consent. It universalised its values of growth and progress into a process of constant change.

The most influential nineteenth-century socialist critic of capitalism was Karl Marx. A radical intellectual, Marx combined a training in German philosophy with an appreciation of the political legacy of the French Revolution and reading of the nascent science of political economy that he supplemented from his own study of the British factory system. With his friend, patron and disciple, Friedrich Engels, who drew both wealth and insight from the cotton industry of Manchester, Marx challenged the springtime of liberal optimism in 1848 with the *Communist Manifesto*. In vivid phrases it enunciated themes that he himself would develop in complex theoretical texts, polemics, journalism and ill-fated schemes, and which his followers in the Communist International would seek to realise. All history was the history of class struggles, and the bourgeois revolution was but the penultimate stage of this historical pattern. The bourgeoisie had broken the fetters on capitalist production, conquered state power for itself and torn asunder the ties of custom, deference, family and culture for 'naked, shameless, direct, brutal exploitation'. The bourgeois revolution centralised political power, concentrated the means of production and reduced all small producers, shopkeepers and peasants to the status of proletarians—in ancient Rome, the lowest class who contributed nothing to the state but their offspring. As the ranks of the industrial proletariat grew, as the victims of capitalism realised their degradation and sought to improve their lot, so they would form a universal class that transcended all divisions of nationality, sex and religion. This class would in turn overthrow the bourgeoisie, abolish private property, take collective control of the means of production and achieve real freedom. Communism would complete history.[5]

The *Communist Manifesto* was at once a political programme and an analysis of the objective laws of history. In contrast with those idealistic philosophers and utopian socialists who sought to redeem human nature, Marx and Engels insisted on the the primacy of material reality as it evolved in a complex and constantly unfolding yet socially determined process. The *Manifesto* summarised the Marxist doctrine of historical materialism in the proposition that 'man's ideas, views and conceptions, in one word, man's consciousness, changes with every change in the conditions of his material existence, in his social relations and in his social life'. The crucial determinant of capitalist social relations was wage labour. Labour was the source of value, capital the product of labour, and profit derived from the extraction of surplus value when owners of capital treated labour as a commodity. This labour theory of value suggested an inherent conflict between the capitalist and the proletariat;

and as the drive for competitive efficiency increased the scale of industry, so the remaining capitalists sought to maintain their profits by increasing their exploitation of labour. The ultimate triumph of communism was thus immanent in the laws of capitalist development:

> The theoretical conclusions of the Communists are in no way based on ideas or principles that have been invented, or discovered, by this or that would-be universal reformer. They merely express, in general terms, actual relations springing from an existing class struggle, from a historical movement going on under our very eyes.[6]

It will be apparent that this science of historical materialism was universal. Across the complexities of human behaviour, the shifting subjectivities and the differences of language, culture, belief and custom, it postulated a common logic leading to a common destination. Capitalism would obliterate all differences. The singular 'man' identified in the *Communist Manifesto* was thus the product of a convergent and irreversible historical process. Marx and Engels were not blind to biological difference, indeed they argued that men's domination of women was a condition of the transmission of property, and they were keen critics of racial oppression; but they treated these and other injustices as corollaries of the class struggle. Nor were they alone in assigning primacy to class. Most nineteenth-century social critics feared the perilous consequences of the great transformation wrought by the market. The replacement of an older, more intimate social order by a vast and impersonal social structure held together by nothing more than the cash nexus was a common preoccupation of their age. But Marx followed the implications of that transition to its logical conclusion. With the final abolition of capitalism, humanity would at last be made whole.

'The Communists', Marx explained in 1848, 'do not form a separate party opposed to other working-class parties'. They were simply the most advanced and resolute section of the proletariat, who pointed out and brought forward its common interests with the particular characteristic that 'theoretically, they have over the great mass of the proletariat the advantage of clearly understanding the line of march, the conditions, and the ultimate general results of the proletarian movement'.[7] Lenin's creation of a separate Communist Party, tightly controlled and utterly opposed to other working-class parties, pressed this advantage to extreme consequences. Working out of the cumulative experience of the socialist movement in the nineteenth century, drawing on the doctrinal disputes within the Second International and always insisting on his fidelity to Marx, Lenin transmuted Marxism into communism.

Marxists held that capitalism could not be reformed, that it would have to be swept away by revolution, and that the state was simply a mechanism 'for managing the common affairs of the whole bourgeoisie'.[8] Even so, they differed from their anarchist rivals in their insistence that the proletariat must form political parties and make use of all available opportunities, including parliaments, to campaign for immediate improvements. The fight for higher wages and democratic reforms would augment their capacity and train them for the battles to come. Capitalism would be overthrown when the economic conditions and the class-consciousness of the proletariat matured—Marx's followers called themselves Social Democrats, as Lenin did, to emphasise that the revolution was not to be the work of conspirators but would be carried out by the great mass of the working class. The actual path of capitalism after 1848, however, presented Marxists with sharp challenges. Economically, its seemingly inexhaustible capacity for further innovation and growth cast doubt on predictions of deepening crisis. Socially, the fact that the middle class and even skilled workers shared in its material benefits belied expectations of two increasingly polarised classes. Politically, the advance of democratic principles and representative institutions provided the state with greater legitimacy. Culturally, the increasing intervention of the state into economic and social regulation softened class antagonisms, while the growth of nationalism as a popular phenomenon undercut proletarian internationalism.[9] By the end of the nineteenth century the member parties of the Second International were growing in membership, capacity and caution, beset by endemic disputes between revisionists and fideists, fatalists and voluntarists, possibilists and impossibilists, as its adherents sought to accommodate these developments.

Lenin's intervention into the debate drew inevitably on his own national circumstances. Russia, ruled by a Tsarist autocracy that refused to tolerate a workers' movement, offered scant opportunity for the sort of democratic activity that was practised by socialists in

Western Europe or Australia. Its economic backwardness, in a country where the great majority worked the land and were only emancipated from serfdom in 1861, made the prospect of a working-class majority long distant. It was hardly surprising that Lenin, writing from exile in Siberia in 1902, should enunciate a conception of the revolutionary party that was small, centralised and imbued with a military discipline, a vanguard party transmitting instructions from its leaders to the rank-and-file membership. His answer to the question *What is to be Done?*, the title of the polemic he wrote in 1902, went far beyond these local circumstances, however, in its rejoinder to the revisionists. Lenin was wrestling with the patently unrevolutionary temper of the workers' movement. Against those who held that the objective circumstances of capitalism would bring workers to revolutionary class-consciousness, he insisted on the need for a more decisive intervention. 'The history of all countries shows that the working class, exclusively by its own effort, is able to develop only trade-union consciousness', and 'trade unionism means the ideological enslavement of the workers by the bourgeoisie'. Equally, those workers who in Western countries elected parliamentary representatives in the hope of ameliorating capitalism were merely succumbing to reformist illusions. Only through revolutionary theory could the workers come to understand the fundamental opposition between their own class interest and capitalism, and that theory could only come from intellectuals such as himself.[10]

From this starting point, Lenin's construction of the Communist Party proceeded. Since a spontaneous movement of workers would fall prey to economism and reformist error, the revolutionary party must be composed chiefly of professional revolutionaries—men and women who devoted their whole time to its activity. They would take up the protests of the workers and all other oppressed groups, participate in every aspect of their endeavours, speak for them, lead them and draw together all the dissatisfactions and protests into a revolutionary movement. This party would consist of both workers and intellectuals, and it would fuse them in a unified whole in which the party would constitute, as it were, a collective worker-intellectual, pure in doctrine, decisive in practice. It would embody the correct consciousness of the workers, irrespective of their actual outlook, because it alone possessed a scientific knowledge. The circumstances of such a party's operation precluded disagreement; the class war did not allow for freedom of criticism. In a subsequent dispute with the Mensheviks—the minority group of the Russian Social Democratic Party—Lenin enunciated his principle of 'democratic centralism' to signify that decisions of the party would be binding on all members.[11]

These ideas, which Lenin urged on all members of the Socialist International, were more novel in their force than their substance. Few of his contemporaries would have dissented from Lenin's proposition that 'There cannot be a revolutionary movement without a revolutionary theory'. Was not Marx himself an intellectual, and was not Marxism a scientific socialism? This, after all, was a recurrent point of contention in their disputes with the anarchists, syndicalists and other champions of spontaneity. Where Lenin differed from other Marxists was in his preparedness to pursue the implications of this line of thought to its extreme end point. His party claimed an absolute authority to activate an otherwise confused or inert mass. He substituted the party for the proletariat—as his sometime critic and sometime colleague Trotsky observed as early as 1904—in order to make politics rather than social location the basis of class identity: thus, just as he described the Australian Labor Party as liberal-bourgeois on the basis of its policies, even though the overwhelming majority of the members were workers, so he claimed that his own Bolshevik organisation, which at this time possessed a minimal working-class membership, was the sole voice of the Russian proletariat.

Unlike those historical materialists who awaited the maturation of social conditions, Lenin was prepared to hasten history. The revolution would not drop into the laps of those complacent leaders of socialist parties in the advanced capitalist countries of the West; indeed it might not begin there at all, for advanced capitalism was a global system of imperial exploitation and the fruits of imperialism blunted the edge of working-class discontent in the capitalist heartlands. It might well be in backward Russia, where capitalism was still new and raw, that the crisis would first arise and the revolutionary party must be prepared to seize the moment of opportunity in order to give shape and direction to inchoate discontent. With the outbreak of the Great War in 1914, and the capitulation of so many Western socialists to chauvinism or pacifism, Lenin developed these expectations into a general appraisal, *Imperialism, the Highest Stage of Capitalism* (1916). True socialists would oppose the war with revolutionary defeatism; they would welcome any movement, whether one of colonial liberation, a peasant rising or a national independence struggle, providing it weakened the imperialist powers.

Then, after the overthrow of the Tsar in March 1917 and the formation of an unstable provisional government, came Lenin's most utopian work, *The State and Revolution* (1917). All states were instruments of class oppression and the dictatorship of the bourgeoisie by means of parliaments must yield to the dictatorship of the proletariat by means of soviets. This workers' state would abolish the principle of the separation of powers, which served merely to frustrate genuine democratic control, so that the representative, legislative, administrative and judicial functions would all be exercised by the soviets during the suppression of the remnants of the old regime and the transition to socialism; but the fact that the ruling class would for the first time be the majority would ultimately render politics obsolete and the new state would accordingly wither away.[12]

The revival of the soviets in 1917 provided the basis of the Bolsheviks' success. Initially the councils of workers, peasants and soldiers assisted the weak and irresolute provisional government to repulse a right-wing military putsch; soon they claimed 'dual power' and ultimately they assumed complete control. The revolutionary programme of the Bolsheviks, 'Peace, Bread and Land', was something less than a socialist, much less a communist policy. It offered an end to Russian involvement in the Great War and a respite from the immense hardship of the war effort, a commitment fulfilled in the Brest–Litovsk Treaty of March 1918, and a redistribution of the great agricultural estates to the peasants who worked them, which was also quickly implemented. But the new regime was forced to fight for its very existence through three years of civil war and foreign intervention. Far from withering away, the new state imposed its dictatorship of the proletariat with increasing rigour to eliminate all opposition. Lenin argued initially that this was a temporary arrangement, the use of state terror justified by the national emergency, and that the Russian Revolution would be followed by other revolutions elsewhere that would bring succour to the Soviet Union. His formation of the Communist International in 1919 proceeded from a growing realisation that this was not happening, and the pitifully thin attendance of delegates from existing socialist parties at its First Congress showed that it would be necessary to create communist parties to constitute it.

The Second Congress of the Communist International thus promulgated in August 1920 the twenty-one conditions for membership. They were uncompromising in their generalisation of Bolshevik tactics for the rest of the world. Every party that wished to join the International had to break completely with reformism, patriotism and imperialism, change its name to the Communist Party, organise itself on democratic centralist lines, drive out all fainthearts and periodically cleanse its membership. Opportunists had to be removed from every responsible position, agitation had to be carried on within the armed forces and a parallel illegal organisation had to be created, for 'in practically every country of Europe and America the class struggle is entering the phase of civil war' and communists could have 'no confidence in bourgeois legality'.[13]

Yet even as the Congress erected these barriers to any rapprochement with the non-communist workers' movements, Lenin was rebuking those doctrinaire leftists in the West who refused to work in trade unions for fear of sullying their revolutionary purity, or participate in bourgeois parliaments lest they encourage reformist illusions. He described such refusal to compromise principles as *'Left-Wing' Communism—An Infantile Disorder* (1920), and the very opposite of Bolshevik tactical flexibility, which required an appreciation of specific national circumstances and a responsiveness to particular historical conditions. This aspect of Bolshevism was perhaps the most difficult for those militant activists in the West, fired by the success of the Russian Revolution, to comprehend. They took that epochal event as a vindication of their own doctrinaire refusal of all compromise, a vicarious justification of the persecution and rejection they had endured. To be told that they must cooperate with the despised reformists or engage in the prosaic activities of the unions affronted both their pride and their conscience. To learn that they should be prepared to dissemble, to manoeuvre, to do whatever was necessary to achieve their object, was an early lesson in communist tactics.

At the heart of communism lay a will for power. Lenin's extreme flexibility of tactics went always with a fundamental intolerance of opposition. Communism was omnivorous, subordinating every aspect of society to the control of the party. Questions of morality were no more immune than religion, philosophy, art or literature to the insistent demand that they serve class interests as determined by the party. The doctrine of historical materialism held that standards of human conduct were determined by social relations. In this sense an ethical code was a product of a class position, and all ethical principles were class specific: hence communists talked of proletarian or bourgeois morality. This left little room for personal accountability, since any actor was directed by forces beyond that individual's control. How else could a capitalist act but selfishly? Why should the perfidious conduct of a Labor politician cause any surprise? Yet communism was a doctrine of emancipation and moral redemption. It employed a language that was saturated in judgements of capitalist evil and proletarian virtue. The party demanded that its members accept the strictest discipline; it expected them to make extraordinary sacrifices for the common good. Australian communists would learn that they must suppress all personal feelings and loyalties, be prepared if necessary to put the interests of the party before family and friends.

It is a common device to explain Lenin by his national circumstances and Leninism by its historical circumstances. Fernando Claudin, a dissident Spanish communist, has written of the way the Bolshevik party was forced to operate as an extra-parliamentary organisation with little experience of the trade union activity that sustained socialist parties elsewhere. 'The circumstances in which this type of party had to maintain its cohesiveness and effectiveness—illegality, repression, the situation of the proletariat as a minority in a peasant and petty-bourgeois milieu . . . —account very largely for the semi-military features of its structure and mode of operation.' He also observed that the civil war intensified these qualities while it robbed the working class of autonomous vitality.[14] Lenin himself became increasingly critical of the failure of the workers' state to wither away, of the corruption, inefficiency and bureaucracy that dogged the new regime. His explanation was the backwardness or lack of culture of Russia, his solution to create new layers of administration wielding still more draconian powers. During his final infirmity, before he died in January 1924, he became alarmed at the concentration and abuse of power by leading party members, especially Joseph Stalin, the secretary-general. Yet Lenin himself was utterly selfless, treating himself and everyone else as an instrument of the cause. His theory of the party was as monolithic as his theory of the state, eliminating all difference, disagreement or human imperfection, reducing every institution of civil society to a lifeless appendage of the dictatorship of the proletariat. He revitalised Marxism with his assertion of the primacy of politics only to abolish politics.

In the immediate aftermath of the Russian Revolution critics condemned communism, as they do now in retrospect, as an atavistic lapse into some pre-capitalist order, either feudalist absolutism or Asiatic despotism. This cannot be reconciled with Lenin's insistently modernist and modernising inclinations. Determined to rescue his own country from backwardness, he sought to leap forward from capitalism to its necessary sequel. It is true that socialism's quest to recover the communal intimacies of a vanished past often involves a rejection of change, but this hardly fits the iconoclastic and innovative zeal of the early Soviet experiment. It is also true that the Soviet success appealed most immediately and directly to those in countries that lagged behind the West, but this was because it offered the promise of joining world history at the next and higher stage. Communism attracted the intelligentsia of the decrepit imperial regimes of Eastern Europe and Asia Minor, the restless former subjects of the Hapsburgs, the Romanovs and the Ottomans. Although their immediate efforts to emulate Lenin proved unsuccessful, the Finn Otto Kuusinen, the Pole Karl Radek, the Hungarian Bela Kun and the Bulgarian Georgi Dimitrov assumed leading positions in the Communist International, and the crescent of countries fringing the western border of the Soviet Union became a communist Pale. Communism appealed also as an advanced variant of the ideology of the West to nationalists in the East, such as the mercurial Indian Manabendra Nath Roy or the dogged Vietnamese Ho Chi Minh, who took up Lenin's critique of imperialism as

The image of a worker striking chains from the globe appeared as the cover illustration on issues of the theoretical monthly, the 'Communist International', which was prohibited from importation into Australia for much of the 1920s. This copy of the familiar image appeared in the Australian newspaper to publicise May Day. The single, heroic metalworker stands for revolutionary proletarians the world over; the links of capitalist oppression are broken over Russia. (Source: 'Communist', 27 April 1923)

a potent weapon in their anticolonial struggle. Within the West it found a response among advanced liberals, who saw its application of collective will to the rectification of society as a fulfilment of the Enlightenment project.

The initial attempts of Lenin and Sergeyev to explain the strength of reformism in Australia supplemented historical materialism with the precepts of Bolshevism. The absence of a genuine revolutionary party deprived Australian workers of any understanding of capitalism. The Australian Labor Party was a 'liberal-bourgeois party', utterly bereft of the organisational rigour of a real socialist party, and Australian trade unions perpetuated the illusions of their members. Beyond this, an Australian working class was still formative. In the absence of heavy industry, the country's wage-earners worked in small enterprises without any clear separation of employer and employee. Many, suggested Lenin, were immigrants from England who expected to improve their lot in the colony. This in turn reflected the historical circumstances of Australia as a producer of primary products for a Britain, which had long enjoyed the status of the workshop of the world, and the correspondingly limited state of local manufacturing, which in turn inclined the labour movement to act as the champion of domestic industry. The infancy of capitalism in Australia, Sergeyev observed, fostered a false consciousness that found expression in racial exclusiveness and a tendency to put national before class interests.

There is much in this analysis that finds support in the analyses of Australian socialists, from Vere Gordon Childe's mordant explanation, *How Labour Governs* in 1923 to Humphrey McQueen's agitated denunciation, *A New Britannia* 50 years later.[15] That gadfly, Donald Horne, would echo Sergeyev's characterisation of 'The Lucky Country' to account for the blissful innocence of his compatriots. Australians did ride on the sheep's back and it long afforded them a remarkably high standard of living. These prosperous colonial settlers provided for their needs with local industries that were small in scale and, at least until the end of the nineteenth century, they were accustomed to a degree of social mobility absent from the more hierarchical European countries. They enjoyed the amenities of liberalism, freedom, the rule of law, representative government and a dense fabric of voluntary associations that sustained civil society; together with the egalitarian ethos, these both sustained and restrained the coercive aspects of the capitalist economy.

The great economic crisis of the 1890s first called these arrangements into question. Strikes, lockouts and mass unemployment gave rise to a language of class, of labour as the victim of capitalism, a response accentuated by the use of police, army and courts to put down union resistance. The novel of labour organiser William Lane, *The Workingman's Paradise*, written in and of the chief confrontation between the shearers and the pastoralists, portrayed a loss of youthful innocence as the serpent of capitalism entered the garden of Eden. The young republican poet Henry Lawson used the same imagery in his lament:

> And now that we have made the land
>   A garden full of promise,
> Old Greed must crook his dirty hand
>   And come to take it from us,

as well as the same militant response:

We'll make the tyrants feel the sting
 Of those that they would throttle;
They needn't say the fault is ours
 If blood should stain the wattle.[16]

In the immediate aftermath of its decisive defeat, however, the Australian labour movement took up the ballot as its preferred weapon. The speedy electoral success of the Labor Electoral Leagues, and their equally quick absorption into the existing forms of parliamentary government, encouraged the belief that labour could civilise capitalism. The various state experiments in public enterprise, industrial arbitration and social protection fostered the attachment of the unions to the Labor Party. As that party sought to broaden support in pursuit of an electoral majority, it jettisoned its earlier flirtations with republicanism, internationalism and millenarian socialism in favour of a more pragmatic moderation. There remained a sense of class difference, a conviction that the division between those who laboured and those who profited from the labour of others marked the moral faultline of Australian society, and a corresponding determination to reduce inequality and eradicate exploitation. There also remained a belief that such abuses were alien to national tradition, Old World evils visited on the New, to be resisted as an unwelcome intrusion rather than recognised and overcome. Class was both a solace and a scourge.[17]

The tiny socialist groups that existed on the fringes of the labour movement thus used a language that was both familiar and foreign to Australian workers. Their denunciation of capitalism spoke to a deep-seated, almost instinctive resentment of the excesses of the market. Their preaching of socialism touched an aspiration to make good the injuries of class and redeem the deprivation, insecurity and humiliation that scarred so many working-class lives. But their insistence on the forcible overthrow of capitalism fell on deaf ears as impractical, indeed unimaginable, in a country that prided itself on its progressive traditions and democratic opportunities. The ASP and SLP operated as ineffective critics of the ALP, arraigning it for its shortcomings but never deflecting it from its course.

The Victorian Socialist Party came closest to mounting an alternative. Formed in 1906 by the charismatic English socialist Tom Mann, it sought to operate as a party within a party: the socialist conscience of the ALP. The VSP grew rapidly to attain a membership of 2000 a year later, and its influence was appreciable; but the tactic of permeating the Labor Party to convert it to socialism soon exhausted the patience of Mann, who turned to industrial activism and departed for Broken Hill. His successor as party organiser was the journalist, Bob Ross, who had little time for revolutionary 'impossibilists' and ensured that the VSP offered a more affirmative message of high-minded endeavour. It thus served as a training ground for activists who leavened the Labor Party with their idealism without ever altering its pragmatism.[18]

The Industrial Workers of the World, by contrast, presented this pragmatic labour movement with a serious challenge. The Wobblies discarded doctrinal declamation in favour of direct action, and in doing so they cut at the distinctive arrangements that linked the trade unions to the Labor Party. The Labor Party had been created by the trade unions, whose continuing affiliation, resources and energies sustained its electoral success, while in turn the state apparatus established as a result of Labor's entry into politics provided a framework in which unions were able to prosper. Now this interlocking relationship was called into question. In the more thoroughgoing Chicago version of Wobbly doctrine, which prevailed in Australia after 1910, the IWW practised revolutionary industrial unionism. It condemned the existing craft unions as ineffective and divisive. It dismissed parliamentary methods and despised Labor politicians. It abhorred the White Australia policy and the protective devices that favoured the European-Australian working-man at the expense of those excluded. It rejected the constraints of industrial arbitration in a succession of major pre-war industrial confrontations that shook the Australian settlement between capital and labour. Above all, Wobblies insisted that the workers would achieve their emancipation themselves. They also refused patriotism, and it was the IWW's opposition to the Great War that provided federal and state governments, mostly Labor ones, with the excuse to suppress the organisation. In their hatred of capitalism and the corresponding odium they incurred, the Wobblies prefigured the communists. With their uncompromising model of working-class self-emancipation, their openness and organisational simplicity, however, the Wobblies were quite unlike the Bolsheviks. Some, like

Tom Glynn, would join the Communist Party of Australia but those who remained communists would have to relearn their politics.[19]

The parliamentary leaders of the Australian Labor Party survived the pre-war strike wave and used the wartime powers of the state to clamp down on the Wobblies. Yet the strains of the war effort, which curtailed working-class living standards and devoured the ranks of the Australian Imperial Force, also brought mounting discontent. The determination of the Labor prime minister, Billy Hughes, to put his proposal to conscript Australians for overseas service to referendum against his party's opposition led, after the defeat of the referendum, to an ALP split. He joined in 1917 with the anti-Labor forces to form a National government that intensified the military endeavour and cracked down on all forms of dissent. Labor, now in opposition, felt the iron heel of the state. Furthermore, Hughes's departure, along with the imperial patriots of the labour movement, shifted Labor's centre of gravity to the left so that industrial militants, such as Jock Garden, Albert Willis and the New South Wales Trades Hall Reds, were encouraged to challenge the dominance of the politicians. The narrow failure of their bid to win control of the New South Wales branch of the ALP in 1919 led to the formation of the breakaway Industrial Socialist Labor Party, and, when it proved ineffective, the decision to establish the Communist Party. Industrial militants also revived the Wobbly project of One Big Union, a unified organisation of workers that would take control of industry. This proposal was formally adopted by a national conference of unions in 1919.[20]

The labour unrest in Australia was part of a broader pattern that enveloped Europe and its dependencies. Four years of killing had brutalised human conduct, embittered social relations, fomented national uprisings, brought down governments. It seemed to many that the collapse of Russia anticipated a more general cataclysm, and responses to the Russian Revolution in Australia, as elsewhere, registered domestic as well as international concerns: thus conferences of the Labor Party in both New South Wales and Victoria congratulated the Russian people on their overthrow of the Tsar at the beginning of 1917 as part of their own call for an end to the fighting.

Then at the end of 1917 came the news of the Bolshevik seizure of power. The government, the media and conservative commentators were hostile from the outset. They dwelt on the wholesale destruction and terror, and worked on popular prejudice with invented stories that the new regime had decreed the nationalisation of women. (It was widely published in the Western press that the Bolsheviks had abolished marriage, ended the sanctity of conjugal relations and made all women available to all men.) Most of all, the Bolsheviks' immediate withdrawal from the war created an implacable antagonism towards the Soviet Union, since it enabled the Germans to transfer their Eastern armies to the Western front and prolong the trench warfare with the Allies that was taking so many Australian lives. The Boche and the Bolshevik were thus linked in the public mind as a common foe. In this initial and powerfully formative reaction, the Russian communists were traitors, their domestic supporters little better than enemy agents. Hence the intervention of the Allies after the Armistice into the Russian civil war in an initial, unsuccessful attempt to put down the communist regime. Hence also the attacks on the left by returned Australian soldiers that punctuated the immediate postwar period, and the right-wing nationalist temper of ex-service organisations that became a persistent feature of Australian public life.

For similar reasons the Australian left responded eagerly and enthusiastically to the news of the October Revolution. Beyond the fact that these obscure revolutionaries were opposed to the war, little was known of them. Tom Barker, one of the twelve Wobbly 'martyrs', was asked by the prison governor in Albury who these Bolsheviks were, and had to confess his ignorance. Wartime censorship meant that Australians had only sketchy, unreliable reports of what was happening in Russia, and it took some time to remedy the dearth of testimony from the protagonists. Peter Simonoff's *What is Russia?* (1919) explained the division between the Bolsheviks and the Mensheviks with a gloss on Lenin's *What is to be Done?* Some fragments of Lenin's own writings began to appear later in 1919, along with translations of statements by Trotsky, Zinoviev, Radek and Bukharin, but so central a work as *State and Revolution* did not appear in Australia until the second half of 1920.[21] Lenin himself quickly became familiar as a mephistophelian presence through garbled newspaper reports, his diminutive figure with its balding pate, fierce eyes and goatee instantly recognisable in photographs and caricatures. But his Western dress set him apart from the undifferentiated mass of his followers as a deranged pedagogue amidst primitive, shaggy *muzhiks*. If the three-year interval between the Russian Revolution and the formation of the Communist Party of Australia confirmed the singular durability of the Soviet model, it also illustrated the distance between the two countries. A star had arisen in the east but who would follow it?

The wider labour movement was divided. Most welcomed the new revolutionary government's declaration of peace. Many discounted the hostile reports of its initial measures in the capitalist press, with one Labor journalist mocking the story of the nationalisation of women:

> In Russia still are lovers—lovers' lies pinched from Above—
> You can lead a man to Russia, but you cannot make him love.[22]

Socialists and industrialists especially celebrated the creation of the first workers' state as an augury of the overthrow of capitalism elsewhere in Europe as well as in Australia—thus *Red Europe* (1919), the report of a radical Labor parliamentarian, Frank Anstey, on his end-of-war tour of the ravaged continent. The leaders of the Labor Party did not. Even if they had shared in the enthusiasm for that prospect, there were immediate practical reasons for them to distance the Australian labour movement from its Russian counterpart. Electoral considerations forced them to maintain support for the Australian war effort, for while the voters had rejected conscription, a subsequent federal election confirmed the tenure of the Nationalist government formed by a fusion of the the non-Labor forces and the ex-Labor conscriptionists. Moreover, Billy Hughes used his popular mandate to excoriate the slightest dissension and characterise any concession to revolutionary internationalism as evidence of Labor disloyalty. The Labor parliamentarians therefore resisted the incursions of the industrialists, rejected the One Big Union, opposed the attempts to commit the party to a socialist objective and, as part of the same defensive moderation, distanced themselves from the Russian Revolution.[23]

The ensuing struggle between the pragmatists and the radicals occupied the Australian labour movement into the 1920s. National conferences of the trade unions and the Labor Party adopted resolutions calling for working-class unity, One Big Union, whole-sale nationalisation of industry, and defence of the Soviet Union. E. J. Theodore, the Labor premier of Queensland, complained at the 1921 federal ALP conference that delegates 'enamoured with the proletariat in Russia and the sentiments of the IWW' had their minds 'saturated with ideals and dogmas that did not belong to Australia'.[24] In fact the decisive influence on these conferences was exercised by socialists who were convinced that communist methods were not appropriate to Australia. Of these the most perceptive was Bob Ross of the VSP, who published his thoughts on *Revolution in Russia and Australia* on the very eve of the formation of the Communist Party of Australia. Ross appreciated the signal importance of the Bolsheviks' success: 'With the Russian Revolution we woke up'. The thrilling grandeur of their accomplishment was 'like an immense lighthouse, set on the highest mountain peak in the world, with inspiring rays sweeping all continents'. Insofar as he understood the Soviet principle, it seemed utterly appropriate; as far as he could judge the operation of the dictatorship of the proletariat—and he set Lenin's justifications alongside the criticisms of Kautsky and other Western European socialists—it appeared justified. His argument was that neither of these two devices, the soviet form of government nor its sweeping powers, was necessary or desirable in Australian circumstances since Australia could achieve its social revolution peacefully.

To establish this claim, Ross traversed much of the ground covered before the war by Lenin and Sergeyev. Australian workers had won sufficient amelioration of their circumstances to justify the methods followed by their industrial and political movement. Taking advantage of their British constitutional heritage, along with their country's youth, to catch capital off guard with their formation of a Labor Party, they had brought about an advanced democracy. Through industrial arbitration they had achieved a higher density of trade union membership than any other country, through the White Australia policy they avoided racial division 'in competition for bread and women'. There was still much to be done, for capitalism continued and many workers still suffered hardship and suppression, yet something distinctive had been secured. This something, which for want of better he named 'Labor Dominance', was an ethos that penetrated into the whole of Australian thought, a national ideal and outlook that permeated even opponents of Labor 'to an extent that would have made their fathers shudder'. It was this that rendered a dictatorship of the proletariat unnecessary in Australia, for it allowed socialists to enlarge freedoms rather than restrict them, to extend trade unions into One Big Union that would take charge of industry, and by such renewed effort to complete the transition to socialism. The more Ross studied Lenin ('and he grows bigger and ever bigger to me'), the more he could see Australia achieving its own social revolution according to its own traditions. This did not exhaust the vitality of the Soviet achievement, which had led the world in the overthrow of capitalism; indeed, its violent revolution made possible peaceful revolution elsewhere.[25]

Ross died in 1931 with most of his hopes confounded. Labor Dominance gave way after the First World War to two decades of conservative supremacy in national politics, punctuated by just two years of Labor government. There was no advance of social democracy, minimal supplementation of public provision and the protective devices that assisted wage-earners were heavily qualified as a new generation of conservatives revised the national settlement. The Labor Party itself drew back from its flirtation with socialism, the One Big Union scheme collapsed and the VSP was abandoned. During the 1920s capitalism extended its grip in Australia, introduced new forms of production and consumption, found new markets, contained its workforce; at the end of the decade, when expansion gave way to severe contraction, it shed workers and cut wages. The advanced democracy became a troubled, deeply divided and fearful dependency, its freedoms circumscribed rather than increased, until in 1939 it plunged once more into a Second World War.

These misfortunes might seem to confirm the earlier predictions of Lenin and Sergeyev. Capitalism had indeed outgrown its infancy in Australia, dispelling illusions that the country was immune from its pernicious effects. The belief that Australian wage-earners could share the fruits of industry with their employers was discredited. The much-vaunted public institutions that were meant to sustain national living standards—arbitration, the basic wage, immigration restrictions, the tariff—failed to do so. The imperial connection provided neither economic nor strategic security. The idea that Australia stood outside the world communist movement, apart from the class struggle, would surely have to be abandoned.

The history of Australian communism is an exploration of these expectations. It is a history of an attempt to realise a political project that was imposed by the logic of history and willed by an organisation of doctrinaire rigidity. Communism broke decisively with the dominant forms of Australian politics. It drew inspiration from events on the other side of the world. It took its instructions from revolutionaries working in utterly foreign circumstances and idioms. Yet it also gathered in local experience and local forms. It harked back to earlier confrontations between capital and labour to establish a line of continuity with earlier rebels. In laying claim to their oppositional practices, communism was itself assimilated. The unintended consequences of Australian communism—its effects on conservative as well as Labor politics, its contribution to trade unionism, its educational contribution, its impact on diverse social movements, intellectual and cultural life, international linkages and polarities—were perhaps of greater long-term consequence, for with the advantage of hindsight, it is easy to see the sheer implausibility of schemes for a Soviet Australia. The challenge is to comprehend what that aspiration meant to the men and women who served it, to ask why Australians gave themselves to such a cause and what happened when they did.

3

Recognition

The coalescence of revolutionary groupings arranged in the spring of 1920 began to break up almost immediately. The foundation conference reconvened twice in November to adopt a programme, constitution and rules. The executive endorsed the branches formed in Melbourne, Perth, Brisbane and Townsville, and in Sydney it authorised the establishment of branches in Newtown and Balmain where former Socialist Labor Party members were keen to join.[1] Existing Australian Socialist Party branches in Sydney, Newcastle and on the New South Wales south coast were also to become branches of the Communist Party—but here already problems arose. When Earsman travelled to Newcastle in November 1920 to speak to potential recruits, he rashly disparaged the ASP and described its three representatives on the provisional executive as 'dangerous individuals who had to be watched'.[2] His suspicion was reciprocated. The Sydney branch of the ASP, which possessed substantial assets (including the Liverpool Street hall), was reluctant to hand control of them over to an organisation in which it had only minority representation; it therefore stipulated that its property would be held in trust for six months. Earsman and Garden, for their part, lacked the numbers to prevail if they sank their group of followers into the branch structure of the ASP; they therefore constituted the provisional executive as the central branch of the new party.[3]

There were further spoils they coveted. The new party needed a newspaper for, as Christian Jollie Smith and Tom Glynn explained on behalf of the provisional executive, 'a party without a Press is like a ship without a rudder'. The plan was to turn the ASP's weekly *International Socialist* into a communist weekly and instal their own editor. This scheme turned on their control of the party, which they put to the test when the foundation conference reconvened for a final session on 11 December. There were just eighteen delegates present and Jock Garden was in the chair. Outnumbered, ex-ASP members Everitt and Reardon proposed the election of a new executive in the new year by a ballot of all members, for this would bring the entire membership roll of their own organisation into play. For precisely this reason, Earsman proposed that the provisional executive continue pending the first proper conference of the Communist Party. After Garden declared Everitt and Reardon's resolution out of order, the conference adopted Earsman's proposal by twelve votes to five. Next, Earsman suggested, they should appoint an editor of the newspaper. 'I think that you are moving a bit too fast', warned Tom Glynn. 'You haven't got the paper yet'. But Glynn was elected editor in preference to Everitt, and arrangements for the transfer of ASP property into the control of the executive were confirmed.[4]

Glynn's warning proved prescient. Four days later Earsman received a letter from Reardon in his capacity as secretary of the ASP informing him that the executive of that organisation had decided to withdraw its delegates. 'The whole of the negotiations', Reardon stated, 'have shown that a definite scheme exists on the part of a dominant section of the Conference, who represent no one but themselves, to subvert the attempt on the part of the ASP to bring about unity, to their own personal ends'. The ASP would therefore go on without them, 'unfettered by the shackles of opportunism', and was immediately adopting the title of Communist Party of Australia (The Australian Section of the Third International). On the first day of the new year this old party with a fresh identity announced itself and a long list of grievances against its false suitor in the pages of its renamed newspaper, *International Communist*.[5] For his part, Earsman put a brave face on the rebuff. Rehearsing his version of the negotiations in the first issue of his organisation's

ᵀᵍᵉ AUSTRALIAN

PROLETARIANS OF ALL LANDS UNITE!

COMMUNIST

Official Organ of the Communist Party of Australia.

VOL. 1—No. 5.   SYDNEY, JANUARY 21, 1921.   PRICE—TWOPENCE

As part of their competition to secure recognition from Moscow and enjoy local legitimacy as the true Communist Party of Australia, the Liverpool and Sussex Street parties both bedecked themselves in the trappings of the 'Communist International'. This early issue of the Sussex Street weekly newspaper sported the hammer and sickle, set in an elaborate frieze of wheat sheafs and laurels taken from Soviet publications. Note the unfamiliar translation of the communist slogan. (Source: 'Australian Communist', 21 January 1921)

organ, the *Australian Communist*, he observed that communist discipline enjoined the acceptance of decisions reached by the majority. The ASP had shown itself impervious to this duty and 'the purging process has to be undergone, sooner or later'.[6]

So there were now two communist parties, each with its own premises, press, adherents and round of activities. Both parties conducted classes and maintained programmes of indoor and outdoor meetings. Both sported the hammer and sickle, both subscribed to the programme of the Communist International. The one that had been the ASP enjoyed the advantages of an established organisation; it owned its own press and meeting hall in Liverpool Street, after which it was commonly known as the Liverpool Street Party (and sometimes as Goulburn Street, the address of its office). Beyond its existing base, however, it showed little sign of progress.

Its rival had to start from scratch. To begin with it printed its newspaper commercially, rented an office in George Street, opposite the Haymarket Theatre, and hired the Concordia Hall in Elizabeth Street for meetings; within three months it moved the office back to Rawson Place and by the end of the year obtained a new meeting hall conveniently adjacent to Trades Hall on the corner of Goulburn and Sussex Streets, after which it was commonly referred to as the Sussex Street Party. But this was not the only tag. Its Liverpool Street critics commonly dubbed it the Rawson Place Party, in reference to the conspiratorial dealings there between Simonoff and Earsman that had brought the alternative party into being, or the Trades Hall Group, to draw attention to its proximity to the site of Jock Garden's machinations.

The Sussex Street party undoubtedly cast its net more widely than the Liverpool Street party. Through Glynn it cultivated former Wobblies; through Garden it had links with the New South Wales Labor Council; through Earsman with the labour college movement; while as a new initiative unfettered by sectarian associations it aroused interest in circles of free-floating radicals in and beyond Sydney. The key members sketched a description of a new kind of revolutionary politics conducted from within the established organisations of the labour movement—even the craft unions—by a new kind of party dedicated to constant agitation. 'The business of the Communist Party', as Jock Garden perhaps tactlessly put it, 'is to get Communists in control of all positions, and to do anything, and everything, to get them there'.[7] Yet the very expediency of the new party's tactics brought immediate difficulties. Tom Glynn, who had already lent his name to the Communist International's appeal to the IWW, was quickly accused by his former comrades of betraying his industrial unionist principles: clearly stung by the accusation, he resigned as editor of the *Australian Communist* on grounds of ill health after just three months in that position. Earsman, on the other hand, was accused by Wobblies, the ASP and the SLP of going soft on craft unionism, while Garden was condemned for 'intriguing and smooging from the Trades Hall to the Pollies'.[8] In short, the Sussex Street communists' attempt to steer a middle line between the industrial unionism of the Wobblies and the political purism of the socialist sects left them open to condemnation from both quarters, while their readiness to grasp at any advantage made a mockery of the claims to constitute a distinctively new revolutionary vanguard.

The accusation of opportunism arose partly from the Sussex Street party's attempt to break the doctrinaire mould of Australian radicalism, partly from the expediency and inconsistency with which the Sussex Street leaders conducted their enterprise. While the term itself was not new, it took on a new salience in the vocabulary of the left after 1920. Hitherto, the charge of opportunism had been levelled at Labor politicians who compromised their principles in pursuit of electoral advantage or trade union officials who sold out their members in industrial negotiation. An opportunist was a back-slider or a renegade from the rigours of the class war. Now there was a new kind of opportunism practised by self-proclaimed revo-lutionaries who rejected industrial and political purism alike in their attempt to gather up the fragments of the revolutionary left into a new kind of radical crusade. These 'unity at any price mongers' were clearly vulnerable to charges of opportunism, yet they combined latitudinarianism with an intolerant suspicion of potential heretics: Jim Quinton, a former Wobbly, came down from Queensland with the intention of promoting unity by joining both communist parties, only to be told he would have to leave the ASP before he could sign up with Sussex Street; Bill Thomas, the lecturer on venereal disease and editor of the Brisbane *Communist*, was turned away after cross-examination by Simonoff and returned to the Liverpool Street outfit. Simonoff himself was chronically conspiratorial, forever 'tell-ing everyone things in whispers and telling each one not to breathe anything to anyone else'; and before the end of 1921 the party expelled Tom Glynn for forming an Industrial Union Propaganda League with his old Wobbly friends, despite his insistence that it was based on the Communist International's industrial programme.[9]

A similar pattern of attraction and repulsion operated in the party executive's dealings with branches. When it convened another unity conference in March 1921, its fresh overtures to the SLP and ASP were rejected. Ernie Judd, the unbending leader of the SLP, denounced the party as a front for capitalist spies and *agents provo-cateurs*, while Reardon returned the ASP invitation with the observation that that organisation no longer existed. Earsman was able to issue conference credentials to local delegates from Sydney, Newtown, Balmain and Darlinghurst, visiting delegates from New-castle, Brisbane, Melbourne and Adelaide, with a proxy from Perth.[10] Yet when Jock Garden and Tom Walsh visited Melbourne in February 1921, they shunned the local branch in favour of more credible hosts such as Percy Laidler, while the fledgling Perth branch criticised the party constitution, and Newcastle and Brisbane pressed for rapprochement with Liverpool Street.[11]

The picture is of a shifting constellation of enthusiasts for different forms of revolutionary working-class politics, drawn by the success of the Bolsheviks in Russia to the prospect of an Australian communist party yet unwilling or unable to sink the differences that defined their distinct forms of activity, and unimpressed by the alternatives—the one a familiar presence decked out in new trappings, the other a motley crew of adventurers. Left to their own devices, the rival claimants might have continued to denounce each other and become just two more sects on the fringes of Australian radicalism. But they were not left to their own devices. For the commitment they made was to a new kind of organisation, international in structure and discipline, and it was to the authority of that organisation that they now turned. While the Liverpool Street party enjoyed the support of most Russian exiles in Australia, the Sussex Street party began with the apparent advantage of Peter Simonoff's sponsorship. Difficult though he could be, he was, after all, the officially accredited representative of the Soviet regime and, at least in 1920, was able to inject the vital ingredient in which Australian revolutionaries were habitually deficient—money. By 1921, however, government surveillance was closing Simonoff's lines of communication to Moscow. Furthermore, a new emissary had arrived in Australia who threatened to upstage him.

Paul Freeman moved, during the war, from Broken Hill to north Queensland. Everything about him was mysterious except for his politics, which were indubitably militant: his name, usually Freeman but sometimes Miller or Cox; his birthplace, which he said was in the United States; even his nationality, either Dutch, Hungarian or possibly German, as the Australian authorities alleged when they arrested him in Cloncurry and deported him in 1919. The United States refused to accept him, so he was shipped back and forth across the Pacific until, after a hunger strike in Sydney, he was despatched to Germany where the government could not prevent his landing. Thence he travelled to Russia, where he made contact with Big Tom Sergeyeff, who was now a member of the Bolshevik Party's Central Committee. Well-connected and resourceful ('he was afraid only of mosquitoes', one Australian colleague recalled), Freeman was entrusted with the mission of organising Australian delegations to the Third Congress of the Communist International and the inaugural congress of the Red International of Labor Unions (RILU), both due in mid-1921. He arrived in Adelaide early in that year with a false passport and a set of conference credentials, and made contact with communists there and in Melbourne as he travelled to Sydney. From March he began publishing a series of articles in the *International Communist* designed to give the impression he was writing from Moscow.[12]

This choice of newspapers was important. Freeman made contact with both the Liverpool and Sussex Street parties to urge that they sink their differences, but he clearly leaned towards the former, which already had a connection with Sergeyev. Furthermore, Freeman's authorisation from the Red International of Labor Unions attracted previously unattached industrial militants into the ASP orbit. So encouraged were Reardon and Everitt by this windfall that they despatched a long message to the executive of the Communist International to press their claims for recognition. All their attempts at unity, they explained, had met with treachery from a group of infantile leftists mired in the outdated bigotry of industrial syndicalism. Their own party was firmly based on the twenty-one conditions laid down by the Second Congress of the Communist International in 1920, and all that was needed to advance the revolution in Australia was £3000.[13]

The new dispensation threatened the Sussex Street group's chief claim to legitimacy, and was one reason for its convening the fresh unity conference in March. Earsman reported to his executive an approach 'by a comrade whose name he was not at liberty to say', and Sussex Street followed this up with a further letter to Liverpool Street taking up Freeman's suggestion of a joint meeting of the two executives. Reardon, however, was now sufficiently confident to rebuff the overture, for Freeman was leaving for Russia the following day, having scattered his invitations so generously that the *International Communist* could boast that three of the party's members would follow him to Moscow, and that 'Comrade Freeman has also accepted credentials as our resident representative at Headquarters'.[14]

Assured by Freeman that the Communist International would

A commentary on the red flag riots in May 1921. This cartoon in 'Smith's Weekly' portrays the attack on the radicals in the Sydney Domain as a salutary lesson. The bearded and tattered Bolshevik lets fall the red flag and his seditious leaflets. (Source: 'Smith's Weekly', 14 May 1921)

reimburse their expenses, a ragtag band of Australians begged, borrowed and jumped ship to attend the world gathering of revolutionaries. They were making a pilgrimage to the first worker's state where the red flag flew over the Kremlin. They were leaving a country where the flying of the red flag had been banned during the war and was still an illegal act of defiance. On Sunday, 1 May 1921, a procession of perhaps a thousand marchers followed a red flag through the city of Sydney to the Domain. Jock Garden spoke first in celebration of May Day, and then Jack Kilburn, the bricklayers' leader and another founder-member of the Communist Party from the Trades Hall Reds. His speech was disrupted by a group of ex-soldiers carrying a Union Jack. The demonstrators seized and burned the hated emblem of imperialism. On the following Sunday an immense gathering, whipped up by the press and primed by a public meeting in the Sydney Town Hall, staged 'an orgy of patriotism'. They converged on the Domain, broke up the platform, where representatives of both communist parties had joined the Trades Hall speakers, and then laid siege to the Sussex Street Party's Concordia Hall. The police closed the evening meeting there. Ernie Judd of the SLP, who had refused to speak on the same platform as the others, was badly beaten and arrested for possession of a revolver.[15] This was only one of many red flag incidents in postwar Australia that attested to the strength of resistance to communism.[16]

Bill Earsman was aware of this resistance to communism in Australia as SS *Themistocles* bearing him and his fellow pilgrim, Jack Howie, made its way across the Indian Ocean. Earsman went as the representative of the Sussex Street party to the congress of the Communist International, Howie as a leading member of the New South Wales Labor Council to the congress of the RILU. With the assistance of the Seamen's Union, they had signed on as members of the crew, and found the conditions less than congenial. The food was poor, the living quarters squalid, and worst of all, the attitudes of his workmates filled Earsman with disgust. The deckhands lived like pigs, stole without compunction, traduced their wives and obstinately insisted that 'when it came to putting bombs under your arse they would have none of it and the old King was good enough for them'. As for the firemen, their language surpassed imagination and some of them would 'do you up for sixpence to get a drink if they were stuck'. Earsman confided to Howie at one point that 'every one of these bastards should be taken out and shot'. Seasick, neuralgic, tormented by the bugs in his bedding, lonely and pining for his sweetheart Christian Jollie Smith, Earsman found his patience with Howie also wearing thin: 'Howie makes me sick the way he guzzles and feeds all day long', not to mention his ability to fraternise with his companions. Earsman's shipboard study of Lenin's *Left-Wing Communism, An Infantile Disorder* yielded the reflection that the master tactician's criticism of opponents was too offensive and antagonistic, a weakness he discerned in himself. Attempts to spread the word among passengers and crew demonstrated the acuity of the self-criticism; for the most part he shunned company. Anzac Day passed at sea with a service at which Earsman spoke up for the red flag. 'Gorblimey, who would take any note of that?' replied a fireman. 'It is only mugs and bastards who talk about Red Flags.' 'All right mate', rejoined Earsman, 'you will see the day when you will raise your hat to the Red Flag'.[17]

They landed in London on 26 May 1921 and proceeded

immediately to the headquarters of the Communist Party of Great Britain. It was not a propitious time: a national lockout of the coalminers was in progress, emergency regulations were in force and leading comrades were in hiding. Earsman was immediately advised to do something about that all-too-conspicuous hat. Still, the vigilance of the authorities produced one useful result: the arrest of one of the Liverpool Street delegates, Jim Quinton, who was picked up while loitering around the docks in Hull and sentenced to three months' imprisonment. Of the two men Freeman had issued with credentials in Adelaide, one was delayed and the other had disappeared. That left three other members of the opposition at large: Alf Rees from Brisbane and Paddy Lamb of Broken Hill, both of whom had been credentialled to the Communist International by Freeman, as well as Freeman himself (who was making his way to Moscow from the other direction, through China and Siberia). There were some additional delegates to the RILU in transit but its congress was not due to begin until July, a fortnight after the opening of the congress of the Communist International, which was the crucial occasion for Earsman's purposes. Earsman also learned that Rees had preceded him through England.[18] To add to his anxiety, he had to wait a week for the next ship that would take him and Howie to Germany, so it was up to his family and the damp cold of Edinburgh before they departed on 2 June. On arrival in Berlin they took in the sights (Earsman thought the Unter den Linden one of the finest thoroughfares in the world, comparable to Princess Street in Edinburgh or even St Kilda Road in Melbourne), arranged visas to the Soviet Union, quarrelled, met other delegates and eventually got away. On 13 June they arrived in Moscow.

This was the third gathering of the Communist International. The first, in 1919, was scarcely more than a gesture of Lenin who had decided that the Socialist International must be replaced because it had betrayed the proletariat by failing to oppose the war with revolutionary leadership. Barely 50 delegates, representing weak and embryonic communist parties, gathered in that year in a Soviet Union wracked by civil war and threatened by the troops of the victorious Allies. Lenin still clung to his conviction that the Russian Revolution was the first of many such revolutions, on which indeed its fate would depend. Revolutionaries from the band of countries to the west of Russia—Germany, Hungary, Austria, Czechoslovakia and the Balkans—shared his optimism. Since the pre-war Socialist International had been the second such organisation (and the successor to that begun by Marx and Engels), the 1919 pilgrims constituted themselves as the Third International. That designation soon gave way to the more expressive Communist International, commonly shortened in the Russian fondness for such contractions to the Comintern.

By 1920, when the Second Congress of the Communist International met, expectations of speedy revolutionary success had been abandoned. While the Red Army had pushed its enemies back from Soviet territory, communists in each one of the Central European countries had met with decisive reverses. Indeed, with the loss of momentum in west, Lenin was more inclined to look east to the countries subjected to European dominion; he now thought their anti-imperial struggles might well prepare the way for communist success in the capitalist heartlands. The emphasis of the Second Congress was on the consolidation of a Third International fully committed to communist principles. Hence more than 200 delegates at the Second Congress from 35 countries adopted the rigorous twenty-one conditions of membership, binding them to a form of organisation dedicated to seizure of power, and then the elimination of parliamentary democracy in favour of soviet dictatorship. Following the Second Congress, moreover, the affiliates in Germany, France and Italy were subjected to damaging splits meant to purge their ranks of moderates and waverers. At the same time, Lenin aimed his tract *Left-Wing Communism*, which Earsman had studied on the voyage to Europe, at those doctrinaire leftists who rejected any involvement in trade unions or parliamentary elections. He drew his examples from Western Europe—though if he had bothered to consider Australia, his strictures might have been applied to both the Liverpool Street communists and the former Australian Wobblies—and his object was to erase all non-Bolshevik traces from the revolutionary left.

A year later the concerns of the Soviet leaders had changed further. The long civil war was over and the exhausted survivors sought respite from the hardships of War Communism. The urgent task of reconstruction demanded a resumption of trade with the capitalist world, and the so-called New Economic Policy adopted early in 1921 allowed market exchange to encourage production of food and other essentials. The 500 delegates to the Third Congress who gathered in Moscow in June 1921 enjoyed special privileges in their dining room at the Hotel Lux, and Earsman supplemented the meals with fruit, vegetables, cakes and lollies bought at Moscow's semi-legal street markets, yet he still felt constantly hungry. He was fortunate that the Congress occurred in the northern summer, for starvation and disease would reach catastrophic proportions as winter set in. He was fortunate also that the Third Congress marked a further shift in Comintern policy. Lenin and Trotsky now regretted the disastrous effects of recent splits, which had reduced the European communist parties to an ineffective rump. Under the slogan of 'Back to the masses', they called for a more defensive consolidation of communist presence in the principal organisations of the working class, which meant a renewed effort in the unions and labour parties—the very course of action that Liverpool Street derided Sussex Street for pursuing. The Australians were by no means the only delegates divided among themselves in 1921: the Germans, the French, and others brought differences created by their recent convulsions, while the Americans despatched rival claimants to the title of the true communists. The Australians, however, were wholly new to this kind of forum.

Earsman immediately began lobbying. His most useful initial contact was Tom Bell, a fellow Scot and a leading member of the Communist Party of Great Britain, who introduced him to both the secretary of the RILU and the credentials committee of the Comintern. Howie and Earsman were accepted with Rees as delegates to the RILU Congress, Earsman given his mandate for the all-important Congress of the Communist International. For the next ten days he worked feverishly to consolidate his advantage. He introduced himself to other delegates, especially the influential Germans whom he thought could be useful allies; attended the preliminary commissions of the Congress and listened to such legendary figures as Lenin, his wife Krupskaya, Trotsky, Zinoviev, Bukharin, Radek, Zetkin and Bela Kun; he wrote and submitted reports on Australia; marvelled at a Red Army parade in Red Square to mark the opening of the Congress, to which he was the Australian representative, and was introduced to Trotsky; pleaded in vain on behalf of the cast-off Peter Simonoff; and endeavoured to stop Howie hobnobbing with Rees. During the rare moments of leisure when he was not washing his clothes, writing up the diary or corresponding with Christian, he struck up a romance with a young German woman.[19]

On 22 June Freeman arrived, apparently friendly but giving little away. Thereafter the contest was intense. First, Earsman discovered that Freeman and Rees had contrived full mandates for the approaching Congress, whereas his own was a lesser, consultative mandate; it took several days of string-pulling to achieve parity. Next it emerged that Quinton's credentials for the RILU as a delegate of the Seamen's Union had been transferred following revelation of his arrest to Rees, an act of betrayal on the part of the union secretary and fellow Sussex Street party member, Tom Walsh. Then Paddy Lamb, the third Liverpool Street delegate, arrived (his forged passport, it was alleged, supplied by John Wren, the sporting tycoon and dubious Labor patron), too late to play a role in the Comintern Congress but in time to attend the RILU Congress as a delegate of the Broken Hill miners. To make matters worse, Freeman was telling influential Comintern officials that Earsman was an anarchist syndicalist, Christian Jollie Smith a bourgeois, Simonoff an incompetent adventurer and their Sussex Street party simply an IWW outfit. With the dispute between the two claimants now well and truly out in the open, Earsman was able to have it referred to a Small Bureau of the Comintern executive at the close of the Congress; meanwhile he resolved to resist the relentless baiting of Freeman. His tactics over the next few weeks were to immerse himself in the business of the Congress, arrogate to himself the role of the senior Australian representative, and leave his opponents to respond as best they could. He quickly sensed the fortuitous change of direction in Comintern policy. He studied the modus operandi of his heroes: Lenin was too scathing; Bukharin, a 'wee jaunty chap', was impressive, but none touched the magisterial Trotsky. He listened to the backstairs gossip and tut-tutted Calvinistically at the sexual immorality. Always at the back of his mind was the uncertainty about Freeman's capacity for mischief.[20]

Freeman's election as an alternative member of the Comintern executive boded ill. Then came an accident that removed Earsman's

worry. On 24 July a party of Comintern delegates on a tour of
inspection of coalmines as the guests of Fedor Sergeyev, now president of the Russian miners' union, were aboard an experimental
train drawn by a propellor-driven locomotive when it left the track.
Sergeyev was one of six killed in the crash, Lamb and Rees were
badly bruised, while Freeman died several days later from blood
poisoning following amputation of a leg. As Earsman reflected, 'It
seems all the ASP delegation is fated. Quinton in gaol. Freeman
dead. Lamb and Rees in bed injured. I am very sorry but thank God
it was not Howie or myself'. Earsman was a pallbearer four days
later as Sergeyev was given a heroes' funeral and buried in the
shadow of the Kremlin; he thought it 'a peculiar touch of fate' that
he should have to deliver one of the eulogies to Freeman when he
was buried two days after that.[21]

So now only Rees and Lamb could oppose Earsman at the Small
Bureau's imminent consideration of the Australian dispute. The odds
evened when a fresh group of Australian trade unionists arrived in
Moscow on 29 July: one of them was Bill Smith, the pliable secretary
of the Victorian railwaymen's union who was immediately furnished
by Earsman with credentials as a Sussex Street communist. Suitably
briefed, he was present at a preliminary meeting of the accredited
Australian delegates—Earsman, Lamb, Rees and Smith—chaired by
a senior Russian comrade with Earsman acting as reporter, which
reached an agreement for ratification by the Small Bureau:

> In view of the fact that there is no difference in principles, program
> or tactics, except differences arising out of local troubles, this meeting
> to-day proposes to the Commission of the Small Bureau to recommend
> an immediate unity of the two parties to take effect before the end of
> January 1922. This unity to take place at a general conference repre-
> senting the two parties.[22]

Such an outcome might seem a triumph of Bolshevik consensus
over reality. There were very real differences of principles and
tactics, if not programme, between the two Australian communist
parties. Earsman himself had told the Small Bureau that the Liverpool Street imposters were 'opposed to the theory of the mass party'
and acted as 'a sect who surround themselves with a halo arising
from the Marxian platitudes which they give lip service to'.[23] But if
the Comintern wanted an agreement then Earsman was happy to

provide it. Principles and tactics, after all, had been the stick with which the Liverpool Street comrades belaboured the Sussex Street opportunists, while Sussex Street was more concerned to get its reluctant spouse to the altar and take possession of the dowry. Moscow was insisting on the first step; he and his associates would take care of the second. He had the additional advantage of acting for all seven Australians who remained in Moscow, as they sought recompense of their expenses; he obtained £500 from Moscow for the costs the two parties would incur in organising the unity conference, and he also established valuable contacts with the German communists as he travelled back to Britain. He left behind the dilatory South Australian delegate, Fred Wilkinson, who as a founder of the Adelaide branch of the Communist Party was clearly aligned with Sussex Street. Wilkinson stayed on in the Soviet Union for eighteen months and ensured that the Comintern officials received Sussex Street's version of subsequent events.[24]

There was further welcome news when Bill Earsman reached England in September: the arrest of Lamb and the consequent exposure of his Liverpool Street contacts to British and Australian security agencies. Earsman had a far more innocent-sounding drop for Moscow's communications to Sussex Street: 'Miss C. J. Smith Ll.B., c/- Rev. T. Smith, The Manse, Coppin St, East Malvern, Victoria', though this too was soon discovered. Earsman again spent time in Scotland where he saw his family, his football team (Hearts) and fellow activists, then embarked for Australia, this time as a passenger. He much preferred that mode of travel, which provided drinks, cards and hi-jinks. Earsman organised several of the shipboard concerts and when 'God Save the King' was played at one of them, he tactfully pretended to faint. Chastised for disloyalty, he found a 'little evasion' saved serious trouble. On his arrival back in Australia the customs confiscated a number of publications in his luggage.[25]

Of the nine Australians who made that trip to the Soviet Union, we have only Earsman's account.[26] Allowance has to be made for his pronounced tendency to present himself as the only reliable revolutionary among fools and knaves. In his diary we see Jack Howie as a man out of his depth, Bill Smith as a dupe, Alf Rees and Paddy Lamb as spiteful plotters brought to heel. Of the political ideals that had brought them all to Moscow there is little: the diary dwells only on their vanity and cupidity and fondness for a good time. The place to which they have come is the site of contrasts: a Tsarist palace given over to proletarian business; lavish concert halls turned into people's palaces; superstition, famine, Russian unpunctuality and backwardness side by side with militant atheism, fervent rhetoric, idealism and ideals made real. Earsman's mode of life becomes almost dreamlike: a round of meetings and discussions and appointments that seldom end before two or three in the morning, interspersed with interminable waiting for a favourable answer. 'Time is of no importance to the Bolsheviks. They work all day and all night. There may be a shortage of food but never of time.'[27]

The evidence from Earsman's diary suggests that this regimen was bad for him, indeed, that it had deeply corrupting effects. He had journeyed to Europe almost as a tourist on a working holiday, tetchy, unsure of himself, missing his lover but wide-eyed and anxious to learn. As he acquired knowledge and expertise, he grew in confidence and vanity. His criticisms were always directed at the laxness and venality of others, for the diary becomes the record of an egocentric monster who projects his own obsessions into the denunciation of convenient miscreants—it becomes a communist variant on James Hogg's *The Confessions of a Justified Sinner*, secure in a Calvinist conviction of the immunity of the elect. Earsman's thoughts of Christian become more perfunctory, replaced by observations of other women in unfamiliar guises: women smoking in bars, women sweeping streets, women accosting him with offers. He is admired for his attractiveness and acquires a red Russian blouse that increases his allure. His esteem for the Soviet leaders is an admiration of their eloquence and insight, but most of all of their potency. So too with the plenipotentiary of Australian communism. He knew what he wanted and he had achieved it: 'I have done my job well', he congratulated himself on the settlement of the Small Bureau decision. To be sure, it was a remarkable performance; heavily outnumbered as the only Sussex Street delegate, he had first of all averted the Communist International's recognition of Liverpool Street, and then set in train a procedure that promised to see them forced into the control of their rivals. 'This appears to be a good bit of business', he told himself, 'and if our party has gone on as suggested, then all is well and we will score and come on top'.[28]

Meanwhile, in Australia, the party had gone on much as before with a round of public activities, lectures, classes and open-air meetings. For all its talk of a new kind of revolutionary agitation, it continued the old forms of socialist propaganda very much as the Liverpool Street party did. A systematic comparison of the work of the two parties in Sydney was compiled by a visiting Queenslander, J. B. Miles, in August 1921. Originally from the Scottish capital of Edinburgh, Miles was a stonemason who emigrated from north-east England to Brisbane in 1913 and on his own admission became 'stuck in the mud politically' until he joined the small Queensland Socialist League in 1918. That group was persuaded by Simonoff, together with the Brisbane branch of the ASP, to throw in its lot with Sussex Street following the foundation conference. A visit from Freeman in the early part of 1921 caused Miles to switch his allegiance, so his visit of inspection of the two Sydney claimants yielded a report that favoured 'Goulburn Street' over 'Rawson Chambers': even so, its description of their activities is instructive. Both parties held street-corner meetings in the city on Friday nights at which they sold their respective weekly newspapers, Goulburn Street vigorously and Rawson Chambers listlessly; both had their platforms in the Domain on Sundays, that of the Rawson Chambers adherents smaller and less successful; both conducted lectures in their halls on Sunday evenings; both ran educational classes. Miles was scornful of the shortcomings of a Sussex Street teacher as well as of the efforts of Adela Pankhurst Walsh as a lecturer in Concordia Hall: 'Mrs Walsh is still sentimental and pacifist'.[29]

There was much that Miles passed over: the links of Sussex Street, through Garden, to the New South Wales Labor Council and its affiliated unions; the fact that Sussex Street still commanded the support of his own Brisbane branch as well as most others; the extension of its influence through the Brisbane fortnightly, *Knowledge and Unity*, as well as its association with the Melbourne monthly journal, *Proletarian*. Nevertheless, the similarity of the public forms of the two communist parties was marked. Their weekly papers, the *International Communist* and the *Communist* (it had recently dropped the national prefix) both offered a mixture of rhetorical uplift and savage invective in blocks of grey letterpress. Their calls to the working class still enunciated the same litany of evils with the same call to salvation. Both were chronically indigent: Carl Baker, the Sussex Street acting secretary and editor of the *Communist*, was able to draw just thirty shillings a week as payment, while Liverpool Street had a mounting debt.[30] Both offered the same beleaguered fellowship of the elect, and both invoked the Russian Revolution as an affirmation of their cause. The lecture on 'War and the Working Class' delivered by Adela Pankhurst Walsh that Miles heard and dismissed as a vestige of pre-communist naivety had been preceded by items sung by the popular Russian choir.[31]

News from the delegates in Moscow was frustratingly sparse, delayed by the poor communications between Russia and Australia, and impeded by the attentions of the security service. Earsman wrote regularly to Christian Jollie Smith and provided reports on the Congress for the *Communist*, but it was not until mid-October that the decisions of the Small Bureau of the Comintern Executive reached Earsman's colleagues in Sussex Street. Hard on the heels of that welcome bulletin came a further message from Earsman in London that reported the arrest of Lamb, regretted 'that the police now have ample evidence that Russia is playing a part in Australian affairs' and warned that 'it will not be very long before you have the police around'. He might have saved pen and ink, for the Australian security intelligence had long been intercepting his own correspondence; it also seems to have had access to his diary.[32] When Freeman departed Sydney on 2 April, he left behind a series of reports on life in the Soviet Union, which were serialised from June in the *International Communist* as if they had been freshly received. The first genuine news of him there was the international press agency's report of his death. Before he was picked up by the English police, Lamb had sent Reardon of the Liverpool Street party a letter relating how Earsman had contrived the outcome of the Small Bureau investigation and advising Reardon to check the credentials of Bill Smith. He somehow managed to get an early passage back to Australia upon his release and reported to Liverpool Street about the time that Sussex Street received Earsman's report.[33]

The last thing the Liverpool Street leadership wanted was another unity conference. Having once escaped the toils of Earsman and Garden, they had no intention of allowing themselves to fall again into the Sussex Street embrace. So when Carl Baker, the acting secretary of the Sussex Street party, wrote to Reardon, the Liverpool Street secretary, to propose that 5 November be fixed as the date for the two organisations to meet and plan a unity conference, Reardon stalled. Acting on Lamb's advice about the crucial role of Smith in Moscow, he had already written to Melbourne for evidence that Smith was a ring-in. Still awaiting that information, he wrote back to Baker on 21 December to decline the invitation: Liverpool Street intended to appeal against the Small Bureau decision on two grounds, first that Smith was not a communist and hence ineligible to serve as a delegate to the Communist International, and second that the Small Bureau was incorrect in suspending the prior affiliation to the International of his own organisation. Earsman, who by this time had reached Sydney, responded by stating he was entitled to issue Smith with delegate's credentials and he challenged Reardon to produce evidence that Liverpool Street was affiliated. Such was the state of play when the Sussex Street party held its first annual conference at the end of the year. (There had been an earlier conference in March 1921, but that had merely ratified the decisions that were to have been taken at the failed unity conference immediately beforehand.) Delegates from Sydney, Balmain, Newtown, a new Trades Hall branch, Newcastle, Melbourne, Brisbane, Cairns and Innisfail heard Earsman's report on events at the Comintern, and sent a delegation to Liverpool Street, without success.[34]

There were worrying signs of setback registered at the conference. The executive complained of carping criticism from the branches. The several Sydney branches were difficult to sustain and the conference resolved to merge them. News from the outlying branches was mixed. Perth was inactive; Adelaide sent a message of support; Brisbane affirmed its loyalty, partly through the work of Peter Larkin, one of a family of Irish rebels, and who had also been active further north; but Melbourne was disaffected. It had begun with more than 50 members, rented a hall in Swanston Street and ran functions most evenings, but this early level of activity quickly ebbed. Of its founders Carl Baker had moved up to Sydney, where he deputised as secretary of the party in Earsman's absence, while Guido Baracchi had sought exile in New Zealand from one of his recurrent romantic intrigues and would shortly leave for Europe. By the end of 1921 the Melbourne branch wanted to merge back into the VSP. Its two conference delegates, Jack Maruschak and May Francis, both thought the lack of unity in Sydney was as much due to Earsman's ambition as Liverpool Street's obduracy, and Francis claimed afterwards that Earsman was so cynical as to celebrate the death of Freeman. The Melbourne branch was wound up soon after their return.[35]

In the face of these difficulties, the imprimatur of the Communist International was all the more important to Sussex Street. If the Liverpool Street members would not agree to a unity conference, it would hold a unity conference without them. The All-Australian Unity Conference duly assembled on 18 February 1922, bereft of ASP representation but gathering Tom Glynn back in along with some other Wobbly remnants, to declare itself the United Communist Party of Australia and send Moscow a full account of how the dutiful comrades had been 'fooled, humiliated and sabotaged' by Liverpool Street.[36] The Liverpool Street party was handicapped by disruption of its correspondence from Moscow, but despatched its appeal against the Small Bureau decision. The Earsman group should have been instructed to join the party with the prior affiliation, argued Everitt, who also provided details of Smith's ineligibility to attend the Small Bureau meeting (for his friend Reardon had since received confirmation from the foundation secretary of the Melbourne communist group that Smith had not taken part in its establishment).[37] It was too much for the exasperated secretary of the Comintern who despatched instructions to Garden and Reardon, reminding them that they had been instructed to resolve their differences by January and demanding that they explain what was happening by return of mail. Six months earlier the Kremlin had been crawling with Australians full of revolutionary zeal. Yet, as the convenor of the Comintern's newly formed Anglo–American Bureau with responsibility for the Australian party remarked, 'The comrades that came here last year voluntarily explained all differences and promised to achieve unity, only to go home and do nothing'. He issued Wilkinson with instructions to convene a new unity conference.[38]

Relief was at hand. Hitherto Reardon and Everitt had commanded the support of ASP membership in their denunciation of the Sussex Street adventurers; now divisions began to open. When the Small Bureau decision first reached Australia, Bob Brodney, who had initiated the ASP's participation in the first unity conference, suggested that unity should be considered anew. Suspended from membership of the Liverpool Street Communist Party (the ASP abandoned that title at the end of 1920) for three months as a disciplinary measure, he appeared to repent but then repeated his error.[39] By March a group of dissidents emerged in the key Sydney branch of the party with allegations of central office mismanagement by Arthur and Marcia Reardon, and against Everitt's conduct of the *International Communist*. The newspaper was deep in debt, and owed Everitt a large sum of money, while ownership of the press on which it was printed had been assigned to him as security, so he controlled the paper absolutely. The dissidents were younger men of radical temper including Bert Moxon, a knockabout with a quick tongue, Tom Payne, a bootmaker drawn from Victoria to the political excitement of Sydney, Gordon Stettler, who became secretary of the Sydney branch, and Bill Thomas, readmitted after an earlier expulsion and indignant because Everitt refused to publish another of his venereal disease tracts. But they were not the only critics of the 'Holy Trinity'. Upon his return from Russia, Alf Rees found the ineffectuality of the Liverpool Street party pitiable. For his part, Arthur Reardon refused to budge an inch to the demands that Liverpool Street rescind its policy against participation in a unity conference with Sussex Street. 'I am not against unity, but against unity by intrigue', he insisted. There were violent rows, accusation and counter-accusation, culminating in a threat by Everitt to sell the press. In retaliation the Sydney branch members quit for Sussex Street, taking with them, under cover of darkness, the furniture, piano and office equipment. The press was too heavy to shift and Moxon wanted to burn it, but wiser caution prevailed and it remained to be sold to a commercial printer. This effectively killed the ASP. Arthur Reardon related its demise to Brodney.

Everything was taken. Piano, forms, platform, partitions, fans, every-thing! Honest men are not wanted in the movement. The slaves do not want them. I have no desire to stand between the slaves and their wishes. The wife is still in a bad way and generally our little world has crumbled to dust about our ears.[40]

A new unity conference was held in July to form a new United Communist Party, though the product was far from united since the former Liverpool Street comrades proved as mettlesome in their dealings with the Sussex Street executive as they had with Everitt and Reardon. Constituting the majority of the Sydney branch of the newly amalgamated parties, the newcomers exercised considerable autonomy in conducting their affairs: they took it upon themselves to discipline and even expel backsliders. With their large book membership (they claimed 175) and a new rule change that gave branches one delegate for every ten members, they were in a position to wield considerable influence at the annual conference due at the end of the year. When the Sydney branch elections went against the executive, the executive charged five of the Liverpool Street mob with various offences, including drunkenness, whispering and alleging that Carl Baker 'was more concerned about a meal ticket than the movement'. Two of these miscreants were expelled. The defiant Sydney members elected them as branch officers. Fur-ther expulsions followed and the Sydney branch retaliated by charging the executive for the use of its hall.

Enough was enough. The executive disbanded the entire Sydney branch and set up a new one to which the rebel members were invited to apply. Some did; the diehards led by Stettler held fast and appealed to Moscow. In the meantime they barricaded themselves in the party hall and broke up the type of an executive statement for the party newspaper. They were cleared out in time for the annual conference to be held in the hall at the end of the year (though one of them assaulted delegates with a length of timber) on the understanding that the 'country' delegates from outside Sydney would adjudicate on the dispute. That part of the conference was chaired by J. B. Miles of Brisbane, who had rejoined the Sussex Street party earlier in the year and was now secretary of the Brisbane branch. This was the second time he had acted as an adjudicator and this time he picked the winning side. The conference endorsed the executive's actions.[41]

All of this would have astounded the officials of the Communist International—not just the unseemly bickering and indiscipline but the very structure of the Australian Communist Party, which remained an organisation constituted along traditional lines, the members organised by locality rather than by workplace, jealous of their rights and delegating only limited authority to the executive. 'Your Party is still weak, your experience of class struggle as a Party still inadequate, your preparedness for taking a lead in the future intensified class fights is still deficient', the executive committee admonished the Australian comrades. Still, the deed was done. A united Communist Party was at last achieved. The patience of the Comintern committee responsible for Anglo–American Bureau matters had been sorely tested: Tom Bell, Earsman's compatriot and friend in court, had pleaded they be given a little more time. The news of success was fittingly given to the Comintern by Earsman, who left Australia in the company of Peter Larkin early in May 1922. In July Earsman was in Berlin and able to pass on a report of the successful unity conference. In August he reached Moscow and gave a first-hand account; on the ninth of that month the United Communist Party of Australia was accorded recognition by the Communist International.[42]

4

Tactics

Recognition came at a price. While membership of the Communist International brought assistance, contacts, prestige, not to mention the heady excitement of participation in the great political experiment of the modern era, it also imposed substantial obligations. The Communist Party of Australia was not simply an affiliate of an international forum where like-minded delegates could pool their experiences and exchange views on policy and methods: rather, it was the Australian section of a 'centralised world party' that invested its Congress and Executive with absolute power over every constituent organisation.[1] Furthermore, the Executive's Anglo–American Bureau was already vexed, not just by the tardiness of the Australian comrades to comply with instructions to achieve unity, but by their laxity in the application of communist principles of political activity.

The Leninist model posited a revolutionary party of a kind unknown in Australia, a vanguard organisation that led the workers in all their struggles, projected its presence wherever they gathered, including in the organisations of the labour movement, in order to unmask the traitorous leadership of that movement and rescue the toiling masses from economism and reformism. This formula challenged the ingrained habits of Lenin's Australian followers. Their rejection of gradualist labourism had led them to repudiate compromise, to maintain the ideological purity of their socialist creeds in tiny, proselytising sects and, in the case of the Wobblies, to counterpose their own industrial organisation against the existing trade unions. The uncompromising tone of the Russian comrades seemed at first to confirm that oppositional stance, for was not the success of the Bolsheviks a vindication of their own vanguard role? It was to combat such attitudes among misguided British revolutionaries that Lenin wrote *Left-Wing Communism, An Infantile Disorder*. Its insistent argument that real revolutionaries did not stand aloof from the forums of the working class but entered them to win over the workers was readily taken up by the Sussex Street communists for use against Liverpool Street's accusation that they were simply opportunists. While Earsman studied an early translation of *Left-Wing Communism* on board the ship that took him to the Third Congress of the Communist International, he found 'good propaganda but nothing new contained in it'. Lenin's arguments seemed to accord with the strategy that he and Garden had been following all along, namely to recruit the ardent revolutionaries into a new party and harness their energies to assist the Trades Hall Reds' campaign to win control of the labour movement. As Earsman progressed further in his reading, his pleasure increased. 'Many familiar arguments are dealt with in a way that is entirely new to me but which I have been acting on.'[2]

Yet, like many polemics, the import of Lenin's tract went further than this. It acknowledged the strength of reformism in countries where the working class had substantial experience of parliamentary democracy and had been able to win a share of the spoils of imperialism. It incorporated his strategic assessment that in the advanced capitalist democracies the postwar revolutionary tide had peaked for the moment, so that further preparation was necessary to win their workers over to communism. It rejected the Wobblies' project of setting up alternative industrial organisations in favour of effort within the existing unions. It construed the labour party as a political form that was fundamentally different from the European social democratic parties, one constituted by its trade union membership rather than a coherent political programme and hence susceptible to 'permeation' or 'boring from within'. It therefore demanded of the newly formed communist parties a degree of discipline and coherence of purpose that they had not previously displayed. Finally, and Lenin did not disguise this limitation even if he was characteristically insistent in his exposition, it relied on its author's second-hand knowledge of the circumstances from which he derived his conclusions: *Left-Wing Communism* drew its estimate of the balance of forces from answers provided to his leading questions by erstwhile British leftists. It was this aspect of the work of the Communist International that made its theoretical practice so susceptible to disputation: not just the reliability of the evidence or the aptness with which reported symptoms were diagnosed, but the inevitable blurring of meaning when a common vocabulary was applied across divergent cultural systems. Lenin found the British (and Australian) form of working-class politics bizarre in their liberalism. Trade unions that were open to workers of all political persuasions sustained a political party that in turn tolerated a remarkable diversity of views. So different was this from the organisational principles with which he was familiar that he underestimated the strength of the British Labour Party's attachment to parliamentary gradualism, and for similar reasons he failed to appreciate the extent of the Australian labour movement's dependence on its privileged relationship with the state.

If the peculiarities of the British puzzled the leading Russian communists (and Lenin had after all studied that labour movement in some depth), how much more paradoxical seemed the circumstances of Britain's antipodean colony. Earlier reports such as that written in 1913 by Sergeyev had suggested that the much-vaunted social laboratory of reformist experimentation was in fact hopelessly backward. It described a class accommodation that was so thorough and complete as to suggest that communists were wasting their time in Australia. The Australian delegates who arrived in Moscow eight years later told a different story. In articles and reports produced at the request of the Communist International during 1921 they dwelt on the radical nationalist tradition, the audacity of the Eureka rebels, the determination of the strikers in the 1890s, the more recent defiance of arbitration tribunals and rejection of conscription. Indeed, so prodigious was their assessment of the class conflict in Australia that foreign readers found it difficult to understand why the local Communist Party was so small and ineffective.[3]

In any event, the way to build the Communist Party of Australia and strengthen its influence seemed clear. It should intensify work in the unions by means of the Red International of Labor Unions, and use the affiliation of unions to the ALP to extend its influence into the Labor Party. As it transpired, neither of these tactics was as straightforward as they appeared to the Comintern. The implementation of both revealed divisions among communists as well as the strength of resistance to them in the Australian labour movement.

The creation of an Australian section of the RILU was entrusted, at the organisation's founding congress in Moscow in July 1921, to Jack Howie. For all of Earsman's difficulties with Howie there, his task seemed straightforward. Howie was a former president of the New South Wales Labor Council and close associate of its secretary, Jock Garden. He returned from Russia, it was said, 'a changed man, abler, straighter and with a better insight into the revolutionary movement'. He also had £300 to help him with the task.[4] His scheme was to secure the affiliation to the RILU of the peak union bodies, the New South Wales Labor Council and its interstate counterparts, a scheme wholly consistent with the methodology of the Trades Hall Reds though scarcely what Moscow had in mind with its slogan of 'To the masses'. The Trades Hall Reds represented a miscellany of craft, industrial and general unions affiliated to the New South Wales Labor Council, which met and had its offices in that ramshackle building in Goulburn Street from which they took their name. Elected as officials or delegates at sparsely attended general meetings of their members, these Trades Hall Reds commanded an uncertain following. By day they endeavoured to organise worksites and improve their members' pay and conditions; at nightfall they gathered in the forum of the Labor Council to pass fiery resolutions against wage slavery.

The scheme to make this body of officials the local arm of the RILU ran into immediate opposition from Tom Glynn. He joined with his former Wobbly comrade J. B. King in October 1921 in the formation of an Industrial Union Propaganda League, based, they said, on the manifesto of the RILU, for the purpose of combatting the sectionalism and craft consciousness of existing unions. The Sussex Street executive denounced this misinterpretation of the purpose of the RILU and expelled them, yet on the eve of the unity

conference of February 1922 accepted them back into the party as
an Industrial Union Propaganda Group and recognised their newspaper, *Direct Action*, as a communist publication. In the same month
the New South Wales Labor Council voted to affiliate to the RILU.
The Communist Party made much of this endorsement from the
largest trade union council in the country, yet in truth it was a
somewhat hollow victory: the Labor Council was a sparsely attended
forum that lacked the membership of key unions, and no other trades
hall elsewhere in Australia followed its lead.[5] Furthermore, Garden's
contemptuous dismissal of rank-and-file industrial organisation
brought angry condemnation from Glynn and King, who terminated
the support for the Communist Party and RILU of their Industrial
Union Group.[6]

This was the final, irrevocable and perhaps inevitable breach,
and the tangible cost was not great since the Wobblies were a
declining force in Sydney. A more serious setback occurred in
Adelaide when, in late 1922, Glynn and King's colleague Charlie
Reeve revived the IWW and precipitated the collapse of the local
branch of the Communist Party.[7] Of greater significance for the
Australian left, in the long run, was the eclipse of the rebel tradition
the Wobblies embodied, a singularly heroic form of workplace
agitation imbued by a rebel spirit that scorned all compromise and
refused the subordination of workers' interests to calculations of
political advantage. It would be almost a decade before the communists rediscovered such forms of obdurate, oppositional militancy,
longer still before they overcame their persistent tendency to impose
political control over industrial activity.

Corresponding weaknesses bedevilled their attempt to enter the
Labor Party. This was an objective that Garden had pursued by one
means or another from the time that he and his Trades Hall Reds
had parted company with it in 1919. They had resigned or been
expelled following their unsuccessful attempt, along with Albert
Willis of the miners, and other industrial militants, to win control
of the New South Wales branch. Their earlier effort to create an
alternative Industrial Socialist Labor Party had failed. Now, through
the Communist Party, Garden tried again. His opportunity arose in
the middle of 1921 when, to heal the divisions and revive its flagging
fortunes, the federal executive of the ALP convened an All-

Australian Trade Union conference in Melbourne. It was a forum well suited to Garden's purposes. The politicians present were anxious to mend bridges with the unions and accepted the proposal that the Labor Party should take as its new objective 'the socialisation of industry, production, distribution and exchange' (even though a federal conference later in that year added the qualification devised by Maurice Blackburn that exempted those enterprises conducted in a 'socially useful manner and without exploitation'). The chief point of contention at the Melbourne conference arose over the revived push for One Big Union as the appropriate form of industrial organisation. Garden no longer pursued that chimera. Instead, he entered into an alliance during the conference with the conservative Australian Workers' Union, which had most to lose from such a scheme and counterposed its own half-hearted alternative by which it would swallow its rivals. Here indeed was a marriage of convenience! The president of the AWU central branch and the dominant figure on the New South Wales Labor Party executive was John Bailey, a bare-knuckle fighter who had hounded the industrial militants out of the ALP back in 1919. Henceforth Garden and the Communist Party would back him in the intense factional conflicts that bedevilled Labor in New South Wales. Such cynical opportunism brought condemnation from Glynn's Industrial Union Propaganda Group, the Liverpool Street communists and his former ally Willis, yet Garden was finally blocked in the pursuit of his objective of readmission to the ALP by his own Sussex Street comrades. As it was reported to the Communist International, following the Melbourne conference an invitation to rejoin the Labor Party was given to the Trades Hall Reds along with the rest of the Sussex Street party, but when Garden reported this offer to the executive they one by one rejected it on the grounds that acceptance would lead to the disintegration of the party.[8]

The episode occurred in mid-1921, before the decisions of the Third Congress of the Communist International, which might well have strengthened Garden's hand, were known in Australia. The Sussex Street party did report the Congress's theses later in the year. As early as 1922 it echoed the Comintern Executive in calling for a united front. The form of this alliance, however, was specified as 'unity in action' rather than communist affiliation to the Labor

Party. Apart from their concern that any application to join the ALP might leave them open to accusations of opportunism, the Australian party leaders simply did not trust Garden. Perhaps they sensed that the strategy of permeating the ranks of the reformists might well overtax their own revolutionary purpose, and that the permeators would themselves be permeated. They certainly feared that Garden was using the Communist Party as a device to re-enter the Labor Party, where his main ambitions lay.[9]

Such was the advice that Earsman took to the Communist International in 1922 and it was badly received. Along with its decision to recognise the finally united Communist Party of Australia, the Anglo–American Bureau of the Comintern was preparing a letter to the Australian comrades that instructed them to apply immediately for membership of the Labor Party. Earsman resisted strenuously. Such a unilateral instruction, he said, was simply holding a pistol to the head of his party's executive and would split the membership. At the very least, he urged, the executive should be given time to prepare those Australian comrades who had devoted their political careers to denunciation of the Labor fakirs for the unwelcome news. A telegram to that effect was despatched to Sydney, while a draft of the letter went off to the praesidium, which passed it across to Karl Radek for a final polish, a fortuitous delegation since items that landed on his desk tended to remain there indefinitely—and there the Australian letter did stay until after the Congress. Even so, the ground for the Australian implementation of the united front was prepared by the appearance of Garden at this Fourth Congress of the Communist International. He was credentialled as a delegate and departed Sydney in early September along with Tom Payne, one of the recent recruits from Liverpool Street. The fact that Earsman had signalled his opposition to the united front just a few weeks earlier makes this hurried addition to the Australian delegation all the more significant. Garden received a full credential as a delegate, Earsman, Payne and another Australian based in the Comintern the lesser consultative ones. Furthermore, Garden arrived in November with a cabled message from the Australian party that cast a cloud over Earsman and, try though he might, the wily Scot could not get his genial compatriot to show it to him.[10]

Bill Earsman's diary entries during this second visit to the Soviet Union reveal new depths of cynical self-absorption. Thoughts of his beloved Christian had given way to Mollie, and in the meantime there were Lola, Wilma and unnamed others in the febrile foreign quarter of Moscow. He had hopes of winning a place on the executive of the Communist International and lobbied assiduously, only to find in the end that Garden would be accorded that honour. He was in touch with Gordon Stettler, the leader of the disbanded Sydney branch of ex-ASP members who had appealed to Moscow for re-instatement to the CPA, but the Comintern Executive knocked that scheme on the head. Earsman's old ally Peter Simonoff was also in Moscow, but had fallen so far from favour that now Bill had to buy the drinks. The Comintern expected Earsman to return to Australia at the end of the Congress, but he had no intention of doing so. Drinking heavily and resorting to casual 'kneetremblers', he declined rapidly. At the end of the Congress he did some work for the Comintern in Germany and in Britain, where he was informed at Australia House that he would not be allowed to re-enter Australia. Back in Moscow by mid-1923, he earned a living as an English teacher at the Military Academy for a year, still censorious, still condemning the opportunists in the party who would use affiliation to the Labor Party for their own ends. He was joined by his wife and children from Melbourne, but she died in 1925; he became an engineering consultant for the Soviet Union, remarried and eventually settled in Scotland where he joined the Labour Party, was elected to the Edinburgh City Council, helped establish its festival and passed out of the history of Australian communism. Few lamented his departure. His lack of scruples and secretive, self-serving habits were unattractive. Yet he has a place in the history of Australian communism, for without those qualities the Communist International would not have endorsed the fledgling party that he assembled.[11]

There was lengthy discussion of the united front during the

Fourth Congress. 'Theoretically', Earsman reported, 'all parties accepted the tactic but not two agreed on the application'. Earsman defended as best he could the Australian party's earlier limited application. But Jock Garden won the limelight and the argument with a speech to the Congress of remarkable audacity. He described a party that was small in numbers but immense in influence: 'The Communist Party in Australia has a membership of nearly one thousand, and yet it is able to direct just close on 400 000 workers . . .' In every union, according to Garden, communist workers served as nuclei to provide leadership and direction. They had linked up the union forces into One Big Union to break down craft barriers and defy the employers. They had exerted their influence at the 1921 Melbourne conference to change the policy of the Labor Party and open its doors to communist affiliation. In short, the Australian Communist Party had 'found the keynote to organisation so far as the Anglo-Saxon movement is concerned'. The speech was a resounding success and won Garden election to the Executive of the International, even though it exaggerated the influence of the party to a ludicrous degree. The party membership, which he put at close to a thousand and the Congress record had at 750, was in fact reported by the acting secretary as 250 and even that figure was too high.[12] The count of 400 000 followers was reached by aggregating inflated estimates of the membership of unions affiliated to the New South Wales Labor Council and the Brisbane Trades and Labor Council. There were no union nuclei. How could there be when the pitifully small number of communist trade unionists concentrated their efforts on manoeuvres at Trades Hall and its adjacent pubs? There was no One Big Union, not least because Garden had joined with the AWU to frustrate it. His speech travestied the prospects of the Communist Party of Australia as well as his own role. 'Why did you do it, Jock?', he was asked when he returned to Australia basking in his celebrity. With a grin and broad wink, Jock answered: 'That's what they wanted'.[13]

Jock lived dangerously. On his way to Moscow he had parted company with Tom Payne (who was travelling on a false passport) to visit family and friends in Scotland, and Tom never recovered the sum of money given to Jock for safe-keeping.[14] After the Congress Jock again interrupted his passage in Scotland. On 10 February an Edinburgh newspaper carried a sensational report from its correspondent on the north-east coast describing remarkable 'Revival Scenes at Lossiemouth' as the Reverend J. S. Garden made hundreds of converts with his fiery sermon, 'Young men, the rapids are below'. Bill Earsman was himself visiting Scotland at the time, and seized on the incident as a means of discrediting the former ally who had so recently eclipsed him. 'I have never trusted him from past association', he claimed, and added that he hoped that 'little bugger Rakosi', the Comintern official (and future Stalinist despot against whom the Hungarians rose in 1956) who had championed Garden at his expense, would be present when he returned to Moscow with chapter and verse of the scandalous incident. Carpeted for his indiscretion, Jock produced an explanation worthy of a character in a John Buchan novel—he presented himself as a white Prester John who put on the dog-collar as a disguise. The Scottish police were on his trail, he said, so that he had adopted the identity of a preacher to throw dust into their eyes. Could he be blamed if his pretence was so effective? There was a grain of truth in this alibi. Jock had returned to his birthplace for a reunion with family and friends. Cutting a fine figure—he was recalled 50 years later for his bright purple cravat—he had at first addressed public meetings as a publicist of Australia as a land of opportunity. It was the concurrent excitement of a religious revival in north-east Scotland that tempted him to display his prowess as a preacher, and he subsequently apologised for his indiscretion, affirmed his fidelity to the materialist conception of history and declared himself 'willing to bow to any discipline'. The Anglo–American Bureau considered his actions foolish but he was too important a figure to lose and no further action was taken.[15]

There were other tall stories told by the Australians at the Fourth Congress. On the evening of 1 December Earsman and Garden were summoned to a private audience with Lenin. As Earsman related the meeting, Lenin listened with close attention to the Australians' account of the changes in the Labor Party and urged the most patient cultivation of its members. He heard of the affiliation of the New South Wales Labor Council to the RILU and declared it a magnificent achievement, warned of the need to prepare thoroughly before risking a seizure of power, and stressed the importance of Australia 'because we all know it as the land of bourgeois political experiments and if a successful social revolution were carried out there, that would be the last straw of the Labor bourgeois politicians smashed'.[16] Earsman also related an earlier meeting with his hero Trotsky at the headquarters of the Red Army. Trotsky asked the Australians how their party had been formed and laughed heartily at the account of the expropriation of Liverpool Street: 'That was real direct action and the party composed of that kind of material is a good fighting C.P'. He paid particular attention to the role of the IWW, for he considered its adherents 'the real proletariat and the real fighters'. Trotsky's partiality for the Wobblies, for those who came to the Communist Party free of the contamination of the 'politicals', was marked. Still, he too pressed the Australians for a statement of their work in the Labor Party and was told that although the party had been bitterly opposed to it and there had been a 'bitter struggle', the members 'now fully understood the full significance of the "United Front" '. Trotsky's interest flattered the Australians; his confidence and elan captivated Earsman in particular: 'You felt the strength and power in every word he uttered'.[17] But according to Tom Payne, the whole meeting was based on a misunderstanding—Trotsky was under the impression that Bill Earsman was the far more important American communist delegate, Max Eastman, and brought the discussion to a speedy termination when he realised his mistake. Payne also gave a different emphasis in his account of the audience with Lenin, whom he thought had quizzed the Australians at length because he was deeply sceptical of Garden's exaggerated claims.[18]

At the conclusion of the Congress the Executive Committee of the Comintern issued its long-awaited letter to the Communist Party of Australia. It pulled few punches. Like other young sections of the Communist International, the letter read, the CPA suffered from isolation, and members worked 'in doctrinaire and sectarian fashion, merely as a means of preserving the purity of their principles'. In particular, 'your press leaves a good deal to be desired'. It was not enough to write clever articles showing up the backwardness of the masses; the paper had to take part in their struggles. Recent developments had confirmed the appropriateness of the Third Congress's call 'To the Masses' against the capitalist offensive, and the subsequent tactic of the united front. The Australian Party should therefore intensify its work in the unions and make immediate application to join the Labor Party, for in Australia even more than in Britain, the Labor Party was a peculiar type of union-based party with a petty-bourgeois leadership that could be unmasked and overthrown from within. 'The United Front is not a peace treaty. It is merely a manoeuvre in the proletarian struggle. It is not an end in itself, but a tool for the acceleration of the revolutionising process of the masses.'[19]

Apprised in advance of the receipt of the letter, the annual conference of the Communist Party of Australia adopted this version of the united front at the end of December 1922. The resolution on industrial policy declared the trade unions to be the 'mass organisations of the working class' and the primary site of the class struggle. Communists were to take up the immediate demands of the workers in ways that would promote class consciousness; they were to encourage the move towards industrial unions but not to split the existing craft unions, and—this final instruction confirming Garden's role—they were to work through the state union councils with the object of aligning Australian trade union policy with the RILU. The resolution on the Labor Party recognised it as the political expression of the Australian working class: 'the aims, ideals, leadership of the Labor Party remain anti-revolutionary because the workers themselves lack class-consciousness'. Only through action would workers gain the experience and understanding necessary to throw off these middle-class prejudices and the reformist leadership, and to this end the Communist Party declared its readiness to support the Labor Party in resistance to capitalist oppression, proclaimed its solidarity with the Labor Party membership and demanded the right to affiliate while at the same time insisting on its own 'independent and revolutionary point of view based upon the unassailable principles of Communism'.[20]

While this was a fair translation of the Communist International's instructions, there was no sign that the larger implications of its criticisms were recognised. The Australian party continued to operate as an association of dispersed branches organised on a residential basis, those outside Sydney in intermittent contact with headquarters; and the Trades Hall rather than factory groups serving as its industrial arm. In Sydney the traditional forms of activity remained much as before: the street meetings with their sale of literature, the evening lectures in the party hall that waxed and waned in attendance, a popular dance on Saturday night and much less popular educational classes that repeatedly had to be revived. The set-piece debate was a political format that continued to pull crowds, so that in August 1923 three communists accepted a challenge from three Protestant ministers to contest the proposition 'That a classless democracy requires for its realisation a Christian dynamic'. Jock Garden prudently occupied the chair.[21] In the same month there was a free speech campaign after the police began breaking up street meetings in the city. Garden, Baker, Howie and Tom Payne were among those gaoled for refusal to pay fines in a traditional form of defiance, and the party was able to mobilise support from the Labor Council, the ALP and sympathetic churchmen in its demand that the established pitches be restored. This was a united front but still of a traditional, restricted and temporary nature.[22]

A communist Sunday school for the young comrades attracted controversy during 1922 when a New South Wales cabinet minister who eventually would be convicted of murder, accused the communists of poisoning the minds of the innocent. Yet in truth the Sunday school merely continued along the lines of earlier socialist children's groups, with dances, songs, classes in nature study and industrial history, and stories that endeavoured to lift young minds 'above the animal plain that some adult minds are satisfied to dwell on'. Branches of a Young Communist League for teenagers were formed in Sydney and Brisbane during 1923, with study classes and social outings. The league also published its own periodical, *The Young Communist*.[23] The party press continued to publish clever articles that dwelt on the backwardness of the masses. Thus the archetypal bonehead worker Henry Dubb, who had his origins in cartoons of the American socialist press, was constantly set right by Australian communists of superior intelligence in dialogues published in the party newspaper, only to remain obstinate in his ignorance, invincible in his lack of class consciousness.

Party membership remained tiny. In a report to the Anglo–American Bureau secretary at the end of 1923, the Australian secretary regretted his organisation still had only 250 financial members. The actual figure was considerably smaller. Since dues had been reduced at the beginning of the year from ninepence a week to sixpence, and the total collected in 1923 was a little over £107, there were on average less than a hundred fully financial members. Three in four candidates for membership were quickly lost, the secretary said.

> They fall out for various reasons, some because we have sought affiliation with the ALP, some because they have been forced to work in centers where no other party members are working, some because they get unfinancial and are unable to devote their time to party activities, others because of indifference, etc.

He listed fifteen groups, several new ones in north Queensland, others in the northern coalfields of New South Wales and the industrial south coast. Most of these were tiny and ephemeral.[24]

Fifteen women members were reported. After some initial attention to capitalism's corruption of sexuality, the party made little effort to recruit women. Adela Pankhurst Walsh had lectured and written in the early days on communism as a force for sexual purity that would free women from the tyranny of lust and the degradation of labour. Her appeal was to women as wives and mothers of the working class, and she vehemently opposed the bourgeois feminism that sought to expand career opportunities for women: 'emancipation does not consist in driving buses and entering munition factories, nor in possessing a latch key or studying the law'.[25] By 1923 she had dropped out of the party and even this circumscribed attention to women's interests had disappeared as the party directed its attention to the masculine arena of industrial politics. The handful of female comrades meanwhile addressed their sisters as backward partners of working men who lacked the class consciousness that came from the factory floor but who might be persuaded to stand by their men. The working-class wife could assist the class struggle so long as she did not carry the sex war into the class war, suggested Christian Jollie Smith, and concluded that it was 'at least twice as hard for a woman to be a Communist as a man'.[26] If the communist was a militant worker, then those who performed domestic labour could at best serve as auxiliaries.

The *Communist* changed its title in June 1923 to *Workers' Weekly*. The change was intended to assist the promotion of a united front, and in response to criticism from Moscow the executive explained that the more forthright bannerhead was unpopular. Circulation rose to 4500, the executive claimed—actual receipts suggest an average circulation of between 2000 and 3000—as some effort was made to popularise the contents in accordance with the Comintern's advice that the party press should 'take part in the daily struggles of the workers' and be a record of 'live activity and example by deed'. Party members offered accounts of their work in the unions and their efforts to permeate local branches of the Labor Party, emphasising the need to consider the views of Laborites and avoid needless antagonism while always seeking to expose the reactionaries 'in their hideousness to the masses'. An impatience with the older declamatory style of socialist propaganda was apparent, as in the self-portrait of a miner on the northern coalfield.

> Many of us do not carry about with us in our heads or our pockets a Cyclopaedia of Marx, and beyond 'Value, Price and Profit' know little of his works (while recognising the absolute necessity for our leaders to have an absolute knowledge of Marx); still, we have brains to understand—that is why we believe in Communism. We are not nice Sunday Communists who attend the Hall in Sydney once every three months.[27]

The mixture of provincial deference and proletarian superiority is striking, if somewhat feigned (for the rhetoric betrays the fluency of a worker-intellectual); the juxtaposition of theory and practice, local activism and guiding doctrine, gives early notice of a persistent tension in Australian communism. At the end of 1922 the party had assumed responsibility for the monthly *Proletarian Review*, dropped its suffix, and moved it from Melbourne to Sydney; under the editorship of Carl Baker it served as a doctrinal primer in the manifold iniquities of capitalism and the laws of history that guaranteed its imminent collapse. Baker, schooled in the soap-box tradition of defiant infidelism and cerebral socialism, also edited the *Workers' Weekly* until September 1923 when H. L. ('Snowy') Denford took over both as editor and party secretary. A knockabout activist who had left school before his thirteenth birthday, and been active both in the IWW and the ASP, Denford was by this time an official of the Ironworkers and one of the Trades Hall Reds. In March 1924 he was succeeded as editor by Jock Garden, who also became the political secretary of the party while Denford continued as financial or organisational secretary.

Garden was the dominant figure in the Communist Party from 1923. He operated out of his Trades Hall premises in Goulburn Street, where an assistant secretary and Albert Willis's daughter, the stenographer-typist, worked in the main room while he used the phone in his thinly partitioned office to conduct his schemes. Guido Baracchi arrived there in 1924 to organise one of the communist united front initiatives, the Workers' International Relief, and observed how Garden was constantly scheming with John Bailey, still his principal ally in the ALP factional infighting. Baracchi was intrigued by Garden's brazen effrontery, his unscrupulousness and generosity, opportunism and courage—'an unmitigated liar who also had his moments of truth'.[28]

Garden opened the united front when he led his Trades Hall communists into the 1923 state conference of the New South Wales branch of the Labor Party. Even by the standards of that body, it was a stormy meeting. The unholy alliance of John Bailey's AWU and the Trades Hall Reds was outnumbered by other union dele-gates (including the miners' leader, Willis) and the parliamentarians, led by the redoubtable Jack Lang. The conference considered Bailey's malpractice in parliamentary preselection ballots and the executive subsequently expelled him. A delegate challenged the presence of the communist union delegates on the grounds that the ALP constitution debarred members of other parties. Willis ruled from the chair that the communists were eligible to attend. With the conference tied on a resolution to allow the Communist Party to affiliate, the chairman exercised his casting vote in favour. Three communists, Garden, Howie and J. J. Graves of the Stovemakers' Union, were elected to the ALP executive.[29]

Willis's support was clearly crucial: although estranged from

Garden, he was still sufficiently sympathetic to the communists to entertain their membership of the Labor Party. Yet almost immediately the Communist Party threw away his support in a display of inept polemics. In a period of shrinking demand for Australian coal and intermittent employment, the owners locked the miners out of a strike-prone Maitland pit. While Willis and the union executive sought to negotiate a return to work, the Communist Party called for an all-out stoppage and accused the union officials of betrayal. No sooner was a resumption of work negotiated in July 1923 than the Communist Party publicised sensational allegations by Bill Thomas, who had now thrown in his lot with Sussex Street and was one of the communist speakers active on the coalfield. Thomas alleged that at the outset of the dispute he had been approached by the Nationalist minister for mines on behalf of an employers' organisation with an offer of £500 if he would advocate violence and implicate the Communist and Labor parties in his activity. According to Thomas, while he was at the office of the employers' association he met Cleeve Ullman, a former member of the ASP employed by the coalminers' union as an advertising canvasser for its newspaper, *Common Cause*. Again according to Thomas, he enlisted Ullman's assistance in playing along with the employers to gather evidence of their perfidy. Thomas duly broke the story, which was taken up in the press and parliament, but Ullman related a different story: he claimed that Thomas had told him he was hard up and had decided to approach the coal owners. For Willis, who accepted Ullman's version of the episode, this was the final straw. He dismissed the communist editor of *Common Cause* for sacking Ullman and withdrew support for the communists in the ALP.[30]

So when the parliamentary wing moved against the communists at the state executive meeting of the ALP, Willis sat on his hands. The state executive voted to expel the communists from the executive and membership of Labor Party. The 1924 state and federal conferences confirmed that decision. In a series of purges the communists were driven out of the local Labor branches. The inquisition conducted by the New South Wales executive tested the resolve of the communists. Some made no bones about their allegiance and were promptly expelled, sometimes taking their Labor branches with them. Others refused to identify themselves in accordance with orders from the party executive, despite the clear instruction from the Comintern that all communists should be forthright in their revolutionary agitation. If the purpose of the united front was to unmask the traitorous leadership of the Labor Party, then in its Australian implementation it seemed that it was the communists who were hiding their true identity. Certainly in arguing the case for affiliation, the Communist Party executive minimised the differences between the two parties: it claimed that both shared the same object, socialism, and differed only over the means of its achievement. Labor needed the communists for they were the best and most reliable fighters.[31]

'You cannot mix oil and water', the Queensland leader E. J. Theodore insisted at the 1924 Federal Conference of the ALP.[32] In retrospect the decision taken at that conference to close the door to communists seems so obvious as to render any close attention to the tactics of boring from within superfluous. No party that sought to win approval from the Australian electorate could afford to be associated with a revolutionary organisation that took orders from Moscow. The circumstances of political life forced the Labor Party to assuage the fears of voters for whom class rhetoric was alarming and the British Empire a bulwark of national security. Labor itself was a coalition of forces, including Catholics who recoiled from the atheist materialism of the communist Antichrist and moderate trade unionists who eschewed industrial militancy for the security offered by state arbitration. Leading communists had reputations as irresponsible adventurers and professional rabble-rousers removed from the enthusiasms, anxieties and modest pleasures of ordinary Australians. All of these truisms have the force of hindsight and in truth they were acknowledged at the time by communist analysis of the unpropitious native environment. Yet the campaign to gain entry to the Labor Party was not wholly quixotic. Labor's composition and character was not predetermined. Still scarcely three decades old, it had cultivated moderation during its pre-war era of electoral success and Commonwealth office. Following the wartime expulsion of its leading moderates over the conscription controversy, it was deprived of success in federal politics throughout the 1920s, and for a time—as the Melbourne conference of 1921 showed—oppositional currents ran strongly. The

1924 decision, then, marked the reversal of that dissident flow at official levels. Henceforth the reformist and the revolutionary streams ran in separate channels.

While the campaign for unity failed to convince the executive of the Labor Party, its effect on communist membership and morale was debilitating. The party executive claimed 115 recruits enrolled during 1924; the financial records reveal a financial membership as low as 75.[33] Nor was the Left Wing Movement it launched in the unions during 1924 any more successful in halting the drift of affiliates out of the New South Wales Labor Council. Garden wrote occasionally to the executive of the Communist International with fresh claims of success for the policy of boring from within, but the Comintern was not convinced. It chastised the Australians for the infrequency of their communications, the lack of information about party organisation, membership and policy, the lifelessness of the occasional copies of *Workers' Weekly* that reached them, and the manifest lack of success. 'Australia is one of the weakest sections of the Communist International', the Executive Committee noted, and 'so long as this silence on your part is maintained, we can never hope to build an effective section of the Communist Party in Australia'. No Australian delegate went to the Soviet Union for the Fifth Congress of the Communist International in 1924; instead Australia was represented by the former English suffragette Dora Montefiore, who had recently returned from an extended stay with family settled in Australia. She had been handicapped by the restrictions the Australian government imposed upon contact with the local comrades but reported that 'I saw enough when in Sydney to realise how grave this muddled situation was'. A Comintern official who made a clandestine tour of Australia at this time to raise funds for Russian famine relief reached the same conclusion.[34]

There were some outside Sydney who shared these misgivings. At the Third National Conference of the party in December 1923 the Queenslanders J. W. Roche and Fred Paterson had wanted a clearer assertion of the communist case against the ALP, and suggested that in their state, where Labor had been in office for seven years, 'the time was opportune for launching an attack'. The suggestion was defeated by sixteen votes to four.[35] Similar criticism surfaced at the party's Fourth Conference twelve months later when

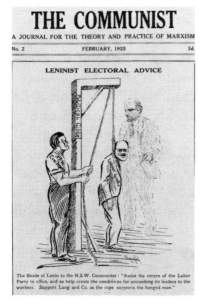

THE COMMUNIST
A JOURNAL FOR THE THEORY AND PRACTICE OF MARXISM

No. 2   FEBRUARY, 1925   3d.

LENINIST ELECTORAL ADVICE

The Shade of Lenin to the N.S.W. Communist: "Assist the return of the Labor Party to office, and so help create the conditions for unmasking its leaders to the workers. Support Lang and Co. as the rope supports the hanged man."

Lenin coined the metaphor that communists would support reformists as a rope supports a hanging man. Here that metaphor is applied to the New South Wales Labor leader Jack Lang, who won office later in that year in an election in which six communist candidates attracted a derisory poll. The ghost of Lenin, who had died the previous year, looks on omnisciently. (Source: 'Communist', February 1925)

Carl Baker denounced Garden's constant intriguing with Bailey and the subordination of communist principles to a strategy that had proved so unsuccessful. He had some support from the Melbourne and Brisbane branches, but was again easily outvoted and removed from the executive.[36] Stung by the criticism, Garden himself signalled the need for more forthright tactics with a denunciation of those party members who had 'hidden every semblance of being a Communist' and subordinated themselves completely to the ideology and methods of the Labor Party. The conference instructed its remaining members in Labor Party branches to declare immediately their membership of the Communist Party and challenge the ALP to expel them.[37] As a further step, the party announced that it would run six candidates in the 1925 New South Wales state election—Garden and Pat Drew in Sydney, Tom Payne and Lionel Leece in Balmain, and H. L. Denford and Nelle Rickie in Botany. Garden, as one of the six, might well have had misgivings since he had to rebut rumours that he was a reluctant candidate. The tortuous qualification the party advanced during the election campaign carries the ring of Garden seeking a bob each way: 'These candidates are put forward, not in opposition to the Labor candidates, but in conjunction with them, in opposition to the orthodox capitalists.'[38] He received just 317 votes. Tom Payne, who might well have won

Labor endorsement for Balmain had he not been expelled as a self-declared communist, drew 191 votes. The Labor Party under the leadership of Lang won the election and not one of the communist candidates saved his deposit. At least Pat Drew kept his sense of humour. Asked how many votes he had obtained in Sydney, he replied, 'Sixteen brother—four more than Christ had to start with'.[39]

Badinage could not disguise the severity of the set-back. In this first test of its electoral popularity, the Communist Party had failed miserably. Furthermore, the anti-Labor forces exploited the communist bogey in federal elections later in the year, bringing new repressive measures and redoubling the determination of the ALP to distance itself from its inconstant and unwanted suitor. The instruction to reveal communist allegiance therefore completed the round of expulsions, just as the threats by the triumphant New South Wales Labor Party to disaffiliate unions with communist officials had a sobering effect on the Labor Council. While Garden remained in the Communist Party, many of his lieutenants did not. Some of these Trades Hall Reds had been open communists and some secret ones; by 1925 the majority came to the conclusion that communism would bring them no benefit in their careers and severed the links—just as Earsman had predicted three years earlier. Garden himself acknowledged after the horses had bolted that the direction 'into the Labor Party' had too easily been interpreted as complete subordination to the Labor Party. The work of the ALP had assumed greater priority than the work of the Communist Party. Its obligations were less irksome, its rewards more enticing. J. J. Graves of the stovemakers was one who opted for the Labor Party along with Jack Beasley of the Electrical Trades' Union, Bob Heffron of the Marine Stewards', Arthur Rutherford of the Saddlers' Union, Jack Kilburn of the Bricklayers' and soon even 'Snowy' Denford, the former Communist Party secretary. These men represented a mixed bunch of trades and differed in their qualities; even so, they included a future leader of the New South Wales parliamentary Labor Party, Heffron, and a Commonwealth Labor Party cabinet member, Jack Beasley. That great Australian party, composed of the ex-communists, was already swelling.[40]

The Communist Party was at a low point. Guido Baracchi had returned to Sydney late in 1924 from Germany, where he had been an editor of the English-language edition of the Comintern's journal, *International Press Correspondence* or *Inprecorr*. He was elected to the Australian party's executive, became editor of its revived theoretical journal, *Communist*, organiser of educational classes in Sydney, and briefly filled in for Garden as political secretary. Baracchi was appalled by the isolation of the party as well as the sectarianism it practised, most notably during the worldwide strike of British seamen in the latter part of 1925 when the communists were at loggerheads with the Seamen's Union, led by Tom Walsh and Jacob Johnson. Walsh (who had parted with the Communist Party) and Johnson (who belonged to a tiny and doctrinaire socialist group) were sentenced to deportation by the vengeful federal government for their solidarity with the British seamen, yet the most that Baracchi could persuade the Communist Party to do was to allow the indigent victims to bunk down in the Communist Hall.[41] In the aftermath of the New South Wales elections he came to the conclusion that it would be better to liquidate the party and concentrate on gingering up the labour movement. An article by him to this effect was included in the December issue of *Communist*, but the executive stopped its publication. His advice rejected, he resigned:

> I feel very much like a man who has just undergone a surgical operation. And this is so because I realise very well that the members of the Communist Party are the best comrades in the movement, although I feel that the Party itself, as an organisation, is such a tragic farce that I cannot bear to be associated with it a moment longer.[42]

The majority of the Melbourne branch, which had reformed in 1924, reached a similar conclusion and also resigned.[43] Among the comrades Baracchi extolled was Tom Payne, whose popularity was such that Baracchi reported Balmain aldermen vying to be seen walking down Darling Street in his company. But at the party conference in December 1925 it was reported that Payne 'did not place much enthusiasm into the election campaign' and dropped his party duties soon after it. He was expelled.[44]

This was the state of affairs that awaited Esmonde Higgins, Baracchi's friend and comrade-in-arms at the University of Melbourne during the anti-conscription struggle. Higgins also returned to Australia in 1924, from England where he had worked for the Communist Party in the Labour Research Department and formed a close friendship with the leading British Communist, Harry Pollitt. His return was arranged by Christian Jollie Smith (a former schoolfriend of his sister, Nettie Palmer), who suggested to Jock Garden that he might revive the Labor Council's defunct Labour Research and Information Bureau in Sydney. Jock liked the idea, but its funding relied on his scheme to win control of the Labor Party so Higgins found himself running it on a part-time basis out of Trades Hall while trying to earn a living as a factory hand. He too was elected to the executive and entrusted with educational and editorial work by a party in which such skills were in short supply. Christian had warned him of the difficulties: 'The movement here is in an extraordinary condition, Guido says unique, most of the rest of us say worse things'. The British party was hardly a model of efficiency, but he was quite unprepared for the extent of the dis-organisation and demoralisation in Sydney, and he poured out his weariness and frustration in letters to Harry Pollitt. In September 1924, he described the party as 'a handful of derelicts marooned away from everywhere, with four-fifths of the Party members only "secret" members as a result of the prohibitions of the Labor Party constitution, and therefore absolutely unreliable'. By March, when the secret members had been instructed to declare themselves, he wrote, 'Things here are awful'. The party was reduced to just 40 active members, 'a couple of handfuls in Sydney, varyingly small handfuls in Brisbane, Newcastle, Melbourne, north Queensland and the three New South Wales coalfields—and that's all'. Squabbling and backbiting was constant. 'Bluff, intrigue, faction, indiscipline, hypocrisy, talk, ineptitude—that is all the poor old Party is able to trade on now.' By the end of July he could stand it no longer and tossed in the editorship of *Workers' Weekly* to chase a job.[45]

There was another observer of the party at its nadir. Christina Stead was working in a city office, having resigned from the New South Wales education department less than three years after she completed teacher training, saving desperately to escape overseas. Through her father, David, who was a scientist, socialist and general enthusiast for good causes, she was familiar with Sydney's radical circle; through her own privations and deep unhappiness she found herself in the inner-city milieu of the communists. Her novel *Seven Poor Men of Sydney* is set during the seamen's strike of 1925 and presents a circle of tormented outsiders who seek through politics and philosophy to assuage their unhappinesses. Written after she reached Europe and drawing on the knowledge of her American communist companion, its overlay of later onto earlier politics makes identification of its characters all the more hazardous, but Guido Baracchi was convinced that he formed the basis of Fulke Folliot, the editor of the party newspaper. Folliot and his wife had independent incomes and had travelled. They worked hard among the seamen and the poorest of Australian workers, and 'carried high the torchlight of their metropolitan culture at the same time, talked Cezanne, Gaugin, Laforgue, T. S. Eliot, Freud and Havelock Ellis'. The party librarian, who works as a printer, is suspicious of such culture: 'There's only one book yew need to know, an' that's Marx, and only one exegesis yew want to read an' that's Lenin on Marx'. The studious German who works alongside him sees Folliot as a romantic: 'It riles me when I see Fulke get up before a body of bleak-faced, whiskered, half-starved men and get off his cheese-cake eloquence . . .' Little Fulke, 'gay, small, plump and mellifluous', addresses party members and British seamen at the Communist Hall, some sleeping with their coats as pillows, and mocks the conservative prime minister, Mr Wellborn, with whom he had been at school (as Baracchi had with Stanley Melbourne Bruce) in a speech that passes high over their heads. The novel shifts about the sprawling city, from inner-city slums in Woolloomooloo to the harbour heads, where Stead spent her childhood, the point of departure from 'Terra Felix Australis, this waste and sleepin' land'.[46]

So at the end of 1925 Guido embarked once more for Europe. On the same liner a leader of the British seamen was being deported, and a long line of waterside workers had assembled to farewell him. As the vessel cast off and the first-class passengers exchanged salutations and streamers with friends on the wharf, the strains of the old Wobbly song could be heard rising over the clamour—sung not sadly as the funereal dirge it sometimes became, but with a jaunty tempo as an affirmation of the rebel spirit:

Hallelujah! I'm a bum
Hallelujah! bum again
Hallelujah! give us a handout
To relieve us from pain.[47]

5

Communism goes bush

By 1925 the hopes of the founders of the Communist Party of Australia were dashed. The coalition of socialists, industrial activists and Trades Hall Reds who had gathered in 1920 under the banner of the Russian Revolution was in disarray. The subordination of older forms of industrial militancy to the new conception of the vanguard party had proved no more successful than the attempt of that party to infiltrate, white-ant and capture the chief organisations of the labour movement. Neither strategy worked because, apart from defects in their execution, both were pulling against an insistent tide. At the end of the war the government had embarked on an ambitious programme of economic development. Overseas borrowing financed rural settlement schemes and associated construction projects; exports of primary products increased; new secondary industries benefited from increased levels of protection to produce new products for domestic consumers; wage rates increased. Poverty, unemployment and chronic insecurity still blighted the lives of manual labourers and their dependants, for the economic change actually reduced the demand for the unskilled, itinerant worker who followed the seasonal patterns of the pick-up, yet the circumstances of such battlers seemed increasingly marginal to the suburban majority. Whereas the communists addressed their revolutionary rhetoric to this sharply delineated audience, the broader labour movement was drawing back from its recent experiments with direct action and anti-capitalist rhetoric into the familiar, safe forms of industrial arbitration and piecemeal reform by electoral politics. With the consequent closure of boundaries that just a few years earlier had been open and fluid, the communists were left as an ineffectual rump. Of the founders, Simonoff and Earsman had left the country, while Garden was drawn in the wake of his Trades Hall Reds towards a necessary accommodation with the state Labor government. Outside Sydney, the turnover of enthusiasts through small and unstable branches that formed and dissolved only emphasised the predicament of Australian communism.

The party was shaped by its beleaguered condition. From its formation it was subjected to the same official surveillance that had operated during the war to censor publications, intercept correspondence, monitor meetings, suborn informants, prosecute speakers, restrict overseas travel and expel aliens. Just as Simonoff had been imprisoned and Freeman deported, so Dora Montefiore was permitted to enter Australia in 1922 only after she surrendered her passport and promised not to engage in communist propaganda. Other communist emissaries during the early 1920s were deported as soon as they were detected.[1] Tom Payne was prosecuted and fined for misuse of a borrowed passport upon his return to Australia from the Fourth Congress of the Communist International. The amended Commonwealth Crimes Act of 1920 codified a number of offences previously dealt with under the emergency War Precautions legislation; under its provisions it was a seditious offence to write, publish or utter words intended to bring the King into hatred or contempt, to excite disaffection against the government or the constitution, or even to promote ill will and hostility between different classes of His Majesty's subjects so as to endanger the peace, order or good government of the Commonwealth. Amendments to the Immigration Act in the same year provided for the exclusion or deportation of any person who advocated the overthrow by force or violence the established government of the Commonwealth, or of any state, or of any other civilised country, with additional legislation to cover passports and registration of aliens. Customs regulations were widened in 1921 to impose the same rubric on the importation of literature; these allowed the Commonwealth to seize a wide variety of communist publications, and by 1926 over a hundred titles were listed. While complete prohibition was impossible to enforce, there was a distinct dearth of Marxist and Leninist texts.[2]

No prosecution for sedition was brought during this period; rather the Commonwealth government exploited the danger of communism to encourage a climate of repressive conservatism. Ironically, it was the notoriety of two non-communists that occasioned a far more intense offensive against the communist menace in Australia. The ex-communist president of the Seamen's Union, Tom Walsh, and its secretary, Jacob Johnson, made easy scapegoats for the recurrent stoppages of maritime transport. Both were born outside Australia, both vehement in their revolutionary rhetoric. In 1925 the Commonwealth government amended the Immigration Act to provide for the deportation of persons not born in Australia who obstructed transport and whose presence was injurious to peace, order and good government. When Walsh and Johnson supported the British seamen's strike in August, they were arrested, brought before a special board and sentenced to deportation. The hearing coincided with a federal election that the government turned into an anti-communist crusade. The prime minister, S. M. Bruce, led off with a warning of how the unions had been captured by 'wreckers who would plunge us into the chaos and misery of class war'. Since the Labor Party was incapable of ridding itself of the extremists, 'the canker of these men advocating Communistic doctrines must be cut out of our National life'. The National Party organisation furnished its candidates with a litany of Bolshevik evils garnished by long quotations of Garden's boasts in Moscow. The government won a decisive victory at the polls, but it was rebuffed by the High Court which in December 1925 found that the deportations were unconstitutional. Bruce therefore turned to a new attorney-general, John Latham.[3]

Latham brought a formidable zeal to his office. A precise, cold man of stern rectitude (he had in his youth worked with Bob Ross in the Victorian Rationalist Society), his experience during the war as a naval intelligence officer and then a participant in the Paris peace conference had convinced him of the gravity of the communist danger to the rule of law in national and international affairs. He worked closely with the Investigation Branch of his department, which carried prime responsibility for political surveillance. He systematically read the files prepared by the head of that section, annotated them and despatched them to the solicitor-general for prosecution. Since the fomenters of unrest were 'not open to intellectual conviction', he reasoned, 'they require criminal conviction'. His redrafting of the Crimes Act in 1926 broadened the definition of unlawful activity and unlawful association to an unprecedented degree. It imposed new penal sanctions on strikers and caused the Communist Party executive to prepare for underground activity. Latham toyed with more drastic measures: his friend Robert Garran, the solicitor-general, had to advise him that even the amended Crimes Act would not justify the closing down of the Communist Hall in Sussex Street.[4]

The increased vigilance of the Australian government coincided with an intensification by the British government of its security measures against Soviet intelligence activities in that country. This severed the lines of communication between the Australian party and the Communist International, and stopped the transfer of money through British banks. Richard Casey, a young protégé of S. M. Bruce who was serving as the Australian liaison officer in Whitehall, sent a regular flow of British intelligence information back to Latham, so that prospective migrants suspected of communist sympathies could be investigated and kept out of Australia.[5] Meanwhile state police forces and municipal authorities imposed a variety of additional restrictions on communist activity, while right-wing movements combined quasi-military preparations with a public crusade against the red menace.[6]

Official repression was a lesser discouragement than the unofficial vilification and harassment, for the usual effect of constant surveillance, censorship and prosecution was to strengthen the conviction of communists that their class war was just and their sacrifices worthwhile. Did not the attention they attracted confirm the significance of this small group of beleaguered activists? More than this, the officers of the Investigation Branch of the Attorney-General's Department echoed the charged imagery of the communists. The activists they described in their detailed files were potent, indefatigable, infinitely resourceful, limitless in their capacity to inflame and suborn loyalties. Noteworthy in the conspiratorial fantasies of the

Investigation Branch was the Secret Seven, 'the most silent, militant and dangerous of the forces now working in Australia'. Despite the name, its membership, according to the Investigation Branch, was elastic and omnipresent, it commanded silent assent by means of the password 'kismet' and used the 'germ cell system' invented in Moscow to worm its way into the unions and the Labor Party.[7]

Here also was a vindication of the party and the demands it imposed. When Guido Baracchi resigned in 1925 he said that the members of the Communist Party were the best comrades in the movement but the party itself a tragic farce. When Esmonde Higgins related the abject state of Australian communism at this juncture, he observed that the dispirited members clung all the more tightly to their identity. 'All we can do is keep chattering the name "Communist Party".'[8] That the name and the identity should have already assumed such talismanic significance is hardly surprising—after all, the competition to secure the title had occupied Australian communists for the best part of two years. Membership of the Communist International and association with its legendary heroes conferred a surrogate prestige on the Australian adherents, just as overseas successes compensated for unavailing local sacrifice. Long before the Australian party adopted the Bolshevik model of organisation, it was extolling the 'marvellous power of discipline' which gave 'life and power' to dormant energies.[9]

The earlier socialist sects had drawn their adherents into an enclosed world of cultural meaning marked out in language and ritual that offered them the reassurance of dogmatic certainty in return for the rigours of evangelical effort. The Communist Party took over that temper but tightened its effects with two additional twists. The first was foreshadowed in the original manifesto of the provisional executive: 'The Communist Party is essentially a fighting organisation and not a debating club.' The success of the Bolsheviks was taken to validate Lenin's insistence on the need to seize the revolutionary opportunity; the split in the ranks of the pre-war socialist international was seen as distinguishing those who made revolution from those who merely talked of one. Earlier socialists had observed ineluctable laws of historical materialism that would in the fullness of social evolution exhaust capitalism and bring the working class to an appreciation of its mission, a process that the socialists might hasten through propaganda and education but could not anticipate until the time was ripe. Comrade History had been their mentor and their solace, as he was for some of the CPA founders—in 1923 a whole issue of the theoretical monthly, *Proletarian*, was given over to an unshakeably fatalist exposition of the materialist conception of history. Stolid Jack Howie was notorious for interrupting party discussion in deeply sorrowful tones with the reminder, 'Ah, no, comrades, we will not decide, mater-r-r-ial conditions will decide'. Henceforth deeds displaced words as the revolutionary hallmark.[10]

If the working class had to be snatched from the grip of economist and reformist illusions and directed into action, it followed that the role of the guiding intelligence was crucial. From the vanguard conception of the revolutionary party came the insistence on a single-minded unity of purpose maintained by an 'iron discipline'. As early as 1921 Australian communists distinguished the military principles of their organisation from the laxity of its predecessors: 'An army is only a body of men before it goes into action', wrote Carl Baker. 'It then depends entirely on its training, its discipline . . .'[11] Just as the new party superimposed the hammer and sickle onto the red flag, so it grafted a martial vocabulary onto classical Marxism. To the sociological categories of the bourgeoisie and the proletariat it added the organisational concepts of the vanguard and the masses, and these in turn generated a veritable litany of infractions that the rank and file must avoid: adventurism and tailism, opportunism and liquidationism. The arcane dialect reassured its users that they were marching to the drumbeat of destiny, even if others could not hear it. Sometimes the language of communism lent itself to unfortunate misunderstanding: thus Guido Baracchi's story of the wife of a comrade who heard her husband described as a fine class-conscious proletarian and rose indignantly to retort, 'I think you're class conscious yourself'.[12] Other phrases, 'the dictatorship of the proletariat' is an obvious example, had resonances that were exploited by those who wished to discredit communism as an alien tyranny.

This was the second novel feature of communism: its foreign provenance. In a period when Australia was retreating into monocultural fortifications, with economic and defence arrangements tied closely to the British Empire as a bulwark against postwar uncertainties, and population policies and cultural institutions designed to resist the menace of cosmopolitan modernity, the Russian Revolution embodied all the evils of the age. It was brutal, atavistic, levelling, irreligious, menacing, licentious. The persistent reports that the communists had abolished marriage and nationalised women in Russia exercised a particular fascination during the immediate post-revolutionary period, speaking to the fantasies of men who upheld monogamy as a bulwark of patriarchal order. The Bolshevik leaders were commonly portrayed as Jewish degenerates with brutal Cossacks at their command; their call for world revolution and colonial liberation threatened a lapse into barbarism. Thus the Nationalist government's 1925 election poster of whiskered Bolsheviks firing into an Australian church and slaughtering the congregation tapped the fear of alien assaults on property, family, Christianity and national security. Such images drew their force partly from Australia's historical location as a colonial nation and partly from racial fears unleashed by the recent war. Their potency was demonstrated in the red flag riots of 1919, when loyalist ex-servicemen attacked the Russian community of Brisbane; in the defence of the Union Jack at the Sydney Domain in May 1921; and in inflammatory confrontations of a similar nature conducted in other parts of the country during the postwar period. They are central to the clash of right and left depicted by D. H. Lawrence in his novel of a postwar Australia in which violence lies close to the surface of a brooding lethargy. The novel, *Kangaroo*, culminates in a pitched battle as ex-servicemen invade a communist meeting:

> The red flag suddenly flashing like blood, and bellowing rage at the sight of it. A Union Jack torn to fragments stamped upon. A mob with many different centres, some fighting frenziedly around a red flag, some clutching fragments of the Union Jack, as if it were God incarnate.

Throughout the 1920s the Nationalist Party fanned the embers with its pamphlet *Under Which Flag?* Should it be the international banner of revolt or the emblem of King and Empire?[13]

Yet the nation that these anxious conservatives defended was only one of several variations on the identity of a country with an ethnic and social composition far more heterogeneous than the repressive monoculturalists acknowledged. The individual communists so far identified in this history attest to a diversity of origins and destinations, with a considerable range of attachments and a keen awareness of international events. The initial local interest in the Soviet experiment is indicated by the sales of left-wing literature in the township of Kurri Kurri on the northern New South Wales coalfield late in 1921. Alongside the sales of Marxist classics—ten copies of Marx and Engels' *Communist Manifesto*, three copies of Marx's *Value, Price and Profit*, one of his *Wage Labour and Capital* and eight of Engels's *Socialism, Utopian and Scientific*—there were 22 copies of the report of the *British Delegation in Red Petrograd*, eleven of *Australia and the World Revolution*, five of Lenin's *State and Revolution*, two of his *Left-Wing Communism* and 21 of Alexandra Kollontai's *Communism and the Family*.[14] Australian communists made no excuse for their decision to take the Moscow road. On the contrary, they rejoiced in the Russian communists' conquest of power, celebrated the transformation of life in the Soviet Union, rebutted all suggestions of error or excess, defended its repression of dissent, and did what they could to collect aid for its reconstruction after famine and civil war.[15]

A common topic for debate during these early years while such orderly disputation between different sections of the left could still occur was 'That the Australian workers to achieve their emancipation must follow the methods adopted by the Russian workers'.[16] The proposition called for a different mode of argument from that which communists used in response to conservative denigration. Many in the labour movement concurred with Bob Ross in his sympathy for the Russian communists in their overthrow of Tsarist autocracy but denial of the relevance of such methods in Australia where civil liberties and democratic practices allowed for a peaceful transition. The usual response was to defend the general applicability of Lenin's analysis of late capitalism while acknowledging that Australia's particular circumstances would affect its implementation. Communists understood the political circumstances not as a refutation of the Leninist insistence on a revolutionary seizure of power—for Australian communists insisted that parliamentary government was a sham, the much-vaunted rule of law a cloak for capitalist dictatorship—but rather as a set of pernicious illusions that bamboozled Australian workers. In this reading of national differences, Russia led the way precisely because of the backwardness of its bourgeois democracy.

Such an estimate reversed the evolutionary perspective of earlier socialists who had assumed that the advanced capitalist countries were pioneering a route that more backward ones would follow. Australia, with its well-established unions and electorally successful Labor Party, had once been regarded as a social laboratory where workers could use their freedom to experiment with devices that would abolish hardship and insecurity. Now that reassuring self-image had to be revised. An early editorial in the party paper, *Communist*, gave this reformulation:

> We in Australia are fortunate. From Australia we can survey the whole world. We can see the revolutionary struggle of the world's proletariat as one standing on a hill and looking down into a valley. We have the writings of Marx, Engels, Lenin and all other Communist writers in our hands. We are able to profit by the experiences of the Russian workers, of the German workers, of the Italian workers, of the English workers, and last but not least, of our own experience.[17]

But perhaps last *was* least. The negligible size of the Communist Party of Australia, its remoteness from the crucibles of conflict and the laggardly course of the class struggle here troubled Australian adherents. Esmonde Higgins pondered the problem for the first time while in England as he considered whether to join the Communist Party of Great Britain. He took as his starting point the belief, so influential among earlier generations of Australian visionaries, that his was a land free of the old-world evils and accordingly able to invent its own future:

> [The] Australia I once regarded as unequivocally lucky in starting free of so many shackles of tradition and free to exploit an infinitely rich and varied land, now seems to me less happy. Some day she will have to shake off capitalism but at present it seems she has to look on while others get their due.

This was an unfortunate good fortune, a land of plenty and opportunity basking in illusory content. Australia had yet to 'go through the capitalist mill'. 'She' (the feminine personification signalled Higgins emotional attachment) was 'too young, lazy, cheerful and smug'.

He concluded that he was unable to 'call myself a Communist because I feel myself an Australian'.[18] A trip to Russia resolved his doubts.

Yet as a member of the Communist Party of Great Britain Higgins merely shelved the problem of Australian communism. When he decided to return, for a mixture of personal and patriotic reasons, his friend Rajani Palme Dutt, the future pontiff of British communism, was scornful: 'Australia is an artificial closed-in box where nothing ever happens or will happen'. Higgins occupied himself on the voyage out in self-scrutiny and study. He re-read his former associate Bob Ross's *Revolution in Russia and Australia* and found it riddled with holes, yet there was still the persistent worry about the basis of Australian communism. 'In England it was easy to feel that there was an obvious necessity for Party work'; in Australia, where conditions were less stringent, it was 'still possible for workers to get something out of capitalism'.[19] Upon his arrival he was struck by the way the Australian labour movement took refuge in nationalism, trade protection and immigration restriction, fostered alliances with local manufacturers and encouraged the illusion that the country could 'reach social salvation' by isolating itself from the rest of the world. Thus the common belief of workers that they could 'purchase paradise on the instalment plan'.[20] Soon he was experiencing at first hand their unresponsiveness to the communist message, and characteristically directed his criticisms inward, to the weakness of the party and its members. It took another newcomer, unencumbered by past Australian associations, Jack Kavanagh, to propose the remedy. Kavanagh, born in Ireland, raised in England, schooled in militancy in Canada, found the Australian working class mired in the past. 'Tradition more than weighs upon them. It smothers, shackles, binds and emasculates them, and one of the first tasks of the militant worker is iconoclastic—to become a wrecker of traditions.'[21]

Kavanagh landed in Sydney on May Day of 1925 and stepped immediately into the vacuum left by the failure of Garden's united front strategy. He appears in Stead's *Seven Poor Men of Sydney* as Whiteaway, a man just come over from Canada who follows Fulke Folliot on the platform of the Communist Hall with the opening words, 'Let's talk about practical things', and within ten minutes has his audience mad with enthusiasm.[22] Kavanagh had been a leading member of the Socialist Party of Canada, which had schooled him in an amalgam of Marx, Engels, Joseph Dietzgen and Jack London, and a founder of the Canadian Communist Party: marital difficulties were the reason for his shift to Australia and he operated at first under an assumed name. Service in the British Army during the Boer War had left a deep antagonism to imperialism, militarism and racism, and as an industrial militant in Vancouver he had strenuously combated anti-Chinese agitation. His extensive experience of the three British Dominions gave him a sharp appreciation of the dynamics of settler capitalism: he quickly dismissed Australia's much-vaunted reputation as a workers' paradise, was scathing in his criticism of the stifling effects on the unions of industrial arbitration—'one is shocked by the docility manifested by the workers' organisations'—and utterly contemptuous of all dealings with the Labor Party. Just as Kavanagh's intractability provided an antidote for Garden's opportunism, so his bearing and conduct offered welcome relief from the disreputable fixer. The pince-nez, round, cherubic face, and care for his personal appearance, the assuredness and directness, all inspired confidence. There was also a flinty self-sufficiency. Kavanagh deferred to no one. In August he was coopted onto the executive; at the end of the year he chaired the party conference.[23]

The 1925 conference picked over the wreckage of the recent election results and the now complete failure to gain entry into the Labor Party. After lengthy discussion it resolved that:

> The action of the ALP in rigidly excluding the Communists from membership in that party has for the time being closed that avenue for our work and the trade union movement will be our most important field for gaining contact with the working masses to expose their reformist illusions, to unmask the reactionary leaders and to influence the workers to the conscious struggle against capitalism.

To this end the conference endorsed the industrial program of a recent conference of left-wing unionists, a £6 minimum wage 'irrespective of sex', a six-hour day, union preference, child maintenance and motherhood endowment. It confirmed the recent appointment of an industrial leader in Sydney to direct the recently formed party groups in key industries.[24]

This seemed to bring Garden's scheming within the Labor Party to an end but almost immediately he was back with a new proposal in response to a threat that the ALP disaffiliate those unions that belonged to the New South Wales Labor Council. This move by the parliamentary wing of the Labor Party against the industrial wing prompted talk of a breakaway industrial labour party, which Garden urged the Communist Party to support. The new executive with Kavanagh as its leading member condemned the proposal.[25] Then the waters were further muddied as the AWU switched its support from Jack Lang to Lang's opponents in the New South Wales parliamentary wing of the Labor Party, and Lang joined forces with Willis and Garden to shore up his position; this unlikely alliance proposed to alter the rules of the Labor Party in order to increase industrial representation. That prospect did interest the communist executive since the new rules would allow unions a free choice of delegates to ALP conferences and thus reopen the door to communists. So Garden secured the backing of the Communist Party, only to drop the vital rule change at a special conference of the New South Wales branch of the Labor Party in November 1926. On 7 December Garden was required by the Communist Party Executive to explain a reported statement in the *Labor Daily* that he was not a member of the Communist Party. On the following day he announced his resignation. Two days later in the *Workers' Weekly* the party announced his expulsion.[26]

So ended the communist career of the last of the party's founders. As secretary of the Labor Council he went on to become Lang's lieutenant, and continued to tap the stream of popular working-class radicalism by promoting Lang's 1930 election campaign with the slogan, 'Lang is Greater than Lenin'. Subsequently he was elected to federal parliament, fell out with Lang, lost his preselection, worked for Eddie Ward in the Curtin and Chifley ministries, was found guilty and then acquitted of corrupt business dealings, ran racehorses as well as an astrology publication, and remained a plausible rogue to the last. His service to the party had hardly been more consistent. But the Communist Party of Australia was not yet rid of Garden. In its radical enthusiasm for peace and an end to imperialist warmongering, the All-Australian Trade Union Conference of 1921 had proposed a Pan-Pacific Trade Union movement. Garden and Earsman had taken up the idea and interested the Communist International in it while in Moscow in 1922. It was scarcely high on Garden's list of priorities though it attracted considerable notoriety in 1925. The Nationalist Party made great play of the threat to White Australia during federal elections in that year with a photograph of Garden, Earsman and Tom Payne alongside Ho Chi Minh and other delegates from India, Vietnam, China and Japan at the Fourth Congress of the Comintern. The *Labor Daily* brazenly denounced the photograph as a forgery and published its own version that cropped Garden and Payne, and disguised Earsman with extra hair and a moustache. Despite pressure from party comrades to affirm the genuine record of revolutionary internationalism, Jock remained silent.[27]

In 1926 the New South Wales Labor Council did persuade another Australian trade union conference to support the formation of the Pan-Pacific Trade Union organisation. A conference of the PPTU followed in China in 1927, and the newly formed Australian Council of Trade Unions agreed to affiliate to it.[28] As the chief Australian figure in the PPTU and editor of its newspaper, the *Pan-Pacific Worker*, Garden was a far more important ally of the Communist International than the tiny Communist Party of Australia was and accordingly he remained a member of the RILU executive despite his expulsion from the party. Furthermore, he arranged for the ACTU to employ an able young communist, Jack Ryan, as its representative on the PPTU secretariat. For that matter, Jack Kavanagh owed his job as an organiser for the Labor Council to Garden.[29] So while Jock was denounced for his vanity, careerism and opportunism, the party gave former comrade Garden considerable organisational latitude. He was allowed to debate his expulsion with Kavanagh (proposition: 'That the present central executive has deviated from the Leninist policy') and the *Workers' Weekly* published several articles from him during 1927 arguing that Australian communists had lapsed into a 'pure infantile sickness'. He was permitted to claim—and it says much for the freedom of discussion at this time that he enjoyed such licence—that the Communist Party was 'suspended in the air' and 'absolutely isolated from the masses'.[30]

It was certainly an attenuated group of delegates that assembled in December 1925. Few of the familiar Sydney members were present after the exodus of the Trades Hall Reds, though a Balmain group of fifteen still operated and Pat Drew had established a new group of eight at Hurstville. There were also two additional groups of Russian and Greek communists, a cricket team of each.[31] From Perth came Christian Jollie Smith's old Melbourne friend, Katharine Susannah Prichard, who had moved west with her husband Hugo Throssell in 1919 and joined the party on its formation, but she and her friend George Ryce were at loggerheads with the other two Perth members who scorned the united front.[32] Melbourne also suffered from chronic factionalism. The branch had re-formed late in 1924 against the opposition of Percy Laidler and other former communists who operated as a Labor Propaganda Group in the unions and ran the Trades Hall's Labor College. Efforts to establish an effective party presence in Melbourne were hindered by conflict between Bob Brodney, now married to May Francis, and Joe Shelley, a German firebrand who had arrived from the west. The Brodneys competed with Laidler to cultivate the united front through educational work (and were assisted by their friendship with the popular Labor leftist Maurice Blackburn), while Shelley, who had been interned during the war for IWW activity, engaged in more forthright agitation among the unemployed. After the Brodneys and their supporters resigned from the new party in April 1925, the rump of some 30 members was completely isolated from the ALP and Trades Hall Council.[33]

There was no delegate from Adelaide to the 1925 conference, that branch having collapsed the previous year. Brisbane again sent J. B. Miles (the observer of Sussex Street and Liverpool Street operations), who, with the recently arrived Bert Moxon, was the driving force in a branch of 35, the largest after Sydney. Queensland presented more favourable opportunities than existed down south since its Labor government, in office for a decade and increasingly dominated by the right-wing AWU, had estranged left-wing unions. In accordance with the united front, Brisbane communists pursued entry to the ALP though the unions, but were repulsed along with their allies at the ALP state conference in 1925. The subsequent disaffiliation of the Australian Railways Union consolidated right-wing control of the ALP in that state and of the Brisbane Trades and Labor Council, which expelled the communists from their office in the Trades Hall.[34] A smaller Ipswich branch of fifteen was formed in 1925 and a tour of northern Queensland by Norm Jeffery as the party organiser resulted in the revival of the Cairns branch (of seventeen) and the formation of a new one in the inland pastoral centre of Blackall (with seven members).[35]

On the New South Wales coalfields small branches had formed at West Maitland, Kurri Kurri and Cessnock but they languished after the communist intervention in the 1923 lockout; there were just six Communist Party members in all three towns by the end of 1925. The arrival of Hetty and Hector Ross brought a few recruits in the Hunter Valley. Hetty was a spirited young schoolteacher, originally from New Zealand where, as Hedwig Weitzel, she had been expelled from the Wellington teachers' college for communist activity; she was posted as a teacher in 1924 from Sydney to Newcastle. Fair-haired and diminutive, a 'Jenny Wren with sparkling eyes', she was indomitable. Hector was a former dancing champion, graceful, idealistic but somewhat humourless ('the noble Hector', she dubbed him) who followed her from Sydney to Newcastle, until they both returned to Sydney in the second half of 1925 to edit the party newspaper and revive the Young Comrades Club.[36] The Newcastle branch (ten members) was represented at the 1925 conference, as was a Wollongong branch of six.

The most successful of these non-metropolitan outposts was Lithgow. With its coalmines, pottery works, meatworks, coke ovens, blast furnaces, steelworks and small-arms factory, this isolated town of less than 10 000 inhabitants was a crucible of interwar industrial expansion. In the miners' lodge Charlie Nelson was the catalyst. He was a Scots hewer steeped in the socialist knowledge of the Plebs

League, an organisation formed in Britain to promote independent working-class education which had been brought with its practitioners to the New South Wales coalfields.[37] Tall, spare, with a jutting chin, Nelson was a fluent speaker and patient proselytiser of the younger men, among them three who would rise to leading positions in the Communist Party. Two were workmates, drawn like Nelson from the British coalfields. Fred Airey, a lanky Geordie who later changed his name to Jack Blake, was just sixteen when Nelson approached him at the pit-cage with a brown-paper parcel and the instructions, 'Don't turn the page corners down'. Inside was a copy of Edward Bellamy's *Looking Backward*, and as soon as Airey finished it, he was given another book to read, and another as Nelson opened a whole realm of ideas to him.[38] Bill Orr, from Lanarkshire in Scotland, was already in his mid-twenties, and more practically inclined than Nelson, but he too had the itch to understand.[39] Orr boarded in the home of Clifton Walker, a railway clerk who later changed his name to Richard Dixon, and was at first inclined to scoff at these earnest young men who gave up their leisure to study in the Plebs League class, but he too was drawn into the party branch and eventually became the most rigidly orthodox of the three.[40]

Other Lithgow members included Jock Lindop and Jock Jamieson, also Scots, and Harry den Hartog, a young Dutchman who had jumped ship in Fremantle in 1923. He came to Lithgow with Jock Jamieson and found work in Hoskins' steel furnace; later he would move to Melbourne, buttle and achieve modest success as an artist.[41] Though den Hartog was a union delegate in Lithgow, the steelworks were less fertile territory for the party, the Ironworkers' Association subject to high turnover and victimisation as its owners sought to compete with the larger and more efficient BHP plant in Newcastle. The party branch was not large, numbering just ten in early 1926, but it benefited from the closeness and intimacy of this working-class locality to build a broader united front. It sustained a breadth of activities beyond most others, and its members showed an imaginative vitality, captured in a contribution to *Workers' Weekly* that imagined a future May Day: Ike the Red returned with his swag to Lithgow to find red bunting sprinkling the main street. When he made his way to the steelworks in search of a job, he discovered the tyrannical foreman was wielding a pick in the pit and Hoskins, the owner, was pushing a broom. His old mate Jock, once a red ragger, now ran the plant on a six-hour shift. It was a scene of happy faces and purposeful labour, until Ike's alarm wakened him for the 11 p.m. shift. 'Comrades', he concluded, 'when will you help to make my dream come true? Join the Communist Party—NOW'.[42]

Some did in other localities as well as Lithgow during 1926, and a few more in the following year as the national party began to make way. It was a slow, faltering progress with more opportunities lost than taken, and many of the initiatives that the party advertised were scarcely more than pious declarations. The basis of activity, as foreshadowed in the resolution of the 1925 conference, was in the trade unions. The emphasis was on rank-and-file agitation on the worksite, in contrast to Garden's previous practice of cultivating the full-time officials who hung about Trades Hall. This change of approach was in accordance with the Comintern's call to detach the workers from the deadening control of their treacherous leaders. The lesson the party drew from Garden's adventurism was that 'certain comrades . . . in their anxiety to gain small successes in the trade union movement' had so neglected the task of militant leadership that they had 'apparently isolated us from the rank and file'. So determined was Kavanagh to guard against this opportunistic tendency that he persuaded the executive in June 1926 to actively discourage members from seeking union office unless there was a clear demand to elect them. 'While little militancy existed the task of Party members was to function as a centre of militancy opposed to the reactionary officials.'[43] The function was to be performed by party members working as 'nuclei' within their workplaces and as 'fractions' within their unions, under the supervision of the executive's trade union organiser. Eight such nuclei were formed in Sydney to cover transport, metal, clerical, clothing, printing and miscellaneous workers, the building trades and the AWU. Only the last two actually functioned. There was also a Trade Union Educational League, established in January 1926 ('Objective: To unite all militant workers in the every day struggle against capitalism'), but beyond Sydney and the coalfields it hardly got off the ground.[44]

An alternative approach to the task of building a broader left-wing industrial movement came from the Lithgow branch, which initiated a Miners' Minority Movement on the British model with which recent immigrants were familiar, a model that emphasised the particular industrial interests of a single occupational grouping. The movement was established in October 1926 with representatives of the three New South Wales coalfields under the leadership of Bill Orr and quickly exerted an influence within the union.[45] The differences in organisation and approach between the communist miners and communist unionists in Sydney were marked and of considerable significance. The miners could contest for control of their union, the party unionists in Sydney could not because Garden's Labor Council was still affiliated to the RILU and thus immune from communist challenge. Kavanagh's rhetoric merely embellished the fact that Garden remained more important to Moscow than the Communist Party of Australia.

The party renovated its own organisation. Members of the executive assumed responsibility for particular areas of activity, training, industrial work, the press, women and internal administration. Norm Jeffery was employed as a national organiser and sent first to Queensland and later New Zealand until lack of money forced his resignation in August 1926. Jeffery was a former Wobbly and founder-member of the party, notable for his bow tie, capable on the soapbox, courageous, a willing workhorse. Tom Wright maintained the executive minutes and correspondence more systematically than they had been, despite his repeated complaints of delinquent correspondents and inactive branches. He was yet another of the Scots who were so prominent in the party's early history: methodical, conscientious and loyal to a fault. The party finally bought its own printing press in 1927. Jack Kavanagh established three classes in Marxist theory early in 1926 and began the preparation of a syllabus that was serialised in the newspaper in early 1927, then revised and published as the *Party Training Manual*. The Young Communist League and Young Communist Children groups, which had lapsed after early activity, were revived.

A women's group was re-established in Sydney in 1926, and in 1927 a women's department of the executive began to organise women's study circles, train speakers, maintain a column in the

The Young Comrades' Club was formed in 1927, reviving earlier initiatives to establish a children's group. The children's corner in the party press regularly used this illustration. In contrast to the adult imagery of a world bound in capitalist chains, here the children from various countries form a circle of friendship around it. (Source: 'Workers' Weekly', 9 September 1927)

newspaper and recruit 'working class women' into a Militant Women's Group on the same united front principles as the industrial fronts. Since potential recruits were 'afraid of the Communist movement', it met in Trades Hall.[46] International Women's Day became part of the left calendar along with May Day, the anniversary of the Russian Revolution in October, Lenin Enrolment Week in January and various other moveable feasts—Hands Off China, rallies against the sentence of death imposed on the American anarchists Sacco and Vanzetti (until those victims of the class war were executed in August 1927), protests against fascist atrocities in Italy and Latvia, prison horrors in Poland, the British government's repression of the General Strike, and corresponding campaigns for the various international appeals of the Workers' International Relief and International Red Aid organisations. The Australians received additional subventions from these auxiliaries of the Communist International, though such payments were often swallowed up in the running expenses of a party that remained chronically short of funds.[47]

From 1927, on the instruction of the Communist International, these activities were coordinated by formal departments of the executive, a political bureau, an organisational bureau, and an agitation and propaganda department, abbreviated to the politbureau, the orgbureau and agitprop. A Control Commission was also created late in 1927 to safeguard the party from splitters and dissidents.

Agitprop, signifying agitation and propaganda, was a new name for the familiar steps whereby the left endeavoured to mobilise support: the initiative with its appropriate 'line' determined within the party and members assigned to its implementation; an organising committee, with a leavening of credible union or Labor Party sympathisers; a rally, with communist and non-communist speakers, leaflets and press articles, leading to the endorsement of predetermined resolutions and demands, all recycling a familiar language of solidarity in the class struggle among greater or lesser audiences. This form of united front activity suffered from an inherent dilemma: for the united front to flourish, it had to allow for diverse views that might well give it a life of its own. That was hardly a danger in these early ventures, since the tight control meant a repetitive, flat sameness. Higgins noted new faces and an increased level of activity when he returned to Sydney in July 1926, but he also observed the mechanical, unthinking nature of the ceaseless tasks, the 'reliance on generalities and jargon learned from *Inprecorr*, that is applicable to European parties but is cant here'. An organiser scarcely exaggerated when he observed that the slogan 'Hands Off—' could be completed by almost any object. The constant round of activity imposed a heavy toll on the desperately small numbers who reassembled so often under different roles.[48]

Still, as older comrades dropped away, recruits took their place. The precise numbers are difficult to establish since (in the absence of financial statements after 1925) branch reports to Sydney and Sydney reports to Moscow are the only available sources, and these always erred on the side of optimism. For what they are worth, the party claimed 300 members by late 1927 and 500 early in the following year, figures which were too optimistic by more than half but indicated the upward trend. Existing branches consolidated, Sydney at 100, Lithgow at 21, Brisbane 30 and Melbourne 36, while there was remarkable growth in north Queensland.[49] Reports of the increased activity in Melbourne can be supplemented by the atmospheric account given 50 years later by Judah Waten in his novel *Scenes of Revolutionary Life*. Waten was a young firebrand and aspirant writer who moved from Western Australia to Melbourne in 1926 and was taken up by Joe Shelley. In contrast with Shelley's report as group leader to the 1927 party conference of trade union work, propaganda activities, regular classes, literature sales, a new headquarters in Russell Street and even a workers' club library, Waten's novel describes a group of beleaguered enthusiasts. He composed his scenes both retrospectively and fictively, in the social-realist mode, through the recollections of an aged communist in an era of yuppie excess who looks back on his youthful dreams. The great majority of the inhabitants of 'dour, hushed Melbourne' during 1927 go about their business, either heedless or hostile; but on the northern fringe of the city centre there is a bohemian quarter of Chinese restaurants, brothels, a temperance hall and evangelical chapels, pawnbrokers and the Salvation Army, and here the communists operate. They declaim and flog the *Workers' Weekly*, argue with the police and hold a concert to mark the hundredth anniversary of Beethoven's death, in a way of life that is quite autonomous and makes no reference to Trades Hall or the Labor Party. They are a disparate group, a frail returned digger, a muscular Scottish blacksmith, an unemployed wharfie, a stern old German woman, a larrikin, and the principal character, a spoiled young man with literary ambitions, all joined by a shared faith in the future.[50]

They were not entirely alone. In 1927 Waten wrote on behalf of the Melbourne branch to Arthur Calwell, then a leading member of the ALP in Victoria, and invited him to lecture on the topic, 'Can a Labor government abolish the capitalist system?'. Calwell made no reply. Yet a year later, when Waten—identified in the press as 'a young curly-headed Russian' with a red handkerchief in his breast pocket—appeared in court on a charge of having distributed communist pamphlets during the Anzac Day procession, he was defended by the then president of ALP state executive, who also paid his fine. Waten's political and literary aspirations were nourished by his discovery of a revolutionary tradition. In Melbourne he knew a chemist whose French father had been a Communard exiled to New Caledonia. He found old English socialists who had known Frederick Engels and William Morris, and sought out former associates of the VSP organiser Tom Mann, and Monty Miller of Eureka fame. Just as the Beethoven centenary that Waten organised sought to ground revolutionary politics in artistic creativity, so his historical interests joined a lineage of heroic struggle to the promised future.[51]

Who were these communists? The evidence is incomplete, the patterns subject to local variation as Waten's sketch suggests. Yet in the shifting mosaic of argument and activity it is possible to discern some recurrent characteristics. The party defined itself by class, sex and race as a movement of Australian male workers, and each of these designations raised issues of political substance in the later 1920s.

What is the social composition of your party, the Australian delegate to the Comintern was asked in 1926? 'The social composition is entirely proletarian', Hector Ross replied. 'There was a bourgeois element but they have entirely left us now.'[52] This characterisation was inherent in the turn to the masses announced at the end of 1925, which heralded a cult of proletarian virtue. It was not altogether new. Communism, after all, rested on a class analysis of politics that contrasted the clear unity of interest of those who lived by the sale of their labour with the weak and vacillating tendency of sympathisers who attached themselves to that cause. A doctrine that placed such emphasis on the extraction of surplus value as the dynamic of history and determinant of class identity caused considerable difficulties for those outside the ranks of the wage-earners: witness Tom Payne, a cobbler, who had to be convinced by Guido Baracchi that he too was exploited by his leather supplier and landlord. In one of his recurrent bouts of self-recrimination, a year earlier Esmonde Higgins, that prisoner of the middle-class conscience, compared his personal frailties with the sterling qualities of the British boilermaker Harry Pollitt. He was lazy, bookish, feckless, untrained in useful skills and susceptible to 'fags, bed, booze'; Harry was confident, shrewd, resourceful and full of 'physical well-being'.[53]

In its literature and iconography the party systematised these attributes ever more insistently into essential differences: the bone-head worker became the instinctive rebel, and Mr Fat the Capitalist was joined in the communist demonology by the timorous, doubting intellectual. The three departed representatives of the bourgeoisie Ross identified in 1926 were Baker, Baracchi and Higgins. Baker, an optometrist, had taken money from customers and done a bunk, 'just when we needed him most'. Baracchi, a man of considerable inherited wealth, stood condemned as a liquidationist, while Higgins had resigned the editorship of *Workers' Weekly* to look for work interstate. This exemplification of the logic of capitalism might seem to exonerate its victim, but Ross was adamant: 'We do not condone his action because he left us at a time when we were fighting very bitterly'. That middle-class communists were unreliable was the chief lesson of the party's early history, an attitude reinforced by Jack Kavanagh's insistence on the necessity of working-class knowledge.

The party inherited a well-established tradition of intellectual improvement, one that combined fiction, verse, philosophy, history and economics as sources of inspiration and understanding. Any serious pre-war socialist assembled a library, read widely and studied the classic texts closely, for knowledge was the key to a new order. Paine, Carlyle, Ruskin, Darwin and Huxley were as influential as Marx and Engels in the project to emancipate humanity from the tyranny of superstition; Shelley, Dickens, Hugo, Zola, Morris, and later, Robert Tressall, Jack London and Upton Sinclair fed the imagination of activists along with William Lane, Henry Lawson and Bernard O'Dowd. The founders of the CPA were steeped in this tradition, and a number had helped to initiate the labour college movement as a vehicle for working-class education. These labour colleges in Melbourne, Sydney and Brisbane, along with the associated Plebs League on the coalfields, fostered an autonomous and politically pointed curriculum in opposition to the reformist Workers' Educational Association and other university extension initatives: thus in 1924 a party member who conducted a Plebs League class at Kurri Kurri reported to the *Workers' Weekly* that his best student had been presented with two volumes of Joseph Dietzgen, the German working-class writer who enjoyed a particular following for his extension of Marxist dialectics into an all-encompassing working-class philosophy.[54]

Even when the labour colleges slipped out of its control in the 1920s, the party continued to employ a similar syllabus in its own classes. Onto a curriculum of the standard editions of the American publishing house Charles H. Kerr, and the textbooks and magazines of the British labour college movement, it simply added Lenin's polemical pamphlets. There was disagreement over the importance of such education. Some objected that 'hair splitting discussions on Marxian Economics' distracted from practical revolutionary activity; others regretted that 'the theoretical side has gone to blazes'. Under the leadership of Jack Kavanagh there was an effort to remedy any theoretical weakness. The party newspaper commenced a monthly 'Theory Page' in 1926; in 1927 it serialised Stalin's codification of *The Theory and Practice of Leninism*; in 1928 the party published its *Training Manual*, adapted by Esmonde Higgins from that of the Communist Party of Great Britain. The change in terminology, from 'education' to 'training', was telling. Classes were now conducted by an 'instructor' and the instructor was himself instructed that he 'must at all times be clear where he is leading the discussion and see that it reaches the right conclusion'. There was still some toleration of diversity. Sidney and Beatrice Webb, G. D. H. Cole and the British ex-communists Mark Starr and Raymond Postgate were listed in class bibliographies along with Lenin, Bukharin and Bogdanov. Vere Gordon Childe, J. T. Sutcliffe and even the Labor renegade W. G. Spence were cited as sources for Australian labour history. But training was single-minded in its emphasis on party needs. The earlier quest for understanding narrowed into a self-sufficient repertoire of the knowledge necessary to be an effective communist.[55]

The simplified and didactic *Party Training Manual* is, however, an unreliable guide to the rich and diverse intellectual culture of Australian communism. Behind it lay a variety of oral and literary practices, allusions and points of reference that sustained the mental world of working-class radicalism in which party members were formed. At a time when few working-class children stayed on at school past their early teens, the inquisitive satisfied their hunger for knowledge with their own reading. Newspapers, magazines, pamphlets and books circulated on worksites; enthusiasms were shared and ideas debated in a community of print. The intense effort to sustain a labour press, the recurrent battles over censorship, the literary endeavours of middle-class reformers and even the arguments over the extent and purpose of public education during the early decades of the twentieth century marked out a cultural contest between the received authority of higher learning and a separately constituted, jealously defended repertoire of knowledge that gave meaning and direction to radical activity.

The communist was also manly. The cult of the resolute proletarian defending his manhood was counterpointed by the persistent difficulty of the party in attracting female comrades and defining their role. 'The conditions under which the working class lived in Australia are relative to the rest of the world so good that Communist work is in general very difficult', explained Hetty Ross in her report as women's organiser to the Communist International in 1927, and added: 'This is specially so among women'. The only evidence she adduced for this assertion was Australian women's enjoyment of the suffrage and the institution of the family wage, which freed most women from wage labour.[56] Communist appeals to women took up their concerns as wives and mothers, about housing, children, prices, in the expectation that 'in this way they will gradually come to take more interest in their own problems and also in those of the working class—of their class—which cannot move forward to emancipation without them'. This final flourish gestured towards the communist doctrine that sexual oppression and class oppression were inextricably linked consequences of capitalism and the resolution of both mutually interdependent, without offering any explanation of what that sexual oppression might be or how emancipation might alter sexual relations. While the party's classes studied Engels on the origin of the family as a means of ensuring patriarchal control over property, the women's group displayed a positive aversion to the distractions of feminism. The role of the working-class woman was to sustain and support the male breadwinner. 'We must make them understand that the woman of the working class has no interest apart from the man worker.'[57] There was even resistance from party members' wives who turned this argument against the activists in the women's group. 'Why should I neglect my family in order to sit at meetings or spout on soap boxes?' asked one. 'I do my duty as a rebel by sympathising in my husband's activity.'[58]

The female activist was a disturbing, transgressive presence in a men's party. Older women performed necessary, unglamorous tasks

WOMEN WORKERS ORGANISE

All workers in the fight for Freedom

An exhortation to the women—described as workers, but inscribed as wives and mothers in this depiction of a communist family group marching resolutely from home. The father's working clothes contrast with the mother's frock. (Source: 'Workers' Weekly', 20 May 1927)

such as housekeeping and literature sales. Certain allowance was made for women publicists with platform skills: Adela Pankhurst Walsh had played this part in the early years and Nelle Rickie, an actress, former member of the VSP and representative of the theatrical employees on the Melbourne Trades Hall Council, took on a similar role when she came to Sydney in 1924. Her dramatic lecture-recitals and short political sketches were popular drawcards in the Communist Hall.[59] Christian Jollie Smith remained an important member, not least because her solicitor's practice provided the party with the legal services it needed so often. Yet she was no longer on the executive and her romantic misfortunes, deserted first by Earsman and subsequently by Carl Baker, are instructive. In both cases the male had a wife and family, and the liaison was a semi-clandestine affair conducted within the shifting, impermanent round of political engagements. While the attitude to such episodes was not restrictive, there was a marked contrast between bohemian mores that flourished within the left and the highly conventional expectations of male comrades in their domestic lives. Communist Party men seldom encouraged their wives to play an active role and were inclined to regard the female comrades as either fair game or dangerous temptresses. Esmonde Higgins's partner, the formidable

Joy Barrington, crystallised these fears with her explanation of why she was unfaithful to Hig—'He doesn't satisfy me'. The same theme recurs in the novel *Sugar Heaven* written by that notorious victim of the double standard, Jean Devanny, and it lies close to the surface of Katharine Susannah Prichard's *Intimate Strangers*.[60]

In both those novels it was the virile Latin who was more attractive than the Australian man. The concern for the purity of the race was a persistent theme of the Australian labour movement, which had made the White Australia policy a central plank of its political platform and treated racial purity as inseparable from the protection of domestic living standards. The Communist Party, as a by-product of that movement and member of an international organisation committed to the unity of the workers of the world, found itself torn between old habits and new loyalties, its difficulties compounded by the fact that it drew support from those manual workers who competed for jobs with the postwar settlers from southern Europe. The numbers of Italian, Greek and Yugoslav immigrants rose sharply from 1924 following restrictions imposed by the United States, and the Ironworkers' Association as well as the AWU (which covered the Queensland sugar industry) were prominent in opposition to them. Thus a communist organiser on the central Queensland coast reported that the locally born cane-cutters were heavily outnumbered by Italians, Greek and Spanish immigrants; a proportion of the newcomers were communists 'but it is necessary for us to control the foreign element as much as possible, for otherwise there may be trouble'. Some early communists denounced all racial discrimination, while others presented immigration as a capitalist plot 'to reduce the workers to a level lower than that of a plantation nigger'. Even a plea for underpaid Aboriginal pastoral workers was coupled with a warning that the employers wished to use the 'backward' and 'primitive coolie races' to drive down the wages of the 'whites'.[61]

By the mid-1920s the party achieved general consistency in its opposition to imperialism and sympathy for native peoples, but its position on immigration remained tortuously qualified because of the fear of Garden and the Trades Hall Reds that their opponents would use the issue against them. Thus while the party denounced the White Australia policy as a cause of working-class disunity, it also rejected 'the importation to Australia of large numbers of coloured workers' and then added the qualification that the threat to employment and wages from cheap labour was colour blind.[62] The result was predictable: allegations from the AWU, Lang and others that the communists were at one with the Nationalist government in encouraging a deluge of aliens, and allegations from the Nationalists, backed by that photo of the eastern delegates at the Fourth Comintern Congress, that the communists were racial traitors. At its 1925 conference the party persevered with equivocation: it condemned foreign immigration as a capitalist attempt to flood the country with cheap labour, described the immigrants as 'an easy prey of the capitalist class', suggested that the RILU could serve as a counter-immigration bureau to dissuade more, and observed that the danger would remain until capitalism was overthrown.[63]

From 1925 the party began to work more systematically among these non-British immigrants. It published appeals in Italian and Greek that warned the recipients of the uses to which they were being put by international capitalism, urged them to insist on full union rates and begged them 'to bear as patiently as possible the racial jibes which are thrown by the stupid elements among the Australian workers'.[64] The formation of Greek and Russian party branches in the same year pursued such a strategy. The results were disappointing. The Russian branch in Sydney broke up within a year, as did the largely Russian branch in Ipswich; the Greek branch in Sydney, based mainly among restaurant workers, survived.[65] Lithgow experienced difficulties also as the steelworks there brought in southern European contract workers. The branch grew to encompass roughly equal numbers of English-speaking and Italian members, a dozen of each, who met as separate groups and were often at loggerheads. 'A definite line of policy must be given to Italians', insisted Kavanagh, who judged the newsheet of the group at Lithgow to display an anarchist tendency and thought its members 'very weak ideologically'. The delegate of that Italian group who attended the 1927 party conference, Comrade Antico, confessed that his compatriots were prone to weakness, in part because they were denied union membership and in part because of the surveillance by the Italian consulate which brought punishment to families back home. 'It is a very unlucky fact that most good members are married', he explained. Antico put the number of Italians associated with the left-wing Trade Union Education League at around 200: 55 in Lithgow, another 55 in Sydney, 35 in Broken Hill, 28 in Wonthaggi, 28 in Corrimal and 15 elsewhere.[66]

The stumblings over race are hardly surprising. The Communist Party was not the first radical movement in Australia to challenge the White Australia policy—the Wobblies were unequivocal in their denunciation of all forms of particularism—but it did so at a time when racial anxieties were increasing. The Great War exacerbated Australian fears of the alien, so that many European nationalities were subjected to new immigration restrictions in the 1920s. Opposition to all forms of racial prejudice, including discrimination against Aborigines, became a consistent feature of Australian communism and one that marked it off from the Labor Party for more than 40 years. The communist insistence on the unity of all workers, regardless of nationality, extended to an affirmation of the inherent worth of all people regardless of race. In Lawrence's novel *Kangaroo*, the communist leader Willie Struthers puts it this way, just as the angry diggers break into the party hall:

> Join hands with the workers of the world; just a fist-grip as a token and a pledge. Take nobody to your bosom—a worker hasn't got a bosom. He's got a fist, to work with, to hit with, and lastly, to give the tight grip of fellowship to his fellow-workers and fellow-mates, no matter what colour or country he belongs to . . . I don't know whether you prefer working in the same imperial slave-gang with Brother Brown of India, or whether you'd prefer to shake hands with him as a free worker, one of the world's workers, but—

This affirmation of comradeship had to be maintained against violent opposition.[67]

Yet in the very way the party discussed 'the Greek problem' and 'the Italian problem' during the 1920s, it signalled its own Australian identity. To be sure it absorbed some immigrants, mainly British but with a striking number of New Zealanders (Hetty Ross, her brother-in-law Jack Loughran, George Winter who worked in the Labour Research Bureau, Andy Barras, a plumber, several other prominent union activists, and by the end of the decade Jean and Hal Devanny), yet this merely emphasised its white Anglophone character. Also evident was a spirited resentment of any suggestion of tutelage. Officials of the CPA were prickly in their dealings with the Anglo–American Bureau of the Comintern, and inclined to bridle at assumptions of superior wisdom, particularly from representatives of the CPGB. 'We quite realise that the revolutionary developments of Australia will follow that of Europe and the East', Jack Howie wrote to the Englishman J. T. Murphy in Moscow, 'and that the main attention of the Comintern must be directed to the imperialist and strictly colonial countries. But are our efforts here ever to meet with anything but complete indifference?'[68] That a movement so cosmopolitan in its origins should have so quickly gone bush was a cause of growing concern to the Communist International.

6

The line straightens

The Executive Committee of the Communist International turned its attention to Australia early in 1926 as the full extent of the problems there became apparent. News of Baracchi's defection, along with the reports of the scheme for a breakaway Labor Party, were probably the cues for its request that the Australians send a representative to Moscow.[1] Hector Ross arrived in April bearing a lengthy report and was subjected to close interrogation, not only about the fortunes of the united front and the organisation of the Australian party, but also about the circumstances of his country, its economy, demography and national traditions. Ross was certainly disconcerted by the extent of the discussion. 'What is the position of the natives of Australia and the natives of New Zealand?' he was asked. 'The Australian natives are not to be reckoned with at all', he replied. None of the members of the Anglo–American Bureau— Comrades Pepper (Pogany, the Comintern representative in the United States), Ercoli (Togliatti, the Italian leader), Rajani Palme Dutt (the Indian–Scandinavian theorist of the British party), Hugo Rathbone (his henchman) and Manabendra Nath Roy (the outstanding Indian revolutionary)—had any prior experience of Australia. They based their conclusions on the testimony of the Australians, partly volunteered and partly solicited, onto which they directed the requirements of the Comintern. It was a process that clearly lent itself to mutual misunderstanding, yet it was a genuine dialogue and Ross was fully involved in the final formulation. The result was the first comprehensive statement of how the Communist International apprehended Australian circumstances, and as such is worth examining at length.

The Australia the Comintern described was a vast, sparsely populated continent 'covered with large-scale cattle and sheep ranches'. While 'small peasant strata are almost entirely lacking', the 'semi-agricultural and semi-industrial workers' (which was how the Comintern designated shearers with smallholdings) constituted 'one of the most important elements among the toilers'. Most of the population was concentrated in 'five or six towns'. The Australian trade unions were exceptionally strong, the level of prosperity high and Australia was the first country to have elected a labour government. Partly because of such 'conditions' and partly as a result of conscious effort by the national bourgeoisie and reformist labour leaders, the Australian proletariat was 'almost completely shut off from the proletariat of other continents'. Isolation maintained the grip of the 'petty-bourgeois minded, craft-narrowed elements' who dominated the Labor Party. 'The slogan of a "White Australia" serves as the rallying cry of all reactionary elements in the labour movement, who are steeped in nationalist ideology, and who seek to isolate themselves in aristocratic arrogance away from the coloured workers and in general from foreign proletarians.' Under these circumstances the Communist Party of Australia had to wage a desperate struggle for its very existence. Its strength lay in the unions and 'grim patience in trade union detail work is one of the most important virtues of the Australian Communists'; but they should not forego their right to belong to the Labor Party simply because its treacherous leaders had expelled them from it. Their tasks were therefore to redouble their efforts to provide a militant lead to workers, to combat reformism and British imperialism, to campaign against the ideology of White Australia and to get a foothold among the foreign-speaking immigrants. 'The Communist Party of Australia can and will become a Communist Party in the true sense of the word when it learns how to combine the fight for everyday demands of the workers with the combatting of the craft spirit of the labour aristocracy, of the ideology of the "White Australia", and of British imperialism.'[2]

This 'Resolution on the Australian Question' was tabled, discussed and adopted by the Australian party at its annual conference in December 1926. The emphasis on the need to shake off complacent insularity and combat both imperial deference and xenophobic nationalism went largely unremarked: the party agreed to campaign against the forthcoming royal visit of the Duke of York and expose the 'dangerous futility' of a White Australia, but its decision to prepare a pamphlet on immigration had still to be implemented a year later. Argument centred on the Comintern's rebuke of the Australian party for neglecting work in the Labor Party. Some delegates wanted a renewed effort for affiliation, others regarded that course as a dangerous diversion of energy. The conference resolved to organise groups of sympathisers inside Labor Party branches, allowing its own members to join these branches only when the executive gave permission and subject to the strict instruction that 'members must at all times affirm their Communist identity unless instructed to the contrary by the C[entral] E[xecutive]'.[3] This final condition, formulated by Kavanagh, was a pointed reminder of Garden's apostasy just three weeks earlier, but it had wider import. For the conference proceedings revealed different understandings of the Comintern's instructions and divergent interpretations of how the united front should be applied in Australian circumstances, differences that would widen over the next three years and absorb the party in an increasingly bitter factional conflict. The authority of the Communist International would be invoked for the eventual resolution of the dispute, and the episode is commonly understood as resulting in the Australian party's final, complete subordination to Moscow, as occurred throughout the communist world during the same period.[4]

The contours of the process are not in dispute. The Communist International was transformed in the course of the 1920s into an appendage of the Soviet Union, the sharp differences and animated debates of the early congresses yielding to conformity at the infrequent later ones, leaving the executive and its administrative apparatus in sole possession of an enhanced authority. Whereas during the early 1920s there were a number of large communist parties capable of independent action, by the end of the decade the International was severely depleted and thereafter it is impossible to identify any initiative of significance that did not originate in Moscow.[5] If the stronger European parties lost their autonomy, the weaker parties of Britain, the United States and Australia were all the more dependent on the support and guidance of the Comintern hierarchy. Until recently the historical literature dealing with these parties was marked by the preoccupations of the Cold War and stressed their supine obedience to a monolithic, totalitarian control; Since the mid-1970s, revisionist social historians have emphasised the interaction of national factors, the force of indigenous considerations of gender and ethnicity, and the variegated nature of lived communist commitment.[6]

That Australian communists accepted the authority of the Communist International is not in dispute. That Moscow determined the outcome of the factional dispute that wracked their organisation during the late 1920s is a gross oversimplification. Two qualifications can immediately be suggested. First, the Comintern's formal authority over this distant outpost was belied by dependence upon it for information, and the instructions that Moscow transmitted on the basis of this received information were in turn susceptible to selective interpretation. It was not until the International was able to train a new generation of Australian cadres (a process initiated when the first group of Australians went off to the Lenin School in Moscow at the end of the 1920s) that mutual misunderstandings narrowed. Until then a selective pattern of communication persisted, the Australians telling the Executive Committee of the Communist International what they thought it wanted to hear, and then taking up those passages of the ECCI's pronouncements that accorded with their own inclinations. The second qualification is a corollary of the first. The local factions appealed to Moscow in their struggle for control of the Australian party, but the issues in dispute were indigenous ones, and are best understood as arising from local circumstances. This can be demonstrated by turning to two specific examples.

The communist group at Lithgow enjoyed particular opportunities to build a united front with the Labor Party. Several of its members were able to attend meetings of the ALP district assembly as representatives of affiliated unions, and they exerted considerable influence on that local body during 1926. In 1927 the eligibility of communist delegates of the Miners' Federation was challenged and a split developed between Labor sympathisers who supported them and opponents determined to expel them: initially the assembly set aside the rule that required all delegates to sign the pledge of loyalty to the ALP, but subsequently it barred Charlie Nelson and the other communists.[7] These party members made no secret of their political identity but others, representing the Federated Ironworkers' Association, did so for fear of victimisation at the steelworks. The CPA executive gave these party ironworkers permission to operate incognito within the ALP but criticised them for standing for union office without declaring their party membership. The issue was raised at a meeting of the Central Executive Committee in August 1927. Lance Sharkey, a new member of the CEC, led the attack. A lift operator and member of the Miscellaneous Workers' Union, who had previously tailed behind the Trades Hall Reds, his new militancy indicated a capacity to sniff the winds of change. Sharkey was supported by Hector Ross, just returned from Moscow and fired with zeal, who insisted that 'this situation arose out of our members functioning in the ALP and is a continuation of the liquidation policy pursued by former members of the Communist Party'. Bill Orr defended his fellow Lithgovians' need to build up the left in the union before they risked victimisation, and he was supported by Jack Ryan and Esmonde Higgins, who had returned from Western Australia. The meeting endorsed Sharkey's criticism by nine votes to three.[8]

Meanwhile a quite different set of circumstances confronted communists in north Queensland. Here the party's presence was episodic, established initially by Peter Larkin during his 1921 visit, re-established by Norm Jeffery in the following year and revived by him once more in his later tour of 1925. The local communists were mostly footloose workers who had little patience for officialdom and a strong preference for direct industrial action.[9] Events in 1925 increased their restlessness. As part of a campaign for a roster system of employment, the local branches of the Waterside Workers' Federation were refusing to load ships during the end-of-year meat-kill and sugar-crush. The employers encouraged local farmers to descend on Cairns and Bowen with firearms, beat up strikers and drive all known reds out of town, and the Labor government did little to prevent these attacks.[10] There was considerable impatience among the unions with the Labor government in Queensland. In 1926 both the railways' and meatworkers' unions withdrew their affiliation to the ALP. In 1927 the state government victimised the building unions in a dispute over public works, and then locked out the railway workers for their support of striking sugarmill workers. These were deeply disturbing events for those in a labour movement where class loyalties commanded a deep, instinctive allegiance. Here were Labor politicians and the ALP executive employing the police and the courts against unionists for giving support to fellow workers in their time of need.[11]

Bert Moxon headed north from Brisbane for a new recruitment drive at this opportune juncture. He found two existing branches— in Cairns and Townsville—each with contingents of militant waterside workers, railwaymen and meatworkers, and formed new ones in the coastal towns of Innisfail, Tully, Lucinda Point and Bowen, along with the sugar townships of Biboohra, Home Hill and Mossman, and the inland mining settlements of Collinsville, Scottsville and Mount Mulligan. Ted Tripp, a young former member of the CPGB who worked as a fitter in the Townsville railway workshop, became secretary of the north Queensland party district. The number of communists enrolled in north Queensland during this period, nearly 200, was far in advance of anything hitherto achieved; their capacity was less certain. Moxon himself reported that the level of political understanding was low, the interest in communist theory even lower: the *Communist Manifesto* was far 'too hard' to use as a textbook in party classes. Relatively few of the recruits were active in their unions, while those who were 'are proving themselves trade unionist first'. Moxon, who quarrelled with even the most sympathetic union officials, astounded some of these recruits when he told them the party took priority over industrial activity. Patterns of work in the region were seasonal, so it would require a concerted effort to stabilise the groups. Still, the lesson that he brought back from the north was clear: both the ALP and the 'left wingers' were worthless, discredited by their actions. The workers were ripe for revolutionary leadership.[12]

The two examples of Lithgow and north Queensland point in different directions. The one suggests the difficulties local communists encountered as they pursued a united front within the established structure of the labour movement under the vigilant surveillance of the party executive; the other reveals an impatience with the united front and a preference for separatist militancy well beyond the writ of the executive. The two tendencies were not restricted to these places; rather they were manifestations of differences within the Australian party that crystallised during 1926 and 1927 into distinct factions. The executive elected at the 1926 conference was led by Kavanagh. He placed primary emphasis on building a party of industrial militants through close attention to organisation and training. He believed the party had to guard against contamination in its operation of the united front, and accordingly placed strict stipulations on relations with the unions and the ALP. In this approach Kavanagh was supported by Moxon and the Rosses. Higgins and Ryan, on the other hand, wanted to pursue the united front more wholeheartedly in order to foster communist influence in the organised labour movement, while the remaining executive members, Wright, Jeffery and Sharkey, were usually somewhere in between. The differences were apparent in a lengthy debate at the executive's August 1927 meeting on the continuing battle between Lang and his opponents for control of the New South Wales branch of the Labor Party. Three alternative theses were proposed, by Wright, Hector Ross and Ryan. The one formulated by Wright wanted the party to back Lang and his Labor Council allies against the AWU and right-wing politicians in the hope of winning rule changes that would allow communists to be elected as union delegates to the ALP conference. Ross contended that there was nothing to choose between Lang and his opponents and consequently 'no working class significance in NSW faction fight', a slogan originally coined by Kavanagh. Ryan, with support from Higgins and Sharkey, based his proposal on the argument that the workers would only come to see the bankruptcy of Labor and the need to overthrow capitalism if communists encouraged them to make demands upon a Labor government. He therefore wanted the party to organise a communist fraction in the ALP and to press for rule changes that would allow them membership. This in fact was done, but the executive also endorsed Ross and Kavanagh's uncompromising slogan by nine votes to four.[13]

Wright was not able to speak to his thesis because he was in Moscow for a further consideration by the Communist International of its Australian section. He said little of the disagreements at home; instead he responded to an assessment of his party's work that was distinctly more favourable than that given a year earlier. If the 1926 'Resolution on the Australian Question' had read rather like a teacher scolding a backward child, this 1927 resolution acknowledged some encouraging signs of more attentive effort. The resolution was drafted by the Anglo–American Bureau (now chaired by the Russian Petrovsky who had extensive experience in the United States and Britain), then amended by the Political Secretariat of the ECCI, where Bukharin and the Japanese leader Katayama as well as M. N. Roy made substantial contributions. It was accepted that 'Australian conditions are not indicative of a revolutionary crisis in the near future'—the working class was only beginning to feel its power and it still lacked experience of Labor in office (Wright objected to this historically inaccurate slight on his compatriots). There was spirited discussion of the status of Australia as an outpost of British and American imperialism (it was an independent bourgeois state, insisted Wright). 'If time is not yet ripe for revolutionary mass action' in Australia, it was all the more important for the party to persist with revolutionary propaganda and agitation. Work within the unions should be pursued: Australian communists should take their place in the front ranks of the workers in every strike and every struggle. The campaign against 'social chauvinism' should be stepped up; communists would insist upon all 'equality of wages, rights and free admittance to the workers of all countries' (here Katayama demurred with the prescient observation that 'I do not think that the Australian workers would approve of this'). Only time would tell whether the Labor Party could be opened to genuine proletarian influence or it would be necessary to found a new party. In the meantime the communists should press their demand for affiliation, not soften in any way their criticisms but rather sharpen them, not fall into the right error of hiding their identity nor the left error of antagonising workers with sectarian revolutionary slogans. To say that 'the Communist Party must understand how to operate the united front tactic suitably' was scarcely to clarify Moscow's expectations.[14]

Tom Wright brought the Comintern resolution back to the party conference in December 1927 along with a Comintern delegate, R. W. Robson of the CPGB. Robson was clearly unprepared for what he found: an executive split into factions, no preparation for the congress, the congress proceedings consumed in factional conflict. He found the calibre of the leadership 'very low indeed', the level of the Australian working class 'very very low'. He fell out with Kavanagh almost immediately and Kavanagh as conference chairman managed to wrong-foot him by announcing his presence to the delegates on the first day. Since his passport would not bear inspection, he had to give an impromptu address and then beat a speedy retreat.[15]

Much of the ensuing debate was taken up with recent executive decisions. First, the Lithgow group appealed against the instruction that its members should identify themselves as communists on the grounds that those who were active in the FIA would lose their jobs. Higgins supported them. The Lithgow group was 'the nearest to achievements in mass work', he contended, and the executive had 'greatly failed the Lithgow group in many of its important activities'. Howie, Jack Ryan and Joe Shelley agreed. Kavanagh rejoined that the most important task was to build up the party, not subordinate it to the pursuit of union office or representation on Labor assemblies, and in this respect the record of the Lithgow group was deficient. Nelson and Bill Orr insisted that the group's main object was to strengthen the industrial movement; Ross replied that their apparent success was gained by stealth. That was too much for Higgins. He observed that two alternative tactics were proposed. The tactic of mass work had brought success in Lithgow, the tactic of separatism employed by Ross during his period at Newcastle had proved utterly fruitless. Lithgow's supporters had the better of an acrimonious debate, but conference endorsed the position of the executive by 24 votes to 18.[16]

Next, Norm Jeffery led an attack on the actions of the executive in the New South Wales Labor Party faction fight. By now this issue was well rehearsed. He and a number of other delegates wanted the party to support the industrialists in the hope of winning new

ALP rules that would allow communists to represent affiliated unions at Labor Party conferences. The executive, still taking its stand on the slogan that Labor's factional struggle had 'no working-class significance', insisted that the Labor industrialists in unholy alliance with Lang were no better than their parliamentary rivals. The debate was notable for the vehemence of the disputation as well as the new alignments it revealed. Bill Orr contended that the actions of the executive were symptomatic of a more general weakness: 'The Party was too much concerned with making the working class understand Communist theory instead of getting them to take an active part in the struggle for everyday demands'. Jack Ryan and Esmonde Higgins concurred. Tom Wright took his stand on the Comintern's recent resolution calling on the Australians to intensify their pressure on the Labor Party. Jack Kavanagh, on the other hand, thought the critics revealed a persistent tendency to submerge the Communist Party into the Labor Party, and the Queensland delegates agreed with him. They carried the conference by 34 votes to seven.[17]

This argument foreshadowed a further disagreement over the executive's new thesis on the Labor Party. Presented by Hetty Ross, it was far more pessimistic about the prospects of radicalising the ALP than the Comintern theses of 1926 and 1927. The ALP was 'purely parliamentary in character'; the possibility that it could be converted into a real workers' party was 'extremely remote'; and those communists who took part in Labor assemblies 'merely serve the purpose of re-attracting dissatisfied workers to the reformist policy of the organisation'. The trade unions, which did not enforce political conformity, were far more propitious sites for communist effort, and activity in the ALP should be restricted to the object of building up the Communist Party. All activity had to be open. There could be no concealment of identity and no participation without direction from the executive. This was far too rigid for Higgins and Ryan. 'Why cut off one of your arms?' asked Ryan. Higgins submitted an alternative thesis that diagnosed increased dissatisfaction with the Labor leadership in a period of intensifying class conflict. 'To this end, the Communist Party must play an active part within the unions and the ALP, seeking in every way, through action as well as propaganda, to increase class consciousness among the rank and file.'

Ross and Kavanagh condemned Higgins's laxity. Tripp, representing the Townsville group, was adamant that the Labor Party was 'reformist right throughout' and communists could not possibly 'smash reformism' by submerging themselves in its organisation. The executive's thesis was adopted by 18 votes to 14.[18]

Running though each of these debates was a clear division of opinion over the means whereby the Communist Party should operate. For several years the party had pursued a united front, with minimal success and without ever clarifying its rationale. Were the unions and the Labor Party susceptible to radicalisation? Could they be drawn to the left? Or was the united front nothing more than a front, a device behind which communists could infiltrate, recruit new members and discredit their opponents? In practice the Australian party had a bob each way, and the returns on each wager were meagre—communists were debarred from the Labor Party, exerted marginal influence in the unions, and had lost as many members to their prey as they gained from it. Kavanagh's impatience stemmed from his conviction that the united front diverted Australian communists from the primary task of building a vanguard party of forthright agitators. He did not specifically repudiate the strategy. Rather, he restricted its operation to certain spheres of activity, principally in the unions, though even there he warned that 'too much attention is paid, in my opinion, to detail [sic] trade union work to the detriment of service to the party'.[19] His critics found those restrictions an impediment to their efforts to build communist support. They argued partly from local experience, partly by appeal to the authority of the Communist International and partly out of their conviction that the Australian labour movement was about to undergo a period of tribulation that would provide new opportunities for the united front. On each of these grounds they were in a strong position. Indeed, the record of the conference reveals that the critics spoke more often and more effectively than the supporters of the executive. Yet they lost.

They were defeated not by argument but by numbers. The rules of the party during this period provided for one conference delegate for every ten members, and allowed groups that could not send their own members to nominate proxy delegates. Bert Moxon, basking in the glory of his tour as organiser in northern Queensland, controlled no less than fourteen of these proxy votes at the 1927 conference, which he distributed among his allies there. The proxies were used both to carry the crucial conference resolutions and to control the ballot for the new executive. There were fifteen candidates for eleven positions. Of those elected, Kavanagh, Moxon, Hector and Hetty Ross were solid supporters of the new line, Higgins and Wright were the only critics, while the remainder were uncommitted; among those dumped from the executive were Jack Ryan, Norm Jeffery and Lance Sharkey.[20]

The factional character of the conference was unprecedented in its intensity, its application to the party organisation wholly new. In clear reference to its divisive effects, Kavanagh closed the conference with an appeal for unity:

> There have been heated arguments in expressing our opinions. This does not mean personalities. A difference exists between our conferences and others—there is honesty in all our arguments advanced for the well being of the Party and the working class movement—not of individuals.[21]

There is no doubt that he was sincere. Kavanagh was pugnacious, dogmatic, egotistical—more than once he was heard to say that he was the only real Leninist in Australia—but he was not vindictive. The allocation of executive duties at the close of the conference attested to the acceptance of differences: Kavanagh was chairman and in charge of trade union work, Wright was secretary, and Higgins in charge of the Agitprop department as well as editor of *Workers' Weekly*. Jack Ryan's wife Edna, who joined the party at this time and ran its Sydney office, has recalled it as a golden age of free debate, with 'no hushing and stifling, no fear of being accused if one proposed a tactic or an idea', an 'open academy' that 'developed what was best for individuals and gave them full opportunity to develop'.

'Am I imagining', she asked herself 40 years later, 'that the socialists, the revolutionaries and the communist leadership of the twenties were people of stature? Most of them had intellectual integrity'. The picture she draws is of young, ardent revolutionaries who asked for no quarter in their heated disputation over priorities and methods, but shared an essential respect for each other's talents and energies. Even the wavering Lance Sharkey, a scruffy, glum, unsociable man who boarded with Higgins and Joy Barrington at Glebe, was included in their fellowship, though recently voted off the executive. The contrast she draws is between this circle of comradeship and Bert Moxon, who represented very different qualities.

> The party was somewhat prim and prissy—we must be genuine workers, belonging to a trade union, and to lead as normal a life as possible in order to belong to and be accepted by the working class. Moxon was an urger, a bit of a larrikin living on his wits—he had the reputation of being able to open any lock. We could be tolerant about him but to have him in the leadership was too much.[22]

This shameless adventurer—Ryan thought him the embodiment of Henry Lawson's Bastard from the Bush—had begun to take himself very seriously. After his scapegrace conduct in the early Sydney branch in 1922, when he had helped carry the furniture from the Liverpool Street party premises to Sussex Street only to stage a further rebellion there, Moxon had moved to Brisbane and joined forces with J. B. Miles. His colonisation of north Queensland gave him a power base among militants who were contemptuous of their Labor government. His impatience with the sort of patient cultivation of a united front practised in Lithgow coincided with Kavanagh's mistrust of any tendency to submerge the party's identity. Even so, their alliance was a temporary one. Kavanagh had little respect for this blustering conman while Moxon, who aspired to Kavanagh's own position as leader, was already courting friends in Moscow.

The decisions taken by the Australian party at its 1927 conference put it to the left of the Communist International. At that time the Comintern still enjoined the Australians to pursue a united front as the appropriate communist tactic in a period of capitalist restabilisation. As the British representative of the Comintern reminded the conference delegates in Sydney, the intense postwar revolutionary unrest had yielded since the early 1920s to a temporary and partial world stabilisation, and that was the reason for cultivating the unions and reformist parties which still commanded the loyalty of the working class. Yet even as Robson spoke, Stalin was announcing to the Fifteenth Congress of the Communist Party of the Soviet Union that a new third period of capitalist crisis had begun, bringing new revolutionary opportunities and new tasks. His reasons for making this announcement arose partly out of the struggle for control of the CPSU (having defeated the left opposition, he was now turning on the right) and partly from the disastrous failures of the united front in various countries. In Britain, the General Strike of 1926 had collapsed in recrimination between communists and the trade union leadership. In China the communists were butchered in 1927 by the armies of the Nationalists, with whom they had been allied in the war for national independence. Earlier the Italian party had failed to avert fascist dictatorship. By the end of the decade the membership and influence of the Communist International had dwindled close to oblivion.

By the time Stalin codified the doctrine of the Third Period (now capitalised to emphasise its decretal status), the international labour movement had passed through a series of phases since the Great War. First was the period of acute capitalist crisis and revolutionary action culminating in the victory of the Soviet Union over its enemies and the establishment of the Communist International. Then in the early 1920s came a period of partial stabilisation when the labour movement was on the defensive and communist parties pursued a united front. Now, in the Third Period, growing imperial rivalry would intensify conflict both between and within the capitalist countries. Capitalists would seek to suppress workers' resistance and put down colonial movements of revolt. In the rising conflict of what they characterised as a battle of 'Class Against Class', the social democrats would be called upon by the capitalists to impose cuts in living standards and to persuade the workers that they were necessary. In doing so they would be exposed as the worst enemies of the working class, as nothing less than 'social fascists'. Stalin's announcement of the Third Period of Class Against Class thus signalled the effective abandonment of the united front.

The turn to the Third Period threw the member parties of the

Communist International into disarray. It was not that they clung to the united front—just as the Australian comrades were exasperated by their failure to win over the unions and Labor Party, so the communists of other countries felt increasing hostility towards the false friends of the workers who spurned or betrayed their own overtures. Furthermore, Stalin's prediction that capitalism was entering a period of global crisis was confirmed by the mounting evidence of trade imbalance, financial instability and lengthening dole queues. The Australian economy, with its heavy borrowing on the international money market and consequent vulnerability to a downturn in world commodity prices, was already under pressure; attempts to restore profitability by an assault on wages and working conditions caused major industrial disputes in key industries from 1928 onwards. To this extent, the new line announced in Moscow accurately embodied their own experience and aspirations. But how was the offensive against the social democratic and labour parties to be conducted? Strictly speaking, the united front was not abandoned, it was recast as the united front 'from below', this signifying the need to detach workers from their treacherous leaders. Yet that formulation hardly indicated the means whereby the communists, who by now were wholly excluded from the organisations they denounced, should effect the necessary internal differentiation. Their perplexity was caused partly by the confusing process whereby the new line was announced during 1928 at the long-delayed Sixth Congresss of the International, where Bukharin (the leader of the right) was still president and tried to play down the change. Within the hall of the Congress his statements were applauded; in the corridors murmurs of his errors presaged Bukharin's subsequent removal and the replacement of all remaining officials who failed to give complete support to Stalin. The Sixth Congress, moreover, introduced a far more rigid regimen, one which formalised a 'strict party discipline and precise execution of the decisions of the Communist International, of its agencies and of its leading committees'.[23]

The unprecedented degree of submission expected of member parties from the late 1920s was a symptom of Stalin's personal authority but it was also something more. The apocalyptic urgency of the Third Period demanded a break with past habits and old faces. The whole tone of communist pronouncements of Class Against

Class, with their insistence on the inexorable logic of class betrayal beneath the benign surface of social democracy and the corresponding emphasis on unmasking traitors, called for new leaders who would exercise new levels of vigilance and impose new standards of obedience. There would be no communist party of any significance outside the Soviet Union that emerged from the Third Period with its leadership intact. The Anglophone parties of Australia, New Zealand, the United States, Canada and, to a lesser extent Britain, all underwent convulsions in which the old leaders were found guilty and removed for the heresy of national exceptionalism.

Three Australians left for Moscow at the close of the 1927 party conference: Moxon, who accompanied Robson as the representative of the Central Executive, and Jeffery and Ryan, who went as delegates to an RILU congress. When the Political Secretariat of the ECCI (chaired by Bukharin, with the British communists Gallacher and Arnot, and the Germans Brandler and Thalheimer) considered Australia in April 1928, it had three reports before it. That of Robson concentrated on the organisational weakness of the Australian party, which it ascribed to factional conflict within the executive while it studiously refrained from political judgement of the issues in dispute.[24] That of Moxon rehearsed the factional history of the party from its foundation through to the recent defeat of the right-wing opportunists. It accused the right of intriguing with Robson as well as of subsequent disruption. The lesson of the past few years, Moxon maintained, was that the Labor Party was no longer a working-class party and that any further support of it by the Australian communist party would be 'next to criminal'.[25] In response, Ryan and Jeffery denied factional opposition and described Moxon's report as 'a series of misstatements and distortions actuated by personal antagonism'. They described the vagaries of the Australian party's implementation of the united front policy in conformity with the policy of the Communist International, explained how Moxon had used proxies to control the recent conference, and reiterated their own programme that would concentrate on building a left-wing movement in the Labor Party in order to expose the reformism of its leadership.[26]

Notably absent from this sheaf of reports as well as from the ensuing ECCI discussion of them was Kavanagh's argument that building a communist party should be the first priority and that

HAILED BY QUEENSLAND WORKERS

Bert Moxon was a delegate to Moscow in 1928. The executive committee of the Communist International accepted his argument that the workers in Queensland were ready to overthrow the treacherous Labor government in that state. The 'Queensland Resolution' is here presented as a dazzling dawn. (Source: 'Workers' Weekly', 14 September 1928)

A PROGRAM OF IMMEDIATE DEMANDS

For Queensland State Elections

concentration on the Labor Party (whether to work within it or to oppose it) was a diversion. His failure to put his own position to the Communist International at a time when that organisation was invigilating its constituent bodies more closely than ever, and when the question of future relations with social democracy was coming to dominate its deliberations, was a costly error. For the resolution adopted by ECCI concentrated exclusively on the Labor Party in Moxon's home territory of Queensland. It took its point of departure from an escape clause in the previous year's resolution when Australian communists had been instructed to continue their efforts in the Labor Party unless and until a genuine left-wing alternative was possible. That possibility was now deemed to have arisen in Queensland because of the reactionary record of the Labor government there, which had already brought the disaffiliation of key left unions. Three or four communist candidates should therefore stand in the state elections due in early 1929; in some other constituencies there should be left-wing ALP candidates supported by 'workers' electoral committees', and elsewhere the Labor candidates were to be pressed, on pain of a campaign against them, to repudiate the past actions of the government and endorse working-class demands.[27]

The 'Queensland resolution', as it became known, was a compromise—as much an attempt to force the Labor Party to the left as an attack on it; more a bridge between communists and non-communists workers than an attempt to stand on a clear communist platform. As such it allowed each of the Australian factions to claim it for their own.

The Australian executive adopted it unanimously. 'The Party has for some time been preparing the ground for a break with the Labor Party and its reactionary Queensland Government', explained the *Workers' Weekly* when it published the 'masterly analysis' of the Communist International. Ryan, Jeffery and Wright joined with Moxon, Miles and Ross to explain why Queensland was peculiarly suited to communist parliamentary candidatures.[28] Arguments arose over the programme of demands that should be put to the Labor candidates, with some suggesting that too moderate a programme would merely confirm the workers in their reformist and parliamentary illusions and others wanting to support the electoral endeavours of the left unions. Those issues were taken back to the Communist International by Higgins (who arrived in Moscow in August 1928 as the Australian delegate to the Sixth Congress), which in turn warned against either too hard or too soft a set of demands, neglect of the left unions or subordination of the party to their campaign.[29]

In short, the implications of the Queensland resolution for the tactics and status of the Australian communist party remained far more ambiguous than the established interpetation of Australian subordination allows. Apparently it was a set of binding instructions handed down from on high. In fact it originated in response to rival claims of local disputants, each of whom appealed for Moscow's support; its authors attempted to find a *via media* between the appellants and, even when pressed, refrained from clarification of the issues that separated the Australian factions. Far from exercising a binding control on Australian communists, the Communist International was still criticised for its neglect. In October 1928 the Australian secretary Tom Wright complained that 'there has been no effective contact with the Communist International'; correspondence was left unanswered, no one in Moscow was responsible for attending to Australian requests, and after Robson's all too brief visit ten months earlier, the need for a Comintern representative in Australia was pressing. The Australians believed they suffered from their inclusion in the Anglo–American Bureau of the Comintern— for much as Australian imperialists believed Whitehall took Australia's attachment too much for granted, so Australian communists felt the CPGB patronised the CPA—and thought that they would be better located in the Eastern Secretariat along with China and Japan.[30] Perhaps they would have, but the primary reason for their inability to get clear advice during 1928 was the political paralysis of the Communist International itself. That the Australians took so long to grasp that fact only underlines their isolation.

Higgins's mission to Moscow illustrates these recondite patterns. He went as a member of the minority faction on the Australian executive, which still defended the united front, through the intervention of his British friends Dutt and Pollitt, who spearheaded the shift to Class Against Class in the CPGB. Assisted by these influential figures in the Anglo–American Bureau, he endeavoured (unsuccessfully) to have the CPA transferred to the Eastern Secretariat.[31] He arrived in Moscow at the very end of the Sixth Congress, too late to witness the bizarre atmosphere in which Bukharin's grudging endorsement of the Third Period was adopted unanimously and then set aside. His own report on the Congress caught the essential components of the new line—the deepening contradictions of capitalism and imperialism, the absorption of social democracy into the capitalist state, the need for an intensified struggle, a united front from below—without any indication how these propositions bore on arguments within the Australian party. Apart from pressing the Comintern to clarify the basis of the electoral programme suggested in the Queensland resolution, Higgins explained why the Australian party could not accept other suggestions the Comintern had made: it could not continue to fetter the Minority Movement for the convenience of the New South Wales Labor Council and hence the RILU, since the trade unions were in urgent need of a militant lead; it could not instruct the Australian office of the Pan-Pacific Trade Union to repudiate the White Australia policy since that would threaten its support from the ACTU. For good measure, Higgins asked the Comintern to explain exactly what was meant by its proposed slogan of 'Australian independence'.[32] Yet again the Comintern assured the Australian party that there was no essential difference between its own advice and the local concerns. Yet again they reassured the Australians of greater support and more regular liaison. Higgins did at least take back £1000, the first injection of funds since the British government had prevented the transmission of drafts through London and sorely needed for the new tasks the Australian party had assumed.[33]

The Communist Party of Australia was conceived in Station House, on the corner of George Street and Rawson Place, close to Central Railway Station in Sydney. Peter Simonoff opened an office there in 1920 as he worked with Earsman, Jollie Smith and Garden to plan the foundation conference. After its foundation, the party leased rooms over the road in Rawson Chambers. Once occupied by trade unions, the refurbished Station House is now leased to business tenants. (Source: Ann Turner)

The propellor-driven locomotive that left the rails on 24 July 1921 when Tom Sergeyeff was host to Australian delegates to the Congress of the Communist International. The fortuitous death of Paul Freeman left Bill Earsman to press the claims of the Sussex Street party to a successful conclusion. (Source: Noel Butlin Archives Centre, ANU K4136)

An early gathering of Sydney communists at Balmoral, on Sydney's North Shore. The variety of the picnickers, young and old, male and female, is striking, and the men's dress varies from winged collars and bow ties to bathing suits. Norm Jeffery, who kept this photo, appears in a striped costume in the back row. (Source: CPA collection, Mitchell Library Pic Acc 6604)

At the end of 1921 Bill Earsman's party acquired a hall in Sussex Street, after which it became known. The sign 'The United Communist Party of Australia' was painted after a conference in February 1922 proclaimed that title. For a decade this was the base of Australian communism; the upstairs hall served as an organisational headquarters, the party's Saturday dance was held there, and on many nights homeless workers bunked down on its floors. (Source: CPA collection, Mitchell Library Pic Acc 6604)

This studio portrait of John Smith Garden was taken in the 1930s, and shows a more carefully groomed Jock than communists and others of his Trades Hall Reds knew during the preceding decade. A born fixer, he was not without principles. (Source: National Library of Australia, NL 21453)

British seamen, prosecuted for participating in the international strike of 1925, march to the magistrates' court in Melbourne; their counterparts in Sydney sheltered in the Communist Hall. Australian maritime workers bade farewell to one seaman who was deported with the song, 'Hallelujah! I'm a bum'. (Source: Geoff McDonald collection, Noel Butlin Archives Centre, ANU K3215)

Jack Kavanagh in 1920. Five years later he stepped onto Australian soil and filled the gap left by the departure of the party's founders. (Source: Jack Kavanagh collection, Noel Butlin Archives Centre, ANU Z400, Box 1)

JOCK GARDEN & CO.   Photo by courtesy " Daily

At the Fourth Congress of the Communist International in Moscow during 1922 the Australian delegates were photographed with a group of Asian comrades. Bill Earsman stands third from the right with Jock Garden on the far right of the same row and Tom Payne seated in front of him. The photograph was published by the Nationalists during the 1925 federal election to embarrass the Labor Party. The 'Labor Daily' cropped Garden and Payne, and disguised Earsman with a moustache, to accuse the Nationalists of forging the genuine photo. Ever the opportunist, Jock Garden let the chicanery go unchallenged. (Source: F.J. Riley collection, National Library of Australia)

May Day in Lithgow, 1927. The workers at Hoskins steelworks march through the town. (Source: Jack Blake)

May Day in Lithgow, late 1920s. Joy Barrington is up on the stump; Jack Blake stands behind her, his head visible above the hat of a female onlooker. The audience in the park is sparse, the masculine ranks of the unionists who marched replaced by an informal circle of men, women and children. (Source: Jack Blake)

In early 1928 Norm Jeffery and Jack Ryan attended a congress of the Red International of Labor Unions in Moscow. Jeffery also participated in a meeting of communist mining representatives. He appears fifth from the right in the back row; Arthur Horner, the redoubtable leader of the South Wales miners, is third from the right in the front row. (Source: CPA collection, Mitchell Library, Pic Acc 6604)

A group of union officials and communist pickets arrested in Sydney during the timberworkers' strike of 1929. Left to right: Jock Garden, J. Culbert, Mick Ryan, E.W. Paton, Jack Kavanagh and W. Terry. Though the strike was faltering by this time, the men regard the camera undaunted. Kavanagh's reputation as a dapper dresser is evident. (Source: F.J. Riley collection, National Library of Australia, PL 667/2)

In 1929 a representative of the Red International of Labor Unions came to Australia to guide the work of the Pan-Pacific Trade Union secretariat. His name was G. Sydor Stöler, but Edna Ryan nicknamed him by his mission as 'Pan'. He appears here on the left of a group. On the right is Esmonde Higgins; his suit betrays the social origins of which he was so conscious. The female in the middle has not been identified. (Source: Esmonde Higgins papers, Mitchell Library, Pic Acc 1303/8)

Harry Wicks in the 1950s. The Communist International sent him to Australia in 1930 and, as Herbert Moore, he supervised the reconstruction of the Australian party. (Source: J.N. Rawling collection, Noel Butlin Archives Centre, ANU N57/2295)

In 1931 J.B. Miles moved down from Brisbane to become secretary of the Australian party. With Lance Sharkey, he exercised close control over its activities for the next two decades. (Source: 'Communist Review', September 1938)

Beneath the surface of this benign neglect, the Australians jockeyed for advantage. In a rare reference to the projection of local differences into the forums of the Communist International, Esmonde Higgins noted that 'Mox' had 'spoiled things in Moscow'. During his visit to the Soviet Union a few months earlier Moxon had promoted himself, on the basis of his success in Queensland, as the Australian comrade best able to make a clear break with the outmoded tactic of the united front. More than this, he damned the 'right-wing oppositionists' collectively and individually in a detailed analysis of the factional composition of the Australian executive that found its way into the Comintern's records. Higgins did not pursue such vendettas (on the contrary, he supported the election of Kavanagh as a candidate member of the ECCI) but he too used his time in Moscow to cultivate 'friends at court'. In clear reference to these activities, the ECCI warned the Australian party: 'care should be taken that questions under discussion must not become the basis for factions and groupings inside the Party'.[34] By that time, in the lead-up to the party conference at the end of 1928, factional conflict was endemic. It split the Melbourne branch. Joe Shelley wrote from Sydney at the end of October to his old friend Jack Maruschak, then in Moscow, to report he had been replaced as Melbourne organiser because of an adverse report from 'that maniac Moxon'—Maruschak prudently forwarded the letter to the secretary of the ECCI.[35] It bedevilled relations between Sydney and Brisbane. Moxon was intriguing in Queensland with J. B. Miles, the secretary of the Brisbane group, and ordered back to Sydney; articles submitted by Miles to the *Workers' Weekly* were rejected.[36]

The conference that assembled in Sydney in December 1928 was the largest ever, though party membership showed no improvement. Sydney had declined from 120 nominal members to 80; Brisbane was up from 14 to 44, though many were unfinancial; both Townsville and Cairns reported a high turnover, and most of the smaller north Queensland groups were defunct. Melbourne, similarly, claimed 48 members but only 15 were up to date with dues; Lithgow had fallen to 12 members and lost its Italian section with the closure of the steelworks, and Perth had 14 book members of whom just four were active. There were new groups in the coalmining towns of Bulli and Cessnock. Lithgow had established an outpost at the nearby cement works, while Broken Hill appeared on the records for the first time. Altogether perhaps 300 individuals professed allegiance to the CPA.

Criticism and self-criticism were the order of the day. In his opening address Kavanagh emphasised that the new tasks for party members during the capitalist offensive would call for a level of discipline, training and revolutionary understanding hitherto unattained. The organiser's report observed the weakness of industrial activity: there was still no effective Minority Movement in Sydney, because the New South Wales Labor Council was still regarded as the arm of the RILU, and in the whole of Australia there were just three communist factory groups. The Lithgow delegates complained particularly of the executive's lack of support for the Miners' Minority Movement, which remained the most productive site of communist industrial activity. Several other delegates criticised the failure to organise the growing numbers of the unemployed, and Lithgow members again complained that the executive had refused to assist a recent hunger march of unemployed miners to Sydney. The secretary also acknowledged the neglect of work among European immigrants, and Hetty Ross as women's organiser lamented the common indifference to the work of the Militant Women's Groups. The party press came in for trenchant comment: it was abstruse, poorly laid out and too far removed from local activity. That it maintained a circulation of nearly 5000 required constant campaigns and absorbed the energies of its sellers.[37]

All in all, the picture presented by executive and local members alike was grim. Hector Ross professed himself 'rather surprised at the mildness of the criticism of the executive' and observed: 'We are not a bunch of supermen, we are only a handful of overworked slaves.' Indeed they were, and the group secretaries presented their own accounts of backward members, contrary members and willing members demoralised by overwork. The Cairns group wanted to ditch its president, who was a professional gambler, but his proposed replacement was too busy in his union. The Brisbane group struggled to maintain viability with at least half its members unemployed. The nomadic habits of the Townsville members made trade union work impractical and left the group in the hands of 'armchair philosophers'. Melbourne comrades were at each others' throats and suffered from what its leader described as a 'very lacka dazical manner'.[38] Yet this ramshackle organisation was proposing nothing less than a systematic assault on the leadership of the Labor Party and the unions.

The resolution on the Labor Party was a compromise, put forward with the unanimous support of the executive as a basis for discussion. It proceeded from the postulates of the Third Period: a severe capitalist offensive, the ALP increasingly aligned with capitalism, the Communist Party therefore assuming leadership of the working class. Even so, it tempered fideism with realism. The workers were coming to see the traitorous role of the Labor Party but were not yet willing to accept the full programme of the Communist Party. Accordingly, they should be presented with a programme of left-wing demands. 'Wherever possible, as in the Queensland State elections, we will put up independent communist candidates or support left-wing workers candidates who support our programme of action.' Where the weakness of the party made this impossible, the party would promote its programme and endeavour to compel Labor candidates to express agreement with it. Finally, while the CPA would no longer seek affiliation to the ALP, it would continue to fight for the right of trade unions to send communist delegates to ALP conferences.[39] The equivocal nature of this resolution, at once condeming Labor and still seeking to influence it, asserting communist leadership while recognising most were still not ready to accept it, allowing that the Queensland resolution might apply beyond Queensland but stopping short of saying so, was plain to the delegates. No one mustered great enthusiasm for the resolution, no one opposed it. There was muted argument over how it should be applied and whether it should have been implemented during the federal elections in the previous month when, for the first time, the wider applicability of the Queensland resolution had been at issue and the executive had belatedly formulated a programme of demands to put to Labor candidates as a condition of support.

The party's own elections gave the clearest indication of the changing disposition of factional alignments. Kavanagh, Wright, Higgins, Jeffery, Hector Ross and Ryan headed the ballot for the executive, followed by Sharkey, Alf Baker, Barras and finally Moxon.[40] Kavanagh and his former critic Higgins had buried their

INDUSTRIAL PEACE, BE DAMNED

The Communist Party campaigned strongly against the Industrial Peace Conference sponsored by the Commonwealth government in 1928 at the suggestion of the employers, and a crowd singing 'The Red Flag' invaded the Sydney session. The image of a muscular militant haranguing an assembled throng before smoking chimneys envisages Lenin's model of the vanguard party. (Source: 'Workers' Weekly', 30 November 1928)

differences, which allowed the re-election of Higgins's close associate Ryan as well as Jeffery, and pushed Moxon into last place. With Miles ineligible for election (at that time members of the executive had to be resident in Sydney), Moxon's only ally on the new executive was Lance Sharkey, who had previously been aligned with the faction that resisted Class Against Class but presented himself at the 1928 conference as its ardent advocate. Sharkey was easily underestimated, a man of limited education who lacked the flair and confidence of other leading comrades and seemed to attach himself to stronger personalities—first Kavanagh, now Moxon—but you underestimated him at your peril.[41]

The other major issue before the party at its 1928 conference was the trade union question. Here too the executive formulated a resolution in the terms of the Third Period. The Australian working class had long basked in illusions of the unique character of its capitalist experience: the isolation from international events, the keen demand for labour, comparatively high living standards and extensive reliance on industrial arbitration all encouraged workers in the belief 'that Australia was the "social paradise", a country to which the laws of the class struggle did not apply, and which would glide peacefully and without any social upheavals into Socialism'. Now, with the looming economic crisis, a general capitalist offensive was under way. Rationalisation, unemployment and anti-trade union measures were destroying the old illusions, while at the same time the government was drawing the unions into the coils of its Industrial Peace Conference. With the right-wing union leaders committed to class collaboration and the ACTU still weak and vacillating, the task of leadership would fall to the the revolutionary left wing under the leadership of the Communist Party. At this point the party executive again baulked at the implications of its own analysis. Despite or perhaps because of its own weak presence in the unions, the Communist Party remained committed to activity within them; for all its denunciation of the trade union bureaucracy, it still hoped to influence the unions through their officials and the peak industrial bodies, the state trades and labor councils and the ACTU.[42] The explanation was simple. The continued affiliation of the New South Wales Labor Council to the RILU was too important to risk by the application of Class Against Class to the industrial field. Except in the case of the miners, whose union was not affiliated to the Labor Council, the Minority Movement therefore remained a lifeless gesture, subordinated to the legacy of the united front.

Almost immediately this vestige of the united front began to break up under the very pressures identified in the communist analysis of the Third Period. As Australia's economic difficulties mounted, the government and employers launched a major offensive on wages and working conditions. The offensive was at once industrial and political, involving legislators, judges and police as well employers, and the conservative federal government opened it with changes to the procedures and composition of the arbitration court as well as the creation of sweeping new penal powers to enforce court awards. It is difficult to exaggerate the significance of these changes. From the turn of the century, the Australian labour movement had used industrial arbitration as a means of gaining recognition and improvement. Through the associated procedures of wage

determination, arbitration served both as a device for the maintenance of living standards and a tangible expression of the belief that
the state could reconcile the claims of capital and labour. All this
was now placed at risk by the conservative Nationalist government,
and with it the attachment of the Australian labour movement to
the arbitration system. But this was not the only consequence of the
assault on existing industrial awards. Since few unions were capable
of resistance in a period of mounting unemployment, and those that
did resist were forced to capitulate, the communists assumed an
increasingly prominent, oppositional position. The bitter industrial
battles fought in 1928, 1929 and 1930 were therefore formative for
a new generation of Australian communists. The defeats suffered by
the strikers, the failure of the unions to protect them and the
conclusions drawn from these events completed the Australian party's turn to the full rigours of Class Against Class.

There were three principal theatres of conflict, each of them
involving a key industry in which large bodies of workers were
starved into submission: first, the maritime industry where the
dispute lasted from September 1928 to mid-1929 and crippled the
Waterside Workers' Federation; then the timber industry where
workers held out from January 1929 to June in Melbourne and
October in Sydney; and finally, the coal industry where the miners
on the northern New South Wales field were locked out from March
1929 to the middle of 1930.

The ports were the first battleground. Here the waterside workers refused to accept a new award, were fined and then replaced by
strikebreakers, who in turn received official preference under the
government's system of licensing workers in the industry. Faced with
these sanctions, both the Federation and the ACTU surrendered,
leaving aggrieved unionists in some ports to maintain their forlorn
cause on picket lines marked by violence, intimidation and victimisation. The Communist Party, which had almost no presence in the
waterside workforce or the union at the time, apart from at some
north Queensland ports, played no part in these decisions, though
the government gave the party prominence when it prosecuted two
leading members for publishing a leaflet, 'Don't Work Black Ships'.
Its direct involvement was restricted to encouragement of the diehards and condemnation of those who betrayed them.[43]

The timberworkers' dispute, on the other hand, brought closer communist involvement. The new award handed down by Justice Lukin in January 1929 was so harsh in its provisions—an increase in hours and reduction in wages—that the ACTU declared it 'the most vicious attack that has been made by the employers through the Arbitration Court on any section of the workers in Australia', and then set out to limit the union response. Under the authority of the ACTU, the New South Wales Labor Council directed the strike in Sydney, confined the dispute to workers in the industry, supervised the picket lines, collected and distributed relief. Jack Kavanagh, as the Labor Council organiser, thus played a key role, and the Militant Minority Movement and Militant Women's Group were both prominent auxiliaries. When Lukin ordered a secret ballot of the striking unionists, it was the Communist Party that arranged the public demonstration in the city where the court's ballot papers were burned along with an effigy of the judge. Of the ballot papers that survived to be counted, 5316 rejected a return to work against 732 in favour. Even as the strike began to fail in Melbourne, there was no weakening of resolve in Sydney. Jock Garden went down to Yallourn to plead for support from the power workers there with one of his characteristically audacious invitations:

> One night out for Yallourn would be more than enough for the employers in Melbourne. One night of darkness in Melbourne and there would be a few more new suits worn in the city. The workers would have a few gold watches too.[44]

Both he and Kavanagh were arrested, convicted and fined under new state anti-picketing legislation. Kavanagh's position was unenviable. As an officer of the Labor Council he was complicit in its refusal to seek a general stoppage of the building industry. He could see that the strikers were doomed: their exhaustion, the depletion of their strike fund, the weight of police repression and the inability of his flying pickets to prevent resumption of work at one mill after another made this inevitable. But for as long as the timberworkers were prepared to fight on, he fought with them and he was not the only activist who believed this forlorn resistance gave pause to other employers who contemplated wage cuts. At the same time the weight of the Third Period's logic allowed for no other explanation of failure other than the treachery of the workers' leaders. Accordingly

Kavanagh made an open attack on Garden for his continued participation in the government's Industrial Peace Conference, and
Garden responded by replacing Kavanagh as Labor Council
organiser. Thus were the predictions of Class Against Class brought
to fruition.[45]

The mining dispute, the last, most savage and prolonged of these
epic industrial conflicts, completed the Communist Party's shift to
a clear oppositional industrial stance. Strictly this was not a strike
but a lockout imposed by the coal owners on the miners of the
northern New South Wales field. The employers' insistence on the
need to reduce production costs could scarcely disguise the implications of their own defiance of the arbitration system, and the
blatant hypocrisy of a government which had enforced the court's
determinations on the wharfies and timberworkers but allowed the
coal owners to escape prosecution only strengthened the communist
argument that the principles of arbitration were a sham, the court
an instrument of capitalist domination. While the policy of the
union executive was to restrict the dispute to the northern field and
seek redress by arbitration, negotiation, or even by direct government intervention (which the Labor Party promised the miners
during the 1929 federal election campaign), the communists sought
to extend the stoppage and bring it to resolution, if necessary by
calling out safety workers and allowing pits to flood. The communists were best represented on the northern field, and through their
Minority Movement they already possessed an influential network
of local lodge officials; in the latter part of 1929 these lodges were
turned into local councils of action, which coordinated community
resistance in the tight-knit pit townships. The failure of the newly
elected federal Labor government to make good its promise to end
the lockout only increased the miners' resentment, and the killing
of a unionist by New South Wales police at Rothbury in December
1929 hardened their determination. The Rothbury mine was opened
by the state government with non-union labour. The Kurri Kurri
pipe band led 10 000 protestors in the small hours of 16 December
up to the pit, where they were ambushed by armed police. Forty
men were wounded; Norman Brown died of a shot in the stomach.

After Rothbury the northern coalfield was an occupied province
on which police detachments conducted a reign of terror. Special

laws forbade meetings of more than two persons. Baton charges, violent assault and arbitrary arrest became habitual. If there was no dramatic influx of party membership, the quixotic courage of its representatives made a deep impression as leading communists journeyed repeatedly from Sydney into the Hunter Valley to stand on the platform with local comrades and endure bashings, fines and imprisonment.[46]

The first national conference of the Minority Movement met in July 1929. Bill Orr reported that the executive of the Miners' Federation had sabotaged the local councils of action and suspended the pickets on the northern coalfield. In the port towns of Queensland, said Ted Tripp, the reactionary union leaders were expelling militants from the trades and labour councils. As chairman, Kavanagh noted the failure of craft unions to support the timberworkers. Despite all these signs of the bankruptcy of union officialdom, the hundred delegates nevertheless resolved to concentrate the energies of their industrial groups on 'strengthening the trade unions'. Beyond that the majority of the party executive (though not Kavanagh) were still unprepared to advance, since to do so would have been to endanger the affiliation to the RILU of the peak union body in New South Wales, Garden's Labor Council, and through Garden, the affiliation of the ACTU to the PPTU.[47] An RILU official had recently travelled to Sydney to insist that this was sacrosanct.[48] The PPTU, after all, linked working-class organisations in China and Japan, as well as those in the extensive East Asian empires of the European powers to their equivalents in Russia, Australia and the United States: it was the most tangible expression of revolutionary internationalism. For all its denunciation of yellow unions and treacherous union leaders, the Communist International therefore made it quite clear to the Australians that these international alliances were more valuable than the tiny Communist Party of Australia. Even the organisation of a national Minority Movement conference had been

In this cartoon produced during the Queensland state election, a worker conveys the Nationalist Party and Labor Party leaders to oblivion. The two politicians are indistinguishable; the avenging worker is a grim and ragged Frankenstein. (Source: 'Workers' Weekly', 3 May 1929)

"WHERE THE HELL'S THE RUBBISH TIP"

opposed by the RILU.[49] At this point, then, Moscow remained an obstacle to the very changes it urged the CPA to adopt.

No one could have predicted the remarkable chain of events that followed. The ruling Australian conservatives, seeking to profit from the turmoil of the strikes and lockouts, changed an industrial offensive into a political controversy, one that soon passed out of their control and turned them out of office. The two main culprits, Prime Minister Bruce and Attorney-General Latham, were brought down by the very spectre of economic misery they had exploited so skilfully before. Having sought and failed to secure additional powers of arbitration to break the strikes, they determined to abandon the jurisdiction, except for the maritime industry, and leave the country's employers a free hand to break the resistance of their workers. They were brought undone by Billy Hughes, the Labor rat and scourge of the communists, who could not resist the opportunity to avenge himself on the prime minister who had supplanted him six years earlier. In September 1929 he persuaded a small group of fellow malcontents to cross the floor and defeat the legislation. The Nationalists immediately called a snap election in which Labor came forward with new confidence as the defender of arbitration and the saviour of the besieged unions. Here were the very circumstances the Communist International had identified as the Third

Period of revolutionary class struggle, the moment at which capitalism fell back on reformists to solve its crisis and communists could at last expose their treachery.

There were only five weeks to polling day and the communist executive's initial decision that it had neither the time nor the resources to stand candidates is readily intelligible. The recent state election in Queensland, in May 1929, had hardly vindicated the exaggerated claims of the comrades there that the workers were ripe for a revolutionary lead. Even though Miles and Moxon worked as full-time organisers for months and drew on every available assistance, the two communist candidates (Miles in Brisbane, Tripp in Mundingburra) and three left-wing candidates (Fred Paterson was one) attracted just 3194 votes between them as the conservatives swept Labor from office. This did not abash the champions of the Queensland resolution. Miles greeted the defeat of the Labor government as a salutary exposure of reformism, and pronounced the party's poll 'satisfactory'. Moxon interpreted the failure of the three left-wing candidates as 'proof in the future that the workers who will follow a revolutionary policy WILL follow the Revolutionary Party—the Communist Party'. In August he called for the application of the 'new line' to every state and to federal politics.[50] Most party members, however, recognised the result as a decisive rebuff to their optimistic expectations and the exultation of some Queensland comrades at the defeat of Labor did not improve their popularity.

Moreover, the Queensland election had exhausted the party's resources. Miles and Moxon were both laid off at the declaration of the poll, and Joe Shelley, sent as replacement organiser to north Queensland, was languishing in Townsville prison as the result of a costly free-speech fight. Party branches in Melbourne, Adelaide and Perth were wracked by dissension, suspension and expulsion. Ted Tripp was due to depart for training at the Lenin School after the Queensland election, but when he arrived in Sydney to receive the money Moscow had sent for his passage, it emerged the executive had long since spent it and in desperation Tom Wright borrowed £65 from Jock Garden.[51] Publication of the party's monthly theoretical magazine had lasped at the end of 1928. There was not even enough money to pay the editor of the *Workers'*

Weekly, and its future was in any case imperilled by an expensive pending libel action. The party, in short, had taxed its members' energies to breaking point. The executive therefore decided that the first priority of the Communist Party should be to defeat the conservatives. The Labor Party was weak and unreliable; its leaders were running away from the class struggle; its candidates should be pressed to support a left-wing programme; but under the circumstances there was no alternative but to urge a vote for Labor.[52]

The decision was immediately challenged by Moxon, who had been brought back to Sydney, and Miles, with whom he remained in regular correspondence. Sharkey joined them in an open challenge, and on 18 September the two dissident members of the executive telegrammed their denunciation of the Australian party's 'right deviation' to the Executive Committee of the Communist International.[53] This was an unprecedented move. In the past, Australian communists had privately canvassed support from sympathetic members of the Comintern, but in violating party rules with an open appeal from a majority decision, the dissidents broke new ground. Even then, the Comintern response drew heavily on advice from the Queenslander Ted Tripp, who had recently arrived in Moscow and fully shared Moxon and Sharkey's zeal for the Third Period.[54] The ECCI instructed the Australian executive that support for the Labor Party would violate the decisions of the Sixth Congress; the CPA must run its own candidates and, in the cryptic phraseology of its telegrammed response, 'MUST COME OUT OWN PLATFORM EXPOSE ARBITRATION AND INDUSTRIAL PEACE COMMON TREACHEROUS ROLE OF BOURGEOIS LABOR PARTY AND REACTIONARY TRADE UNION BUREAUCRACY STOP'. The message reached the Australian executive on 26 September, just sixteen days before election day. It briefly indicated, again by telegram, that there was no time to stand candidates. The ECCI reiterated its earlier instructions, also by telegram. On 8 October Moxon and Sharkey cabled Moscow that their proposal to implement the Comintern instructions had received no support, and a further flurry of telegrams followed.[55] By now the ECCI had despatched a lengthy Open Letter for circulation to all Australian members and a special envoy who was to guide the Australian party. The Open Letter would not arrive until the very eve of the annual party conference at the end of the year, but a final telegram, sent on 18 October, put the defiant Australian executive on notice:

> PARTYS DUTY AS SOLE PARTY WORKING CLASS CONDUCT INDEPENDENT CLASS POSITION OPPOSITION LABOR PARTY TRADE UNION BUREAUCRACY STOP FIRST CONDITION SUCCESSFUL CONDUCT THIS POLICY RUTHLESSLY COMBATING RIGHT WING DEVIATIONS OWN RANKS BY INTRODUCING STRONGER WIDE SELF CRITICISM STOP . . . STRAIGHTEN PARTY LINE ACCORDANCE DECISIONS SIXTH CONGRESS TENTH PLENUM AND STRENGTHEN PARTY LEADERSHIP.[56]

While it was too late to obey the first instruction, the further injunctions could not be ignored. On 25 October, just a week after Labor won the election, the *Workers' Weekly* opened a 'free discussion of the problems of the party'. It continued for two months and was the last discussion of its kind in the party press for several decades. Among the questions Higgins, as editor, posed at the outset were 'is there a Right danger in the Party?', and three weeks later he reminded members that it was only one of a number of urgent questions—to no avail, since it was the only question members wished to discuss.[57] Their overwhelming response was in the affirmative, and the formulation of the question probably ensured that it would be, for no one wanted to be a champion of the right. Over the course of the discussion the logic of the Third Period came to prevail as party members outbid each other in left virtue. They did so, it should be noted, of their own volition. While publication of the ECCI Open Letter on 6 December informed them where their duty lay, the pattern of conformity was already well established. It is possible to suggest reasons for the voluntary compliance with the new line. The Wall Street Crash on 24 October 1929, demonstrating the severity of the international financial crisis, confirmed earlier predictions of a major depression. The inability of the new federal Labor government to end the lockout of the miners or protect many more workers from layoffs added daily to the plausibility of the Third Period diagnosis. But circumstantial explanations such as these fail to capture the underlying tone of the discussion, which was recriminatory, impatient, enclosed in a logic that understood worse to mean better, verging on a chiliasm of despair that saw past failure as the harbinger of future success.

At the outset of the *Workers' Weekly* discussion Higgins also expressed the hope that 'no comrade should yield to the temptation to score personal points' or 'give any encouragement to factionalism'. Most yielded eagerly in a flurry of recriminations over who should accept responsibility for the party's record in the Queensland and federal elections. Publication of the ECCI's Open Letter, including the statement that 'the decision of your Central Committee to support the Labor Party in the last elections is clearly a glaring example of grave Right deviation deserving the clearest condemnation', only intensified the preoccupation with settling old scores. Moxon called the executive 'anti-Comintern, anti-working class, oppositionist and cowardly'; Wright condemned his 'lying and unscrupulously factional character'.[58] Every failure in the performance of the party was attributed to political deficiency, every deficiency deemed the result of a culpable personal weakness. It was in vain that Wright and others pointed out the sheer logistical limitations of a tiny, impoverished organisation, for that merely confirmed the defeatism that must be expunged. Self-criticism had become obligatory and the executive now accepted the Comintern's Open Letter as 'a necessary corrective to serious mistakes'.[59]

The critics extended their allegations of political error and personal failure into a vulgarised class analysis. They spoke from a position of proletarian virtue as militant activists in the field; they portrayed the leaders of the party in Sydney as overly respectable pedants who lacked real contact with the class struggle and were hopelessly out of touch with the revolutionary temper of the workers. Higgins, the editor of the *Workers' Weekly*, was particularly susceptible to this charge. In a notable polemical open letter to the CEC written on the eve of the conference, Moxon alleged that his 'only real qualification is that he spells well'. Hence Higgins's reasoned objections to the wild allegations against the leadership could be swept aside as confirmation of his non-working class character. 'What effrontery!' Moxon admonished him. 'It doesn't fit this time, Comrade Higgins, because the right wingers are going to be replaced by proletarian communists, yes, even if their spelling is bad.'[60]

Notwithstanding its contrition, the annual conference was conducted in an atmosphere described by Higgins as 'absolutely poisonous'.[61] The report of the outgoing executive attempted to explain the errors to which it now confessed: the party had not appreciated the implications of the Third Period; it had mistakenly believed that Australian workers were not ready to discard their attachment to the Labor Party, but now appreciated the new line. Moxon and Sharkey presented a minority report that raked over the failure to oppose Labor in the federal elections, criticised the party's conduct in the timberworkers' and coalminers' disputes, and found a persistent pattern of right deviation. It was clear from the outset that they would prevail. One delegate after another condemned the 'rank cowardice', the 'treachery and bankruptcy' of the communist leadership. On the second day of the conference a cable was received from the ECCI, reminding delegates that their task was to subject recent policy to 'the severest criticism' and describing the actions of the executive dissidents as 'perfectly sound and necessary'. Kavanagh remained defiant; Hector Ross, Jack Ryan and Tom Wright responded to the wilder accusations against them; Higgins mixed rebuttal with self-reproach. J. B. Miles took the high ground to warn against attribution of failure to executive errors alone: 'The whole Party has been off the revolutionary line'. To bring them back onto it, Moxon proposed a slate of candidates for the new executive that included just three of the outgoing members: himself, Sharkey and Barras. All but three of his list were duly returned, and the only survivor of the discredited leadership was Higgins. On 30 December the self-styled Praesidium of the Communist Party of Australia, Moxon, Miles, Sharkey, and two of their closest support-ers, despatched a telegram to the secretary of the Communist International: 'ANNUAL CONFERENCE GREETS COMINTERN DECLARES UNSWERVING LOYALTY NEW LINE'.[62]

7

Bolshevisation

The Australian party made its unswerving loyalty to the new line of the Communist International quickly apparent. From the beginning of 1930 the executive embarked on a course of absolute fidelity to the politics of the Third Period. It gave constant and uncritical support to Stalin's actions in the Soviet Union: the breakneck industrialisation, the collectivisation of agriculture and the purges and show trials that accompanied them. It reproduced his strident denunciations of the imperialist powers and exhorted workers to defend the Soviet homeland from imminent assault. It heralded the world crisis of capitalism as the harbinger of a revolutionary upsurge. It construed fascism and social democracy alike as devices to which the capitalists resorted in their attempt to avert the crisis—hence the social democrats were now social fascists, a term that meant little in a country where few recognised the Labor Party as the local form of social democracy, but was promulgated regardless—and it sought to expose the reactionary nature of both. It therefore embarked on a strategy of defiant confrontation of the authorities and unrelenting opposition to the Labor Party and the trade unions. It imposed an iron discipline on its own adherents, who were expected to make any sacrifice, endure any hardship, accept any risk, in the service of the party. The Communist Party of Australia had come late to the Third Period and it now embarked on a frenzy of activity designed to provide revolutionary leadership to the victims of the crisis, workers, unemployed workers, the poor and dispossessed, in the struggle of Class Against Class.

Circumstances lent plausibility to the new line. The federal Labor government that won office in October 1929 was confronted almost immediately by the breakdown of the international financial system and paralysis of world trade, with domestic consequences that a debtor country heavily reliant on its export industries was powerless to withstand. As wool and wheat prices tumbled, and loans were called in, many farmers walked off the land. Falling sales, business failures, wage reductions and lay-offs extended the misery to towns and cities. Thus began what would become known as the Great Depression, though at the time it seemed more like collapse. It was an economic crisis of unprecedented severity that engulfed Australia along with every other capitalist country, and its effects persisted for years. It was a social crisis that upset established patterns of production and consumption, overwhelmed entire communities and strained the relationships that gave order and meaning to collective life. And it was a political crisis that swept away elected governments and threatened to extinguish democratic freedoms.

Unable to prevent the economic disaster, incapable of dealing with its budgetary consequences, the national Labor government succumbed to internal division and was voted out of office at the end of 1931. The inability of federal Labor to protect jobs was matched by the failure of Labor governments in South Australia, Victoria and Western Australia, and later in New South Wales and Queensland, to provide more than the most meagre relief to the victims of the Depression—the wage-earners who were thrown onto the scrap-heap, the families deprived of an income, the young people who had no prospect of finding a job, the growing army of destitute, homeless and desperate Australians. Their rising discontent brought street protest to every Australian city, which in turn was answered by police repression and the mobilisation of right-wing organisations to suppress the left. The capacity of the trade unions had been sapped by the defeat of the waterside and timberworkers, so that when the miners were bludgeoned into submission the effective resistance of the industrial labour movement was exhausted.

According to the Communist Party every one of these developments confirmed the logic of the Third Period. The poverty of the countryside, the cuts imposed on wage-earners, the misery of the unemployed, the weakness of the Labor Party and the unions, the brutality of the police and the outrages of the paramilitary right, all were consistent with revolutionary crisis. In the first flush of its supremacy, the new leadership exulted in the beleaguered condition of the party. A constant round of activism, street demonstrations, confrontations with the social fascists, expulsions, bashings, arrests and repeated gaol sentences, all validated the line. Even as it fought to survive, the party drove out any who hesitated to make such gestures of defiance most of which were futile as they were destined to be ignored by workers. For a brief moment, the logic of Class Against Class pushed Australian communism to the verge of insurrection.

'Moxon tends to be hysterical, acts as though he were in the midst of a battle in which instant action was of vital importance.' Jack Kavanagh made the observation in his diary in February 1930, just a few weeks after Bert Moxon assumed the post of party secretary and plunged into precipitate implementation of the new line. Moxon had immediately turned the *Workers' Weekly* over to reports of a general capitalist offensive upon workers in all industries, along with repeated explanations of how the treacherous social fascists were sapping resistance. The newspaper's tone of desperate urgency transmuted any wage cut or work speed-up into a symptom of the impending crisis, any communist activity into evidence of a rising revolutionary tide. The forms of communist activity it held up for emulation were stridently confrontational, accusatory, defiant, irreconcilable. Every rebuff it suffered, every failure to answer its shrill proclamations, became further confirmation of the bankruptcy of the reformists. 'The correct appreciation of social fascism', Moxon predicted, 'will forge the party into a steely power to meet the coming decisive class battles'.[1]

The steel was forged on the northern coalfield where, after nearly a year of defiance, the miners were in a desperate condition. All savings were exhausted, the local co-ops had long since emptied their shelves. The federal Labor government had failed to end the owners' lockout, the conservative state government had despatched large squads of police to open pits with volunteer labour and stopped unemployment relief, the craft unions had surrendered and the central council of the Miners' Federation still refused to extend the dispute to other fields. As soon as he assumed control of the party, Moxon despatched leading comrades to Maitland, Cessnock, Kurri Kurri, Weston and the other mining townships, with strict orders to defy the bans on public assemblies and conduct themselves without regard to their personal safety.

The Hunter Valley thus became a testing ground for party members in the new rigours of Class Against Class. Dozens were arrested, charged and convicted for offences ranging from intimidation and assault to vagrancy, profanity and insulting policemen.[2] The party insisted that members should refuse to be bound over or pay fines: 'gaol must be accepted if only to prove that such institution cannot deter or intimidate the real revolutionary workers'. It held Joe Shelley up as a model of 'Communist defiance' when he was charged with incitement to murder in a speech given to a meeting in Kurri Kurri on 8 January. 'I am a Communist', he declared at the trial. 'I hold that force, violence and energy are the essence of progress and as such are necessary.' Sentenced to two months hard labour, he refused to enter into a bond of good behaviour and was given another three months. A local communist, Bill Laidlaw, responded similarly when convicted of insulting police from the same platform four days later with the words, 'They are so low, they could crawl under the belly of a snake and still have a bit to spare'. He chose to serve a fortnight in gaol rather than pay his fine and since a good behaviour bond would have required him to desist from public speaking, he accepted an additional four weeks.[3] The party celebrated its martyrs and it singled out particular comrades for martyrdom. Moxon sent many of the old executive for spells of duty on the coalfield; he accused one of sounding the retreat as the union executive prepared to conclude the forlorn resistance, and even ordered Esmonde Higgins to use force if necessary to prevent union officials from putting its proposals to a mass meeting of miners. Of the 3000 present, Higgins judged that perhaps a dozen would have backed him.[4]

The defeat of the miners, the last of the major work groups to have resisted the employers' drive at the end of the 1920s, demonstrated the depleted condition of the Australian labour movement. As the Depression intensified, no union was able to withstand the insistent downward pressure on wages and working conditions. Yet Moxon's repeated exhortations to smash the capitalist offensive by 'ruthless exposure' of the Labor Party and the trade unions, a project which belied their enfeebled condition as well as that of his own party, culminated in April 1930 with a directive for nothing less than a general strike: 'Workers of Australia, the hour has struck— fight as one man. Smash capitalism in a mass strike.'[5] Not one worker responded to the party's call and not one communist seriously expected them to do so. The directive was aimed at Moscow, not Australia; for while the new executive undoubtedly enjoyed the approval of the Communist International, it had yet to make good its undertakings of unswerving loyalty to the new line. Its need to consolidate control over the Australian party and its determination to break utterly with the old ways both required the most credulous revolutionary rhetoric.

Breaking with the old ways meant discrediting the old leadership. Jack Kavanagh still enjoyed the respect and companionship of prominent comrades such as Esmonde Higgins and Joy Barrington, Jack and Edna Ryan, Tom Wright and his future wife Mary Lamm, who clustered in the inner suburbs of Glebe and Newtown, close to the party headquarters, and sustained much of its activity. His residual influence was apparent when he topped the poll in elections to the New South Wales state and Sydney district committees conducted shortly after the national party conference. He and Jack Ryan showed no signs of remorse, and Kavanagh was said to have boasted that the new national leadership would not last six months; yet neither man could be attacked without serious risk of collateral damage since Kavanagh enjoyed a strong personal following on the New South Wales Labor Council, which remained a valuable affiliate of the Red International of Labor Unions, while Ryan was still the Australian organiser of the RILU's Pan-Pacific Trade Union

Secretariat, to which both the Labor Council and the ACTU were affiliated. Even in full flush of the Third Period, the Communist International was reluctant to sacrifice these valuable footholds in the Australian labour movement. Moxon proceeded, nevertheless, to do so.

On 6 February 1930 he accused Ryan of 'perpetuating the reformist illusion' with an article Ryan wrote in the *Pan-Pacific Worker* that attributed the persecution of the miners to the Nationalist New South Wales government and a notice in the same journal that donations to a defence fund for Indian prisoners should be sent to 'the counter-revolutionary Garden'. Flimsy though these charges were, they sufficed to achieve Moxon's purpose, as Ryan disdained to answer them. He was accordingly expelled from the party later in the same month, on the very eve of the ACTU congress in Melbourne. The timing was unfortunate. At that congress the ACTU's link to the PPTU came under sustained attack from right-wing delegates; Ryan was excluded from the communist fraction of five inexperienced delegates who voted against a compromise resolution, and by a narrow margin the congress then rejected further affiliation.[6] Moxon reported Ryan's expulsion to the ECCI by telegram and lamely sought its immediate advice about the implications for the RILU and PPTU. The Comintern Executive's response to his message is not known but its displeasure can be gauged from a subsequent comment that the expulsion was 'inexpedient' and Moxon's apologetic justification that Ryan was 'unreconcilable'. Ryan himself reported his travails and their larger consequences in a letter to Lozovsky, the secretary of the RILU, who lobbied on his behalf in Moscow. If he had been prepared to recant his errors, he would undoubtedly have been readmitted. But as he remarked, it was obvious that the Australian party must be making 'remarkable strides' if it was able to expel one of its most active members out of 'personal animosity'.[7]

Moxon conducted his campaign against Kavanagh more circumspectly. The former leader retained the confidence of party members in Sydney, as the recent election of the district committee demonstrated; he still believed that the recent change of national leadership was a temporary reverse and that his supplanters would quickly discredit themselves. Moxon therefore sought to detach Kavanagh from his base of support by despatching him to the provinces. To do this he had to assure Kavanagh that he bore no grudges. Kavanagh was justifiably sceptical of Moxon's disavowal of the insistent rumours that he was 'head hunting', but perhaps too ready to interpret the new party secretary's simulation of conciliation as a sign of weakness: 'He is afraid to push too far', Kavanagh noted in his diary. So he allowed himself to be sent out of Sydney on missions that were designed to discredit him. First Moxon directed Kavanagh to the northern coalfield and then accused him of going there without permission. Next he ordered Kavanagh to Adelaide to supervise the party's campaign in the state elections. Kavanagh found the theoretical level of the South Australian comrades low, and no wonder, since the branch there had only just been re-established, but was censured by the Central Executive Committee in his absence for perpetuating reformist illusions in the campaign literature.[8]

He returned to Sydney in April to find the Sydney district branch in uproar. An aggregate meeting in the previous month, called by the CEC to explain the expulsion of Ryan, had produced open criticism of the party leadership; Tom Wright was reported to have said that 'The CEC is a gang of nincompoops led by the nose by Moxon'. The CEC interpreted such frankness as a 'glaring example of the flagrant opposition to the New Line' and convened a further aggregate meeting in April, with one of its own members, Ted Docker, in the chair. Docker, a Sydney carpenter and early member of the party who had emerged as a particularly zealous enthusiast for the new line, wielded his authority with relish to chastise the branch and replace dissident members of its committee. When he denied Kavanagh a hearing, Joy Barrington called him a Mussolini.[9]

At this inauspicious point in the new regime, the representative despatched by the Communist International arrived in Sydney in April 1930. His name was Harry Wicks, though in Australia he used his Christian names, Herbert Moore, and also the pseudonyms Simpson and 'XYZ'. He was an American, who had gone to Moscow in 1929 as part of a delegation of the Communist Party of the United States of America, which itself had fallen into the error of national exceptionalism in resistance to the new line of the Third Period. Lovestone, the United States party leader, had been denounced by Stalin and expelled, but Moore submitted and was now sent to root out the same error in Australia. Tall, commanding, with a square-shaped, close-cropped head that reinforced a barrack-room manner, he immediately imposed his authority on the Australian comrades. Kavanagh, who resisted him from the outset, claimed to have recognised him from an earlier American encounter as a member of the Ku Klux Klan. That seemed an extravagant allegation but Moore was ultimately expelled from the American party as a spy and subsequent evidence suggests that he was an undercover agent for anti-communist organisations for the whole of his party career.[10]

Moore took up the campaign against the party rebels as an object lesson in Bolshevik discipline. His method of imposing control was far more subtle than the bluff and bluster of Moxon, for it involved the systematic use of a new punishment known as self-criticism. Self-criticism was a form of public confession in which the errant communist publicly acknowledged his or her failings and undertook to eradicate them. In rebuking the Australian party for its deviations from the line in 1929, the Communist International had instructed the leaders to embark on a cleansing process of self-criticism and Moxon had endeavoured to comply, with limited success. Moore insisted. Within two weeks of his assumption of control, the *Workers' Weekly* announced 'Self-Criticism as a Means of Winning the Masses'. He straightaway summoned the oppositionists in the Sydney branch to appear separately before him and accused each of failure to carry out particular tasks in an appropriate manner. Joy Barrington had already been expelled for calling Docker a Mussolini, but then appealed to the state committee, which reinstated her. She now came before Moore and the CEC, and was forced to apologise for 'an impermissible attack upon the leadership of the Party'. Upon signing a public undertaking that she would henceforth submit herself to revolutionary discipline and join the struggle against 'all who continue to follow my former wrong line', he allowed her to remain. Among the other dissidents to follow her example was Tom Wright. He would become at once the most pliable and the most steadfast of party functionaries, a striking example of the restorative powers of self-criticism.[11]

Ryan and Kavanagh were harder to crack. Moore sought out

Ryan and urged him to apply for readmission. As he related their private meeting, Ryan declared that he wanted to be in the party but that 'many comrades have it in for me'. Moore replied that 'personal considerations cannot enter into the work of the Party. It is purely a political question.' (Ryan's impish aside that he knew Moore must have arrived in Australia because of a split infinitive in a recent party manifesto suggested that personalities were not so easily suppressed.) In any case, Ryan's utility was declining as the communists widened the breach with Garden and the New South Wales Labor Council by setting up their own fraction of the RILU and seizing control of the Australian office of the PPTU, so that by 1931 the Labor Council was not even a nominal ally. Before that final breakdown in relations between the communists and the erstwhile Trades Hall Reds, Moore had, in any case, convinced the ECCI that Ryan was incorrigible since he still refused to make a confession of his errors.[12]

It did not stop there. Edna Ryan, Jack's wife, was called upon to repudiate his opposition. Initially torn between attachment to the party and loyalty to Jack, she allowed the *Workers' Weekly* in early 1931 to publish a statement that she was not associated with his anti-party activities. In a cruel twist, she was then denounced by her former friend, Mary Lamm, for a defiant speech given at a women's meeting and ordered to appear before the party's disciplinary tribunal, the Central Control Commission. Jack Loughran, another old comrade, interrogated her.

> It was hard to believe I was being carpeted by that Irishman who could be so funny, full of humour and repartee—one of the enjoyable members of the group. He was sour, bitter and quite ridiculously authoritarian and judicial. I did not try very hard, I did not plead . . . If I ever received an official notification of the result, I do not remember it. It was over and I never went back.[13]

Kavanagh was also resistant. He first came before Moore and the CEC for his conduct at the Sydney branch meeting in April 1930 and for criticising Moxon's rash call for a general strike. The Third Period was still not operating in Australia, Kavanagh told his critics, and there was not yet sufficient resistance among Australian workers to justify its tactics. It was 'a serious error', he insisted, 'to issue a call that would bring our members out of industry and sacrifice them needlessly'. Moore appealed to Kavanagh as a leading member of the party to reconsider his position. 'We don't want to discipline members to the limit', he claimed, and Kavanagh's cooperation was all the more important because the executive was 'not as strong as it ought to be'. Kavanagh was unimpressed. He observed in his diary that 'Self-criticism is intended primarily for those who do not kowtow to the CEC'. Later in the same month he allowed himself to be elected to the chair of an unemployed conference in place of the party nominee. In the following month he again accepted nomination at the Labor Council in an election of delegates to the RILU conference in Moscow, despite instructions from Moxon and Jeffery to withdraw. That he attracted as many Labor Council votes as the two party candidates, Sharkey and Docker, only aggravated his offence. The CEC discussed this serious infraction and Moore made clear how it was to be treated. 'Will we expel him? No. He is a leader so we deal with him in a different way. We do not expel him at once. We kill him politically.'[14]

They did so by pressing home the duty of self-criticism. Kavanagh appeared before the Central Control Commission on 26 May charged with his conduct at the Labor Council, his persistent questioning of party policy and his attacks on the CEC 'for indulging in self-criticism'. The last of these charges occasioned fierce disputation. Kavanagh contended that the constant rehearsal of errors and failures had a demoralising effect on members, just as the emphasis in the party press on the defeats and betrayals of the workers dampened the spirits of readers so badly in need of encouragement. If differences between leading members arose, they should be resolved internally and not by public confessions that could only damage the party's credibility. For the Central Control Commission, however, self-criticism was a necessary safeguard against the pernicious errors that sprouted in a malign environment: 'Such criticism must be for the purpose of searching out the roots of such errors in order that they may be exterminated from the working class soil. Even more, it must absolutely destroy the soil from which such poisonous things spring.' It deemed Kavanagh's aversion to public confession a form of petty bourgeois individualism and warned him that a failure to submit would place him outside the party.[15]

For almost half a year Kavanagh fulfilled his obligations. While privately contemptuous of the new leadership's empty gestures, he publicly stated he had been wrong and that he now accepted the new line. He took classes for the party, he addressed meetings both in Sydney and on the coalfields, he served a spell in Long Bay prison for holding a street meeting, he read Katharine Susannah Prichard's novel *Working Bullocks* ('story is realistic but grammar is poor') and he stood for the party in the electorate of Newtown during the 1930 New South Wales state elections. But as the date set for the next party conference drew closer he was once again under attack, this time for his role in a demonstration at the Sydney Town Hall on 7 November to mark the anniversary of the Russian Revolution.[16] Moxon ordered Kavanagh, who was one of the party speakers at the Town Hall, to attack the new state Labor government and Kavanagh refused. When inflammatory oratory from Norm Jeffery and Moxon resulted in a baton charge and arrests, Moxon led the crowd to Trades Hall, where further arrests were made. Moxon claimed that he stood on a windowsill and urged the crowd to avenge their mates, and that Kavanagh held them back. Kavanagh claimed that he had simply drawn public attention to the presence of *agents provocateurs*. Even though he had been warned by Esmonde Higgins that this time Moore and Moxon were after his head, he responded hotly to allegations of cowardice. It was a trumped-up charge, he insisted, and in any case it was 'un-Marxian' to suggest one man could have prevented the workers from attacking the police. Arraigned before the Central Control Commission for his conduct on 7 November, he remained defiant:

> A Communist Party is not an association of Pharisees which excuses its sins by blackening the sins of others, nor is it yet an association of sadists taking pleasure in self-flagellation for the sake of manifesting its humility and by the same action its supreme egotism.

The commission recommended his expulsion, the CEC enumerated twenty instances of slander, defiance and sabotage, expelled him and warned all party members against further contact.[17]

There was a protracted sequel. Kavanagh and Ryan applied repeatedly over the following years to be readmitted to the party. Ryan would not confess his errors and was rebuffed; Kavanagh did and was placed on probation, but he never managed to effect the level of abasement the party demanded and was ultimately deemed beyond redemption in 1934.[18] To relate the full process of degradation to which he was subjected would take a history of Australian communism into a cul-de-sac; he was a negligible force after 1930, and the space given already to this squalid vendetta might seem excessive. It is significant, however, as an illustration of how the new leadership imposed its authority. The campaign against Kavanagh was at once an eradication of the old and an imposition of the new. Through the public humiliation of its most reputable figures, an organisation that had once allowed vigorous debate and open discussion of differences was reconstituted as a conventicle of rigid conformity. The obligation to engage in self-criticism drove party discipline into the very fibre of the party's being, and removed all grounds of principled dissent. However ritualised its performance, whatever reservations a practitioner might harbour, the public recital of error sapped the capacity for independent judgement—thus, even though Kavanagh resisted, hedged and protested, repeated subjection to the device eventually broke his resolution. More than this, self-criticism dissolved old loyalties by turning friends into accusers. As Higgins observed in a letter to Harry Pollitt, the members of the executive 'behaved like jackals towards Kavanagh', and in rounding on him so savagely to save themselves from the same fate his former comrades forfeited their own self-respect.[19]

Kavanagh's friends turned upon him as part of their own self-criticism during the pre-conference discussion that opened in October 1930. Its limits were made clear from the outset: there was to be 'no repetition of last year's purposeless wrangle' and 'no space will be found for letters questioning the correctness of the line'. Every contributor was to keep in mind the importance of self-criticism and even though most complied, Moore drew attention to the silence of Kavanagh, Ryan and Higgins. The approaching annual conference intensified the fervour of Class Against Class, and Moxon and Moore issued repeated calls for violent confrontations with the police. A series of street actions that followed the demonstration of 7 November resulted in so many gaol sentences that the conference set down for the end of the year had to be postponed until Easter of the following year.[20]

By then there was another victim of Moore's authority. From the time he assumed the Australian leadership, Moxon's habit of cabling the ECCI for advice whenever he encountered a set-back had made a poor impression in Moscow, as did his seeming incapacity to exercise authority without resort to expulsions. His profligacy with the large sums of money that the Communist International sent to Australia in 1930 was legendary, and an inability to delegate tasks exacerbated his administrative deficiencies. At the end of 1930 Moore relieved him of his duties as party secretary and sent him to Melbourne, where he again failed to fulfil expectations. In a characteristically madcap maneouvre designed to win control of the unemployed organisation created by the Trades Hall Council in that city, he directed the local branches of the communist body to join it. He was brought back to Sydney to express contrition at the party conference for his right-wing opportunism and assigned to other duties. Moore found Moxon bereft of judgement. 'You only came upon [Class Against Class] by accident', he told Moxon, 'because being a leftist . . . you would inevitably hit upon the right line of the Comintern some time or other'. Now that the Australian party was fully committed to that policy, Moxon's reckless impetuosity no longer compensated for his organisational shortcomings. Briefly he accepted demotion and remained a member of the central committee, but before long he tried to retrieve his fortunes with an appeal to the Comintern against the alleged anarcho-syndicalism of his supplanters. The ploy had succeeded in 1929; when he tried it again in 1931 it brought his demise.[21]

Moore was grooming a new leadership. The two young Lithgow comrades, Cliff Walker and Fred Airey had been sent for extended training at the International Lenin School along with a Victorian, Vic Varty: to avoid recognition by the security forces, they would return as Richard Dixon, Jack Blake and Len Donald. Lance Sharkey and Bill Orr also visited the Soviet Union as delegates to the Fifth RILU Congress in August 1930. Orr, the secretary of the Minority Movement, was confirmed there as the party's leading industrial organiser. Sharkey's ascent has been noted already: he was awkward, uncouth, slow in thought and hesitant in speech, still feeling his way as a dialectician and a public figure but with a growing firmness of judgement. He became editor of the *Workers' Weekly*, clearly destined for even greater eminence. But not yet. It was J. B. Miles who was brought down from Brisbane to serve as party secretary.[22]

Miles had been an important member since the early 1920s, but his distance from party headquarters meant that he could make only occasional direct interventions into national affairs. Now, on the eve of the party conference, he moved his family down from Brisbane. He was in his early forties, older than the others, and readily assumed his new authority. Once Jack, henceforth he was known as 'JBM' and cadres would afterwards refer to him as 'the Old Man'— but not in his hearing. A demanding patriarch, he applied a rigid Scots propriety to revolutionary purposes. His caution, frugality, attention to detail were all qualities that the Australian party had lacked. He, more than anyone, built it into a coherent, durable entity—at a heavy cost. Jean Devanny, with whom he began a clandestine and stormy relationship, found him tense, volatile, cutting, with a powerfully intuitive intelligence. 'He's got exceptional capacities', a visiting European comrade told her, 'but he's too hard on the comrades. He hurts too often and too much.'[23]

The deferred tenth party conference set down for December 1930 met as the Tenth Congress in April 1931 and completed organisational changes Moore had begun during the previous year. The former state branches were now reconstituted as districts. Originally there were eight: Sydney, the south coast and the New South Wales hinterland became Number 1 District; Newcastle and the Hunter Valley, Number 2; Queensland, Number 3; Victoria and the Riverina, Number 4; South Australia and Broken Hill, Number 5; Western Australia, Number 6, Northern Territory, Number 7 and Tasmania, Number 8. In 1933 north Queensland became Number 9 District. Each district was divided into sections, also enumerated, and each section into factory and street units. At every level a committee supervised the work of the subordinate level; the district committee supervised the work of the sections and the section committee supervised the work of the local members. All communications were hierarchical, and members were forbidden to communicate across this vertical structure. In place of the central executive committee, there was now an enlarged central committee which in turn was led by a smaller political bureau (or politbureau) and a secretariat of just three members.[24] At the Tenth Congress Moore introduced further refinements. The outgoing central committee elected a praesidium which nominated an examination committee to consider nominations for election to the new central committee.[25] This method of controlling elections henceforth applied at all levels of the party and effectively suppressed democratic choice of representatives.

There were some complaints at the congress about the Communist International's dictatorial 'Instructor' and his methods. Ted Tripp had returned from the Lenin School in 1930 in the expectation of speedy advancement but was already on the outer, probably because he had met American students there who regarded Moore as a 'huge joke'. Tripp told the congress delegates that Moore had told him to feign friendship with Kavanagh in order to discover his plans, but he drew the line at 'pimping'. Charlie Nelson from Lithgow claimed that he was told to toe the line or his head would come off. Jack Loughran, the most outspoken of the dissidents, suggested that 'the Party is being reduced to a party of gramophones that will only play one record—it must be "Moore's Melody" '. The great majority accepted the new regime. One comrade told Tripp that 'Inside and outside the Party he must be prepared to obey the Party and even if it is your own mother, you must pimp on her if necessary'. Ted Docker insisted 'There is no room in the Communist Party for slight differences of opinion—we must be on the line completely'. Moore, who had opened proceedings with an address lasting four hours, congratulated the Australians on a 'better discussion, more Bolshevik', one that had 'annihilated' the arguments of the dissenters. 'We are going to have one monolithic whole', he predicted.[26]

The first congress of the Australian party was also its last annual gathering. In its place there would be regular meetings of the party plenum (which consisted of the members of the central committee and other nominated participants) or extended sessions of the central committee (enlarged with leading district officials), usually at quarterly intervals. Full transcripts of these proceedings of the plenums, which usually occupied two or three days, and even of the central committee, were produced to enable Moscow to invigilate the work of the Australians. The next congress, Moore explained, would not meet until the Communist International judged that a change of line made it necessary. His work completed, Moore left Australia in July.

Moore's reorganisation of the Communist Party of Australia was foreshadowed in a lengthy ECCI letter sent to the party in October 1930, 'Resolution on the Situation in Australia and the Tasks of the CPA', which restated the postulates of the Third Period. The growth of mass struggles against the bourgeoisie showed that all the features of the general crisis of capitalism were manifest in Australia, completely destroying the theory of Australian exceptionalism advanced by former leading comrades. The task of the party was to provide independent leadership against the social fascist Labor government, Labor Party and trade union bureaucracy, partly by industrial demands and partly by organisation of the unemployed. Admonitions against trailing behind the workers were balanced with warnings against sectarianism and also (this a clear rebuke to Moxon) perpetually calling for strikes without adequate preparation. The Australian party must be a 'broad mass organisation' and not an 'isolated adventurist group'. To this end the ECCI set out the national, district and local structure, with a strong emphasis on factory groups as befitted a party of the revolutionary proletariat, and on the Minority and the Unemployed Workers' Movements as the means of extending party influence throughout it. These and other mass organisations were to be controlled by fractions of party members under the careful supervision of the party.[27]

The meagre resources of the Australian party strained its capacity to implement these instructions. Throughout 1930 the membership remained tiny: the various districts reported 486 members at the end of the year, a twofold increase over twelve months. The Tenth Congress in April 1931 enumerated 1135 members, and a subsequent membership campaign lifted the total to 2021 by July. In December 1931 there were 2093 members, and a year later 1929. Based on the returns of district committees anxious to report success, all of these figures have to be treated with scepticism. As Moore cautioned in 1931, 'Let us not fool ourselves. A good part of the increase exists on paper and on paper only.' One district organiser admitted at the end of that year that less than a quarter of the nominal membership in his state 'participate to any extent in the life and work of the Party'. Many of those signed up at public meetings or recruited in membership drives during the early 1930s remained purely nominal members; others failed to pay their dues, dropped out or were expelled. The national organiser noted a persistent pattern of recruitment and failure to retain recruits. The statistics were unreliable because 'the large percentage of unemployed members and the movement of these members from place to place and their consequent falling into inactivity are difficult to tabulate'. He was able to identify two features of the membership: just 518 of the 1929 on the books in December 1932 were in employment and only 216 were women. Both features were pronounced in other membership reports: just 9 per cent of the Victorian district membership were in employment at the time of the Tenth Congress and 10 per cent were women; six months later in New South Wales the corresponding figures were 13 and 8 per cent. This was an organisation of unemployed men.[28]

A census of the delegates who attended the Tenth Congress provides further insight into the Australian party's social composition. Of 60 delegates who provided information, there were sixteen miners, eleven labourers, five building workers, three railway workers and three waterside workers, two each from the sugar and textile industries, two intellectuals, a butcher, a baker and a miscellany of manual occupations other than candlestick-maker. Seven were women. Twenty-nine were born in Australia, twelve in England, seven in Scotland, four in Ireland, two in New Zealand and the remainder hailed from Wales, Holland, Finland, Poland, Patagonia and New Guinea. Twenty-six were employed, 23 unemployed and the remaining eleven worked for the party or other organisations. At a time when nearly 30 per cent of the country's trade union members were out of work, the number of unemployed communists at the congress was disproportionately high, but a much higher proportion of the delegates packed a work-lunch than the membership at large. It is hardly surprising that the number of factory units were pitifully small, or that the women's section remained little more than a pious aspiration.[29]

When the new leadership took control the *Workers' Weekly* was

In 1930 Lance Sharkey assumed control of the party paper at a time when sectarian excess, lack of money and legal proceedings threatened its future. Its banner was now in heavy capitals and flanked by the party badge. (Source: 'Workers' Weekly', 17 March 1930)

faced with imminent closure as the result of the libel action begun in 1929. Christian Jollie Smith negotiated a settlement with the help of a donation from Guido Baracchi, the usual standby, but the printing plant remained under threat of seizure for debt. Editions of the newspaper appeared in 1930 without illustrations because the blockmaker refused further credit, and with prominent notices rebuking district committees because they owed large sums on their bulk orders. The circulation was given as 10 000 in January 1931, a suspiciously round number; 9997 a year later; and 11 463 by the end of 1932.[30] A monthly *Woman Worker* commenced in 1930 and the *Young Worker* in 1931 as journals of the women's section and the Young Communist League, but both suffered from parlous finance and irregular publication. Re-establishment of a theoretical journal, the *Labor Review*, had to wait until 1932 and it mostly reprinted articles from *Inprecorr*. *Red Leader*, the newspaper of the Minority Movement, appeared in 1931 along with *Soviets To-day*, which was produced by the Friends of the Soviet Union. These were two of many auxiliary bodies through which the party implemented Class Against Class: the League Against Imperialism to campaign against the oppression of colonial people; International Class War Prisoners Aid and Workers' International Relief to provide legal and material support to the victims of the class war; the Unemployed Workers Movement to rally its Australian victims; and, briefly, a Workers' Defence Corps to provide physical protection.

Each of the 'fraternal' organisations had its own headquarters and leadership, published its own literature and convened its own annual conference. Each was designed to draw class-conscious workers into revolt, to detach them from the grip of social fascism and lead them to communism. Each enjoyed its moments of success when it sparked the popular discontent with the effects of the

Depression. The problem was to reconcile autonomous vitality with party control. Characteristically, an impressive list of names adorned the letterhead of these communist fronts, but a party official directed their activity, and fractions of party members ensured that the directions were implemented. All too often, their zealotry would reduce the auxiliary to a mere reflex of the party itself, smother broader participation and perpetuate the dependence on the flagging energy of overworked comrades. Such was the Bolshevik organisation created out of the Communist Party of Australia in the early 1930s.

8

Class Against Class

In early 1931 Fred Airey made his way to the Lenin School. Disembarking in Italy, he travelled to Berlin, where the German party had organised his entry into the Soviet Union. He found the party headquarters on the Wilhelmstrasse inspiring, a great fortress protected by a steel door. On his return two years later, all had changed. Hitler was chancellor, his stormtroopers were everywhere, and Airey was under strict instructions to stay out of trouble, so he 'went back to the station and bloody well stayed there until my train left'.[1] The failure of the German left to prevent Adolf Hitler's march to power is a turning-point of twentieth-century history. The two working-class parties, the social democrats and the communists, both with a large following and considerable resources, allowed their mutual antagonism to take precedence over the threat from the right. Each blamed the other for the national malaise that made the authoritarian programme of the Nazis so plausible. Even as Hitler snuffed out the political freedom afforded by the Weimar Republic, they were unable to unite for its defence.

Historians affix much of the blame for this ruinous division on the communist policy of Class Against Class. By abandoning its earlier call for a united front and by heaping abuse on the social democrats, the Communist International made cooperation impossible. The policy postulated a deepening crisis in which capitalism would cast off its democratic trappings in order to crush working-class resistance to the growing misery. As popular discontent mounted, the reformists would stand revealed as the false friends of the workers. The very term social fascist obliterated any distinction between reformism and reaction. To suggest that one was preferable to the other was to fall into the error of the lesser evil; indeed, communists were expected to strike the main blow at the social democrats in order to hasten the polarisation of Class Against Class. Hitler quickly demonstrated that there was indeed a greater evil, a regime that simply suppressed the labour movement, but by the time the communists grasped that reality it was too late. Their fortress on the Wilhelmstrasse had fallen.

Australia had its admirers of Hitler and Mussolini. In the depths of the Depression popular movements formed in opposition to the existing political parties, critical of the democratic forms of Australian government, impatient with the licence given to left-wing agitators. Some of them had links to clandestine paramilitary organisations that were prepared to defend God, King and Empire by force if that became necessary. It turned out not to be necessary. The Labor government in Canberra reluctantly accepted the inevitability of harsh economic measures, and maintained sufficient discipline over its more radical members until they were implemented. It was not until 1931 that growing internal dissension brought down the Scullin government, and by then a revitalised conservative party was ready to take office. In New South Wales the demagogic Labor premier Jack Lang rode the wave of working-class radicalism with his denunciation of the federal Labor government's economic measures and defiance of their implementation in his state, but he submitted meekly to his dismissal in May 1932. Both during the lead-up to the fall of the Scullin government in late 1931 and the destabilisation of the Lang government in early 1932, politics spilled onto the streets with clashes between the left and the right that threatened a crisis such as those that had ended capitalist democracy in Germany and other countries. In Australia, however, the crisis quickly passed.

The measures taken by the Labor Party in response to the Depression were wholly consistent with the arguments of Class Against Class. From its initial inability to end the lockout of the miners in 1929 through to its final defeat over a proposal to finance unemployed relief work in 1931, the Labor government failed utterly in its election promise to get the country back to work. Hamstrung by its lack of a Senate majority, dependent on the cooperation of the states, it was a weak and ineffective administration. Efforts to ameliorate economic hardship were undone by its acceptance of cuts in public expenditure dictated by the banks. Under the Premiers' Plan it negotiated with the states, all outlays were reduced, including pensions. The state Labor governments followed Canberra in reducing their own social expenditure and consequently offered only the most stringent emergency relief to the mounting numbers of unemployed. The strategy the Commonwealth reluctantly adopted was for Australia to trade its way out of the Depression by reducing all costs, public and private, which effectively abandoned Labor's commitment to the regulatory devices that protected the standard of living. The Arbitration Court made an across-the-board cut in the basic wage. Employers followed with their own assault on wages and conditions. The politicians upheld, and the police and the courts enforced, the laws that maintained their property rights.

It is easy to criticise the political folly of Class Against Class. By directing a small number of diehards onto a collision course with every significant body in the country, it condemned them to severe retribution. Worse than that, its absolute hostility to the Labor Party and the unions cut the Communist Party off from exerting influence within those organisations as both began to draw back from the measures taken in 1930 and 1931. But desperate times bring desperate measures. For those who practised Class Against Class, it was no abstract analysis. The class war was apparent to them as a daily reality. The boss who held the whiphand and used it without restraint, the local officer who determined whether or not they would be given a bag of rations, the union secretary who refused to take up their grievances, the Labor parliamentarian who insisted that nothing more could be done—these were its forms. If you didn't take up the battle of Class Against Class, the other class would walk all over you.

Through its newly refashioned organisational structure, the party therefore engaged in battle. It lost many more engagements

The Boss's Box of Tricks

An Arbitration Court judge prepares to stab a worker in the back while the social-fascist demagogue distracts his attention at the behest of the capitalist. The worker is upright and vigilant; the spanner in his hand suggests a capacity to defend himself as the Third Period demanded. (Source: 'Workers' Weekly', 20 March 1931)

than it won, and frequently the result of Class Against Class was to to maroon the Communist Party in isolated outposts of militant endeavour; but it persisted, and by trial and error gradually began to modify its tactics. So too did its opponents, and the patterns of activity reveal a dialectic of initiative and response. This can be illustrated by turning to the three principal sites of communist activity: in the workplace, among the unemployed and on the hustings.

In its industrial campaigns the party aimed to unite workers in resistance to the employers' assault on wages and working conditions. In keeping with the new line, the Communist Party now regarded all trade union leaders as accomplices of the employers. 'All tendencies and hang-overs of trade union legalism must be annihilated from our ranks', proclaimed the Minority Movement in 1931.[2] The effect was to estrange those few left-wing unions, such as the Australian Railways Union, which had previously offered some

MIGHT!!

OUR CLASS HAS THE POWER—IT WILL DEVELOP THE WILL!

In this early 1930s illustration, the worker is a behemoth. The emphasis on brute force is heightened by the absence of any suggestion as to where his hammer will fall or how it will ease his anguish. (Source: 'Workers' Weekly', 7 March 1930)

support for the party. Communist condemnation of the New South Wales Labor Council and violent denunciation of the ACTU poisoned relations with even the most sympathetic union officials, who dismissed as utterly unrealistic the insistent demands for strike action against new awards in the railways, the metal, meat and other industries issued by an organisation that lacked any presence within them. Repeated disturbances at meetings of the trades hall councils in Sydney, Melbourne, Brisbane and Adelaide during 1930 and 1931 resulted in the suspension of communist delegates and the closure of public galleries.

Under these circumstances the Minority Movement functioned as an industrial opposition group that counterposed its own revolutionary demands to the treachery of the officials. It operated outside the union structure, typically in factory committees, and its roneoed job bulletins were as antagonistic to the union secretary as they were to the management—it was at this juncture that J. B. King and a sprinkling of erstwhile Wobblies drifted into the party.[3] The circumstances of the period undoubtedly exacerbated that style of oppositional militancy. Party activists were sacked as soon as they were identified; union officials afforded them scant protection and frequently colluded in their dismissal. Those members who survived in employment were marginal, transient workers thinly scattered across the transport, construction, mining and metal industries, given to disruption and walk-off in the absence of sustained organisational presence. While the Minority Movement was ostensibly aimed at broadening the struggle, it suffered from an insistent circumscription of activity in accordance with the party's rejection of 'trade union legalism'. Membership of the Minority Movement remained small: 3000 were claimed in 1932.[4]

At a national conference of the Minority Movement at the end of 1931, Bill Orr introduced the first cautionary note. He advised that it was important for militants to base their campaigns on bread-and-butter issues, and wrong to neglect opportunities to use union meetings in order to reach workers. Union officials should be criticised for their policies, not their positions, and random abuse lent weight to reformist allegations that the communist 'propaganda was merely anti-union'.[5] Orr, who took over as national organiser of the Minority Movement after he returned from the Fifth Congress of the RILU in 1930, played a crucial role in the reorientation of communist activity in the early 1930s. Strongly opposed to the policies of the Third Period during the protracted debates of the late 1920s, he accepted the decisions of the party's conference at the end of the decade as binding and never disputed the new line. His comrade, Charlie Nelson, president of the Lithgow state mine lodge, did and was expelled in 1932 for his 'anti-party and anti-working-class attitude'.[6]

Orr stood third in seniority to Miles and Sharkey on the central committee and was the party's authority on industrial issues. A man of nervous intensity who burned the candle at both ends, he brought an evangelical fervour to the party's denunciation of the union leaders—as a young man he had aspired to become a missionary, and when his devout Scottish mother first heard him expound the gospel of secular salvation she was moved to declare 'what a fane meenister oor Wullie would have made'. Just as Orr's background as a miner and lodge official tempered intransigent opposition to all traces of 'trade union legalism', so the devolved structure of his union and the close solidarity of its constituent mining communities channelled his energies into the resuscitation of existing institutions. He was assisted in the conduct of the Minority Movement's weekly newspaper, the *Red Leader*, by Esmonde Higgins, who shared his sympathies for patient, practical activity. The publication in the *Red*

Leader of an 'Agit-Prop Corner' with its exegesis of 'Unfamiliar Terms Explained' went some way to translate the arcane vocabulary of the Third Period—'bureaucracy', 'social fascist', 'right opportunism', 'left sectarianism', 'reactionary', 'pseudo-left'—into a language more accessible to the uninitiated.[7] Under his encouragement, party members set out to build the Minority Movement by selling the *Red Leader* and distributing factory bulletins—if need be outside the workplace beyond the notice of the foreman. They were prepared to hold their meetings at the factory gate, where the risk of victimisation was reduced, and to seek to build up support within the union before proposing strike action.

In only one instance did the party manage to go further and establish a breakaway union, as most other communist parties did during this period. The Pastoral Workers' Industrial Union (PWIU) emerged in 1930 out of a strike by shearers against a new award handed down in July that cut the old rates by up to a quarter. The consistent failure of the Australian Workers' Union (AWU) to protect the interests of its members in the wool industry fanned the discontent of a rank-and-file movement, which in December 1930 established the new union. Senator Arthur Rae, a veteran socialist long since expelled from the AWU, was president and Norm Jeffery secretary. The PWIU remained a small union, with several thousand members at most, who fought to organise shearing sheds in New South Wales and Queensland in the face of victimisation, arrest and violence from vigilantes. Faced by the combined force and active collusion of the AWU, the graziers' association, the state police and the Commonwealth government, its survival for seven years testified to members' resolution. Nor was it a purely communist union. The party had frequent occasion to criticise the PWIU for failures and deviations from the line. Nevertheless, it was the closest the Australian party came to the policy of dual unionism that the Communist International encouraged during the Third Period.[8]

The rural crisis also provided the Australian party with an opportunity to extend its presence in the bush. The collapse of the export market hit farmers hard, especially wheatgrowers and other small producers engaged in more intensive forms of agriculture, who had little capital and relied on good prices to service their mortgages. In accordance with the instructions of the Communist

International, the CPA established a new agrarian section in 1930, again headed by Jeffery, to link the farmers' misfortunes to the exploitative logic of finance capitalism and encourage them to fight foreclosures and resumptions. Mistrust of the Money Power ran freely among the cockies and bush battlers, many of whom had strong sympathies with the labour movement. Albert Robinson, who would become a communist organiser, was just one rural militant who took up a smallholding because he was blacklisted by the employers of his north Queensland region; similarly, Laurie Jarmson, a Shetlander who joined the Party in the early 1920s, ran a few hundred hens on wasteland outside Newcastle for three years because he was marked out as an activist in the Carpenters' Union.[9] Such refugees from the labour market imbued some local producers' associations with an anti-capitalist temper, and poultry farmers' associations would eventually become one of the more unlikely communist redoubts; but rural discontent more commonly found expression in populist ideologies of a more insular and conservative kind—the Australian kulaks regarded the communist agitator no more fondly than they did the foreign bondholder. Larger farmers' organisations remained firmly on the non-Labor side of the political divide, linked through the Country Party to the conservative coalition and as antagonistic to the left as other employers' bodies.

It was among the unemployed that communism found readiest response during the Depression. This was a general feature of Western communist parties and Moscow recognised it with the declaration of International Unemployment Day on 6 March 1930, 25 February 1931, 25 February 1932 and 27 February 1933. The phenomenon was not new—throughout the 1920s there were never less than 100 000 members of the Australian workforce in search of jobs—and in each of the major cities fragmentary organisations, loosely connected to the trade unions, had employed the time-honoured devices of the street march and the public remonstrance to press the authorities to make good the deficiencies of the labour market. Now, as unemployment became a mass phenomenon, these cast-offs grew into an army, and makeshift bodies previously on the margin of the labour movement became central to its political concerns.[10]

The Communist Party turned its own unemployed groups into a national Unemployed Workers' Movement in 1930. Its first major conference in June of that year began with a hunger march from the coalfields to Sydney that was marked by arrests, a police raid on the party headquarters where the hunger marchers were billeted, a three-day gathering notable for communist attacks on the Labor Council delegates, and then a city demonstration that swelled the numbers in police cells. Kavanagh, who chaired one session of the conference in the absence of the party nominee, observed that its poor organisation and sectarian tone destroyed any chance of union cooperation, and in the immediate aftermath of this inauspicious launch a number of Sydney branches of the UWM went over to the Labor Council's own Unemployed Workers' Union.[11] The same pattern of rivalry between the communist Unemployed Workers' Movement and the non-communist alternative organisation set up by trades halls councils was quickly replicated in Melbourne, Brisbane and other cities.

Street protest, the customary form of unemployed activism, remained the principal communist tactic in the first phase of the UWM. A series of demonstrations in Sydney culminated in November 1930 with mass arrests at city rallies, and then a march on Parliament House where Moxon and others were taken into custody. In Melbourne an earlier unemployed rally on the steps of the Victorian Parliament House in October, called to protest against the state Labor government's replacement of food vouchers with direct issue of rations, turned into a vicious melee that resulted in nearly 60 arrests. In Adelaide in January 1931 the UWM organised a march to the city from Port Adelaide to protest against a government decision to substitute mutton for beef in the food ration. The ensuing 'Beef Riot' hospitalised seventeen, including ten policemen, and brought twelve arrests. Not to be outdone, the Darwin unemployed marked the new year with an occupation of the government offices, over which they raised the red flag; the police evicted them

and incarcerated their leaders. In Perth there was a major distur-
bance outside the Treasury building in March 1931, resulting in ten
arrests and nine admissions to hospital. Each of these demonstrations drew large numbers into the city centre and in each case the
demonstrators came prepared for trouble, with truncheons and
banner poles for use against batons and mounted police.[12]

These mass rallies were deeply disturbing of established
attitudes. The comfortable and secure Australians who had previously extended charity to the deserving poor were now confronted
with the importunate demands of a milling throng. Those displaced
wage-earners who had previously recoiled from the humiliation of
such dependence were now presented with an alternative response
to their predicament. The immediate official reply to the emergency,
the creation of municipal depots for the distribution of rations,
served as focal points for communist agitation. By haranguing the
queues, distributing handbills, chalking the footpaths and publicising
their city rallies, the UWM mounted a significant challenge to
control of public space. But the consequences of such activity were
costly to both the unemployed, who forfeited all sympathy in the
one-sided press coverage of the violent confrontations, and to the
Communist Party, which suffered damaging reprisals. By the end of
1930 most of the national leadership was in Sydney's Long Bay
prison. In Melbourne, following the October demonstration, the
police raided the Communist Party hall and a number of other
addresses to round up all known communists. Similar police action
in Adelaide and Perth crippled the UWM there.

An alternative tactic became increasingly common. The founding conference of the UWM had resolved to prevent the eviction
of unemployed workers and their families. The first attempt to
implement this decision, at the Sydney suburb of Clovelly in July
1930, was inauspicious—a police spy gave advance warning and
framed the organisers—but anti-eviction activity gave the authorities
far more difficulty than the city rallies. It took place in working-class
neighbourhoods and drew on the solidarity of residents with the
tenant against the landlord. It offered little advance notice: the
appearance of the bailiff could be answered by the rapid assembly
of pickets in advance of the police. It was an effective deterrent
since the UWM was prepared to destroy a property rather than

allow it to be repossessed. The terrain, away from the open spaces where police could use their horses, was also more advantageous for defensive resistance. Finally, it enjoyed considerable popular legitimacy in its assertion of the right to shelter over the the claims of property: the sight of an evicted family's meagre possessions dumped on the footpath was perhaps the most emotive image of the Depression. 'The first eviction I saw', recalled the artist Noel Counihan, who joined the Communist Party in 1931, 'had a devastating effect on me'; the experience 'finished the capitalist system as far as I was concerned'.[13]

The success of anti-eviction activity, which quickly became common in all cities, was evident in amendments to tenancy legislation in New South Wales in 1931 and new provisions for rent assistance in Victoria in 1932. Such victories did not reduce the incidence of evictions, however, and there were major confrontations in Sydney during 1931 after the political bureau pronounced the anti-eviction campaign 'the main point of struggle'. Clashes in the Sydney suburbs of Redfern, Glebe, Leichhardt, Bankstown and Newtown in May and June of that year developed into warfare. In these suburbs activists answered the threat of eviction of unemployed tenants by occupying the residence in strength and turning it into a garrison. They boarded up windows, fortified the entrances with barbed-wire entanglements, laid in supplies of missiles and in at least one case invested the property with explosives. The police in turn laid seige to the house, turned away food supplies and drove off sympathetic local residents before eventually storming the residence with firearms. In every case the police prevailed. Some of the defenders were shot, all of them were badly beaten. So heavy were the casualties that by the end of June the political bureau had to caution restraint.[14]

Similar incidents occurred in other cities. Brisbane's fiercest battle was fought in September 1931, and in the Newcastle suburb of Tighes Hill there was a particularly violent affray in June 1932 when the police turned on local residents who sought to assist those inside the beseiged house. These and other set-piece engagements were difficult to sustain. Occupation of a house surrendered the advantage of mobility, and almost invariably ended in beatings and wholesale arrests. Sometimes widespread community sympathy augmented the original action, as in Newcastle where the mayor headed a defence committee and an outspoken Anglican priest, Ernest Burgmann, denounced the police brutality at Tighes Hill: after 22 of the defendants were acquitted, charges against the remainder were dropped. In the absence of local support of that kind, however, unemployed activists were always vulnerable to reprisal.[15]

The same was true of agitation among the homeless unemployed who took to the track. This was a common experience, especially for the young and unattached, who would team up in small groups to seek casual jobs or handouts from farmers, eking out a hand-to-mouth existence as they roamed the country. Their displacement and humiliations, the daily fight for survival, the brushes with local police and the dodging of railway police fostered a distinctive ethos that is registered in novels such as Kylie Tennant's *The Battlers* and the autobiographical account of Frank Huelin, '*Keep Moving*'. Huelin, a young immigrant from the Channel Isles, arrrived in Australia just as the Depression hit and was one those it turned to communism, for communism provided the more resourceful and spirited of the bagmen with purpose and companionship. As he narrates his experiences, communism preserved some basis for fellow-feeling and mutual support among outcasts who otherwise turned in on themselves and against each other.[16]

The UWM had most success in channelling the discontent of the itinerant unemployed when they gathered seasonally in rural centres and pressed demands for assistance. Such aggregations, however, raised fear and resentment that anti-communists were quick to exploit. In the irrigation town of Mildura, for example, townspeople sided with the police in hostility towards the itinerant unemployed who camped on the banks of the Murray. At the end of 1931 they broke up a UWM meeting, hospitalised the organiser and seven other comrades, and forced the visiting speaker, Ted Tripp, to flee to safety.[17] In the pastoral centre of Bourke, armed squatters and land agents swept down on an unemployed camp in the riverbed, and ordered the UWM members from the town. At Cairns in the following year, locals evicted several hundred unemployed men from their quarters in the showground in a ferocious assault; communists hid out in the bush for weeks afterwards.[18]

Then there were the shanty towns created on wastelands within the cities. Here homeless families would gather, build humpies or shacks with scrap iron, bagging or flattened tins, and try as best they could to make do. These camps lacked basic amenities, they were rife with poverty and disease, and yet their inhabitants sustained a collective existence. They entertained themselves, restrained domestic violence, organised working bees to kerb and gutter the footpaths, and agitated for the provision of water and sanitary services. Above all, they fought for recognition. The formation of a UWM branch was a natural extension of such activity, even though it might lapse as the immediate grievance disappeared and the particular enthusiasts moved on.[19]

The Depression aroused acute discontent because the provision for support of the unemployed was so rudimentary. There was no system of public welfare and only Queensland had unemployment insurance. Elsewhere it was intermittent relief work for male breadwinners, meagre issues of food and clothing for their dependants, work camps and rations from rural relief depots for the single unemployed. Sometimes the UWM sought to apply familiar methods of collective bargaining. At Bulli on the south coalfield of New South Wales the replacement of local relief committees by state officials, who used police to identify applicants, triggered a boycott of the dole offices in May 1931. On the northern coalfield the issue of a new relief registration form, designed to tighten eligibility requirements and cut recipients from the dole, launched a communist campaign in October 1932 to burn the offensive questionnaire. Neither of these unemployed 'strikes', for that was the model they followed, was successful but both attracted considerable publicity. A similar outcome awaited the several hundred men who marched on Perth in September 1932 to protest against the hardship of their conditions in the unemployed camps on Frankland River. Their leaders were arrested and their demands refused. The same pattern was repeated in relation to other UWM activity elsewhere, and with little more to show for it. 'But we felt we've got to make a stand', as one activist put it, 'Do something! Don't cop it passively'.[20]

Towards the end of 1931 the party secretary warned members that a 'serious sectarian condition' was impairing the work of the Unemployed Workers' Movement. 'Where the UWM is not stagnant, it is declining.' While noting that anti-eviction struggles had mobilised large numbers in defence of the unemployed, Miles criticised members for their antagonism to other bodies that offered assistance: 'the organisation had become divorced from large numbers who had been compelled, through sheer poverty, to rally to the charity organisations'. Too many comrades who spoke at meetings of the unemployed were concerned to display their revolutionary credentials to the disregard of the 'concrete problems of the unemployed'. In too many localities the local committee of the organisation had 'dwindled to a small communist sect calling itself a branch of the UWM'. The politbureau ordered the Workers' International Relief to establish kitchens for the unemployed and 'overcome the sectarian tendency of just howling for revolution'.[21]

Miles' strictures recognised the fragile character of communist activity among the unemployed. It was difficult to maintain the UWM: active members fell away under the rigours of their duties, and recruits were easily disheartened by the regimen of protest and punishment. His diagnosis is less persuasive, if only because it was his own organisation that maintained tight control of the UWM. It had insisted that the UWM was a protest and not a relief organisation. It imposed a didactic routine. One activist recalled meetings of the district committee of the UWM in the Hunter Valley, where the party cadre 'would give a political report that took you from the Arctic to the Antarctic' in an exhaustive survey of the world capitalist crisis. 'We'd start at seven o'clock at night, and at nine o'clock we were only at the equator on the way down.' The validity of the Communist International's line was not in question. 'Brilliant bloody analysis', the activist found it, 'but I used to keep thinking: how do you get that back to the rank and file?'[22]

It was the party, also, that imposed the sectarian policies that restricted the UWM's appeal. Communists were quick to single out the Labor Party and the unions for betrayal of the unemployed. The major demonstrations in Sydney, Melbourne and Adelaide in the summer of 1930 to 1931 were all directed at Labor administrations, indeed the election of a Labor government in New South Wales in November 1930 triggered a new round of unemployed protests designed to discredit Jack Lang as premier and Garden as secretary of the Labor Council. For similar reasons, the UWM kept up an unrelenting hostility to the bodies for the unemployed created by the trade unions, even when the demands of such bodies coincided with its own. In Melbourne the UWM responded to the refusal of Trades Hall Council to allow it representation with repeated disruption of council meetings and, when a subsequent raid on the barricaded entrance was repulsed by police, with denunciation of 'the vermin' inside doing the bosses' work.[23] The frequent invasions of meetings of trades hall councils in other cities alienated delegates to the point that UWM delegations were forbidden further entry to the council meetings. The obligation to discredit the social fascists ensured that what was intended as a front organisation remained narrow in its political base. It had been established with Senator Arthur Rae as president and a brace of federal Labor parliamentarians on its executive; by 1932 the ALP forbade its members any association with the UWM.

As a front organisation the UWM was intended to extend the influence of the Communist Party, to tap the discontent of unemployed workers, draw them into action around their immediate concerns, lead them in activities that would demonstrate the futility of reform, and ultimately recruit them to the revolutionary cause. The details of party membership presented in the last chapter suggest that such a process occurred: of the several thousand who joined the party in the early 1930s the overwhelming majority were out of work. Yet CPA members represented only a fraction of the numbers the UWM mobilised. The actual membership of the UWM is difficult to estimate: a local branch could form, enrol as many as 500 members, and pass out of existence in the space of a year. The finances of the organisation suggest that only a minority kept up the minimal dues. But if nominal adherence and some participation in UWM activity are taken as a test, then the 30 000 members claimed in 1932 are a fairly accurate measure.[24]

UWM members sustained a multitude of endeavours that are difficult to incorporate into a national survey such as this. Here the UWM arranged for an unemployed family to keep a roof over its head; there it persuaded local shopkeepers to meet the needs of a group of homeless men struck off rations; elsewhere it provided warmth and fellowship to the outcast. The Brunswick branch of the UWM ran a successful weekly dance with an entrance charge of just threepence, which was less than the price of a bottle of milk; from the proceeds and with the help of sympathetic businessmen, it provided free lunches for the children of the unemployed.[25] In such localised activities arising out of the direct needs of the unemployed the UWM achieved a success it never managed in the more dramatic engagements when the state was able to bring its force to bear on a concentrated target. Yet paradoxically it was the acts of defiance that gave hope and strength to the unemployed in their daily perseverance. The forlorn heroism of the diehards, the acts of quixotic bravery, the very sectarianism that Miles deplored kept the flame of rebellion burning through the Depression.

The revolutionary politics of the Communist Party in the Third Period placed particular emphasis on elections. Since the internal struggle that led to the adoption of Class Against Class had arisen out of the party's attitude towards the ALP in the 1929 federal election, it is hardly surprising that the new leadership should insist on standing candidates against Labor wherever possible. The argument in 1929 had turned on whether the workers had sufficient experience of Labor in office to appreciate its treachery. The Depression provided plentiful experience. A federal Labor government from 1929 to the end of 1931, and state governments in New South Wales (1930–32), South Australia (1930–33) and Victoria (1929–32) proved no more capable of protecting jobs, and scarcely more generous to the jobless, than their conservative counterparts.

The pattern of Australian politics during the Depression was indeed unstable. No government that went to the polls in the early 1930s, with the exception of the Nationalists in Tasmania, survived the judgement of the electors. The dissatisfaction of conservatives with their own loss of national office, the fear of growing social unrest and a growing impatience with the results of democracy found expression in extra-parliamentary organisations that took the threat of communism as justifying emergency measures. The All For Australia League, established at the beginning of 1931, quickly enrolled more than 100 000 members. Behind it stood the secret armies, composed largely of ex-servicemen, that began skirmishing with communists. This phase of right-wing mobilisation peaked during 1931 in direct action against the left as seen in the terrorism at Mildura and Bourke. The formation of a new party, the United Australia Party, and its election to national office in December 1931, confirmed the conservative renewal.

The dissatisfaction of the labour movement, on the other hand, weakened the Labor Party. It suffered defections from its right wing, including that of two Labor premiers, and Lyons, the federal Treasurer, who became the leader of the new United Australia Party. The New South Wales Labor leader, Jack Lang, took his state branch out of the ALP, and his supporters in the federal parliament left the Labor caucus. Socialisation units agitated within the Labor Party in this and other states for more radical solutions to the crisis. Despite these developments, the Communist Party kept up an unremitting hostility to Labor. There was in fact considerable sympathy between communists and members of the socialisation units at a local level. Jack Hughes, a leading member of the units in Sydney, recalled how they and the communists would protect each others' stumps from right-wing attack. Communists attended unit meetings and one of them, Tom Payne, formally proposed that the units accept the need for a revolutionary seizure of power. Yet the party leaders condemned the socialisation units vehemently, and following the rejection of Payne's proposal, ordered him and all members to break with the socialisation units.[26] A similar response followed the dismissal of Jack Lang by the governor of New South Wales in May 1932. This constitutional coup produced jubiliation on the right, profound indignation on the left. It occasioned what might well have been the largest ever political meeting in Australian history, a gathering organised by Jock Garden at Moore Park and attended by at least 200 000 supporters. The Communist Party's response was to distribute leaflets denouncing Lang as a stooge, 'the chief force holding the radicalised workers in check and keeping them from the path of struggle against capitalism'.[27]

Lang was an old adversary of the communists, his denunciation of the silvertails and British bondholders a calculated appeal to populist sentiment. Even so, he undoubtedly tapped a substantial vein of radical sentiment. Yet in the context of the Third Period, the communists interpreted such elements as 'left social fascism', serving only to perpetuate the reformist illusion and thus constituting a further extension of the capitalist conspiracy. The 'social fascists' themselves remained the principal opponent, against whom the 'main blow' must be directed, and any suggestion that they constituted a 'lesser evil' than the conservatives was a deviation from the line. As fascism was deemed the form of class rule to which capitalists resorted in the final phase of their era, so social fascism was the form assumed by social reformism in that period of decline. The valency of this new communist terminology is striking. Earlier they had spoken of 'Labor fakirs', a term popularised by the Wobblies and other militants, and signifying a false friend of the workers. Literally the Arabic word *fakir* meant a poor man, more specifically a Muslim religious mendicant; the homonym *faker* suggested the insincerity of the Labor politician who feigned sympathy with the workers in order to attract their support. A social fascist, on the other hand, was more than a charlatan. He was a betrayer, a saboteur and, now that circumstances demanded, a repressive enemy. The main blow directed against him was designed to expose his true role. Mostly the blow was verbal, though on occasion it was physical. Communists (led by those who had been batoned at the Trades Hall in the previous year) rushed the official platform at the Yarra Bank in Melbourne on May Day 1932 and assaulted the Labor leaders, but this was an unusual occurrence and recognised by the party as damaging to its cause. It certainly was—the Trades Hall Council refused to participate in May Day for decades afterwards.[28]

More generally, the Communist Party chose elections as the most suitable occasions to campaign against Labor. The purpose of communist electoral activity was to popularise Class Against Class and offer working-class voters an opportunity to express their rejection of social fascism. The results were extremely discouraging. In its initial venture, the South Australian state elections in April 1930, where Kavanagh directed the party's campaign, two Communist Party candidates attracted 696 votes. In the New South Wales state election in October 1930 there were no less than 51 communist candidates—probably a quarter of the membership in the state was pressed into service—and they won 10 445 votes, less than

1 per cent of the statewide tally. The two northern coalfield electorates of Kurri Kurri and Cessnock were most responsive, with over
a thousand CPA votes in each, but in inner Sydney the tallies of
251 in Newtown and 143 in Glebe were disappointing and those in
the affluent Lane Cove (24) and North Sydney (23) derisory. The
federal election of December 1931 saw ten communists stand for
the House of Representatives and four for the Senate. The best
lower house results were obtained in the coalfield electorate of
Hunter and some inner-Melbourne areas, but the total vote was only
8511. The Senate candidates, who drew from a wider pool, won
29 443 votes, but Queensland, where the communists received 2.32
per cent of the poll, was the best state result. Subsequent efforts
were marginally better. Thirty-eight communists stood in the New
South Wales state election of 1932 and won 12 351 votes; six in
Queensland and one in Victoria in the same year polled 1057 and
953 respectively; three in South Australia in 1933 improved the
result there to 1908; and two stood in Western Australia for the
first time, attracting 442 votes. Results in local government elections—the party ran 120 candidates in New South Wales in
1932—were of the same exiguous order.[29]

Election campaigns made heavy demands on the party's scant
resources. Federal candidates were required to lodge a deposit, and
most states had a similar requirement; a communist who made the
payment in Victoria testified to the astonishment of the electoral
officials as he counted out the sixpences and threepences.[30] New
South Wales, where the party made the most of free candidature,
set a deposit of £25 after the 1932 election. Then there was the
cost of literature and venues for campaigning, the calls on party
members to speak and canvass, and the demoralising effect of
repeated rebuffs. The very act of seeking parliamentary election was
difficult to explain for a party that insisted parliamentary democracy
was merely a cloak for capitalist dictatorship. The executive often
had occasion to correct comrades for their mistaken campaigning.
They were to put forward a platform of workers' demands but not
mislead the workers into believing those demands could be met.
They were not to say that the election of communists would make
no difference, but neither were they to encourage the illusion that
the bourgeoisie would permit communists to win control of the

state. They were to oppose the social fascist Labor Party absolutely but not to overlook fascist non-Labor. With these tortuous distinctions the communists offered themselves to the voters. Their venture onto the hustings and the stark rebuffs they encountered illustrated the difficulties of leading Class Against Class.

The Depression communists

The Depression occupies a special place in twentieth-century history as a time of extremity. It brought acute distress, rancour and division that took capitalism closer to breakdown than before or since. With the advantage of hindsight, most economic historians mark the Depression of the 1930s off from the profligate excesses of the preceding decade, and see it yielding gradually to a hesitant recovery, with a resumption of growth and stability only after the necessary lessons were learned and the appropriate methods of economic management adopted in the 1940s. This retrospective periodisation misses the desperate uncertainty felt by people at the time of a slide towards an abyss. It loses sight of the continuities and cuts across lines of cause and effect that interwar critics of capitalism discerned. In the diagnosis advanced at the time by the Communist International, capitalist competition generated a growing imperialist rivalry that brought war in 1914 and revolution in 1917. After these cataclysms there was a temporary respite and then a renewed, deeper and more general crisis that intensified hardship, exacerbated international tension and compelled a final choice between revolution and war.

The dire predictions of the Third Period turned out to be too fatalistic. A second world war did follow the Depression, and it generated a new wave of revolutions, but capitalism survived and ultimately triumphed. Looking back over the interwar years, a distinguished communist historian suggested recently that the entire period from 1914 to 1945 might more aptly be characterised as the Age of Catastrophe. He sees the First World War and its revolutionary legacy as crippling the world economy, sweeping away colonial empires and overthrowing democracies, until a temporary and bizarre alliance of liberal capitalism and communism formed to win the Second World War and usher in a Golden Age of plenty. In this reading of the political economy of the twentieth century, the peace terms imposed after 1918 fatally impaired earlier patterns of international trade; by the late 1920s stocks built up by primary producers, such as Australia, swamped the costive market; once commodity prices collapsed, there was a general retreat into economic nationalism that intensified the contraction, so that world trade fell 60 per cent in the years 1929 to 1932. Deflationary remedies, balanced budgets and the absence of welfare expenditure deepened and prolonged the slump while they sapped the very foundations of government.[1]

Such an interpretation accords with the popular memory of the Depression. 'Depression!', a bushworker interviewed 40 years later exclaimed, 'I never knew nothing else! The 1920s was just as bad.' For many Australian manual labourers, jobs were scarce long before the Wall Street Crash of October 1929 signalled the collapse of the world financial system. These Australians continued to hunt for work long after the unemployment rate peaked at 30 per cent in 1932. Not until 1937 did national output regain its 1928 highpoint, and even then a quarter of a million Australians were still out of work. For those caught up in this Depression it had no clear beginning and no decisive end. It was a condition that suspended the passage of time into an indefinite waiting. It broke up families, embittered breadwinners, demoralised school-leavers. It marked its victims for life.[2]

The circumstances of the Depression were stamped on those it made into communists. Few, if any, had regular employment and most were out of work for years. They knew hardship not as a temporary misfortune, but as a constant condition, and the experience never left them. Their rejection of capitalism was no rhetorical gesture, it was a visceral hatred of a system that imposed hunger and humiliation, stunted lives and treated humans as outcasts. For these recruits, the class war was a daily reality. The police, the courts, the press upheld the claims of property over the most basic of all human requirements, the need for food, clothing, shelter and dignity. To submit was to abandon hope and succumb to despair, to resist and fight was to affirm one's self-respect and concern for others. Some who had prior involvement in Labor politics turned in disgust from the utter failure of the ALP to protect its supporters. Les Barnes was an unemployed printer from the inner-Melbourne suburb of Brunswick who regarded himself as an instinctive social democrat for whom the Soviet model of a revolutionary under-ground had little appeal, but he embraced communism in 1932 because 'the Labor Party was doing nothing', the Communist Party 'at least was doing something'. Carl King, a canecutter, gave the Labor Party away in the same year that the Queensland Labor government blacklisted a group of relief workers who had simply asked for proper pay.[3]

Others were too young, too unsettled or too preoccupied with immediate concerns to have had any involvement in politics before they were caught up in the novel forms of collective endeavour. Ernie and Lila Thornton were in their mid-twenties, living in inner Melbourne and moving accommodation every few weeks, when they joined in 1931. He was a boy migrant from Yorkshire who became involved in the local UWM and was badly knocked about by the police. She was a local girl horrified by the 'red raggers' until she accompanied him to the Yarra Bank and heard their orators promise to end greed and want. The need for such mutuality was never more urgent, and Lila Thornton found that the Depression did in fact 'make people share', just as it convinced her of the need for the compulsory sharing of communism. Joe Carter, from the New South Wales rural town of Moree, was barely in his teens when he began to carry his swag during the early 1920s. He was an instinctive rebel, quick with his fists, and fought a contractor during the shearers' strike of 1930 from which the PWIU emerged. It was in 1931, when he arrived in Lithgow, that he joined the party. 'Why did I become a communist?' he later asked, and recalled the humiliation of beg-ging for food, 'the way they used to look at ya', and the indignities of working with the boss 'right over the top of you'. To turn the question around: 'Why wouldn't I be a communist?' But there was more to it than this, as he himself suggested with his recollection of the warmth and purpose of the Lithgow party comrades. Human warmth seems conspicuously absent from the rigorous communism of Class Against Class, but with half the town on the dole, Carter found a complete absence of prejudice against the unemployed: 'Lithgow, to me anyway, would be the greatest workers' town I've ever been in in my life.' After finding construction work in Port Kembla, Carter saved his wages to buy a passage to Spain and fight in the International Brigade. The pattern here is of an instinctive belligerence channelled into disciplined, collective militancy.[4]

Regardless of background, the commitment to communism was not made lightly. A panel of senior comrades subjected the applicant for membership to a searching interrogation. Bill McDougall, an itinerant Scots immigrant, was drawn to the party as a result of his involvement in the unemployed demonstrations in Sydney during 1930. Bert Moxon and two members of the district committee quizzed him. The question that stumped McDougall was why the Communist Party and not the Labor Party? He knew the answer instinctively, for it sprang from his recent activity and was manifest in his very application to join, yet how could he express it in the requisite formula before he was drilled in the vocabulary of Class Against Class? Fortunately, one of the district committee members filled the doctrinal gap for him and he was accepted. Others were treated more abruptly. Flo Davis, a deserted wife working in Brisbane pubs, dressed in her best clothes to appear before the district committee only to be told, 'Come back when you know a bit more'. Ted Bacon, a young public servant in the same city, suffered the same fate: 'Come back when you grow up'. Johnno Johnson scraped through his rigorous examination by the north Queensland district committee: 'God, the things they asked you'.[5]

The recruits who survived such scrutiny accepted the iron discipline of the party as a necessary condition of the class war. The Depression communist was hard, unyielding, capable of enormous self-sacrifice, indomitable. 'Compromise' and 'conciliation' were terms of disapprobation in the party lexicon; 'annihilation' of the enemy was the object, to be achieved by 'ruthless exposure' of all faint-hearts and 'liquidation' of any personal reservations. The stri-

INSPECTING THE GUARD.

Herb McClintock arraigned social fascism in a cartoon drawn for the first issue of 'Strife'. The 'basher squad' of the Victorian police parades for inspection by a generic capitalist, with an ineffectual Labor member of parliament trailing in his wake. At this time of heightened police brutality, the Labor Party held office in Victoria. (Source: J.N. Rawling collection, Noel Butlin Archives Centre, ANU N57/1994)

dent tone of communist agitation certainly increased the incidence and severity of official repression. The party fell prey to the comforting delusion that its success could be measured by the hostility it attracted. In January 1930 the prominent Queensland communist Fred Paterson was charged with sedition for a speech in the Brisbane Domain where he allegedly urged workers to take the law into their hands. While he was acquitted, another Queenslander, Bob Bossone, was found guilty of the same crime later in the year for declaring, 'To Hell with King. To Hell with the Union Jack. The Red Flag is what we want to see flying here.' Bossone then had to endure a scalding in the party press for entering into a good behaviour bond.[6]

State governments employed a variety of laws to quell demonstrations and deter participants. Unlawful assembly was the most common charge, frequently supplemented with loitering in a public place, offensive behaviour, insulting police, resisting arrest, or assault. The increasing prosecution of activists for vagrancy turned an economic condition into a political offence since in a period of mass unemployment very few of those the police picked were able to demonstrate 'lawful means of support'. To add insult to injury, the police accused one communist seized in a house raid in the Melbourne suburb of Newport, where at least one in every four adult males was unable to find a job, of 'dodging work', and he was

sentenced to six months' imprisonment. In another Melbourne case
the magistrate made it clear that the offence consisted not in the
indigency of the defendant but in his party activity. Jack Stevens,
the party organiser in Western Australia, was gaoled in 1931 on a
charge of being a person of 'evil fame'.[7]

The states also introduced special laws during the Depression
that augmented police powers to prevent public gatherings. They
formed special police squads to maintain surveillance over communists, break up street protests and put down resistance to evictions.
These squads gained a fearsome reputation for brutality. They also
exchanged information with the Investigation Branch of the Commonwealth Attorney-General's Department, which continued to
gather anti-communist intelligence. The election of a federal Labor
government in 1929 had been expected to curb the Investigation
Branch's activities; in May 1930 it was even rumoured that its budget
would be cut from £10 000 to £3000. But customs officers continued
to seize communist literature and over the next few months the
Investigation Branch coordinated raids on communist headquarters
in Sydney, Adelaide and Melbourne.[8] Postal officials destroyed 2000
copies of the *Red Leader* in 1931 on grounds that the Postmaster-
General refused to divulge despite repeated questions from Eddie
Ward, a sympathetic federal parliamentarian.[9] Newspapers, pamphlets and handbills were a particular target of police action, and
printing presses were often confiscated.[10]

In the first flush of enthusiasm for Class Against Class the party
expected members to prove their revolutionary mettle with a reckless
contempt for the restrictions on their activity. They mounted the
stump, spoke out, took the beating and served the time. The charge
of cowardice Moxon levelled at Jack Kavanagh for supposedly holding back workers from attacking police outside the Trades Hall on
7 November 1930 was the most damaging of all the accusations
against him. Following that affray, Moxon directed a series of
further confrontations. On Friday 14 November the Women's
Group defied a police ban on a city march. Twelve were arrested,
the formidable Joy Barrington twice: when first bundled into the
back seat of a police car she escaped from the other side and resumed
her attack on the police. A week later Moxon himself was arrested
after he urged the crowd to break through barriers in front of the

New South Wales state parliament. He appeared in court in full revolutionary fig, his head swathed in bandages, and was sentenced to two weeks' imprisonment. Along with ten UWM members serving stiff terms for their part in the Clovelly anti-eviction campaign, this November action brought the number of incarcerated Sydney communists to more than 50, and most embarked on a hunger strike until the party called their action off in December.[11]

Hard cases received special attention. Bill Laidlaw, a miner who had been convicted of insulting police at Kurri Kurri in January 1930, was one of those arrested on the hunger march from the Hunter Valley to Sydney in June; in August he was gaoled for three months as the result of a dispute with the owner of a city restaurant where he was working; the court was told he had not worked underground for five years. Joe Shelley was another arrested during the hunger march. He had served three months in Townsville in 1929 for his part in a free speech campaign (and would have done time in Melbourne a year earlier for insulting the police had not Guido Baracchi paid his fine) before his conviction for incitement to murder on the northern coalfields in 1930. He completed that five-month sentence just in time to be arrested on the hunger march. The party then put Shelley onto a coastal steamship as its maritime organiser, but he was sacked and threatened with deportation as soon as he was identified in 1931. Later in the same year he was set upon by thugs when speaking in Katoomba, New South Wales; the local policeman arrested him and a further two months' hard labour followed. A small boy who witnessed the incident recalled Joe Shelley, 'bloody but unbowed', 'tough as Stalin's nails'.[12]

For a time the party flirted with reprisals. There was talk in 1930 of armed resistance on the northern coalfield, of sabotage of the power supply in Adelaide where the port and its surrounds were under police occupation as volunteer workers were introduced to the wharves, and even of a general uprising in Broken Hill.[13] The Australian delegates to the RILU Congress in August 1930 boasted of these designs and were chastened to discover that the Comintern disapproved. To embark on such romantic escapades in the absence of far greater support than the party enjoyed, they were told, was dangerous folly. While communists were revolutionaries who sought to overthrow capitalism by force, they abjured terrorism and condemned random acts of violence. Such unscientific blows in the class war were ill-directed and self-defeating, a symptom of the impulse to revolt that in the absence of Bolshevik discipline found expression in anarchosyndicalist spontaneity such as had brought the Wobblies undone. Sharkey and Orr returned from Moscow with clear instructions to halt such plans and thereafter the Australian party eschewed them. The same held for individual acts of violence. Mick Ryan, who abandoned the Labor Party to become a leading figure in the UWM, issued a public repentance in 1931 for his action in assaulting a Labor organiser, 'Plugger' Martin, at the ALP's Sydney office. Martin was a notorious bully and had besmirched Ryan's reputation with sexual tittle-tattle; but the 'correct Communist line of action', Ryan recognised, was to 'maintain the utmost self-control in all situations'.[14]

In 1930 the party also formed a Workers' Defence Corps. Composed initially of ex-servicemen, and organised along conventional military lines into companies and platoons, it was to provide protection to the pickets, eviction resisters, speakers and demonstrators so sorely in need of such assistance. On the northern coalfield these formations achieved some initial success against the far-flung police detachments that guarded the pit-heads from angry miners, but the police hit back with massive reinforcements. Operating out of fortified camps, special detachments used motor transport to descend *en masse* upon their adversaries. Subsequently the WDC adopted a more flexible form of organisation, better suited to 'guerilla warfare', with units of no more than eight members. The defensive purpose suggested by the title of the Workers' Defence Corps is nevertheless significant. Despite flirtation with stronger measures—Sharkey claimed the miners' contingent of the Corps obtained two machine guns—communists remained defiant rather than insurrectionary, incurably majoritarian even though they constituted only a tiny minority, convinced that capitalism was doomed and that their own resolution in its death throes would win the support of the working class. The object of the WDC, then, was to afford the necessary protection to working-class activists in their legitimate activities.[15]

Even this proved a hazardous business. In New South Wales, where the WDC originated, state legislation forbade unauthorised paramilitary drilling: the leaders were marked men. Those members who were found with weapons—batons and coshes were most common—incurred heavy penalties. The WDC also attracted some desperate types. Among its Sydney ranks was a group of Irish descent, well versed in the traditions of the republican army, who acquired a cache of police revolvers and a store of gelignite from the coalmines. They were preparing to invest a house at Bankstown under order of eviction when the police stormed it. Several of the defenders received bullet wounds, others were hospitalised by beatings administered afterwards at the police station when those arrested were handcuffed, then bashed senseless. An Aboriginal party member, Dick Eatock, got eighteen months and his brother Noel two-and-a-half years for a later WDC action in Glebe.[16]

The Bankstown eviction case occurred in 1931, when the Communist Party came under fierce assault, more general and more violent than it had so far encountered. The attack came from the paramilitary bodies, formed largely from ex-servicemen, that had sprung into existence during the 1920s to uphold national and imperial interests against the threat from the left. Initially they operated in a clandestine fashion, drilled under cover of darkness and held themselves in readiness for the moment of need. The mounting difficulties of the federal Labor government in dealing with the country's financial crisis, the return of Lang to office in New South Wales at the end of 1930 after three years in opposition, and above all the communist agitation among the unemployed, convinced these conservatives that the moment had arrived. From 1931 members of the New Guard in New South Wales, the League of National Security in Victoria and equivalent bodies in other states began to appear in force. The Victorian organisation called out its rural detachments to prepare for an uprising in March 1931, probably in response to the communist International Unemployment Day, though the hard-faced men who dug trenches and patrolled their towns through the night were taking no chances and in several instances locked up the local Catholics as an additional security precaution. In the cities these clandestine organisations presented themselves as defenders of law and order who would assist the authorities in their enforcement of the public peace. At a communist demonstration at the Sydney Town Hall in April 1931 against Joe

Lyons, the former Labor treasurer who was preparing to go across to the conservatives, a police officer asked a returned serviceman to hold one demonstrator while he apprehended another, and the helpful volunteer obliged by punching his charge unconscious. At a street meeting in the Melbourne suburb of Fitzroy, custodians of conservative honour threatened to knock a member of the Young Communist League off his box for insulting Lord Baden-Powell. Two constables in the crowd stepped in to arrest the young communist for offensive behaviour.[17]

With the formation of the United Australia Party in May and the growing paralysis of the hopelessly fragmented federal Labor government, such events became increasingly common. In swollen numbers and with the clear approval of the press, detachments of the secret armies broke up communist meetings. Typically, the New Guard members would howl down the speaker, sing loyal refrains (which had a practical as well as a patriotic purpose, as they served to distinguish foe from friend—any man who did not remove his hat for the National Anthem was a red) and then set upon their opponents. 'Nothing more lethal than a pick handle', was their commander's instruction, though he 'noted with amusement many a bulge on the hip'. His men did not always prevail, especially when they ventured into working-class neighbourhoods where their flash cars and prosperous appearance made them conspicuous, but they undoubtedly increased the hazards of left-wing activism. The growing incidence of street violence bore disturbing resemblance to the rise of fascism in Germany, Austria and other countries at this time, as did the sympathy of many police and magistrates for the right-wing combatants. Australian communists noted the similarities, but at least initially they did not cause any reconsideration of tactics. Rather, the fact that the police in New South Wales and Victoria were administered by state Labor governments confirmed communists in their belief that social fascism was responsible for their persecution. 'The correctness of Communist theory is again demonstrated in the unity of the social-fascist and fascist forces in the present anti-working class offensive.'[18]

The wave of anti-communism swept the countryside. The assault on the UWM in Mildura on 1 November 1931 and Bourke a fortnight later were followed by similar actions in northern Victoria and western New South Wales. Again there was a consistent pattern. A town meeting of 'concerned citizens' would deliver an ultimatum that all communist activity must cease. Those who resisted were beaten, then taken onto the highway and told to keep walking. One activist had the word RED burned onto his forehead with acid. Other unemployed residents were rounded up and made to affirm their loyalty. Police intervened only when this wholly illegal action threatened to turn into a lynching, at which time they would arrest the victim. Moxon was one of those arrested at Bourke, and he served ten days for speaking without a permit.[19]

The federal election, which followed the fall of the Labor government at the end of November, extended the right-wing offensive. Communist candidates for the Senate were prevented from campaigning in rural centres in both Victoria and New South Wales. In Sydney a number of municipalities announced a ban on all communist activity which the New Guard enforced with renewed rigour. At Lane Cove, Bondi, Drummoyne, Darlinghurst and King's Cross large crowds gathered to close down communist meetings. Sometimes they gave notice of their intention to the police, who then escorted the communists from the locality; sometimes they instigated a brawl, which almost always resulted in arrest of communists. Mark Gosling, the minister in Lang's cabinet with responsibility for the police, both deprecated and abetted the anticommunist offensive. He insisted that the New Guard had no authority to prevent public meetings; he also published a list of the names and domestic addresses of all known Sydney communists.[20]

The Lang government itself came under increasing attack from the New Guard in the early months of 1932. Apart from the celebrated incident when one of its officers, Francis de Groot, slashed the symbolic red ribbon across the Sydney Harbour Bridge with his sword before the premier could cut it with ceremonial scissors, there were raids on Labor meetings and even an assault on Jock Garden in his home. This final frenzy lasted until the governor finally dismissed Lang from office and the electors returned the United Australia Party, and again it occasioned pitched battles between left and right. The fear and hatred of the unemployed turned respectable middle-class men into thugs who invaded working-class neighbourhoods to clean up the reds, a challenge the communists met with equal resolution. The battle of Bankstown, on the night of Friday 26 February 1932, was perhaps the most celebrated encounter. When a motorised column of several hundred New Guards attempted to stop a meeting of the UWM, they were beaten off in savage fighting, their cars put out of action: 'the hoods were ripped to pieces, windscreens were smashed, side windows in the sedans were holed, and tyres were damaged'.[21]

In the course of the federal election the United Australia Party made much of the communist threat. Upon its accession to office at the beginning of 1932 it reimposed a more intense censorship of imported communist material and implemented a number of new measures. In February the postmaster-general refused mail delivery of communist newspapers. In April the Commonwealth deported a German-born party member upon the expiry of his imprisonment for crimes committed in the Adelaide beef riot. In May the attorney-general introduced new amendments to the Commonwealth Crimes Act which made it an offence to provide assistance to an unlawful association, and widened the definition of an unlawful association to include any body that encouraged 'the overthrow by force of violence of the established government of a Commonwealth or of a State or of any other civilized country or of an established government'. He then prosecuted the publisher of the *Workers' Weekly* for soliciting funds for the party.[22]

The court convicted the publisher and sentenced him to jail, but the High Court overturned the conviction on the grounds that the appeal was for an auxiliary body, which could not be assumed to share the revolutionary aims attributed to the party. The prosecution thus failed on a technicality and left the party free to continue, but the threat of further prosecution hampered its activities. The ban on postal transmission of newspapers caused an immediate drop of circulation (that of the *Red Leader* fell immediately from 8000 to 3500) and was costly to circumvent. The threat of prosecution of the party's Sydney landlords under the Crimes Act deterred other property owners from allowing communists to rent premises or hire meeting places, while a proposed amendment to the Commonwealth Arbitration Act, which would have deregistered any union linked to an illegal organisation, forced the Australian Railways Union to withdraw from its proposed affiliation to the Red International of

Labor Unions. The government's augmented power to deport naturalised Australians for membership of an illegal organisation hung over the heads of many activists. Party members were also prevented from attending international congresses by cancellation of their passports, and several public employees who visited Russia as delegates of the Friends of the Soviet Union were sacked upon their return.[23]

Even these measures did not satisfy the more virulent anti-communists who bombarded the attorney-general with reports of red outrages and demands for summary justice. John Latham, who resumed the office of attorney-general in the Lyons ministry, had to remind one particularly insistent Sydney businessman that while he had redrafted federal laws on crime, customs, postal services, immigration and naturalisation, the rule of law still required evidence to secure a conviction—and he also called for a security report on his vexatious correspondent. Latham continued to chafe, nevertheless, against the constitutional limits on federal jurisdiction, and repeatedly asked the states to use their own untrammelled constitutional powers to simply close the party down. Victoria obliged him with its ban on the use of rail transport for communist publications; New South Wales toyed with the possibility of a more comprehensive Disloyalty Act.[24]

Restrictions on public assembly remained the chief curb on communist activity. With the return of conservatives to government, the right-wing thugs faded away; the police remained and tightened their control. The effects were severest in Victoria, where the commander of the secret army, Major-General Thomas Blamey, doubled as the commissioner of police. He had used a special squad to stop all marches and meetings in the city of Melbourne, an object achieved during 1931, and obtained additional powers in 1932 from the new UAP state government to break up suburban street meetings. Some municipal councils forbade such meetings and some, especially inner-suburban Labor councils, allowed them; Blamey now overrode the local authorities to close down pitches in Carlton, Prahran, Footscray, South Melbourne and Brunswick, which traditionally served soapbox orators on a Friday night. In the face of growing protest from the Free Speech League, the chief secretary agreed in March 1933 to amend the law so that such meetings could be held where they did not obstruct traffic. Blamey, however, continued to enforce the old law, even in Phoenix Street, a cul-de-sac off Sydney Road in Brunswick.

The free speech fight became concentrated on Brunswick and brought many arrests. It culminated on the evening of Friday 19 May, when Noel Counihan volunteered to defy the ban from inside a lift cage bolted to a cart padlocked to a verandah post along Sydney Road. His friend 'Shorty' Patullo would climb on top of a tram to harangue the crowd and distract the police while the deed was done. Both of these young men were recent recruits to the Young Communist League, single and sufficiently reckless to accept the inevitable consequences. Counihan was able to speak for fifteen minutes and connect the free speech campaign to the plight of the unemployed, the rise of fascism and the ambitions of the war-mongering imperialists before the police battered a hole in his cage. Patullo was quickly chased up an alley and shot in the thigh. Both were arrested and convicted, though Counihan's subsequent appeal succeeded on a legal technicality. He found so many free-speech victims in Pentridge that there was a large Marxist study class. Further arrests continued for another two months before the legislative amendment conceded by the chief secretary came into force. It was the campaign of the Free Speech League, a campaign involving both communists and Labor Party members, that determined the outcome: the subsequent dramatics were strictly an epilogue, a result of Blamey's determination to win the battle of Phoenix Street and the resolution of the communists that he would not. A statue in Sydney Road now marks their ultimate victory. It is a bell-shaped cage, draped in a cloth, but above it a bird sings its freedom.[25]

In Sydney there was a similar campaign of even greater longevity against a ban on the sale of literature or collection of money at the Domain. Sunday afternoon at the Domain was a time-honoured fixture for espousers of causes in Sydney, its location on the edge of the city centre well suited to attract passing spectators. Communists had held public meetings there since the party's formation, so the party took up the restrictive regulations introduced early in 1934 as a major challenge. International Labour Defence, the successor to the International Class War Prisoners' Aid, organised a team of speakers who reached back into the party's past: Jack Howie, now of the ALP, Jim Quinton, on behalf of the ALP's Socialisation Units, Paddy Drew, still a communist but representing the Labor Council. It must have felt like old times as the police drew batons and made 25 arrests. For more than a year the campaign continued and the toll mounted. Jean Devanny was one of those who once more served time in the cause. 'I'll go again if the Party decides that way, Tommy', she told Tom Wright, 'but I dread the thought of it'. Yet again she was convicted, only this time the party paid her fine.[26]

A recurring motif in communist history is the spy. Ever since the party had come into existence the Commonwealth Investigation Branch, state police and employers' organisations had gathered information by attending meetings and planting agents in party branches. In the desperate circumstances of the Third Period, when the party was waging the war of Class Against Class, this infiltration took on an augmented significance. Spies gave warning of activity that relied on surprise if it was not to be suppressed; they urged members to commit crimes, and they framed them for crimes they did not commit. Communists endured great hardship during the Depression. They accepted the physical danger attached to their duties and were prepared if necessary to break the law, but the presence of enemies within their ranks was peculiarly unsettling.

In 1930 the party executive discussed how to deal with a spy who had been discovered in Sydney. He was a Melbourne man named Mulholland, who had hung about the party bookshop with bottles of beer in his pocket, boasting of his contacts. 'There are probably spies in the Party', Herbert Moore allowed—and well he might, since he was one himself. 'Some of them will be found out soon, some of them later, but no spy lasts very long.'[27] Some were readily identified by their appearance. The policeman who turns up at an early conference of the UWM at the Trades Hall in Judah Waten's novel, *Time of Conflict*, is a dead giveaway: 'his sports coat was spotless, his trouser cuffs weren't frayed and his open-necked shirt was white with a kind of whiteness no unemployed man in the single men's house ever achieved'. Stan Moran, a leading member of the UWM in Sydney, claimed that he spotted an infiltrator when he looked down at his boot and saw 'NSW Police Department' stamped on it. Others came to light when an interstate comrade recognised them. The South Australian member Tony McGillick arrived in Sydney for the UWM conference in June 1930 and identified among the unemployed delegates billeted in the party hall a police spy who had secured a shop for Adelaide communists at cheap rental, which proved to be a police trap. Another, Constable Cook, disclosed his true identity when he appeared in court to give evidence against communists in the Clovelly eviction case of 1930.[28]

Others again betrayed themselves in a momentary lapse, such as a New South Wales policeman, Parsons, who joined the party in January 1931 and worked with Jean Devanny in Workers' International Relief. He was energetic, punctual, cheerful, no task was too difficult, but as Devanny was travelling with him to a lunch-hour meeting and he asked her a question about an eviction the party planned to contest, she experienced a moment of revelation:

> . . . out of the blue, absolutely without reason, there came over me a queer feeling. I turned and looked at him. Our eyes met—and in the depths of his, as plainly as if reflected in a mirror I saw him in the uniform of a policeman.

The feeling passed, the idea seemed ridiculous. Devanny reported it nevertheless to a district committee member and he laughed that next she would accuse him of being a spy. Moxon also claimed later that he had reported his suspicions of Parsons and been censured for 'raising doubts about a good proletarian'. Then in June Parsons approached a comrade and suggested the party take reprisals for the police shootings at Bankstown by mining another house at Guildford with explosives. The Control Commission immediately expelled him. Some days later he turned up at the party hall in Sussex Street and was confronted by the aggressive Sam Aarons, whose parents had been founder-members in Melbourne and who had joined himself when the Depression ruined his chain of shoe repair shops in Sydney. Parsons drew a revolver, arrested Aarons for insulting language and made his final exit. Devanny claims that when next she saw him, on duty in uniform, he flushed and averted his face.[29]

It was at this time also that the party press began to carry lengthy reports of treachery in the workers' state. Imperialist agents were destroying livestock to create food shortages. The great Five Year Plan for modernising Soviet industry was being sabotaged by foreign technicians. The founder of the Red Army, Leon Trotsky, expelled from the party in 1927 and deported in 1929, was conducting a campaign of vicious lies against the party leadership. Former leaders such as Zinoviev, Kamenev and Bukharin were revealed as counter-revolutionary plotters. If these illustrious Old Bolsheviks could turn out to be traitors, how could the tiny Australian party remain pure?[30]

At least one other spy at Sussex Street went undetected. Alf Baker was the business manager of the *Workers' Weekly* who handled its subscriptions and also kept the membership records of the party. He was a member of the central committee, though he seldom participated in its business, for he was one of those industrious, unassuming functionaries who are to be found behind the scenes of any voluntary organisation. He earned his living as a postal worker, and came and went according to his shift, working in a little office alongside the meeting room that was kept securely locked. Then one day in 1938 Baker failed to turn up, and was never seen again. He was, it transpired, a detective sergeant.[31]

The forms of organisation and activity the party assumed during the period of Class Against Class were shaped by the environment in which it operated. The rigid hierarchical structure, the iron discipline enforced by expulsions and reinforced by self-criticism, afforded some protection against the fierce hostility members encountered. The secrecy reduced the exposure to spies. The prohibition of dissent and ban on factional activity were checks on error or disruption. At the same time these devices perpetuated the beleaguered condition of the party, holding it in a state of tension where mistakes were repeatedly discovered and dangerous tendencies constantly had to be rooted out.

The party made demands that taxed even the most ardent. In an open letter to the communist parties of capitalist countries at the beginning of 1930, the ECCI observed that while the new tasks of Class Against Class would require some cleansing of the ranks, no general purge was required. Frank self-criticism and careful examination of the party's ranks, from the top down, would be more appropriate since the difficult conditions that these parties were encountering provided 'a fundamental guarantee against the entrance into the party of careerists and placehunters'.[32] This was certainly true of Australia and yet the party took to the task of cleansing itself with profligate relish. Andy Barras, a member of the central committee, Gordon Kilpatrick, until recently organiser in Western Australia, and E. W. Paton, a prominent Sydney member, were all expelled early in 1930. Unlike another victim, Jack Ryan, they were not accused of political errors; rather, they were deemed to have failed in the tasks they were allocated. A similar fate befell Judah Waten, who had moved from Melbourne to Sydney to work on the staff of the *Workers' Weekly*. He left Sydney, and was suspended for twelve months for not obtaining leave. Others were deemed to lack Bolshevik courage: one Melbourne member was expelled for cowardice when he failed to defend party speakers against 'organised thuggery'.[33] Even the indomitable Joe Shelley would fall victim to this allegation when, between prison terms, he failed to combat the right wing in Lithgow. Called before the Control Commission and instructed to offer self-criticism, he placed his party card on the table and walked out. The party removed him from the central committee and then allowed him to resume his exertions on its behalf on the waterfront. Within a year he was severely censured for a breach of discipline and sent back to Lithgow.[34]

These exemplary lessons in party discipline were imitated across the country. Districts and sections demonstrated their rigour by expelling members for any laxity in the performance of duties, any infraction of discipline. Indeed, the party units displayed greater severity than the national executive, which was more likely to extend clemency to an offender who expressed contrition. The pages of the *Workers' Weekly* carried dozens of brief announcements sent in by local secretaries that recorded the expulsion of this coward or that traitor. The practice became endemic until Sharkey, the editor, announced at a party plenum in December 1932 that it should cease. 'All these small, trivial expulsions do not improve the tone or level of the Party organ. As a general rule it is only when someone of mass standing in the movement has to be expelled or criticised that we should give space.' The incessant purges also stunted the party's growth, as the national secretariat noted in a review of progress in the three months after this plenum. In some sections the number of expulsions exceeded recruitments, and it was made clear that such indiscriminate bloodletting was to cease: 'expulsions must only be resorted to in cases where comrades bring discredit to the Party or where they persist in carrying on a line in opposition to the Party line'.[35]

A similar tendency to go to the extreme bedevilled the other technique of party discipline, self-criticism. Initially employed for the condign punishment of right opportunists such as Ryan and Kavanagh, it was quickly given general application. Under the supervision of Herbert Moore, leading members outbid each other in proclamation of their errors, the better to establish their integrity. 'Discipline presupposes the existence of conscious and voluntary submission', Comrade Stalin laid down, 'because only a conscious submission can become a discipline of iron'. To submit was to cast off all personal feelings of friendship or antipathy. A comrade who resented the authority of another, or allowed personal loyalty to come before duty to the party, or attributed his own treatment to malice, was succumbing to the heinous sin of petty-bourgeois individualism. 'A Communist has only one supreme loyalty and that is to the Communist Party and the Communist International', Sharkey insisted at a party plenum. 'If he is doing something out of loyalty to other comrades, he wants to drop that point of view. We have no personal ties in the Communist Party.' But excessive self-criticism could be just as debilitating as wholesale expulsions, a danger the party recognised when it warned against 'the penitential form of the confession with its *mea culpa, mea culpa*'. In the ritualised form it so often took, self-criticism served also as a form of self-aggrandisement, the mock humility merely drawing attention to the refractory materials from which the party was constructed.[36]

In both these disciplinary devices the Australian party implemented the forms of Bolshevik practice and drew back from the full consequences of such a regimen. A similar pattern was apparent in the party's response to official repression. The Third Period postulated a confrontation with capitalism in its hour of crisis. No alleviation of the misery of its victims could be expected. Social fascism, the twin of fascism, would throw off the cloak of democracy as discontent grew. In their direction of the revolutionary struggle, communists could expect no quarter and must be prepared to continue their struggle under conditions of illegality. With the election of the UAP federal government at the end of 1931 and the amendments to the Crimes Act in 1932, that prospect seemed imminent. The party prepared to go underground with a cell system of clandestine members, safe addresses, hidden printing presses, secret communications and other security techniques to avoid detection.[37] Australians had scant familiarity with such 'conspiratorial work', as it was called, and little attraction to it. They found it hard enough to follow the limited security measures that were introduced into party life at the time: the use of pseudonyms, the frequent changing of meeting places and the discouragement of casual conversations among members. As the party recognised, such measures negated the efforts to popularise the cause and establish a communist presence in factories and working-class neighbourhoods. In smaller towns such subterfuges were in any case impossible, as a Toowoomba comrade pointed out to the Queensland district secretary in forthright terms: 'Oh, don't be so fucking stupid. Everyone knows my name's Cliff Jones. How can I run round this town telling them I'm someone else? You must be bloody stark staring mad down in Brisbane.'[38]

The tight security also changed the character of the party. It reduced opportunities for general discussion and widened the gulf between the ordinary party members, who necessarily remained open in their activity, and the full-time organisers and leaders, who would periodically disappear from view and consequently became more remote, inaccessible, cloaked in an aura of mystery. Herbert Moore had introduced the clandestine procedures to the first of the party plenums, the enlarged gathering of the central committee that met every few months and lasted several days. Gil Roper, a recent Adelaide recruit who attended this new kind of national assembly in 1930, was astonished that each session reassembled at a new meeting-place announced at the close of the previous one. As party secretary, J. B. Miles tightened the format. Delegates were henceforth identified in minutes by letter or number (Miles was 1, Sharkey 2) and a neophyte who was so indiscreet as to carve a hammer and sickle on a table incurred his wrath. Some members relished their notoriety in an atmosphere of imminent illegality and proposed that the party should treat any prohibition on its activities with the same defiance members displayed when brought before the courts to answer individual charges. In fact the Australian party contested the federal government's use of the Crimes Act, and made full use of the very legal system it denounced to restrict the impact of the legislation.[39]

The experience of the Australian party during the Third Period replicated that of other communist parties. They too embarked on the extreme policies associated with Class Against Class at a time of acute economic crisis, social distress and political instability, and they too encountered a heavy-handed response from the governments they sought to overthrow. All of them underwent a similar process of 'Bolshevisation', one that installed new leaders, new structures and procedures designed to ensure fidelity to the instructions of the Communist International. In Australia, the cumulative effect of its beleaguered condition and the iron discipline was to remake the Communist Party of Australia into a party like no other in the country's experience of radical movements. Demanding absolute obedience, it treated anything less as treachery:

> In a critical period such as the present when the Australian party is called upon to steel itself against the blows of the capitalists it is vital that the party preserves its unity and bolshevik fighting qualities by combating all those elements who attempt, through various activities, to carry on disruptive and provocative work inside the party.

Hence, in the stark formulation of J. B. Miles, 'We do not allow dissension in the Communist Party'.[40]

It is clear how the practices of expulsion, self-criticism and secrecy assisted Miles to stamp out dissension, and it is tempting to see them as mere devices whereby he and his colleagues imposed an absolute authority over the membership. But this view hardly allows for the leaders' own misgivings about the uses to which the practices were put, and it exaggerates the degree of control they were able to exercise in the early years of their leadership. Sharkey acquired eminence only after his return from the Soviet Union at the end of 1930; Miles' pre-eminence began several months later. For some time afterwards they had to deal with criticisms and challenges. Arguments over the correct interpretation and implementation of Class Against Class arose at every major gathering of party members up to 1935. The leaders' persistent recourse to self-criticism and expulsion was not simply a manipulation of party discipline to serve their own interests. The limits they imposed on its application suggest, rather, a recognition of the damaging effects of excessive zeal. It is to these internal controversies, with their interplay of ideology, aggrandisement and exigency that we now turn.

At the party congress in Easter 1931 the opposition was led by two members of the central committee, Jack Loughran and Esmonde Higgins, and two other leading party members, Ted Tripp and Charlie Nelson. Their chief grievance was the stifling of discussion under the dictatorial regimen imposed by Moore. Loughran's animosity towards Moore was shared by Tripp, who had encountered him while in Moscow in 1929 and learned from American students at the Lenin School of his shady record and ultimate expulsion from the American party. Higgins's contribution to the pre-congress discussion had been censored (it consisted of 'lies and slander', said Sharkey), while Nelson resented the threats of decapitation made against him. Their arguments against party policy were more muted. Criticism of the party's campaign in the New South Wales state elections in October of the previous year, ostensibly on the grounds that 51 candidates were excessive and too many of them were of poor quality, was as far as they would take their doubts about the new line. In response they were accused of wanting the election of a Labor government, which amounted to right opposition to the new line. Most denied the accusation, though Tripp and Higgins argued that the return to office of Jack Lang did provide the party with opportunities to expose the illusions of reformism. This was the heresy of the 'lesser evil', which made them no better than 'agents of the left social fascists', according to one of the many delegates who denounced them. Duly admonished, they were then invited to offer self-criticism. All but Higgins did so and were restored to their positions, Loughran on the Control Commission, Nelson and Tripp on the central committee. Even Higgins, who was dropped from the central committee, took up an editorial post on the *Red Leader*.[41]

Some prescient delegates to the Tenth Congress discerned a left as well as a right danger in the party ranks. Moxon was the only representative of it identified at that time, but six months later—and after the Eleventh Plenum of the ECCI clearly warned against it—J. B. Miles found leftism to be rampant. It was apparent, according to Miles, in the failure of the UWM to take up the 'concrete problems of the jobless' (an early example of this dreadful adjective and many of his readers must have wondered if he was proposing to feed the unemployed from cement mixers), in its inappropriate use of revolutionary slogans and in sectarian attitudes that isolated communists from the masses. Miles's criticism of the work of the UWM was aimed at Jack Sylvester, its charismatic national organiser. Sylvester was an English immigrant based in Balmain, educated, articulate and by no means submissive to the leadership. Miles did not name him and Sylvester did not participate in the ensuing discussion. But Jack Hitchen, a forthright south-coast miner, took the bait and suggested that the critics of the UWM were afraid of its revolutionary policies. Jack Kavanagh also weighed in with a criticism of any softening of unemployed militancy, and was duly taken to task: 'Comrade Kavanagh is replacing his right views with the left variety, once again proving the close affinity of right and left deviations'. The campaign against sectarianism (by now clearly established as a synonym for leftism) widened to take in all areas of party activity, and district committees admonished themselves for their past failures.[42]

Number 4 District proved most prone to sectarianism; indeed, Victoria emerged at this point from its earlier torpor to become the region of fastest growth and greatest turbulence. The party there had attracted a number of young recruits of a particularly ardent disposition. Moore visited Melbourne during 1930 and found a district committee composed of young, inexperienced comrades who 'in their enthusiasm were anxious to discover all sorts of real and imaginary right deviations'. Moxon's subsequent spell of duty there did little to curb their enthusiasm. Early in 1932 the national leadership removed two of the most impetuous, Arthur Marshall (he used the pseudonym King) and James Higgins (he had led the raid on Trades Hall in September 1931 with the declaration, 'There'll be Soviet power in Melbourne tomorrow') from the district committee. Under the cloak of self-criticism these former New Zealand hotheads were said to have demonstrated 'anarchist dishonesty to try to discredit the leadership of the Party'. In April Marshall accused the central committee of 'criminal right opportunism'. He and Higgins were expelled, along with Moxon who had persisted with his leftism. Hitchen followed some months afterwards when he said the party had become lost in a 'jungle of left Social Fascist activity'.[43]

The Victorian district secretary, Dinny Lovegrove (he used the name Jackson), was the next to challenge the leadership. He had opposed the more reckless escapades of Marshall and Higgins, and was not responsible for the assault on the Labor platform at the Yarra Bank on May Day 1932; that was the work of Jean Devanny, a visiting speaker, and Les Cahill, probably a police spy. But he kept up a confrontational style of street action that the Sydney leaders increasingly discouraged, notably in the rally he organised to mark the fifteenth anniversary of the Russian Revolution in November 1932. In defiance of police commissioner Blamey's ban on city demonstrations, the celebrants gathered in Melbourne's commercial centre to sing 'The Internationale'. Blamey met them with 22 mounted troopers, 30 police on motorcycles, 50 in plain clothes and 100 in uniform. As Ralph Gibson, the secretary of the Friends of the Soviet Union recalled, 'there were enough Party members and non-Party stalwarts to require continuous police bashing from the starting-point outside the Capitol Theatre to the Temperance Hall in Russell Street, which was booked for the final rally'. Gibson was one of many arrested.[44]

Both Lovegrove and Thornton were young, unemployed zealots who took readily to the rigours of Class Against Class. Both combined courage and organisational flair with a hectoring manner that brooked no contradiction. Lovegrove's erratic judgement and autocratic manner caused the Sydney leadership increasing concern during 1932. He expelled his chief local rival, Ernie Thornton, along with Thornton's supporters in the Yarra section of the district, based on Richmond and Collingwood, where the party had made greatest progress. Tom Wright came down from Sydney to investigate the numerous complaints against Lovegrove and tried to mediate the dispute, but Lovegrove derided the central committee as too respectable and timid.[45]

On behalf of the entire district committee, Lovegrove and two other Victorians took a comprehensive bill of charges against the central committee to a plenum at the end of 1932. It accused the Sydney leaders of failing utterly to take advantage of the splendid objective conditions to build the party, of persistent opportunism, of liquidating the UWM, of capitulation to capitalist legality in their response to the Crimes Act prosecution of the publisher of the *Workers' Weekly* and, among many other sins, of disgracing the party's reputation with the Saturday night dances it held in the Sussex Street hall. The hall was described as 'little more than a brothel' that attracted the lumpen-proletariat, beer and prostitutes. Leading Sydney members were even alleged to have brought their pyjamas with them to the dances—the reasons for such modesty are unclear. The description of these dances given in Judah Waten's novel, *Time of Conflict*, suggests they did indeed attract the larrikin pushes from nearby Pyrmont, Darlinghurst and Surry Hills, and it is possible that he had taken back such stories when he returned to Melbourne at the end of 1930.[46]

The Victorians gained no support from the other delegates, and offered abject self-criticism before the plenum concluded. Yet upon returning to Melbourne, Lovegrove retracted his retraction. J. B. Miles and two other members of the central committee then convened a special meeting of the district committee and expelled Lovegrove along with five other members of that state executive. 'These waverers and fainthearts, these opportunists and slanderers' were duly denounced in the party press and cast into outer darkness. It was an extraordinary performance, both by the Melbourne rebels in so comprehensively misjudging the mood of the national delegates, and on the part of the central committee in affording them such publicity. 'Why do we give so much space', *Workers' Weekly* asked, 'to these relatively unimportant people who are already discredited?'

> The answer is that such discussions of deviations and opportunist distortions have a very great educational value, clarifying the Party line and raising the political level of the membership, exposing the basis of the different deviations that occur from time to time and carrying on the ideological fight on two fronts, against right and 'left' opportunism for the Leninist line of the Comintern.[47]

As well as providing educational value, such episodes reminded members of the constant need for vigilance against error. It was by no means easy to steer a middle course between the left and right deviations, for to avoid the error of left adventurism was to risk lapsing into the error of right tailism (tailism was another of the neologisms introduced at ths time to suggest lagging behind the revolutionary masses). At one moment the party suffered from bureaucratic inertia, at another from excessive spontaneism. An enlarged meeting of the central committee during 1932 saw so many errors laid bare that one comrade suggested, 'We have surely exhausted the possibilities of making any new ones'.[48] Errors were generally evident in retrospect, when a shift in the line turned adherence to the line into deviation from it. Since, by the rules of the party, discussion was limited to the application and implementation of policies that were binding on all members, disagreement was seldom expressed openly but rather suggested obliquely by placing stress on particular phrases and judging other malefactors against them. The chief lesson of these public challenges, with their associated self-criticism and expulsions, was that a prudent member backed the line of the central committee.

Some of those expelled from the party during this period lost contact with it and with left-wing politics altogether. Others found their way back in, for with all its faults it offered an organisational framework and sense of revolutionary purpose they could not find elsewhere. In 1933 an alternative became available when a group of former communists established a Workers' Party of Australia (Left Opposition). Jack Sylvester was its principal figure. Recently expelled, the former national organiser of the UWM retained a strong following in his own suburb of Balmain, and he found additional support among the unemployed activists in Glebe angered by the party's failure to support the casualties of the unemployed protest campaign there. That failure in turn was a result of the CPA's insistence on absolute control of unemployed activism: unable to control the Glebe branch of the UWM, it left the members to their fate. One of Sylvester's followers was Laurie Short, also expelled from the Young Communist League in December 1932 for corresponding with another YCL member in Melbourne in support of Ernie Thornton when he was expelled during the Victorian factional conflict—a remarkable pairing since the political careers of Thornton and Short would remain entwined for a quarter-century, the one as the communist secretary of a major trade union, the other as his anti-communist nemesis. At this time Short was friendly with Jack and Edna Ryan, who lent him radical newspapers from America, including those produced by followers of Leon Trotsky, the former colleague of Lenin defeated and deported by Lenin's successors. In exile, Trotsky's left opposition to the Soviet leadership gave rise to Trotskyism, a doctrine that linked Stalin's abandonment of the ideals of the Russian Revolution to betrayal of the world revolution. Trotskyists regarded the Communist International as a sham, an organisation dominated by authoritarian opportunists who slavishly followed the Soviet leaders. These ideas formed the basis of the new Workers' Party's manifesto, and in its monthly newspaper, the *Militant*, it sought by constant criticism to provide a revolutionary alternative to an Australian communist party 'floundering in a morass of political ineptitude'.[49]

If the Workers' Party had been able to attract even a modest proportion of those driven out of the Communist Party at this time, it would have presented a formidable challenge. In the event Ted Tripp and Arthur Marshall were its most notable recruits. The Ryans, Jack Kavanagh and Esmonde Higgins followed it with interest but did not join. (Kavanagh's statement at a meeting of the

Friends of the Soviet Union (FOSU) that he did not consider Trotsky 'an absolute counter-revolutionary' was the basis of his final expulsion from the party in 1934.) Dinny Lovegrove and James Higgins formed their own Trotskyist group in Melbourne and achieved some success with the Dole Workers' Union they organised as an alternative to the communist UWM, but that soon faded away and Lovegrove eventually moved into the Labor Party where he would become a formidable anti-communist organiser. In Western Australia an unemployed activist, Sid Foxley, planned a Workers' Party upon his expulsion from the Communist Party at this time, but that also came to nothing.[50]

Champions of inexpediency, dogmatic to a degree, the Australian Trotskyists spent as much energy in internal disputation as they did in invigilating the errors of the Communist Party. For the time being Trotskyism remained more a term of abuse for CPA members than a serious challenge. Communists accused Sylvester, Tripp, Short and Marshall of offences ranging from pimping for the police to sexual depravity. During 1933 the *Workers' Weekly* dwelt so insistently on their crimes that it eventually conceded, 'Some comrades may wonder if we are not giving too much space to the insignificant clique of renegades'. As deviators they were contemptible, as informed critics of the Soviet Union they were intolerable. Hence communists were instructed to 'place your heels on the heads of these snakes'. The analogies between communists' own status as political pariahs and the treatment they accorded the Trotskyists passed unacknowledged.[51]

One of the few adherents of the Workers' Party was John Anderson, professor of philosophy at the University of Sydney. Anderson is best known as a libertarian, Andersonianism as an intellectual tradition mistrustful of all doctrines of secular meliorism and especially the tyrannical egalitarianism of Marxists. But in 1927, when Anderson arrived in Australia from his native Scotland, he was strongly sympathetic to communism. Writing as A. Spencer, he contributed articles to the *Workers' Weekly* and the monthly *Communist* from that time. At the end of 1929 he lent clear support for the turn to Class Against Class and subsequently attended the party plenum of Easter 1930. An admiring Moxon declared him the party's 'Theoretical Adviser'.[52]

Such sympathies brought conservative odium but Anderson displayed courage in the face of threat of dismissal from the university. His close association with Moxon, however, antagonised other communists. Kavanagh, Moxon's predecessor at the helm of the CPA, resented the professor's prestige with the fierce resentment of a proletarian autodidact. Miles, Moxon's successor at the party helm, suspected him with a self-righteousness fully the equal of his compatriot. He pounced on articles Anderson contributed during 1932 to the magazine of the Labour Club at the University of Melbourne, *Proletariat*, for their unproletarian qualities. Anderson, never one to duck a challenge, responded with citation of Lenin's *What Is To Be Done?* to remind Miles of the role of intellectuals in the revolutionary party. He also contrasted the open discussion that had occurred in 1929 with the distortions, personal abuse and suppression of dissent that accompanied the eclipse of Moxon—or rather, which were introduced by Moxon, Kavanagh observed in his annotated copy of Anderson's remonstrance. Finally, Anderson suggested that the party was exhibiting a 'fear of spontaneity' that was 'a sign not of leadership but of bureaucracy'. Miles instructed Lovegrove, then the Victorian district secretary, to suppress this further contribution to *Proletariat*. To Anderson's allegation that he was 'playing the schoolmaster', Miles insisted that the party was 'teacher and leader', and had to be safeguarded from the impositions of 'university men'. 'How dare a mere proletarian', he continued with heavy irony, 'tell a university student, graduate, or what not, that he is in the baby class?' Having published his suppressed article as a pamphlet, Anderson became a founder-member of the Workers' Party. He continued to denounce the Stalinist betrayal of revolutionary socialism and to uphold Trotsky's fidelity to the emancipatory project of communism until some years later when he concluded that both Lenin and Trotsky were themselves complicit in the despotism of the party. Like Short and Lovegrove, his initial enthusiasm for Class Against Class produced a subsequent reaction into first left and then right opposition to communism, but always marked by their distinctive intolerance of the politics of the broad left.[53]

Anderson's unrepentant intellectualism was a singular instance of resistance to the insistently proletarian temper of communism during the Depression. The appearance of communists at the

University of Melbourne signalled the first stirrings of a new constituency; the title of their magazine and the criticisms it drew from the party leadership testified to the suspicion of these new adherents. The earlier inconstancy of Guido Baracchi was recalled when his application for readmission was rejected in 1932, even though he was conducting classes for the party and frequently dipped into his pocket to assist it. Esmonde Higgins, who also ran party classes and edited the *Red Leader*, was removed from the central committee in 1931. These intellectuals with their precious consciences were inherently unreliable, their training in bourgeois knowledge a source of confusion and error. The theory that the party esteemed was a theory grounded in practice, a working-class doctrine accessible to workers who applied themselves to its mastery. 'Where did I get my knowledge from?' Miles asked at a national plenum in 1932. 'Amongst the workers and from books . . . I did not have the advantage that you people have got. It is not a question of a different brain box, but a question of determination to get to know.'[54]

The middle-class recruit to communism underwent a testing ordeal. It was a perilous business to declare your commitment, as the University of Melbourne communists discovered in 1932 when three of their number were thrown into the lake by right-wing hearties. In the same year communists appeared on the Sydney campus as guests of that university's Labor Club to show a film, *In Lenin's Country*, on the fifteenth anniversary of the Russian Revolution, only to be chased down Parramatta Road by loyalist undergraduates.[55] The student radicals encountered a daunting hostility. To be middle-class and become a communist was to give up comfort and leisure, to incur social ostracism and jeopardise a career. This experience of crossing a line, of making an irrevocable choice, is exemplified in Ralph Gibson, the son of the professor of philosophy at the University of Melbourne and with his own expectations of an academic life. The comfort and prestige mattered little to Ralph, who was the most selfless of men and all the more impregnable to doubt in his luminous intensity. Yet after he rejected the offer of a university lectureship late in 1931, he sat in front of the postbox for twenty minutes before he finally inserted his letter of application for party membership.[56]

The Melbourne physician Gerald O'Day described his conver-

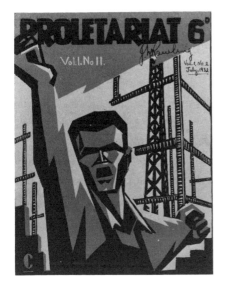

The Labor Club at the University of Melbourne established its magazine 'Proletariat' in 1932. Noel Counihan's powerful cover illustration for the second issue employed the common device of a declamatory militant male worker, one fist raised, the other cocked. The girders of the construction site suggest the building of a new order. (Source: J.N. Rawling collection, Noel Butlin Archives Centre, ANU N57/2114)

sion, also in the depths of the Depression, as the result of a search for understanding of why hunger and hardship afflicted so many of the patients he treated despite the country's natural wealth. He had come to the party through the FOSU and lost a position at St Vincent's hospital and much of his private practice when he did. 'Aided by the knowledge of five languages, and the scientific instruction that had enabled me to gain the degree of Doctor of Medicine', he pressed on to discover the answer in the writings of Karl Marx and the example of the Soviet Union.

> For all these reasons I deemed it my duty to join the Communist Party; and with all my power to aid the liberation of humanity from the economic slavery that prevents the full blossoming of the precious individuality of each and every one.

Within twelve months he was confessing his failures to the party plenum. Charged with offensive behaviour for his part in the Melbourne march to mark the fifteenth anniversary of the Russian Revolution, he had failed to carry out the instructions of the district committee on the conduct of his case and instead had withdrawn his allegations of police thuggery. 'As a bourgeois intellectual', he conceded, 'I have tendencies towards individualism, right opportunism and being undisciplined'.[57]

University-educated communists such as Gibson and O'Day were rarities in the early 1930s. The ferment of war and revolution, which had drawn such middle-class rebels as Prichard, Jollie Smith, Baracchi and Higgins to embrace communism, yielded in the later 1920s to a febrile stability. As initial expectations faded and the party retreated into the familiar rituals of a sect on the fringes of the labour movement, it lost its wider appeal. Those children of the middle class who rejected the conservatism of their parents turned to various forms of modernism or bohemianism, but not to the drab rigidities of communism. Now, with the onset of profound capitalist crisis, communism appealed to a new generation of dissidents. They included James Rawling, an arts graduate from the University of Sydney; Dave Morris, a bachelor of engineering from the University of Queensland; Ted Bacon, a part-time arts student at the same campus; Len Fox, a Melbourne schoolteacher; Joan and Alan Finger, respectively MA and MBS from Melbourne; and Lloyd and Edgar Ross, sons of the veteran socialist Bob Ross: like Esmonde Higgins, Lloyd Ross was a Melbourne history graduate. Such recruits brought valuable skills to the party. They had technical expertise. They could write, some were effective public speakers, with an appropriate adjustment of diction to a working-class audience, and most could be entrusted with organisational tasks. Bill Orr first encountered Ralph Gibson on a visit to Melbourne and judged he posessed 'certain organisational and administrative abilities that can be utilised for the Party'. Those who became full-time party workers tended to be assigned to front organisations—in Gibson's case the Friends of the Soviet Union, which flourished under his control and reached out to progressive circles beyond the organised labour movement—and excluded from central political or industrial responsibilities. They were expected to demonstrate their credentials, to accept hardship and danger, to undertake whatever was demanded of them. 'Gibson was loyal, but that was about all you could say', Miles opined when he went down to Melbourne to expel the Loveday group. Tom Wright thought him a 'good fellow, always working', and regretted that Lovegrove's successor was inclined to dictate instructions to Gibson just as Lovegrove had bullied O'Day. They also made effective election candidates: O'Day attracted more than 2500 votes in a by-election for the Legislative Assembly electorate of Carlton in 1932, and 27 309 as the Senate candidate in Victoria in 1934 in the same election in which Gibson polled nearly

5000 House of Representative votes in the federal electorate of Flinders.[58]

Even in this electoral activity, however, the non-working class communist was unreliable, and none more so than the Queenslander Fred Paterson, who in 1944 would become the party's only member of parliament. From straitened origins, he had proceeded by scholarships to the University of Queensland, where he was a champion athlete, and then after First World War service, to Oxford as a Rhodes scholar. There he abandoned theology and on his return in 1923 joined the Communist Party. He left it in 1925 (for similar reasons as Baracchi, namely that the CPA was so weak that it was better to concentrate on the ALP) but remained active in the left; stood as one of the left-wing candidates in the 1929 Queensland state election; and rejoined the party shortly before he was tried for sedition in 1930. By then he was completing legal studies, and he represented himself as well as many of the victims of official repression in Queensland in the following years. Both as a lawyer and a communist, Paterson retained the high moral principle and service of others that had seen him train for the Anglican priesthood—and perhaps the same need to hold to a faith, however much he might question points of doctrine. Shifting to Townsville in 1932, Paterson built up a strong personal following that was apparent in the growing number of votes he attracted in successive municipal, state and federal elections. But he remained resistant to the electoral implications of Class Against Class. In his view a Labor government was preferable to a conservative one, if only because 'the quickest and most effective way of destroying confidence in the Labor Party was to be obtained by the return of Labor to power'. On the eve of the 1932 state election Paterson even suggested the party offer to exchange votes with Labor to defeat the conservative government there. He admitted that the Labor executive would reject the offer but argued that in doing so it would commence the process of detaching sincere workers from the bureaucratic leadership.[59]

This was the argument of the 'lesser evil', the very argument that had brought the old leadership undone in 1929, and Paterson was ordered to retract it. He did but was criticised by his district committee for right opportunism and failure to denounce social fascism with sufficient ardour. This he would not do to the party's satisfaction, not even when J. B. Miles travelled north to instruct him to engage in self-criticism. The district plenum met in 1933 and repeated the call. Still Paterson persisted with his 'usual petty bourgeois, individualist, liberal defence of not being convinced and feeling hypocritical if he spoke against his convictions'. That he was allowed to remain in the party was probably due to a combination of circumstances: local popularity, distance from Sydney and the fact that he did not propagate his heresy. 'We considered that by putting him forward as the candidate we would reach thousands of people we would not reach if we put forward someone else', was how the district secretary explained the decision to run Paterson for the mayoral contest in Brisbane in 1934, but 'we are watching closely for any deviation' and 'explaining his errors to the workers'. Paterson remained adamant and discreet, a solitary instance of the irrefragable communist intellectual.[60]

The party cultivated an identity of proletarian virtue. Its forms of reportage, the stories it told about itself in the party press and the vocabulary it used to tell them, built up a composite self-image of resolution, solidarity, endurance. The communist both shared and transcended the circumstances of his class, responded to hardship and maltreatment with anger and channelled that anger into purposeful collective action. Persecution only hardened him. This codification of masculine capacity and masculine control raised problems of class and gender that the circumstances of the period aggravated. In depriving so many men of their status as breadwinners, the Depression took from them the very basis of their class identity and imposed heavy strains on the established gender roles within the working-class family. Women and children fell back on charitable assistance. The inability to provide robbed a man of his pride, his companionship and even his very manliness.

In its response to these strains during the first, most reckless, phase of Class Against Class, the party seemed to fracture conventional boundaries of male and female activity. The Sydney women who were so prominent in the street protests of 1930 were trespassers, their turbulence deeply disturbing of conventional expectations of feminine decorum. In holding their own demonstration in November of that year they created pandemonium: the public spectacle of women wrestling with police amidst city traffic, resisting arrest and shouting their defiance, was profoundly iconoclastic. By their unruliness both then and later in prison they were challenging codes of masculine chivalry, forcing the authorities to employ the same severity against them as it used against men. The circumstances of the Third Period allowed a new role. Women were no longer supporting men in industrial dispute, though that conception of the female activist as an auxiliary who sustained and assisted the militancy of her husband still persisted in the women's department of the party and restricted its appeal. Instead, these women engaged in the campaigns against fascism and social fascism in their own right. They took up the protest against unemployment as a phenomenon that affected them directly and they underwent the same hazards in their activity. Prominent party women, such as Joy Barrington and Jean Devanny, gained a reputation as firebrands, undaunted by repeated convictions, uncompromising in their militancy. Joy was the larger and better able to acquit herself in physical confrontation. Jean was more frail and perhaps more daunting in her fury.

They were also notorious for their transgressive personal lives in a party dominated by men with sexual double standards. After an initial flurry of controversy, the early Communist Party avoided discussion of sexual politics. Initially it had responded to anticommunist allegations of the nationalisation of women with its own claims of capitalist debauchery, whether in Adela Pankhurst Walsh's denunciations of sexual commerce or Bill Thomas's illustrated warnings of veneral disease; but these quickly gave way to an uneasy silence. On the one hand there was the predatory behaviour strikingly demonstrated by Bill Earsman, on the other the repressive avoidance best illustrated by Bob Ross when he congratulated Guido Baracchi on his marriage: 'Well, I suppose it solves the sex problem'. It didn't, either for Guido or many other party members of the 1920s who sought a freer, less circumscribed morality based on sexual equality. That generally tacit and informal ethos was repudiated in the 1930s, as the party proclaimed a far more conventional morality, and yet men continued to use their authority and prestige to establish claims over younger female comrades. A Queensland communist woman has recalled how Jack Henry, the district organiser, used to 'pick off' female recruits at party dances; when she taxed him with this behaviour he replied that 'what he did outside was his own business'. But his business was also party business: applicants for membership in Queensland were asked not just about their class origins but whether they had venereal disease. Furthermore, when Jean Devanny inserted a priapic and readily identifiable Jack Henry into the manuscript of *Sugar Heaven*, he threatened to resign unless it was altered.[61]

This aspect of Australian communism would rigidify as Miles and Sharkey imposed their own libidinous sanctimony on the party during the 1930s, but was evident even while Moxon's madcap approach held sway. He warned delegates to the Tenth Congress of 'wrong ideas about freedom' that resulted in 'promiscuity in sex relations'. Since women were more politically backward, he held, such 'degeneracy' discredited the party. His own subsequent defection was attributed to the influence of his wife who was said to have insisted he quit the party—in fact she remained an active member long after he left. Lindsay Mountjoy, an equally ardent enthusiast for the Third Period, employed similar conceptions of female licence and feminine restraint in her speech to the congress. She said that the sexual indiscretions of party women caused working-class wives to stop their husbands from joining the party: 'We must remember the Communist Party is not a bohemian club'. Several years later, when her husband was organiser in Western Australia, she lamented his philandering with party women.[62]

A similar pattern of licence and control marked the party's attitude towards single men. The strains that the Depression imposed on the family increased the incidence of separation and desertion; young men without a job were unable to establish households of their own and were often forced out of the parental home. The party recruited from such resentful outcasts, and used them as its 'shock troops', as one UWM organiser put it, in more desperate endeavours. 'They were daredevils, political bushrangers, so to speak, but for a worthy cause.' Some established communal households in inner-city terraces, and were available to protect speakers from attack or to offer resistance to eviction against police assault. These were the barracks of the Workers' Defence Corps, which the authorities regarded with particular alarm. Through their relief regulations the state governments employed strategies of isolation and dispersal to break up congregations of unattached, unemployed men. It confined them to labour camps on the outskirts of cities or despatched them to rural areas where they could draw rations on condition that they keep moving.[63] Such circumstances brought out the best and worst in human nature. Rejection and constant hardship stripped away the outward forms of civilisation.

At the party congress in 1931 Charlie Nelson complained that a comrade sent from Sydney to Lithgow to stand as parliamentary candidate in the 1930 state election had made a poor impression because of his impoverished appearance. He did not even possess a shirt. A former Wobbly observed at that time that the party leaders in Sussex Street seemed to believe that the use of soap and water amounted to a 'bourgeois deviation'. This image of the party under Moxon's leadership as a 'a party of the unwashed' suggests the problematic character of the Depression communist. For those formed in an earlier tradition of working-class radicalism, the activist commanded the respect of workers through an exemplary self-respect. Unemployment weakened that moral order, refashioning its victims as rejects and depriving them of both the capacity and the desire for such respectability. Jack Kavanagh's pride in his personal appearance made some think he looked like a businessman; Moxon's larrikin style was deemed that of the lumpen-proletariat. The term was German in origin, *lumpen* meaning rags, used by Marx to signify the vagrant or criminal underclass who were uninterested in collective revolutionary endeavour. The issue that troubled communists was whether the army of single, itinerant, unemployed men constituted an advanced segment of the working class, the unemployed workers as they were designated, or a distinct stratum of rootless and refractory outcasts. The problem the party faced in concentrating its work among them was how to speak in their idiom without succumbing to their indiscipline. It was a problem nicely captured in Frank Hardy's semi-fictional account of the battle of Cairns, where the daredevil agitator Jack McCormack provokes the townspeople and the party member Snowy Hall deprecates his speech as sectarian. Snowy wants an organising committee, Jack is 'a bloody anarchist' who insists on self-management. Jack hoists a red flag, Snowy seeks a compromise. But they both stand together in the final confrontation and they both get a beating.[64]

Under the direction of Miles and Sharkey, the party moved away from the confrontational style of unemployed agitation cultivated by Moxon. 'The workers got the impression that in order to get into the UWM you had to bash and you had to be bashed', Miles observed of the earlier dispensation. The forms of activity he encouraged were more orderly, more closely tied to immediate needs, directed more to the unemployed worker and his family than to shifting assemblies of homeless men. Just as party members were to be scrupulous in sexual conduct, so they were to attend to their personal appearance. Such bagmen as Jack McCormack came to be seen as deficient in the qualities the party needed as the Australian economy slowly recovered, leaving a residual core of long-term unemployed. Their very rebelliousness unfitted them for party work, Richard Dixon told the central committee. Like the libidinous women, these men manifested a 'degeneracy', except that in this case the symptoms were not hyperactivity but work-shy torpor. They had been deprived of work for so long that they had lost the vital qualities of the worker. Thus Dixon's conclusion: 'We have to recognise that any individual who is working under a boss has to work quickly, etc., and in his party work he carries the same method into the work and also the discipline that he learns in the factory'.[65]

Discipline was an essential feature of the Depression communist. The British Marxist Perry Anderson has observed that 'The Comintern remains to date a sociologically unique phenomenon, as an organisation which commands an absolute loyalty, a disciplined fidelity, amongst its constituent national sections'. From 1930 the Communist Party of Australia adopted an iron discipline that was alien to the indigenous political culture, one that subordinated it to a nominally international organisation that was itself subjected to the control of the Communist Party of the Soviet Union under the dictatorship of Joseph Stalin. Stalin's dictatorship was enforced through purges, show trials, executions and state terror. But in Australia communist discipline was exercised in circumstances where its distinctive sanctions were absent. As Anderson asks, 'What is the nature of a Stalinist party in a society in which that party enjoys no form of political coercion, administrative power, or any other form of physical duress over its membership?'[66] An answer has to account for a relationship between party and membership that was at once voluntary and obligatory, imposed and accepted.

The structure, machinery and essential techniques of party discipline have already been considered. The rules of the Australian party mirrored those of the Comintern, creating a hierarchical organisation that subordinated members to leaders and placed careful restrictions on the election of the leaders—but no one had to become a member. The operation of the party demanded absolute obedience and left no room for disagreement or debate—but as Lenin's term 'democratic centralism' indicates, it was the members who legitimated their submission. Any infractions incurred the sanctions of self-criticism or expulsion—but no one was prevented from leaving. Those who did leave attracted stories of personal weakness or scandalous misconduct. The charge of cowardice levelled at Kavanagh was an example; embezzlement was a more common allegation, used against both Moxon and Tripp—but a party as small and isolated as the Australian one could scarcely ensure that such calumnies achieved the wide circulation on which their efficacy depended.

Perhaps the most striking feature of this disciplinary regime is the acceptance of it. There were very few prominent party members who willingly parted company with the party as it entered into draconian excess during the Third Period. Tom Wright, Norm Jeffery, Hector Ross and Hetty Weitzel were among the discredited exponents of the old line who quickly yielded to the new. Jack Kavanagh resisted longer, but submitted to discipline more than once before he was finally pushed out. Joy Barrington performed her penance, Esmonde Higgins accepted his demotion. Jack Ryan made three attempts for readmission but was debarred by his cursed personal pride, Edna Ryan tried to hang on. Old warhorses such as Joe Shelley and Jack Loughran endured their humiliation; even Young Turks like Jack Sylvester and Ted Tripp did not abandon the party until all hope of rehabilitation was gone.

Why did such aggrieved victims persist? It was certainly not for comfort or advantage. Party duty was onerous, demanding, constant. The new leaders affected a hardness, an impersonal driving rigour that made few concessions to personal needs or human warmth. An unemployed activist who joined the party at this time had occasion to admire a sunset and was advised by a member of the Victorian district committee: 'Comrade if you've got time to watch sunsets you're not doing as much Party work as you should be doing'.[67] The anecdote, related 40 years afterwards, uses a different tone from contemporary parlance. The form of communist reportage during the Depression, the vocabulary of the platform and newspaper that carried over into minutes and even private correspondence, allows for only a certain kind of political response to the demands and impositions. It praises defiance, rebukes failure, judges individuals as they conform or fail to conform to expectations in a limited range of settings with predetermined roles. It says little of the peculiarities of those who perform those roles or of their human capacities.

Among these communists there are very few of the memoirs wherein those who saw that frame of reference collapse rethought the impulses that moved them in their earlier enthusiasm. The nearest account of this kind we have for the Depression communists is the autobiographical account of Jean Devanny, begun in the early 1940s when she was expelled from the party, completed in the 1950s when she had resigned after rejoining. Her perspective is different from the outlook of those who adapted to the Bolshevised party, for she was one of the Third Period recruits. She arrived in Sydney from New Zealand in 1929. Her children, Pat and Karl, joined the YCL, her husband Hal, the Communist Party. Pat travelled in 1931 to the Soviet Union for training at the communist youth school. Jean hung back, all too conscious of the demands that membership would make on her as an experienced speaker and how those demands would take her from writing. It was her participation in one of the street demonstrations in November 1930, and subsequent conviction and imprisonment, that impelled her to apply for party membership. She was told she would be on probation for three months because she was a writer: writers were a 'declassed element'. Her wealthy friend Marion Piddington warned her, 'Jeanie, you are not tough enough for them. They will break you. Mark my words, they will break you.' Eventually they did, as the narrative relates, but the need to join prevailed and the pleasures of belonging sustained Jean Devanny through hardships imposed on her and difficulties of her own making. To one of her many stories of such exploitation, she appends the explanation: 'The sense of consecration was still strong within me—and I still hugged to myself that warm, wonderful feeling of belonging'. So did others, tougher but no less compassionate than her.[68]

10

Towards the united front

The onset of the Third Period brought a sharp change in the tactics and temper of the Communist International, one marked by internecine argument and recrimination as the capitalist democracies plunged into crisis. The new communist leaders accentuated the discontinuities to exorcise all remnants of reformism and opportunism. The abandonment of the Third Period, by contrast, came slowly and unevenly. There was no declaration of a Fourth Period, no repudiation of errors or replacement of those who had made them. Rather, as the Depression eased and levels of production and employment slowly recovered, communists reoriented their activity back to workers in the workplace. This recovery was fragile. The Depression had strained, perhaps irreparably, the institutions of the liberal order—an order marked out by progress, liberty, elected governments, free trade, peace, international cooperation—and many who abandoned those broken idols turned to the antithesis of liberalism, fascism. Communists had previously regarded fascism as a device to which capitalists resorted when the usual forms of constitutional government failed them, but as fascists stamped out freedom in one country after another, it became all too clear that there was indeed a difference between fascism and capitalist democracy. As the the fascist powers threatened to engulf the world in a new war, communists reoriented their politics from revolutionary opposition to progressive alliance. The policy of Class Against Class, with its vehement opposition to social as well as capitalist democracy, yielded to a united front for the defence of a people's democracy.

Historians of communism locate this change as occurring between the years of 1933 and 1935, and key the new policy to the response of the Soviet Union to crucial international events. At the beginning of 1933 Hitler came to power in Germany. Within weeks he used the burning of the Reichstag to justify the suppression of the German Communist Party. The trial of its leaders and Georgi Dimitrov, the head of the European bureau of the Comintern, heralded a Nazi crusade against communism. After Hitler's suppression of communists came the suppression of social democrats, and as early as March 1933 the ECCI called for an alliance to meet this right-wing assault on the left. Subsequent fascist coups in Austria, Latvia and Bulgaria magnified the threat to the Soviet Union on its western border, while the Japanese invasion of Manchuria created a new threat in the east. In France, meanwhile, there was an augury of a new alignment as communists joined socialists on the streets of Paris in February 1934 to throw back a fascist march on the Chamber of Deputies—this, the first demonstration of the effectiveness of the united front, prepared the way for similar alliances elsewhere. Later in the same year the Soviet Union joined the League of Nations, which had been created in 1919 by the victors of the First World War to legitimate their division of spoils and was described at the time by Lenin as 'a thieves' kitchen'. In 1935 there were further Soviet accommodations to the exigencies of world politics, as Stalin called for the League to impose sanctions against fascist Italy because of its invasion of Abyssinia, and then entered into a mutual defence pact with France. At its Seventh Congress in 1935 the Communist International acknowledged the political corollary of these strategic changes: no longer social democracy but fascism was the main enemy of the workers' state and of workers all around the world. The need to resist fascism required a united front of the labour movement, reformist as well as revolutionary, in concert with all progressive forces.[1]

In itself the call for a united front was not new. Throughout the Third Period communists had called for a united front from below that would detach workers in trade unions and social democratic organisations from their treacherous social fascist leaders. The qualification 'from below' was all important: those discredited opportunists who had been brought to account at the Australian party conference of 1929 were deemed to have pursued a united front from above, and thus to have perpetuated the reformist illusion. Herbert Moore had insisted at the 1931 congress that the chief blow must therefore be directed at the social fascists who posed as friends of the workers. This attitude was first modified at the party plenum at the end of 1932. Following the Twelfth Plenum of the ECCI held two months earlier under the shadow of Hitler's rise to power in Germany, the Australian party declared that social fascism was no longer the chief danger. Rather, the capitalist class was the main enemy, the social fascists provided its chief support and the correct way to expose them was not sectarian abuse but 'clear, simple and concrete exposure of the reformist leaders'.[2]

Then came Hitler's success and the Comintern's call in March 1933 for a united front with the Socialist International. It was heavily qualified. The ECCI considered it 'possible to recommend' to its constituent units that they 'refrain from making attacks on Social-Democratic organisations' providing the social democrats joined in a campaign of resolute opposition to the common threat. The Australian party published the Comintern statement alongside its own. The capitalist offensive against working-class living standards, the repressive measures of conservative governments, the continued activities of the New Guard and the growing threat of war all required 'a common united front struggle'. The Communist and Labor parties should organise joint committees of action and if the Labor Party agreed to abandon 'all class-collaborationist policies', the Communist Party would 'renounce attacks on the Labor Party leaders during common action'.[3]

This initial Australian overture was perhaps even more grudging than that of Moscow. Given that the New Guard was rapidly dwindling into irrelevancy, it placed greater emphasis on economic and political circumstances that were hardly different from those that had been used to justify Class Against Class. It was directed both to the executive of the ALP and 'to all Australian workers', and its call for committees of action continued the emphasis on a united front from below. In the same breath that it appealed to the Labor Party for unity, the statement rehearsed at length the perfidious record of the Labor leaders in fomenting disunity. The party leadership was worried that the Communist International's new line—and Miles recognised that it signalled 'a very distinct change from the attitude toward the social democratic parties during the third period'—might cause 'a lot of confusion in the Party'. Right opportunists would take comfort from it, the leftists who had so recently disrupted the party plenum would seize on it as a vindication of their allegation of a right danger. A week after it appeared, the Australian party made clear that while it would forego attacks on the Labor Party and unions during common action, communists would continue to criticise them if they shrank from what was needed. 'We must distinguish between criticism and attacks', the party stipulated. Nor were communists abandoning their estimation of the Labor Party and union leaders. 'We continue to regard them as Social Fascists . . . and arising from this the task of the Party is to expose and isolate them from the working class.'⁴

It is hardly surprising that the ALP dismissed such a mealy-mouthed offer, just as the Socialist International rejected the appeal of the Communist International. Throughout 1933 the Comintern floundered as it sought to comprehend the nature of fascism, a generic term that it had applied indiscriminately across national and political boundaries and now attached primarily to the German National Socialists. Attempts to analyse the Nazi Party in class terms, as the last resort of finance capital as it sought to suppress the political contradictions of late capitalism, failed utterly to recognise the malign force of an ideology that subordinated class to race. The derangement that would culminate in the Final Solution lay outside the Enlightenment framework of progress that communism shared with capitalism. The Thirteenth Plenum of the ECCI at the end of the year still attributed the success of the fascists to the treachery of the social fascists. Hence at its own Fourth Plenum in April 1934 the Australian party declared that as capitalism intensified its assault, the Labor Party deceived and disarmed the working class. 'This means that Communists in their propaganda, agitation and everyday work among the masses must direct the main blow against the Labor Party, which paralyses the working class in face of the advance of Fascism and the approach of war.' Members should seize on anti-fascist and anti-war sentiments of workers to put forward proposals for united struggle, around the decidedly unrevolutionary slogan 'lighten the workers' burden', but must appreciate that the united front led 'to weakening not strengthening of reformism'. While the emphasis was still on the united front from below, in order to separate the workers from the social fascists, it was important to avoid 'replacing of careful analysis with abuse of the Labor Party'. As Richard Dixon explained at a subsequent meeting of the central committee, when Labor Party members heard themselves described as social fascists, they were hardly amenable to a united front. It was not abuse that was needed but 'a positive concrete programme' that would more effectively serve the ideological struggle against reformism.[5]

This was the policy the Communist Party took into the federal elections of September 1934, in which it opposed 21 Labor candidates and helped defeat several of them as the conservative Lyons government renewed its majority. Yet a month later J. B. Miles announced that the party was again to approach Labor with united front proposals. Once more a joint campaign for improved living standards, opposition to war and resistance to fascism was proposed. This time the appeal was directed to the ALP Federal Executive and a meeting sought between the two bodies: 'Comrades, we are addressing this appeal for united activity to you in all earnestness and sincerity, prompted only by the desire to advance the fight of the whole working class in its struggle against Fascism and war'. Almost immediately, however, the party had to explain to a puzzled correspondent that the proclamation did not signify that the Labor leaders had lost their social fascist spots. The purpose of the appeal was to win 'reformist workers' for joint action that would eventually draw them to accept the 'full programme of the socialist revolution and the proletarian dictatorship'. The correspondent was not alone in his puzzlement. When Miles explained the new approach to the Labor Party at a meeting of the central committee, a leading Victorian member confessed that he would have to go back and remove a common misapprehension: 'I think generally throughout the Party it has been considered only as a left manoeuvre to attack and expose the social fascists'. Miles corrected him. He added that while the previous campaign for a united front had lasted only a few weeks, this time it would have to be sustained in order to demonstrate to the workers who were the real splitters and disruptors of the labour movement.[6]

The ALP's inevitable rebuff revealed a continuing uncertainty about whether the united front was to be effected from above or below. At a central committee meeting in February 1935 Sharkey said the object was a united front from below and the offer of a united front from above merely a device to facilitate it. Miles, who had recently returned from Moscow where the issue had still be resolved, said the purpose was to 'disintegrate' the Labor ranks in order to deliver its working-class members to the revolutionary movement. Subtlety was needed to widen differences within the Labor Party between its left wing (there was no more talk of left social fascism) and its right. Consequently the Communist Party decided to direct second preferences to the Labor Party—under the slogan 'The Stronger the Communist Party the Stronger the Labor Movement'—in state elections held in Victoria, New South Wales and Queensland during the first half of 1935. Furthermore, the Australian party began for the first time to signal its interest in building a broader class alliance 'between the workers, farmers, civil servants, middle classes, intellectuals' who would rally around the campaign against fascism and war.[7]

The final enunciation of the united front at the Eleventh Party Congress at the end of 1935 came, then, after an erratic series of swerves that moved towards and shied away from the ultimate destination, an accommodation with the nonrevolutionary majority of the labour movement. The Seventh Congress of the Communist International in August 1935, when Dimitrov laid down that 'the main and immediate task of the international labour movement [was] to establish the united fighting front of the working class', determined that the persistent reservations would no longer apply. 'We have not to think of it in the manner we thought of it previously', Sharkey, the chief Australian representative at the world congress, explained to the delegates at the subsequent national congress. The expectation that reformists would be won over to revolutionary communism continued, the duty to expose sabotage remained, but Australian communists were to work with, to seek affiliation to, and if necessary to send members into the Labor Party to secure the united front.[8]

No-one at the congress challenged the final flowering of this new strategy. Jack Loughran had observed imprudently at the central committee meeting in June that it marked a shift to the right, and was removed from both the Central Control Commission and the Number 1 District Committee as well as the congress. 'I know Lenin as good as you', he told Miles, who warned him that if he did not cease criticising, 'his political corpse is going to be stretched on a marble slab along with that of Kavanagh'.[9] The corpse of Kavanagh was an embarrassing presence in party discussions of the united front during 1935. Was not the adoption of the united front a belated recognition that he had been correct in 1929? Much ingenuity was needed to show that the shift to Class Against Class had been a necessary step in the creation of a real communist party and that it was only because the Australian party had established its independent leadership of the working class that it was now able to respond to the new circumstances. Even so, Miles was concerned that another laggard in Class Against Class, Fred Paterson, would think that he had been right in his 'lesser evil' arguments of 1932 and Miles had been wrong.[10]

Miles was always loath to concede errors. As one long-suffering comrade put it, a party member could have any opinion as long as JBM agreed with it.[11] The maintenance of such inflexible rectitude in dealings with the Labor Party fatally compromised the united front from the outset. By the end of 1935 communists had cast off much of their former sectarian abuse of the Labor Party and the trade unions. They had come to appreciate that strident denunciation of Labor politicians and union officials alienated many of the activists they were trying to reach, and that some of those leaders of the reformist labour movement were themselves at least as advanced as the workers they represented. It was clearly impossible for the communists to erase the epithets they had levelled at the social fascists, but if Labor Party cooperation was to be obtained then at least some acknowledgement of those past excesses was needed. Far from apologising for past hostility, however, the party leadership suggested repeatedly as it moved reluctantly towards the new policy that it was simply a new means of achieving the old objectives. Communists grossly underestimated the legacy of ill-will and mistrust that they had incurred, and every state branch of the ALP remained adamant in rejection of the united front proposal. Thwarted in their direct approach, communists therefore relied on other avenues to build support. By far the most fruitful was the unions.

In their application of Class Against Class to industrial activity communists had regarded trade unions with the same animosity they had expressed towards the Labor Party. The Minority Movement kept up a constant criticism of all union officials for holding back workers from contesting the lay-offs, wage cuts and speed-ups that occurred in every sector of the workforce. But with few communists in employment, their attempts to lead such resistance through factory committees that issued violent denunciations of both the boss and the union in roneoed bulletins, and backed them with unofficial stoppages and walk-outs, ended almost invariably in sackings and victimisation.

Bill Orr, the organiser of the Minority Movement, continued during 1932 and 1933 to argue for greater attention to unions. Communists could not expect trade unions to serve the needs of the working class, because the reformist bureaucracy would use any means to retain control of them, but they should seek to win over the rank and file. Slogans that suggested unions were obsolete were counter-productive, and dogmatic 'anti-official' allegations were to be avoided. Orr took particular exception to those militants who attempted to exclude trade union officials from strike committees, and persuaded the Anglo–American Bureau of the ECCI to his position on a visit to Moscow in October 1932. The turn back to the unions was evident in the decision of the Australian politbureau at this time that 'leading members be assisted to become financial and carry on work in the unions to which they belong'.[12] Both the *Workers' Weekly* and the *Red Leader* introduced columns that examined the job bulletins issued by party factory units and Militant Minority groups, praised those that offered practical leads and condemned others for indulging in random abuse. There were hundreds of these ephemeral bulletins, and they are an underused source of radical, demotic culture. Each consisted of a page of roneoed foolscap, issued irregularly, which mixed revolutionary exhortation with pithy anecdote and pungent commentary on the pretensions of the pannikin boss. Their very titles are as expressive of local and occupational identities as of industrial militancy: the *Crib Can* (Cessnock MM), the *Darg* (Richmond colliery group), *Line of Load* (Broken Hill party section) and the *Plod* (the South Mine group); the *Red Signal* (Brisbane railway group) and *Railway Rebel* (Jolimont workshop); the *Newtown Footboard*, the *Punch* and the *Live Wire* (tramways depot groups); the *Galvaniser* (Lysaght's group) *Never-Tyre* (Goodyear's factory MM), *Borthwick Bovril* (a meat-workers' group) and the *Abattoirs Blade*, subtitled *To Cut Deep into Capitalism and Expose its Rotten Inside*.[13]

During this period the Minority Movement was able to report some successes as particular work groups began to offer resistance to employers. Textile workers struck against the new Bedeaux system, which intensified their work process; meatworkers came out in protest against introduction of the analogous 'chain' system of slaughtering; metal miners in several Queensland towns sought improved wages. Typically, militants initiated these disputes through mass meetings of the workers and spurned all compromise. Jack McCormack, who led the battle of Cairns in 1932, had served two months for blowing up a railway bridge to assist a successful wage claim by Queensland copper miners in Dobbyn and Mount Oxide earlier that year.[14] More often than not, however, in the absence of durable structures capable of sustaining resistance, the strikers' solidarity crumbled and the union regained control from the local body.

At the same time as the Communist Party first approached the Labor Party for a united front, in April 1933, the *Red Leader* published a similar appeal to the ACTU, the state industrial councils and all unions. While it would not 'forego our right of critical analysis of the work of reformists in general', the Minority Move-ment proposed cooperation between its rank-and-file committees and the unions in a joint campaign against fascism and economic hardship.[15] The peak union bodies dismissed the proposal, as the ALP had done, but it was far harder for them to proscribe such alliances. Whereas the Labor executive could declare participation in the Communist Party or its various fronts incompatible with membership of the ALP, union rules did not usually allow that blanket proscription. Members of the Minority Movement were entitled to take part in the affairs of the union to which they belonged, and they increasingly began to contest elected union positions. With so few communists in unions, this proved a slow process. The national conference of the Minority Movement at the end of 1933 was attended by 123 union delegates, drawn from 43 unions. The party's claim that they had been elected by 2000 unionists representing 30 000 workers revealed the hollowness of this *modus operandi*: militants either secured the mandate of a thinly attended union branch meeting or convened their own meeting at the factory gate to declare themselves delegates. These militants remained impatient with the irksome restrictions trade unions imposed on their members, the cumbrous structures of authority and subordination of members to full-time officials, as well as with the impediments that arbitration imposed on direct industrial action.[16]

Even so, the party was committed to building its presence in the unions. As economic conditions began to improve and wage-earners looked to win back the ground they had lost in wages and working conditions, the limits of reliance on workshop committees became clear: these unofficial groups of activists exhausted their energies in the initiation of disputes that the officials would then settle. Thus came the recognition that 'The trade unions are the key to the whole present situation in Australia and we can capture a number of trade unions in this country'. Richard Dixon sought to put a Third Period gloss on the emergent strategy in a central committee discussion of industrial policy with his suggestion that communists should seek to achieve control in order to drive reformists out of unions. Orr disagreed: the object was to win over the reformists and defeat the reformist leaders. Hence his insistence that success in trade union and industrial work lay in the ability of communists 'not to be carping critics as we have been in the past, but in our ability to properly study the conditions of the workers we are working amongst'. He spoke from a position of strength, and not just because Moscow shared his interpretation. At the beginning of 1934 he had been elected general secretary of the Miners' Federation.[17]

It is difficult to exaggerate the importance of this breakthrough. It was achieved in a direct ballot of all members of the Miners' Federation by 6321 votes to 4818 and attested to Orr's assiduity— while Minority Movement organiser he rode his motorcycle to almost every pit in New South Wales. Beyond the revival of the left in its traditional strongholds, the northern and western districts of New South Wales, it signalled growing support in isolated and previously quiescent mining towns, such as Collinsville in Queensland and Wonthaggi in Victoria. It gave the Communist Party leadership of a major national union, consolidated later in the year when Orr was re-elected secretary and Nelson (who rejoined the Communist Party in 1933 at the instigation of Orr) elected president, and a corresponding influence in the wider labour movement. More than this, it validated Orr's strategy of prosecuting vigorous, concerted campaigns around the immediate concerns of union members. Bread-and-butter issues was the standard formula, though crusts-and-dripping was perhaps a more apt description of the conditions suffered by miners and their families with low wages, speed-ups, accidents, large-scale unemployment and victimisation all common at this time.[18]

The new style of militancy was exemplified at Wonthaggi, an isolated town in rural Gippsland where more than a thousand men worked underground in a state-owned coalmine. They downed tools in March 1934 over the victimisation of union members arising from the insistent pressure of the management to reduce labour costs. The distinctive feature of this strike was the fusion of union militancy with communal forms of support. A large committee with wide representation of both moderates and Minority Movement members organised specialist subcommittees. The Propaganda Committee sent speakers out as far afield as Western Australia to explain the miners' case. The Relief Committee collected thousands of pounds (Orr won the support of all union lodges, while other industrial organisations also donated funds) and gathered relief in kind, including that given by local farmers. A butchering department, a vegetable department, a boot repair depot, a sewing centre, hairdressing salons and foraging parties catered to residents' needs. The Entertainment Committee held concerts, dances, socials and sports competitions. The women of the town formed their own committee in support of the miners. In the fourth month of the stoppage the union elections were held and the communist Idris Williams led a slate of successful Minority Movement candidates. Williams, a future national president of the Australian coalminers, had become a pit-boy in his native Wales at the age of thirteen and lost a leg in the First World War before coming to Wonthaggi. Just as Orr and Nelson brought with them the egalitarian zeal of the Scottish mining community, so Williams provided a tangible link to the radical fervour of the South Wales valleys. The Minority Movement itself expanded in the course of the dispute from 70 to 400 members. The state minister responsible for the mine was Robert Menzies, dismissive of the miners' claims but increasingly anxious to settle the strike before he moved into federal politics. He pronounced the new union executive 'more reasonable' than its predecessor and capitulated in July.[19]

Communists made significant progress at this time in one other industry, the railways. The most radical state branches of the Australian Railways Union (ARU) were in Queensland, where railway workers had disaffiliated from the ALP in the 1920s, and New South Wales, under its redoubtable state secretary Arthur Chapman, though both had been subjected to communist criticism at the height of the Third Period. The Minority Movement worked in the railways through shop committees, which changed their orientation during 1933 and 1934 from independent activity to closer involvement in the union. They were rewarded in 1935 with the election of Lloyd Ross as state secretary in New South Wales after the death of Chapman. He was the elder son of Bob Ross and pursued a similar style of socialist fellowship as a tutor in the Melbourne Labor College and then the Workers' Educational Association, before he took up the post. Ross explained his subsequent decision to join the Communist Party 'partly because of being associated with them in being elected secretary, but mainly because they were the only group within the ARU that sat down and discussed the problems of the ARU'. Like Orr, Ross reinvigorated his union with campaigns to improve its organisation, efficacy and range of activities.[20]

The party's new approach to industrial work, which brought initial success in the mining and rail transport unions, was uneven in its application and results. Those industries that employed large groups of manual workers who had traditionally sustained a class-conscious solidarity were still quiescent, the numbers of trade unionists reduced well below their former strength by the combined effects of unemployment and the owners' preference for non-union labour. The party made little headway in the Waterside Workers' Federation and efforts to loosen the grip of the existing leadership of the Seamen's Union proved unsuccessful when the Commonwealth government joined with the shipowners to crush a strike organised by a communist rank-and-file committee in 1935. The Pastoral Workers' Industrial Union was going backwards, the building trades were rife with non-unionists, the Meat Industry Employees' Union was crippled by its earlier defeat. More encouraging were the advances in the public transport industry, with gains in the Australian Federated Union of Locomotive Enginemen paralleling those in the Australian Railways Union, and a strong showing of Minority Movement activists in the Victorian branch of the Australian Tramways Employees' Association.[21]

Elsewhere the growth of communist influence was slower, uneven, appreciable in local campaigns that are difficult to summarise, but cumulatively of decisive significance. By holding down wages and refusing to restore the cuts imposed earlier in the Depression, wage tribunals encouraged local forms of disputation. In exploiting their strategic advantages during the Depression, employers created the conditions for a more aggressive approach to industrial relations that transformed previously conservative trade unions. In the metal industries, for example, the Amalgamated Engineering Union pursued wage claims with increasing militancy. The Federated Ironworkers' Association (FIA), so weak in the early 1930s that a member described it as a 'secret society', began to challenge conditions in the Newcastle and Port Kembla steelworks. Communists established their influence in these unions at the branch level, seeking election as delegates before they contested executive positions. Ernie Thornton's election as Victorian organiser of the FIA in 1935 marked their progress, as did victories in the craft unions in both Newcastle and Port Kembla.[22]

By 1934, then, the Communist Party was committed to extending its influence in unions. The example of Wonthaggi, the first major victory since the onset of the Depression, demonstrated what could be achieved when strike action initiated by party members was backed by a union executive and sustained by the broader union movement. Conversely, the party observed that in other disputes where militants were able to initiate a stoppage, reformist officials would quickly reimpose control. Strike committees were 'temporary and episodal', Dixon observed, unions were 'permanent'. He and other party leaders chastised the Minority Movement for its continuing neglect of unions. Orr estimated that as many as half of the Minority Movement's 3000 members were not financial members of their unions, and many still gave the impression that they were 'out to destroy the trade unions'. These rebukes and those of the Comintern and RILU raised concerns about the Minority Movement. It was designed to appeal to all militants but made the same demands of recruits as of party members. It was meant to extend the party's influence—to serve, as Richard Dixon put it, as 'a transmission belt through which we can connect the Party with the class'—but its active membership was in fact no larger than that of the party. Miles drew the obvious conclusions. The Minority Movement was too narrow and sectarian, the very 'absurdity of the name' suggested that it had outlived its purpose. Dixon explained that communists no longer wanted a militant minority movement, they needed a 'majority movement'. This 'dialectical change from quality into quantity', as he described it, rendered the Minority Movement superfluous. The party itself assumed direction of industrial activity and supervised the efforts of members organised in factory units and trade union fractions. The *Red Leader*, its very title judged unsuitable to the majoritarian aspirations of the united front, ceased publication in July 1935.[23]

The task of transforming the Minority Movement into a majority movement proved difficult. Its workshop committees, originally focal points of militant agitation against both the bosses and the trade union bureaucrats, had to be redirected into ancillary units that would link the party to the union. Instead of fomenting discontent, they were to channel workers' demands into union campaigns. Rather than contest union elections where they lacked majority support, they were to support candidates from outside the party and even the Minority Movement if need be: 'We must run people on their merits'. As the groups achieved majority support in their workplaces, they were instructed to affiliate union branches directly to the movement and end their separate existence. In Wonthaggi the results were disturbing. A Minority Movement group of 400 was liquidated. The Communist Party branch of 52 members itself fell away to 33 in the absence of a forum for communist activity in the union.[24]

The turn to the united front in their industrial work posed new difficulties for communist activists. They were to take up the immediate concerns of their workmates but not to foster economist illusions. They were to encourage proletarian solidarity at home and abroad, to take up the dangers of war and fascism, but not to move too far ahead of the union membership. They were to combat conservative, defeatist officialdom without lapsing into sectarianism. A historian of British communism has described the stance as revolutionary pragmatism, and it certainly required communist unionists to stay light on their toes as they balanced shopfloor activism with the wider culture of trade union loyalties, wresting advantages out of the capitalist system they proposed to abolish.[25] They achieved success in struggle yet suffered their most serious reverses when an ill-judged industrial campaign ended in defeat. The trick was to find the auspicious moment when a lead appropriate to the particular circumstances might find a response.

Such a moment came on the canefields of northern Queensland in 1934. The sugarcane industry employed several thousand cane-cutters and millhands, who were covered by the Australian Workers' Union. On the eve of the 1934 season party workers began agitating for the cane to be burned before harvesting to prevent the transmission of Weil's disease, a lethal illness spread by rats urinating in the plantations; the growers opposed burning because it reduced the sugar content, and scaled down the pay for cutting burnt cane. In the absence of union activity, local rank-and-file committees were formed and by striking they achieved higher cutting rates. The AWU retaliated with threats to expel the communist leaders of these committees, Jack Henry and Jim Slater of Tully, Les Sullivan of Goondi, Doug Olive of Ayr, Carl King of Mourilyan and Pat Clancy of Ingham. All were impressive organisers, none more so than Jack Henry who combined industry, acumen and presence. A large, imposing man, he commanded attention in any company. The local party leaders wanted to break with the AWU, but the central committee insisted they carry on the fight within the union.[26]

This proved extraordinarily difficult. The AWU dominated the Labor government in Queensland, and used both the state industrial court and the police against the rank-and-file committees when the campaign resumed in the 1935 season in response to the union's refusal to seek burning orders. This time the strike committees had broadened to include representatives of the Italian canecutters (whose presence in the industry was resisted by the AWU) to organise distribution of relief and sustain morale. 'Bandera Rosa' accompanied 'The Red Flag' and 'The Internationale' in the strikers' concerts. 'War On All Rats!', declared the banners they carried on marches. Women's auxiliaries assisted with relief activities and helped to break down the sexual tensions generated by the high numbers of single men and exacerbated by ethnic jealousies. Jean Devanny's novel *Sugar Heaven* suggests how erotic and political desire flowered in the lush tropical paradise and how the flames of political activism consumed the detritus of capitalist impurity. In the end, however, the AWU divided the strikers and defeated them. After six months of defiance, the last districts capitulated at the end of 1935.[27]

'The main lessons we learned from the strikes', Jack Henry reported to the party congress in the immediate aftermath, 'is that immediately we must attack against the union, exposing them to the mass of workers . . . and we must have a broad central leadership'. The mistake, Carl King suggested later, was to have established a Sugar Workers' Rank and File Committee, 'which made the AWU more bitter against us because they thought we were going to tear a lump out of the AWU'. Both appraisals testify to the difficulties of pursuing a united industrial front with a hostile partner. The central committee had in fact intended to lead the sugar workers out of the AWU if it could unite them.[28] The insistence of party leaders that they were offering the reformist trade unions a united front from above in order to facilitate a united front from below, and that they reserved the right to oppose class collaboration, was belied by the disparity in size between the two parties. Well might the AWU dismiss the party's proposals at this time for an agreement between its pastoral division of 30 000 members and the PWIU's 500, especially since the very *raison d'être* of the PWIU was to offer an alternative to the AWU.[29] For other unions to entertain seriously such an alliance it was necessary for the communists to build their strength by undermining the very officials with whom they sought an accommodation. The united front thus involved both criticism and reconciliation; through local campaigns around immediate issues, it brought an uneven but perceptible accretion of influence. Sharkey's formula of offering a united front from above in order to achieve a united front from below captured only one aspect of the industrial policy that the party adopted by 1935: in practice Australian communists were also pursuing the united front from below in order to facilitate a united front from above.

The success of the united front is commonly represented as broadening the ambit of communism from the narrow confines of the Third Period. An oppositional sect of mostly unemployed workers in the first half of the 1930s is contrasted with the larger, more diverse movement that reached out in the second half of the decade to engage with progressive groups in a range of common concerns.[30] It is undoubtedly true that the united front took the party into new associations and that growth enabled it to sustain a level of activity beyond its earlier capacity. In relating the transition in these terms, however, there is a danger of oversimplification. Third Period communism carried proletarian struggle into a number of fields of practice. The richness of activity around the united front was always constrained by party control. The move from the one to the other brought significant reorientation that closed off certain political forms while it opened up new ones.

An early casualty was communist work among the unemployed. It was noted in Chapter 8 how the party leadership moved as early as the end of 1931 from a style of confrontational activism, now deemed 'sectarian', in favour of attention to the 'concrete problems of the unemployed', especially questions of relief. The Unemployed Workers' Movement yielded to a series of organisations more closely modelled on unions (the Relief and Sustenance Workers' Union was one of these), which employed analogous methods of collective representation to press the authorities for a better deal. The party abandoned its reckless street demonstrations and paramilitary support of eviction resistance. More than this, it discouraged the acts of defiance whereby the militant unemployed drew attention to their plight. The smashing of city shop-windows, the ordering of an expensive meal in a restaurant and then instructing the proprietor to charge it up to the premier—these demonstrative exercises in political street theatre were now condemned as anarchism, symptomatic of the insubordinate temper that had overtaken Sylvester, Lovegrove and other renegades. Those households of single unemployed, such as Sylvester had encouraged in Sydney's Balmain as an experiment in alternative communal practices, lapsed. The constantly moving army of men and women on the track were no longer flag-bearers of proletarian revolt; they were maimed victims of capitalism, to be redeemed by the discipline of wage labour. 'The Communist Party cannot be based on bagmen', Miles told the Eleventh Congress. The Number 2 District organiser insisted that all members, even those on the dole, must keep themselves 'clean and presentable', and remember the party was not a 'philanthropic society for the rehabilitation of the demoralised'. Tom Hills, a Port Melbourne activist who lost his job as a wharfie in the 1928 strike and did not get it back until 1937, put the change of policy more succinctly: henceforth it was 'faces to the factory and arseholes to the unemployed'.[31] The unemployed workers became a substratum of the working class, their lack of employment an injury that maimed them as much as it disgraced the society in which they lived.

The change in mood is apparent in the writing of Eleanor Dark, who was perhaps the most politically sensitive of the novelists of the 1930s. The daughter of a Labor politician, she initially explored the predicament of the educated woman imprisoned by domestic responsibilities in loveless marriages. *Waterway*, a novel located in the same setting as Christina Stead's *Seven Poor Men of Sydney*, connects this search for fulfilment to the politics of the recovery. It takes a day in the lives of a group of people living in Watsons Bay: a reactionary businessman, his dissatisfied socialist wife, her irresolute, searching younger sister, a rich hedonist suitor, and his embittered, unemployed childhood friend. It is a novel of movement, along the waterway to the city, and of dislocation, between idle pleasure and desperate squalor. There is a quickening interest in new possibilities, captured in snatches of conversation overheard on the ferry ('You get a man like Lenin once in a . . .') but the older forms of proletarian protest occur offstage as the shouts of an unemployed demonstration invade a beauty salon, until the demonstrators are caught up in a society wedding and violence erupts.[32]

As if anticipating this outcome, the party drew back from the Depression excesses of unruly women and returned female comrades from the streets to more circumscribed sites of activity. Through the Women's Department of the central committee, which replaced the Militant Women's Groups in 1930, and its newspaper *Working Woman*, female organisers had sought to mobilise women around the issues of employment, unemployment and domestic life. The paper's title and the pamphlet that publicised the decisions of the Tenth Congress, *Women in Australia: From Factory, Farm and Kitchen*, stressed the class character of this programme. It was vehemently opposed to the middle-class women's organisations. At the same time it asserted the special needs of working women, calling for comprehensive social services, including day nurseries, and for access to birth control and abortion. *Working Woman* also published selections from Alexandra Kollontai's *Communism and the Family*, which argued that the emancipation of women from economic dependence on men would liberalise marriage and free women in their family and personal lives.[33] Endeavours to promote such a programme were sporadic, however; indeed it received most publicity from conservative feminists who put sexual immorality at the forefront of their anti-communist crusade. The number of female communists remained pitifully small, just 200 at most, and as a proportion of the party membership they actually fell. The Women's Department organisers, Annie Isaacs, Jean Thompson and Hetty Weitzel (no longer Ross as she had reverted to her maiden name) complained regularly at party plenums of the neglect of work among women; the male district secretaries would just as regularly offer their excuses and do nothing. Working women's conferences lapsed after 1932; the women's section of the UWM collapsed in the same year.[34]

A new emphasis was apparent at the Fourth Plenum in 1934, where Jean Thompson linked recent Comintern statements to the revival of work among women in the Australian party. She also corrected past errors. 'Many weaknesses and wrong ideas were in evidence among the women during the textile strike', which had recently swept through the industry in New South Wales and Victoria, 'particularly in their attitude towards the men, which led to division in their ranks'. Her cryptic remarks have to be supplemented with an editorial in the *Red Leader*, criticising the Minority Movement's rank-and-file committees, which had initiated the walk-outs from the textile factories, for their sectarian antagonism to male union officials.[35] This kind of separate industrial activity, applauded by *Working Woman* when women textile workers had previously employed it, was now discouraged. The rank-and-file committees of women workers were displaced by women's auxiliaries, first formed in the ARU in 1934 and then extended to the mining and other unions. The woman as militant worker relapsed into the helpmate supporting her husband. *Working Woman* changed in the same year from a newspaper to a magazine, more domestic in orientation, less concerned with industrial campaigns than with life in the Soviet Union and the issues that affected women as wives and mothers.

'Why is it that so few comrades have drawn their wives into the Party?', asked the Victorian party paper at the end of 1934. The most common answer, it reported, was that women were too busy with household tasks to become involved, and that many were hostile to a cause that robbed them of their husbands to the detriment of family life. Such comrades should learn that 'their wives are just as important to the Party as themselves'. They should take on some of the domestic duties in order to free their wives to participate. This exhortation was characteristically directed to the man as the mentor; and while it sought to break down domestic inequality, it assumed that the domain of politics lay outside the home.[36]

At the 1934 plenum Thompson also criticised the 'tendencies in articles on birth control clinics to neo-Malthusism'—the fallacy, attributed to the English economist Malthus, that capitalist crises could be solved by family limitation. Kollontai's emphasis on sexual liberation gave way to Clara Zetkin's interview with Lenin, reprinted in the *Communist Review* in 1935, in which he admonished Kollontai for suggesting that in communist society the satisfaction of sexual desires would be as simple and perfunctory as drinking a glass of water. The central committee sent out a circular, drawing attention to Lenin's rebuke—'Will the normal man in normal circumstances lie down in the gutter and drink out of a puddle, or out of a glass with a rim greasy from many lips?'—and warned against 'loose practices'. Miles repeated the warning at the Eleventh Congress in 1935: 'Bolshevism demands a steel-like character and that has to apply on sex questions as well as on other questions'. Just as the party had cleared out 'those who had become degenerate through unemployment', so it had cleansed its ranks of bohemians with their 'pseudo-advanced ideas'. The party Edna Ryan had known at the beginning of the decade, one in which sexual freedom was practised and a drag queen was welcome as a member, gave way to one in which any leading member had to consult the central committee before entering or leaving a relationship. In place of libertarianism there was now a double standard that blamed the female for irregular sexual liaisons—or failure to submit to them, as one young comrade discovered when denounced by a male comrade she had rebuffed; the central committee refused her appeal as it was based on 'personal matters'. Jean Devanny, who witnessed the case, remained defiant in her insistence on sexual autonomy, but she herself had to submit to the strictures of her secret lover, Jack Miles.[37]

The party's youth work followed a similar course. Third Period communism regarded the young as an important constituency, and well it might with so many school-leavers unable to find a job. During the early 1930s the Young Pioneers encouraged children to challenge authoritarianism in schools, communist Sunday schools offered a secular alternative to the teaching of the churches, and the Young Communist League defied conventional mores with campaigns against the 'patriotic bunk' of the Boy Scouts.[38] All these organisations remained tiny in membership (though for communist children such as Laurie and Eric Aarons they served as a political nursery), not least because of the vigilance of their gatekeepers.

When 15-year-old Audrey Blake applied to join the YCL in 1932, three young men interrogated her on her 'social origin' and attitude to Trotskyism. She did not understand the first question and was relieved to hear that her father's job as a sheetmetal worker qualified her as proletarian.[39]

The stern oppositional stance and rigorous invigilation of members softened with the turn to the united front, though member numbers still remained small. Miles returned from a visit to Moscow in early 1935 with instructions to build up the YCL as a broad-based organisation of young workers, only to find that its journal, the *Young Communist*, had expired in his absence. Sharkey also called for a broader approach through campaigns on such issues as bathing dress regulations, and castigated the YCL for regarding these as 'beneath the dignity of Marxists'. The new organiser agreed that the YCL had isolated itself from the 'normal life of youth'; there was too much discussion, too little sport, games and entertainment.[40]

Third Period communists also paid greater attention to the issue of race. Earlier, the Australian party had endeavoured to comply with Comintern instructions to oppose the White Australia policy, but this was as much a therapeutic as a strategic directive, intended to break down the conservative isolation of the Australian working class. With the onset of the Third Period, Moscow stressed the need to provide assistance to oppressed colonial peoples in their struggle for independence. Among the catalogue of oppression publicised through the League Against Imperialism, the party stressed the misdeeds of the Australian colonial administration in the mandated territory of New Guinea. Above all, Australian communists concentrated on their own internal colonialism. The programme entitled 'Struggle Against Slavery' that the party published in 1931 defined the Aborigines as the most exploited Australians, the 'slaves of slaves'. They were the victims of 'mass physical extermination', abused by pastoralists and police, denied the most basic human rights by their official protectors. Previously the revolutionary movement had overlooked their plight, henceforth 'no struggle of the white workers must be permitted without demands for the aborigines being championed'. The party's immediate demands were of two kinds. One was emancipatory, demanding full equality of economic, social and political rights, equal pay, abolition of the protection boards and an 'absolute prohibition of the kidnapping of aboriginal children'. The other involved recognition of Aboriginal autonomy with land rights, separate social services controlled by Aborigines, and preservation of 'native culture'.[41]

In this and subsequent statements the party worked with a particular conception of the Aborigine that was both racial and cultural. Even though there were communists of Aboriginal descent in both Sydney and Perth, they were not identified as such. To have done so would have been considered discriminatory and inconsistent with the principles of working-class equality. Equally, there is no evidence to suggest that Aboriginal party members sought such identification. The identity was reserved for those indigenous Australians in the rural hinterland and far north of the country, who were denied such incorporation into the labour movement. Communists understood these Aborigines as lying within the ambit of revolutionary politics as a special kind of victim of capitalism, a 'doubly exploited worker', mistreated even by the white worker. From this understanding they proposed the two lines of political action, though seldom recognising their divergence. One line would remove the barriers between Aborigines and other victims of capitalism to absorb them as proletarians within the revolutionary movement. The other would accept and preserve their special status. The reasons for this duality lie partly in the evolutionary historical logic of Marxism and partly in the particular understandings of the members who took up Aboriginal issues. Moxon initiated the 1931 programme. He found immediate support from Norm Jeffery, whose work as rural organiser had brought him into contact with Aboriginal activists; from Mick Sawtell, a former Wobbly now based in Sydney who had worked in the Northern Territory; and from Tom Wright, whose interest had begun when he had worked in the bush and was rekindled by correspondence with Olive Pink, one of A. P. Elkin's anthropology students undertaking fieldwork in central Australia. Communists set great store by anthropological knowledge. Just as the Soviet Union was deemed to have recognised, honoured and reconciled its constituent nationalities, so a Soviet Australia would use the science of anthropology to preserve its native race's 'primitive culture'.[42]

The party's agitation was shaped also by the diverse forms of

Aboriginal politics. In the 1920s an Aboriginal organisation based in northern New South Wales had put forward demands for land rights as the basis of economic and cultural independence, and its influence was apparent in the party's 1931 programme. During the 1930s new Aboriginal groups began to contest the discriminatory regime with demands for full citizenship. Tom Wright had closest contact with these activists and rallied support for them within the New South Wales Labor Council. Meanwhile, in the Northern Territory, there was a series of frontier clashes between whites and Aborigines that raised different issues. Communists in the south joined with anthropologists, church leaders and humanitarians to arraign the hypocrisy of a capitalist order that unleashed police expeditions and imposed capital punishment on natives 'steeped in their own tribal organisation', who 'from their own understanding had committed no wrong'. A public campaign in 1934 against one notorious case in 1934 brought Mick Sawtell and the organiser of the party's International Labor Defence organisation onto the platform with Mary Gilmore, an Anglican canon, Professor Elkin and a solitary Aboriginal representative. Party members in Western Australia also assisted Aboriginal groups with their submissions to a state royal commission in the same year.[43]

Yet the party was not free from racism. While Richard Dixon was at the Lenin School in Moscow, and worked during the summer of 1932 on a collective farm, he remarked that he was 'as black as a nigger' and was hauled over the coals for his linguistic lapse. In 1934 the *Workers' Weekly* rebuked 'Comrades [who] still use the terms "Pommie", "Dago", "Nigger" and so forth'. It was a party of increasing ethnic diversity in which such language no longer passed without censure. There were growing links between Australian communists and radical associations formed by southern European immigrants, such as the Melbourne Greek Democritus Club and Italian Matteotti Club; the former supported a Greek party unit and the latter gave way at this time to a *Gruppo Italiano contro la Guerra e il Fascismo*. In Melbourne and Sydney Jewish settlers from eastern Europe formed branches of the *Gezerd*, a support organisation for a Jewish homeland in the Soviet Union, and many of them were drawn into the Friends of the Soviet Union and had other contacts within the party.[44] Newcomers such as Itzhak and Manka Gust, who came to Australia from Poland via Palestine and Belgium at the beginning of the decade, gravitated quickly towards the Melbourne branch of the FOSU. While their secular anti-Zionism was atypical of most Jewish immigrants from Central Europe, this beleaguered outpost of international communism provided them with an immediate point of reference for their political sympathies as well as unqualified acceptance—Itzhak's memoirs suggest the complete absence of anti-semitism.[45] More generally, fascism's glorification of racial purity imbued anti-fascism with a strong internationalist tone. The party took a strong stand against xenophobia in the Weil's disease strike in north Queensland. Its Western Australian members showed particular courage in defending Italian and Yugoslav miners during the Kalgoorlie race riot of 1934.[46]

The campaign against fascism changed in character during the first half of the 1930s. Initially the party's domestic offensive against social fascism was of primary significance, and auxiliaries such as International Class War Prisoners' Aid and Workers' International Relief ministered to its casualties. With the conservative resurgence at the end of 1931, the party established a United Front Against Fascism (UFAF) and, as the new federal government unveiled its battery of measures against the party, there was an Anti-Illegality and Workers' Press Defence Committee. The ICWPA and UFAF in turn merged during 1932 into International Labor Defence. Alongside these bodies, all domestic in orientation despite their qualifying adjectives, were the League Against Imperialism (LAI) and the Friends of the Soviet Union (FOSU). The LAI conducted campaigns of denunciation of the bloody record of the major capitalist powers in their Asian and African colonies; the FOSU provided an international counterpoint, celebrating the achievements of the workers' homeland.

With the fall of Germany to the Nazis and the mounting international tension, the LAI turned itself into the Council Against War. The change was consummated at a National Anti-War Congress in Sydney from 30 September to 2 October 1933. It was a conspicuous success, by far the most encouraging exercise so far in the emergent strategy of the united front. Trade union leaders and prominent church figures joined more than 500 delegates at the Paddington Town Hall to denounce the warmongers. At this point

Torchlight Procession

CENTRAL SQUARE

AUGUST 1st, 8 p.m.

International Day Against
War and Fascism

Smash War Plans!

The Movement Against War and Fascism began in 1933 and quickly attracted greater support than other communist front organisations. This early poster sees the threat of war as primary, the British Empire as its chief impetus. (Source: J.N. Rawling collection, Noel Butlin Archives Centre, ANU N57/2263)

the opposition to war had a sharp revolutionary edge, indeed the indignant denial by the conference organisers that it was simply a communist front was scarcely assisted by the president's opening call that delegates sing 'The Internationale'. 'This council is not pacifist', insisted the president, the railway leader Arthur Chapman. 'It realises that war may be thrust upon us and does not object to fight for the workers . . .'[47]

The party's continued attachment to the strategy that the Bolsheviks had employed in the Great War, one that had turned an imperialist war into a revolutionary war, handicapped the Council Against War after its initial success. Most Australians construed proletarian internationalism as unpatriotic, the Leninist doctrine of revolutionary defeatism as treachery. But that doctrine lapsed as the Soviet Union sought protection from the German threat in collective security arrangements with its former enemies. The Communist International now drew a distinction between the fascist and non-fascist powers. It was the fascist regimes that were the instigators of war and workers might be justified in defending their countries against the fascist aggressor. The redesignation in 1934 of the Council Against War as the Movement Against War and Fascism (MAWF) signalled this new orientation, as did its formation of a Returned Soldiers section. Previously those comrades who had fought in the Great War had kept quiet about it. There were some exceptions, most notably Katharine Susannah Prichard's husband, Captain Hugo Throssell, VC, who in the immediate aftermath of the war renounced his martial glory, but he was a genteel cuckoo in a proletarian nest. Persecuted anti-conscriptionists were the radical heroes of the 1920s; military service was regarded within the left as a sign of gullibility, suggesting you had been duped by jingoism. Now party members came forward with their battle honours: John Simpson of the central committee was revealed as John Simpson DCM MM and the leader of the communist Returned Soldiers section; Jack Zwolsman, an unemployed stalwart in Adelaide, was once again Sergeant-Major Zwolsman MM and a champion breast-stroke swimmer.[48]

Even so, the MAWF struggled during 1934 to establish its credibility. Belligerent in its anti-war propaganda, dismissive of pacifists, contemptuous towards those who suspected its intentions, at the end of the year it even threatened to turn on its most prominent church supporter, Ernest Burgmann, for his insistence on the 'renunciation of war as an instrument of political policy altogether, both international and inter-class'.[49] It was revived by its opponents. The MAWF planned a second National Anti-War Congress for Melbourne in November 1934 to coincide with the visit of the Duke of Gloucester and an entourage of imperial dignitaries to open the Melbourne Shrine as part of the state centenary. Police Commissioner Blamey was determined to frustrate the plans and twice pressured municipal councils to cancel bookings for hire of their town halls; eventually the Victorian Council of the MAWF secured the use of the Port Melbourne Town Hall. Blamey also learned through a police spy that the World Committee Against War was to send a delegate, a man apparently called Ewart Risch. The Commonwealth Investigation Branch established from British sources that Risch was in fact Egon Kisch, a prominent Czech writer and publicist, who played up to his soubriquet of 'The Rampaging Reporter from Prague'. Acting on this information, the minister for the interior made a declaration of exclusion against Kisch under the Immigration Act. Kisch was prevented from landing when the ship on which he was travelling reached Fremantle in October. At Melbourne he jumped onto the wharf, broke his leg, and was put back on board. At Sydney he was released as the result of a court

ATTEND CONGRESS

AGAINST WAR & FASCISM

"Millions for Armaments while Millions Starve"

PORT MELBOURNE

TOWN HALL,

NOVEMBER 10 and 12

The Movement Against War and Fascism was twice refused the use of town halls for its congress in 1934 before it secured that at Port Melbourne. The John Bull figure in the top segment of the illustration signifies the British military advisers who attended the centenary celebrations; the destitute family below is their victim. (Source: J.N. Rawling collection, Noel Butlin Archives Centre, ANU N57/2258)

application, rearrested and given a dictation test (under the Immigration Act an applicant for entry could be tested in any European language and since Kisch was fluent in several, he was tested in Gaelic). Having failed the test he was charged with being a prohibited immigrant and sentenced to six months' imprisonment. After he was released on bail, the High Court set the conviction aside (on the grounds that Gaelic was not a European language). Further proceedings resulted in a sentence of three months' hard labour. Again he was released on bail and negotiations with the Commonwealth resulted finally in remission of the sentence, payment of his costs and voluntary departure on 11 March 1935.[50]

While the Australian government's attempt to exclude Kisch was initiated by the minister for the interior, it fell to Robert Menzies as attorney-general to pursue it through the courts. At the end of 1934 Menzies succeeded John Latham (who went on to the High Court bench) as the federal member for Kooyong and the champion of the Melbourne establishment's stern and unbending conservatism. Both men had risen from modest origins through success at the bar, and both acquired a deep reverence for the law as a force for certainty and stability, a tangible expression of the derivative English traditions that they had absorbed, and a bulwark against the levelling change and disorder they came to associate with communism. Both

Left: The feud between Menzies and Australian communists began even before he entered federal politics in 1934. As Commonwealth attorney-general, he introduced amendments to the Crimes Act in 1935 that would have imposed new press controls; the legislation was abandoned in the face of public protest. Counihan places Hitler on a plinth alongside Menzies and both give the Nazi salute. (Source: 'Workers' Weekly', 25 February 1936) Right: Menzies's entry to federal parliament was made possible by the retirement of John Latham to the High Court. In October 1935 he became chief justice. Counihan recalls in this cartoon that as attorney-general, Latham revised the Crimes Act in 1926 and 1932 to facilitate prosecution of the Communist Party. Behind him, Hitler appears envious of the prim Australian's success. (Source: 'Workers' Weekly', 27 March 1936)

affected a patrician style, Latham colder and more aloof than the urbane Menzies. In this early test of his federal ambitions, however, Menzies was humiliated. At every point the judges had rejected his strategems. To add injury to insult they found a distinguished group of Caledonians in Sydney to be in contempt for their denunciation of the High Court's determination that Gaelic was not a European language. Menzies departed Australia before Kisch to seek solace in the Royal Jubilee celebrations in London. First the Wonthaggi miners, now this foreign red-ragger: Menzies' antipathy to communism was developing into a feud.

His inept handling attracted far greater publicity than the MAWF could have hoped for. Kisch's dramatic entry made front-page news. The draconian use of the law brought widespread criticism (the respected Congregational minister, Albert Rivett, died after addressing a protest meeting at the Sydney Domain in November 1934, in what a supporter called following 'the Galilean to the end of the last mile'), and once the courts freed Kisch on bail, he addressed large audiences all over the country. There was also another banned congress delegate, the New Zealand communist Gerald Griffin. He entered Australia behind sunglasses and under the assumed name of Dodds; later he travelled from Melbourne to Sydney disguised as a Salvation Army officer. At an overflowing meeting in the West Melbourne stadium—secured by the MAWF activist Mary Wren from her father John, who had usually employed his considerable influence in the labour movement against the left—Griffin stood up to briefly reveal himself. The police pounced, only to arrest the wrong man. The campaign on behalf of Kisch and Griffin was undertaken by Christian Jollie Smith and served by the radical lawyers A. B. Piddington and Maurice Blackburn; it attracted able young journalists such as John Fisher (son of a former Labor prime minister), Edgar Holt and T. M. Fitzgerald. A Kisch Reception Committee, headed by Katharine Susannah Prichard, included E. J. Brady, Louis Esson, Vance and Nettie Palmer, and gave rise to the Writers' League. The reception concerts featured contributions from Greek, Italian, Yugoslav, Jewish, Russian and Aboriginal performers, emphasising the internationalism of the campaign against war and fascism. The Victorian Council Against War and Fascism drew in students from the university, a development that was noticed when an organiser took a stencil down to be roneoed by the South Melbourne organiser of the Unemployed Workers' Movement. 'Why can't the fuckin' Anti-War Movement get a bloody duplicator of their own? They've always got plenty of the sons and bosses of the bloody Boss class hanging around their office.'[51]

This was hardly fair to Len Fox and Dorothy Alexander, who assumed organising positions in the Melbourne office. Both came from comfortable families, and were educated at private schools and university; neither showed any regret for the sacrifices they made as they abandoned professional careers. Rather, they worked with extraordinary patience and good humour to build a united front broad enough to encompass working-class organisations and what were now described as the 'progressive' sections of the middle class in the face of conservative vilification and proscriptions imposed by the Labor Party.[52] Maurice Blackburn and Catherine Clarey, the wife of the president of the Melbourne Trades Hall Council, were among those expelled from the ALP for their association with the MAWF. Neither were the MAWF organisers helped by the party's close invigilation of their activities. They were expected to follow every twist of Soviet and Comintern policy. Rawling, MAWF national secretary, was carpeted for resisting the turn to the League of Nations, when the Soviet Union called for League sanctions against Italy for its invasion of Abyssinia in 1935. There is some evidence to suggest the central committee was anxious to wind up Kisch and Griffin's protracted legal challenges, and that it was the secretary of the International Labor Defence who stood out in defiance; this stalwart who preferred mass pressure to lawyers was expelled from the party in 1936.[53]

There was a further consequence of the mounting communist alarm about the war danger. While the Soviet Union sought collective security from the threat posed by the fascist powers, it harboured a deep suspicion that it would be left isolated to fight a new war. If so, what was to prevent the capitalists and militarists from joining in an anti-communist alliance and turning their own armed forces on the workers? To guard against these perilous possibilities, the Communist International instructed member parties to infiltrate their countries' military forces. Agitation and organisation of the ranks would provide a safeguard against their use for foreign aggression or domestic repression. Just how seriously the Australian party took these instructions it is difficult to establish. While the party's plans for underground operation included military infiltration, its archives provide no evidence that this was accomplished. The Australian armed forces, on the other hand, took the threat very seriously. In calling on the government in 1934 to outlaw communism, the army chief of general staff alleged widespread subversion. So, too, the Investigation Branch of the Attorney-General's Department claimed in its regular reports that a special apparatus of the Communist Party was gathering military intelligence for transmission to Moscow. It named Miles, Dixon and Sam Aarons as the controllers of the operation, with Joe Shelley as the

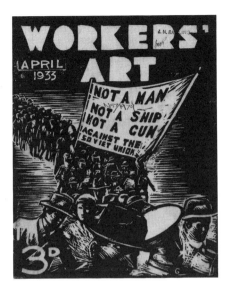

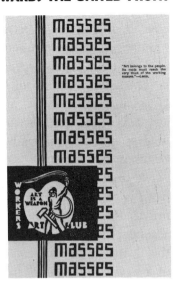

Left: The first issue of the magazine produced by the Sydney branch of the Workers' Art Club. The linocut illustration combined an anti-war message with defence of the Soviet Union. In contrast with similar images in the 1920s, the mood of the demonstrators is more subdued, their politics more defensive. (Source: J.N. Rawling collection, Noel Butlin Archives Centre, ANU N57/1979) Right: The reverse cover of the first issue of 'Masses' uses a Leninist epigraph and the motto of the Workers' Art Club: 'Art is a Weapon'. Against an artist's palette, a worker holds aloft the torch of knowledge. (Source: J.N. Rawling collection, Noel Butlin Archives Centre, ANU N57/1967)

The familiar figure of the worker with hammer, reworked in 1932 for the first issue of the Melbourne Workers' Art Club Magazine, 'Masses'. The aesthetics of the body are now of greater concern, despite the anatomical impossibility of the stance, and the grip half-way up the shaft robs the gesture of menace. (Source: J.N. Rawling collection, Noel Butlin Archives Centre, ANU N57/1958)

courier. But this is inconsistent with all that is known of communist espionage: such prominent leaders would not have been associated with so risky an enterprise, while Shelley was far too unreliable to be entrusted with so important a responsibility—his notoriety and German origins made him a plausible villain but an implausible agent. Not for the last time, it seems that the communists and their professional adversaries had a mutual interest in exaggerating their common concerns.[54]

A final illustration of the reorientation effected by the united front is offered by changes to the experiments in proletarian culture initiated during the Depression. In 1927 Judah Waten had organised a concert in the party hall in Melbourne to mark the centenary of the death of Beethoven. Three years later he wrote the manifesto of a new revolutionary magazine, *Strife*, that was to be launched at the demonstration of the Melbourne unemployed in October 1930:

> 'STRIFE' is another force added to the world-wide movement to uproot the existing social and economic order of chaotic and tragic individualism . . . 'STRIFE' is an organ of the new culture, destructive and constructive, a culture ploughing deep into the roots of life, and, as such, condemns and rejects all manifestations in form and content of the social disorder we oppose.

Strife never appeared—a blasphemous poem by Brian Fitzpatrick caused the confiscation of the issue—but the editorial signalled a new political aesthetic among young artists and writers. They provided the impetus for the Workers' Art Club, formed in both Sydney and Melbourne in 1931, which took as its slogan Lenin's dictum, 'Art is a weapon'. The club offered literature readings, art and drama classes, film and lecture evenings to a predominantly unemployed audience. The approach was strongly influenced by the experiment in Proletcult conducted in the early years of the Russian Revolution, at once liberating culture from the rarified forms imposed by the capitalist division of labour, and placing it at the disposal of a revolutionary movement. Hence club members assisted with the design of factory bulletins and painted banners for street marches, such as the heavily stylised portraits of Marx, Engels, Lenin and Stalin that Noel Counihan created for the 1932 May Day march in Melbourne.[55]

The Workers' Art Club was quickly beset by dispute. In Sydney

This photograph of hunger marchers from Cessnock was made into a postcard. A small group of men with their belongings slung over their shoulders make their way off a ferry on the road to Sydney. (Source: CPA collection, Mitchell Library, Pic Acc 6604)

An unemployed march through the streets of Sydney in November 1930. The banner of the International Class War Prisoners' Aid draws attention to the heavy toll of arrests, which by the end of the month saw most of the party leadership in gaol. (Source: J.N. Rawling collection, Noel Butlin Archives Centre, ANU N57/2344)

A press photograph of the 'beef riot' in Adelaide, January 1931, when police and unemployed marchers fought a pitched battle in the city streets. (Source: Jack Kavanagh papers, Noel Butlin Archives Centre, ANU Z400/3)

Shanties of the unemployed on Sydney Harbour. This photograph appeared in the Sydney 'Sun', 4 May 1931. (Source: Jack Kavanagh collection, Noel Butlin Archives Centre, ANU N57/2348)

Communists used typewriters and Gestetners to produce hundreds of local bulletins. 'The Tocsin' was the 'official organ' of the Balmain branch of the Unemployed Workers' Movement. (Source: J.N. Rawling collection, Noel Butlin Archives Centre, ANU N57/2027)

Most bulletins used a simple bannerhead, some were more ambitious. This one, the work of a party factory group at Bonds' factory, evokes the work-skills of the industry. (Source: J.N. Rawling collection, Noel Butlin Archives Centre, ANU N57/1952)

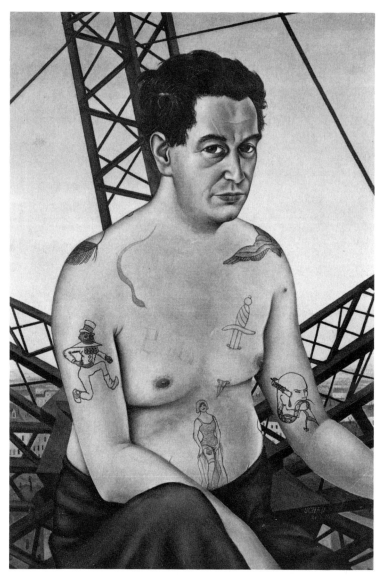

During his Australian tour in the summer of 1934–35, Egon Kisch became familiar as a stout, middle-aged man with a bristling moustache and voluble demeanour. In this portrait painted some years earlier by a German artist, Christin Schad, he is clean-shaven, watchful and covered in lurid tattoos. The girders behind him heighten the effect. (Source: Hamburger Kunsthalle)

Kisch's last speaking engagement was on the Esplanade in Perth. At the end of a dry summer, Kisch perches on a conventional podium flanked by calico banners. (Source: J.N. Rawling collection, Noel Butlin Archives Centre, ANU N57/2353)

The success in the Miners' Federation built on extensive activity in the local lodges. The occasion and location of this display are unknown. The banner copies the earlier depiction of a proletarian hero striking the chains from the globe and quotes the closing words of the 'Communist Manifesto'. Note the ropes to stabilise the banner. (Source: Australasian Coal and Shale Employees' Federation, Noel Butlin Archives Centre, ANU K2472)

The Italian invasion of Abyssinia in 1935 was the first of a series of incidents of international fascist belligerence that culminated in the outbreak of World War II. In this Sydney demonstration, the banner depicts a composite representation of Italian and German militarism. (Source: J.N. Rawling collection, Noel Butlin Archives Centre, ANU N57/2355)

In September 1936 Ralph Gibson attended the World Peace Congress in Brussels, and returned to publicise the International Peace Campaign in Australia. He was seen off from Melbourne by two stalwarts of the Movement Against War and Fascism, Len Fox (in the middle) and Dorothy Alexander, whom he married upon his return. The banner suggests he was bound for Geneva, but the Congress was subsequently transferred to Brussels. (Source: Gibson papers, National Library of Australia, MS 7844)

Australians in Spain, some carrying flags and some wearing berets. From left to right, Jim McNeill, Charles McIlroy, Charlie Riley, Charlie Walters, Jack Franklyn and Joe Carter. (Source: Laurie Aarons)

Four Australian nurses, en voyage to Spain, were met at Melbourne in October 1936. The nurses, from left to right, were Una Wilson, Mary Lowson, May MacFarlane and Agnes Hodgson. A.F. Howells flanks them in the right of the picture. Behind them can be seen Len Fox, Helen Baillie, Dorothy Alexander, Joyce Metcalfe and Nettie Palmer. (Source: Laurie Aarons)

A group of Australians in Barcelona, December 1936. The four Australian nurses are joined here by Aileen Palmer (far right), and John Fisher (the taller of the men) to farewell Jack 'Blue' Barry (third from the left). Barry was killed on the Madrid front soon after. They stand before the Hotel Colòn, which displays portraits of Lenin and Stalin, on the Plaza di Cataluna, the headquarters of the combined Socialist and Communist Party of Catalonia. (Source: Amirah Inglis)

THEIR HOUR OF TRIUMPH

"The torture of a thousand cuts."

George Finey's cartoon for the 'Labor Daily' portrayed a worker tortured by capitalists. A singular figure, he is powerless to prevent the draining of his life force by sinister, knife-wielding plutocrats. An exhibition of Finey's work at the Workers' Art Club in 1932 was criticised by the central committee for depicting unemployed workers too pessimistically. (Source: 'Labor Daily', 8 October 1931)

Jean Devanny ran afoul of the central committee in 1932 for allowing George Finey, the club's art director whose biting renditions of hardship in *Smith's Weekly* still shock the viewer, to mount an exhibition that portrayed unemployed workers too pessimistically. A similar attitude is apparent in the response of Tom Wright to Noel Counihan's early drawings of the unemployed as maimed victims of capitalism: 'Why don't you draw something beautiful?' Beauty was scarcely the primary objective of the cartoons that appeared in the party press at this time, which depicted massive proletarian heroes with superhuman physiques in violent acts with fist or sledgehammer. Counihan's response to the grim reality of the Depression would be reworked in later canvasses, such as *At the Start of the March, 1932* (1944), in which a bedraggled man, woman, child and babe-in-arms stand before a line of static, sullen figures while the crumpled banner is raised off to the far corner. The twisted, malnourished anguish of the child, the mis-shaped, burdened but enduring adult bodies are portrayed with a compassion that orthodox communists found difficult to accept. One dismissed the Melbourne members of the Workers' Art Club as 'a pack of petit-bourgeois degenerates'.[56] In

Sydney a party critic condemned as politically naive the production by the club's theatre group of two plays written by Nelle Rickie. Devanny appealed for greater sympathy and argued that a recent dramatisation of *The Ragged-Trousered Philanthropists*, that deeply pessimistic English novel of socialist martyrdom, was itself 'politically incorrect' (in what appears to be the first use of that phrase in this country). After other members of the club weighed in with their estimations of communist theatre, the party pronounced that Devanny was too 'liberal and conciliatory' in her attitude towards 'artistic sectors of the middle strata'. She remained unrepentant: 'Until our movement learns to welcome and utilise the technique of sympathetic fellow-traveller [a very early Australian example of that term also] artists, our art will remain maimed and halt'.[57]

But already the party was reaching out to precisely such sympathisers and moving from a sharply oppositional conception of proletarian culture to a more generalised idea of culture as a progressive force. As it did so, the artistic experiments of the early 1930s gave way to the more conventional forms of social realism. In the first issue of *Strife*, Judah Waten had stressed the iconoclastic immediacy of revolutionary writing:

> Facts are the new literature. The proletarian writer will break with the sickly plots, tremulous love chirpings, ecstasies, love triangles and individual heroisms of the writers of the past. He will work with facts. He will not worry too much about form; he will transcend the antiquated forms of the past, to create a new form based on facts.

Other contributors to the publications of the Workers' Art Club had explored a different kind of prose to portray the effects of the Depression. Here the derangement of human lives produced a fragmentary and disjointed surrealism:

> A strange madness is this chasing of phantom dreams, and the shadows of unreality dim the eyes of the dreamers. Somnambulists treading softly in a busy thoroughfare, muttering incoherently of the night at high noon.

The verse forms were declamatory, violent in their obliteration of human kindness:

> Now work for the dole, you bastards,
>   Take that gleam of hope from your eye.

Just work for the dole, you bastards
　Or watch your children die.
We've got batons and bullets, you bastards,
　We'll see you all toe the line.
But we'd keep you down much better
　If it weren't for these communist swine.[58]

Now challenge softened into portrayal, art as a weapon gave way to art as homily, and there was a turning back to literary traditions. The enlistment of Henry Lawson as a popular writer was an early example: it was stated in 1934 that he lacked a clear understanding of class struggle but depicted working-class life with 'sympathy for toilers'. The same claim also indicated a growing interest in the Australian experience as a site of cultural politics. The Workers' Art Club was replaced by broader bodies such as the Writers' League, formed during the visit of Egon Kisch as the Australian section of the Writers' International. The League stressed its 'broad and non-sectarian nature', and pursued a united front with progressive liberals in campaigns such as that conducted by the Book Censorship Abolition League during 1935.[59]

The Third Period party had applied the principles of Class Against Class to a range of sexual, racial, international and cultural issues. On each of them it took up a revolutionary stance that was starkly confrontational, juxtaposing capitalism's manifold evils with a communist solution in order to expose and polarise two alternative orders of value. With meagre resources to support its endeavours, the articulation of this comprehensive proletarian position was necessarily programmatic, but even in its beleaguered isolation there could be no mistaking the party's intention to replace one form of class rule with another. The united front brought a more pragmatic, less confrontational approach based on strategic alliances as a different kind of politics, an approach that sought common ground both within and beyond the labour movement, and replaced the earlier revolutionary separatism. Communists did not abandon their aspirations to leadership of the working class or their conviction that the workers must prevail over their class enemies, but they now saw those goals as the correlates of campaigns for peace, freedom, emancipation of the oppressed and enrichment of human life. Defensive in its historical origins, affirmative in its purpose and manipulative in its execution, the change affected them as much as their new allies.

The change called for a different style of party work, less declamatory and more persuasive. It demanded additional qualities of its members beyond the reckless courage of the street activist or the indomitable defiance of the shopfloor activist. A leading Bolshevik elucidated the expectations:

> The most valuable quality in a Party worker is the ability to work with enthusiasm in an ordinary humdrum situation, and overcome, day in and day out, one obstacle after another; the ability to preserve his enthusiasm in face of the obstacles with which practical life confronts him daily, hourly, and to let the humdrum, cumbrous obstacles develop and strengthen his zeal; the ability in this day-to-day work to keep in mind and never lose sight of the ultimate aims for which the Communist movement is fighting.[60]

The party's leaders sought to build a membership of sufficient size to sustain the united front, sufficient patience to attend to its practical, everyday tasks and sufficient ardour to ensure its communist character. They paid close attention to both numbers and provenance of members, using this information as an index to evaluate the work of the district committees. Statistics were kept for male and female members, those in work and those who were union members, those in factory and those in street units.

At the end of 1932 there had been 1929 members on the books. By mid-1934 there were 2371, and the congress at the end of 1935 enumerated 2873, though only 1674 were financial. Number 1 District based on Sydney remained the largest (1048 in 1935), but the Victorian Number 4 District (683 in 1935), the Hunter Valley Number 2 District (317 in 1935) and the new Number 9 District created in north Queensland (361 in 1935) were expanding most rapidly. In the same year Number 3 District in south Queensland (255) and Number 6 in Western Australia (130) showed signs of growth; South Australia (57), Tasmania (21) and the Northern Territory (no return) still languished. The composition of the party was revealed by the preponderance of what it called 'street units' over factory units. A census in mid-1935 found that there were 230 of the residential groups and only 118 factory units. Less than half the membership was employed, just over a thousand belonged to trade unions and only half of these belonged to factory units. There were just over 200 country members and about the same number of women.[61]

The performance in parliamentary elections offered some encouragement. The party's 21 candidates won 47 499 votes for the House of Representatives in 1934 against 8511 for its ten candidates in 1931, and 73 506 votes for six Senate candidates, more than double the earlier tally. In state elections in New South Wales, Queensland and Victoria during 1935, the CPA achieved significant increases on the 1932 results, with greatest support for candidates in the coalfield districts of New South Wales and northern electorates in Queensland. But the Senate performance, where communists won 2.23 per cent of the national vote (3.26 per cent in Queensland), was the highest aggregate percentage and represented a meagre return on the 400 000 manifestos, 500 000 how-to-vote cards, 15 000 posters and the heavy expenditure of effort such election campaigns entailed. Since the primary purpose of electoral activity was to build the party, the gap between voters and members emphasised the magnitude of the communist task.[62]

It is difficult to discern in these figures a clear vindication of the party's new direction. The auxiliary organisations of the united front did provide fertile ground for recruitment, but turnover remained high. It was estimated that half of those signed up in these years were lost almost immediately and the central committee rebuked those comrades who 'appear to think that the party is a big sieve'. Yet the party's procedures required that new members serve a term of probation, and it was the secretariat that purged the ranks with periodic instructions that all unfinancial members be struck off the books—a South Australian delegate told a plenum in 1934 that if the requirement were enforced in his state it would liquidate the party. Finance remained a constant problem. The larger part of members' dues went to the district committee and the central committee, leaving units with a constant battle to make up the funds needed to sustain their activities.[63]

Despite these difficulties there was an appreciable growth of the party's presence and level of activity. In 1934 it shifted the national headquarters from the dingy hall in Sussex Street to new premises in George Street and then around the corner to Hay Street, only a short distance for members to carry the tables, chairs and office equipment but an expressive move away from the old associations with the 'Hungry Mile' along Darling Harbour to the bustle of Central Railway Station. The party now maintained offices in each of its district centres, along with separate premises for the auxiliary organisations. The Anvil Bookshop in Sydney was joined by the International Bookshop in Melbourne, the Anvil in Brisbane, the Radical in Perth and a crop of suburban Workers' Bookshops that sprang up from the middle of the decade.[64]

In 1933 a publishing company, Modern Publishers, was established to produce local editions of communist works that were prohibited by the Commonwealth customs. At that time Itzhak Gust was the Australian agent for the Soviet English-language publishers, and distributed a range of magazines and books. In 1934 the party acquired the agency from him and the import restrictions eased to allow party bookshops to distribute a growing range of Soviet, British and American material.[65] The party specialised in the production of pamphlets, which were especially suited to its purposes. Cheap, portable, timely and pointed, they circulated in bulk. In 1934 a new monthly theoretical journal began, the *Communist Review*, filling a gap that had been left with the discontinuation of the earlier *Communist* in 1928. Some districts even began publishing their own papers. The Western Australian *Red Star* appeared first in 1932 as a roneoed news-sheet to circumvent the ban on mail and railway distribution of the *Workers' Weekly*; it became a printed paper from August 1933. Victoria established the *Workers' Voice* in September of the same year. South Australia over-reached itself with *Struggle*, which began in November and lasted only a few months. The *Workers' Weekly* itself obtained an expensive new press and typesetting machine in 1934 and from 1935 appeared twice a week.[66]

Changes in layout and content of the newspapers followed the new orientation. In 1933 and again in 1934 the Communist Inter-

With the growth of the party in the 1930s and its cultivation of the popular front, the heavy banner on 'Workers' Weekly' became more restrained, the hammer and sickle stylised as a semi-tone. (Source: 'Workers' Weekly', 17 May 1935)

national criticised the *Workers' Weekly* for a lack of accessibility. Leaving aside the logistical constraints (members outside Sydney often complained of the neglect of their news, while the editorial staff grumbled of the infrequency and late arrival of interstate reports), the publication at that time was not so much a newspaper as a party bulletin. Miles acknowledged that it carried 'certain articles necessary for the Party that cannot be put in very simple language that would appeal to workers'. By 1935 those internal needs were met through the *Communist Review* and an improved system of organisational circulars. The redesigned *Workers' Weekly* was pitched at a broader readership. A lighter typeface and bolder headlines, and a less crowded page with more illustrations set off the more buoyant tone. There was irreverent commentary on topical events and greater coverage of sport, mainly boxing. The paper still carried lengthy reports of meetings and resolutions, and occasional rebukes and admonitions, but now they were flanked by reports of success in this union or swelling support for that campaign. A gallery of prominent party activists was created, each with a standard photographic portrait, the collar-and-tie or neat open-necked shirt favoured by Queenslanders, well-groomed hair and resolute expression conveying youthful vigour. Conspicuously absent were the arguments, the doubts, the reports of expulsions and other signs of difference. The same appearance of purposeful unanimity was served by the growing use of communist ritual on public occasions. The party song 'The Internationale', the salute (the clenched fist), the use of agitprop chants and other distinctive devices affirmed the esprit de corps of a disciplined army of class warriors.[67]

Perhaps the most telling sign of growth was the increase in the number of full-time organisers. Even South Australia, a district of

80 members teetering on the edge of insolvency, had four of them in 1935. The Communist Party, now fully Bolshevised, was a cadre organisation. The cadres (the term was military in origin, meaning an establishment of officers) played a crucial role in transmitting the decisions of the central bodies to the local units. Each was assigned a particular area of responsibility but during these transitional years moved frequently from one district to another—thus Jack Blake took up work in national headquarters after returning from Moscow before shifting to Melbourne in 1934, where he joined Len Donald to take charge of Number 4 District. It was Donald, himself with a newly minted name, who met the former Fred Airey at Spencer Street Station with the news that henceforth his name would be John D. Blake. Jack asked what the 'D' stood for. Desmond. 'I said, for Christ's sake, I draw the line at that.'[68]

Blake and Donald were two of a dozen or so Australians trained during the 1930s at the Lenin School in Moscow, in a wide-ranging syllabus that included political economy, historical and dialectical materialism, the history and practice of the Communist Party of the Soviet Union and the International. Jack flourished at his studies, Len hated them; on one occasion Jack had to retrieve the copy of Marx's *Capital* that Len had thrown out the window. Len Donald was a wild man who, whenever he could lay his hands on a few roubles, would take Jack out to buy some 'peasant's nightmare' and get stuck into it; drink would eventually get him into trouble as district secretary. But he was doggedly loyal and his organisational capacities were well matched to Blake's incisive intelligence. Working under them was a dozen or so cadres with specialist tasks, in a pattern followed in other districts. Since the party had yet to establish its own national school, most cadres prepared with a stint of supervised work at the party headquarters in Sydney.[69]

Miles and Sharkey attached the utmost importance to the cadre ranks of the party. One persistent problem was their financial support. Some received a 'sustenance grant' from the party that was never generous and always uncertain. Others relied on public sustenance, and were liable to go back to paid work at the expense of their political duties. There was a tendency also for the organisers to spread their energy too thinly and to shift from one activity to another in response to Sydney's latest instruction. This habit of acting as a 'fire brigade', as one organiser put it, drew condemnation from Richard Dixon, the assistant secretary who in his colourless efficiency reinforced the party's turn to a more bureaucratic routine. He was now third in seniority and bereft of both the vices and virtues of his two superiors, a loyal functionary trained in Moscow with no prior political experience and no engagement in activity beyond the ambit of the organisation. It was Dixon who insisted that organisers had to know how to delegate. 'If you go into a factory you do not find that the boss does all the work', he observed in a disturbing analogy, 'but we have this position in the party'. The cadres stood at a crucial intermediate position in the hierarchical structure of the party. They attended the plenums and enlarged meetings of the central committee to report on how they had implemented previous instructions and to learn new ones. There was a tendency for them to disguise lack of success with fulsome support of the party line. Miles coined the phrase 'fossilised bureaucrats and chatterers' at one such gathering to describe this tendency—and the term was immediately parroted by those at whom it was levelled.[70]

The turn to the united front was completed at the Eleventh Party Congress in December 1935. Miles and Sharkey had clarified the Australian party's line in visits to the Soviet Union. The worldwide threat of fascist belligerence and the need to defend democracy made working-class unity imperative; the party was to seek affiliation to the ALP and launch a public campaign to overcome the resistance of the Labor leaders. As part of this campaign Miles would have to come out 'before the party and working class as leader of the party'. For more than a year he had been underground, appearing only at closed party forums and working mostly from home, with Jack Simpson acting as go-between for the party secretary and the cadres. This reclusiveness allowed Lance Sharkey to steal a march at the earlier Congress of the Communist International where he represented the Australian party. The Australians were to have a member of the new Comintern Executive Committee, a high honour indeed and the first time it had been paid them since Garden and Kavanagh's brief moments of glory. Sharkey convinced the other Australian delegates, Ted Docker and Stan Moran, who were in Moscow at the Lenin School, that Miles was a family man who couldn't travel, so he should fill the position. An astonished Comintern official asked, 'What, is there a split in your party?'[71]

Miles was now to play a different role, that of the general secretary, a position equivalent to Comrade Stalin. This new status required a strong and resolute figure who could be invested with the exemplary qualities of a proletarian patriarch. A similar cult of the leader had already arisen around the general secretaries of other communist parties, such as Harry Pollitt in Britain and Maurice Thorez in France. Jack Miles lacked their physical presence and could match neither their qualifications as industrial activists nor their patriotic status (anyone who heard him could detect his Scottish origins) but the Australian central committee determined he 'has these characteristics that are essential to a leader of the working class', and subsequent party publicity provided him with them.[72]

The cultivation of a public face of Australian communism did not obviate the need for secrecy. Whereas Third Period communism had sought to achieve the greatest possible impact, making up for its lack of numbers by shouting its presence, united front communism pursued a quiet effectiveness. In 1930 Moxon had instructed members thus: 'If a number of young workers leave a trade union meeting together, they should march in closed ranks, sing revolutionary songs, cheer for the revolution, and if curious passers-by stop and join them, then one of the comrades should make a speech'. In 1935 Miles laid down as an elementary rule that members should 'come to a meeting place on time and get right into it, when it is dispersed go away in small numbers and get right away'. The change registered a reorientation of tactics, methods and expectations. Adversarial communism yielded to affirmation, confrontation to the patient cultivation of alliances; and recognition that workers in dire distress were not necessarily the most advanced, altered the whole style of party work.[73]

The Party congress accepted all these changes without demur. Jack Loughran, the sole dissident, had been excluded and was dismissed in his absence by Miles as 'a silly old man'. The congress was notable also for the allocation of time limits to speakers. Sharkey was given an hour for his report on the Seventh Congress of the Communist International, Miles two hours for explaining the tasks of the Australian party. Politbureau members and officials of the larger districts had 30 minutes, lesser district representatives and central committee members twenty minutes, and all other delegates just ten. At the opening session Jack Blake announced the composition of the praesidium that would guide the election of new officials. It had three honorary members: Comrade Thälmann, the German party leader 'whose name is symbolical of the spirit of the German working class and toiling people of that country against fascism'; Comrade Dimitrov, who had defied Hitler from the dock of a Nazi court, was now president of the International, and 'whose name is inseparably connected with the struggle of the working class throughout the world against fascism and against war'; and finally 'he whose name is connected with the strivings of the working class throughout the world . . . the great leader of the Bolshevik Party, Comrade Stalin'. The delegates stood to applaud.[74]

11

Communism by fronts

By 1935 the Communist Party of Australia was committed to the cultivation of strategic alliances. Initially it sought a united front of all sections of the labour movement; subsequently it extended the boundaries to pursue a broader alliance still, a popular front of workers, farmers and the middle class. Both the united front and the popular front had defensive and offensive aspects. The fronts were to save freedom and world peace from fascist belligerence, a menace that imperilled all workers and all people, but a successful resistance to fascism and war required an aggressive resolve that only communists could provide. Following Dimitrov's definition at the Seventh Congress of the Communist International in 1935, the party now understood fascism to be the most imperialist, reactionary and chauvinist wing of finance capital, and this provided the 'objective basis' for a coalition across class lines, yet it followed from the same characterisation that the final defeat of fascism would entail an abolition of the class order from which it emerged.

The word 'front' has various usages. One meaning is a line of battle which troops extend to face the enemy, and this was how communists presented the united and popular fronts. But the word can also suggest an outward appearance serving to conceal ulterior motives, and this was how opponents interpreted communist activity in the second half of the 1930s. For some participants these were years of common engagement in a life-and-death struggle to preserve liberty, a moment of truth when the choices became clear and idealists could act in concert. For others it was the time of falsity and pretence—of what W.H. Auden called 'the necessary lie'—that led, in 1939, to the ultimate communist betrayal and war.

Ralph Gibson, who had joined the party in the depths of the Depression and experienced the full rigidities of Class Against Class, looked back on the mid-1930s as a time of transition, 'a period when the Left was trying to break out of its narrow bounds'. Audrey Blake, another Depression communist, observed in her memoirs that the aim of the party's 'fronts' (renamed 'fraternal organisations' now that the term front had to serve a larger purpose) was 'to extend the space in which the Party could work'. Len Fox, who was drawn into the party in 1935 through activity in the Movement Against War and Fascism, quoted Gibson's statement in his own memoirs, *Broad Left, Narrow Left*. Fox was exemplary of those drawn to communism in the period. A science graduate, a poet and a progressive educationalist, he travelled to Europe in the early 1930s and returned to Melbourne 'feeling that the greatest service anyone could render Australia would be to carry it a warning of the dangers of fascism and of the world war which must come soon if fascism were not checked'. He was as selfless in that cause as Ralph and Dorothy Gibson, with whom he worked in the MAWF, and carried the same devotion into his party work. His memoirs chart a conflict between the broad and narrow forms of communism that he encountered, a difference suggested by two of the chapter titles, one recalling the 'Warm, Human People' engaged in its campaigns, another the narrow and dogmatic 'Men at the Top' who directed them.[1]

The 1930s began in mass unemployment and ended in mass destruction. They are sometimes described as the Devil's Decade after the dictators who first extinguished freedom in their own countries and then embarked on wars of extermination that ended in Auschwitz and Hiroshima. The events of this Devil's Decade can be recited chronologically as a succession of international crises brought on by the fascist regimes. In 1931 Japan began its assault on China with the annexation of Manchuria. In 1935 Italy invaded Abyssinia. In 1936 Hitler remilitarised the Rhineland and entered

Noel Counihan frequently drew for the communist press during the 1930s. His depiction of the popular front shortly after its proclamation at the Seventh Congress of the Communist International takes the successful defence of French democracy in 1934 as a model that alarms Hitler. The idealised figure is again a giant male worker, but more controlled than the brutal representations that had appeared in the earlier period of Class Against Class. (Source: 'Workers' Weekly', 21 February 1936)

into an anti-Comintern pact with Japan; Italy joined them the following year. Also in 1936, the Spanish generals staged an uprising against the elected government, and were assisted by Italy and Germany to prosecute a civil war that ended in 1939 with fascist victory. In 1937 Japan invaded China. In 1938 Hitler seized both Austria and the German-speaking areas of Czechoslovakia; the following year he annexed the remainder of Czechoslovakia, while Mussolini took Albania. In every one of these acts of aggression the League of Nations proved ineffective; at each moment of crisis the governments of the major non-fascist countries took refuge in appeasement or isolation, thereby clearing the way for the next outrage. Not until Germany invaded Poland in the autumn of 1939 did the Western powers make a stand, and by then it was too late. War began between the Allies and the German Reich in 1939. Mussolini's declaration of war in 1940, Germany's attack on the Soviet Union and Japan's strike against American military bases in 1941 completed the descent into global war.

Arising out of economic hardship and social discontent, channelling popular discontent with capitalist democracy into authoritarian nationalism, exalting the unity of the corporatist state and refusing class or any other form of disunity, fascism posed a fundamental challenge to communism. In adapting the methods of mass mobilisation, it unleashed revolutionary violence against the left. Alarmed by the strategic threat of fascism on both its western and eastern borders, the Soviet Union pursued collective security agreements with the capitalist powers. From its initial interpretation of fascism as a symptom of general capitalist crisis, after 1935 the Communist International recast the phenomenon as a new and distinct malignancy. In his speech to the Seventh Congress of the Communist International, Dimitrov insisted that:

> The accession to power of fascism is not an *ordinary succession* of one bourgeois government by another, but a *substitution* of one state form of class domination of the bourgeoisie—bourgeois democracy—by another form—open terrorist dictatorship. It would be a serious mistake to ignore this distinction . . .[2]

The absolute opposition of communism to capitalism thus yielded to a tripartite configuration of capitalism, communism and fascism, and the search for common ground on which the first two might repulse the third. From condemnation of democratic illusions the Communist International turned to the defence of freedom; onto revolutionary internationalism it grafted progressive national traditions. For Len Fox, as for others engaged in such endeavours, these realignments allowed the left to shake free of its narrow confines and draw men and women of good will into a broader range of activities.

The threat of fascism rescued communism as an international movement. The attempt during the 1920s to extend the Soviet model of revolutionary socialism had failed. The Depression benefited the right rather than the left. The effect of fascism in the 1930s was to force communism and liberal capitalism into an alliance against a common enemy, an alliance that neither would have chosen but was forced upon both. The strategic importance of the Soviet Union and the organisational capacity of the Comintern made communism an indispensible component of this alliance and, as Eric Hobsbawm has observed, 'The logic of this situation was so compelling that even the two years when Stalin reversed the anti-fascist policy could not weaken it'.[3] It was thus during the Devil's Decade that communism began the ascent that brought it to its highest point of support and influence. Such was the success of communism's front activities, so pervasive was temper of engagement, that the 1930s are also remembered as the Red Decade.

The Red Decade was a product of the same world events as the Devil's Decade, for the conservative appeasement of the fascists broke down the barriers between progressives and revolutionaries. But the imposition of the strategic interests of the Soviet Union, as determined by its ruthlessly pragmatic and deeply suspicious ruler, onto the policies of the Communist International produced fatal contradictions. The Communist International rallied to the defence of the Spanish Republic; it sent money and medical supplies, it enrolled volunteers into the International Brigade, many of whom died in battle. But it also turned on those Stalin deemed to be Trostkyists, and its commissars murdered their anti-fascist rivals. The Soviet Union appealed to the Western powers for sanctions against acts of international aggression and mutual defence pacts, but it also recruited spies to gather military and security information for use against them. Communists in Australia and other countries campaigned against their governments' policy of appeasing the fascist regimes in their belligerent demands, until August 1939 when Hitler and Stalin divided Poland and the Baltic states between them.

At least until that final betrayal, idealists such as Len Fox could not or would not see the subjugation of an international movement to partisan considerations. The broad left achieved its breadth partly by drawing Australians into world affairs and partly by connecting those affairs to a larger and more diverse domestic audience. The fascist aggressors cast a long shadow that extended over Australia. The Australian government cooperated with Mussolini's officials to maintain surveillance over anti-fascist Italians in Australia; it accepted the request of the German government to prevent anti-Nazi agitation here and it set tight restrictions on the entry of Jewish refugees from Hitler's pogrom. Boycotts of the shipment of strategic materials to Japán brought Australian trade unionists into direct conflict with the Commonwealth. From the Kisch affair onwards, the anti-communist and pro-appeasement policies of the conservative federal government provoked protests against censorship and repression, and attracted wider circles of church people, civil libertarians, intellectuals, men and women from outside the traditional confines of the labour movement. Paradoxically, the party's industrial base became even more important. Since the Labor Party remained adamant in its rejection of the united front, the unions were the sites of communist activity for both international and domestic campaigns, the institutional bases from which the party was able to exert its influence. Yet the rapid progress of communist trade unionists in the second half of the 1930s was based above all on their ability to improve their members' wages and working conditions, to soften the stringencies of capitalism and to make the institutions of capitalism serve their needs. The Red Decade consolidated Australian communism as a party of doctrinaire pragmatism.

The failure of the Communist Party's renewed appeal to the Labor Party at the end of 1935 for a united front caused no surprise. Its campaign to unify the labour movement against fascism and war proceeded, therefore, through the trade unions and front organisations such as the Movement Against War and Fascism. Here it met with immediate setbacks. In October 1935 the party announced its support for international sanctions against Italy in response to the Italian invasion of Abyssinia. In this it followed the lead of the Soviet Union, and in doing so encountered sharp opposition both within and beyond its own ranks. Some party members found difficulty in aligning themselves with the imperialist powers, for at this time the British as well as the Australian government supported the League of Nations' call for sanctions although the Australian government quickly backed away from this position in favour of appeasement. The central committee emphasised 'the need to distinguish between the support of the capitalist class and that of the working class for sanctions'. Some non-party pacifists believed that such action increased the danger of war, but the party stressed that sanctions were the best chance of preserving peace.[4]

Many in the broader labour movement combined elements of both anti-imperialism and pacifism with a more general hostility to foreign entanglements that was rooted in memories of the conscription referendums during the First World War and the divisions those controversies had opened in the Labor Party. Others followed the lead of the Catholic church in support for Italy. Maurice Blackburn was the only member of the federal Labor Party who broke ranks to support the Lyons government's Sanctions Act in November 1935. Furthermore, the ACTU Congress later in the same month rejected arguments in favour of sanctions put by Lloyd Ross, Bill Orr and Ernie Thornton. By 78 votes to 41 congress declared its 'uncompromising opposition to the policy of applying sanctions' on the grounds that 'the delegating of powers or authority by organised Labor to the representatives of capitalistically controlled Governments . . . would amount to the betrayal of the cause of the workers'.[5]

Blackburn's defiance of the Labor caucus and his prominence in the Movement Against War and Fascism brought immediate retribution. In September 1935 the State Executive of the ALP, which had established its own Labor Anti-War Committee, declared that no loyal member of the ALP could be associated with the MAWF. In October it gave its members until 15 November to sever the connection. On Armistice Day Blackburn spoke at the Yarra Bank for the Victorian Council Against War and Fascism (VCAWF), adamant of the need for 'a wider anti-war, anti-militarist movement than can be got within the confines of any one party'.[6] On 6 December the state executive expelled him and a number of other Labor activists. This was a serious blow. Before the rupture two leading members of the Communist Party in Melbourne had met privately with Percy Clarey, Albert Monk and Don Cameron, the principal officers of the Melbourne Trades Hall Council. They were encouraged to hear that the trade union officials agreed on the desirability of a united labour movement. But when they next met, the Trades Hall Council had determined that no affiliated body could remain a member of the VCAWF and any prospect of a united front vanished. The VCAWF responded with a proposal for a joint conference with the Labor Anti-War Committee, but this compromise was rejected. The national committee of the MAWF counselled submission, the Victorians argued for defiance and claimed that most of their union affiliates were not prepared to break the connection with the VCAWF. In April 1936 (conveniently before the Easter state conference of the ALP which the union delegates would otherwise have attended) the Melbourne Trades Hall Council suspended the affiliation of the ARU, the Wonthaggi miners, the FIA, the Locomotive Engine Drivers' Union, the Teachers' Industrial Union and the Ballarat Trades and Labor Council.[7]

With a number of other unions and a score of Labor Party branches affiliated to it until it was proscribed, the Victorian section of the MAWF had made the greatest progress, and the attack on it indicated the difficulties the party encountered as it sought a united front. There were particular opponents in Victoria. Dinny Lovegrove, the former communist who in 1935 became secretary of the Labor Anti-War Committee, was a bitter adversary. A group of Catholics who had formed around the Campion Society in 1931 and who espoused the corporate state as a bulwark against Godless communism, wielded increasing influence in the Victorian labour movement. The Labor Party expulsions and the Trades Hall Council disaffiliations were part of an intense factional struggle within the Victorian labour movement at this time, marked by sectarian divisions between the Catholic right and their moderate or left-inclined Protestant opponents. The cautious overtures of the THC officers to the communists were an episode in this contest, the subsequent rift an illustration of the handicap suffered by Labor activists who associated with communists. Rather than the industrial wing of the labour movement facilitating a united front of the Communist and Labor parties in the cause of peace, the communist bogey had damaged industrial unity and isolated the VCAWF. The party's central committee recognised as much when it instructed left-wing unions to abandon their links with the VCAWF and the Victorian district to strengthen communist fractions in ALP branches.[8]

In New South Wales the circumstances were more propitious. There, Lang's control of the Labor Party and Labor Council rested on a narrow base of trade union officials, the so-called inner group, who maintained control by ruthless manipulation of the party rules Lang had devised. During 1935 Lang came out in opposition to sanctions against Italy. He used the *Labor Daily* to damn the communists and insisted that Australia must remain resolutely free of all foreign entanglements. In 1936 he led his State Labor Party back into the federal ALP, and thereby buttressed its isolationist stance. But his attempts to wrest control of the radio station 2KY from the Labor Council and strengthen his grip on the *Labor Daily* brought him into conflict with the Miners' Federation (which had put up money for the paper) and a growing number of other unions. Jock Garden, now a federal member of parliament, and his successor as Labor Council secretary, R. A. King, led a challenge to Lang that gathered momentum. To its surprise, the Communist Party found itself once more allied with Garden—'a very shady gentleman', as Richard Dixon described him, 'as big a political crook as Lang', insisted Sharkey—in a struggle that strengthened the left in the Labor Council and would ultimately clear a space for a united front with the New South Wales branch of the Labor Party.[9]

Not yet, however, and in the meantime Labor in that state remained as hostile to the united front against war and fascism as in Victoria. Elsewhere the efforts to win the Labor Party over to a more resolute anti-fascist foreign policy met with mixed results. South Australia was most amenable, but its labour movement was a negligible force.[10] In Queensland and Western Australia, where Labor held office, communists were kept firmly at arm's length. Nationally the MAWF languished. A united front of the Australian labour movement remained blocked by the organisational resistance of the Labor Party. Under these circumstances the communists turned their attention to a popular front. The popular front, conceived as a more general alliance of the working class with other classes, held out the attractive prospect of greatly widening the resistance to war and fascism, and held the tactical advantage that the additional components were not bound by the same disciplinary control as bound Labor Party members and affiliates.

The transition from united front to popular front began in Melbourne on Armistice Day 1935 at the very anti-war rally that occasioned Blackburn's expulsion from the Labor Party. At that rally the VCAWF joined with religious and other anti-war organisations to form a United Peace Council. This in turn became the World Peace Congress Committee, which sent delegates to a World Peace Congress in Brussels in September 1936. Following the congress, the International Peace Campaign (IPC) was established in Australia, which convened the national Peace Congress in Melbourne in 1937 attended by more than 800 delegates. The breadth of the World Peace Congress, which was chaired by the ageing British conservative politician, Lord Cecil, was matched by its Australian counterpart, which included representatives of the churches, the

League of Nations Union, the United Association of Women and the Australian Natives' Association among its office-bearers, and featured a string of judges, bishops, academics and businessmen as patrons. This International Peace Campaign was clearly much more than a communist front. The pacifists who attended its Melbourne congress were far more insistent in their opposition to war than the communists, and party members of the IPC state committees repeatedly complained of the difficulty of converting anti-war sentiment into anti-fascist action.[11] Ralph Gibson had detected the same underlying differences at the founding congress in Brussels. There the IPC adopted a four-point programme: recognition of the sanctity of treaties, reduction of armaments, a strengthened League of Nations and collective security. But some argued that the sanctions imposed by a strengthened League of Nations would increase the danger of war, while others greeted the appearance of the Spanish communist delegate Dolores Ibarruri (who as La Pasionaria became the most celebrated champion of the Spanish Republic) with the bellicose chant, 'Guns for Spain! Planes for Spain!'[12]

The Spanish Civil War, which had begun less than two months earlier and would continue until 1939, fractured the illusions of peace through collective security. It demonstrated the subservience of the League of Nations to the major powers and their policy of non-intervention that denied support to a lawfully elected government yet allowed Italy and Germany to send guns and planes to the fascist insurgents. While pacifists sought peaceful resolution, the Communist International raised volunteers to fight: 'I fight against war—with war', declared Sam Aarons, one of the Australian communists who joined the International Brigade.[13] Spain thus became the testing ground for the larger conflict that would follow, the European cockpit in which fascists and communists did battle.

In 1936 the Spanish Republic was just five years old and still seeking to establish its legitimacy over deeply conservative opponents. The civil

They shall not pass!

HELP
the Spanish People
to Defend Themselves
against the Attack of
FOREIGN FASCISM

They are Fighting
FOR DEMOCRACY
FOR PEACE
FOR YOU!

Send Food!
Send Medical Supplies!
Send Money!

A poster produced by the Victorian Council Against War and Fascism in the early stage of the Spanish Civil War. (Source: J.N. Rawling collection, Noel Butlin Archives Centre, ANU N572271)

war began as a military uprising led by General Franco, who used Moorish troops and drew on Falangist (the Falange was the Spanish fascist movement) and clerical support against the electoral success of a popular front government. The popularity of the front was indisputable: it stretched from moderate republicanism to communism and well beyond to include Trotskyists and anarchists. Initially the war was marked by mass killing on both sides, as the stronger local force put down the weaker and settled old scores. This phase produced atrocities against the Catholic church, which was a powerful institution of the *ancien régime*, as well as clerical complicity in atrocities against the left, and the religious dimension inflamed the divided responses in Australia to news from Spain. Subsequently the rebels controlled the north and west of the country, the government the south and east, and the war was fought on shifting fronts as the military tightened its hold and began to push, slowly but inexorably, into government-controlled territory. The left strongholds of Catalonia and Aragon were gripped by a revolutionary euphoria which saw peasants seize estates from their landlords and workers turn the city of Barcelona into an anarchosyndicalist commune until the Communist Party imposed its own control. In 1937 German planes bombed the Basque capital of Guernica and the rebels won control of the industrial north. By 1938 the rebels had cut the country in two. At the beginning of 1939 Barcelona and Madrid fell and the war was over.

Australians made up a tiny fragment of the volunteers who enlisted in the International Brigade, some 40 out of a total close to 40 000. They provided about the same proportion of nurses, administrators, drivers, journalists; altogether perhaps a score of the 20 000 foreign non-combatants who assisted the Republic. Their Spanish Relief Committee raised about £17 000, probably a smaller proportion of total foreign aid though still a remarkable sum. Even when allowance is made for disparities of population, the Australian contribution was more modest than that of Britain, the United States or Canada, which raised its own Mackenzie-Papineau battalion, whereas the Australians were mostly scattered throughout the British battalion. There were particular reasons for the limited response. Most Australians knew little of Spain, and many of those who did supported the insurgents. The long distance from Spain and restrictions imposed by the Australian government made it necessary for volunteers to make their way to Britain—sometimes posing as tourists, more often working their passage or even bunking down as stowaways with the assistance of a ship's crew—and then evade the blockade imposed on Spain.[14]

The heroism of Australian volunteers was repeatedly connected to national traditions. Jack ('Blue') Barry, who had been a militant in the Pastoral Workers' Industrial Union, died in 1937 during the defence of Madrid. A New Zealand journalist remembered him as a 'sturdy, sandy haired working man who grumbled cheerfully and blasphemously about the non-arrival of food as I have heard Australian and New Zealand shearers grumble hundreds of times, and then met his death covering a retreat alone, with all the gallantry of the Anzacs in 1915'. Ted Dickinson, a former Wobbly who had been gaoled in 1928 for his part in the maritime strike, was captured in the Jarama Valley near Madrid during the same campaign and faced his captors with defiance. 'If we had ten thousand Australian bushmen here we'd have pushed you bastards into the sea', he was said to have told them. They put him up against a tree and shot him. An RSL journal responded to the story with the tribute: 'Whatever one may think of the merits of the cause in which they are serving, it is gratifying to learn that the old strain of Gallipoli and Poziers is running true to form'. Though Dickinson was in fact an Englishman and had returned there some years earlier, the line

Ted Dickinson's execution by Franco's troops at Jarama was often recalled, as was his fearless defiance of the executioners. This cartoon misspells his name and extends his martyrdom into a refusal to submit to fascist militarism. (Source: 'Workers' Weekly', 27 August 1938)

drawn here runs from the First World War to the opening phase of a second, and the Australian volunteers in Spain constitute an advance contingent in fight to defend freedom from fascism that would continue until 1945. 'I wouldn't mind dying for democracy', was the explanation given by an unemployed Tasmanian volunteer, Charlie Walters, while Charlie Riley, a gold miner from Tennant Creek, said that 'Adolph the Butcher had got right under our skins'. Some Australians, such as Ron Hurd, a tough communist seaman who had boxed professionally, were keen to fight. Other volunteers, such as Lloyd Edmonds, who had attended the Victorian Socialist Party's Sunday School with Hurd and was expelled from the ALP in 1935 for membership of the VCAWF, were drawn more by a feeling of obligation. When Jack Stevens died fighting in 1938, Katharine Susannah Prichard remembered the earlier hardship he had experienced as party organiser in Western Australia. 'Shabby and hungry, he struggled against tremendous difficulties', including six months' imprisonment, and throughout remained 'honest, unobtrusive, loveable, sterling'. The emphasis here is on selfless dedication to a universal cause.[15]

La Pasionaria's slogan, '*No Parasan*—They Shall Not Pass', became the catchcry of the defenders of the Spanish Republic. Neither the volunteers nor their Australian supporters admitted to any reservations, not even when the Spanish communists turned on the other parties of the left, or the political commissars of the International Brigade began to weed out unreliable elements. 'Barcelona Crushes Trotsky Fascists', was the headline over the *Workers' Weekly*'s account of the repression of the anti-Stalinist *Partido Obrero de Unificacion* (POUM) in May 1937. The article described a foul gang of fifth columnists under the control of Trotsky's agents who were in secret communication with Franco; in fact the POUM were so resolutely independent in their fight against Franco that they had fallen out even with Trotsky. This ruthless and mendacious surveillance affected a party of four Australian nurses who were given a 'rousing Red Flag farewell' from Sydney in October 1936. They were under the leadership of Mary Lowson, a party member, and they included the forthright Agnes Hodgson, who had no prior contact with the left and was motivated simply by liberal humanitarianism. Her fluency in Italian and distaste for bombastic political ceremony soon brought her under suspicion from zealous communists. When the group arrived in Spain, her three colleagues were posted to the International Brigade hospital at the front but Hodgson was left behind in Barcelona. Lowson made no reference to this contretemps when she returned to Australia in 1937 to publicise the cause. Nor did Australians learn of Bill Belcher, who had the misfortune to enrol in an anarchist militia, was arrested by the communist security and eventually released only through the intervention of the British consul. While Aileen Palmer admitted privately that there were 'many shades of grey in the Spanish war', she condemned the 'dirty work' of the POUM and accepted the need for 'strict discipline'.[16]

Australians did not lack their own sources of information about Spain. In the Queensland sugar districts there were Spaniards who received Spanish newspapers, and several of whom returned to fight against Franco. There were journalists such as Alan Moorehead (correspondent for the pro-republican London *Daily Express*), John Fisher (his father Andrew was the prime minister at the outbreak of the First World War who had promised Australia would send its last man and last shilling) and Rupert Lockwood. All three young men had been drawn to the anti-fascist cause by Egon Kisch, and their reports from Spain were informed by the same commitment.[17] Fisher was not the only example of a generational shift: Portia Holman, the daughter of the former Labor premier of New South

Wales who had ratted with Hughes during the First World War, was a medical worker in Spain; Richard Latham, on whom his vehemently anti-communist father John doted, drove a truck for a humanitarian relief organisation. Then there were Vance and Nettie Palmer, who at the outbreak of the civil war were living in Catalonia with their daughter Aileen; she remained in Spain with a British medical unit while they returned to Melbourne to organise support through the Spanish Relief Committee. There were films, brought from Spain and taken around Australia by the University of Melbourne Labour Club communist, Ken Coldicutt, as national film organiser of the Spanish Relief Committee. There were scholars, such as Max Crawford, who had begun an intensive study of Spain's quest for freedom before he took up the chair of history at the University of Melbourne at the beginning of 1937, and who joined other academics in public support of the Republic.[18]

Throughout the conflict, the Australian government maintained a policy of 'strict neutrality and non-interference in the internal affairs of a foreign country'. Public opinion divided sharply at the edges between champions of the Republic and supporters of Franco, with a large and generally inert middle ground. Like the Communist Party, the Catholic church saw Spain as a battleground in a larger struggle, and even before the outbreak of the civil war it had condemned the secular policies of the Republic. The Australian hierarchy responded to an appeal from the Spanish bishops in July 1936 with unqualified support for the rebellion. A stream of publications described communist atrocities, the execution of priests and violation of nuns, with lascivious outrage. The papal encyclical *Divini Redemptoris* issued in March 1937 (it sold 87 000 copies in Australia) linked 'the fury of Communism' in Spain, the destruction of churches and the 'indiscriminate slaughter' of clergy, to the urgent struggle between the promise of the Redeemer and the satanic scourge of atheistic communism. In the eyes of Bishop Gilroy, who would become Australia's first native-born cardinal, General Franco was 'a man who seemed to be raised up by Almighty God'.[19]

The most celebrated confrontation between the two sides—it has been recalled by Manning Clark, among others, as a formative moment of political awakening—occurred in the public lecture theatre at the University of Melbourne in March 1937. Three members of the Campion Society, including the young B. A. Santamaria, affirmed the proposition 'That the Spanish Government is the ruin of Spain' in a debate with Nettie Palmer and two communists, Gerald O'Day and Jack Legge, an undergraduate science student. The theatre was packed by members of the Catholic Young Men's Society, who joined their champions in the cry, '*Vivo Cristo Rey*' at its conclusion. Similar debates followed elsewhere but it was more common for Catholic supporters of Franco to break up meetings of the Spanish Relief Committee. Thus two months later they descended on the Adelaide Town Hall, where a dozen speakers were billed in an appeal to assist the Spanish people. The first speaker was my grandfather, the Reverend Aubrey Stevens of the Congregational Church. He was heard in silence, but after him the president of the the South Australian branch of the ALP was drowned out by booing and cat-calls.[20]

Catholic opposition to communism was not new but anti-communism in Australia had not previously achieved such popular and systematic character. During the 1920s conservative politicians had exploited the red scare with material provided by the security service and encouragement from employers' groups and the press, but the influence of such professional publicists as Tom Walsh and Adela Pankhurst Walsh was restricted. Their apostasy and extreme conservatism had discredited them in the eyes of the labour movement, and the anti-communism preached by Adela's Women's Guild of Empire was as fanciful as Millicent Preston Stanley's similar work for the Sane Democracy League. The New Guard and other secret armies had assumed mass proportions in their anti-communist drive during the political instability of the early 1930s, but these again were external and antagonistic to the labour movement. Spain altered these alignments, for adherents of Catholicism comprised a substantial proportion of the labour movement and, as the principal Catholic anti-communist, B. A. Santamaria, has observed, 'it was the conflict of ideas generated by the Spanish Civil War which in Australia transformed the Catholic attitude to Communism from generalised opposition to passionate resistance'.[21]

The appearance in 1936 of the newspaper he edited, *Catholic Worker*, and the establishment in 1937 of a National Secretariat of Catholic Action to be conducted by another layman and himself, signalled a new emphasis on anti-communist agitation and organisation within the labour movement, as critical of the injuries of capitalism as it was of communist false remedies. Very quickly these Catholic activists, distinguished by their black-and-white badges with the holy cross, became prominent as anti-communist shock-troops at public meetings in Melbourne. Ernie Thornton warned the central committee as early as April 1936 that the *Catholic Worker* was exercising 'a big influence on the situation in Victoria. There is quite a big proportion of Catholic workers in the trade unions and they have been aroused by the *Catholic Worker*.' From outside Victoria, as well, communist organisers reported that Catholic Action was mobilising support in trade unions (the state mine lodge at Lithgow was an early example) to defeat communist delegates and officials.[22]

There was an additional dimension to this Catholic activism. During the 1930s a number of Protestants were drawn to the peace movement. In New South Wales the Anglican warden of St Paul's College at Sydney University, Arthur Garnsey, was president of the International Peace Council; in Victoria the Methodist minister Palmer Phillips occupied the same position, and representatives of the Student Christian Movement, the YMCA and the YWCA attended its meetings. While the bulk of the Protestant laity remained anti-communist, those clergy who were most engaged in the churches' social mission often entered into dialogue with communists and communism. The Irish-born Harry Gould, who became a full-time party worker at this time with special responsibility for theoretical work, likened these progressive Protestants to eighteenth-century deists, who treated Christianity as an ethical code stripped of its supernatural trappings. He had in mind such figures as Ernest Burgmann, who in 1934 became Bishop of Goulburn. Burgmann's earlier experience in the Newcastle diocese during the Depression had not faded and in 1936 he declared that capitalism was 'warfare, naked and unashamed'. His outspoken radicalism and sympathy for the Soviet Union earned him the reputation of the 'Red Bishop'—an Australian equivalent of the notorious 'Red Dean' of Canterbury and naive apologist for Stalin, the Reverend Hewlett Johnson—but Burgmann's purpose is more accurately captured in his own formulation as 'the Christianising of Communism'. Similarly, Farnard Maynham, the Vicar of St Peter's, led members of that church in

East Melbourne in a quest for Christian socialism that was intensely sacramental in liturgy and theology. While a few of the Protestant clergy joined the party, the great majority associated with its campaigns were following their own stars.[23]

More striking is the growing prominence of ex-Catholic communists. Initially, the Communist Party had inherited the rationalist temper of the socialist and radical left. Its founders were thoroughgoing materialists who dismissed the Christian dogma of salvation by faith—derided by the Wobblies as 'pie in the sky'—for its quietism. Irish adherents such as Jack Loughran, who ran the party bookshop in Sydney, and Mick Healy, who took on the same task in Brisbane, were militant atheists. There were members from a strong religious background, but typically evangelical Protestantism: Jock Garden and Bill Orr had preached for nonconformist sects; Bill Gollan and Jack Hughes, notable recruits of the 1930s, were brought up in the Salvation Army. The sprinkling of Jewish communists had little to do with religious observance. Former Catholics, on the other hand, were trained in a confessional faith that was not so easily set aside. In a number of cases, youthful piety as an altar boy preceded a prolonged crisis of faith; typically, their turn to communism caused lasting family tension, especially as communism and Catholicism became sharply polarised.

To Catholics, who felt keenly their own minority position in Australia, the alignment of Protestants against Catholic Spain hardened sectarian divisions. During his national tour after the party's Eleventh Congress, J. B. Miles encountered this phenomenon, particularly in Queensland where the Labor Party was close to the Catholic church. In response to Archbishop Duhig's repeated attacks on Godless communism, he sought to play down the question of religious belief:

> We are not concerned at the moment with the question of how the world came into existence or what will happen when we pass away. We are concerned with the things that happen here and now—in decent wages, living conditions, in defence of our democratic rights, with the preservation of peace.

The central committee also advised its districts that they should be careful in responding to the Catholic campaign. Catholics made up 'a considerable proportion of the working class', and it was important to concentrate on the church's alliance with fascists, 'making it clear that we are not specifically attacking the faith and doctrines of the Catholics as a religion'. Lance Sharkey's pamphlet, *An Appeal to Catholics*, sought to reassure Catholics that there was freedom of worship in Spain as well as the Soviet Union, and that there were many Catholic republicans. He also countered the ethnic division that underlay religious sectarianism in Australia with an appeal to his fellow Irish-Australians' love of freedom and rebel spirit.[24]

This was a far cry from the militant atheism that communists had proclaimed in the 1920s, and some party members found it hard to practise. Dr Gerald O'Day, a former Catholic, had inflamed the Melbourne debate on Spain with his anticlerical jibes. In response to the pro-Franco speakers' allegations of republican attacks on the church, he asked 'What harm ever came to anyone through perse-cuting the Catholic Church?' O'Day wrote afterwards that Catholic supremacy 'resulted invariably in stagnation and illiteracy'. He joined a materialist refutation of religious belief to a trenchant class analysis of religious practice.

> The Communists reveal the historical and economic roots of religion. Religion (i.e. the religious ideas, institutions and practices) is regarded by them as a man-made thing, a portion of the superstructure built by man on the basis of the productive forces.

The church was supported by the ruling class because it 'helps to keep the oppressed masses from the struggle for a heaven on this earth'. It flourished amidst poverty, unemployment and superstition; hence 'with the end of capitalism the end of religion begins'. Miles might have had O'Day in mind when he cautioned against communist use of such aphorisms. Rationalism was but another strand of religious sectarianism, he declared, and 'we are not going to succeed in the course of mass work . . . if we come out under the slogan "Religion is the opium of the people"'. Comrade Marx, the author of this slogan, was not available to be set straight by the Australian party secretary, and neither was Comrade O'Day prepared to desist. On another occasion, asked what he would do if Stalin invaded Australia, he returned the question: 'What would you do if the Pope raped your mother?'[25]

Neither the conciliatory nor the aggressive presentation of com-munist religious policy mollified those Catholics in the labour movement who shared their church's opposition to the Spanish Republic. Amid heated argument in the state branches of the ALP, the federal leader, John Curtin, maintained a policy of non-intervention. A special congress of the ACTU in July 1937, on the other hand, adopted a resolution moved by Lloyd Ross of support for the Spanish government, and by 79 votes to 48 congress also reversed the ACTU's previous opposition to collective security. This resolution, which was proposed by the secretary of the New South Wales Labor Council with the support of Orr, Ross, Thornton and Garden, coupled 'German and Italian aggression in Spain' with German aggression in Central Europe, 'directed finally towards Russia', and Japanese aggression in China, which threatened both the Soviet Union and Australia. It supported the principles of the Brussels Peace Congress, and urged a 'united effort of all working-class bodies'. It was by far the most encouraging advance to date in the Australian campaign for a united front.[26]

Japan's invasion of China in July 1937 brought a significant extension of the campaign against fascism and war. The pretext for this belligerence was the Chinese Nationalist government's failure to suppress communism, and it was accompanied by mass executions by the Japanese military of Chinese civilians in the coastal cities. The rape of Nanking at the end of the year joined Guernica as a symbol of militarist brutality. The party revived its Hands Off China Committee, which worked along similar lines to the Spanish Relief Committee, and raised funds to send an ambulance and other medical assistance to the victims. The substantial trade links between Australia and Japan also allowed the communists to push for economic sanctions. In October 1937 the ACTU called on Australian consumers to boycott Japanese goods. From January 1938 members of the Waterside Workers' Federation (WWF) began to refuse to load shipments of scrap iron for export to Japan. They secured the endorsement of the New South Wales Labor Council and ACTU executive, but were forced to lift the ban in May when the Commonwealth government threatened to apply the provisions of the Transport Workers Act and de-license the WWF.[27]

There was an encouraging success at the end of 1937. A British cargo vessel, the SS *Silksworth*, under charter to a Japanese company and with a predominantly Chinese crew, docked in Newcastle to take on coal. When members of the crew approached local communists with allegations of mistreatment, the maritime unions and Newcastle Trades and Labor Council declared the ship black. The ship's captain initiated court action against the crew and had 30 of them arrested, but another six had been taken by the communists into hiding in Sydney. Their plight occasioned large protest meetings in both Newcastle and Sydney, and highlighted the fact that the ship was bound for Japanese-occupied China with a cargo of wheat. The Chinese consul and many Chinese-Australians supported the campaign for the crew's release. After blaming their plight on 'the extreme element', the Australian government eventually arranged for the prosecutions to be withdrawn and paid the crew's passage to the Philippines. The crucial factors in this successful campaign were the solidarity across racial lines, so often a point of division, and the determination of the unions to maintain their industrial action. There was an attempt to 'sneer at the trade union movement', said the communist district secretary 'with the inference that the Chinese were people lower than Australians', but 'here was collective international action, an example of the way the masses could unite against aggression'.[28]

A year later the Port Kembla branch of the WWF refused to load pig-iron on another ship bound for Japan, the SS *Dalfram*. The decision was a local one, taken on the initiative of the communist secretary of the WWF branch, Ted Roach, against the policy of the National Executive, which feared that the combination of the Transport Workers Act and BHP (the company that produced the iron) was too powerful. But the Port Kembla wharfies were backed by the local labour movement and held firm—even when BHP shut down its steelworks, the members of the Federated Ironworkers' Association and other unions maintained support for the ban. Robert Menzies, as Commonwealth attorney-general, proceeded to Wollongong under heavy police escort to rebuke the strikers, and Roach told him that 'This pig iron will be used to slaughter our own women and children, and raze our own cities to the ground in Australia, in the same way as in China today'.[29]

Menzies already bore the reputation of an appeaser of the fascist regimes, if not a sympathiser, because of his complimentary comments about Hitler's Germany, and it was a communist orator working on the Sydney wharves, Stan Moran, who now dubbed him 'Pig Iron Bob'. His declaration of the licensing provisions of the Transport Workers Act brought wide criticism, including from Isaac Isaacs, the former governor-general, who said that the coercion of the waterside workers was 'dictator's rule'. The ACTU affirmed its support for the principle that 'there should be no export of war materials to countries engaged in a war of aggression', and the government's insistence that the trade should continue undoubtedly increased union mistrust of its domestic and external intentions. In the end, the nine-week strike ended in a truce: the government lifted the provisions of the Transport Workers Act and agreed to reconsider an embargo on the export of war material, while the Port Kembla waterside workers loaded the ship.[30]

Apart from its exploitation of the draconian powers of the Transport Workers Act to bar workers from their industry, the government also resorted to censorship during the Port Kembla dispute. The Sydney radio station 2KY (by that time under left-wing control) broadcast allegations of government interference with union telegrams and telephone calls. In retaliation, the postmaster-general ordered engineers to cut the connection between the studios and the transmitter, and refused to re-establish the connection until the station apologised. This was not the first case of censorship of radio broadcasts. Earlier in 1937 a state manager of the ABC had ordered the deletion of passages critical of Hitler and Mussolini from an educator's address on Machiavelli and modern dictators; in the following year a member of the Spanish Relief Committee was told to omit the word 'German' from a reference to the bombing of Guernica, and Alf Foster, a Victorian county court judge and member of the International Peace Campaign, was prevented from speaking on censorship. There was also the refusal, at the request of the German government, to allow public performances of the anti-Nazi play *Till the Day I Die*, by Clifford Odets. These prohibitions brought protests from the Australian Council for Civil Liberties, which had evolved from the Book Censorship League, and affronted a growing body of progressive middle-class opinion. Indeed, by joining the infringement of civil liberties to appeasement of the dictators the Lyons government seemed almost deliberately to foster the politics of the broad left.[31]

The Axis powers certainly showed a remarkable blindness to Australian sensitivities. At the end of 1937 the Italian government sent a battle cruiser, the *Remo*, on a good-will voyage to New Zealand and Australia. Local Italian anti-fascists had previously distributed leaflets to passengers and crew on visiting Italian liners, and this warship's recent involvement in the blockade of republican Spain and bombardment of Barcelona made it a natural target for protest. When similar literature was smuggled on board *Remo* after it berthed in Melbourne in February 1938, a ship's officer ordered ratings to seize a local Italian taxi-driver, Ottavio Orlando, in the mistaken belief that he was the leader of Melbourne's *Gruppo Italiano* against war and fascism, Frank Carmagnola. Other members of the Italian navy drew knives in an Italian club in Carlton and smashed the club's picture of Italian volunteers in the International Brigade. Orlando was beaten and interrogated on board the *Remo* in the presence of an officer of the Commonwealth Investigation Branch, and Attorney-General Menzies's insistence that the branch had given no names or descriptions to the Italian officers failed to placate indignation. Several thousand people demonstrated at Station Pier against the warship. Similarly, the MAWF organised protests and pickets against the Nazi representative Count von Luckner, who was another guest of the Australian government in 1938.[32]

In contrast to the welcome given these fascist emissaries, the Commonwealth government showed scant sympathy for their victims. It maintained strict controls over the entry into Australia of Jewish refugees. Even after *Kristellnacht* on 9–10 November 1938, when the Nazis unleashed mass destruction of Jewish property, Prime Minister Lyons insisted on a limit of 5000 Jewish immigrants a year, subject to special landing fees. In this he was supported by some in the Labor Party who regarded the refugees as a threat to Australian workers, and some Catholic publicists who dwelt on the communist proclivities of 'world Jewry'. It was the conservative president of the Victoria Legislative Council who went furthest in his warning of 'slinking, rat-faced men' who were turning Carlton into a ghetto of sweated industry. Against all of them the Communist Party waged a campaign to discredit anti-semitism and pressure the government to liberalise its immigration procedures. Previously there had been a limited Jewish membership of the Communist

Party of Australia—Sam Aarons and his mother Jane, Judah Waten, Nattie Seeligson, and Itzhak and Manka Gust in Melbourne, Annie Isaacs, Sam Lewis, Bella Weiner and Harry Gould in Sydney, were perhaps the most prominent—but by 1937 Jewish groups of the party were established in Sydney and Melbourne with fruitful connections to Jewish cultural bodies and community organisations.[33]

Even the communists eventually faltered in their campaign for the Spanish refugees. By 1939 there were several hundred thousand of them, mostly held in camps in southern France, early victims of the plight that would afflict so many millions more men, women and children rendered stateless by the enforcement of political conformity by so many regimes in the latter part of the century. The Australian government provided the shamefully small sum of £3000 for their assistance. The Spanish Relief Committee, which was still collecting donations, also pressed for admission of Spanish refugees to Australia but some of its state branches worried that this might antagonise Australian unionists. The campaign languished, the donations declined and activity fell away. The outbreak of the Second World War effectively ended the work of the Spanish Relief Committee.[34]

Just as the ALP's refusal of a united front encouraged the communists to make a popular front the basis of their campaign against fascism and war, so in its domestic campaigns the Communist Party increasingly emphasised a popular alliance. This was a gradual and partial reorientation on the part of an organisation that remained overwhelmingly proletarian in its membership, leadership and outlook, and by its rapid progress in the trade unions was still hoping to win over the Labor Party. Both the fronts, the united front and the popular, were foreshadowed at the Seventh Congress of the Communist International. They were not seen as mutually exclusive, and the formal distinction between them was probably lost on many members: Guido Baracchi found when he took over party classes in

Sydney in the second half of 1938 that most did not know the difference between the united front and the popular front.[35] The difference in composition—a united front of the working class, a popular front of the working and other classes—was qualified in both cases by the historically ordained mission of the working class in the final overthrow of capitalism and the leading role allocated to the party in that necessary outcome. More significant was the alteration of emphasis and tone, from the stress on a separate and self-sufficient working class in conflict with the capitalist ruling class to the common endeavours of men and women, workers by hand and brain, wage-earners and farmers, artists and intellectuals, all striving for a more harmonious, richer and fuller life.

It was a member of the Anglo–American Bureau of the Communist International who first drew the Australian party's attention to the full implications of the popular front. Writing as S. Mason in the Comintern bulletin *Inprecorr* in July 1936 on 'The Next Task of the Australian Communists', he stressed that the imminent danger of war required 'a real popular people's front programme'. This in turn entailed a different orientation than that pursued by the Australian party: 'The question for us at the present moment is not proletarian revolution versus war, but peace or war; not Soviet power versus bourgeois democracy but . . . the extension of bourgeois democracy'. Mason's identity remains a mystery, a mystery compounded by the fact that J. B. Miles later used the same pseudonym (as a play on his former occupation as a stonemason). That this Mason was not Miles quickly became evident during the recriminations his article caused once it was put before the party in the *Communist Review*. Lance Sharkey used Mason's article to criticise Dixon's tardiness to embrace the popular front, and though the diligent assistant secretary took the blame, Sharkey was for the first time challenging the party secretary, Miles. Mason's strictures were so pointed that Miles offered abject self-criticism at the next meeting of the enlarged central committee, which resolved on a substantial alteration of the party's electoral activity. Paradoxically, the insistence that the Australian party reorient its politics to the popular front meant working for a Labor government. To assuage the fears of the Labor Party and improve the prospects of Labor defeating the Lyons government, the party withdrew all but two of its candidates from the 1937 federal elections and campaigned for a 'common front of the workers, farmers and middle class against reaction'.[36]

Not all accepted the abrupt change of tack. A Queenslander suggested it would dismay the workers in that state who had lost patience with its reactionary Labor government. Ernie Thornton told the central committee in the immediate aftermath of that election, which Labor lost, that 'it would be a very big mistake if we ever allowed ourselves to forget that we are a class party and a revolutionary party, as seems to be the case in a lot of our propaganda'. Guido Baracchi, readmitted to the party in 1935, harboured misgivings about the persistent tendency to 'dissolve the proletariat in the people'. Mason's instructions were in any case soon countermanded by his successor as secretary of the Anglo–American Bureau, Andre Marty, the ruthless French commissar of the International Brigade. At a meeting of the committee in September 1937 he taxed the Australian representatives, Dixon and Orr, with the Australian party's failure to take a more independent electoral position and brushed aside their explanation that it had been determined for them by Mason. 'The article by Mason was bad. I don't know why Mason had the idea of writing such an article. The comrade who is responsible is removed from our apparatus.' In any case, he continued, 'The responsibility for this line is only the responsibility of the Central Committee of the Australian Party. An article by Mason is not sufficient. The leadership of the parties are not babies.' Dixon's chagrin is easily imagined.[37]

In any case, Australian communists were now fully committed to the Popular Front, and its urgent necessity was the dominant theme of the Twelfth Party Congress in 1938:

> A People's Front against poverty and sorrow, for prosperity and happiness; against reaction and fascism, for progress and democracy; against the instigators of war and their friends in this country, for a lasting peace and security.

These polarities provided the coordinates of a popular alliance that would incorporate 'workers, farmers, teachers, civil servants, doctors, other professional workers and small businessmen, Catholics and Protestants'. Dixon was even able to quantify 'the progressive and democratic people' as constituting 90 per cent of all Australians. In this vein the preamble of the new constitution adopted at the Twelfth Congress defined the Communist Party as:

> . . . a working-class party carrying forward the best traditions of Australian democracy, the struggle against convictism, for self-government, at Eureka the fight for social reforms, against military conscription and peace. Upholding the achievements of democracy and standing for the right of the majority to direct the destinies of our country, the Communist Party fights with all its strength to unite the masses to resist any and every effort, whether it comes from abroad or within, to impose upon the Australian people the arbitrary will of any selfish minority group, or party, or clique. It is devoted to the defence of the immediate interests of the workers, farmers and middle class against capitalist exploitation.

To further emphasise the democratic basis of the popular front, Jack Blake declared that the party had no intention forcing socialism on Australia. That would require majority support and Australians were not ready for it. 'Let it be known definitely once and for all that the Communist Party is not and never has been an advocate of force and violence.'[38]

The new emphases of the popular front were served by material that contrasted the economic interests of the masses against the greed of a parasitic minority. In 1936 the party demonstrated the feasibility of its demands for increased wages and shorter hours by detailed analysis of business profits. For the 1937 federal election, James Rawling produced the leaflet *Make the Rich Pay*, which publicised the twenty families who controlled so much of the country's industry along similar lines as the French party's exploitation of their country's 200 richest families. Rawling also wrote *Who Owns Australia?*, which showed the the narrow concentration of national wealth in the hands of a 'modern feudal aristocracy' who lived in palaces alongside 'horrible and soul-destroying slums'. From an earlier political economy that used the labour theory of value to show how all profit derived from the exploitation of wage-labour and argued that the logic of capitalist accumulation would necessarily reduce the middle strata to the ranks of the proletariat, the party now championed farmers, shopkeepers and small business against an oligopoly of large Australian companies characterised by interlocking directorates and links into conservative politics.[39] The change was at once a move towards careful empirical research into company registers conducted by experts who invoked the authority of massed facts, and an adaptation of the techniques of public relations. As Lloyd Ross told the central committee, 'Simplification, illustration, reiteration—the methods of the successful advertiser—must be applied to our propaganda'.[40]

A further extension of this popular front literature was the practical blueprint. Ralph Gibson's *Socialist Melbourne* (1939) is a striking example of the genre in its description of how his city would appear to a future visitor: the modernised public transport system, the new schools, the People's Bank and the new People's University, the Richmond slums replaced by housing estates, the Pelaco factory on the hill now a community centre, the Toorak mansions across the river made into rest homes for the workers, the red flag flying over Parliament House. To go inside a factory was 'a new and wonderful experience. One felt as if one had walked into a club rather than a factory.' Gibson reported both changes and continuities. Pentridge Prison was no more, crowds at the Melbourne Cricket Ground were down because new sporting facilities allowed much greater popular participation, but the churches in Collins Street were still free to operate. It was a 'new Melbourne, very different from the Melbourne that we know', and yet 'eminently realisable' and even likely to be realised in the immediate future. This is not so much a utopian work in the pre-communist millenarian tradition of William Morris, or like an earlier Melbourne utopia imagined by the anarchist bookseller David Andrade, a genre that heightened the contrast between what was and what could be, as rather a readily recognisable account of a familiar place enhanced by an expanded range of communal amenities.[41]

The most striking feature of popular front communism was its cultivation of national traditions. This strategy was equally true of other communist parties. The American communist party at this time constructed a progressive lineage that ran from Jefferson and Paine to Jackson and Lincoln: 'Communism is the Americanism of the twentieth century', declared its party secretary, Earl Browder. In Britain communist writers including the expatriate Australian Jack Lindsay turned, as earlier radical movements had done, to the past in order to connect Wat Tyler, the Levellers and the Chartists to the contemporary defence of liberty: 'Whatever was good in British traditions', Harry Pollitt told the CPGB Congress in 1937, 'the National Government had abandoned and betrayed'. In France the Communist Party revived the rich revolutionary heritage of the Republic to declare itself 'the heir of the Jacobins'.[42] The difficulty for Australian communists was that their own popular memory was so exiguous. The radical nationalists associated with the *Bulletin* in the closing years of the last century had celebrated convict martyrs and defiant diggers. Bob Ross of the VSP had commemorated the Eureka rebellion with his study published in 1914, and the epic event was recalled intermittently during the 1920s.[43] Little remained of such history by the 1930s, not least because early Australian communists regarded it with suspicion for perpetuating romantic national illusions, though Bob Ross's son Lloyd would publish his study of the utopian socialist *William Lane and the Australian Labour Movement* in 1937 and the first instalment of Brian Fitzpatrick's radical interpretation of Australian history would appear in 1939.[44] The key figure in the Australian party's construction of a popular national tradition was James Rawling, who worked in Sydney as the party's researcher and the national secretary of the MAWF. An interest in Australian history, stimulated by the teaching of Professor Arnold Wood at the University of Sydney in the 1920s, found expression in a miscellany of articles on popular resistance in the colonial era published from the early 1930s in the *Workers' Weekly*, the *Red Leader* and the *Communist Review*. His incomplete *Story of the Australian People*, issued by the Modern Press in irregular instalments from 1937, shows the clear influence of Wood in its emphasis on the convicts as wronged victims of a bloody penal code and the emancipists' struggle for freedom against autocracy and squattocracy.[45]

Until communists became interested in the popular front, these enthusiasts evoked little response. In 1934 Lloyd Ross tried to interest the labour movement in the centenary of the transportation of the Tolpuddle Martyrs, with limited success. Later in the same year Rawling drew attention to the eightieth anniversary of the Eureka Stockade, but the party did nothing to commemorate it. Two years later, however, J. B. Miles reported to the central committee that he had recently been in Ballarat and visited the site of the stockade as well as the museum that held the flag and other relics of the diggers' rebellion. He was 'compelled to realise . . . the need to study Australian history'. Almost immediately the *Workers' Weekly* responded by hailing the Eureka rebellion and the anti-conscription struggles of the First World War as 'true expressions' of 'real Australian traditions'. The 'self-styled patrons of the rich families who at present control Australia' had claimed a monopoly of patriotism but a suitably nurtured appreciation of the past showed that 'the Communists today are the real inheritors of the true Australia, of the fathers of democracy, of the Dunmore Langs, Parkeses and Wentworths'. The pen of Rawling was clearly apparent in the claim that:

> True Australianism has always been a dominant mode in the history of this country; in the early struggle against the oppressions of the governors, against convictism, for the extending of democratic rights and in countless battles of the worker for betterment in their working and living standards.

Hence in late 1936 the party organised a procession through the streets of Sydney to mark the twentieth anniversary of the first conscription referendum, with six of the twelve 'martyred' Wobblies present along with a selection of other celebrities in the battle against conscription. At the same time as they celebrated 'the heroism of the men who were brave enough not to fight', communists reclaimed the Anzacs for their enlarged radical nationalist pantheon. These volunteers had been manipulated and misled, but they 'thought they were dying for liberty' and it was anti-militarism rather than militarism that was true heir to the Anzac tradition.[46]

Sharkey clarified the object of this patriotic initiative. It was Dimitrov, he told the central committee in November 1936, who had pointed out the great success of fascism in 'playing upon national feelings and grievances', deep-rooted emotions that communists had neglected. Henceforth all parties must therefore develop 'the national traditions of the people'. 'We are the real Australians', Dixon responded the following year, 'the inheritors of everything that is good and decent in the history of Australia'.[47] In this spirit the party contested the celebrations in 1938 to mark the sesquicentenary of British settlement, which it justifiably feared would foster 'an incorrect view, an anti-working-class view, of

The Stalinist terror demonised Trotsky as the evil genius behind every trace of opposition. When the communists turned on the Spanish POUM, they accused Trotsky of sabotaging the defence of Spain in order to assist the fascists. This malicious caricature gives him Nazi insignia and emphasises his Semitic features. (Source: 'Workers' Weekly', 10 August 1937)

Australian history'. The official re-enactment of the landing of Governor Phillip affirmed the imperial purpose of colonisation and eliminated the convicts while it brushed lightly over the original inhabitants. In contrast, communists assisted the Aboriginal Day of Mourning and Protest, and took a leading role in the counter-celebrations organised by the New South Wales Labor Council. This 'Pageant of Labor' showed a convict flogging, persecution of Aborigines, the Eureka rebels, alongside other tableaux emphasising the achievements of the toilers. Mourning and protest had their place but the popular front required an affirmative note; as the party organisers put it, 'because of mass participation we must have a positive attitude'. Thus the party's own float contrasted a 'Gallery of Honour' (Marx, Engels, Lenin, Stalin, Harry Pollitt, Tom Mann, Mao Zedong, Harry Bridges, La Pasionaria) with a 'Rogues Gallery' (Hitler, Mussolini, Franco, a Japanese militarist, Chamberlain, Lyons—and Trotsky).[48]

For Leon Trostky such endeavours were a capitulation to national chauvinism and a betrayal of proletarian internationalism. Australian communists did warn against xenophobia. The central committee advised in 1937 that the campaign against Japanese aggression should draw a clear line 'between the Japanese fascists, militarists, imperialists, the government, which are planning war, and the Japanese people', so that any suggestion of a 'yellow peril' should be rejected absolutely.[49] In practice the distinction between a people and its government was often lost. Again, the communists' cultivation of progressive national traditions was not exclusive. As the Gallery of Honour suggested, Australians were encouraged to celebrate a number of revolutionary heroes who embodied the best traditions of their countries—thus the party's campaigns against racism in the United States, fascist aggression in Spain, and imperialism in India introduced Australians to a diverse repertoire of progressive patriotism, while figures such as Paul Robeson and Jawaharlal Nehru were incorporated into the experience of the left. Even so, the the popular front elevated nationhood as a category and nationalism as an ideology. Front communism sought to tame the savage beast that the fascists had set loose, to reclaim patriotism as a force for good by emphasising the national qualities of the parties that comprised the Communist International. But the beast would not be tamed. National antagonisms erupted into a new world war, the Communist International dissolved and eventually even communist countries confronted each other across national boundaries.

The popular front attracted appreciable numbers of writers, artists and intellectuals for the first time to communism. There was a perceptible quickening of cultural life in Australia in the second half of the 1930s that was apparent both in new levels of activity and a restless impatience with older forms. For many of the creative younger generation who came to adulthood during the decade, witnessed the collapse of the old society and felt the dangers of fascism and war, communism seemed the only realistic alternative.

Even those who did not submit to the demands of party membership were drawn into its ambience of cultural engagement.

A popular front emphasised broad alliances and inclusive forms of organisation. The Writers' League, formed in 1935 as a 'broad and non-sectarian' body, turned itself into the Writers' Association after Nettie Palmer attended the Paris Congress of Writers for the Defence of Culture Against Fascism in 1937, and in the following year it merged with the Fellowship of Australian Writers, which embraced all but the most decorous *litterateurs*. The theatre groups associated with the Workers' Art Club reformed in Sydney and Melbourne as the New Theatre to attract a younger generation of urban progressives. The communist artists combined with others impatient with the stultifying conservatism of the academy to form the Contemporary Art Society in 1938.[50] These realignments did not remove the commitment to an alternative, experimental culture that challenged restrictive forms and practices. Communist artists at this time continued to work mainly in linocut or graphic media rather than paint, and to draw cartoons, illustrate magazines, design pamphlet and book covers, produce stage designs and banners. The New Theatre took drama back from the open platform to the proscenium arch, but its productions still involved non-professional actors, producers and designers, using stylised sketches in a documentary and didactic mode, and commonly called on audience participation. The party opened the gates of cultural access, encouraging its members to participate. Branch life in itself trained communists in reading, writing, speaking, editing.[51]

Noel Counihan took his pencil to the countryside when he and Judah Waten set off north from Melbourne in the winter of 1935. Waten had been expelled from the party once more as the result of 'petty bourgeois irresponsibilities', and he proposed to act as Counihan's manager and hunt out country notables prepared to sit for caricature portraits that could be exhibited and sold. Through Albury, Wagga Wagga, Tumut and Goulburn (where Bishop Burgmann welcomed them with stately courtesy) they proceeded with sufficient success to clear their pub bill and move on. Christmas found them in Sydney, where Noel met Stan Cross and George Finey. In the new year it was on to Orange, Tamworth, Armidale and Brisbane, where they befriended Raphael Cilento. This was fortuitous. Cilento, the director-general of medical services in Queensland, was an influential patron who helped them sell a substantial proportion of the portfolio. But he was also the honorary Italian consul and at a celebratory meal the guests fell out with their host over Mussolini. Thus ended the *Wanderjahr* and there was just enough from the proceeds of the Brisbane exhibition to pay their passages back to Melbourne.[52]

At the All-Union Congress of Soviet Writers in 1934 the leading party authority on culture, A. A. Zhdanov, took Stalin's description of writers as 'engineers of human souls' to codify the artistic doctrine of socialist realism, a heightened realism that faithfully rendered the heroic struggle of the working class to help it achieve its appointed goal. In the communism of the popular front, artists and writers were to cast off narcissistic aestheticism and take their rightful place alongside the only truly creative class, the proletariat. Socialist realism, with its insistently political message, is seen by some literary critics as an incubus on the creative imagination of Australian communist writers such as Katharine Susannah Prichard. Her earlier novels such as *Working Bullocks* (1926) and *Coonardoo* (1929), with their rich vitality and sensuality, are compared with those written after she had returned from a writers conference in the Soviet Union in 1933, in which the class struggle takes precedence over human subjectivity.[53] This view has been contested, partly on the grounds that Zhdanov's speech was not published in Australia during the 1930s and the term 'socialist realism' not commonly used until after the Second World War; but it was certainly promulgated earlier and its effects were readily apparent in a range of contemporary statements. That it stultified artistic creativity, at least in its initial impact, is equally dubious as the denial that it was promulgated.[54]

Writers such as Alan Marshall and John Morrison were publishing at this time vignettes of working life in party newspapers and journals, fragments of experience and action in which the short sentences, direct diction and urgent immediacy blurred the distinction between fiction and documentary. There was a close relationship between such prose and the experimental genre of reportage, which was a new form of journalism strongly influenced by Egon Kisch and characterised by one of its Australian practitioners, Tom Fitzgerald, as 'a report plus atmosphere, comment and deduction';

not 'copy-cat realism' but 'lessons for human progress'. Then there were political novels such as John Harcourt's *Upsurge* (1934), a jagged distillation of events in Western Australia in which 'the story and actual fact walk hand in hand'. The Melbourne New Theatre's play *Thirteen Dead* (1937), based on a recent underground explosion at the Wonthaggi state mine, used a similar technique of 'dramatic reportage' to drive home the lesson that capitalism destroyed lives in its compulsive drive for profits. As David Carter has suggested, such writing deliberately challenged literary convention; its politicisation of the text was such that it 'entails thinking of propaganda, not as bits of political rhetoric insufficiently made over into art, but as an available narrative strategy'.[55]

In their laconic intimacy, the short stories of Marshall and Morrison resemble those of Henry Lawson, who was championed by the Fellowship of Australian Writers during the 1930s just as enthusiastically as he was claimed by the Communist Party. The more direct influences on writers of the left came from abroad: Dos Passos, Hemingway, Steinbeck and the *New Masses* magazine, Gide and Malraux, Gorky and Sholokhov. Among the members of the Writers' League in Melbourne, in fact, there was resistance to the minority of enthusiasts—Frank Huelin, Len Fox, Arthur Howells—who advanced claims for an Australian literary tradition: when one member introduced the work of Joseph Furphy, hardly anyone else knew of him. The more established figures associated with the literary popular front—Vance and Nettie Palmer, the Essons, Miles Franklin, Marjorie Barnard and Flora Eldershaw—appreciated only too well how fragile was the space occupied by Australian literature. In the satirical novel on the sesquicentenary written by Miles Franklin and Dymphna Cusack, *Pioneers on Parade* (1939), we see the snobbish denial of convict origins as an obstacle to the development of an independent Australian civilisation. It is in the native soil and from those who who mixed their sweat and tears with it that these radical nationalists expected a real culture to grow. Both the fiction and the art of the later 1930s moves from the stark depiction of embattled labour, alternatively crushed or heroically defiant, to a more affirmative rendition of popular endeavour from early pioneering days to the present, a collective memory gathered into a narrative of progress.[56]

As communists ventured out from their oppositional fastness, they encountered a new constituency that responded less to national traditions or local concerns than overseas influences and international issues. A younger generation of educated Australians who came to adulthood in the 1930s rejected the enclosed conservatism of their parents. They looked outwards, past the mental boundaries of the British Empire, to new centres of energy and innovation. Few of these restless, enquiring young men and women were drawn to the dogmas of communism in its proletarian Australian accents, which sounded no less parochial to ears attuned to cosmopolitan modernism, but they were attracted to the cultural ambience of the left. They did not suffer acute material distress, since their professional qualifications and intellectual skills afforded reasonable comfort, but they were appalled by the misery, the waste, and perhaps most of all the sheer irrationality of the capitalist Depression. By contrast the Soviet Union appeared efficient, purposeful, progressive. Its heroic feats of construction appealed to technicians, its mass programmes of literacy and culture to teachers. For those who watched with alarm the march of the fascist dictatorships, and the pusillanimity or worse of the bourgeois democracies, communism seemed the only realistic alternative. Such dissident middle-class sympathisers did not easily adapt to the demands of party membership but they swelled the popular front.

This altered climate of opinion especially affected journalists, just as they shaped it. The dark machinations of diplomacy, big business, spies and treachery crossed the genres of reportage, travel writing and the thriller, so much so that the writings of Graham Greene, Eric Ambler and Ernest Hemingway became emblematic of the decade. Journalism was at once glamorous and seedy, competitive and world-wearily cynical, its privileged access to events constrained by media proprietors deeply complicit in the structures of power. In Melbourne Keith Murdoch assembled a remarkable combination of youthful talent for his Herald and Weekly Times chain—Brian Fitzpatrick, John Fisher, John Hetherington, Kim Keane, Clive Turnbull; Edgar Holt, Frederick Howard and Douglas Wilkie from England; and later James Aldridge, Rupert Lockwood and Alan Moorehead. As Moorehead recalls:

Nearly all of us were left wing and we glowed with hate for Mussolini

> and the up and coming Hitler. We read such books as John Reed's
> *Ten Days That Shook the World* and Sholokov's *And Quiet Flows the Don*
> . . . Every one of us I suspect was secretly planning or already working
> on a novel.

The view here is outwards, and most of these journalists would try
their hand abroad; some, like Moorehead, never returned. Earlier,
as undergraduates, these ambitious young men affected a style of
raffish sophistication. On the Melbourne campus there was Cyril
Pearl, who became an editor for the Packer press in Sydney, and
Alwyn Lee and Sam White, both briefly party members, who cut
their teeth on the Labour Club's magazines, *Proletariat* and *Stream*,
before departing for careers overseas. Sam eloped with Mary Wren,
as Alwyn Lee had decamped to Sydney with Guido Baracchi's wife.[57]

Stream, a volatile mixture of Lenin, Joyce and Pound, gave way
in the later 1930s to the sober exhortations of the *Left Book Club
News* and the monthly club selections in their uniform livery, brick
red for the hardbacks, tangerine for limpcover editions. The Left
Book Club was a significant extension of the popular front. Established in Britain by the left-wing publisher Victor Gollancz, it
provided members with cheap editions of works concerned with
fascism, the threat of war and poverty. Gaetano Salvemini's *Under
the Axe of Fascism* and Robert Brady's *The Spirit and Structure of
German Fascism* were complemented by Edgar Snow's *Red Star Over
China* and Hewlett Johnson's *The Socialist Sixth of the World*. The
party promoted the Left Book Club in Australia both in the trade
unions and through encouragement of club groups that met to
discuss the books and participate in progressive politics. The central
committee advised that it was important for party members to play
an active role in these suburban groups, and to 'guide the political
line'. By 1938 there were 4000 Australian members, an *Australian
Left News* and a full-time organiser.[58]

The Australian Council for Civil Liberties was another forum
for progressive activity. Formed in Melbourne at the end of 1935,
it took up political censorship, the use of the Crimes Act against
communist activity, the attack on Ottavio Orlando and the plight
of refugees from fascism. Its secretary and moving spirit was the
radical intellectual Brian Fitzpatrick, who was more closely aligned
with the left than some of the professors and lawyers who swelled

its list of office-bearers found comfortable. While Fitzpatrick recruited such allies as Judah Waten and Rupert Lockwood, his object in constructing what he described hesitantly as a 'United Front (mmm?) of liberals, C.P. and subsidiaries, and all unionists' depended upon his own ability to secure 'their co-operation in semi-darkness'.[59]

'The middle class appreciates strength in the uncertainties and wants to be on the side of the millions—whether the millions of the people or the pounds of the millionaires depends largely on the working class.' This appraisal from Lloyd Ross captures the lingering communist suspicion of the new social constituency it cultivated for the purpose of a popular front. The middle class fitted awkwardly into a Marxist class analysis based on relations of production, as its intermediate status suggests. Members of the middle class were regarded as waverers in search of certainty and in need of firm proletarian guidance. Ross cited the example of Frank Dalby Davison who, as president of the Fellowship of Australian Writers, had initiated the merger with the Writers' Association, and described him as 'somewhat of an intellectual ne'er-do-well and political libertine'. Those middle-class progressives who were drawn to the Communist Party had to overcome their instinctive liberal inhibitions. In 1936, when a Melbourne newspaper was conducting one of its periodical communist witch-hunts, an earnest correspondent demurred:

> There are few thinking people today who do not admit that we need some change in our social system. History shows that progress is only made by a handful of enthusiasts propagating their particular doctrines. If we give full freedom to these movements right and truth must prevail.

The correspondent was Wilfred Burchett, another of the questing Australians drawn to investigative journalism by the example of Kisch. Burchett has recalled that when he applied to join the party at this 'stage of mental, moral and ideological development' he was 'repelled' by the violent language of the *Communist Manifesto*. Evelyn Shaw, who abandoned legal studies for art, found the dictatorship of the proletariat an obstacle when she joined in 1937.[60]

A notable proportion of the recruits to the Communist Party at this time were women, for the popular front provided greater opportunity for female activity than the earlier, insistently masculine proletarianism of Class Against Class. The male leaders of the popular front party also encouraged a broader participation. According to Mary Wright, who had helped organise the party demonstration for International Women's Day in 1935, it was Jack Miles who asked, 'How long are you going to keep it to yourselves?' No matter that he had previously instructed the party women to stick to the straight and narrow. The organisers duly approached a number of women's groups, including the Federation of Women Voters and the United Association of Women, all of which it had previously condemned as mere apologists for bourgeois feminism. At the party congress in December 1935 it was reported that an approach had been made to the United Association of Women's redoubtable Jessie Street but that she had taken fright. However, her support was secured for an enlarged Women's Day in 1936, and this provided the basis for communist participation in her campaign for equal pay for women, and for mobilisation of community groups in campaigns to improve family services. In the same year the party's monthly, *Working Woman*, was abandoned and replaced by *Woman Today*, which enlarged the ambit of female interests with articles on fashion, mothercraft and family health as well as women's careers. To the woman worker and woman as auxiliary to her worker-husband, were added the woman writer, the woman as peace activist, the progressive woman.[61]

The change proceeded from the party leaders' recognition that 'our percentage of women members is so appallingly weak', and it entailed no reconsideration on their part of the subordination of gender to class. Party women felt their inequality keenly, and in subsequent autobiographical writings they are acutely aware of the double standards that operated under the aegis of a puritanical party of universal emancipation; but there is little of such questioning in the contemporary party record. Many of the women recruited into the party in the 1930s had independent careers: of those who have recorded their memories, Marie Gollan, Jess Grant, Joyce Batterham and Flo Davis were teachers; Bernice Morris and May Pennefather were nurses; Justina Williams a journalist; Betty Roland a playwright; Mona Brand an advertising copywriter; Evelyn Shaw an artist; Audrey Blake a shop assistant; Joan Goodwin an unemployed graduate. Such a sample is manifestly skewed towards those best able to articulate their experience, but it does suggest some instructive patterns. Typically women were drawn into popular-front activity before they joined the party, and brought to their communist commitment a level of education and a breadth of experience beyond the organised labour movement. Some became full-time party or union organisers, others worked in a part-time capacity. All remained in subordinate positions.[62]

Some were young. Daphne Gollan joined the party in 1938 while still in her teens and studying part time at the University of Sydney and working at the Mitchell Library. Her account combines youthful engagement with mature reflection. She joined, she recalls, because the Communist Party seemed the only political organisation that stood actively for socialism and against fascism; but she admits the additional attraction that she found it 'shocking and conspiratorial'. Her problem on joining the party 'was that of all women in organisations in which they are greatly outnumbered: overshadowed development'. The limits of her experience in the public domain were narrower than those of men; much of her activity was mediated by men, and having found her own way into the party she was 'speedily headed off, cornered and captured'. When war came and it was necessary for her to adopt a pseudonym, she put forward Cleopatra Sweatfigure. 'That's enough, comrade. We are not joking', a member of the central committee told her. In fact, she insists, she was not joking. 'The colours of life were very bright then.'[63]

One field of women's activity was the youth movement. From its parlous condition in the early 1930s the Young Communist League quickly applied the strategies of the popular front to youth activity. A National Youth Congress in Sydney in September 1935 attracted 71 delegates from church organisations and university student clubs, who formulated a Declaration of the Rights of Australian Youth. This in turn resulted in the Australian Youth Council, one of the genuinely popular fronts. The YCL itself was reorganised by Jean Devanny's daughter, Pat, who had recently returned from the Lenin School well-trained in such work. Her bulletin, the *League Organiser*, provided members with exhaustive advice on how to cultivate support. An article on 'How to Work in a Cricket Club', for example, explained the need to be a good sport, to mix with all your team-mates but pay particular attention to the captain, and to point out the class significance of sport as opportunity arose. Through the Workers' Sports Federation, well-organised Easter and Christmas camps and local YCL clubs offering games and dances, the party attracted larger numbers of teenagers.[64]

Upon her return from Moscow in 1938, Audrey Blake took charge of the party's youth work in Melbourne and greatly expanded its scope. Its Workers' Sports Federation was on a scale far larger than in other cities, its holiday camps grew to a peak attendance of 2400. The winter programme in that year included football, netball, table tennis, boxing and gymnastics ('To win in the class struggle we have to keep fit'), dramas, dances and rallies, classes in history, political economy, cookery and public speaking, conducted tours of the *Herald* office in Flinders Street, Parliament House and the city courts. She described it as a 'movement for peace, freedom and progress'; it might equally be seen as a regimen in progressive civics. Even so, the title of the organisation remained an obstacle to the aim of building a large, anti-fascist alliance of youth, and in 1939 it was reformed as the League of Young Democrats. The popular magazine *Pix* provided an illustrated report of the league's premises, two floors and the basement of the Tattersall's building in the city, with a gymnasium, a cooperative cafe, even a printery, a place humming with purposeful activity.[65]

The popular front undoubtedly struck a chord among many Australians who had not previously been associated with the left. Its internationalism appealed to those who were alarmed by world developments, its affirmative nationalism attracted those weary of the insular colonialism that dominated Australia between the wars. The appeal to middle-class progressives, artists and intellectuals seemed to weaken the class barriers that had dominated the country's political life, and to provide the labour movement with an infusion of new energy. But as Len Fox's formulation suggests, the broad left was in tension with the narrow left. The Communist Party, the most rigidly proletarian of political parties, might have relaxed its dogma but it certainly did not relax its control and it is to this interplay of the narrow with the broad that we now turn.

12

Growth pains

Communists made significant advances in trade unions during the later 1930s. After the initial breakthroughs in the Miners' Federation and the Australian Railways Union, Ernie Thornton was elected secretary of the Federated Ironworkers' Association, and Tom Wright secretary of the Sheet Metal Workers' Union in 1936. Jim Healy won the same position in the Waterside Workers' Federation in the following year, while party members consolidated leadership of the Seamen's Union and made appreciable gains at state and branch level in a number of other unions. Midway through 1937 the party was able to report to the RILU that 29 of its members occupied full-time union posts. In the two centres of heavy industry, Newcastle and the Wollongong region of New South Wales, the trades councils were said to be 'under Party leadership', and a 'decisive' influence was claimed for communist delegates and their allies in the New South Wales Labor Council. Its Victorian counterpart proved more resistant but by this time the party could usually count on support from about one-third of the delegates to the Melbourne Trades Hall Council, and in Queensland the left was not far short of a majority on the Brisbane Trades and Labor Council.[1] The efficacy of the united front was apparent at the National Congress of the ACTU in 1937 as the mining and transport delegates, the secretaries of the New South Wales and South

Australian Trades Hall councils, even the secretary of the ACTU itself endorsed the resolution in favour of collective sanctions, which communists moved and the congress adopted by 79 votes to 48.[2]

Across a complex diversity of industries and occupations with their own distinctive characteristics, it is possible to identify some common patterns. First, communists achieved success by taking up the industrial demands of union members and prosecuting effective campaigns for better wages and conditions. In contrast to earlier pronouncements of an acute capitalist crisis that allowed no possibility of improvement, the party now accepted a partial economic recovery was under way. The recovery was fragile and incomplete, the world economy beset by fierce rivalry between the leading capitalist powers with intensified exploitation of their domestic workers and colonial markets. Dixon presented a Report on the Economic Struggle and the Tasks of the Communists in the Trade Unions to the Eleventh Party Congress in 1935 that attributed the increase in production from the depths of the Depression to 'an increase in the exploitation of the workers by increasing the intensity of labour'. The task of the party was to lead resistance to the speed-ups and to demand that workers receive higher wages.[3] It was a timely initiative. While national output increased after 1933 to finally attain pre-Depression levels by 1937, wages still lagged behind profits. In 1933 and again in 1934 the Arbitration Court rejected union applications to restore the basic wage it had cut in 1931; its 1937 supplementation fell a long way short of the ACTU's submission. With the unions thus baulked by the national wage tribunal, militants in particular industries were able to persuade their workmates to turn instead to direct bargaining with employers; with the partial recovery, employers were more likely to yield to such union action.

Second, the seeds of of communist success had been sown some years earlier as the party turned from dissident agitation to involvement in union affairs. In the New South Wales Teachers' Federation, for example, communists had worked during the early 1930s through an Educational Workers' League, which counterposed a radical conception of working-class education to the apolitical, professional concerns of a union executive dominated by headmasters. From 1934 the militants concentrated on a campaign to restore salaries, and gradually, as this industrial strategy altered the character of the federation, communist teachers such as Hettie Weitzel won executive positions. The larger concern with the class character of education was now pursued through the union in popular front initiatives such as the Conference on Education for a Progressive, Democratic Australia organised in 1938 by Sam Lewis, the former secretary of the Educational Workers' League and the driving force of the new teachers' unionism.[4]

The number and duration of industrial disputes increased steadily from a lowpoint in 1933 to a new peak in 1938. Not all of them were led by communists, but the party's application of its new industrial strategy brought immediate results. In January 1936 the Port Kembla (NSW) branch of the Federated Ironworkers' Association imposed a ban on overtime in the BHP works there. A tenweek stoppage and deregistration of the union followed the sacking of a union delegate. The immediate outcome was a compromise— the company agreed to reduce overtime, though not to reinstate the communist delegate—and it was followed by growth of union membership, election of communist officials, further union gains in subsequent action and a greatly improved national award in 1939. It was this momentum that carried Ernie Thornton to national leadership of the FIA and established his union as a pacesetter in the new militancy.[5] He had been put into the union as Victorian organiser in 1935 and his election as national secretary a year later was followed by the success of communists in two key branches: Scottish Pat McHenry, the 'Grey Ghost', in Port Kembla, and Welsh Charlie Morgan in Newcastle.[6]

Thornton rose quickly to become perhaps the most celebrated of the communist union leaders by the end of the decade—when he failed by just twelve votes to secure the presidency of the ACTU. A stocky, powerful man with a 'flashing sabre-toothed tiger grimace of a smile', he exemplified the qualities of the party industrialist: warm-hearted, generous, combative, domineering. With aggressive leadership he transformed a loose, ineffectual federation into a large, centralised and remarkably successful fighting organisation. A paper membership of 10 000 in 1935 increased to more than 20 000 by 1939 and doubled again by 1942, as the members secured greatly improved pay and conditions. Thornton had a reputation for strikes.

His forthright statement to his union's federal council, 'We made strikes our business', became notorious and indeed the FIA repeatedly confronted BHP and the owners of smaller foundries and workshops with threats of direct action to back its demands. But he was also adept in using industrial tribunals to achieve improved awards: during his first year as national secretary he appeared in no less than 27 such cases. Disputation, negotiation and arbitration constituted a repertoire of tactics, and while communist union leaders placed emphasis on the first, they owed their success to orchestration of all three. Thornton proclaimed that 'a union official who is not prepared to lead men out on strike is not fitted for his position'; but added 'so also is an official who, when the time for retreat has come, has not the courage to fight for his policy'. The proclamation emphasised both the responsibilities and the prerogatives of leadership, a role that Thornton assumed perhaps too readily, for he would later be denounced for rigging union ballots. This charge is difficult to sustain for the 1930s and is belied by the clear evidence of support in mass meetings. He typifies the communists who with the recovery from the Depression made the transition from unemployed agitation to union leadership—tough, intelligent, prickly, turbulent men who had battled all their lives for a job and a fair go. They were prepared to stand up to anybody on behalf of their members, and the members in turn stuck by them with a fierce loyalty.[7]

Meanwhile, in the Miners' Federation, Bill Orr and Charlie Nelson joined safety issues and hours of work to wage demands in a log of claims that they served on the coal companies in 1937. After the union stopped production at selected pits, the dispute was taken to arbitration and the owners agreed to restore the wage cuts they had imposed in the 1929–30 lockout.[8] There was also the lengthy campaign conducted by the New South Wales branch of the Australian Railways Union for a shorter working week, sick pay and leave entitlements, benefits gradually won by different sections of the union by dint of protracted local endeavours led by the state secretary, Lloyd Ross.[9]

A third feature of communist industrial activity is apparent in these examples—a patient, flexible, strategic prescience. Far from storming the industrial barricades, communist union activists were prepared to bide their time, mix direct action with recourse to arbitration, and work towards attainable objectives. Their campaigns were preceded by careful analysis and painstaking preparation; they laid the ground with workplace meetings, and used their own union publications, the party press and the mass media to build popular support for their demands. These tactics acknowledged a crucial fact: a small, highly disciplined party operating on a slender base of members in any single industry depended of necessity on the support and cooperation of a larger mass of non-communist union members. There were perhaps 3000 communist workers by the late 1930s in a workforce a thousand times that number. Beyond this, however, the communist union officials who had experienced the futility of precipitate militancy during the Depression were seized with the lessons of earlier defeats. The chief of those lessons was not to start a strike you could not win. The force of that maxim was driven home by the mixed fortunes of communists in the maritime transport industry.

The party had long held great expectations of the Seamen's Union. Unsympathetic shipping companies, harsh working conditions, cramped accommodation and the draconian discipline of shipboard life all fostered a rough-and-tumble militancy among the workers in this vital transport industry. Ever since the union's national secretary, Tom Walsh, had quit the the party in the early 1920s, communists endeavoured to re-establish control of the union, but had repeatedly failed to dislodge Walsh's successor, Jacob Johnson, from the union headquarters in Sydney. Johnson and the branch secretaries in Melbourne and Brisbane were adherents of the rigidly doctrinaire Socialist Party of Great Britain, which allowed no compromise in the class war, and enforced the union rules as strictly as they upheld the letter of impossibilist Marxism. With decisions taken at monthly stop-work meetings, however, there was scope for local action, so as prosperity returned, ships' crews began to demand piecemeal improvements. One such dispute escalated in August 1935 into a general stoppage, opposed by Johnson and led by the militants in Sydney under the leadership of Joe Keenan, a Scottish party member whose fiery oratory was well suited to the open union forum. When the arbitration court handed down a new award that reduced special rates and introduced penal clauses to curb strikes, the seamen again overturned the officials' instructions in favour of a general stoppage. Although the Commonwealth government applied the licensing provisions of the Transport Workers' Act to authorise non-union labour, the seamen held firm, and in late December 1935 at a large stop-work meeting they replaced Johnson as general secretary with Keenan. The Communist Party invested considerable effort into support of the seamen's action. Keenan's success, coinciding with the party congress, brought paeons of praise for 'one of the most capable agitators and mass leaders'. The delegates elected him to the central committee.[10]

Within two months the strike was broken and Keenan discredited. The fault was not his alone: Johnson used the courts to cling to office, the shipping companies used the licensing provisions to man their ships with volunteers, the miners voted overwhelmingly against their union executive's recommendation to support the seamen, and the ACTU refused assistance. Nevertheless, Keenan's decision in February to urge a return to work played into the hands of the former officials, who now became firebrands to discredit him for selling the union out. 'The seamen are really somewhat different to other workers', J. B. Miles lamented, 'they are most unruly'. Other leading party members added that they were 'anarchistically inclined and very left'; one claimed their main argument was arsenic—'they wanted to poison the volunteers'. But Keenan carried the blame for failing to understand the importance of collective action, and was further accused of dissolute laxity in portside pubs and brothels. In mid-1936 the political bureau decided to look elsewhere for leadership of the seamen and removed him from the central committee.[11]

The strategy of communists in the other major maritime union, the Waterside Workers' Federation, offers an instructive contrast. Here too the ravages of the Depression and the legacy of the government's licensing provisions had created deep divisions in the workforce: union members had to accept second or even third preference at the daily pick-ups behind members of the scab unions formed during the strike of 1928–29. Under these circumstances the conservative union leadership resisted all calls for precipitate strike action. Jim Healy offered a new approach. Healy, the president of the Mackay branch of the union who only joined the party in 1934, hailed from Manchester in England and had arrived in Queensland a decade earlier. He was a large, slow-talking pipe-smoker with a shrewd grasp of the limits of sectional militancy. In a series of articles in the *Workers' Weekly* under the heading 'What Is Wrong with the Waterside Workers' Federation' and directed at party members and sympathisers in the industry, Healy argued that unity of the workforce was the key to improvement. In 1937 he transferred to Sydney and at an interstate conference of the union later that year proposed a national campaign to win back some of the conditions lost over the past decade. A subsequent ballot installed him as general secretary.[12]

Healy immediately began rebuilding the federation. He established a union newspaper, along the same lines as those of the miners' union and the ARU, to publicise union issues. He toured the branches to persuade militants that they must accept the former strike-breakers into their ranks in order to present a common front to the employer, no easy matter in close, portside communities where memories were long and the hatred of scabs was intense. One of the Port Melbourne party wharfies recalls Healy's compelling argument:

> You've been hitting 'em on the head, you've been chasing them, you've been shooting at 'em. You've thrown them over bridges. You've done everything possible to get rid of 'em but they're still here! Now the only way we can get rid of them is to absorb them into the Federation.

Healy was quite prepared to resort to industrial action—the campaign against trade with Japan saw branches of the federation repeatedly tie up ships during 1937 and 1938—but he was wary of engaging in such action without clear, immediate and attainable objectives. He glossed the party's standard condemnation of industrial arbitration with acknowledgement of its utility: 'We can expect little or nothing from the Arbitration Court . . . On the other hand, what little it is possible to gain from such a Court can only be gained by workers organised in industrial strength.' He eschewed the general strike and usually retreated in the face of threats to invoke the Transport Workers' Act in order to keep his union's strength intact.[13]

Such pragmatism, willingness to learn from mistakes and preparedness to withdraw when necessary characterised communist activity in other industries. It was apparent in the mixed fortunes of the miners. During 1935 Orr and Nelson opened a campaign against mechanisation. They blamed the spread of coal-cutting machinery for increased accidents, wage reductions and loss of employment, and announced the union would prevent any 'further introduction of mechanical appliances'. But when the lodge members of those pits most directly affected by mechanisation refused to implement the union ban, the leaders beat a hasty retreat. Instead, they made the increased productivity of the industry the basis for a general log of claims that brought the new award of 1937; and while they backed these demands with stoppages of selected pits, they insisted that such lightning strikes were 'not a continuation of the anti-mechanisation campaign'.[14]

Similarly, the members' rejection of their call at the beginning of 1936 for a general strike in support of the seamen inhibited Orr and Nelson from repeating such acts of solidarity. Communists had long since abandoned calls for general strikes, and henceforth they were reluctant even to embark on sympathy strikes. Indeed, as they consolidated their influence within trade unions, they turned away from workshop committees and other such mechanisms to coordinate action across organisational divisions that the Minority Movement had promoted during the Third Period. The change of communist strategy has been criticised as a shift to sectional militancy, but this is to lose sight of the coordinating role of the party itself. The party encouraged worker solidarity, and actively promoted union amalgamations; but its efforts to develop industrial campaigns always centred on the official peak bodies, the state trades hall councils and the ACTU.[15]

The party central committee recognised in 1936 after the Miners' Federation refused to support the seamen that 'The decision of the miners represents a set-back which will require much intense work'. Union secretary Orr was inclined to blame other comrades for such setbacks. He was especially critical of party members in the Newcastle district for neglecting to take up union campaigns in the lodges, while they in turn criticised his own failure to consult. The district organiser complained that 'Comrade Orr is inclined to be neurotic owing to overwork and nerve trouble, and he is prone to bite your head off'. The fact that the union office was in Sydney and that Orr boarded in pubs while working there did not help. But the politbureau backed the union secretary, and agreed with him that the setbacks were the result of the 'inadequate reaction of the Communist Party in localities'. As for the grumblings of his failure to consult, 'leaders in the field must see when overburdened central leaders need protection from carping criticism'. Only in 1939, when the strain on this gifted, driven man, who had given so much to the Communist Party as well as to his union, became apparent in alcoholic binges, did the party leaders intervene. At their insistence he undertook to get into the field more often.[16]

The tension between communist union officials and local activists became more pronounced with the party's successes, especially when officials imposed their own strategic pragmatism on more headstrong union members. In 1936 militants in two small Victorian coalmines defied Orr's instructions and stopped work in pursuit of their claims. Orr blamed party members in nearby Wonthaggi for the action, which he said had flooded the pits with scabs. Charlie Nelson went down there to assist the striking unionists to retrieve their jobs. Those at the Sunbeam mine at Korumburra did so by occupying the mine in a dramatic operation portrayed in the film *Strikebound*, while the Wonthaggi miners marched on the other mine and defied armed guards to persuade the non-unionists to cease work. Even then, Orr was critical of the Victorians' audacity. 'I was concerned at the time that it might have been a boomerang against us, but they succeeded in holding the pit for 15 hours', he said—in fact the Sunbeam miners had barricaded themselves underground for more than two days.[17] When communists schooled in the iron discipline of the party's democratic centralism came to union office, they had to adjust to the very different forms of democracy that obtained among a diverse membership. They extolled mass activity in the expectation that it would follow their lead. They legitimated their leadership in rank-and-file support on the assumption that they could channel the instinctive impulses of workers into purposeful action.

Not all party unionists subscribed to industrial pragmatism. Thornton, of the Ironworkers, frequently championed traditional forms of militancy. The golden rule of any strike, he told the Eleventh Congress in 1935, was to 'knock the first scab over'. He continued on subsequent occasions to lament the moderation of front communism and the party's eschewal of class conflict. 'Where are our agitators in the Communist Party who can really stir up the people?', he asked a plenum of the central committee in 1937. Two years later he compared the gradualism of the ARU and the Miners' Federation with the combativeness of his own FIA. Miles rebuked him for his intemperance, but he was not alone in his misgivings about the reliance on industrial tribunals for piecemeal and painfully slow improvements. The ARU had to wait three years for settlement of claims it submitted in 1937. Having secured its first round of wage increases in 1937, the Miners' Federation's second round log of claims lodged in the same year dragged through the industrial tribunal until 1940. Orr himself appreciated the dampening effects of such displacement of energy. He observed at the central committee in 1937 that 'There is perhaps less mass agitational work . . . than at the time when our party membership was only ten per cent of its present size'.[18]

The consolidation of communist industrial activity posed even more sharply the perennial question of how to reconcile revolution and reform. The party held that capitalism could not satisfy workers' needs, yet the essential function of the unions was to make it do so. Leninism sought to resolve the contradiction by grounding trade union campaigns for better wages and conditions in a proper appreciation of the class struggle, and communists were therefore expected to guard against what were termed 'economist' illusions by drawing out the essential political lessons of every industrial campaign. The Communist International saw economism (or its left variant, anarchosyndicalism) as a persistent tendency of the Australian party, where practically 'the whole leadership is composed of trade union functionaries', who 'have not time for studying the political questions' and were more concerned to lead industrial campaigns than build the party. The Australian leaders themselves warned periodically against the same tendency. Orr told delegates to the Eleventh Congress that 'We must remember that we are not in the struggle merely for the sake of the struggle, to win an extra sixpence, etc., but that we are in there as revolutionaries'. J. B. Miles observed in 1938 that 'We are better trade unionists and our trade union numbers are greater, but too many who could do so without risk do not appear as Communists, while others overlook or submerge political questions under purely trade union problems'. Jack Blake went even further at the Twelfth Congress in the same year when he warned against the conventional demarcation of the political and industrial wings of the labour movement. The trade unions, he insisted, had keen interest in the struggle for peace and progress, so 'to term such a movement an industrial movement could only tend to narrow its scope and hinder its full development'.[19]

This larger purpose was served by a renewed emphasis on research, education and publicity. All of the major communist unions employed research officers to assist in the preparation of claims, and in union publications these officers habitually linked the conditions of the industry to the larger economic and political circumstances. All of them encouraged working-class education, none more assiduously than the ARU which appointed Gordon Crane, a Communist Party member, as national education organiser responsible for a wide-ranging syllabus. All established union newspapers were conducted by talented journalists, and these traversed both national and international issues. A single issue of *The Railroad*, the publication of the New South Wales branch of the ARU, saw the union general secretary editorialising on the united front, reviewing a compilation of Lenin's articles on Britain, scripting a dramatic presentation of the life of Lenin and presenting a chant for the release of Thälmann.[20]

Yet the politicisation of trade union activity brought its own problems. During the latter part of the 1930s the party's opponents alleged repeatedly that the party was imposing its own extraneous concerns on union members. Whether it be the denunciation of fascist belligerence in a union newspaper, union affiliation to a communist fraternal organisation or industrial action in support of an international campaign, the communist union officials were accused of putting political considerations ahead of the members' interests. Party members usually tried to answer such charges by showing the necessary connection between the industrial and the political. The *Silksworth* dispute, in which the maritime unions took up the master's victimisation of the Chinese crew of a vessel that happened to be bound for Japan, provides a good example of the efficacy of such linkages: 'Never had he met better unionists', said the Newcastle Trades Hall secretary of the Chinese seamen.[21] In its cultivation of the united and popular fronts, however, the party was inclined to minimise its distinctive purpose. Thus the resolution adopted in 1937, 'The Stronger the Communist Party the Stronger the Labour Movement', said that:

> . . . every Communist is to be looked upon as the best trade unionist, eliminating every remnant of appearing as an opposition force in the unions, and declaring publicly (and this should be the content of our everyday work) that the Communist Party does not interfere in the internal affairs of the unions.[22]

This was a long way removed from the recent rigours of Class Against Class, and it was a disingenuous description of an organisation that still organised its industrial members in union fractions under party direction. The interests of Australian workers did not stop at the factory gate, nor was their concern restricted to the size of their pay packet. Communists leavened the union movement with energy, resolution and breadth of purpose. But the web of loyalties that joined communist and non-communist workers remained fragile.

In opening the campaign for the united front, the party had expected that its growing industrial influence would yield a commensurate political influence. The structure of the Australian Labor Party, to which affiliated unions contributed substantial resources and in which they were well represented, seemed to offer the opportunity to push out from the workplace. Communist trade unionists were not themselves eligible for membership of the Labor Party, but they were able to throw their union delegations at Labor conferences behind moves to break down the ALP's isolationist foreign policy, to strengthen the left in local Labor branches, to contest right-wing control of state and federal executives, and to exert pressure on the parliamentary Labor Party for a united front.

The expectation came closest to realisation in New South Wales, where the left continued its campaign to unseat Jack Lang and his 'inner group' who ran the state Labor Party. The critics were known as the 'industrialists' because of their base in the Labor Council, but Lang's autocratic conduct and continuing feud with the federal ALP enabled them to win over a growing number of local Labor branches. Their challenge culminated at an unofficial state conference in early 1938 with the election of an alternative state ALP executive under the parliamentary leadership of Bob Heffron, who had been one of the Trades Hall Reds associated with the Communist Party in the early 1920s, before he drifted away and entered parliament in 1930. His defection now from Lang's inner group showed which way the wind was blowing. The industrialists had recently won control of the *Labor Daily* and radio station 2KY. Lloyd Ross's younger brother Edgar moved from editing the Miners' Federation's journal, the *Common Cause*, to join other party journalists on the staff of the *Labor Daily*. Under the management of Charlie Nelson, the paper was renamed the *Daily News* in 1938 and held a circulation of 40 000. In August 1939 the federal executive of the ALP convened a state unity conference, which in turn confirmed the victory of Heffron and the industrialists.[23]

Jack Hughes and Wally Evans, respectively the vice-president and secretary of what was now recognised as the New South Wales branch of the Labor Party, would both subsequently declare their membership of the Communist Party. Hughes, an official of the Clerks' Union, had in fact joined the party at the end of 1935 along with Bill Gollan, a leading member of the Teachers' Federation, and other ALP radicals. On the instructions of the party leaders, they kept their allegiance private so that they could continue to work in the Labor Party along with Lloyd Ross. It was not an arrangement likely to convince non-communists of the bona fides of the united front, and these undeclared communists chafed at their inability to participate in party life, but needs must go where the devil drives.[24]

New South Wales was a special case, the gains achieved there made possible by the split in Labor ranks. Elsewhere, the growth of communist influence in unions affiliated to the ALP produced a strong resistance. As party secretary, J. B. Miles renewed the appeal for a united front with a letter to the federal secretary of the Labor Party in November 1936 applying for affiliation. He received no response until April 1937 when the federal executive rejected the application. In a resolution formulated by that resolute anti-communist, Arthur Calwell, it declared the Communist Party an 'anti-Labor political organisation' in direct conflict with the policy, platform and constitution of the ALP.[25]

This fresh rebuff presented the party with a quandary. In pursuit of the United Front it had cultivated closer relations with members of the Labor Party. Communist sympathisers had been directed to join and work for unity within local Labor branches. Even before the Eleventh Congress in 1935 suggested that party members also might be sent into the Labor Party, the politbureau conducted regular discussions with a communist fraction of the New South Wales ALP state executive. In 1936 the party's rural organiser claimed that whole branches in regional towns of that state had been formed by communists, while Jack Blake estimated that twenty of the 60 local Labor branches in Victoria were under party control.[26] But as soon as these units of the united front showed their colours, as they did in Victoria by affiliation to the MAWF, they risked expulsion. Initially the communist leaders expected them to run the risk. During 1936 the party repeatedly warned against sacrificing principles to expediency and reminded sympathisers as well as followers that the achievement of a united front would require exposure of the anti-communist Labor leaders. Communists therefore regarded the fierce battles within Labor ranks as a healthy sign. That attitude changed, however, as the urgency of international considerations was driven home. The threat of fascism and the danger of war demanded the defeat of the Lyons government, which in turn required the election of Labor to office. In a discussion with the Anglo–American Bureau of the ECCI in Moscow in mid-1937, Richard Dixon stated that a split in the Labor Party had at all costs to be averted. At the Twelfth Party Congress in the following year he said that even though the Labor leadership still clung to isolationism, the task of the party was to provide 'constructive criticism'.[27]

The implications of this position were played out during the federal elections of 1937. As early as 1936 the party put forward the slogan 'Down with the Lyons Government'. Following the pointed advice of the Comintern official who wrote as S. Mason in the *Communist Review*, the politbureau decided early in 1937 to throw its weight behind Labor. 'Comrades, the role of reformism is no longer the same', J. B. Miles told the central committee in March 1937. 'Reformism is no longer the chief social prop of capitalism.' The urgent need for working-class unity in defence of democracy made a Labor government imperative. The party therefore resolved to withdraw all its Senate candidates and run just two members for the House of Representatives in the elections that were due in October, so that it could assist Labor to office. Miles, who had been brought reluctantly to this position himself, characteristically presented it as a vindication of the leading role of the party: since the masses were moving left, the party could only remain ahead of them if it dropped its opposition to the Labor Party. Explaining the decision to readers of the *Workers' Weekly*, Jack Blake was more prescient: 'there may be some comrades who will develop the idea that this line worked out by the central committee is a right-wing deviation'.[28]

There were such comrades, especially in north Queensland where the Communist Party had grown rapidly to challenge, if not surpass, the number of Labor Party adherents. The party section in Cairns objected strongly to the decision not to run a communist candidate for the federal seat of Kennedy. In Townsville, where Fred Paterson was to contest the seat of Herbert, the section criticised the party's general support for Labor and recorded its 'resentment at the way the change was forced on the membership'. Other northern sections also rejected national policy. The comrades in the tropics had a reputation for independence, so a recent decision to reduce them to a sub-district under the control of Brisbane did not improve their temper. Even after Jack Henry, who had recently taken up duties there as district secretary, forced compliance at an aggregate meeting in Townsville, resentment lingered. Pat Clancy, the northern sub-district organiser, resigned in protest, while Paterson continued to state his opposition through the party's north Queensland paper, the *Guardian*, which he edited. Miles explained to the central committee that the north Queenslanders were 'very radical' but suffered from an 'anarchical tendency'. To raise their level of political understanding he did permit two of them to publish temperate criticism of the party's election policy in the *Communist*

Review, then sternly corrected their misconceptions and reminded all party members that 'the discussion should be confined to consideration of how to apply the line'. A further contribution from Mount Mulligan, which observed that 'Comrade Miles' reputation for annihilating comrades who criticise the line of the Party is well known', did not appear. Of all the critics, Paterson attracted Miles's greatest ire. He was a lawyer, not a worker, and a liquidator. 'The trouble with Comrade Paterson is that dialectics is a completely closed book to him and always has been.' The politbureau withdrew his endorsement, and only restored it when Jack Henry guaranteed Paterson's loyalty.[29]

The other communist candidate was Ralph Gibson, who stood in the Victorian seat of Flinders, which included Wonthaggi. Party members in that state readily accepted the instruction to work for a Labor victory, indeed Len Donald and Jack Blake had great difficulty in persuading the local comrades to contest state elections held just three weeks before the federal ones. Donald claimed that there were more than a dozen branches of the Labor Party in Victoria ready to declare support for communist affiliation, but since that would have weakened Labor on the eve of the election the communists were instead working for Labor candidates in 'unofficial joint and parallel campaigns'. Such was their enthusiasm for the united front that they came under criticism for opportunist tailism. The leaders in Sydney judged that their election poster with the slogan 'RIP UAP, Vote Labor' gave no indication of the role of the Communist Party. Worse, in giving the impression that 'we are just foisting ourselves upon the Labor Party', it weakened rather than strengthened the united front, since it would lend credence to conservative allegations of the 'Red Bogey' and force the Labor Party to attack the Communist Party. All these predictions were fulfilled. Lyons did allege that the Labor Party was infiltrated by communists; Curtin did insist that Labor had no truck with them. To prove it, he cited the last federal election when communists had opposed his own party and, he claimed, attracted sufficient votes to defeat several Labor candidates. Communists responded with their own psephological analysis to buttress the claim that their preferences actually assisted Labor.[30]

The two communist federal candidatures were premised on the judgement that they offered a good prospect of success. Paterson came closest with 12 523 votes, about half those won by the successful Labor candidate. His 21.2 per cent of the total poll compared well with the 24.5 per cent he had attracted in a by-election for the smaller state seat of Bowen in 1936, which increased in the 1938 state election to 29.3 per cent. Gibson's tally of 4630 in Flinders, 9 per cent of the poll and 120 fewer votes than he had attracted in 1934, was a major disappointment. Along with the poor showing in the state elections when two communist candidates received 5700 votes, the Victorian result vindicated local critics, led by Thornton, who rose up in condemnation of Len Donald as district secretary and forced his transfer to Sydney. The party also put up four candidates for the New South Wales elections in March 1938, who attracted just over 10 000 votes. 'The Communist Party is a Labor Party—a Labor Party of a new type', Miles told the voters of Bulli in a radio broadcast. Eight communists stood for the Queensland parliament in the following month, and none came close to Paterson's level of support. The Western Australians contested the state seat of Fremantle in 1939 and mustered a derisory 308 votes. Well might the ECCI conclude that 'our comrades are recognised as good trade unionists, but politically our comrades are not recognised'.[31]

They had greater success in local government, especially in localities where they enjoyed close relations with Laborites. In Number 2 District the party negotiated a united front to contest the Lake Macquarie shire council elections in 1939 and campaigned vigorously among the miners, the unemployed and retired workers, small farmers and even the surf clubs. A majority of united front candidates were returned, the sole communist candidate only narrowly defeated. In the same year Fred Paterson was elected to the Townsville city council and Jim Henderson to the Wangaratta shire council in north Queensland, which encompassed the coalmining town of Collinsville.[32]

The Communist Party of Australia embraced the pro-Labor policy in 1937 because it believed Labor could win. Enormously encouraged by the electoral successes of the popular front in France and Spain, the Australians thought they could both assist and benefit from a Labor victory. They overlooked the crucial difference between those examples of the electoral popular front, where the danger of fascism was such that communist, socialist and radical parties entered into formal agreements to repulse it, and their own unrequited overtures to a parochial Labor Party whose leaders saw nothing to gain and much to lose from any such alliance. The non-Australian members of the Anglo–American Bureau were more sceptical, and rebuked the Australians for mechanical application of a tactic that called for wholehearted enthusiasm—thus the ECCI criticised Miles and Sharkey for cutting short the party's discussion of its election policy.[33]

Beyond such defects in implementation, however, there remained the stubborn fact that the Labor leaders did not want communist assistance. The Australian communists thus found that their subordinate position circumscribed any capacity to influence the Labor Party. Having renounced open antagonism, they were left as unwanted advisers, forever holding back their censure in order to sustain a non-existent partnership. As the Communist Party grew, this problem became more pronounced. In the immediate aftermath of its defeat in the 1937 federal election, Sharkey observed that the Labor Party was 'drifting onto the rocks', so that communists would have to help rebuild it. The party criticised John Curtin, the federal leader, for his cautious moderation but forbore from actions that might have endangered his position. It denounced the Labor premiers who spurned all offers of cooperation, but always stopped short of action that might split Labor or damage its popular standing: 'It is not the Labor Party as such we are fighting, but some of the reactionary right-wingers'. Communists had opened the campaign for a united front in the expectation that they could exert their considerable influence in the labour movement to win the Labor Party. As Bill Orr put it, by 'pulling strings in the trade unions and labour leagues' they would make the ALP amenable to their objects. Instead, by the end of the decade they found themselves accommodating their own policies to Labor's internal dynamics. Even as they pressed Labor to abandon its isolationist foreign policy, the communist leaders raised a moistened finger to test the wind lest they damage the illusory united front.[34]

A popular front called for a popular party. After 1935 the members of the central committee vied with each other to tell cautionary tales of the misplaced rigour that marooned Australian communism. One related a meeting of a party unit at Lithgow. It opened at 7.15 p.m. with the secretary reading through the correspondence. Then the five members present related their various activities: this one had to prepare the factory bulletin, another was responsible for finance, yet another had to arrange for sale of literature. Then there were social activities to organise, trade union business to consider, study classes that needed evaluation, the agenda of the next meeting of the Trades and Labor Council to be discussed, and so on. 'We learned that most of the comrades were in difficulties with their wives and had domestic troubles, and were also in trouble because they were unable to carry out all their party tasks.' The meeting finished close to midnight with much of the work still to be transacted. Another member of the central committee observed that the majority of recruits passed quickly out of the party. As soon as they signed the application form they were immediately weighed down with duties: 'We are apt to have arbitrary demands for activity and dues payments, and so-called deadheads are wiped off wholesale'.[35]

After 1935 the party began to recruit a higher proportion of white-collar workers, public servants, professionals and intellectuals; the unemployed members were returning to industry and no longer able to sustain the same level of activity. Lance Sharkey recognised the altered circumstances in his appeal to 'Join the Communist Party':

> You will not be asked to expose yourself to victimisation, nor have to spend all your time on Party work. The Party is 'growing up' and the old harmful 'leftism', as it will, in inner-Party life of the past, has been largely abolished.[36]

In his reply to the discussion before the Twelfth Party Congress, J. B. Miles noted 'remnants of an old sectarian defect, the idea that so-and-so is not developed, not a Communist, not up to a standard set by our stick-in-the-mud members'. He accepted that the new members had neither the time nor the resolution of the older diehards, and in any case the need to popularise the party called for a different style of work. There was no longer the same imminent threat of illegality or fear of victimisation, so that party members could now work openly as part of a 'people's movement'.

This lifting of the clandestine veil was a necessary condition of the popular front, heralded by Miles's own emergence from secrecy in 1935 and subsequent national tour. The party had previously drawn comfort from its semi-legal status, and counted the efforts to repress it as evidence of its importance, but that notoriety no longer suited the changed aspirations. It therefore commenced legal proceedings in May 1935 to compel the government to lift the ban on transmission of its publications. The action was joined by the Commonwealth, and occupied Fred Paterson and Clive Evatt for more than a year, but eventually it became clear to the attorney-general, Robert Menzies, that it was likely to succeed and he arranged for a settlement. The postal ban was lifted, and although federal and state agencies continued to hamper the party's activities, the danger of illegality receded.[37]

Party officials took advantage of the changed circumstances to lighten the load. Ralph Gibson, who was notorious for his own breakneck tempo, reported in 1939 that 'We do not do disciplinary driving as we used to do in Victoria and do not crack the whip as we used, but in place of that we have to produce amongst the Party members a real desire to be active'. As exhortation replaced peremptory instruction, party work was turned into a form of voluntary endeavour invested with transformative qualities. Thus Jean Devanny celebrated the 'unconquerable optimism, indefatigable zeal, flaming enthusiasm' of the stalwarts who stood at the factory gates or knocked on doors to peddle the party's newspapers; this was a constant, time-consuming task, and the frequent rebuffs had a debilitating effect on morale but Devanny assured the canvassers that 'every paper sold is a block of granite in the building of a Soviet Australia'. Similarly, a contributor to the pre-congress discussion in 1938 scattered capital letters as he anticipated the superhuman intelligence that would guide its work: 'Soaring like an Eagle, Keen-eyed and Far-visioned, High above the Sparrow-like Policy of Isolation and Sectarianism of the Leaders of the ALP . . . Congress will trace from its mountain eyrie of Marxism-Leninism the path that Labor must travel in order to reach its goal'. If ordinary members became accustomed to such overblown rhetoric, they were more likely to translate it into demotic idiom: thus the celebrated valediction of a stalwart from the inner suburbs of Melbourne, 'See you this arvo at the demo; up the revo!'[38]

One aspect of party life did not diminish. Early in 1935 the central committee announced a year of intensive study of Marxism-Leninism to remedy the indifference to theory that it saw as an ingrained national weakness. Party education was systematised around core texts, Marx and Engels's *Communist Manifesto*, Marx's *Wage-Labour and Capital* and *Value, Price and Profit*, Lenin's *What Is To Be Done?* and *State and Revolution*, Stalin's codification of Lenin and other exegeses. All recruits were expected to undergo training in classes that were conducted by senior members under the supervision of two new epigones, E. W. (Ernie) Campbell and L. H. (Harry) Gould. They also prepared a new training manual that blended dogmatism with patient endeavour. Its emphasis was on organisation rather than theory, and its exposition of the principles of activity elaborated the understanding needed for patient construction of the popular front. 'A mistake, a bad statement, a failure to carry out work, even hostility to the Party, does not necessarily mean that the person is "no good".' On the other hand, 'The Party is not weakened, but strengthened, by removing members who are incorrigible'. The object was practical dogma, 'revolutionary zeal combined with American efficiency'.[39]

Campbell, a Sydney recruit trained at the Lenin School, laid out communist doctrine as a set of syllogisms, finished and complete, which allowed no uncertainty and were able to encompass every eventuality. Gould was an Irishman who had spent time in the United States and began his party career with a flurry of heroically proletarian doggerel verse. He became the director of the party school, long foreshadowed and finally realised in a twelve-week intensive course undertaken in 1938 by twenty hand-picked students, who included Doug Gillies from South Australia, Ted Bacon from Queensland and Max Thomas, an unemployed activist turned printer. It was held in a block of flats at Kingsford, and attended by Sharkey and Dixon.[40]

The limitations of this party training are readily apparent. It replicated Stalin's schematic rendition of Lenin, who had himself rigidified the frequently speculative formulations of Marx and Engels into the language of a military manual. From time to time Australian communists talked of the need to speak more intelligibly. 'We are not a sect', insisted one in 1937, and should take care to use 'the language of the masses'. Harry Gould urged members to keep in mind the fresh faces in the audience in order to repeat the same leaden exhortation to 'speak in the language of the masses'.[41] In 1939 a party member took the creation of the party's national school as an opportune moment to call for a more substantial, 'painstaking overhaul of our language'. He argued that since communists were the inheritors and guardians of 'real human tradition', they should make 'purity of language' a matter of honour. As examples of the hackneyed phrases and lurid jargon that disfigured communist usage, he cited 'granite foundations', 'cohorts of reaction', 'the vile conduct of the Trotskyists', 'capitalist pimps' and 'fascist hordes' as well as the fulsome terms of endearment for party leaders. A number of members agreed with him. James Rawling did so as a linguistic conservative who objected to the errors of style and taste, the exaggeration, bathos and grammatical faults in party newspapers; others were more concerned with the habitual parroting of 'Communese', which acted as a barrier between communists and non-communists. Steve Purdy, for the central committee, defended the 'Leninist-Stalinist' vocabulary and also put the case for neologism: 'Advanced politics cannot be adequately voiced by conservative language'. Harry Gould suggested the critics suffered from a 'bourgeois intellectualism' and reminded them that 'In the beginning was the deed'.[42]

This was a rare instance of open debate of an issue that simmered in party circles. Communist rhetoric codified an understanding of politics that enclosed its practitioners within the certainties of language. It fired their enthusiasm and validated their heroic zeal, but it also separated them from non-initiates. Communist education systematised this understanding into a comprehensive philosophy. It provided intellectual justification for the arcane terminology but taxed the capacity of many. The inner mysteries of dialectical materialism, which was meant to animate an otherwise inert mechanism of base and superstructure, simply baffled many of those to whom it was expounded; witness the Newcastle maritime worker who proudly announced that he had been reading all about this 'diabolical materialism'. Yet the party's theoretical practice should not be dismissed too glibly. With all of its oversimplifications, it provided communists with a means of understanding their politics, a concentrated capacity for strategic analysis of the alternatives with which they were presented, and an ability to situate themselves in a larger historical perspective. More than this, it was their own proletarian knowledge. That provenance greatly enhanced communism's appeal since it presented a systematic alternative to the received knowledge and culture, an alternative that banished all traces of intellectual inferiority. You did not have to master such a system of ideas to feel its power.[43]

The growth of the party nationally was slow but appreciable. In early 1936 there were 3000 members on the books, a slight advance on the position at the time of the Eleventh Congress; by the middle of the year the number had fallen to 2700. Then came a significant lift, to 4124 at the beginning of 1937, and that level was maintained over the next two years. The proportion of unemployed members declined, those in unions increased. There were more women members, perhaps 15 per cent of the total by the end of 1937, and the number of middle-class recruits was apparent in the increase of street units at the expense of factory units. A new spurt of growth meant that the central committee issued 4421 cards in mid-1939.[44]

The pattern of growth is clarified by communist fortunes at the state level. In 1937 the party accepted the state boundaries as the basis of its own districts, reunited Broken Hill and the Riverina with Numbers 1 and 2 Districts in New South Wales, and joined Numbers 3 and 9 Districts in Queensland. New South Wales remained the party's home base, closely supervised by the Sydney-based politbureau, free from the deviations and factional tendencies that beset other states. It held its numerical supremacy with 1850 members in 1939.

Victoria, on the other hand, was a recurrent object of criticism. It had grown during the mid-1930s, to 683 members in 1935 and 950 in 1937, but never managed to throw off a reputation for unreliability. In 1935 Richard Dixon observed that 'the Melbourne comrades draw up beautiful plans of work' but never realised them and instead abused the central committee for their own failures. Part of the difficulty was the collision of powerful personalities. Two

Moscow-trained comrades, Len Donald and Jack Blake, had been sent down from New South Wales to provide direction. Donald, the loyal larrikin, was a first-class organiser and a terrible public speaker; Jack Blake was a powerful dialectician but utterly bereft of small talk. Together, they made a good team. However, they clashed repeatedly with the turbulent Ernie Thornton, who enjoyed considerable latitude as a leading union official and was permitted to carry the Victorian banner in repeated outbursts at central committee meetings in Sydney. In 1937 Blake left for the Soviet Union to represent the Australian party. In his absence, Thornton used the failure of the recent parliamentary campaigns to mount a coup. Abandoned by Miles, Donald confessed to bureaucracy, passivity, personal degeneracy and resistance to criticism, and was transferred to Sydney. He continued to serve the party faithfully but Blake thought he was never the same. He drank more, lost his perkiness, 'he didn't have the heart'.[45]

Thornton had little time for the niceties of the popular front. An instinctive militant who had left school at thirteen, he resented intellectuals: when Brian Fitzpatrick once told him he split his infinitives, he retorted he did not know what an infinitive was and indicated he thought that the blame lay with the grammar. Relations with Ralph Gibson, who replaced Donald as Victorian district secretary, remained strained and it was perhaps as well that Thornton shifted to Sydney in 1939 to base himself at the FIA national office. Gibson might be taken as an extreme example of the Melbourne radical tradition—earnest, improving, closely engaged in civic life, intellectually serious and sometimes censorious of the hedonism up north—that party leaders in Sydney found quite alien. 'Once and for all', Miles castigated him before the central committee as he reported on local ructions, 'we want to get rid of this situation that keeps on developing in Victoria'. Party membership there had slipped by this time to 860.[46]

Meanwhile, as noted earlier, Queensland rehabilitated itself from laggard to pacesetter. Where there had been 616 members in 1935, 361 north of the tropic and and 255 south of it, by 1939 there were 1220. With the turn to the fronts the improvement of the party's fortunes was dramatic: a rump of unemployed activists in Brisbane at loggerheads with the labour movement became a large, influential body of activists in unions that chafed against an unresponsive state Labor government. In early 1936 the district secretary confessed that 'twelve months ago if we had gone near Trades Hall we would have been assaulted'; by 1939 his successor could advise the politbureau that the party controlled the Brisbane Trades and Labor Council.[47]

It was further north that communism came closest to constituting a genuine mass movement. With their own regional newspaper and extensive involvement in local life, these communists provided impetus and direction for regional aspirations. They were both class warriors who fought absentee owners, union officers down south and Brisbane bureaucrats, and civic leaders of isolated occupational communities which had to create their own amenities. Thus they combined oppositional and affirmative roles. In the coalmining town of Collinsville, for example, the union officials, the cooperative society, the volunteer ambulance and even the local Caledonian society turned out to welcome J. B. Miles during his 1936 national tour. Collinsville sustained four Communist Party branches and just one ALP branch; 48 per cent of its voters supported Paterson for state parliament in 1938, while in neighbouring Scottsville the figure was 75 per cent.[48] The sugar and meatworkers, the railwaymen and wharfies in the larger coastal towns, all sustained a combative militancy. The Spanish Civil War and other anti-fascist campaigns had special appeal for Italian and Spanish immigrant families in the canefields. The party also assisted local Aboriginal initiatives and in 1936 even supported a four-month strike of Torres Strait Islanders working in the pearling industry. When Ralph Gibson went on a national tour on his return from the International Peace Congress in 1937, he remarked how the movement 'suddenly leaps into life when you get north of Townsville'.[49]

The red north sent a succession of able organisers down south, first Jack Henry in 1937, then Les Sullivan, Jim Slater and Albert Robinson; and no wonder, since they brought a distinctive elan that was captured in Jack Henry's boast to a Brisbane cadre, 'They're the *real* mass leaders'—he had what struck her as the 'queer idea that if you were from south of the Tropic of Capricorn you weren't a mass leader'. These men, and they were emphatic in their masculinity, carried with them a reputation for anarchism, a common party term of disapproval mixed with grudging admiration, which in this case signified a devil-may-care impatience for the constraints of officialdom. In Brisbane Ted Bacon thought the impetuosity arose from the fact that so many of the Queensland party members were seasonal workers—shearers, canecutters, mill-hands, meatworkers, wharfies—in a frontier setting free of the constraints of more settled regions. They certainly enjoyed a reputation for irreverence. 'We were larrikins', boasted the Toowoomban Claud Jones, 'bush larri-kins' with 'a militant don't-give-a-bugger attitude. If you were out of a job, you didn't get all upset and get ulcers, you'd go get a quid or thieve a quid or go to a two-up game or something else.' He liked to relate the occasion when J. B. Miles told him, 'The trouble with you, Jones, you're too much of a larrikin', and he replied, 'A few more fucking larrikins and less theoreticians, and we might get somewhere'.[50]

Western Australia also made ground. The 130 members in 1935 increased to 350 by 1939. Many of the recruits had spent their formative years in the Depression, sometimes on the dole and sometimes eking a living from casual work. As they found their way back to employment, these Depression communists began to challenge the entrenched moderation of the state Labor government and the compliant union officials who were its chief clients. Other party recruits were university students or young urban professionals, impatient with the provincial complacency and drawn to the Inter-national Peace Campaign, the Workers' Art Club, the Left Book Club and the Modern Women's Club established by Katharine Susannah Prichard. The substantial southern European communities living on the goldfields or working market-gardens around Perth contributed further recruits. The long distance from the eastern states also gave party members a relative autonomy. Only Wilfred Mountjoy, the district secretary, had substantial experience of national affairs, based on his apprenticeship at the national head-quarters in Sydney in the early 1930s. Katharine Susannah Prichard, a revered but somewhat remote figure, as the customary non-con-traction of her name suggests, alone possessed the prestige to challenge his authority, and she did so in missives to the central committee that warned of his drinking and unreliability. The politbureau left him in charge.[51]

South Australia, by contrast, languished. Party membership had declined from 53 in 1935, of whom perhaps 40 were financial, to 31 active members in 1936 and to a mere 20 in 1937. Some improvement began with the arrival from Melbourne of Alan and Joan Finger in 1936. Both university graduates, they had greatest success in building up the peace movement and Left Book Club with a number of middle-class recruits, including Elliot Johnston, a lawyer, and two sons of E. S. Kiek, the principal of the Congregational theological college. By 1939 there were 105 members of the party. The few union members were prominent in a local labour movement remarkably free of the divisions that characterised the eastern states. Tom Garland, who represented the Amalgamated Engineering Union, served a term as president on the Trades and Labour Council before becoming state secretary of the Gas Employees' Union in 1937, and Joe Flanagan, a tramway worker, was also president of the TLC in 1938. But they were too few to establish more than a personal following.[52]

Tasmania and the Northern Territory remained backwaters, despite spasmodic attempts to revive them. In 1935, when there were 21 members on the books in Tasmania, the party Secretariat attempted to explain that the Third Period was over and the islanders should stop abusing the workers; in particular, Sydney implored, 'avoid using unnecessary adjectives' in your leaflets. Number 8 District duly considered the advice and reported that the reason for its minute size was 'the crooks and sabotagers' who disrupted its work. Esmonde Higgins provided Sydney with a first-hand report when he went to Tasmania in 1936 as a WEA tutor. He found just ten active members, who seemed incapable of any collective activity beyond denigration. The 36 members recorded in 1939 were far less significant than sympathetic union officials such as Bill Morrow, the state secretary of the ARU.[53]

Party finances grew with membership, but remained precarious. Dues were set at sixpence per week for employed members and threepence for unemployed members. These membership fees were low, less than the cost of admission to the cinema, football or cricket, but most could afford no more. Some of the income from dues was retained for local or district use, some remitted to national headquarters. In 1939 the party's national budget provided for expenditure of £2725; of this £750 was for sustenance payments to party workers, £600 for propaganda, £350 to subsidise the *Workers' Weekly*, £250 for repayment of loans, and lesser sums for rent, office expenses and fares. Income from dues was expected to amount to £1680, and the balance would be made up of special levies and donations. But all of the states were behind with their dues payments, an endemic condition. At the local level we get a glimpse of the exigencies from a financial statement of the Sydney eastern suburbs section in 1936. There were 290 members who paid £8/3/- per week in dues (indicating that some were contributing more than sixpence). The income was split in four unequal parts, among the unit, section, district and central committee, which left the section £2 for its own needs. It expended £10 per week on rent, office expenses, and the support of four party workers (each of whom had to get by on a meagre weekly allowance of 32s 6d). The deficit was made up by collections, socials, raffles and donations.[54]

The burden of such special fund-raising was extraordinary. In 1936 the party raised £5000 in addition to ordinary dues. The north Queenslanders independently put together £1500 to establish their newspaper in that year while the Victorians issued £2150 in party bonds to purchase a new press for theirs. Some of the party's schemes were distinctly dodgy. One section organiser in Sydney ran a book on horse and dog races, and his own rake-off only came to light when he bought a house. Party cadres could hardly expect to become homeowners: Lance Sharkey's level of sustenance payment as party president, raised to £4/10/- a week in 1939 and still below the basic wage, made him the highest paid functionary of all. Communists in trade union posts usually enjoyed a better salary but paid a proportion of it directly to the party. The party had to borrow to acquire its Sydney headquarters, and borrow again to finance the purchase of new printing equipment. Guido Baracchi was the principal shareholder of the holding company for the party press, though when the *Workers' Weekly* moved in 1939 from its George Street premises to take up the offices at Rawson Place newly vacated by the Miners' Federation, it benefited from the union's generous terms.[55]

It is difficult to establish the level of foreign subsidy. The records of the Communist International and the files of Australian intelligence disclose various payments to Australia from the time of its formation, but neither source is sufficiently systematic to allow the calculation of reliable aggregate figures. During the 1920s it was possible to make financial transfers from Moscow to Sydney, via London, but this channel closed in the late 1920s. Australian delegates to the Soviet Union requested and sometimes received subventions. Higgins is reported as bringing back £1000 from the Sixth Congress of the Communist International in 1928, and Sharkey returned from Moscow with £720 in a money belt in 1930, which combined two six-month instalments of a monthly subsidy of £60 for the Pan-Pacific Trade Union Secretariat and £60 for the work of the Australian party. Bill Orr received £300 for the Minority Movement on the same visit and a further £260 by courier in 1931. Jack Ryan had previously obtained £170 for the PPTU, Jean Devanny received a cheque from London for nearly £200 for Workers' International Relief in 1931, and Ted Tripp claims that he was handed nearly £1000 for International Class War Prisoners' Aid by a representative of the Communist International in London at the same time.[56] These payments were intended to sustain the work of front organisations at a time when the party itself was indigent, and frequently they were diverted to defray the party's most pressing debts—not the least of J. B. Miles's service to the Australian party was his capacity to manage its finances so that it lived within its means. Irregular remittances continued during the 1930s, sent by individual draft from London to a cooperative third party here, but Australian intelligence was convinced that they amounted to no more than £500 per annum.[57] The celebrated Moscow Gold, which might have contributed a substantial proportion of the Australian party's income when it was on its uppers, was a negligible factor now that it flourished.

A number of the organisational changes were introduced in the late 1930s to simplify the party's cumbrous structure and thereby increase its appeal. At the 1938 Congress the old district committees became state committees, and the units became branches; the intermediary level of the section had been abolished in 1937. The change from district to state was merely nominal, but that from unit to branch aggregated small groups into larger ones, mostly based on residential location but also allowing for common-interest groupings.

There was keen debate about the name of the paper when the party decided to abandon the title 'Workers' Weekly', and further argument about whether it should identify itself as a communist publication. This first issue of the 'Tribune' describes itself as 'the people's paper'. The cartoon in the top left-hand corner was taken from the British 'Daily Worker'. (Source: 'Tribune', 1 September 1939)

Even the terminological changes marked a turn by the party towards familiar forms, as did the renaming of the party's newspapers. In June 1939 the Victorian *Workers' Voice* became the *Guardian*. As early as March 1938, a new title was canvassed for the *Workers' Weekly*, ostensibly on the grounds that it was no longer a weekly publication. Eventually the alternatives narrowed to *Tribune* or *Clarion*, both appropriately radical yet unspecific. Consultation established members' clear preference for the former; there was then further discussion whether the renamed paper should identify itself as a publication of the Communist Party. Eventually the politbureau decided 'there was no principle in the matter' and the secretariat should make a decision once the paper's layout was determined. The *Tribune* first appeared on 1 September 1939, the bannerhead shorn of its hammer and sickle, and identifying itself simply as 'The People's Paper'.[58]

The party also glossed its rules on democratic centralism. The rules had previously favoured the centralism at the expense of the democracy, prescribing a 'unified, firm discipline' and enjoining 'rapid and precise execution' of directives. The changes introduced at the Eleventh Congress emphasised the democratic basis of such authority, provided for 'free and positive discussion' in reaching decisions, and set down the accountability of all officials to representative assemblies. This was scarcely an accurate description of how the Australian party actually worked. Its national congress, nominally the supreme body, met only three times during the 1930s. Constituted by delegates elected by state conferences, its composition and agenda were in fact closely prescribed from above. The central committee it elected was also determined in advance, and it too became a passive, acquiescent assembly as its numbers grew: that elected at the Twelfth Congress in 1938 had 29 members. Real authority rested with the politbureau, which also expanded to seven permanent and three candidate members by 1938. All of these were full-time party or trade union functionaries, and the seven permanent members—Miles, Sharkey, Dixon, Wright, Orr, Docker and Simpson—had all occupied leading positions since the beginning of the decade. Dixon was assistant secretary to Miles, and Sharkey was styled party president. In a party attempting to re-invent itself in a more popular idiom, the signs of ossification were clear.

The pattern was replicated at each level of the party's work through the full-time party workers. They supervised, invigilated and drove every aspect of communist activity. The number of these cadres was never precisely calculated, but cannot have been less than 50; even the stripling Western Australian District supported four of them. Their frequency in a party so relatively small astonished the ECCI, which sensed that they both sustained and enclosed the Australian party. Sometimes Moscow called for a reduction of numbers and sometimes for an improvement in their quality: in 1937 it stipulated that every cadre should enjoy the confidence of 'the common people'.[59] The nature of cadres' duties imposed a heavy strain that a single example must illustrate. Bob Cram was born in Newcastle in 1906 and completed an apprenticeship as a carpenter before moving to Sydney. He joined the party in 1926, became a full-time worker and was elected to the central committee. In 1934 he was sent back to Newcastle as party organiser and guided its revival there. But by 1939 he was in serious trouble. With a sick wife, six children to support and mounting debts, his party work suffered. Cram interpreted the politbureau's strictures criticising him for not making greater progress as an attempt to isolate him, and alleged that Ted Docker, who was sent up from Sydney to remedy the weaknesses, was spying on him. He therefore resigned from his post and returned to work as a builder. This was perhaps an unusual example—the party accepted the resignation and lent Cram the working capital for his new venture—but it illustrates the confluence of personal and political difficulties.[60]

The authority of the cadre rested on something more than the party rules. Daphne Gollan captures one aspect of it in her

The cult of the leader transformed the party secretary, J.B. Miles, from a quiet dogmatist into an inspiring proletarian patriarch. Jean Devanny hailed a 'political genius' with a 'deep tenderness underlying' his hard exterior. Counihan's caricature sharpened Miles' features to suggest a sympathetic perspicacity. (Source: 'Communist Review', January 1939)

observation that 'these men lived isolated lives of unremitting work, much of it routine, for which they were paid a pittance'. She also notes the consequent danger of corruption in the sense of power that 'flowed from the deference with which we listened to them'. Members such as Gollan appreciated the extraordinary sacrifices the party functionary made, and respected such self-denial of worldly comforts, yet these same admirable qualities also exposed the cadre to the temptations of hubris. Austerity could isolate the cadre, dedication could confine him within a habitual round of activity, doctrine could become a substitute for creative endeavour. The party functionaries certainly cultivated an air of infallibility. Just as the party line was never wrong—rather, objective conditions had changed—so the expositors of the line embodied a collective infallibility. As so often, Guido Baracchi caught this reification of a constantly shifting yet always binding warranty when he implored that 'we find some other expression for the wretched term "Party line", which suggests something to be toed, or something to be negotiated as a tight-rope, or something to be sold as a commodity'. The line had to be toed, negotiated and sold, but behind it lay the force of experience, the habit of authority.[61]

The deference to which Gollan refers was cultivated with augmented assiduity in the later 1930s. From the time of J. B. Miles's national tour it became customary to greet him with special salutations; a banner inscribed with his name was flying at the Sydney Domain when he returned there in August 1936. Profiles of Miles and Sharkey presented them as both ordinary and extraordinary. Miles was portrayed as a slight man with a Scottish burr, a 'hard-clamped aggressive mouth' softened by the 'twinkle deep back in the eyes' (and this was how Noel Counihan's caricature portrayed him to readers of the party press). He smoked and drank in moderation, was not a teetotaller but objected to 'drinking to the detriment of the Party'. He worked a twelve-hour day but relaxed with popular cinema, where he preferred Joe Brown to Clark Gable and Popeye to Hollywood he-men, as well as light fiction. 'It's a big jump from Lenin to Edgar Wallace but I do it, easily.' Jean Devanny went further in an encomium written for the women of Bulli when Miles stood for that state electorate in 1938:

> I have known many men in politics and literature and art, but judged from every point of view, J. B. Miles stands out among the biggest, in artistry, in principle. To hear him analysing a situation, stripping every unessential from it, laying bare its core, is an experience a Communist can never forget.

The hyperbole, and the choice of expression, is startling. Elsewhere Devanny recorded the coldness and anger with which her secret lover treated her, his puritanism and contempt for culture. Yet here she hailed him as a 'political genius', the pride and champion of all women, with a 'deep tenderness underlying that often biting tongue': all who went to him in their trials felt his 'grandeur of character'.[62]

Something similar occurred in the profile of Sharkey. He was presented as a son of the soil, steeped in communist theory, yet always a man of the people. The list of his virtues was directed so unerringly to his limitations as to suggest parody. It was noted that 'like all the leaders of our Party, Comrade Sharkey was temperate in his habits'; in fact his binges in Moscow were notorious. He was a brilliant mass agitator; actually his oratory was leaden. He had an instinctive genius; yet when he took up Lenin's favourite pastime of chess, lesser party members had to be careful to lose. Perhaps these pastiches passed over the heads of these victims; in any event, their status in party assemblies was inviolable. Thornton, the most audacious of the notables, was brought before the politbureau for displaying insufficient respect at the party congress in 1938. He explained that he had made jokes at Sharkey's expense because of the party president's 'seriousness', which exacerbated his own 'lackadaisical attitude'. After appropriate self-criticism he was warned not to repeat the offence.[63]

13

The socialist sixth of the world

The Australian party's veneration of its leaders was modelled on the Soviet adulation of Stalin, and this reached new extremes as the CPSU general secretary consolidated his domination over every aspect of Russian life. Stalin's decisive influence on the policies of the Communist International has already been noted. He determined the turn to the extreme policies of Class Against Class at its Sixth Congress in 1928, and then the belated turn back to the anti-fascist front in 1935; he imposed the party rules that turned democratic centralism into centralised control, and enforced a regimen of unquestioning obedience, self-criticism and expulsions. In 1939 he would cynically abandon the anti-fascist alliance for an accommodation with Hitler; in 1941 the German invasion of the Soviet Union would result in unprecedented slaughter; in 1943 Stalin would dissolve the Communist International as an empty token of goodwill towards his capitalist allies. Only after his death in 1953 could his successor Khrushchev reveal his crimes, and even then many Australian communists refused to believe them. Stalin's dark shadow falls as a curse across the entire history of communism, and all attempts to lift that curse have failed.

The coinage of the term 'Stalinism' was an attempt to exorcise it. Originally employed by Leon Trotsky and others driven out of the communist movement by Stalin, 'Stalinist' is a recurrent epithet in the reflections of those Australian communists whose testimony informs this history, as they looked back in old age on the ruined cause they had served so ardently. In identifying Stalinism as the source of error they refer to a combination of attitudes and habits derived, by compulsion or emulation, from the Soviet leader that vitiated their endeavours: manipulativeness, mendacity, suspicion, intolerance, ruthlessness. Trotskyist and other left critics would go further and apply the attribution to the whole of the communist movement Stalin directed, one that put party before class, expediency before principle, the deformation of socialism as practised in the Soviet Union over revolutionary ideals. This emphasis on a single individual sits ill with the Marxist method of historical materialism. It makes Stalin the scapegoat for consequences that have emerged repeatedly in communist regimes. It disregards the recurrent tendency for the communist parties of other countries to throw up their own leaders who practised the same lethal megalomania: Mao Zedong, Kim Il Sung, Nicolae Ceausescu, Pol Pot. Most contentiously, it exonerates Lenin from the enormities of Marxism-Leninism.

Lenin played no part in the construction of the couplet. That was a project supervised by Stalin, just as the preservation of Lenin's embalmed body in a mausoleum in Red Square served as a relic for the posthumous cult that Stalin fostered as Lenin's heir. Nor would Lenin have recognised Stalin's codification of *The Foundations of Leninism*, with its reduction of fluid, contingent arguments into a closed system in which every component had a single, fixed meaning. Like the other leading Bolsheviks, Lenin underestimated the crafty Stalin until it was too late to dislodge him from the post of party secretary. A cosmopolitan intellectual immersed in world affairs, Lenin regarded the provincial zealot as a useful functionary. His own party name, Lenin, was taken from the river Lena; Stalin's was a boast, the man of steel. Lenin seized power in the expectation of world revolution and then had to improvise support for a vast and impoverished federation of pre-capitalist peoples; Stalin captured control over the Communist International and made it into a tool of Great Russian interests.

The overwhelming difficulty facing the Bolsheviks in the aftermath of their revolution was backwardness. The civil war had destroyed industry and reduced agriculture to starvation levels. The temporary solution they adopted in the early 1920s was to encourage private production of food by peasants on smallholdings, but this began to break down because of the inability of factories to produce sufficient manufactured goods to entice rural producers to sell their agricultural goods in the cities. Stalin's solution when he came to power at the end of the decade was to embark on breakneck industrialisation and collectivise agriculture. Under the Five Year Plan introduced in 1929 he conscripted labour into vast construction projects. Coalmines, steel furnaces and mills, power plants and engineering works were created almost from scratch, while in the countryside 25 million peasant holdings were gathered into just 200 000 collective farms. Every unit in this centralised economy had to meet its production quota, and all that was left over from subsistence levels of consumption was directed back into further growth. Such a system was primitive, inefficient and always prey to corruption. Established at the expense of immense disruption and acute famine, it achieved its rapid growth by constant driving and speed-ups, which in turn were obtained by a combination of exhortation and terror. The Third Period of Class Against Class augmented the Soviet fear of enemies without and within. Extension of the class war into the countryside unleashed mass killing of the *kulaks*. Yet this breakneck economic transformation was accompanied by a cultural revolution that exalted the heroic capacity of the people, and there is unmistakable evidence of a genuine popular support for Stalin's leadership. He demanded long toil for low pay, but he offered a job, food, clothing, subsidised housing, education, and hope for a better future. He oppressed workers and he exalted them, ignored their privations and yet ruled in their name.

By the mid-1930s the worst rigours of collectivisation and enforced industrialisation were easing, and with them passed the last vestiges of revolutionary egalitarianism. Stalin now waged war on the dreamers with show trials of Old Bolsheviks and mass purges that reached far down into the party. The new Soviet constitution he introduced in 1936, with its sham democratic provisions and guarantees of freedom of speech and assembly, 'only in accordance with the interest of the workers and for purposes of strengthening the socialist system', abandoned any lingering expectation that the communist state would wither away to a stateless society. Stalinism meant a powerful, unlimited state, with centralised bureaucratic planning and enforced unanimity; it abolished civil society, allowed no genuinely representative institutions, no intermediary between the rulers and the ruled. Like its creator and namesake, it was both triumphal in its patriotism and intensely suspicious in its constant vigilance. An officer of the dreaded security police boasted during the height of the terror that 'If Marx fell into our hands, within a week we would have him admit to being an agent of Bismarck'.[1]

The Soviet Union had served as both model and guide to the Australian party during the 1920s, but for most members it still remained a distant presence. During the 1930s the gap closed. Organisations such as Friends of the Soviet Union propagated more systematically the achievements of the socialist sixth of the world, which stood in stark contrast to the capitalist heartlands. These were faltering, beset by crisis, racked by conflict; it was advancing, unified and triumphant. This Soviet utopia was eminently practical, dominated by the realisation of great plans, the construction of gargantuan buildings, factories, dams, monuments in steel and concrete to a new kind of civilisation. New media, such as Soviet cinema and shortwave radio broadcasts from Moscow, brought heroic images and celebratory reportage of this prodigious success to sympathetic Australian audiences. More Australians travelled to the Soviet Union and participated in a carefully controlled itinerary of political tourism. As the Communist International exercised a more regular supervision of the Australian party, so Soviet communism pressed more heavily on the loyalty of its members.[2]

As befitted an important party auxiliary, the post of national organiser of the FOSU was entrusted to leading comrades. Jack Morrison, later manager of the International Bookshop in Melbourne, was the first, followed by Ted Tripp after he returned from the Soviet Union late in 1930, then by Sam Aarons, and then Bill

Thomas, the veteran party journalist. To its monthly publication, *Soviets To-Day*, were added the news weekly *Moscow News* and the glossy *USSR in Construction*, a colour pictorial of colossal engineering triumphs and sturdy pulchritude. Local branches of the FOSU organised lectures and socials, marked key anniversaries and events in the Soviet Union's revolutionary history and generally promoted its benefits.

Membership of the FOSU fluctuated according to the efforts of organisers. It was never a mass organisation, but formal membership mattered less than friendship. Sympathy and support for the Soviet Union might lead to recruitment to the Communist Party of Australia, but that too was a secondary objective. Rather, the FOSU sought to break down the popular antagonism, the strategic alliances and economic blockades that threatened and isolated the Soviet Union, as well as the torrent of adverse publicity that discredited it. Especially after Stalin achieved supremacy, it responded to the fear of attack with an insistently affirmative message. Insofar as it offered a critique of capitalism, it did so by presenting the Soviet Union as an exemplar of progress that others might follow. In the circumstances of the Depression this meant stressing the benefits of a planned economy over the anarchy of capitalist markets, as in the 1932 pamphlet *Contrasts* published by the FOSU in Adelaide, which set out the advantages of production for public benefit rather than private profit, work for all instead of mass unemployment, good working conditions instead of wage cuts and sweating, systematic public welfare rather than the dole. Written by a recent party recruit in response to a local anti-communist jeremiad, it projected a complete solution to local ills onto a distant workers' paradise.[3]

The FOSU also organised tours of the Soviet Union. Earlier visits by Australian union leaders had occurred under the auspices of the Red International of Labor Unions and the Pan-Pacific Trade Union, but from the early 1930s a regular routine became established.[4] A contingent consisting principally of union representatives would arrive in the northern spring and depart several months later seized with enthusiasm for what they were shown. The first such delegation set off from Australia in March 1932. To prepare its members for what they would find, Itzhak Gust accompanied them on the voyage and taught them Russian history as well as a few words of the language. To coach them in their intended roles of proselytisers of communist achievement, the Soviet hosts asked them before they returned to prepare a report of their impressions. The guests duly set down what would become a standard inventory of attractions: good working conditions, excellent schools and hospitals, a high standard of cultural and social life, emancipation of women from domestic drudgery, freedom for national minorities, the impressive evidence of construction and 'the faith of the people in the leadership of the Communist Party'. There was one dissident who contrasted the enthusiasm of the people with the long food queues, and concluded from the trains full of impoverished peasant families that the pace of collectivisation had been too rapid, but his reservations were brushed aside.[5] The chief controversy arose instead when, upon return to Australia, one of the delegates was barred from returning to his job in the Victorian Railways and another, Beatrice Taylor, was sacked from the New South Wales teaching service for her public praise of the Soviet accomplishment. This became a regular hazard for subsequent delegates, in addition to the difficulty of obtaining passports for travel to Russia and the seizure by Australian customs officers of literature, slides and film that the delegates brought back to Australia.[6]

These trips generated a considerable volume of books, pamphlets and articles over the course of the decade. At once travel writing and tract, the literature reveals some common themes and instructive variations. Trade union delegates characteristically judged the Soviet Union against the conditions with which they were most familiar. Thus *Red Cargo*, the report of a 1934 visit by Jim Healy and another wharfie, gave a detailed account of port operations in Odessa and Leningrad, praised the provision of clothing, canteens and clinics, the participation of women in the industry, and the management consultation with the union. The Australians did not ignore Soviet weaknesses—both the ports they inspected required greater mechanisation—but laid particular emphasis on permanency of employment in the Soviet Union, in contrast to the chronic insecurity of the Australian workforce, and on the gains in productivity that went with the better working conditions. From this detailed consideration of their own area of interest, the authors worked outwards to the general amenities of Soviet life: the provision of

Jim Healy and Ben Scott reported their impressions of the Soviet Union in the pamphlet Red Cargo, published by the Friends of the Soviet Union in 1935. The two were representatives of the Mackay and Sydney branches of the Waterside Workers' Federation, and their report concentrated on the maritime industry. The design and typography contribute to the tone of triumphant modernity. (Source: National Library of Australia)

housing, education, health care, sporting and cultural facilities. 'It only remains with the workers of Australia', they concluded, 'to do all that lies in their power to prevent any attack on this great country, the first workers' country'. Healy joined the party upon his return to Australia. In similar vein the Melbourne tramworker, who was one of eight miners and transport workers to visit in 1935, emphasised the rapid strides in urban public transport in his glowing account of the new Russia. Another, a north Queensland worker, found the fact that there was 'no crawling for tips' as remarkable as the new Moscow underground. He also lent authenticity to his testimony with some parochial touches: 'There is something they call black bread. I call it poison.' A Wonthaggi delegate perhaps strained credulity with his claim that 'the drink problem was being tackled in the right spirit' with the provision of mineral water.[7]

For the party faithful the pilgrimage to the Soviet Union possessed an augmented significance. Here was the word made real, the vindication of their own embattled status and the augury of their future success. Their reports paid greater attention to the legendary sites of revolutionary history in Leningrad and Moscow, the Winter Palace, Lenin's mausoleum, Red Square. A highlight of the tour was the May Day parade, a mass choreography of Soviet power as an endless procession of workers, peasants, troops, artillery and tanks passed before the party leaders. 'At six o'clock in the evening', wrote Prichard, 'they were still moving in dense dark streams with their scarlet banners flying, along the river banks, white with snow'. The spectacle moved one Australian who in 1934 witnessed this 'kaleidoscope' of 'the achievements of seventeen years of Soviet power' to wonder 'how long it will be before we will be witnessing a similar spectacle—from the GPO steps in Martin Place'. Tony McGillick, who became FOSU organiser in 1938, wrote similarly of his visit in that year. 'The Soviet people, clear-eyed, strong in body and mind, proudly march on from victory to victory.' Sam Aarons's mother Jane returned in 1934 from her second tour of the Soviet Union to a poem that contrasted Russian achievement with the tawdry trappings of Victoria's sesquicentennial celebrations:

> You've returned to us from Russia
>   Where life is sane and whole,
> And not one Worker's unemployed
>   And no-one's on the dole.
>
> You've returned to us from Russia
>   And your coming's a rebuke,
> For all we have to show you
>   Is a warboat and a Duke.
>
> And lollysticks and pylons
>   And Union Jacks as well,
> You've left an earthly paradise
>   To come back to a Hell.[8]

A third category of visitor was the fellow-traveller, a term that came into vogue during the period of the popular front to describe those who shrank from joining the Communist Party and all that membership entailed, yet sympathised with its apparent ideals. Such sympathisers were important for at least two reasons. First, they provided independent corroboration of communist claims. Second, they were more likely to reach a wider audience than party members, whose own testimony generally went unreported in the mass media. (Katharine Susannah Prichard did arrange for serialisation in the Melbourne *Herald* of an account of *The Real Russia*, but Keith Murdoch terminated the arrangement midway through her 'provocative' reports.)[9] The Soviet Union lent itself to the yearnings of progressives, who saw it as a demonstration of the efficacy of state planning, as well as to idealists, who could project upon it their schemes for the regeneration of humanity. Neill Greenwood, the professor of metallurgy at the University of Melbourne, attended a conference at Kharkov late in 1932 and contrasted the scientific advances there with the neglect of science in the West. The crucial difference was the alignment of Soviet science with popular needs and aspirations:

> Having passed through Canada, USA and England on the way to Russia, and having seen in those countries helplessness and despair— just the same as had been left behind in Australia—the unparalleled enthusiasm and optimism of Russia came as a refreshing change.

Harold Woodruff, head of the bacteriology department at the same university, spoke similarly of his visit a year later: 'Their educational system, medical services and housing arrangements were irreplaceable'.[10]

The prominent feminist, Jessie Street, found the same validation of her expectations when she travelled to the USSR for the first time in 1938. On the morning after her train crossed the Polish border, she awoke and pulled up the blind to rejoice at the sight of women working alongside men on track maintenance. Then followed inspections of creches, factory nurseries, maternity clinics, and the discovery that gender equality brought 'a completely different set of moral values'. She returned 'convinced that the new way of life which they were developing in the USSR would put an end to the exploitation of man by man, and of women by men as well'.[11]

The glowing reports of Greenwood and Street are similar to those of celebrated European and American visitors to the Soviet Union during the 1930s. George Bernard Shaw, the Webbs, H. G. Wells, Lion Feuchtwanger, Heinrich Mann, a whole gallery of non-communist intellectuals wrote glowing accounts of Stalin and his achievements. The question that arises out of this mass of testimony is how the evils of the regime can have escaped the visitors. For some Western critics, the fellow-travellers were gullible dupes, flattered by the attention paid to them, mesmerised by power, allowing their impatience with human imperfection to exalt an odious despot. For some post-Soviet Russians who have read their apologias, the fellow-travellers were deliberate falsifiers. These charges imply that the evils of Stalin's Russia were clearly visible. In fact, the visitors inspected a carefully chosen set of showplaces. They did not speak the language and were reliant on translators. Their access to people was restricted. They knew little Russian history and took the evidence of fresh construction, modern amenities and naive enthusiasm as indices of progress. Furthermore, they were profoundly unfamiliar with the politics of communism and had little interest in acquiring an understanding. Neither Greenwood nor Street, nor the other Australians who extolled the achievements of the Soviet Union, were interested in the works of Marx or Lenin, much less in joining the Communist Party of Australia.[12]

The Soviet miracle culminated in the prodigious achievements of a Donbas coalminer, Alexi Stakhanov. Inspired by a speech of Comrade Stalin on the need to apply socialist zeal to practical tasks, Stakhanov applied himself to the improvement of coal production. As he explained to the All-Soviet Union Central Council of Trade Unions, meeting at the Moscow Palace of Labour in 1934, 'I was always a good worker, and used to produce 14 tons of coal in a day. However, on the day on which I descended the shaft to operate the new methods, I produced 102 tons of coal.' Stakhanov's achievement was extolled by Stalin, his methods were taken up by whole detachments of Stakhanovites and applied throughout Soviet industry. These methods, which applied indomitable enthusiasm to the performance of simplified, repetitive tasks, were well suited to the management of a command economy as it built up heavy industry and drilled an inexperienced workforce in the techniques of mass production. More than this, they provided the template for a socialist work ethic that would produce 'a people of a new and special type', people who would find joy in labour. Stalin told the same assembly that heard Stakhanov, 'It is very difficult, comrades, to live on freedom alone'. In the schema that now guided communist policy, socialism was a higher stage of historical development than capitalism because it superseded the antagonism between the owner of capital and the seller of labour. As the first socialist society, the Soviet Union would necessarily triumph over its enemies by out-producing them. Stakhanov provided the model 'hero of labour' who would ensure this victory.[13]

The Australian party's celebration of Stakhanov sat awkwardly with its fierce opposition to the introduction of similar methods to Australian industry. After all, Orr and Nelson's campaign against mechanisation of the coal industry had singled out for criticism the very techniques that Stakhanovites employed: the simplification of the work process at the expense of craft skills, the application of new technology to intensify the tempo of work, the setting of higher quotas and extension of shift work, the payment of bonuses for results. If these methods were dangerous in Australian pits, were they not equally dangerous in the Donbas ones? If the drive for greater efficiency increased the exploitation of Australian workers, did not the same process oppress their Soviet counterparts? Party leaders sought to rebut such comparisons by emphasising the different provenance of the Stakhanov movement. It was not a capitalist speed-up but a 'grand upsurge of socialist initiative, bursting all the bonds and limitations imposed in class society'. It was not exploitative but a 'sane and rational' augmentation of productive capacity that demonstrated socialism was 'immeasurably superior' to capitalism. J. B. King, the former Wobbly who had led resistance to the efficiency experts in Australia during the First World War, returned from several years as a mine engineer in the Soviet Union in the early 1930s to lecture on the achievements of the Stakhanovite movement. The Australian party adopted the same methods of 'shock work', and 'socialist competition' in its own work, as one branch challenged another to recruitment contests or newspaper sales drives.[14]

A persistent theme in Australian reportage of the Soviet regime was the enthusiasm of its people. For party members and fellow travellers alike, it was this manifestation of popular support that validated the communist experiment. Professor Greenwood contrasted the 'unparalleled enthusiasm and optimism' of people from all walks of life in the USSR with the 'helplessness and despair' of those in capitalist countries. Katharine Susannah Prichard was struck most of all with the energy of those she met during her trip in 1934: '. . . how people work and study and amuse themselves so indefatigably was a mystery to me'.[15] These claims—and almost every visitor of the 1930s offered variations upon them—challenge the image of Soviet life that is now dominant, one of long-suffering victims of a brutal dictatorship which squeezed out all initiative and spontaneity, and left only cynicism and passive conformity. However, such imagery is reinforced by the final collapse of the Soviet Union, when a generation who had known nothing else but economic inefficiency, obsolescent technology, corruption and indifference finally turned their backs on the sterile state ideology that no one, not even the *nomenklatura*, could any longer believe. That outcome, in turn, shapes a historical literature that has always been subject to partisan considerations. Those opponents who allowed the Stalinist dictatorship no redeeming virtues, for so long confounded by the persistence of the Soviet regime, now triumphantly deride the revisionists who insisted that it had enjoyed a measure of popular support.[16]

Then as now, critic and supporter alike place undue weight on this aspect of the Soviet regime. Each treats democracy as the inseparable companion of liberty. The opponent of communism sees its denial of even the most basic freedoms manifested in the absence of popular support, while the defender takes popular enthusiasm as indicative of a liberatory dimension. Yet the history of the twentieth century has surely weakened the common nexus the disputants assume. In the Nazi stronghold of Nuremberg in the 1930s, the countryside of China during the Cultural Revolution of the late 1960s, the Iranian capital of Tehran a decade later, we surely see variant forms of popular tyranny. As the product of an intensely ideological movement that allowed no alternative to its claim to interpret the will of the people, the Russian Revolution is prototypical of such mass mobilisations. Above all, it came first. Leaving aside the French Revolution of 1789, to which argument by analogy repeatedly returned, there were no modern precedents to guide discussion of the paradoxical trail it blazed. Libertarian in its goals, authoritarian in its methods, it plunged a backward society into civil war and then forced it into rapid modernisation. International in its scope, increasingly national in its calculations, it resolved its contradictions by inflaming passions and inculcating terror. The purges of the party's ranks, the Great Terror that carried off real and imagined opponents, and the show trials that paraded former leaders to confess their treachery, these were something more than measures of repression whereby the Soviet leadership consolidated its supremacy. Rather, they involved the population at large as active participants.

Australians who spent long enough in the Soviet Union to experience this regimen were troubled by its contradictions. As foreign residents they enjoyed certain privileges, but they entered more fully into Soviet life than could the members of the delegations who were escorted around selected showplaces. Stan Moran and Ernie Campbell enjoyed far better food than the ordinary Muscovite while students at the Lenin School in 1934, but they still found the diet extremely hard. Almost by definition, such longer-term residents were politically trustworthy. Even a non-party member such as Betty Roland, who accompanied Guido Baracchi to the Soviet Union in 1933, felt she was 'participating in a great historical event'. They lived in Moscow and Leningrad for more than a year, he as a translator, she as a journalist then a typist, and Roland's diary recorded the 'contrast between the optimism here and the pessimism of the outside world'. The diary also expressed the contrast between privilege and hardship, the cynicism of party notables and the kindly, warmhearted, patient Russian people. She witnessed a local form of political interrogation, the *chistka*, and observed that 'the all-powerful Party has its terrifying aspects and even Guido seems a little shocked by this ruthless treatment of a loyal member'. She befriended an English communist, Freda Utley, whose Russian Communist Party husband fell under suspicion and would perish in a labour camp; and she observed that Katharine Susannah Prichard, who visited them in 1933, was beset by misgivings. Prichard's subsequent account of that trip, written after she returned to Australia to find her husband had taken his life, gave no hint of any such doubt. For that matter, Roland joined the Communist Party after she returned to Australia.[17]

Another Australian resident was Audrey Blake, who lived in Moscow with her husband Jack from 1937 to 1938, when he was the Australian party representative and she worked for the youth section of the Communist International. This was at the height of the terror, when, besides the millions who were summarily arrested, convicted and executed or simply disappeared, the remaining Old Bolsheviks were made to confess their crimes in show trials. In August 1936 Zinoviev and Kamenev had been tried, along with fourteen others, and executed for their self-confessed crimes against the the revolution. Radek and sixteen others were similarly found guilty in January

1937 (though Radek himself was temporarily spared to denounce others), and in March 1938 Bukharin followed with twenty more. Audrey Blake's retrospective vignette evokes the 'strange atmosphere' in which she lived and worked. At the Hotel Lux on Gorky Street, where the foreign communists resided, one after another of the rooms was sealed after its occupant disappeared. The very official who warned her not to mix with the Russians was himself arrested as an enemy agent a week later. She claims to have felt no sense of personal danger—indeed she and her husband 'felt safer than we did at home where we were unceasingly proclaimed "the enemy" '—and suggests that all the 'big tragedies' of the Stalinist era were enacted 'silently, outside our purview', yet the papers of the time were dominated by the trials of the Old Bolsheviks. With her faith in the revolution and the party unshaken by her own brushes with authority, she insists that 'we didn't feel in danger since we knew we weren't spies or agents'.[18]

Jack Blake's memories have a similar quality. He would eventually become one of the most thoroughgoing critics of Stalinism, a phenomenon he came to appreciate was lodged deep in the communist project. Furthermore, he was one of the few Australians to learn Russian and undoubtedly appreciated the nightmare quality of the purges. As his and Audrey's neighbours in the Hotel Lux disappeared, he recalled that he believed they 'must have been agents and spies' and that 'I didn't worry because I knew I wasn't'. Yet at the back of his mind was the knowledge that 'if I'd been snatched away', only Audrey would have known of his innocence. 'In Australia, if word had got back that Blake was arrested because he was a spy or whatever, people would have accepted that he must have been.' Upon his return to Australia he cited the courtroom confessions of the Old Bolsheviks as conclusive evidence of their guilt. There was no terror in the Soviet Union but rather a 'spirit of freedom, joy and happiness', not sympathy for the Trotskyite 'agents of fascism' but relief they had been unmasked, no personality cult but rather love and admiration for the 'genius' of Stalin.[19] Another party member celebrated him in verse:

> They fear him, the silent one, the unscrupulous one.
> For he is no vain scribbler, no vain talker, no senseless screecher,
> He is more powerful than they.

He, the big-hearted one, the inviolable will of the Party,
Has mastered their weapons, has excelled . . .[20]

The evils of the Stalinist terror weighed like a nightmare on the minds of the survivors. Its effects fatally impaired communism's claims to be a movement of liberation, and resisted every effort to explain or justify them, including Khrushchev's official apology in 1956. Frank Hardy's novel *But the Dead Are Many*, written nearly 40 years after the terror, relates the personal and political disintegration of two ageing Australian cadres, each obsessed with the fate of Nikolai Buratakov, whose own confession for the sake of the party to the crimes he did not commit infects one and then the other with guilt and morbid despair. The character of Buratakov is based on Nikolai Bukharin, whose trial Jack Blake had attended (and when the novelist quizzed this eyewitness, it puzzled Blake that Hardy was most interested in Bukharin's appearance). The first of the Australian cadres is based loosely on the party organiser Paul Mortier, who was only nineteen when Bukharin was executed, but became deeply troubled by Khrushchev's revelations and eventually took his own life. The second allows Hardy himself to offer a retrospective penance. Hardy came late to such an acknowledgement of Stalin's murderous legacy, but every Australian communist had to make her or his own accommodation with it.[21]

For those prepared to attend to it, there was no lack of evidence. Foreign correspondents reported the mass arrests, reputable independent commentators cast doubt on the show trials. The problem was that the admirers of the Soviet Union were so habituated to anti-communist slanders that they usually ignored the contradictions and dismissed the objections. Nettie Palmer thought the similarity of the confessions offered by the accused had a 'sinister sound', but Ralph Gibson attributed her doubts to 'Trotskyist tendencies'. Gibson's own pamphlet *Freedom in the Soviet Union*, written before the trials, established a framework in which the apparent freedom of the capitalist West was illusory, the supposed lack of freedom in the Soviet Union in fact the basis of a fuller freedom. Thus comforted, Baracchi could describe the Australian press's reportage of Radek's downfall as an 'excretion of anti-Soviet filth'. Having crossed swords with Radek during the 1920s, he had no doubt that the impudent intriguer was guilty of the crimes of which he was accused. It was a 'tragic irony of history' that such 'social scum' rose to the surface 'just at the moment when the working people of the Soviet Union have written their socialist conquests into the most democratic constitution in the world'. Evident here also was the need of middle-class intellectuals such as Baracchi to affirm their own reliability: he could readily understand the process whereby such figures could end 'on the wrong side of the class struggle, since I have experienced its initial stages in my own person'. Is there perhaps also a wrestling with doubts sown during his recent experiences in the Soviet Union? On his own subsequent admission, he was deeply disturbed by a letter Freda Utley sent him after her husband was taken by the NKVD, and he had taken that letter straight to Richard Dixon 'and told him that it troubled me'. Such frankness can hardly have eased Utley's plight.[22]

In the earlier period of Class Against Class there was an acknowledgement of resistance to communism in the Soviet Union. The Australian party justified the 'repressive measures' that accompanied forced collectivisation in the early 1930s as 'necessary for the successful carrying out of the tasks of the proletariat'. Thus the introduction of an internal pass system was aimed at exercising a 'better control over anti-social, criminal, kulak and similar elements' whose 'social parasitism' weakened 'labour discipline'.[23] This ruthless rationalisation of class warfare yielded in the changed climate of the popular front to claims of socialist triumph and complete unanimity of purpose marred only by the treachery of leading Old Bolsheviks. The allegations against Zinoviev, Kamenev and Bukharin and other veterans mindful of Stalin's own modest role in the Russian Revolution, as well as his debasement of its principles, distracted attention from the scale of his purge of the party ranks. Under the direction of the head of security, N. I. Yezhov, hundreds of thousands of Soviet citizens were arrested, executed or despatched to labour camps in Siberia during the later 1930s in a process so indiscriminate that it coined the term *yezhovschina*.

The Australian party avoided mention of the *yezhovschina*. Not once did it question the guilt of those subjected to the show trials or express the slightest reservation about Stalin's murderous regime. In response to an article in a Sydney newspaper on the terror, Jack Blake's predecessor as Australian party representative in Moscow claimed that the population were at 'fever heat' against Zinoviev, Kamenev and their gang of Trotskyist wreckers. On the eve of Bukharin's trial, the *Workers' Weekly* assured its readers that 'the world will hear the story of the guilt of these mad monsters from their own lips'. 'Shoot the mad dogs', it quoted Lenin's widow, who was herself under threat of Stalin's vengeance. This brutal language of exposure, liquidation and annihilation had been introduced in the period of Class Against Class, along with the practice of self-criticism that seemed to authenticate the confessions of the Soviet victims. Initially the words functioned as political hyperbole; ultimately they desensitised those who used them to the atrocities they licensed. Just as some of Stalin's former colleagues were so habituated to the rhetoric of vilification that they expected to the last to be spared the executioner's bullet, so Australian communists seemed oblivious of the enormity of the regime they lauded and the brutalities they imitated.[24]

Jack Blake was questioned closely in 1937 by the ECCI about party members' attitude to the Moscow trials. He advised that 'some of the rank and file' did not 'understand' them. 'That is, they read from press publicity in the capitalist press to the effect that two old Bolsheviks [Zinoviev and Kamenev] were being edged out.' More than once the Communist International had to instruct the Australian party that it was giving insufficient coverage to the trials. The Australian central committee in turn had to instruct the districts to explain the traitorous role of the defendants, and to link their crimes to Trotsky. The Australian politbureau had to instruct the party press that 'much more Soviet feature material' had to be produced. The reluctance of Australian communists to discuss the trials, let alone acknowledge the *yezhovschina*, was essentially pragmatic. There is no evidence of disagreement or opposition; rather, members shied away from a subject that most Australians found deeply disturbing, one that confirmed their worst fears of communist dictatorship. Jack Miles's caveat when arranging for an announcement of expulsion of a party miscreant in 1937 has a chilling quality. 'We realise that the statement must be careful. We are not yet in the USSR and not yet the ruling party and cannot handle this the way they handle the trial of Trotskyists in the Soviet Union.'[25]

A principal means of instilling proper appreciation of these events was through the *History of the Communist Party of the Soviet Union*.

Prepared under the personal supervision of Stalin and issued in Russia in 1938 to replace an earlier history, it became the standard textbook for party classes.[26] Through it party members learned the rudiments of Marxism-Leninism, and came to understand that Stalin had stood at Lenin's shoulder during the long preparation for the Russian Revolution. With shameless effrontery, it then cast Stalin as the constant guide through subsequent travails as one after another traitor sought to derail the building of a socialist society. The subtitles of the last chapter, covering the years from 1935 to 1937, marked out the seeming completion of this goal: 'Second Five Year Plan Fulfilled Ahead of Time. Reconstruction of Agriculture and Completion of Collectivization . . . Stakhanov Movement . . . Rising Standard of Welfare. Rising Cultural Standard . . . Eighth Congress. Adoption of the New Constitution . . . Liquidation of the Remnants of the Bukharin–Trotsky Gang of Spies, Wreckers and Traitors to the Country . . . Broad Inner-Party Democracy.' But there was one discordant element. Under the subtitle 'Beginning of the Second Imperialist War', the *History* noted that 'the fascist ruling circles of Germany, Italy and Japan' had already opened their 'brutal war of unmitigated conquest at the expense of the poorly-defended peoples of Abyssinia, Spain and China'. This was but a preparation for their drive against the capitalist democracies, which was likely to bring them into armed conflict with the ruling circles of Britain, France and the United States. 'Clearly, the USSR could not shut its eyes to such a turn in the international situation . . .' The prediction was scarcely made than it was fulfilled, ending the period of the popular front and plunging the Australian party once more into crisis.[27]

14

War

Throughout its campaign against fascism and war, the Communist International remained mistrustful of the intentions of the non-fascist powers. On each occasion that Germany, Italy or Japan committed a new act of aggression, the governments of Britain, France and the United States failed to resist. The reasons for British and French appeasement of the dictators, and American isolationism, escaped the intensely suspicious Stalin: he was convinced that the capitalist statesmen wanted to manoeuvre Germany into war with the Soviet Union. The Munich agreement of September 1938 intensified his mistrust. In response to a German threat of war, the British and French heads of governments met there with Hitler and Mussolini, and ceded part of Czechoslovakia to Germany, this in spite of Soviet support for the Czechs. Hitler's assurance that he would respect what was left of Czechoslovakia was speedily broken in the new year, yet Britain and France continued to resist proposals from the Soviet Union for a mutual defence agreement.

For similar reasons Australian communists suspected the government of their country. The UAP–Country Party coalition led by Joseph Lyons was at least as reluctant to confront the fascist powers as Britain was, and its failure to respond to the growing international crisis contributed to its collapse at the beginning of 1939. Robert Menzies, who assumed leadership of the UAP following the death of Lyons and became prime minister in April, was hardly a resolute anti-fascist. During his visit to Europe in 1938 he had aligned himself clearly with the appeasers of Hitler and Mussolini, expressed sympathy for Germany's territorial aspirations and said there were 'credit entries in the Nazi ledger'. He had no truck with fascism in English or Australian trappings, for he thought its florid ideology and illiberal excesses 'not suited to the British genius', but he was a selective cultural relativist, willing to allow the legitimacy of such right-wing movements and quite unprepared to extend a similar understanding to communism. 'There is a good deal of really spiritual quality in the willingness of young Germans to devote themselves to the service and well-being of the State', he pronounced upon his return from Berlin. To the end, he hoped to avert war with Germany.[1]

Many Australians were suspicious of Menzies, and the Communist Party warned that he would use the war threat to suppress the labour movement. The great danger of a military build-up by a conservative government was that it could be used against the people and for purposes of imperial aggression against the Soviet Union. The party still argued that Australia should form part of a collective security agreement against the fascist Axis, but this would require a new, popular and progressive government, with voluntary and democratic defence forces, elected officers and representative committees of service personnel. In the meantime, the central committees instructed party units to send members into the military and civilian defence organisations.[2]

One of Menzies's first measures was a National Register of all males between the ages of 18 and 65, which communists believed he would use for both military and industrial conscription. They were by no means alone in this view. The Labor Party opposed the legislation, and the ACTU declared a boycott of the register. With substantial opposition to the National Register from the Australian Council for Civil Liberties and other liberals, the campaign to refuse to complete the registration forms seemed fertile ground for the popular front and the party tilled it enthusiastically. Unfortunately, John Curtin, the federal Labor leader, spoiled the harvest. He disagreed with the boycott and obtained sufficient concessions from the government (including a register of wealth as well as manpower)

A poster produced during the campaign to boycott the national register in 1939. The coalminers are the victims, and Menzies the villain. (Source: J.N. Rawling collection, Noel Butlin Archives Centre, ANU N57/2275)

to persuade the ACTU executive to call it off at the end of June 1939. This presented communists with a dilemma. The ACTU's backdown could be challenged if three of the state industrial councils voted to continue the boycott, and communist delegates calculated that was possible, but such a challenge would deepen divisions in a labour movement already beset by argument between isolationists and supporters of collective security. Communist leaders concluded that the cost of intransigence would be too great since it would isolate the party, and reluctantly instructed members to desist. It was not a popular decision: the Victorians called it a retreat and wanted to continue the campaign, and Dixon had to go down to Melbourne to explain that 'to lift the boycott was not in the nature of a retreat, but rather to compromise, which are two different things'. As for those diehards who wanted to burn their registers, Sharkey warned that 'burning the forms was an expression of contempt and it would be used as a flagrant disregard of the law'. So it would have been, but was not that the very reason for a revolutionary movement?[3]

This first switch of communist policy in 1939 was rapidly followed by another, this time determined in Moscow. Following his seizure of Czechoslovakia in March 1939, Hitler turned to Poland.

While Menzies declared that Germany had a case for sympathetic consideration of its territorial claims on Poland, Britain and France began negotiations with the Soviet Union to prevent German aggression against its eastern neighbour. The negotiations dragged on through the northern summer, hindered by the reluctance of the two Western governments to agree to the comprehensive defence guarantee that the Soviet representatives sought. The Australian party welcomed the prospect of such an agreement, which would vindicate its call for collective security and discredit the appeasers, but became increasingly concerned with the reluctance of Britain and France to conclude it. Then, in late August, came the news that instead the Soviet Union had entered into a pact with Germany.[4]

The Nazi–Soviet pact bound the two signatories to neutrality if either were at war. Ostensibly it was merely a non-aggression agreement, and welcomed by the Australian party as a contribution to world peace. As was explained in the communist press, the Soviets had won a great victory and forced Hitler to seek terms; the arrangement did not cut across a more comprehensive defence arrangement with Britain and France, and should in fact force these recalcitrants to join the anti-fascist alliance.[5] In fact the pact included secret clauses that gave a free hand to Germany in eastern Poland and Lithuania, and to the Soviet Union in western Poland, Latvia, Estonia, Finland and a portion of Rumania. It thus secured Germany's eastern flank and left that country free, as in 1918, to direct its full military capacity to the west, only this time from a position of much greater strength. Why did Stalin do it? He was undoubtedly terrified that he would be left to fight Germany alone. It is also true that the pact confined the ensuing war initially to Europe, since the German agreement with the Soviet Union discouraged Japan from continuing hostilities with the Red Army in Mongolia past the end of the month—a respite that Australian communists stressed in their justifications of it. But this could hardly disguise the shock of such a sudden and cynical change. The Soviet Union, which had insisted that fascism was the overriding danger to world peace, now stood back to allow Nazi Germany to go to war. 'The pact with Germany marks a certain change', the Australian party central committee advised its state committees, 'a change dictated by the circumstances of the situation'. Immediately it detected 'signs of opposition amongst the masses to the pact'. On the night the news of the Nazi–Soviet pact reached Australia, J. B. Miles was due to speak in north Queensland; he was prevented from speaking and the noticeboard advertising the meeting was hacked to pieces with an axe. Among sympathisers and members the effect was profound. You might reconcile yourself to the pact and rebut the hypocritical recriminations of apologists for appeasement, but you could no longer see the politics of the left with quite the same hopeful idealism as during the years of the popular front.[6]

Further surprises followed. Britain and France declared war on Germany when it invaded Poland at the beginning of September, and Menzies announced that Australia was accordingly at war. The Communist Party immediately welcomed this declaration of war against Germany, and pledged its support for the defence of freedom from fascist aggression. In a statement issued to the press a few days later, it reiterated the importance of assistance to 'the Polish people in their struggle for independence against the savage Nazi fascists. We stand for the full weight of Australian manpower and resources being mobilised for the defence of Australia, and along with other British forces for the defeat of Hitler.' Yet within three weeks the *casus belli* had disappeared. 'Poland has ceased to exist', announced *Tribune* on 22 September, after Germany completed its conquest of the western half of Poland and the Soviet Union, exercising the secret clause of the Nazi–Soviet pact, occupied its eastern half. Henceforth there was no more talk of this victim of fascist aggression, but rather celebration of its liberation from domestic tyranny by the Red Army. That this liberation was imposed at the point of a bayonet and accompanied by mass executions and deportations was not disclosed in the Australian party's faithful recital of Soviet propaganda.[7]

With the occupation of eastern Poland, the Baltic states and territory in the Balkans, the Soviet Union regained the land it had lost in the First World War. Furthermore, in a German–Soviet Treaty of Friendship, Co-operation and Demarcation, signed at the end of the month, the two powers cemented their bloody cooperation; Lithuania was transferred to the Soviet sphere of influence in return for Polish territory. Stalin's initial justification for his accommodation with Hitler shifted quickly from a necessary tactical manoeuvre to an act of principle: the war became an imperialist war and then a war in which the Allies were the aggressors. His abandonment of the last vestiges of anti-fascism presented Western communist parties with severe difficulties. Both the French and the British parties were beset by internal divisions and mass resignations before they came reluctantly into line.[8] The Australian party, by contrast, dutifully accepted each new instruction from Moscow without question. On 4 October the ECCI chastised the Australians for regarding the war as an anti-fascist campaign; on 6 October the central committee informed members of 'a change in our tactics' that called for peace. On 3 November the ECCI sent a new message calling for outright opposition to the imperialist conflict; on 6 November the politbureau complied and *Tribune* declared the war in Europe to be 'an unjust, reactionary imperialist war'. From criticising the Labor Party in September for opposing the overseas despatch of Australian troops, the party insisted before the end of the year that Australians must have nothing to do with the conflict. Even such ready compliance did not satisfy the ECCI, which expected member parties to acknowledge their errors. Miles complied with this instruction, also with the explanation that the Australian party had been led astray by its anti-fascist fervour: 'Instead of approaching the problem in a dialectical fashion, we did so from a one-sided anti-fascist fashion'. Blunt Sam Aarons objected that such self-recrimination would only 'play into the hands of the enemies who have been endeavouring to create the idea of confusion'. Miles and Sharkey sought to convince him of its necessity, but this discussion resulted only in agreement not to press disagreements to open discussion.[9]

The bewildered loyalty of the Australian party is illustrated in the recollections of Les Barnes, a leading Victorian member. On the day that news came of the Nazi–Soviet pact he and Nattie Seeligson were due to address a public meeting in the Melbourne suburb of Hawthorn; they were dumbfounded and found difficulty in answering the numerous interjectors. A few days later at the party hall in the city the party speakers reassured the audience that the pact would secure peace, and yet at the end of the week Germany attacked Poland. During the weekend of 2–3 September Australians waited anxiously on the German response to Britain and France's ultimatum, and yet on the Sunday afternoon Ralph Gibson again insisted that war could be averted. That night the state committee met at the Hawthorn home of Ted Laurie, a recent recruit. Most were convinced that war was inevitable but Ralph still insisted anti-fascist resolution would deter Hitler. At 8.30 there was knock on the door and Mrs Laurie entered: 'I'm sorry to disturb you but war's been declared'. There was a stunned silence as Les reflected how all that the communist movement had worked for was now lost. Ralph recovered first, gave a quick grin and 'proceeded to develop a wholly new thesis' that the war was an imperialist war between democratic imperialist and fascist imperialist camps and that the duty of members was to support the Allies. A month later, Richard Dixon came down from Sydney and the state committee agreed 'we were on the wrong track' and the war was an imperialist conflict pure and simple and the party must call for peace. As Barnes recalled, 'It was a difficult year'.[10]

The remarkable cohesion of the Australian party was strained only by a further action of the Red Army. In late November the Soviet Union sought to complete its seizure of the spoils allowed it by Germany with occupation of Finnish territory on its northern border close to Leningrad. The Finns resisted and in fierce fighting inflicted heavy casualties on the Red Army before weight of numbers finally prevailed in the new year. The Soviet justification for this aggression, duly repeated by the Australian party, was that Finland was a reactionary vassal of imperialism to be used as a springboard for an invasion of the USSR, but some found such a patently contrived rationalisation of Soviet interests too much.[11] Jim Rawling, who was editor of the Movement Against War and Fascism magazine, *World Peace*, felt that it betrayed the principles of proletarian internationalism, a betrayal he traced back to 1935 when the Communist International began to distinguish between 'good' and 'bad' capitalist powers according to the strategic interests of the Soviet Union. In mid-December the politbureau discovered he was about to publish an attack on the party in the January issue of the magazine and immediately expelled him. 'An "intellectual", a non-proletarian, he is of the type that has frequently deserted the Revolutionary movement in times of stress', explained *Tribune*. He responded with a statement of his criticisms in a leaflet, *J. N. Rawling Breaks With*

Stalinism, and at this point seemed headed in the direction of the Trotskyist Communist League (as the ex-communists who had formed the Workers' Party renamed themselves in 1938), which was active in its condemnation of the Communist Party for betraying Leninist anti-war principles. But within three months Rawling had transmuted his revolutionary internationalism into anti-communist patriotism with pro-war articles in the *Sydney Morning Herald*.[12]

Rawling refused to identify who had written the censored article but leading party members believed it was Guido Baracchi. He had resigned his post as assistant editor of the *Communist Review* in October when it supported the imperialist war, and was equally critical of the switch to advocacy of an imperialist peace. His deviation from the line on the outbreak of the war became apparent to the party class of University of Sydney undergraduates he took, one of whose members resigned from the class while the others were solemnly warned by Ted Docker that they should expunge their tutor's heresies from their minds.[13] After Rawling's expulsion, Baracchi was called in and questioned at length. Yes, he conceded, he had lent books to Rawling but then he had also lent a book by Trotsky to Sharkey. Yes, he had corresponded with the ex-communist leader Jack Kavanagh, who had written to criticise his tasteless sneers in the *Communist Review* at the fate of Radek, and yes, he had come to doubt the veracity of the Moscow show trials. Yes, he had had dealings with Jack Ryan, Gil Roper and other ex-party Trotskyist renegades, but he would like a fortnight to consider before he agreed that Trotsky was 'a foul counter-revolutionary'. Yes, he had growing doubts about the party's repeated tacking to the shifts in Soviet foreign policy, but he would like a fortnight to resolve his attitude to the party. Remarkably, he was granted his two weeks, and several weeks more while he composed a vast screed that caused his expulsion. To the announcement in *Tribune* in February 1940, and the charge of 'political and moral cowardice', he replied with his own open letter to party members that compared his record of forthright anti-war agitation in the First World War with the far more cautious conduct of J. B. Miles.[14]

Betty Roland, his partner, also left the party at this time. In a letter of resignation she explained that her disillusionment had begun with the party's abandonment of militant industrial leadership several years earlier and that she had not attended branch meetings for some time, but the final break was still difficult for 'the complete loss of faith is a very devastating thing'.[15] The party responded by ordering the New Theatre not to produce her plays. Several other members also sent letters of resignation marked by bewilderment over the sudden changes in the party's war policy, and some— including two Sydney organisers—simply dropped away. Party auxiliaries suffered substantial defections and the International Peace Campaign broke up in disarray over the Soviet attack on Finland.[16]

Most stuck to the party, if only because of the severe difficulties it encountered at this time. The announcement of the Nazi–Soviet pact had brought angry criticism and there were assaults on communist speakers in the first few days of the war, but the Soviet attack on Finland unleashed a far more sustained hostility. By the closing weeks of 1939 organised violence against the party's open-air meetings became commonplace. In Melbourne, for example, members of Catholic Action attacked the usual Collingwood pitch with stones and smashed the platform. Party members found a nearby open site and carefully cleared it of all missiles in order to complete the next meeting. In Newcastle the New Lambton branch moved its street meetings to the footpath in front of a shop with a large plate-glass window to avoid the same hazard. Elsewhere, members and sympathisers reinforced their security arrangements for public meetings that were repeatedly under attack.[17]

The principal confrontations occurred at the central sites. Trouble began in the Sydney Domain on Sunday 3 December, immediately following the Soviet action against Finland, when members of the audience took exception to communist justification of it. There were similar incidents over the next two weeks, provocatively reported in the Sydney press. Then on 24 December a group of soldiers seized and burned the party flags, the red one decorated with hammer and sickle as well as the blue one with the southern cross. The cause of their action appears to have been criticism of military recruitment, as Lance Sharkey made a public statement repudiating such epithets as 'five bob a day murderers' and insisting that the party wanted better conditions for the Second AIF. Even so, the presence of these young soldiers, on leave from their training camps and in search of excitement in the city, introduced a disturbing element. They were egged on by Harold Thorby, the deputy leader of the federal Country Party, which was already demanding the suppression of the party. Thorby was present at the Domain on the following Sunday when a crowd of 15 000 gathered to follow the action. There were twelve speakers, since the strain of addressing such a large audience without a microphone quickly exhausted an orator, and this time the party platform flew no flags. The appearance of the chairman, Norm Jeffery, was greeted with a shower of tomatoes and the singing of the national anthem. Party members responded with a clenched-fist salute and rounds of 'Solidarity for Ever'. Repeated charges by soldiers in uniform brought eight arrests. There was further trouble on the first Sunday in 1940 when one of the speakers said that half the Second AIF were economic conscripts, but thereafter the attendance and the turmoil temporarily ebbed.[18]

In Melbourne a similar pattern of escalating violence reached its peak sometime afterwards, and the close similarity of incidents there and in other state capitals suggests that reportage from Sydney served as a model. On Sunday 11 February a group of servicemen alleged they too had been described as 'six bob a day murderers' (the base pay for privates remained five shillings a day but the government increased their allowances at the end of the year) and broke up a communist meeting at the Yarra Bank. Ralph Gibson wrote to the daily press to state that the party had the highest respect for recruits, 'who, we believe, joined the AIF in sincere desire to defend Australia from fascism'. Notwithstanding his statement, men in uniform hooted, counted out and threw stones at communist speakers on the following Sunday until an all-out brawl ensued. In Brisbane it was again the war against Finland that provoked increasing opposition at the party's Saturday night open-air meeting in the city, culminating in running streetfights on 10 and 17 February. By this time attacks on communist speakers in suburban and rural locations had become ubiquitous.[19] Later, in April, as Hitler launched his western *blitzkrieg*, there was a further escalation. On the evening of Wednesday 3 April some 50 soldiers attacked the Communist Hall in George Street, and on the following Sunday a larger group besieged the building. That was followed by renewed attacks on the communist platform at the Domain until, on Sunday 26 May, more than 200 soldiers declared they would wreck the party premises unless mates arrested earlier at the Domain for assault were released. On several occasions soldiers down from Puckapunyal training camp invaded the city premises of the League of Young Democrats in Melbourne.[20]

The extent of antagonism towards communists is not easy to gauge. Party members recognised some familiar adversaries sooling the soldiers, who in any case were frequently in trouble during their Sunday leave in the city and found the party a conveniently legitimate target for hooliganism. Members of Catholic Action, which itself was by no means in favour of Australian participation in a European war until it became clear that the Soviet Union would not be an ally, also took advantage of the party's anti-war policy to escalate attacks upon it. Clearly, these anti-communists were able to work on a substantial body of opinion that regarded the party's opposition to the war as unpatriotic, its constant justification of the Soviet Union's ruthless conduct as disloyal. Yet communists were far from alone in criticising Australian war policy. After their speedy invasion of western Poland, the German armies paused. While Britain and France rejected Hitler's offers of peace in October, their armies made no effort to engage the enemy and remained behind their western defences; at the beginning of April 1940 the British prime minister declared that Hitler had 'missed the bus'. While the Australian government enlisted 20 000 men in the AIF and prepared to despatch them overseas, its efforts to prepare the country for a sustained effort were weak and dilatory; shortly after he declared Australia to be at war with Germany, Menzies advised that at home it would be 'business as usual'. He also ruminated in a confidential letter to the Australian high commissioner in London that he could see little to be gained and much to be lost by a war fought over a dismembered central European country for which 'nobody really gives a damn'.[21] The Labor Party accepted its own leader's support for the war with limited enthusiasm, and still opposed sending forces overseas.

During this 'phoney war' there was substantial industrial conflict. In March 1940 the miners went on strike against an arbitration ruling that denied surface workers the 40-hour week won by the union's earlier campaign of 1938. The communist leaders of the Miners' Federation initiated the strike and the party put considerable effort into support for the miners as their stoppage continued into April and May; the ACTU also backed their demands. Employers felt no obligation to suspend their own hostilities: BHP, for example, took advantage of the coal shortage to retrench workers from its Newcastle steelworks, and thus get rid of a list of communist employees provided by the Commonwealth Investigation Branch. Menzies repeated his appearance the previous year at Wollongong, when he had insisted that the wharfies load pig-iron to Japan, with a trip to the Hunter Valley to explain personally that it was now the miners' patriotic duty to accept the ruling of the court and produce coal. Not until 16 May was a settlement negotiated.[22]

Dissatisfaction with the war came to a head in the Labor Party at the New South Wales State Conference in Easter 1940. The conference restated the ALP's opposition to imperialism, declared that the present war was 'being pursued in the interests of big finance and monopolies', and called for an immediate end to hostilities. In itself, this resolution merely affirmed the isolationist current that still ran strongly in the labour movement. A similar declaration failed by only two votes at the ACTU congress a fortnight later when Ernie Thornton proposed it; but it was accompanied at the ALP State Conference by a further resolution drafted by the three leading communist members of the New South Wales Labor Party, Lloyd Ross, Jack Hughes and Bill Gollan. By 195 votes to 88, the conference resolved its additional opposition to 'any effort of the anti-Labor government to change the direction of the present war by an aggressive act against any other country with which we are not at war, including the Soviet Union'. This 'Hands Off Russia' resolution, as it became known, brought a storm of criticism. Lang immediately reformed his own anti-communist Labor Party, which once again divided the federal parliamentary ranks. The Federal Executive of the ALP ordered the resolution be struck from the records and in August suspended the New South Wales executive.

The ousted executive in turn established its own State Labor Party, known as the Hughes–Evans party after its two best known members. While it retained a substantial following, the State Labor Party lacked any parliamentary representation and even communist unions such as the ARU, the FIA and the miners, failed to affiliate to it. Meanwhile the party reverted to the language of the Third Period in its denunciation of the 'social fascist' Labor Party. The conclusion is inescapable that Australian communists' subservience to Stalin's wartime foreign policy undid all the gains they had made in the Labor Party with the anti-fascist united front.[23]

Between the passage of the 'Hands Off Russia' declaration and the reconstruction of the ALP in New South Wales, and between the beginning of the miners' strike and its abandonment, the course of the war changed completely. In April Hitler invaded Denmark and Norway, in May he advanced into the Low Countries, in June France capitulated. Henceforth Britain stood, with its dominions, alone. In the east Stalin again took advantage of the Nazi activity to occupy the Baltic states and the Romanian provinces of Bukovina and Bessarabia. The phoney war had ended, a fight for survival took its place, and all talk of peace ended. Australian communists had made some headway in the early months of 1940 with their denunciation of the war, their industrial campaigns and criticism of war profiteering. From the middle of the year the environment was far more hostile.

At the outbreak of the war, when the government armed itself with sweeping powers under a National Security Act, Menzies gave assurances that political freedom would be sacrosanct. A number of local councils quickly introduced prohibitions on communist meetings, arrests and prosecutions under state laws increased, plainclothes agents became more common at party meetings, but in general Australian communists were permitted to continue their usual activities. Apart from imposing a ban on flags in the Domain, the non-Labor government of New South Wales resisted calls to prohibit communist gatherings there, and for the most part the police quelled the disturbances even-handedly. The Queensland Labor government was perhaps the most intolerant with its threat to ban public meetings unless the party undertook to cease all 'anti-British' statements. By comparison with France, which had speedily arrested communist deputies and banned protests, the measure of civil liberty preserved here was considerable. In January 1940 Menzies called a conference of all state police commissioners, the heads of the intelligence sections of the three armed forces, and H. E. Jones of the Investigation Branch. The military intelligence services wanted the suppression of the Communist Party. Apart from the communist anti-war propaganda and discouragement of enlistment, they alleged there was a concerted attempt to infiltrate the armed forces, weaken morale and undertake sabotage and espionage.[24]

There is no doubt that the Communist Party directed members to enlist. This tactic had begun well before the outbreak of war and was linked to the party's campaign to democratise the armed forces so that they could not be used against the left. In this endeavour it had little success. A group of communists was formed in the navy and struck for better conditions shortly before the war, but the leader turned out to be a security agent. Far from infiltrating the senior service, in the late 1930s the party served as an escape route for naval ratings who wished to terminate their long term of enlistment: since possession of communist literature was an offence punished by discharge, a regular trickle of disenchanted ratings passed through the Anvil bookshop in Sydney. A number of members joined the Second AIF upon its formation, for at that point the party actively supported the war effort, but they were usually discharged as soon as they were identified as communists; one in Melbourne got as far as the embarkation wharf before he was sent home. 'Don't be confused if the man you are asked to keep an eye on is outwardly a good soldier', the *Military Manual for Dealing with Subversion in the Armed Forces* warned. 'The Communist Party doesn't pick fools or known bad characters for their agents.'[25]

Once the party turned from support to opposition to the war, open enlistment ended and in any case there was a slackening of recruitment as by this time the army had largely filled its modest initial quota of trainees. Henceforth the party press began to publicise the poor conditions of the training camps and the dissatisfaction of the men. A subsequent defector has claimed that as branch secretary he was instructed to select a member for a revolutionary nucleus in the armed forces, and that these infiltrators attended a special party school where they were taught to stir up trouble, nurture incipient mutiny and encourage desertion. There is no evidence of any such instruction, and in any case the communists in uniform needed no special training in the agitation they fostered in the summer of 1939–40. Rather, they took up the issues of pay and conditions precisely as they would have done in civilian employment and the effect of such trade union tactics, which secured improvements in food, clothing, leave and wet canteens, seems to have been a reduction rather than an increase in discontent.[26]

There is no evidence of sabotage.[27] As for the accusation of espionage, there is the substantial and in my judgement persuasive evidence of radio traffic between Moscow and a KGB officer in the Canberra embassy of the Soviet Union from 1943 onwards that reveals a senior member of the party was collecting political and military intelligence for the KGB. But that embassy was not established in 1940, when the available means for sending information from Australia to Russia were still rudimentary. For that matter, none of the Australian communists who are known to have entered the armed forces in 1939 occupied ranks that would have given them access to any significant military intelligence.[28]

The Commonwealth Investigation Branch was not persuaded by the military claims and the report of the security conference recommended a strengthening of controls rather than a complete prohibition that would merely provide communists with additional publicity. Menzies thought the report superficial but accepted its recommendations. In early February his government acquired power under the National Security Act to call up newspaper copy before publication; two days later it ordered the editor of the Victorian communist paper, the *Guardian*, to submit copy for inspection.[29] The prime minister was pressed to do more when he reformed his government in March 1940 to take in the Country Party. Both the leader of the Country Party, Archie Cameron, and his deputy, Harold Thorby, argued publicly for a ban on communist activity. In early April the government prevented the broadcast by radio station 2KY of *No Conscription*, a play by Rupert Lockwood. The first meeting of the new coalition Cabinet resolved to close the communist press. Under regulations issued on 23 April 1940 the government strengthened its powers of censorship: communist publications were already prevented from reporting on the war, and henceforth they were not to comment on industrial disputes. So sweeping was the censor's blue pencil that the May issue of the *Communist Review* appeared with the Sermon on the Mount as the principal article: 'Blessed are the peacemakers' was its only reference to the war, while publication of Henry Lawson's 'Faces in the Street' was deemed too inflammatory. Shortly afterwards, the government ordered eight communist newspapers and journals (as well as the Trotskyist *Militant*) to cease publication and instructed five union papers to remove communists from all editorial positions or suffer the same fate. On the same day the government acquired the power to prevent known communists from holding union office. On 27 May cabinet resolved to declare all communist organisations illegal.[30]

In answer to a parliamentary question that day, the prime minister said that he anticipated being able to make a statement on the matter within 24 hours. In fact it took more than a fortnight to alert the state premiers so that their police forces could prepare to take action, and the necessary regulations under the National Security Act were not promulgated until 15 June. They allowed the government to declare illegal any organisation it deemed to be 'prejudicial to the defence of the Commonwealth or the efficient conduct of the war', to confiscate its property, prevent it from raising funds or holding meetings, and prosecute anyone in possession of its publications. In the meantime the party leaders, advised by a worker in the government printing office and by police sympathisers, completed preparations begun sometime earlier. On 11 June the central committee ordered local officials to issue no more dues stamps and remove the party name from receipt books; all members were to destroy their membership cards and 'sentiment must not be allowed to interfere in the carrying out of these instructions'.[31]

On the night of Saturday 15 June 1940 police raided the party's offices and the homes of all known members. They took away truckloads of documents, books and pamphlets from the national office in Sydney, and the Melbourne and Brisbane state offices. All assets were confiscated, the presses, the furniture, everything. The operation involved simultaneous searches of hundreds of addresses in every state and every major town in the country—there had probably never been a police activity of this kind on the same scale—and was inevitably attended by slips and mishaps. Bill and Marie Gollan were living in Cessnock and had burned all papers, but their sister-in-law arrived with a copy of the illegal *Tribune*, which had to be smuggled out to the privy. In Queensland Ted Bacon was not at home when the police called early on the Sunday morning. The caretaker of his block of flats told them he was at Mass, then replaced the incriminating books on Ted's shelves with his own westerns. The police also descended on the state tax office, where Bacon worked, and wanted to take the contents of his desk, but were sent away by the horrified office head. Laurie Aarons and his wife had been playing cards at his father's place on the Saturday evening and heard the next day that Sam had been raided. 'Our noses were a bit out of joint', Laurie recalled, because he and his wife had been overlooked, but he subsequently heard that the police had searched the shop in Banksmeadow, Sydney, where they had previously lived. The prominent communist union leaders were apparently immune. Ernie and Lila Thornton hosted a party at their place in Coogee on the night of the raid, and most of the guests went home to find books missing.[32]

In their zeal some police took the most unlikely publications and overlooked more obvious candidates for confiscation. Works by any Russian author, even Tolstoy or Dostoevsky, were likely to go, and the raid on the New Theatre in Sydney even netted Shakespeare among the 600 playscripts that were carried away, yet more than one member claimed to have passed off the *History of the Communist Party of the Soviet Union* (which used the abbreviation CPSU on the spine) as a record of the Commonwealth Public Service Union. Mick Ryan and Jess Grant had hosted a party meeting in their home that Saturday afternoon before the evening raid and Jess had a correspondence book in the lounge room; when the copper picked it up it fell open at the divider headed 'Housewives' Organisations' and he tossed it aside as harmless. Guido Baracchi had laboriously packed and carted his library to a safe address but Betty Roland lost the Russian-language contract for a production in Leningrad of her play *A Touch of Silk*. In Melbourne the police went systematically through Ted Laurie's possessions and took a stapler. They knocked on the front door of Clarrie and Barbara Boyd's house, politely lifted their hats, then took away every book with a red cover.[33]

Sometimes the police action was amicable, sometimes it was not. The tiny miner's cottage of Annie and Sam Graham in Kurri Kurri, New South Wales, was raided at two in the morning. She had already stored the party material and left only a pile of *Soviets To-Day* for the police. The local copper had great difficulty in gathering up the heavy, shiny magazines since, as Annie appreciated, 'they're buggers of things to pile on your arm and carry', so he asked if he could take them in a port. She angrily refused. 'Look, there's hundreds of men in this town haven't had a job for years, but if they were offered your job tonight, they wouldn't bloody do it. It would be beneath them to do such a rotten, dirty, bloody job as you're doing.' Eleanor Dark's novel *The Little Company* has a defiant Sydney intellectual spreading 'a veil of comedy over the whole ugly business'. He invites the police into his library, watches them confiscate *The Wealth of Nations* and pass over a textbook on dialectics ('Not that, food', the sergeant instructs the constable); but his companion is less sanguine, 'conscious all the time of this democracy as a fraying rope, snapping strand by strand' and aware that such raids were not always so innocuous.[34] In Queensland, where the Labor government took the opportunity to crack down on its left critics, the raids were less discriminate and more violent. In some country centres the police were vindictive: in Ballarat, Victoria they destroyed the hats of Ted Rowe's wife on the grounds that they might conceal seditious material.[35]

The repression was greatest in Western Australia, where an ambitious detective-sergeant took advantage of the national security regulations to anticipate the crackdown. His name was Ron Richards, better known as the Black Snake or Ron the Con, who would become deputy director of the postwar Australian intelligence service and chalk up a number of successful operations, including the defection of the Soviet diplomat, Vladimir Petrov. Richards used both bluff and cajolery to break down the defences of his victims. He affected a mutual understanding, hinted at the mutual advantage of shared confidences, switched easily from threat to promise. Not even his own colleagues were privy to his intentions. Before the outbreak of the war he had cultivated the friendship of Bill Mountjoy, the state secretary of the party, who accordingly regarded the instructions to prepare for illegality as unnecessary. A police raid on the party office in London Court therefore netted extensive details of members' names and addresses. In subsequent actions, all before 15 June, Richards rounded up all the leading party members but Mountjoy. Arthur Rudkin, the editor of the *Workers' Star*, was charged with publishing information that might be useful to the enemy, namely an article on gas masks based on information from a British scientist that had recently been classified. He was gaoled for four months. William Dean, party treasurer, was sentenced to six months for notes on gun emplacements on Rottnest Island. Kevin Healy, who replaced Mountjoy as secretary, got three months for possession of a party newsletter, as did Paddy Troy, a member of the state committee. Altogether, more than a dozen party members were arrested and convicted, including Jack Simpson, who was sent across from Sydney to take over as secretary after the initial raid.[36]

Outside Western Australia there were few arrests at this stage. The purpose of the declaration of illegality and the raids of 15 June was to disarm the party, to deprive it of capacity to oppose the war, rather than to make martyrs of its members. Stronger action followed but only because the raids failed in their purpose.

There is a tendency in the reminiscences of Australian communists about their wartime underground activity to exaggerate the effectiveness of the party's arrangements. The central committee had repeatedly given warning of the need to prepare, to keep no unnecessary records, to install flatbed presses or duplicators in safe premises and build up stocks of paper, to break large branches into smaller cells and disguise meetings as social occasions, to avoid recognising members in public, and of various other precautions. Yet when Eva Bacon arrived in Australia from Vienna in 1939, she found Australian communists' understanding of how to work illegally quite rudimentary. She immediately set down her knowledge of such activity as a sort of manual for party members in Brisbane, and one of them showed the document to a journalist, who published it in *Truth*. For that matter, the authorities' enforcement of illegality struck a woman who had undergone the attentions of the Austrian and then the German secret police as 'a complete joke'. The experience of her future husband, Ted, illustrates the national weakness. He had advance warning of the declaration of illegality from contacts— including, he claimed, Major Wake, the head of the Brisbane office of the Investigation Branch—yet on the night of the raids he had left an extensive library of Marxist literature at his home. The various stories of correspondence and address books snatched from under the eyes of the ignorant clodhoppers have a similar quality of naivety.[37]

The most comprehensive overview of how the Australian party fared as an illegal organisation is that of Wally Clayton, who was in charge of the arrangements. He was originally a New Zealander who later worked as a travelling salesman while serving as a party organiser for Len Donald in Victoria, where one comrade remembered him constantly coming and going on his motorcycle with instructions. In 1939 Clayton moved to Sydney to work as circulation manager for *Tribune*. Some time in that year, he has stated, he was called to appear before Dixon and Sharkey and told to take charge of the central committee's preparations for illegality. He immediately set about arranging secret residences, meeting places, transport, stores, printeries, a vast apparatus of facilities that enabled the party leadership to function uninterrupted. He safeguarded the party's records and funds, eliminated all attempts at infiltration, set up meetings for Miles and Sharkey, even arranged for them to receive medical treatment.[38] This triumphant account of a successful task was related comparatively recently, for Clayton spent much of his subsequent life avoiding publicity. He was underground from 1940 to 1943 and again from 1947 to 1954, and the habits of secrecy became ingrained. He was also pursued by Australian security and subjected to enormous pressure after 1954, accused of being the Australian spymaster who had gathered secrets from a circle of informants for the KGB. Clayton has never admitted these allegations, but their effects are apparent in his account of how he outwitted the security services and the police in 1940. He finds vindication in his sterling service during the party's hour of need.[39]

Clayton's version exaggerates his accomplishment. He says that when he took charge of underground work, no preparation had been made; it had. He says that he had no guidance beyond an article in *Inprecorr* and had to devise the arrangements himself; the Australian party had circulated manuals that set out the basic principles since the early 1930s. He claims that he went underground well before the police raids; he was found on the evening of 15 June hiding in the lavatory of a party member's house in Petersham with a copy of the *History of the Communist Party of the Soviet Union*.[40] He presents a picture of tight security in which the only victims of official surveillance were some inexperienced and 'very liberal underground workers'; in fact the conditions of party work were difficult and dangerous. Many members came to grief. Just how many is not certain. The commonly accepted figure of 50 convictions for offences against national security regulations is almost certainly too low: the Council for Civil Liberties recorded nearly that number of cases, and the Commonwealth archives contain files for many other raids, arrests and prosecutions of both prominent and obscure communists.

Even when elaborate preparations had been laid, they were imperilled by inexperience or carelessness. The principal cadres were to move interstate, where they would not be so easily recognised. Ralph Gibson planned to travel to Brisbane in a series of car and train journeys, but on the night of 15 June he almost ran into the hands of the police at the Melbourne offices. In Brisbane the printing press had been secreted on a poultry farm and Albert Robinson, the editor, turned up while the police were questioning the farmer; fortunately they did not recognise the interloper. Les Barnes had bought a flatbed press for use in Melbourne and carefully arranged for a carrier to transport it to its secret location; the carrier turned out to be a former printer who knew Les, and some time later the military intelligence came looking for him. These presses were troublesome items, partly because they were so noisy when operated and partly because they were such a magnet for the police. Even to move them was a hazardous business, as the Melbourne comrades discovered when they were assisted in doing so by a curious policeman. In smaller cities and towns, where everyone knew everyone else, secrecy was especially difficult. Barbara Boyd, who went to Western Australia as an organiser after the leading members were jailed, remarked that in a place like Perth it was dangerous to be seen lumping a Gestetner. The party took pride in the fact that it continued to produce its newspapers and pamphlets, sometimes defiantly sporting such publishers as T. Gracchus of Cato Street, John Fairfax at the address of the *Sydney Morning Herald*, or the Dimitrov Press at the offices of the UAP; but their publications appeared less frequently, in abbreviated form and cost a number of arrests. When the *Communist Review* reappeared after the press was reestablished in defiance of the ban, it boasted that 'we were never so free as now when we have no freedom', but this was after an interval of six months and in a greatly reduced format.[41]

After a publication was printed, it had to be distributed. Sale or possession of communist literature was an offence that brought sentences of three to six months, more frequently in Western Australia than in other states but sufficiently often to make it a risky undertaking. Even to post placards or paint slogans after dark required a team of three: one to hold the material, one to wield the brush and one to act as cockatoo. Lil Davis, a much loved battler of inner Sydney, was caught letter-boxing pamphlets for lack of this precaution. She was also placed at risk by the presence of a security agent in her party group. We know about him because he was detected—really, he gave himself away, since he arrived knowing no one, kept asking for the names of paper sellers, and most tellingly, he owned a car. This infiltrator was quickly turned out but others were more skilful in their camouflage. As a result the police were able to pounce on party meetings, even those disguised as picnics or parties, arrest the members and find incriminating material. A year after the party was declared illegal, *Tribune* still had to warn members that 'many prosecutions are still the result of holding illegal publications which could have been passed on or otherwise cared for'. The party was, of course, banned from holding public meetings and speakers who appeared on some other platform might still be prosecuted for breach of the national security regulations. Those apprehended were commonly invited to enter into a bond to observe the regulations for the duration of the war. Phyllis Johnson's refusal to do so when she was prosecuted for an anti-war address at the Domain cost her a month in Long Bay prison. Fred Paterson, on the other hand, did sign a bond when he was convicted for an anti-war statement made at a Townsville city council meeting.[42]

Not all of those apprehended were prosecuted and not all of those prosecuted were convicted, for the close scrutiny of lawyers revealed loopholes in the myriad regulations issued under the authority of the National Security Act, which the government in turn attempted to close with further regulations. The case of George Wallis, a leading Tasmanian communist, attested to the assiduity of the authorities. In May 1940 the police raided his Sandy Bay boarding house and seized a duplicator. On 15 June they again ransacked his room and took away communist publications. In October 1940, January and February 1941 there were further raids and following the last of the raids he requested, as was his right, a list of his seized possessions. He was then arrested and charged with living without lawful means of support, a charge the Hobart magistrate dismissed since Wallis had both money and a job.[43]

One other offence put a large number of party members away— the offence of alien status. Communists were by no means the only offenders, indeed they were outnumbered by German and Italian settlers who actively identified with the Nazi and fascist regimes. The individual determinations whereby the Australian government interned several thousand settlers of enemy origin in the first year of the war were based partly on evidence of such loyalties and partly on a range of other kinds of political activism. Left-wing sympathies or even a record of involvement in a trade union frequently caused internment, despite the fact that such individuals were clearly opposed to the governments of their country of origin. That Italy entered the war just a few days before the Communist Party was declared illegal seems to have resulted in Italian communists being treated as doubly disloyal, for they were singled out for special attention. Many of these anti-fascist Italians suffered violence within the internment camps, and at least one was killed.[44]

Two more communists were interned in 1941 in controversial circumstances. Horace Ratliff was a Gallipoli veteran and jack-of-all-trades; Max Thomas was an unemployed relief worker who had gone into the printing industry. They went underground in June 1940 and lived in a secluded cottage at Bonnet Bay, which lay on a tributary of the Georges River on the southern outskirts of Sydney, and used it both to produce literature and hold meetings. In November 1940 the police raided the cottage and charged the two men with possession of papers, a typewriter and a Gestetner. Both refused to give a bond to obey the national security regulations and were sentenced to six months hard labour, which Ratliff served at Bathurst and Thomas at Goulburn. Upon his release in May 1941, Thomas returned to his wife and children at Kogarah and found work on the *Daily Mirror*. On 14 June he and Ratliff were interned in Holdsworthy military camp, at the order of the minister of the army, on the grounds that they were active members of an illegal organisation and had refused to give an undertaking to obey the national security regulations. On 2 July Ratliff and Thomas began a hunger strike to draw attention to their case. On 19 July they broke the strike to give evidence in an appeal against the minister's decision, held in a hospital where they had both been taken in a seriously weakened condition and tempted with chicken broth. The appeal was rejected and they resumed the fast. Their case was first publicised in the newspaper of the State Labor Party, and propelled by protest meetings outside the internment camp where POWs responded by singing 'The Red Flag' and 'The Internationale' in their own languages. The Council for Civil Liberties organised a petition for their release. A newly formed Civil Rights Defence League, chaired by Frank Dalby Davison and with Marjorie Barnard and Miles Franklin among its patrons, dwelt on the injustice. Unions staged a round of protest strikes. Eventually the men accepted the advice of the New South Wales Labor Council to abandon their hunger strike and were released when the Labor Council provided sureties for them.[45]

This, the only occasion on which the government used its full powers against individual party members, indicates the means whereby the party was able to carry on its work. The term 'underground' gives a misleading impression. Only a small minority of leading members actually went into hiding and even they would surface periodically as parliamentary candidates or for some other public occasion before disappearing once more from view. One member of the New South Wales police has recalled his Sunday afternoon duties at the Sydney Domain as a shorthand recorder of party speakers. He was instructed to follow Lance Sharkey, 'and

Silksworth Chinese Sailors Arrested

Chinese sailors from the Silksworth outside Newcastle Trades Hall during the week-end.

The spokesman of the crew, a detective, and a policeman outside the Trades Hall.

FASCISM IS WAR

GUERNICA
MADRID
CANTON
NANKING

BOYCOTT JAP GOODS

STOP EXPORTS TO JAPAN
BUILD THE COMMUNIST PARTY

The Silksworth tied up at the silo wharf. Above: One of the many posters in Steel-street. Sketches of Hitler, a Jap, and Mussolini are seen against a bar sinister. Right: Silksworthies following police into the Trades Hall.

The strike by Chinese crew of a ship carrying wheat to Japanese-occupied territory coincided with a campaign to boycott Japanese products. (Source: 'Newcastle Morning Herald', 19 October 1937)

Registered at the G.P.O., Sydney, for transmission through the post as a periodical.

January, 1939 *Kembla Iron Not For Japan* SIXPENCE

The refusal at the end of 1938 by members of the Waterside Workers' Federation at Port Kembla to load pig-iron for export to Japan brought on a major confrontation with the Commonwealth government. Three members of the union pose here in cheerful resolution with the subject of the dispute. (Source: 'Communist Review', January 1939)

A studio portrait of Katharine Susannah Prichard, a founder member of the party in Western Australia and the most revered of the communist writers. (Source: Prichard papers, National Library of Australia MS 6201/12/2)

Communists first achieved positions of national leadership in the unions in 1934 when Bill Orr was elected secretary of the Miners' Federation, to be followed later in the year by Charlie Nelson, who was elected president. At the general council of the Federation in 1935, Orr is third from the right in the front row and Nelson fourth from the left. Between them is their longstanding rival and ally, 'Bondy' Hoare. (Source: Australasian Coal and Shale Employees' Federation, Noel Butlin Archives Centre, ANU K2434)

The Townsville party branch, June 1940. It was in north Queensland that the party made greatest strides in the second half of the 1930s, but the composition and demeanour of this assembly belies the area's reputation as a site of footloose hard cases. (Source: Laurie Aarons)

F.O.S.U. State Conference
February, 1936

The Friends of the Soviet Union became one of the most important of the party's auxiliary organisations during the 1930s. This record of the Victorian state conference in 1936 shows the platform and the floor. (Source: Ralph Gibson collection, University of Melbourne Archives)

A mass choreography of Soviet power, the May Day parade in Moscow was the highlight of a visit to the USSR in the 1930s. 'How long will it be before we will be witnessing a similar spectacle—from the GPO steps in Martin Place?', asked an Australian delegate the year after this picture appeared. (Source: 'Soviets To-Day', September 1933)

Katharine Susannah Prichard's visit to the Soviet Union in the winter of 1933–34 was overshadowed by the suicide of her husband back in Australia. Prichard's account of the trip, 'The Real Russia', allowed none of the misgivings that Betty Roland claims she confided while in Moscow. In this record of an inspection of a collective farm, a boy shows her his model areoplane. (Source: Prichard papers, National Library of Australia MS 6201/12/2)

A demonstration in support of Ratliff and Thomas, location unknown but possibly outside the Holdsworthy army base in New South Wales. The demonstrators march line abreast in good cheer and are better dressed than before the war. (Source: CPA photographic collection, University of Melbourne Archives)

everywhere Sharkey spoke we went'. A superior taught him 'fifty or sixty phrases in the Communist jargon', which he duly transcribed, but no prosecution followed.[46]

The great majority of Australian communists went about as before, more circumspectly perhaps, but with their identities and allegiance known to neighbours and workmates. Since all party activity was illegal, it had to be conducted in a clandestine fashion, yet the object of communism as a popular movement required that it maintain a visible presence. This objective was assisted by recourse to other organisations that retained their legal status. The Friends of the Soviet Union, for example, was never suppressed, though its monthly magazine was banned and other publications heavily censored. The League of Young Democrats remained a legitimate organisation until February 1941, and was then able to transfer its activities into the youth wings of sympathetic unions. New organisations were established, most notably the Legal Rights Committee, as surrogates for those proscribed. The party made considerable use of the State Labor Party in New South Wales and its newspaper, now renamed *Progress*, for the conduct of public campaigns. Most of all, it relied on its substantial presence in the unions. For all of its denunciation of industrial fifth columnists, the government's war effort relied on the cooperation of key unions such as the miners, the wharfies, the seamen, railway workers and ironworkers, and it was loath to antagonise them with action against their elected leaders. These officers were exempted from the police raids on 15 June because, as one of them put it, there was 'a sort of agreement that nothing could be done to trade union officials'.[47]

There are no membership records for this period and the circumstances make it difficult to determine just how the party fared. From subsequent comments, it seems likely that the party lost some of its members and recruited very few new ones, though those who remained were spurred on by the conditions to work with a particular intensity. The frequently repeated statement that the outlawed party grew fails to distinguish between its extremely difficult circumstances as an illegal organisation opposed to the war and the subsequent change of fortunes when it supported the national war effort. Lance Sharkey later stated that there was 'a drift out of the party' in the first year of illegality.[48]

Nevertheless, the heavy-handed repression seems to have allayed the doubts that many had felt about the bewildering earlier switches in party policy, and to have overridden anxiety about the military success of Hitler. Ralph Gibson has claimed that after the ban, public opinion became friendlier to the party, and there is some evidence for this. In federal elections held in September 1940 communists standing as independent candidates polled surprisingly high tallies. Fred Paterson received 11 104 votes (18.3%) in Herbert, and Gibson himself 5175 (9.1%) in Yarra. Others standing for the State Labor Party in New South Wales also did well: Bill Gollan 12 956 (25%) in Hunter, Rupert Lockwood 8555 (14.9%) in Martin, Jack Hughes 6211 (10.6%) in Reid. This election revealed growing dissatisfaction with a government that was beset by internal dissension, tainted by a record of appeasement and infirmity of purpose. This was the period, also, when the New Theatre presented its satirical revue, *I'd Rather Be Red*, to packed audiences for four months:

> There'll always be a Menzies,
> While there's a BHP
> For they have drawn their dividends
> Since 1883.

along with the confession of a censor:

> Oh years ago I gave some dough
> To the funds of the UAP,
> But I suffered defeat in a certain seat,
> So Menzies said to me:
> 'You haven't got the nous of a mouse or a louse,
> Or the brains of a chimpanzee.
> You weren't even meant for parliament
> So a censor you can be.'[49]

The Queensland elections six months later suggested a comparable antagonism towards the Labor government in that state, as many who had chafed at the compromises associated with the united front readily accepted the reversion to forthright denunciation of the Labor Party: Paterson, with 47.3 per cent of the vote in Bowen, narrowly failed to win election and several other party members attracted a respectable tally. Sympathy for a plucky underdog probably compounded doubts about the conduct of the war.[50]

If the conditions of illegality failed to eradicate communism, they pushed it into a narrowly agitational role and hindered any real consideration of strategy. A national congress was clearly impossible, and even central committee meetings were difficult to arrange. Messages had then to be relayed interstate by couriers in ways that did not allow for discussion or feedback. Communication with Moscow was also difficult since the cable service used to send or receive policy announcements in 1939 was no longer available, and at crucial junctures in the course of the war leading Australian comrades simply had to improvise their response. The one constant was that Stalin was right. Just as his pact with Germany had outwitted the imperialists and kept the Soviet Union out of the war, so a similar agreement with Japan in 1941 should be supported by all workers: 'since the continued advance of socialism and the security of the land of socialism is in the interests of all toiling people, no genuine socialist can doubt the value of the pact'. The war was nothing more than a contest between two camps of imperialists and 'the Soviet Union takes advantage of the conflicts between the rival imperialist gangsters'.[51]

For Australian communists this meant an absolute rejection of the war and a return to the extreme abuse of the Third Period against those in the labour movement who supported it. Jack Lang, John Curtin, even a 'liberal flunkey' like Bert Evatt or that courageous civil libertarian Maurice Blackburn, were once again 'the Labor servants of imperialism'. Miles and Sharkey exhumed Lenin's 1913 characterisation of the Labor Party as 'a liberal party of expanding capitalism', now turned into 'a handmaiden of the warmakers'. The party again talked of a united front from below, rather than from above, and a people's government that would restore peace. It continued to urge the replacement of the Menzies government by a Labor one, but only so that the treacherous Labor leadership would 'expose itself in office' and 'hasten the end of reformism'. It constantly drew attention to the horrors of war, the needless slaughter and the rampant profiteering. Yet its slogans— 'Make the Rich Pay for the War', 'Strike for More Pay', 'Don't Work Overtime'—were scarcely the stuff of revolutionary defeatism.

Rather, they represented a remarkably conventional programme of industrial militancy. Conversely, the call for 'A People's Government and Peace' was scarcely a realistic way of dealing with a German leader who was sweeping all before him.[52]

Indeed, the more closely the Australian party's attitude towards the war is examined, the more stilted its conformance to Stalin's instructions appears. It was not that it resisted the twists and turns of Soviet diplomacy, though it is noticeable that the Australians never suggested that the Allies were the aggressor, as Stalin himself argued in 1940. Australia was one of the most compliant sections of the Communist International in its acceptance of the dictum that there was nothing to choose between the two capitalist blocs since they were both equally belligerent, just as predatory in their treatment of colonial peoples, alike in their fundamental malevolence to the workers' homeland. But to suggest that the Allied powers were no better than the Axis ones was not to favour Hitler, as Stalin did; it was rather to claim that the British and French ruling class had been hoist on its own petard. There was certainly a case to be made against the selective moral indignation of the Allies and the inability of the Australian government to provide genuine national leadership. There could be no justification for Stalin's utterly unprincipled opportunism. The long-term effects of the party's subservience to Soviet policy in the period 1939–41 would return in the Cold War to haunt Australian communists.

The immediate equivocations arose from the local attempts to suggest that in championing the interests of the Soviet Union, communists were also serving the real interests of the Australian people. Thus the CPA claimed that the two countries would both benefit from peace since each would avert the death, destruction and danger of invasion that war entailed. Its propaganda dwelt particularly on the threat from Japan. If the Australian communists presented the conflict in Europe as irrelevant to Australian security and of real concern only to conservative Anglophiles, it also warned that a Pacific war would threaten national survival. Hence the ambiguity of its criticisms of the war effort, with the persistent implication that the Menzies government was incapable of rising to the fascist threat. Even as Australian communists condemned the war, there remained a strong anti-fascist undertow, a conviction that the hypocritical appeasers would not, as well as could not, fight a real anti-fascist war. The term 'fascism' was dropped by Stalin when he entered into his agreement with Hitler, and generally eschewed by the Australian party, but its continuing presence in the minds of local communists is clearly discernible. Without the participation of the Soviet Union, Paterson argued early in 1941, the war was not against fascism but a contest for world domination by the 'kings of finance and industry'.[53]

The strains of these rationalisations began to tell on some of the party's leading unionists. Lloyd Ross accepted the twists and turns of 1939, took his turn on the Domain platform and led the debate on the 'Hands Off Russia' resolution at the New South Wales Labor Party conference in Easter 1940, but he found increasing resistance among the members of his state branch of the ARU to the campaign of industrial militancy. His own doubts about communist characterisation of the war as imperialist came to a head when Paris fell in mid-1940, and he held back from support of the breakaway Hughes–Evans State Labor Party. By August he was arguing that the labour movement had to take up the struggle against fascism and turn out Menzies for a Labor government committed to a popular war effort. In early September the party expelled him as a ' "middle class" intellectual' who had gone over to 'the camp of the class-collaborators'.[54] Some time earlier Bill Orr had resigned his position of secretary of the miners' union, finally falling victim to the bottle, and he was removed from the party central committee along with Mountjoy, the disgraced Western Australian secretary, and two other 'deserters'. The president of the Miners' Federation also fell by the wayside in the following year. As federal attorney-general, the seemingly ageless Billy Hughes had established a slush fund to counteract the efforts of the communists and promote industrial cooperation. Charlie Nelson and the president of the northern district of the miners' union, who both accepted payments, gave an undertaking in early 1941 that the miners would refrain from stoppages in order to 'assist Australia in the war emergency'. Nelson also had a problem with alcohol; the party observed that 'No doubt Charlie got down to "fundamentals" in the bar of Parliament House', and washed its hands of him.[55]

These defections did not alter the party's anti-war resolve and there is little evidence of defections among the communist union membership. Lloyd Ross was placed under considerable pressure from the left in his union. The executive of the Miners' Federation repudiated the statements of Nelson and his colleague, and communist candidates replaced both of them in subsequent union elections. The wharfies and seamen continued to conduct industrial campaigns, while the ironworkers embarked on a dozen significant strikes between October 1940 and May 1941, with general success and significant increase in membership. In 1941 publicans in north Queensland even alleged that communists had organised a union boycott that forced them to lower the price of beer.[56] The ACTU continued to suspect the intentions of the government, and Menzies was still unable to reach agreement with the unions for wartime organisation of industry. The picture that emerges is of ingrained antagonisms between an industrial labour movement with accumulated grievances and a government unwilling to acknowledge them and thus unable to secure their wholehearted support. If few accepted the communist argument that this was a war that did not concern Australian workers, they were not yet persuaded that it justified the sacrifices demanded of them.

The war continued to go against the British and Australian forces. In 1940 the *Luftwaffe* pounded British cities. In 1941 the *Panzerkorps* came to the rescue of the Italians in North Africa and drove the Allies back towards Egypt. In the same year the Germans swept down through the Balkans, and Australian communists once again reviled Churchill, the architect of the Gallipoli sacrifice of 1915, for his despatch of Australian forces to a bungled and costly defence of Greece. Now the master of western Europe, Hitler was already planning a further strike which could only be in the east. During the early months of 1941 Churchill warned Stalin that he was in danger; the Australian party construed his warnings as an invitation to Hitler to attack the Soviet Union, which was unthinkable. Even as German reconaissance aircraft flew over Soviet territory, it insisted that the 'provocateurs' would not succeed. The Red Army was invincible. The Soviet Union was not afraid of Germany, nor would it provoke that country. As late as 22 June 1941 communists described the rumours of an impending onslaught as 'a compound of imperialist hatred of the Soviet Union, British plans to switch the war and wishful thinking'.[57]

On that very day Hitler launched Operation Barbarossa and the German forces advanced deep into Soviet territory. Before the end of the year, the Japanese attack on Pearl Harbour would open the Pacific theatre of the war and Hitler's generals would be within sight of the Kremlin. With the attack on the Soviet Union, the war changed irrevocably and with it the communist war policy. 'The Soviet cause is the cause of working people everywhere,' proclaimed J. B. Miles, and called on the workers to rally to its support. The change was immediate and untroubled by any acknowledgement of past mistakes. 'The Wise, Farseeing Stalin' had anticipated all. On this unshakeable note Australian communism entered into a new era.[58]

Conclusion

With the opening of the Great Patriotic War, the history of Australian communism enters a new phase. Overnight the party became a supporter of the war, which it now proclaimed to be a people's war against fascism and for a new social order. Profiting from the close relationship between the new Labor government and the unions, in which the party had a strong role, it quickly recovered lost ground. By the time its legality was restored, at the end of 1942, it had trebled its membership over that in 1940 and by the close of the war there were more than 20 000 Australian communists. This period of unprecedented prestige and influence was brief, however, and yielded soon after the war to further conflict and controversy. The onset of the Cold War returned Australian communism to a beleaguered state from which it never recovered. There would be a further round of hostilities against the Chifley Labor government, a resounding victory against Menzies's second attempt to outlaw communism, and new accusations of treason. The party would assist colonial independence movements, contest the Western military alliance, justify every twist and turn of Soviet foreign policy. It would open major industrial campaigns, sustain a range of political and cultural endeavours, cultivate alliances and denounce rivals, suppress internal dissent, fall into disputation, divide and decline. The history of communism up to the Second World War is on an upward trajectory, that afterwards is one of protracted decline.

It is in the nature of history to disguise hindsight as inevitability.

This history has emphasised the adverse circumstances, the problems that confronted Australian communists and the internal weaknesses that afflicted their organisation in its first two decades, conscious always that in the end they were unsuccessful. Furthermore, it is not just their eventual failure that overshadows this early history but the manner of their passing. For in the end they were not defeated but rather succumbed. Some fell by the wayside, to be sure, and some retreated into an imaginary world in which time stood still and Khrushchev had never revealed Stalin's crimes, but the best of them remained true to their ideals, confronted the past as well as the future, and continued to organise and agitate. Whether or not they retained a formal connection, the CPA remained their party. Time did not so much vanquish the obduracy and ardour of these ageing comrades so much as it thinned their ranks, depleted their audience and removed the landmarks of their politics. As in Eastern Europe and the Soviet Union, there was no last heroic stand but an accumulation of failures, a growing realisation that the cause could not be salvaged. They did not yield to their enemies, they terminated the party as defiantly as they had created and sustained it.

But if the crooked path of history had not swerved in 1941 to revive the prestige of the Soviet Union, if the Red Army had not prevailed over the German *Wehrmacht* and if Marshal Stalin had not survived to project his model of Soviet power onto postwar circumstances, then radical energies would surely have taken a different direction. If the Australian Communist Party had not continued past 1941, if like the Wobblies its wartime suppression had broken it up so completely that an alternative working-class radicalism emerged in its place, how might its activity up to that point be assessed?

The older way of writing communist history, as a story of virtue rewarded, error punished and paradise postponed, clearly will not do. It is now apparent to all but those impervious to reason that the communist project itself was deeply flawed, that it nurtured tyranny within its emancipatory scheme. It gathered its adherents from particular segments of Australian society, the ardent, the outcast, the restless and dissatisfied; it gave them companionship, hope, purpose, and demanded much in return. It channelled their energies into a politics that pursued freedom through discipline, sought to mend social division by means of class war, appealed to altruism and worked with ruthless single-mindedness. Some fideists would still attribute the failure of Australian communism to opportunism and error, misapplication of working-class energies and betrayal of socialist principles, but that diagnosis is now confounded by what has followed the dissolution of communism. Their immanent critique cannot explain the far more conclusive failure of all attempts to supplant or replace communism with an alternative form of revolutionary class politics, let alone the more general decline of the labour movement. Communism might well be implicated in the collapse of socialism, but it is hardly responsible for the dwindling of class loyalties.

It will not do, either, to place the blame on the leaders. The party's hierarchical structure and subordination to Moscow, its rules of democratic centralism and intolerance of dissent, the authoritarian practices and personality cult that developed around prominent cadres, all undoubtedly disfigured Australian communism. Its lack of success has often been related in these terms. Thus Alastair Davidson presented it as the product of an indigenous radical tradition that succumbed to the deadening effects of Stalinism, which in turn committed Australian communists to modes of politics that were utterly inappropriate to Australian circumstances. Others have depicted the Communist Party of Australia as an army of lions led by asses, an organisation that attracted some of the finest men and women of their generation only to expend their enthusiasm in a tragic misapplication of effort. Thus Len Fox contrasted the 'Warm, Human People' who sustained the party and the cold, dogmatic 'Men at the Top' who directed them. There is much in the historical record and popular memory to support such a picture. So many of the recent memoirs set the courage, the generosity and exuberance of ordinary members alongside the cynical, grudging solemnity of those who directed them. So much of the history related here reveals errors of calculation and execution. From Earsman and Garden through to Miles and Sharkey, Australian communism seemed peculiarly suscep-tible to intriguers, adventurers and petty despots who stamped their own shortcomings upon the better impulses of the ordinary activist. My narrative has provided plentiful evidence of the failures of judgement, the squandering of opportunities and ruthless enforce-ment of discipline by the party leadership.

Yet I have also observed that the apparent conformity was far from complete. Australian communists did not simply take orders from Moscow; they drew support and guidance from the Communist International, they appealed to it and they used it to settle their own disputes. They did not merely imitate the Soviet model; they projected onto it their own aspirations. Nor did the leaders of the Australian party invariably direct the members to sectarian abuse or hold them back from practical endeavour; at crucial junctures we have seen the central committee tempering the excesses of doctrinaire local activists. Furthermore, the leaders did not command the absolute obedience that the party's rules suggested. The fact that the national executive had to keep intervening, straightening the line, replacing cadres, attests to the persistence of powerful contrary tendencies. The stress on a monolithic organisation characterised by iron discipline is indicative not of a docile obedience but rather of its composition of activists inclined to communism by a spirit of rebellion—determined, headstrong and refractory men and women who did not easily receive orders.

The communist party was a party of a new type, a disciplined army of the active members of the working class involved in every aspect of its collective effort and educated to see its true nature and implications. It was not a mere aggregation of groups and individuals but a unified whole, a collective intelligence capable of understanding and guiding the working class in its immediate situation, as it performed the necessary tasks towards its appointed historical mission. This communist party as conceived by Lenin was utterly remote from the Australian experience of the trade unions and Labor Party. The story of Australian communism in the 1920s is of a small, localised organisation that sought to create such a role for itself and repeatedly failed to do so, kept alive only by its association with an international movement and the periodic influx of new leaders with new strategies. In the 1930s there was an appreciable extension of membership and influence as communists found a role, first among the unemployed and then in the workforce. The party itself achieved an organisational coherence and stability that enabled it to transmute the directives of the Communist International into effective action. But by this time communism was no longer a politics of Leninist revolutionary internationalism, it was rather a Stalinist instrument of Soviet state power and strategic policy. The Australian party was not a fusion of theory and practice, it was a structure led by full-time communist functionaries and trade union officials.

In the course of its growth and consolidation Australian communism altered. It began in the socialist *demi-monde*, operating out of a shabby hired hall and reliant on open-air gatherings to spread its message; by the end of the 1930s there were communist headquarters in every city, hundreds of suburban branches conducted their regular 'cottage meetings', and major political initiatives were launched in town halls. Initially the party produced a four-page weekly newspaper; after less than two decades it outpublished any other Australian political party. In 1920 it had a toe-hold in the Sydney Trades Hall; by 1939 it was an active presence in every major union, and communist-led unions were far ahead of non-communist ones in their capacity for research, publicity and in industrial effectiveness. The early meetings of the Communist Party of Australia heard musical performances and songs from the Russian choir; soon it sustained a whole spectrum of alternative cultural activity. Its domestic and international concerns, at first barely programmatic, touched almost every aspect of public life.

With augmentation of capacity came changes in composition, practice and self-understanding. Communism found its initial support within the familiar social constituency of Australian radicalism, where the ranks of the unskilled, casual and often itinerant workers met the radicalised craft worker or self-employed tradesman seized with dissident purpose. The early communist activist might be a militant agitator fresh from the Wobblies, or a salaried union official attached to the Trades Hall Reds, or even one of the younger, middle-class and university educated enthusiasts such as Baracchi, Higgins and Jollie Smith. He, more often than she, was likely to be an immigrant estranged from the national exclusiveness of the Australian labour movement: all but one of the six party secretaries during the first two decades had reached adulthood before coming to the country. We might describe this early communist movement as a combination of outsiders—battlers, dissident labour activists, the *déclassé* petit-bourgeoisie and newcomers. The volatility of such a combination was apparent in the recurrent, acerbic and typically personal divisions over the party's purpose and policy. Two decades later, however, there was general agreement that the coalition had consolidated into a monolith, a stable proletarian party with a measure of middle-class support.

As Australian communism redefined its social base, so its language and imagery changed. Initially it presented itself as the champion of the oppressed, giving guidance and inspiration to the downtrodden wage-slave, calling on men to reclaim their manhood, and women to refuse the moral degradation of capitalist exploitation. The emphasis here was on the class war to repair the injuries of class, to restore and make whole. With the onset of the Depression the temper of Australian communism shifted from vulnerability to defiance. After the defeat of the labour movement in the strikes and lockouts of the late 1920s, mass unemployment brought a tone of irreconcilable difference, a rhetoric of unbending resolution and violent confrontation. Then, with the movement back into work and the growth of communist union activity, the language of defiance shifted once more to a language of power. The party was now an agent of improvement and advance, providing practical leadership for wage-earners and speaking for the Australian people in the defence of their freedoms. In their trade union work as well as in campaigns for a popular front against fascism and war, communists cultivated alliances that would increase their own capacity to direct and control.

The party that emerged from these changes was larger, broader and stronger than the tiny, beleaguered organisation formed twenty years earlier. Although it lost some adherents in the course of its transformations, it held most and gathered in many more. By the end of the 1930s the essential features of its membership were clearly established. It was a party of workers in which all other social groups played a strictly subordinate role. While the salaried, the self-employed, the farmers and shopkeepers, lawyers, doctors, teachers, journalists, writers and artists who attached themselves to it had their own spheres of activity, which in turn served the purposes of the popular front, they were expected to accept the leading role of the working class. Australian communism had some impact on interwar cultural life, but little on the country's intellectual institutions, for the number of university educated members was tiny and the party absorbed all their energies. Ralph Gibson and Lloyd Ross taught for the Workers' Educational Association before they joined the party, Esmonde Higgins did so after he left, but there were no communist academics other than John Anderson, whose ill-starred intervention into the party's affairs confirmed members' suspicion of halls of learning. It is noticeable that those Australians who contributed to Marxist theory at this time, such as V. G. Childe and Jack Lindsay, went overseas to do so. Not until after the Second World War would Australian communism enter into academic life here.

This is not say that the Australian party neglected theory. On the contrary, it regarded itself as the informed intelligence of the working class, channelling instinctive desire into understanding and action. It did so on the basis of Marxist theory as grasped and realised by Lenin, then codified by Stalin. That an originally critical analysis degenerated into dogma never entirely negated the potency of this cognitive process. Against the older forms of working-class organisation, the trade union and the Labor Party, whose pragmatism bound their deliberations to the logic of the market and the ballot box, communism provided a powerfully coherent alternative. It was crudely instrumental, often specious and opportunist in its rationalisation of sudden changes of the line, but it proceeded from a process of systematic deliberation that worked from its own texts, its own vocabulary and knowledge.

The party's growth sustained and enclosed the membership. From the very beginning its oppositional role imposed strains on adherents that were most likely to be withstood by supportive networks of comrades. In the first decade, only Sydney maintained an organisational continuity and it was in the inner suburbs of Sydney that these patterns of comradeship first developed: contiguity, friendship, shared interests, mutual assistance. The Saturday evening dance in the Communist Hall that so affronted the Melbourne puritans provided more than financial support. During the 1930s similar networks developed in other cities and regional centres, and the growing range of party activities and pastimes, the housewives' groups and youth centres, the Workers' Sports Federation and the New Theatre, provided popular front communism with a broader locale. The autonomous forms of party life both connected members and separated them. They were at once community leaders and yet different from their workmates and neighbours, exemplary workers and atypical enthusiasts. The Leninist model of a unified, disciplined body of revolutionaries acting as organic working-class intellectuals produced the figure of the Australian communist who enjoyed respect as a wise, disciplined outsider.[1]

Yet by 1939 it was apparent that this Australian communist was not in fact a revolutionary. The growth of the party, its strong presence in the trade unions and extensive participation in a whole range of public activities made it a part of civil society. It continued to contest exploitation and injustice, to agitate for change and improvement, to counterpose Soviet achievement against capitalist barbarism, but it did so from within, seeking to extend its own disciplined unity to the rest of the working class and thereby bring order and purpose to the whole of national life. By background and temperament, the Australian communist was a radical and a militant, a nay-sayer and a troublemaker; by training and conviction that person was an organiser and improver. The party channelled the spirit of rebellion into obedience, banished transgression, imposed regularity: of all sins in the communist lexicon, that of anarchy was the most reprehensible. Its emphasis on unity, firmness and control, its mistrust of spontaneity and local initiative, gave it a formidable capacity to direct campaigns and to withstand campaigns against it. The very qualities that enabled it to withstand illegality during the Second World War fatally compromised its revolutionary mission. Unlike the Wobblies, those unbending rebels who owed allegiance only to their principles, disdained all subterfuge and were ground under the iron heel, the Communist Party of Australia tied its fortunes to a foreign dictatorship, persisted with its own iron discipline and survived. Embattled and defiant, it still expected to keep its appointment with history.

Endnotes

The sources on which this study is based are identified in the endnotes. Most are listed in *Communism: A Resource Bibliography*, compiled by Beverley Symons with the assistance of Andrew Wells and Stuart Macintyre, and published by the National Library of Australia in 1994. This bibliography provides a comprehensive guide to the manuscripts sources, communist and other contemporary publications, as well as memoirs, oral histories, secondary works, research dissertations and other materials. Although I have drawn on some additional works, principally outside the ambit of Beverley Symons's compilation or produced after she completed her guide, they are too few to warrant separate listing.

The abbreviations used in the endnotes for organisations, publishers, libraries and archives are listed in the table of abbreviations.

The Australian records of the Communist International are indicated by the abbreviation CI. These records are held in Moscow by the Russian Centre for the Preservation and Study of Documents of Recent History. A microfilm copy of the records for Australia was deposited in the Mitchell Library by Barbara and Geoffrey Curthoys. The records use three numerical citations: the first is the number of the collection (the *fond* in Russian), the second gives the number of the series (*opis*) and the third the number of the file or folder (*delo*). The Mitchell Library has divided the microfilm into ten reels, classified as FM4 10415-24.

Where no repository is indicated for documentary sources, correspondence, taped interviews or transcripts, the item is in my possession.

Introduction

1 *History of the Communist Party of the Soviet Union (Bolsheviks)* (Moscow: Foreign Languages Publishing House, 1939); L. L. Sharkey, *An Outline History of the Australian Communist Party* (Sydney: Marx School, 1944); E. F. Hill, *Commu-*

nism and Australia: Reflections and Reminiscences (Fitzroy, Vic: CPA (ML), 1989);
W. J. Brown, *The Communist Movement and Australia: An Historical Outline*
(Haymarket, NSW: Australian Labour Movement History Publications, 1986);
Workers News Editorial Board, *Betrayal: A History of the Communist Party of Australia*
(Marrickville, NSW: Allen Books, n.d.); Tom O'Lincoln, *Into the Mainstream: The
Decline of Australian Communism* (Westgate, NSW: Stained Wattle Press, 1985).

2 Stan Moran, *Reminiscences of a Rebel* (Chippendale, NSW: APCOL, 1979);
Edgar Ross, *Of Storm and Struggle: Pages from Labour History* (Sydney: APCOL,
1982); John Sendy, *Comrades Come Rally! Recollections of an Australian Communist*
(Melbourne: Nelson, 1978); Bertha Walker, *Solidarity Forever!* (Melbourne:
National Press, 1972).

3 Beverley Symons, *Communism in Australia: A Resource Bibliography* (Canberra;
NLA, 1994).

4 Alastair Davidson, *The Communist Party of Australia: A Short History* (Stanford,
California: Hoover Institution Press, 1969).

5 Oriel Gray, *Exit Left: Memoirs of a Scarlet Woman* (Ringwood, Vic.: Penguin
Books, 1985); Dorothy Hewett, *Wild Card: An Autobiography 1923–1958* (Ring-
wood, Vic.: McPhee Gribble/Penguin Books, 1990); Daphne Gollan, 'The
Memoirs of "Cleopatra Sweatfigure" ', in Elizabeth Windschuttle (ed.), *Women,
Class and History: Feminist Perspectives on Australia 1788–1978* (Melbourne:
Fontana Books, 1980), pp. 313–29; Bernice Morris, *Between the Lines* (Colling-
wood, Vic: Sybylla Press, 1988); Amirah Inglis, *The Hammer & Sickle and the
Washing Up* (Melbourne: Hyland House, 1995); Joyce Stevens (ed.), *Taking the
Revolution Home: Work Among Women in the Communist Party of Australia
1920–1945* (Fitzroy, Vic: Sybylla Press, 1987); Audrey Johnson, *Bread and Roses:
A Personal History of Three Militant Women and their Friends 1902–1988* (Suth-
erland, NSW: Left Book Club, 1990); Bernard Smith, *The Boy Adeodatus: The
Portrait of a Lucky Young Bastard* (Ringwood, Vic.: Penguin Books, 1985); Roger
Milliss, *Serpent's Tooth: An Autobiographical Novel* (Ringwood, Vic.: Penguin
Books, 1984); Dorothy Hewett, *Chapel Perilous* (Sydney: Currency Press, 1972).

6 These and the sources subsequently discussed are listed in Symons, *Communism
in Australia: A Resource Bibliography*.

Chapter One   Foundation

1 Guido Baracchi's account of the cockroaches is in his memoir 'The Twenties',
Baracchi papers (NLA MS 5241, folder 44).

2 Roneoed circular dated 22 October 1920, in Socialist Labor Party records
(NLA MS 2576/4) and Hancock papers (ML MS 772/11).

3 That of Baracchi is held by Ann Turner; that of Norm Jeffery by John Sendy.

4 Involvement in the formation of the CPA is attributed to a host of individuals
who make up the Investigation Branch's Summary of Communism 1922–23
(AA, A6122, item 111).

5 J. Normington-Rawling, The Communist Party of Australia to 1930, Work in
Progress Seminar, ANU, 4 May 1962; Brodney, Recollections, Brodney papers
(SLV MS 10882/3).

6 *International Socialist*, 4 January 1919.

7 Eric Hobsbawm, *Age of Extremes: The Short Twentieth Century 1914–1991*
(London: Michael Joseph, 1994), ch. 2.

8 *International Socialist*, 10 January 1920.

9 See Bede Nairn's entry for Garden in the *Australian Dictionary of Biography*,

vol. 8, pp. 614–17. The best treatment of the Trades Hall Reds is by Miriam Dixson, Reformists and Revolutionists: An Interpretation of the Relations between the Socialists and the Mass Labor Organisations in New South Wales, 1919–27, PhD thesis, ANU, 1965, chs 1–3.

10 *To the I.W.W. A Special Message from the Communist International* (Melbourne: Proletarian Publishing Association, 1920); the foreword is dated 15 September. See generally Ian Turner, *Sydney's Burning* (Melbourne: Heinemann, 1967); Verity Burgmann, *Revolutionary Industrial Unionism: The Industrial Workers of the World in Australia* (Melbourne: CUP, 1995).

11 Joy Damousi, Socialist Women in Australia, c. 1880–1918, PhD thesis, ANU, 1987, ch. 7; Peter Morrison, The Communist Party of Australia and the Radical-Socialist Tradition, 1920–1939, PhD thesis, University of Adelaide, 1975, App. 3; Verna Coleman, *Adela Pankhurst: The Wayward Suffragette 1885–1961* (Melbourne: MUP, 1996), chs 11–12; Adela Pankhurst Walsh to Tom Walsh, n.d., Walsh papers (NLA MS 2123/61).

12 He is recalled in Bob Brodney's Recollections, Brodney papers (SLV MS 10882/3); the expulsion is recorded in the minutes of the VSP, 8 November, 2 December 1920 (NLA MS 564/1/6).

13 Ann Turner, Independent Working Class Education in Australia, 1917–29, MEd thesis, University of Melbourne, 1981, ch. 2 and her entry on Earsman in *ADB*, vol. 8, pp. 403–4.

14 *ADB*, vol. 11, pp. 641–2; Investigation Branch, Summary of Communism, p. 103 sets out the circumstances of the allegation.

15 The criticism was by Ray Everitt in *International Socialist*, 26 July 1919. Earsman's letters to Baracchi of 12 and 19 August 1919 describing these manoeuvres were copied by the censor (AA MP 95, item 169/41/90).

16 W. P. Tuitene, interviewed by J. N. Rawling, Rawling papers (ANU N57/299) and Simonoff's report to the People's Commissariat of Foreign Affairs, November 1921; I am grateful to Greg Pemberton for providing me with a copy.

17 Eric Fried, 'The First Consul: Peter Simonoff and the Formation of the Australian Communist Party', in John McNair and Thomas Poole (eds), *Russia and the Fifth Continent: Aspects of Russian–Australian Relations* (St Lucia, Queensland: UQP, 1992), pp. 110–25.

18 *Communist*, 23 September 1921. Many years later Earsman presented a similar account in a letter to John Playford, 9 October 1958, Rawling papers (ANU N57/234).

19 Investigation Branch, The Secret Seven, Summary of Communism, pp. 132–3; see Fiona Capp, *Writers Defiled* (Ringwood, Vic.: McPhee Gribble, 1993), pp. 15–26.

20 *International Socialist*, 2 October 1920.

21 Minutes of conference called by Central Executive Committee of the ASP, 30 October 1920, Hancock papers (ML MS 772/9). Reardon's version is repeated by J. N. Rawling in his unpublished history, Communism Comes to Australia, vol. 1, p. 72, Rawling papers (ANU N57/1).

22 *International Socialist*, 6 November 1920.

23 Communist Party of Australia, *Manifesto to the Workers of Australia* (Sydney: CPA, 1920).

24 Drusilla Modjeska and Marjorie Pizer (eds), *The Poems of Lesbia Harford* (Sydney: Angus & Robertson, 1985), p. 81 and introduction by Modjeska.

25 *Communist*, 19 August 1921.

26 *International Socialist*, 4 January 1919.

27 *Australian Communist*, 24 December 1920.

28 William Lane, *The Workingman's Paradise: An Australian Labour Novel* (Brisbane: Dunlop, 1892).

29 W. J. Thomas, *Venereal Disease: A Social Problem* (Sydney: self-published, 1922).

Chapter 2   What was to be done?

1 'Labour Government in Australia', in *Lenin on Britain* (London: Martin Lawrence, 1934), pp. 91–3. The provenance of the article, first published in *Pravda* on 13 June 1913, and its subsequent redactions are discussed by Rick Kuhn, 'Lenin on the ALP: The Career of 600 Words', *Australian Journal of Politics and History*, vol. 35, no. 1 (1989), pp. 28–49.

2 Jurgen Tampke (ed.), *Wunderbar Country: Germans Look at Australia, 1850–1914* (Sydney: Hale & Iremonger, 1982); Crauford Goodwin, *Economic Enquiry in Australia* (Durham, North Carolina: Duke University Press, 1964), ch. 11.

3 Tom Poole and Eric Fried, 'Artem, A Bolshevik in Brisbane', *Australian Journal of Politics and History*, vol. 31, no. 2 (1985), pp. 243–54.

4 'Australia, the Lucky Country', translated by Poole and Fried in 'Artem, A Bolshevik in Brisbane'.

5 'Manifesto of the Communist Party', in Karl Marx and Frederick Engels, *Selected Works* (Moscow: Foreign Languages Publishing House, 1951), vol. 1, p. 35.

6 ibid., pp. 44, 49.

7 ibid., p. 44.

8 ibid., p. 35.

9 Leszek Kolakowski, *Main Currents of Marxism: Its Rise, Growth and Dissolution. Volume 2. The Golden Age* (Oxford: Clarendon Press, 1978), ch. 1.

10 V. I. Lenin, *Selected Works in Three Volumes* (Moscow: Progress Publishers, 1970), vol. 1, pp. 143, 151.

11 'One Step Forward, Two Steps Back' (1904), in ibid., p. 431.

12 A. J. Polan, *Lenin and the End of Politics* (London: Methuen, 1984).

13 'Conditions of Admission to the Communist International', in Jane Degras (ed.), *The Communist International 1919–1943: Documents*, vol. 1 (London: OUP, 1956), pp. 166–72.

14 Fernando Claudin, *The Communist Movement from Comintern to Cominform. Part One: The Crisis of the Communist International*, trans. Brian Pearce (New York: Monthly Review Press, 1975), p. 104.

15 Vere Gordon Childe, *How Labour Governs*, first published 1923 (Melbourne: MUP, 1964); Humphrey McQueen, *A New Brittania: An Argument Concerning the Social Origins of Australian Radicalism and Nationalism* (Ringwood, Vic.: Penguin Books, 1970); Donald Horne, *The Lucky Country: Australia in the Sixties* (Ringwood, Vic.: Penguin Books, 1964).

16 'Freedom on the Wallaby' (May 1891), in Henry Lawson, *Poems* Colin Roderick (ed.) (Sydney: John Ferguson, 1979), pp. 50–1.

17 Stuart Macintyre, *The Labour Experiment* (Melbourne: McPhee Gribble, 1989).

18 G. C. Hewitt, A History of the Victorian Socialist Party 1906–32, MA thesis, La Trobe University, 1974.

19 Verity Burgmann, *Revolutionary Industrial Unionism: The Industrial Workers of the World in Australia* (Melbourne: CUP, 1995).

20 Ian Turner, *Industrial Labour and Politics: The Labour Movement in Eastern Australia 1900–1921* (Canberra: ANUP, 1965), chs 7–8.

21 Roger Coates, 'Lenin's Impact on Australia', *Australian Left Review*, no. 24 (April–May 1970), pp. 26–32.

22 Quoted in Edgar Ross, *The Russian Revolution: Its Impact on Australia* (Sydney: SPA, 1972), p. 15.

23 Patrick O'Farrell, 'The Russian Revolution and the Labour Movements of Australia and New Zealand', *International Review of Social History*, vol. 8 (1963),

pp. 177–97; Frank Farrell, *International Socialism and Australian Labour: The Left in Australia 1910–1939* (Sydney: Hale & Iremonger, 1981), chs 1–2.

24 Quoted by L. F. Crisp, *The Australian Federal Labor Party 1901–1951* (London: Longmans Green, 1955), p. 280.

25 R. S. Ross, *Revolution in Russia and Australia* (Melbourne: Ross's Book Service, 1920), pp. 6, 7, 30, 46–7.

Chapter 3   Recognition

1   Correspondence with the Melbourne, Perth, Brisbane and Newtown branches during December 1920, and with an Adelaide branch on 27 January 1921, is in CPA records (ML MS 5021 ADD-ON 1936, box 4).

2   *International Communist*, 1 January 1921.

3   Minutes of recalled conferences, 6, 13 November 1920, and executive meetings 23, 29 November, 6, 11 December 1920, Hancock papers (ML MS 772/9).

4   Minutes of recalled conference, 11 December 1920, supplemented by further account reported in *International Communist*, 1 January 1921.

5   Reardon to Earsman, 14 December 1920, reprinted in *Australian Communist*, 24 December 1920, and *International Communist*, 1 January 1921.

6   *Australian Communist*, 24 December 1921.

7   T. Glynn, 'Communists and Industrial Unionism', *Australian Communist*, 31 December 1920; W. P. Earsman, 'The Communist Party and Industrial Unionism', *Australian Communist*, 14 January 1921; J. Garden, 'The Pure and Simple "Communist": An Elementary Lesson in Communist Tactics', *Australian Communist*, 22 April 1921.

8   Donald Grant and Douglas Sinclair, open letter to Tom Glynn, *International Communist*, 19 March 1921; letter from Charlie Reeves in ibid., 26 March 1921; articles by Brodney and Everitt in ibid., 9, 16, 30 April 1921. See Verity Burgmann, *Revolutionary Industrial Unionism: The Industrial Workers of the World in Australia* (Melbourne: CUP, 1995), ch. 15.

9   Sussex Street executive minutes, 22 January 1921, Hancock papers (ML MS 772/9), and Liverpool Street executive minutes in *International Communist*, 5 February 1921; letter from Thomas to friends in Brisbane, n.d. [early 1921], Comintern records (CI 495/94/17) and Christian Jollie Smith to Earsman, 8 July 1921, Investigation Branch report (AA, A981, COM 10); *Communist*, 11 November 1921.

10 Judd to Earsman, 16 March 1921 (NLA MS 2576/6); conference minutes, 25 March 1921, Hancock papers (ML MS 772/9).

11 Executive minutes, 22 January, 26 February 1921, Hancock papers.

12 Investigation Branch, Case of Paul Freeman (AA, A3932); notes by J. R. Rawling, Rawling papers (ANU N57/239); Bertha Walker, *Solidarity Forever!* (Melbourne: National Press, 1972), pp. 178–81; 'Two Class War Fighters Remembered', *Workers' Weekly*, 23 July 1926. The first of Freeman's articles was 'Moscow Calls to Australia's Trade Unions', *International Communist*, 12 March 1921. His deportation is discussed by Ray Evans, 'Radical Departures: Paul Freeman and Political Deportation from Australia Following World War One', *Labour History*, no. 57 (November 1989), pp. 16–26.

13 Everitt and Reardon to Central Executive Committee of the Communist International, 22 March 1921, Comintern records (CI 495/94/6).

14 Sussex Street executive minutes, 1 April 1921, and correspondence, 5, 8 April 1921, Hancock papers (ML MS 772/9), supplemented by statements by Garden

and Baker, *Communist*, 24 June 1921; *International Communist*, 7, 28 May 1921. See also the copies of the correspondence sent with an explanation by Reardon to the Communist International, 15 April 1921, Comintern records (CI 495/94/6).

15 *Communist*, 6, 13 May 1921; *International Communist*, 7, 14, 21 May 1921; *Sydney Morning Herald*, 7, 9 May 1921; there is a verbatim report of the May Day meeting in Investigation Branch's Summaries of Communism 1920–7 (AA A8911, item 154) and also that of Norm Jeffery, CPA records (ML MS 5021, box 83). See also Andrew Moore, *The Secret Army and the Premier: Conservative Paramilitary Organisations in New South Wales 1930–32* (Kensington: NSWUP, 1989), pp. 39–41.

16 For others see Raymond Evans, *The Red Flag Riots: A Study of Intolerance* (St Lucia, Qld: UQP, 1988), and Bobbie Oliver, *War and Peace in Western Australia: The Social and Political Impact of the Great War 1914–1926* (Nedlands, WA: UWAP, 1995).

17 Earsman diary, 8, 10, 16, 17, 23, 25 April, 9, 15, 22 May 1921, Earsman papers, University of Edinburgh Library Special Collections; I am grateful to Ann Turner for providing me with a copy.

18 Earsman diary, 26 May–2 June 1921; entries for Quinton and Rees in Investigation Branch, Summary of Communism, 1921–23 (AA, A6122, item 111); and Lamb's progress through Britain was reported to the Australian government on 20 July 1921, Hughes papers (NLA MS 1538/21/143–6). The misfortunes of the Adelaide delegates are described in the diary of Ted Moyle (in possession of Jim Moss), and by John Playford in History of the Left Wing of the South Australian Labor Movement, 1908–36, BA Hons thesis, University of Adelaide, 1958, pp. 42–3.

19 Earsman diary, 12–22 June and his report to the executive of the Sussex Street party, Hancock papers (ML MS 772/9), reprinted in *Australian Left Review*, no. 27 (October–November 1970), pp. 2–19; Earsman to Praesidium of the Third International, 16 June 1921, Comintern records (CI 495/94/6); Earsman to Simonoff, 11 August 1921, Earsman papers.

20 Earsman diary, 23 June–23 July, and his report, which differs in important respects from the diary. The progress of the other delegates is recorded in Investigation Branch, Summary of Communism 1922–23, pp. 66–8, 91, 99 (AA A 6122, item 11).

21 Earsman diary, 25, 28, 30 July 1921.

22 Earsman's report to the Small Bureau on behalf of the Australian delegates, dated 5 August, Comintern records (CI 495/94/6); diary, 1–5 August 1921; letter to Sussex Street executive, 2 August 1921, Hancock papers (ML MS 772/9). See the Investigation Branch report on Smith (AA A6122/40, 111), and Geoff Bullen, 'William Smith—Bohemian Socialist', *Recorder*, no. 56 (February 1972), pp. 10–12.

23 Additional confidential report to CEC of CPA, n.d. CPA records (ML MS 5021, box 82).

24 See especially Wilkinson's articles in *Inprecorr*, vol. 1, nos 15, 17 (9, 16 December 1921), and the report of the Anglo–American Bureau, 6 April 1922, Comintern records (CI 495/72/2). There is an account of Wilkinson's departure from and return to Adelaide in the diary of Ted Moyle.

25 Earsman to Executive, Comintern, 12 August 1921, and to Rakosi, secretary of the Comintern, 4 September 1921, Comintern records (CI 495/94/6); diary, 6 August–4 December 1921, and Investigation Branch, Summary of Communism 1921–23, pp. 26–36. The arrest of Lamb and the confiscation of his passport are the subject of an Investigation Branch report (AA A981, COM 10), which also contains a copy of Earsman's letter to the Comintern Secretariat

giving the new address. A report to the prime minister on 9 March 1922 also reveals the Investigation Branch had access to his diary; Hughes papers (NLA MS 1538/21/196–200).

26 Two delegates of the Seamen's Union submitted a report to their union but they arrived after the Congresses; Walsh papers (NLA MS 2123/61).

27 Earsman's diary, 15 June 1921.

28 ibid., 5 August 1921.

29 'Who Are the Communists? The Result of an Investigation', supplement to *International Communist*, 24 September 1921. For Miles's loyalties, see his letter to A. T. Brodney, 21 May 1921, Rawling papers (ANU N57/270), and also *Communist*, 30 September 1921. He described his wartime inactivity in 'This is J. B. Miles', *Communist Review*, vol. 4, no. 2 (February 1937), pp. 6–10.

30 C. W. Baker to D. Rosen, 7 November 1921, Brodney papers (SLV MS 10882/5/9).

31 *Communist*, 19 August 1921.

32 Earsman's articles began appearing in the *Communist*, 26 August 1921; the result of the Small Bureau hearing was reported by the acting secretary of Sussex Street, 20 October 1921, Hancock papers (ML MS 772/9), and his letter from London, 7 September 1921, is attached to the acting secretary's report. The Investigation Branch's Summary of Communism 1921–23 quotes from both correspondence and diary.

33 Freeman's articles began appearing in *International Communist* from 6 June; his death was reported on 6 August 1921; Lamb to Reardon, n.d., Hancock papers (ML MS 772/9) and Investigation Branch report on Lamb (AA A6122/40, 111).

34 Baker to Reardon, n.d.; Reardon to C. E. France, 14 October, Reardon to Baker, 21 December 1921, Earsman to Reardon, 27 December 1921, Hancock papers (ML MS 772/9); minutes of the Annual Conference, 27–29 December 1921, Hancock papers (ibid.).

35 Earsman to Francis, 13 December 1921, and Francis, Notes, n.d., Brodney papers (SLV MS 10882/5/10); May Brodney [Francis] to Baracchi, Baracchi papers (NLA MS 5241); minutes of the Annual Conference, 22–29 December 1921.

36 Minutes of the Unity Conference, 18–19 February 1922, Hancock papers (ML MS 772/9); C. W. Baker to Executive Committee of the Communist International, February 1922, Comintern records (CI 495/94/6).

37 Everitt to Executive Committee of the Communist International, 7 February 1922, Comintern records (ibid.), drawing on letter from C. E. France to Reardon, 4 January 1922, Hancock papers (ML MS 772/9). The controversy over Smith continued in *Communist*, 20 January 1922 and *International Communist*, 29 January 1922.

38 Kuusinen to Garden and Reardon, 10 April 1922, Comintern records (CI 495/94/11), and minutes of the Anglo–American Bureau, 15 June 1922, Comintern records (CI 495/72/2).

39 Reardon to Brodney, 17 October 1921, Brodney to Reardon, 7 February 1922, and to Alf Rees, 25 April 1922, Brodney papers (SLV MS 10882/1/1).

40 Minutes of the Sydney branch of the ASP, 16 February–20 June (ML MS 2389/1); Rees to Brodney, 16 April, 3 May 1922, E. L. J. to Brodney, 16 May 1922, Reardon to Brodney, 18 June 1922, Brodney papers (SLV MS 10882/1/1); and Tom Payne, interviewed by Andrew Reeves and Ann Turner, 17 May 1976 (NLA).

41 Minutes of the combined Sydney branch of the CPA, 24 July 1922– 24 January 1923, CPA records (ML MS 2389/1); minutes of the Unity Conference, 15–18 July 1922, and minutes of the First Annual Conference of the United CPA, 23–28 December 1922, CPA records (ML MS 5021 ADD-ON 1936, box 1);

statement by executive in *Communist*, 1 December 1922 and report of the executive to ECCI, 26 January 1923, Comintern records (CI 495/94/19); Investigation Branch, Summary of Communism, pp. 205–17.

42 Minutes of the Anglo–American Bureau, 15 June, 4 July, 8 August 1922, Comintern records (CI 495/94/11 and 72/2); Earsman to Comintern, 22 July, Comintern records (CI 495/94/11); his report to CPA, 10 December 1922, and ECCI to the United Communist Party of Australia, 25 December 1922, Earsman papers.

Chapter 4   Tactics

1 The augmentation of the authority of the Congress and Executive by the Fourth Congress of the Communist International is documented in Jane Degras (ed.), *The Communist International 1919–1943: Documents*, vol. 1 (London: OUP, 1956), pp. 436–42.

2 Earsman diary, 8–9 May 1921, University of Edinburgh Library Special Collections.

3 See the reports of Earsman, 12 July 1921, Bill Smith, 17 August 1921, and Jim Quinton, 29 September 1921, Comintern records (CI 534/7/1; 495/94/6).

4 *Communist*, 25 August 1922.

5 Raymond Markey, *In Case of Oppression: The Life and Times of the Labor Council of New South Wales* (Sydney: Pluto Press, 1994), p. 190.

6 *Communist*, 11, 18 November 1921, 10, 14 February, 7 April 1922; *Direct Action*, February 1922, and Glynn to Earsman, 7 March 1922, CPA records (ML).

7 John Playford, History of the Left Wing of the South Australian Labor Movement, 1908–36, BA Hons thesis, University of Adelaide, 1958, ch. 2.

8 Anglo–American Bureau meeting, 6 April 1922, Comintern records (CI 495/72/2); the reservations of Sussex Street are apparent in the editorial in *Communist*, 8 July 1921, while Garden's account appeared in the party monthly, *Proletarian*, August 1921. See generally the *Official Report of the All-Australian Trades Union Conference* (Melbourne: ALP, 1921); Ian Turner, *Industrial Labour and Politics: The Labour Movement in Eastern Australia 1900–1921* (Canberra: ANUP, 1965), ch. 9; and Miriam Dixson, 'The First Communist "United Front" in Australia', *Labour History*, no. 10 (May 1966), pp. 20–31.

9 *Theses on Tactics Adopted by the Third Congress of the Communist International* (Sydney: CPA, 1921), and ECCI directives on the united front, 18 December 1921, reprinted in Degras (ed.), *The Communist International*, vol. 1, pp. 307–16; *Communist*, 24 March, 9 June 1922.

10 Minutes of the Anglo–American Bureau, 8, 10, 11, 24 August 1922, Comintern records (CI 495/72/2); Earsman diary, 7–11 August, 9 November 1922, and report by W. P. Earsman, 13 December 1922, Earsman papers and CPA records (ML MS 5021, box 82); credentials letter, 1 September 1922, Comintern records (CI 491/1/353); and Earsman's articles in *Inprecorr*, vol. 2, no. 63 (1 August 1922) and *Communist*, 1 September 1922.

11 Earsman diary, 10 August, 14 October, 18 November, 5, 20 December 1922, 10, 22 January, 21 February, 4 April, 14 June 1923, 14 August 1924; entry by Ann Turner in *ADB*, vol. 8, pp. 403–4.

12 *Fourth Congress of the Communist International: Abridged Report* (London: CPGB, 1923), p. 291; Earsman to Kuusinen, 4 February 1923, and general secretary of CPA to Comintern, 'Reporter for the Colonies', 2 November 1923, Comintern records (CI 495/94/17, 19). The minutes of the Second Conference,

23–24 December 1922 give a membership of 128, though this figure omits the former ASP members of the Sydney branch who might have added as many as 75; CPA records (ML MS 5021 ADD-ON 1936, box 1) .

13 Garden's speech reported in *Inprecorr*, vol. 2, no. 116 (22 December 1922), pp. 968–70, and *Fourth Congress of the Communist International*, pp. 230–2; J. N. Rawling, Communism comes to Australia, p. 118, Rawling papers (ANU N57/1).

14 Tom Payne, interviewed by Andrew Reeves and Ann Turner, 17 May 1976 (NLA).

15 *Scotsman*, 10 February 1923; Earsman to ECCI, 16 February, 16 March 1923 and diary, 22 February, 22 March 1923; Garden to ECCI, 17 July 1923; Bob Stewart to Communist International, 11 September 1923, Comintern records (CI 495/94/17, 23 and 117); Arthur Hoyle, *John Smith (Jock) Garden (1882–1968): A Political Biography* (Canberra: self-published, 1984), pp. 47–8, who draws on Lossiemouth testimony. More than a decade later, as a Labor member of the House of Representatives, Garden rebutted conservative accusations of communist irreligion with the claim that he was 'holding a mission in the north of Scotland' in 1922, 146 *CPD* p. 341 (27 March 1935).

16 Earsman, 'Lenin and Australia', typescript, n.d., Earsman papers.

17 ibid.

18 Tom Payne, address to Victorian branch of the ASSLH, n.d. Payne's version is retrospective, hostile and dubious.

19 The letter was published in *Communist*, 23 February 1923.

20 Minutes of the First Annual Conference of the United CPA, 23–8 December 1922, CPA records (ML MS 5021 ADD-ON 1936, box 1); the relevant resolutions were published in *Communist*, 22 December 1922.

21 *Workers' Weekly*, 27 July 1923.

22 *Workers' Weekly*, 17, 24, 31 August, 7 September 1923.

23 *Communist*, 10 June 1921, 5, 19 May 1922; *Sydney Morning Herald*, 4 October 1921, Sydney *Sun*, 17 May 1922 for the attack by Ley; Annie Allison to Executive Committee of the Young Communist International, 18 March 1923, Comintern records (CI 533/10/1). See *ADB*, vol. 10, pp. 97–8, for the minister, T. J. Ley, and see generally Ray Sutton, Labour Movement Youth Organisation and Policy in Eastern Australia, c.1918–c.1939, PhD thesis, ANU, 1990, ch. 1.

24 H. L. Denford to R. Stewart, 2 November 1923, Comintern records (CI 495/94/19); and his report as financial secretary to the Fifth Conference of the CPA, 26–8 December 1925, CPA records (ML MS 5021 ADD-ON 1936, box 1).

25 'Capitalist Home Life and Communism', *Australian Communist*, 7 January 1921. See Joy Damousi, *Women Come Rally: Socialism, Communism and Gender in Australia 1890–1955* (Melbourne: OUP, 1994), chs 5–6.

26 'Woman's Approach to Communism', *Communist*, 18 August 1922, and resolution to establish women's groups in minutes of the First Annual Conference of the United CPA, 23–28 December 1922 CPA records (ML 5021 ADD-ON 1936, box 1); see also Hetty Weitzel, 'Women of the Working Class. Why They Are Not Yet in the Movement', *Workers' Weekly*, 16 November 1923; and Joyce Stevens (ed.), *Taking the Revolution Home: Work Among Women in the Communist Party of Australia 1920–1945* (Fitzroy, Vic.: Sybylla Press, 1987), pp. 24–5.

27 *Workers' Weekly*, 6 July 1923.

28 Baracchi, 'The Twenties', Baracchi papers (NLA MS 5241, folder 44).

29 The complex factional patterns of the New South Wales branch of the Labor Party have been treated at length by D. W. Rawson, The Organisation of the

Australian Labor Party 1916–1941, PhD thesis, ANU, 1954, ch. 5; Miriam Dixson, Reformists and Revolutionaries: An Interpretation of the Relations between the Socialists and the Mass Labor Organisations in New South Wales, 1919–27, PhD thesis, ANU, 1965, chs 5–6; Heather Radi and Peter Spearritt (eds), *Jack Lang* (Sydney: Hale & Iremonger, 1977), chs 3–4; Bede Nairn, *The 'Big Fella': Jack Lang and the Australian Labor Party 1891–1949* (Melbourne: MUP, 1986), ch. 3; and Jim Hagan and Ken Turner, *A History of the Labor Party in New South Wales, 1891–1991* (Melbourne: Longman Cheshire, 1991), part 2. The underlying dynamics are best treated in Miriam Dixson, *Greater than Lenin? Lang and Labor 1916–1932* (Melbourne: Melbourne Politics Monograph, 1976).

30 *Workers' Weekly*, 13, 20, 27 July, 3 August, 12 October 1923; *Daily Telegraph*, 3 August 1923; *Common Cause*, 26 September 1923; W. J. Thomas, *A Red Revolution for £500! An Account of the Weaver–Thomas Conspiracy Case* (Sydney: Sydney Printing House, n.d. [1923]). See Edgar Ross, *A History of the Miners' Federation of Australia* (Sydney: Australasian Coal and Shale Employees' Federation, 1970), pp. 318–20.

31 The *Workers' Weekly* published 'Twelve Reasons Why the Labor Party Should Allow the Affiliation of the Communist Party' in a series of articles from 1–29 February 1924.

32 Quoted by Ross McMullin, *The Light on the Hill: The Australian Labor Party, 1891–1991* (Melbourne: OUP, 1991), p. 134.

33 Financial secretary's report to the Fifth Conference of the CPA, 26–8 December 1925, CPA records (ML 502 ADD-ON 936, box 1).

34 ECCI to CPA, 18 August 1924, Comintern records (CI 495/18/229); Garden to Piatnitsky, 26 August 1924; Montefiore to Albert Inkin (a CPGB member in Moscow), 1 February 1925 Comintern records (CI 495/94/26); and Investigation Branch, Summary of Communism 1922–23, pp. 281–2 (AA A6122, item 111). The visit of Rubin Herscovici is the subject of an Intelligence Branch file (AA A8911, item 154).

35 Minutes of the Third Conference of the CPA, 22–27 December 1923, CPA records (ML MS 5021 ADD-ON 1936, box 1).

36 Minutes of the Melbourne branch, 7 January 1925; Brodney to Garden, 7 January 1925, and Christian Jollie Smith to Brodney, n.d., Brodney papers (SLV MS 10882/5/11).

37 Minutes of the Fourth Conference of the CPA, 26–28 December 1924, CPA records (ML MS 5021 ADD-ON 1936, box 1); *Workers' Weekly*, 19 December 1924, 9 January 1925.

38 *Workers' Weekly*, 9 January, 20 February 1925. Alastair Davidson, *The Communist Party of Australia: A Short History*, (Stanford, California: Hoover Institution Press, 1969) p. 33, and Frank Farrell, *International Socialism and Australian Labour: The Left in Australia 1919–1931* (Sydney: Hale & Iremonger, 1981), p. 65, both suggest he was the originator of the decision.

39 *Workers' Weekly*, 5 June 1925.

40 Garden's report to the Fifth Conference of the CPA 26–28 December 1925, CPA records (ML MS 5021, ADD-ON 1936, box 1); see Dixson, 'Reformists and Revolutionaries', ch. 6; Davidson, *The Communist Party of Australia*, ch. 2.

41 Baruch Hirson and Lorraine Vivian, *Strike Across the Empire: The Seamen's Strike of 1925 in Britain, South Africa and Australasia* (London: Clio Publications, 1992), esp. ch. 6; Brian Fitzpatrick and Rowan Cahill, *The Seamen's Union of Australia 1872–1972: A History* (Sydney: SUA, 1981), ch. 9.

42 Baracchi to Tom Wright, 9 December 1925, Comintern records (CI 495/94/26); letter from Baracchi to *Labor Daily*, 24 December 1925; 'The Twenties', Baracchi papers.

43 Minutes of the Melbourne branch, Brodney papers, as in note 36.

44 Baracchi, interviewed by Miriam Dixson, 11 July 1962; Minutes of the Fifth Conference of the CPA, 26–28 December 1925, organising secretary's report, as in note 40.

45 E. M. Higgins, 'Moralisings while on SS *Baradine*, June–July 1924', Rawling papers (ANU N57/174); Christian Jollie Smith to Higgins, 9 January, 18 July 1924, Higgins papers (ML MS 740/11); Higgins to Pollitt, September 1924, 25 March 1925, Higgins papers (ML MS 740/4, 7) and *Workers' Weekly*, 31 July 1925. The figure of 40 members is attributed to him by Baracchi, interviewed by Miriam Dixson; in an interview with J. N. Rawling, 11 February 1952, Rawling papers (ANU N57/198), Higgins suggested there were 129 members.

46 *Seven Poor Men of Sydney*, first published 1934 (Sydney: Sirius, 1981), pp. 57–8, 125, 148, 172–4, and Hazel Rowley, *Christina Stead: A Biography* (Melbourne: William Heinemann, 1993). Baracchi's self-identification is noted in David Walker, 'Guido Baracchi', *Overland*, no. 97 (December 1984), p. 16.

47 Baracchi, 'The Twenties'.

Chapter 5   Communism goes bush

1 Report on 'The Communist Menace in Australia', Latham papers (NLA MS 1009/27/120–62).

2 Minutes of the CPA Central Executive, 2 March 1926; minister for trade and customs to secretary of the CPA, 22 November 1926, CPA records (ML MS 5021 ADD-ON 1936, box 4) and report to Comintern, 15 April 1926, Comintern records (CI 495/72/14); Frank Cain, *The Origins of Political Surveillance in Australia* (Sydney: Angus & Robertson, 1983), chs 6–7; Sam Ricketson, 'Liberal Law in a Repressive Age: Communism and the Law 1920–1950', 3, *Monash University Law Review* (1976), pp. 101–33; Laurence W. Maher, 'The Use and Abuse of Sedition', 14 *Sydney Law Review* (September 1992), pp. 287–316.

3 David Carment, 'Sir Littleton Groom and the Deportation Crisis of 1925: A Study of Non-Labor Response to Trade Union Militancy', *Labour History*, no. 32 (May 1977), pp. 46–54; Bruce's speech and the Nationalist handbook are in the Latham papers (NLA MS 1009/26/1, 9).

4 File on the Crimes Act Amendment Bill, which includes Latham's second reading speech, Latham papers (NLA MS 1009/27/1); Garran to Latham, 9 November 1928 (AA A467, item SF42/64).

5 Despatches from Casey (AA, A467, SF42/64); see Christopher Andrew and Oleg Gordievesky, *KGB: The Inside Story of its Foreign Operations from Lenin to Gorbachev* (London: Hodder & Stoughton, 1990), pp. 82–4; Francis Beckett, *Enemy Within: The Rise and Fall of the British Communist Party* (London: John Murray, 1995), ch. 2.

6 The extensive literature on these movements is listed in Andrew Moore, *The Secret Army: Conservative Paramilitary Organisations in New South Wales 1930–32* (Kensington: NSWUP, 1989).

7 Investigation Branch, Summary of Communism, 26 July 1922 (AA A1979/199), and H. E. Jones, 'Communism in Australia', 22 June 1927 (AA A467); see also Fiona Capp, *Writers Defiled* (Ringwood, Vic.: McPhee Gribble, 1993), pp. 15–26.

8 Higgins to Pollitt, 22 March 1925, Higgins papers (ML MS 740/7); for Barracchi, see chap. 4, note 42 *supra*.

9 Jock Garden, 'In Soviet Russia', *Workers' Weekly*, 22 June 1923.

10 *Australian Communist*, 24 December 1920, and *Proletarian*, no. 29 (June 1923); Howie reported by Baracchi, 'The Twenties', Baracchi papers (NLA MS 5241, folder 44).

11 Baker, 'Building a Communist Party', *Communist*, 29 July 1921.

12 Baracchi, 'The Twenties'.

13 For the first of these incidents see Raymond Evans, *The Red Flag Riots: A Study of Intolerance* (St Lucia, Qld UQP, 1988); D. H. Lawrence, *Kangaroo*, first published 1923 (London: Ace Books, 1961), p. 307; the pamphlet *Under Which Flag?* (Sydney: Nationalist Federation, 1928) is discussed by Andrew Lee, Nothing to Offer But Fear? Non-Labor Electioneering in Australia, 1914–54, PhD thesis, ANU, 1997, ch. 4.

14 Frank Sheridan to A. T. Brodney, 20 November 1921, Brodney papers (SLV MS 10882/5).

15 See for example, the defence of the trial of the socialist revolutionaries in *Communist*, 7 November 1922, and of religious leaders, 6 April 1923.

16 This was the proposition advanced by Carl Baker and opposed by J. B. King in August 1922; see *Communist*, 11 August 1922.

17 *Communist*, 15 July 1921; the editorial was by Carl Baker.

18 Autobiographical notes, 1920, in Higgins papers (ML MS 740/4, item 19).

19 Rajani to Salme Dutt, n.d. [February 1924], Dutt papers, CPGB archives, Manchester, UK; I owe this quotation to Kevin Morgan; Higgins, 'Moralisings', June–July 1924, Rawling papers (ANU N57/174).

20 Higgins, 'Australia the Superior', *Communist Review*, no. 2 (February 1925), pp. 12–13, quoted by Rick Kuhn who takes Higgins's phrase as the title of his study, Paradise on the Instalment Plan: The Economic Thought of the Australian Labour Movement between the Depression and the Long Boom, PhD thesis, University of Sydney, 1985, p. 15.

21 *Workers' Weekly*, 8 January 1926.

22 *Seven Poor Men of Sydney*, first published 1934 (Sydney: Sirius, 1981), p. 174.

23 J. K., 'The Australian Labour Movement as Viewed By an Outsider', *Proletarian*, n.s. no. 8 (August 1925), pp. 15–16. See David Akers, The Making of a Marxist: Jack Kavanagh, 1879–1914, paper presented to third national conference of the ASSLH, Newcastle, 25 June 1993, and 'Rebel or Revolutionary? Jack Kavanagh and the Early Years of the Communist Movement in Vancouver, 1920–1925', *Labour/Le Travail*, no. 30 (Fall 1992), pp. 9–44; Margaret Sampson, Intellectual History from Below? The Diary of Jack Kavanagh, unpublished paper, History Department, University of Newcastle, 1989; and the Investigation Branch file on Kavanagh (AA A467).

24 Minutes of the Fifth Conference of the CPA, 26–28 December 1925, CPA records (ML MS 5021 ADD-ON 1936, box 1).

25 Minutes of the Central Executive of the CPA, 4 January 1926, CPA records (ML MS 5021 ADD-ON 1936, box 3); *Workers' Weekly*, 15 January 1926.

26 *Labor Daily*, 6 December 1926; *Sydney Morning Herald*, 8 December 1926; *Workers' Weekly*, 10 December 1926; the fullest treatment of these complex events is Bede Nairn, *The 'Big Fella': Jack Lang and the Australian Labor Party 1891–1949* (Melbourne: MUP, 1986), chs 6–7.

27 Arthur Hoyle, *John Smith (Jock) Garden (1882–1968): A Political Biography* (Canberra: self-published, 1984), p. 64; Frank Farrell, *Inter- national Socialism and Australian Labour: The Left in Australia 1919–1939* (Sydney: Hale & Iremonger, 1981), pp. 89–90.

28 *Report of the Third All-Australian Trade Union Congress, 7 August 1926*, (Sydney:

New South Wales Labor Council, 1926); see the lengthy intelligence report (AA A981); and Farrell, op. cit., ch. 5.

29 Esmonde Higgins, interviewed by J. D. B. Miller, 26 January 1952, Rawling papers (ANU N57/198).

30 The debate with Kavanagh was reported in *Workers' Weekly*, 24 December 1926; Garden's articles appeared 27 May–24 June 1927.

31 *Workers' Weekly*, 7 August 1925 reports their formation. Membership figures come from a report by the CPA to ECCI, 14 April 1926, Comintern records (CI 495/94/26).

32 She explained the divisions in *Workers' Weekly*, 31 July 1925 and minutes of the conference; see also Justina Williams, *The First Furrow* (Willagee, WA: Lone Hand Press, 1976), pp. 84–97.

33 Branch minutes and correspondence, Brodney papers (SLV MS 10882/5/9, 11).

34 *Workers' Weekly*, 11 December 1925; K. H. Kennedy, 'The Anti- Communist Pledge Crisis', in D. J. Murphy et al. (eds), *Labor in Power: The Labor Party and Governments in Queensland 1915–57* (St Lucia, Qld: UQP, 1980), pp. 369–81.

35 *Workers' Weekly*, 16 October 1925. His recollections of the tour appear in Andrew Moore (ed.), *The Writings of Norm Jeffery* (Campbelltown, NSW: Sydney Branch of the ASSLH, 1989), pp. 25–30, based on manuscript in the Gilmore papers (NLA MS 727/8/51).

36 For Hetty Weitzel, see J. C. Beaglehole, *Victoria University College* (Wellington: New Zealand University, 1949), p. 191; Martin Sullivan, 'Hetty Ross Formerly Hetty Weitzel', *Hecate*, vol. 22, no. 1 (1996), pp. 127–38; and Ross Edmonds, *In Storm and Struggle: A History of the Communist Party in Newcastle 1920–1949* (Newcastle: self-published, 1991), p. 11.

37 *ADB*, vol. 10, pp. 675–6, and profile by Edgar Ross in *Communist Review*, vol. 4, no. 10 (October 1937), pp. 44–8.

38 Jack Blake, interviewed by Laurie Aarons, August 1979 (ML) and information given to me, July 1997. Airey assumed the name of Blake when he returned in 1933 from training in the Soviet Union.

39 *ADB*, vol. 11, pp. 98–9 and profile in *Workers' Voice*, 14 September 1938.

40 Richard Dixon, 'Early Years in the Party' in *Australia Left Review*, no. 48 (September 1975), pp. 48–54. Walker assumed this name when he returned at the same time as Blake from the Soviet Union.

41 Harry den Hartog, interviewed by Frank Strahan and Andrew Reeves, 4 September 1982 (UMA).

42 Ike the Red, 'Ten Years On—Will This be So?', *Workers' Weekly*, 21 May 1926.

43 *Workers' Weekly*, 8 January 1926; CEC report to groups, June 1926, CPA records (ML MS 5021 ADD-ON 1936, box 4).

44 Minutes of Sixth Conference of the CPA, 26–28 December 1926, CPA records (ML MS 5021 ADD-ON 1936, box 1).

45 CEC report to groups, October 1926, as in note 43.

46 Militant Women's Group report in minutes of the Seventh Conference of the CPA, 24–28 December 1927, pp. 50–1, CPA records (ML MS 5021 ADD-ON 1936, box 1). Copies of the group's bulletin, *The Woman Worker*, are in the Kavanagh papers (ANU P12/2/6). See also Audrey Johnson, *Bread and Roses: A Personal History of Three Militant Women and Their Friends 1902–1988* (Sutherland, NSW: Left Book Club, 1990), ch. 1.

47 See, for example, the protracted requests of the International Secretariat of International Red Aid for an account of the expenditure of £600 sent as three months' running expenses (CI 539/3/232).

48 Higgins to Pollitt, 30 August 1926, Rawling papers (ANU N57/158); Rawling, Communism Comes to Australia, p. 256 (ANU N57/1).
49 These membership figures come from minutes of the 1927 conference, and two reports to ECCI, one by Herbert Moxon and the other by a Comintern representative, R. W. Robson, Comintern records (CI 495/94/41, 42); there are minor discrepancies.
50 Judah Waten, *Scenes of Revolutionary Life* (Sydney: Angus & Robertson, 1982).
51 Judah Waten, 'Seventy Years', *Overland*, no. 86 (December 1981), pp. 16–18.
52 Report by Ross to British Secretariat, 15 April 1926, Comintern records (CI 495/72/114).
53 Tom Payne, address to Victorian branch of the ASSLH, n.d.; E. M. Higgins, 'Moralisings while on SS *Baradine*, June–July 1924', Rawling papers, (ANU N57/174). The correspondence is noted in Kevin Morgan, *Harry Pollitt* (Manchester: Manchester University Press, 1993), p. 121.
54 *Workers' Weekly*, 11 April 1924. For Dietzgen and this intellectual culture, see Stuart Macintyre, *A Proletarian Science: Marxism in Britain 1917–1933* (Cambridge: CUP, 1980); for the labour colleges, Ann Turner, Independent Working Class Education in Australia, 1917–29, MEd thesis, University of Melbourne, 1981; and for the reading history of the Australian labour movement, Lucy Taksa, 'Spreading the Word: The Literature of Labour and Working-Class Culture', in John Shields (ed.), *All Our Labours: Oral Histories of Working Life in Twentieth Century Sydney* (Kensington, NSW: NSWUP, 1992), pp. 64–85.
55 *Workers' Weekly*, 16 May, 19 September 1924, 3 June–14 October 1927; *Party Training Manual* (Sydney: CPA, 1928), p. 6.
56 Report on work among women in Australia, 23 September 1927, Comintern records (CI 495/94/35).
57 Hetty Ross, 'The Women of the Working Class', *Workers' Weekly*, 28 May 1926.
58 E. Reynolds, letter to *Workers' Weekly*, 11 March 1927.
59 See the report in *Workers' Weekly*, 24 April 1925, and the biographical sketch in Joy Damousi, Socialist Women in Australia, c. 1890–1918, PhD thesis, ANU, 1987, pp. 304–5; Rickie was one of the six parliamentary candidates in 1925. See generally, Joy Damousi, *Women Come Rally: Socialism, Communism and Gender in Australia 1890–1955* (Melbourne: OUP, 1994).
60 As recalled by Edna Ryan in Joyce Stevens (ed.), *Taking the Revolution Home: Work Among Women in the Communist Party of Australia 1920–1945* (Fitzroy, Vic.: Sybylla Press, 1987), p. 125. Jean Devanny, *Sugar Heaven* (Sydney: Modern Publishers, 1936); Katharine Susannah Prichard, *Intimate Strangers* (London: Cape, 1937)
61 *Communist*, 28 July 1922; *Workers' Weekly*, 12, 26 January, 28 September 1923.
62 *Workers' Weekly*, 23 January 1925.
63 Immigration policy resolution in minutes of the Fifth Conference of the CPA, as in note 24; the resolution follows closely Jack Kavanagh's analysis of 'The Immigration Menace', *Workers' Weekly*, 7 August 1925.
64 This from a leaflet issued in north Queensland, reported in *Workers' Weekly*, 3 July 1925; a similar appeal to Italian timberworkers in Western Australia appeared in the same newspaper on 31 July 1925.
65 Peter Alexanders, interviewed by Stelios Korbetis, 24 January 1987, was a founder-member.
66 Minutes of the Seventh Conference of the CPA, 24–28 December 1927, pp. 38–40, CPA papers (ML MS 5021 ADD-ON 1938, box 1). This early phase of Italian communist activity in Australia seems to have escaped the notice of historians; see Gianfranco Cresciani, *Fascism, Anti-Fascism and Italians in Australia, 1922–1945* (Canberra: ANUP, 1980), p. 117.

67 Lawrence, *Kangaroo*, p. 305.
68 Howie to Murphy, n.d. [1927?], Comintern records (CI 495/94/43).

Chapter 6   The line straightens

1 Baracchi's resignation was reported to ECCI on 24 January 1926 and the cable requesting an Australian representative was received on 8 February, Comintern records (CI 495/94/26); CEC report to groups, February 1926, CPA records (ML MS 5021 ADD-ON 1936, box 4). The Comintern correspondence is also contained in an Investigation Branch file (AA A467).
2 Minutes of the Bureau, 22 April, 20 May 1926, Comintern records (CI 495/72/114) and 'Resolution on the Australian Question', Comintern records (CI 495/2/57).
3 'The Political Situation and Our Attitude to the ALP', in minutes of the Sixth Conference of the CPA, 25–28 December 1926, CPA records (ML MS 5021 ADD-ON 1936, box 1).
4 Thus L. L. Sharkey, *An Outline History of the Communist Party of Australia* (Sydney: Marx School, 1944), pp. 20–3 presents the issue as a fight against the heresy of Australian exceptionalism, while from a Trotskyist perspective Tom O'Lincoln, *Into the Mainstream: The Decline of Australian Communism* (Westgate, NSW: Stained Wattle Press, 1985), p. 36 emphasises the importance of the Kremlin. Alastair Davidson, *The Communist Party of Australia: A Short History* (Stanford, California: Hoover Institution Press, 1969), pp. 48–51 sees the episode resulting in 'rigid Comintern control'. J. D. Blake, 'The Australian Communist Party and the Comintern in the Early 1930s', *Labour History*, no. 23 (November 1972), pp. 38–47 disputes this interpretation. Peter Morrison, The Communist Party of Australia and the Radical-Socialist Tradition, 1920–39, PhD thesis, University of Adelaide, 1976, ch. 4, and Barbara Curthoys, 'The Communist Party and the Communist International (1927–1929)', *Labour History*, no. 64 (May 1993), pp. 54–69 provide more nuanced accounts.
5 Among the substantial body of work on the International, Franz Borkenau, *World Communism: A History of the Communist International* (Ann Arbor: University of Michigan Press, 1962), Julius Braunthal, *History of the International. Volume 2: 1914–1943* (London: Thomas Nelson, 1967), E. H. Carr, *The Bolshevik Revolution 1917–1923*, vol. 3 (London: Macmillan, 1953) and *Socialism in One Country 1924–6*, vol. 3 (London: Macmillan, 1964), and Fernando Claudin, *The Communist Movement from Comintern to Cominform. Part One: The Crisis of the Communist International*, trans. Brian Pearce, (New York: Monthly Review Press, 1975) are of particular value.
6 In an extended review of the revisionist works, Theodore Draper, 'American Communism Revisited', in *A Present of Things Past: Selected Essays* (New York: Hill & Wang, 1990) defends the earlier view, while the alternative position is surveyed in Michael E. Brown et al. (eds), *New Studies in the Politics and Culture of U.S. Communism* (New York: Monthly Review Press, 1993).
7 Minutes of the CEC, 15 April 1927, CPA records (ML MS 5021 ADD-ON 1936, box 3); *Workers' Weekly*, 3 June, 15 July, 5 August 1927.
8 Minutes of the CEC, 20 August 1927.
9 The Investigation Branch compiled detailed reports on these activists in 1922 and 1925 (AA A6122, item 135).
10 *Workers' Weekly*, 13, 27 November, 4, 11 December 1925; see Andrew Moore (ed.), *The Writings of Norm Jeffery* (Campbelltown, NSW: Sydney Branch of

the ASSLH, 1989), pp. 27–9; Anne Smith, 'McCormack, Rymer and the Bowen Industrial Trouble, 1925', in *Lectures on North Queensland History*, no. 4 (1984).

11 K. H. Kennedy, 'The South Johnstone Strike and Railway Lockout, 1927', *Labour History*, no. 31 (November 1976), pp. 1–13. The best account of political currents in Queensland remains E. M. Higgins's, The Queensland Labour Government, 1915–1929, MA thesis, University of Melbourne, 1954.

12 Moxon's report in minutes of the seventh Conference of the CPA, 24–28 December 1927, pp. 25–9, CPA records (ML MS 5021 ADD-ON 1936, box 1); *Workers' Weekly*, 16 July–21 October 1927 *passim*, and issues of *Solidarity*, the strike bulletin of the Townsville group, September 1927, Kavanagh papers (ANU Z400, box 4).

13 Minutes of the CEC, 20 August 1927, as in note 7.

14 Minutes of the British–American Bureau, 3, 4 August, and Political Secretariat of ECCI, 10, 14 October 1927 (CI 495/72/27 and 495/3/39–40); part of the resolution appeared in minutes of the Seventh Conference of the CPA, 24–28 December 1927, pp. 12–15, as in note 12.

15 Robson's report to Political Secretariat of ECCI, 20 April 1928, Comintern records (CI 495/3/63) and letter to 'Bob' [Stewart?], 30 January 1928, Comintern records (CI 495/94/41).

16 Minutes of the Seventh Conference of the CPA, 24–28 December 1927, pp. 36–9, 61–5, as in note 12.

17 ibid., pp. 66–70.

18 ibid., pp. 75–8.

19 See his chairman's address to the conference, ibid., p. 2.

20 ibid., p. 61. Other accounts, including those of Blake and Curthoys (cited in note 4), state wrongly that Higgins was removed.

21 ibid., p. 80.

22 Edna Ryan, typed notes on Alastair Davidson, *The Communist Party of Australia*, Kavanagh papers (ANU P12/9/2), supplemented by her contribution to Joyce Stevens (ed.), *Taking the Revolution Home: Work Among Women in the Communist Party of Australia 1920–1945* (Fitzroy, Vic.: Sybylla Press, 1987), pp. 120–36, and written communication to me, 23 June 1994.

23 Statutes adopted at the Sixth Congress, in Jane Degras (ed.), *The Communist International 1919–1943: Documents*, vol. 2 (London: OUP, 1960), pp. 464–71.

24 Robson to Kuusinen, 19 April 1928, and report, 18 April 1928, Comintern records (CI 495/94/41).

25 Moxon, 'Report of the Representative of the CC of the CPA on "Party Factions" ', 7 April 1928, and statement to secretariat, 20 April 1928, Comintern records (CI 495/94/42).

26 'Report of Comrades Jeffery and Ryan on the Position of the Communist Party of Australia', 10 April 1928, and further reports, 18 April 1928 (ibid.).

27 The resolution was adopted by ECCI on 27 April 1928, Comintern records (CI 495/3/64).

28 'Communist Party and Queensland Labor Party', *Workers' Weekly*, 20 July 1928, and subsequent articles, 27 July, 3, 17, 24, 31 August, 14 September 1928.

29 'Report of the Representative of the CPA on Matters Arising Out of the CI Letter and Resolutions', 6 September 1928, and CEC of CPA to ECCI, 20 September 1928, Comintern records (CI 495/94/42, 44); ECCI, 'To the CEC of the Australian Party', 2 October 1928, CPA records (ML MS 5021 ADD-ON 1936, box 8). Higgins's subsequent report to the CEC on the Congress, dated 20 December 1928, is in the Rawling papers (ANU N57/371).

30 Wright to ECCI Secretariat, 21 May 1928, 2 October 1928, Comintern records (CI 495/94/43, 495/6/16).

31 Dutt to Pollitt, 6 January 1928, Pollitt to Dutt, 13 February 1928, Dutt papers (CPGB archives, Manchester, UK).

32 Higgins's report to the CEC of the CPA, 20 December 1928, CPA records (ML MS 5021 ADD-ON 1936, box 3), and report to the Eighth Conference of the CPA, 22–27 December 1928, together with his handwritten notes, Rawling papers (ANU N57/370).

33 ECCI, 'To the CEC of the Australian Party', 2 October 1928, CPA records (ML MS 5021 ADD-ON 1936, box 8).

34 Higgins to Pollitt, n.d. [September 1928], Higgins papers (ML MS 740/7); the document prepared by Moxon is in Comintern records (CI 495/94/41); Higgins's reference to 'friends at court' is in a letter to Robson, 21 February 1929, Comintern records (CI 495/94/52), and see also the remarkably well-informed report based on British intelligence sent by R. G. Casey to S. M. Bruce, 21 February 1929, (AA A467). The ECCI warning is contained in the letter to the CEC of the CPA, 2 October 1928, as in note 33.

35 Shelley to Maruschak, 31 October 1928, Comintern records (CI 495/94/44).

36 Minutes of the praesidium meeting, 12 November 1928, and of the CEC, 3 December 1928, CPA records (ML MS 5021 ADD-ON 1936, box 3).

37 Minutes of the Eighth Conference of the CPA, 22–27 December 1928, *passim*, Rawling papers (ANU N57/370).

38 ibid., p. 19 and attached group leaders' reports.

39 ibid., pp. 23–4.

40 ibid., p. 29. cf. Davidson, *The Communist Party of Australia*, p. 50, who suggests Moxon and Sharkey were dropped.

41 Kavanagh, 'Pages from Party History', Rawling papers (ANU N57/250).

42 Minutes of the Eighth Conference, pp. 29–31 and Kavanagh's appended trade union report; the resolution appeared in *Workers' Weekly*, 11 January 1929.

43 Director, Investigation Branch to Secretary, Attorney-General's Department, 5 October 1928 and Latham to solicitor-general, 6 November 1928 (AA A467); and Miriam Rechter (Dixson), The Strike of Waterside Workers in Australian Ports, 1928, and the Lockout of Coalminers in the Northern Coalfield of New South Wales, MA thesis, University of Melbourne, 1957.

44 *Sydney Morning Herald*, 8 May 1929; the earlier Sydney demonstration was reported in the same paper and the *Labor Daily* on 28 March 1929.

45 CEC minutes, 11, 18 February 1929 (ML MS 5021 ADD-ON 1936, box 3) and report in *Sydney Morning Herald*, 23 February 1929; *Workers' Weekly*, 30 August 1929 and *passim*. The weekly bulletins of the Timber Workers' Disputes Committee in New South Wales, the *Picket Line*, 19 June–17 October 1929, Kavanagh papers (ANU P12/2/4), give a clear account of Kavanagh's strategy. See Miriam Dixson, 'The Timber Strike of 1929', *Historical Studies Australia and New Zealand*, vol. 10, no. 40 (May 1963), pp. 479–92.

46 See, in addition to Rechter, 'The Strike', Robin Gollan, *The Coalminers of New South Wales: A History of the Union 1860–1960* (Melbourne: MUP, 1963), ch. 9; and Edgar Ross, *A History of the Miners' Federation of Australia* (Sydney: Australasian Coal and Shale Employees' Federation, 1970), chs 13–14.

47 Report of the All-In Conference of the Militant Minority Movement, 19–20 July 1929, p. 9, CPA records (ML MS 5021 ADD-ON 1936, box 16). Norm Jeffery described the differences within the CEC on the appropriate strategy for the Minority Movement in an earlier report, 20 February 1929, and enlarged on the issues in a letter to the RILU, 16 May 1929 (CI 534/7/4).

48 The importance of this factor is set out in Frank Farrell, 'Explaining Communist History', *Labour History*, no. 32 (May 1977), pp. 1–10, and Moscow's priorities were also noted by the Investigation Branch (AA A981). Barbara Curthoys, 'The Comintern, the CPA and the Impact of Harry Wicks', *Austra-*

lian Journal of Politics and History, vol. 39, no. 1 (1993), p. 24, identifies the RILU official as G. Sydor Stöler, but does not recognise him as 'Pan', a name she misattributes to A. Lozovsky, the general secretary of the RILU (p. 27). It was Edna Ryan who named the visitor 'Pan' because his mission was to establish the *Pan-Pacific Worker* (personal communication, 28 June 1994) and there were several references to his mission at the Ninth Conference in December 1929. He wrote in this journal and in *Inprecorr*, vol. 9, nos 23, 66 (17 May, 29 November 1929) as 'Carpenter', but *Inprecorr*, vol. 9, no. 62 (1 November) has an Australian article by Stöler.

49 Wright to Lozovsky, 26 September 1929, Comintern records (CI 534/7/4).
50 Miles, 'The Challenge to Capitalism and Reformism', *Workers' Weekly*, 31 May 1929; Moxon, 'After the Queensland Elections', *Workers' Weekly*, 24 May 1929, and 'Communist International New Line Correctly Applied', *Workers' Weekly*, 9 August 1929.
51 Tripp to Rawling, 21 January 1963, Rawling papers (ANU N57/109).
52 CEC minutes, 15 September 1929, and letter to groups, 16 September 1929, CPA records (ML MS 5021 ADD-ON 1936, boxes 3, 4); see election articles in *Workers' Weekly*, 20, 27 September 1929.
53 Letters from Moxon and Sharkey to CEC, 16, 22 September 1929, CPA records (ML MS 5021, ADD-ON 1936, box 8), and copies in Comintern records (CI 495/94/52). The correspondence between Moxon and Miles is in a separate file of the CPA records (ML MS 5021 ADD-ON 1936, box 28).
54 'Report by Comrade Clayton [the pseudonym of Tripp] on the Present Situation in Australia Comintern records, September 1929' (CI 495/94/52) and a further submission to ECCI, 20 September 1929, Comintern records (CI 495/3/162). Tripp recounted his advocacy in Moscow in an interview with J. N. Rawling (ANU N57/109) and his diaries for the period are in the Tripp papers (UMA).
55 The telegrams are held in the minutes of the CEC, CPA records (ML, as in note 53), and copies are contained in Comintern records (CI 495/72/52–3).
56 Political Secretariat of ECCI, Comintern records (CI 495/4/3).
57 *Workers' Weekly*, 25 October, 15 November 1929.
58 *Workers' Weekly*, loc. cit., and 6, 27 December 1929.
59 CEC to Anglo–American Bureau, 16 December 1929, Comintern records (CI 495/94/61).
60 Moxon, letter from Melbourne, 12 December 1929, Brodney papers (SLVMS 10882/5 /10)
61 Higgins to Harry Pollitt, 21 March 1930, Comintern records (CI 495/94/61).
62 Minutes of the Ninth Conference of the CPA, 26–31 December 1929, pp. 40, 43, 64–5, CPA records (ML MS 5021 ADD-ON 1936, box 1); telegram from ECCI in *Workers' Weekly*, 10 January 1930; telegram to ECCI in Comintern records (CI 495/94/53).

Chapter 7   Bolshevisation

1 Kavanagh diary, 20 February 1930, Kavanagh papers (ANU Z400, box 1); *Workers' Weekly*, 14 March 1930.
2 Andrew Metcalfe, *For Freedom and Dignity: Historical Agency and Class Structures in the Coalfields of NSW* (Sydney: Allen & Unwin, 1988), ch. 9 includes a table summarising the charges and convictions. Christian Jollie Smith undertook

more than 250 defences on behalf of the CPA; 'Notes on Cases for IWCPA', n.d. [1932], Thorne papers (ANU P15/8).

3 *Workers' Weekly*, 17, 31 January 1930; *Cessnock Eagle*, 24 January 1930, quoted in Ross Edmonds, *In Storm and Struggle: A History of the Communist Party in Newcastle 1920–1940* (Newcastle: self-published, 1991), p. 55; *Sydney Morning Herald*, 13, 16 January 1930.

4 See J. D. Blake, 'The Australian Communist Party and the Comintern in the Early 1930s', *Labour History*, no. 23 (November 1972), p. 45, and Higgins to Pollitt, 21 March 1930, Comintern records (CI 495/94/61); Moxon's accusation about the lockout in *Workers' Weekly*, 21 November 1930.

5 *Workers' Weekly*, 14 March, 4 April 1930.

6 Copies of letters from Moxon to Ryan, 6, 10, 19 February 1930, Kavanagh papers (ANU P12/3/7/1–3); *Workers' Weekly*, 28 February, 21 March 1930; *Sydney Morning Herald*, 28 February 1930; Frank Farrell, *International Socialism and Australian Labour: The Left in Australia, 1919–1939* (Sydney: Hale & Iremonger, 1981), ch. 7; Jim Hagan, *The History of the ACTU* (Melbourne: Longman Cheshire, 1981), pp. 94–5.

7 CEC to ECCI, 24 February 1930, Comintern records (CI 495/94/61); Moxon to ECCI, 13, 19 March 1930, Comintern records (CI 495/94/61), and ECCI Resolution of the Situation in Australia and the Tasks of the CPA, November 1930, Comintern records (CI 495/4/63), and also in the Report of the Tenth Congress of the CPA (ML MS 5021 ADD-ON 1936, box 1); Ryan to Lozovsky, 9 March 1930, Comintern records (CI 534/7/5) and quoted in Melbourne *Argus*, 4 March 1930. Copies of the correspondence between Ryan and the CEC are in the Kavanagh papers (ANU P12/3/7). See also Barbara Curthoys, 'The Comintern, the CPA and the Impact of Harry Wicks', *Australian Journal of Politics and History*, vol. 39, no. 1 (1993), pp. 23–36.

8 Kavanagh to CEC, 29 January 1930, Comintern records (CI 495/94/61) and also in Rawling papers (ANU N57/251); Kavanagh diary, 31 January 1930, as in note 1.

9 Moxon to ECCI, 19 March 1930; *Workers' Weekly*, 21 March, 25 April 1930; CEC minutes, April 1930, CPA records (ML MS 5021 ADD-ON 1936, box 3).

10 Descriptions of Moore come from Gil Roper, interviewed J. N. Rawling, 1961 (ANU N57/291), and Edna Ryan, personal communication, 23 June 1994; Bernard K. Johnpoll and Harvey Klehr (eds), *Biographical Dictionary of the American Left* (New York: Greenwood Press, 1986), pp. 414–5.

11 Barrington to Esmonde Higgins, n.d. [19 April 1930], Rawling papers (ANU N57/158); *Workers' Weekly*, 25 April, 6 June 1930; Moore to ECCI, 25 July 1930, Comintern records (CI 534/7/5).

12 CEC minutes, 4 May 1930; Moore to RILU, 25 May, 25 September 1930, Comintern records (CI 534/7/5, 6); ECCI to Moore, 21 November 1930, Comintern records (CI 495/4/65).

13 Moxon to PB, 28 January 1931, state correspondence and reports, CPA records (ML MS 5021 ADD-ON 1936, box 4); *Workers' Weekly*, 20 March 1931; Edna Ryan, personal communication, 23 June 1994; Joyce Stevens (ed.), *Taking the Revolution Home: Work Among Women in the Communist Party of Australia 1920–1945* (Fitzroy, Vic.: Sybylla Press, 1987), pp. 120–36.

14 CEC minutes, 26 April, 24 May 1930, as in note 9; Kavanagh diary, 22 May, 22 June 1930, as in note 1.

15 'Censure and Warning of Com. Kavanagh', *Workers' Weekly*, 6 June 1930.

16 In 1917 Russia was still using the Julian calendar, so 15 October in Russia was the equivalent of the West's 7 November.

17 *Workers' Weekly*, 5 December 1930; correspondence between Kavanagh and

CEC, and subsequent appeals to the Tenth Congress of the CPA and the ECCI in the Kavanagh papers (ANU P12/3/1–5), Rawling papers (ANU N57/251, 375) and Comintern records CI 495/94/61. J. N. Rawling's unpublished history, Communism Comes to Australia, pp. 349–65, Rawling papers, ANU N 57/1, provides a detailed narrative.

18 An application of Ryan was reported in *Workers' Weekly*, 2, 16 September 1932. Kavanagh submitted a long statement of self-criticism to *Workers' Weekly*, 4–18 September 1931, and was then put on probation for a year; the probation was extended a further year in September 1932, and in September 1933 he gave further assurances. He was expelled in June 1934. Kavanagh to CCC, 18 September 1932, and CCC to Kavanagh, 26 September 1932, 21 September 1933, 16 May 1934, Kavanagh papers (ANU P12/3/4/4 and P12/3/5/4); Workers' Weekly, 29 June, 20 July 1934.

19 Higgins to Pollitt, 11 January 1931, Rawling papers (ANU N57/198).

20 *Workers' Weekly*, 3 October, 5 December 1930.

21 *Workers' Weekly*, 21 November 1930; Moxon was quoted by Jeffery in the minutes of the Tenth Congress of the CPA, April 1931, CPA records (ML MS 5021 ADD-ON 1936, box 1), and his organisational faults were discussed in a separate organisational session, Comintern records (CI 495/94/20); there were further accusations at the closed session of the CC plenum, 2 January 1932 (AA A 6335, item 31). See also Beris Penrose, 'Herbert Moxon, a Victim of the "Bolshevisation" of the Communist Party', *Labour History*, no. 70 (May 1996), pp. 92–114.

22 It has been suggested that Moore proposed Sharkey as the new party secretary and that Christian Jollie Smith, no longer an active member but still very influential, objected; Rawling, Communism Comes to Australia, p. 367.

23 Biographical details from J. B. Miles, interviewed by Roger Coates, 12 January 1965; Carole Ferrier (ed.), *Point of Departure: The Autobiography of Jean Devanny* (St Lucia, Qld: UQP, 1986), p. 157.

24 Moore to Organisation Department, ECCI, 25 September 1930, Comintern records (CI 534/7/5).

25 Minutes of the Tenth Congress of the CPA (transcript is marked 11.45 a. m. Monday).

26 ibid., and Tripp interviewed by Rawling, Rawling papers (ANU N57/109); Moore's address was published as *Australia and the World Crisis* (Sydney: CPA, 1931).

27 CI 495/4/63 and also in minutes of the Tenth Congress, as in note 21. A delay in the receipt of this letter was a contributory factor in the postponement of the congress.

28 Moore to ECCI, 10 November 1930, Comintern records (CI 495/7/5); minutes of the Tenth Congress and Moore's statement in the minutes of the organisation session, p. 76, Comintern records (CI 495/94/20); *Workers' Weekly*, 29 May, 31 July, 27 November 1931, 15 January 1932; Organisation Report, 31 December 1931, CPA records (ML MS 5021, box 82); Third Plenum of the CC 25–27 December 1932, p. 135, CPA records (ML MS 5021 ADD-ON 1936, box 3).

29 *Workers' Weekly*, 17 August 1931.

30 Jollie Smith to A. T. Brodney, 19 September 1929, Moxon to Brodney, 17 February 1930, Brodney papers (SLV MS10882/5/11). Circulation reported to Third Plenum of the CC, p. 156, as in note 28. At the Eleventh Congress of the party in 1935, Sharkey as editor sharply reduced the circulation figures for the early 1930s.

Chapter 8   Class Against Class

1 Jack Blake, interviewed by Laurie Aarons, August 1979 (ML) and by me, July 1997; copies of CIB files in Blake papers (ML MS 5971/1/4).

2 *Red Leader*, 23 October 1931. A report of the Minority Movement conference is in Comintern records (CI 534/7/7).

3 *Workers' Weekly*, 10 October, 21 November 1930, 13 February, 10 April 1931.

4 ECCI to CC of CPA, 22 October 1932, CPA records (ML MS 5021 ADD-ON 1936, box 8); see also Alastair Davidson, *The Communist Party of Australia: A Short History* (Stanford, California: Hoover Institution Press, 1969), pp. 56–60. There are few studies of industrial activity in the Third Period, though individual union histories contain some information. L. J. Louis, *Trade Unions and the Depression: A Study of Victoria 1930–1932* (Canberra: ANUP, 1968), and Joanne Scott, 'Don't Cop it Passively': Strikes, Lockouts and Unemployed Protests in Queensland 1929–39, BA Hons thesis, University of Queensland, 1990, chs 1–2 are useful state accounts. The minutes of the Second National Congress of the MM, December 1933, CPA records (ML MS 5021 ADD-ON 1936, box 16) provide a good retrospective view.

5 *Red Leader*, 15, 22 January 1932; and report of conference, Comintern records (CI 534/7/7).

6 *Workers' Weekly*, 6, 13 May 1931, 8 July, 26 August 1932; *Red Leader*, 13 July, 17 August 1932; *Sydney Morning Herald*, 1 August 1932; minutes of the PB, 26 September 1931, 4 May, 24 June 1932, Comintern records (CI 95/94/70, 95); minutes of the Third Plenum, 25–27 December 1932, p. 168, CPA records (ML 5021 ADD-ON 1936, box 3).

7 The series of articles appeared in Red *Leader*, 27 July–14 September 1932; on Orr, personal communication from Bob Gollan.

8 *Workers' Weekly*, 8, 15 August 1930, 9 January, 16 October 1931. See Andrew Moore, 'The Pastoral Workers' Industrial Union', *Labour History*, no. 49 (November 1985), pp. 61–74, and Alastair Davidson, The Communist Party of Australia 1920–35: Policy and Organisation, PhD thesis, ANU, 1966, pp. 371–86. There are extensive records of the PWIU collected by an agent of the New South Wales Graziers' Association in the records of that organisation (ANU E256/261).

9 Robinson in Wendy Lowenstein, *Weevils in the Flour: An Oral Record of the 1930s Depression in Australia*, rev. edn (Newham, Vic.: Scribe Publications, 1989), pp. 148–50; Jarmson, interviewed by Laurie Aarons, 19 July 1981 (ML).

10 E. H. Carr, *The Twilight of the Comintern, 1930–1935* (London: Macmillan, 1982), pp. 38–9; Wray Vamplew (ed.), *Australians: Historical Statistics* (Sydney: Fairfax, Syme & Weldon Associates, 1988), p. 152. The traditional forms of unemployed protest are described in Stuart Macintyre, *Winners and Losers: The Pursuit of Social Justice in Australian History* (Sydney: Allen & Unwin, 1985), ch. 4. The two best accounts of unemployed activity in the Depression are Judy Mackinolty, Sugar Bag Days: Sydney Workers and the Challenge of the 1930s Depression, MA thesis, Macquarie University, 1972, and C. J. Fox, Unemployment and the Politics of the Unemployed: Victoria in the Great Depression 1930–37, PhD thesis, University of Melbourne, 1984.

11 Minutes of the OBU of Unemployed and UWM, 1928–32, CPA records (ML MS 5021 ADD-ON 1936, box 16); Kavanagh diary, 20, 28 July, 1 August 1930, Kavanagh papers (ANU Z400 box 1); *Workers' Weekly*, 1, 8 August, 24 October 1930.

12 For Sydney, *Workers' Weekly*, 14, 21, 28 November 1930. For Melbourne, *Workers' Weekly*, 31 October 1930; *Argus*, 24 October–3 November 1930;

C. R. Walker, 'The Fight of the Unemployed', *Pan-Pacific Worker*, vol. 3, no. 12 (1 December 1930), pp. 359–61, and Louis, *Trade Unions and the Depression*, pp. 169–70. For Adelaide, *Workers' Weekly*, 16 January 1931; Adelaide *Advertiser*, 10 January 1931, and Ray Broomhill, *Unemployed Workers: A Social History of the Great Depression in Adelaide* (St Lucia, Qld: UQP, 1978), pp. 176–9. For Darwin, a report of the Department of Home Affairs (AA A31/4202). For Perth, *Workers' Weekly*, 13 March 1931; *West Australian*, 7 March 1931; transcript of interview with Sid Foxley, 28 October 1970, Battye Library (PR 6361/2); Geoffrey Bolton, *A Fine Country to Starve In* (Nedlands, WA: UWAP, 1972), pp. 146–57, and Sandra Wilson, 'Police Perceptions of Protest: The Perth "Treasury Riot" of March 1931', *Labour History*, no. 52 (May 1987), pp. 63–74.

13 *Sydney Morning Herald*, 29 July, 20 August 1930 on the Clovelly case; Counihan quoted in Judy Mackinolty, 'Meeting Them at the Door: Radicalism, Militancy and the Sydney Anti-eviction Campaign of 1931', in Jill Roe (ed.), *Twentieth-Century Sydney: Studies in Urban and Social History* (Sydney: Hale & Iremonger, 1980), p. 210, and also in Bernard Smith, *Noel Counihan: Artist and Revolutionary* (Melbourne: OUP, 1993), p. 87.

14 Minutes of the PB, 13 May, 20 June 1931, Comintern records (CI 95/40/70); *Workers' Weekly*, 26 June 1931; *Red Leader*, 2 October 1931 and the report by Christian Jollie Smith, 'Notes on Cases for ICWPA', n.d., Thorne papers (ANU P15/8)'; Mackinolty, 'Meeting Them at the Door'.

15 Joanne Scott, ' "A Place in Normal Society": Unemployed Protest in Queensland in the 1930s', *Labour History*, no. 65 (November 1993), pp. 136–49; Ross Edmonds, *In Storm and Struggle: A History of the Communist Party in Newcastle 1920–1940* (Newcastle: self-published, 1991), pp. 43–6; Sheilah Gray, *Newcastle in the Great Depression* (Newcastle: City Council, 1989); Peter Hempenstall, *The Meddlesome Priest: A Life of Ernest Burgmann* (Sydney: Allen & Unwin, 1993), pp. 145–7.

16 Kylie Tennant, *The Battlers* (Sydney: Angus & Robertson, 1941); Frank Huelin, *'Keep Moving': An Odyssey* (Sydney: ABS, 1971).

17 *Workers' Weekly*, 6, 13, 20 November 1931, 5 August 1932; *Argus*, 2, 14 November 1931; *Sunraysia Daily*, 2 November 1931; Tony McGillick, *Comrade No More: The Autobiography of a Former Communist Party Leader* (West Perth: self-published, 1980), pp. 73–6; and 'Down with Fascism', leaflet issued by Mildura section (CI 495/4/130).

18 George Bliss, 'The Battle of Cairns', in Len Fox (ed.), *Depression Down Under*, 2nd edn (Sydney: Hale & Iremonger, 1989), pp. 85–92; Brian Costar, 'Controlling the Victims: the Authorities and the Unemployed in Queensland during the Great Depression', *Labour History*, no. 56 (May 1989), pp. 1–14.

19 Vera Deacon, 'Making Do and Lasting Out', in Fox (ed.), *Depression Down Under*, pp. 95–119; Karl Strom, 'Slacky Flats', *Australian Left Review*, no. 85 (Spring 1983), pp. 46–52.

20 *Workers' Weekly*, 16, 23 May 1931, 4, 11 November 1932; *Red Leader*, 16 November 1932; Len Richardson, *The Bitter Years: Wollongong During the Great Depression* (Sydney: Hale & Iremonger, 1984), ch. 4; Gray, *Newcastle in the Great Depression*, pp. 46–8; Justina Williams, *The First Furrow* (Willagee, WA: Lone Hand Press, 1976), pp. 123–30 and 'The March from Frankland River' in Katharine Susannah Prichard, *Straight Left*, ed. Ric Throssell (Sydney: Wild & Woolley, 1982), pp. 23–34; George Bliss in Lowenstein, *Weevils in the Flour*, pp. 173–7.

21 'Sectarianism—Our Approach to the Masses is Incorrect', *Workers' Weekly*, 20 November 1931; minutes of the PB, 13 May, 28 November 1931 (ML MS

5021 ADD-ON 1936, box 15) and Industrial Report to Plenum, 31 December 1931 (ML MS 5021, box 82)

22 Jim Comerford, quoted in Metcalfe, *For Freedom and Dignity: Historical Agency and Class Structures in the Coalfields of NSW* (Sydney: Allen & Unwin, 1988), p. 105.

23 *Age*, 18 September 1931; *Red Leader*, 25 September 1931; Ralph Gibson, *The People Stand Up* (Ascot Vale, Vic.: Red Rooster Press, 1983), p. 53; Louis, *Trade Unions and the Depression*, pp. 183–4.

24 Membership reported in ECCI letter to CC of CPA, 22 October 1932 (ML MS 5021 ADD-ON 1936, box 8); see also organisational report for 1931 and UWM minutes as in note 11, 3 January 1932.

25 Les Barnes, recorded April–May 1991.

26 John Hughes, interviewed by Laurie Aarons, September 1980 (ML), and by Ken Mansell, 7 May 1983 (ML); Robert Cooksey, *Lang and Socialism: A Study in the Great Depression* (Canberra: ANUP, 1971), ch. 3. Payne rejoined the CPA in 1932 on the insistence of the PB; see minutes, 27 February 1932, as in note 6.

27 *Workers' Weekly*, 10 June 1932. Bede Nairn, *The 'Big Fella': Jack Lang and the Australian Labor Party 1891–1949* (Melbourne: MUP, 1986), pp. 284–5 describes the protest meeting, and Miriam Dixson, *Greater than Lenin? Lang and Labor 1916–1932* (Melbourne: Melbourne Politics Monograph, 1976) explores his popular appeal.

28 *Workers' Weekly*, 6, 13 May 1932; *Red Leader*, 11 May 1932; *Argus*, 2, 3 May 1932; Gibson, *The People Stand Up*, p. 54.

29 The aggregate statistics appear in Colin A. Hughes and B. D. Graham, *A Handbook of Australian Government and Politics 1890–1964* (Canberra: ANUP, 1968); see also Peter Morrison, The Communist Party of Australia and the Radical-Socialist Tradition, 1920–39, PhD thesis, University of Adelaide, 1976, pp. 400–3.

30 Alf Watt, *Reminiscences of Sixty Years in the Communist Movement in Australia* (Surry Hills, NSW: SPA, n.d. [1987]), p. 14.

Chapter 9   The Depression communists

1 Eric Hobsbawm, *Age of Extremes: The Short Twentieth Century 1914–1991* (London: Michael Joseph, 1994), ch. 3.

2 Harry Hartland in Wendy Lowenstein, *Weevils in the Flour: An Oral Record of the 1930s Depression in Australia*, rev. edn (Newham, Vic.: Scribe Publications, 1989), p. 47; Wray Vamplew (ed.), *Australians: Historical Statistics* (Sydney: Fairfax, Syme & Weldon Associates, 1988), pp. 133, 152.

3 Les Barnes, recorded April–May 1991; Mona Frame (ed.), *Wherever the Struggle: The Story of Carl King* (Campbelltown, NSW: Sydney Branch of the ASSLH, 1991), pp. 14–16, and Carl King, interviewed by Ken Mansell, 5 May 1983 (ML).

4 Lila Thornton, quoted in Robert Murray and Kate White, *The Ironworkers: A History of the Federated Ironworkers' Association of Australia* (Sydney: Hale & Iremonger, 1982), p. 87, and interviewed by Ken Mansell, 3 May 1983 (ML); Joe Carter, interviewed by Laurie Aarons, 1986 (ML).

5 Bill McDougall, typescript, n.d., in possession of Laurie Aarons; Flo Davis quoted in Audrey Johnson, *Bread and Roses: A Personal History of Three Militant Women and Their Friends 1902–1988* (Sutherland, NSW: Left Book Club,

1990), p. 109; Ted Bacon, interviewed by Laurie Aarons, n.d. (ML); Johnno Johnson, interviewed by Ken Mansell, 5 May 1983 (ML).

6 *Workers' Weekly*, 14 February, 3 October 1930; Laurence W. Maher, 'The Use and Abuse of Sedition', 14, *Sydney Law Review* 287–316 (September 1992).

7 *Argus*, 4 January 1931, 22 October 1932; Justina Williams, *The First Furrow* (Willagee, WA: Lone Hand Press, 1996), pp. 100–01.

8 *Argus*, 10 May 1932; H. E. Jones to Secretary of Attorney-General's Department (AA A981, item COM part 1); see also Frank Cain, *The Origins of Political Surveillance in Australia* (Sydney: Angus & Robertson, 1983), pp. 244–5, and Robert Haldane, *The People's Force: A History of the Victoria Police* (Melbourne: MUP, 1986), p. 217. Peter Coleman, *Obscenity, Blasphemy, Sedition: Censorship in Australia* (Brisbane: Jacaranda Press, n.d. [1963]), pp. 112–13 notes that the Scullin government did restrict the scope of the prohibition of the importation of seditious literature.

9 132 *CPD*, pp. 334, 812, 1402 (30 September and 16, 30 October 1931).

10 See, for example, the seizure of a press at Kurri Kurri used to produce the *Militant Miner*, reported in *Sydney Morning Herald*, 3 March 1930; the conviction of two Melbourne men for printing leaflets, *Argus*, 31 March 1931; the confiscation of a press in Melbourne, *Argus*, 20 January 1932. The conviction of a party member in Sydney for distributing handbills produced on a roneo machine was set aside on appeal financed by the firms that sold such machines; Jollie Smith, 'Notes on Cases for ICWPA', n.d. [1932], Thorne papers (ANU P15/8).

11 *Workers' Weekly*, 14 November–19 December 1930; *Working Woman*, December 1931; *Sydney Morning Herald*, 29 November 1930. Carole Ferrier (ed.), *Point of Departure: The Autobiography of Jean Devanny* (St Lucia, Qld: UQP, 1986), pp. 124–8, and Grace Peebles in Johnson, *Bread and Roses*, pp. 32–6 provide direct testimony.

12 *Workers' Weekly*, 1 August 1930, 25 December 1931; *Sydney Morning Herald*, 30 August 1930, 17 December 1931; 132 *CPD*, pp. 923–64 (14 October 1931); Roger Milliss, *Serpent's Tooth: An Autobiographical Novel* (Ringwood, Vic.: Penguin, 1984), pp. 76–8.

13 The preparations for armed force and sabotage were discussed in the closed session of the CC plenum, 2 January 1932 (AA A6335, item 31) and there is some corroborative evidence. The South Australian action was reported by the premier (*Argus*, 5 September 1931) and confirmed by Tony McGillick, *Comrade No More: The Autobiography of a Former Communist Party Leader* (West Perth: self-published, 1980), pp. 54–6.

14 'Comrade Ryan Realises Own Error', *Workers' Weekly*, 2 October 1931; though in an earlier article, 'Plugger Gets Plugged', 18 September, the paper had justified the action. See also the report of the assault on Martin in *Sydney Morning Herald*, 16 September 1931, and minutes of the PB, 26 September 1931, Comintern records (CI 95/94/70).

15 The WDC was preceded by a Labour Volunteer Army, formed in 1927 to protect pickets on the northern coalfields, and revived as the Labor Defence Army under the auspices of NSW Labor Council in January 1930. It was known briefly as the Workers' Defence Army before assuming its standard name in mid-1930; *Workers' Weekly*, 17, 24 January, 28 November 1930; *Sydney Morning Herald*, 20 January 1930; Sharkey to Lozovsky, n.d. [June 1930], (CI 534/7/5). The Investigation Branch claimed the WDC published its own bulletin, the *Red Fist* (AA A467, bundle 21, SF7/2), but I have not seen a copy.

16 *Red Leader*, 19 October, 26 April 1933. The depositions of those beaten in the Bankstown eviction incident are in the Thorne papers (ANU P15/8); Johnson, *Bread and Roses*, pp. 38–43 discusses the Irish section of the WDC, which also

figures in the debate at the closed session of the CC plenum, 2 January 1932, as in note 13.

17 *Argus*, 10 March 1931; *Sydney Morning Herald*, 28 April 1931. See generally Michael Cathcart, *Defending the National Tuckshop* (Fitzroy, Vic.: McPhee Gribble, 1988), and Andrew Moore, *The Secret Army and the Premier: Conservative Paramilitary Organisations in New South Wales 1930–32* (Kensington: NSWUP, 1989).

18 Eric Campbell, *The Rallying Point: My Story of the New Guard* (Melbourne: MUP, 1965); pp. 70, 107–8; editorial, *Workers' Weekly*, 27 November 1931. See also the leaflet, 'A Call to Action by the Workers' Defence Corps', dated 23 October 1931, Comintern records (CI 495/94/56).

19 *Argus*, 23–25 November 1931; *Sydney Morning Herald*, 13–17 November 1931.

20 *Argus*, 14–15 December 1931; *Sydney Morning Herald*, 28 November–16 December 1931; *List of Names of Certain Communists in New South Wales*, announced in the Legislative Assembly on 1 December and published as a separate parliamentary paper on 23 December 1931.

21 *Workers' Weekly*, 4 March 1932, Sydney *Sun*, 27 February 1932; Keith Amos, *The New Guard Movement 1931–1935* (Melbourne: MUP, 1976), pp. 70–1.

22 *Workers' Weekly*, 25 March, 13 May, 1932 and AA A1931/8304; 134 *CPD*, 1140–2, 1156–76 (23 May 1932); see Geoffrey Sawer, *Australian Federal Politics and Law 1929–1949* (Melbourne: MUP, 1963), pp. 55–7.

23 *Workers' Weekly*, 9, 30 September 1932, 7, 14 April, 12, 26 May, 21 July 1933; *Red Leader*, 4 September 1931, 1 June, 10 August 1932, 10 May 1933; *Sydney Morning Herald*, 2 April, 25, 26 October 1934; *Argus*, 26 April, 29 September 1932; See Cain, *The Origins of Political Surveillance*, pp. 245–50; and Peter Morrison, The Communist Party of Australia and the Radical-Socialist Tradition, 1920–39, PhD thesis, University of Adelaide, 1976, pp. 334–41.

24 There is a large file of letters calling for a ban on communism (AA A1606, file B5/1) and Latham's exasperated reply was to a persistent correspondent, H. C. Cropper (AA A432, item 1933/152). His pleas to the states were in 1933 (NLA MS 1009/53/73) and 1934 (AA A467, bundle 28SF10/15).

25 *Workers' Weekly*, 24 June 1932, 3, 24 March, 7, 12 April, 26 May, 30 June, 4 August 1933; Noel Counihan in Wendy Lowenstein, *Weevils in the Flour*, pp. 390–6; Bernard Smith, *Noel Counihan: Artist and Revolutionary* (Melbourne: OUP, 1993), pp. 91–5; C. J. Fox, Unemployment and the Politics of the Unemployed: Victoria in the Great Depression 1930–37, PhD thesis, University of Melbourne, 1984, pp. 565–87; Cecile Trioli, Unemployment and Local Resistance: The Free Speech Fights in Brunswick During the Depression Years 1930–33, BA Hons thesis, Deakin University, 1990.

26 *Workers' Weekly*, 16 March, 31 August, 10 October 1934, 18 January 1935; *Red Leader*, 28 March, 11 July 1934, 16, 30 July 1935; *Sydney Morning Herald*, 26 February, 12 March 1934; *Fascism in the Sydney Domain* (Sydney: International Labour Defence, 1934); Ferrier (ed.), *Point of Departure*, p. 166.

27 CEC minutes, 4 May 1930, CPA records (ML MS 5021 ADD-ON 1936, box 3).

28 Judah Waten, *Time of Conflict* (Sydney: ABS, 1961), pp. 166–7; Stan Moran in Lowenstein, *Weevils in the Flour*, p. 212; McGillick, *Comrade No More*, p. 49; *Workers' Weekly*, 22 August 1930; report of Control Commission to ECCI, 8 January 1932, Comintern records (CI 495/94/94).

29 Ferrier (ed.) *Point of Departure*, pp. 134–5; Moxon to 'Frank', n.d., Comintern records (CI 495/94/94); *Sydney Morning Herald*, 30 June, 2 July 1931; *Workers' Weekly*, 19 July 1931.

30 The vilification of Trotsky and the Left Opposition had begun in 1928. The allegations of sabotage and conspiracy began with 'Soviet Arrests British Agents'

and 'Counter Revolutionaries Sentenced in Moscow', *Workers' Weekly*, 7 November, 12 December 1930.

31 The story was given to me by Edna Ryan, personal communication, 23 June 1994, and he was identified as Detective Sergeant Whitlock by John Johnson, interviewed by Ken Mansell, 5 May 1983 (ML). Baker's name first appeared in the *Workers' Weekly* on 25 June 1926 and was removed on 25 October 1938. In 1936 Miles described him as the party's 'best routine worker'; CC minutes, 10–12 April 1936, [p. 224], CPA records (ML MS 5021 ADD-ON 1936, box 4).

32 'Political Letter of the ECCI', *Workers' Weekly*, 16 May 1930.

33 *Workers' Weekly*, 31 January, 2 May 1930, 23 January, 12 June 1931; CEC circulars, 10, 18 March 1930, Comintern records (CI 495/94/61). The CEC minutes, 4 May 1930, record that Waten was convalescing from tuberculosis but in fact he went to England at the end of the year; see his application for readmission, 5 March 1957, Jack Hughes papers (ML), and Jack Beasley, *Red Letter Days: Notes from Inside an Era* (Sydney: ABS, 179), pp. 103–4.

34 Minutes of the PB, 13 May 1931, 22 July 1932, Comintern records (CI 95/94/70, 95); Shelley to 'Comrades', 6 August 1932, Comintern records (CI 534/7/8).

35 Minutes of the Third Plenum, 25–27 December 1932, p. 85 and minutes of the PB, 28 April 1933, CPA records (ML MS 5021 ADD-ON 1936, box 3); *Workers' Weekly*, 5 May 1933.

36 The passage from Stalin's authoritative codification of communist doctrine, *The Foundations of Leninism*, was quoted in *Workers' Weekly*, 10 March 1933. 'Censure and Warning of Com. Kavanagh', *Workers' Weekly*, 6 June 1930; Sharkey in minutes of the Third Plenum, p. 59; *Workers' Weekly*, 3 October 1930.

37 Miles in minutes of the Third Plenum, 25–27 December 1932, p. 21; 'War and Illegality', instructions issued by the CC, n.d., Rawling papers (ANU N57/384); and ECCI to CC of CPA, 22 October 1933, in ECCI letters, CPA records (ML MS 5021 ADD-ON 1936, box 8). R. Cram described the techniques of conspiratorial work in 'Organisational Questions', *Communist Review*, vol. 1, no. 8 (November 1934).

38 Claude Jones recalling his elder brother, interviewed by Laurie Aarons, June 1980 (ML).

39 Transcript of interview with Roper by Rawling (ANU N57/291); Miles in minutes of the Fourth Plenum, 1–2 April 1934 [p. 94], CPA records (ML MS 5021 ADD-ON 1936, box 3).

40 *Workers' Weekly*, 4 March 1932; Miles in minutes of the Third Plenum, p. 63, as in note 35.

41 Minutes of the Tenth Congress of the CPA, April 1931, CPA records (ML MS 5021 ADD-ON 1936, box 1); Tripp told J. N. Rawling of his knowledge of Moore in an interview in 1961, Rawling papers (ANU N57/109).

42 E. H. Carr, *The Twilight of the Comintern 1930–1935* (London: Macmillan, 1982), ch. 2; *Workers' Weekly*, 20, 27 November, 11, 25 December 1931.

43 Moore to organisation department CEC, 7 June 1930, CPA records (ML MS 5021 ADD-ON 1936, box 3); *Workers' Weekly*, 15, 22 April, 30 September 1932; W. Orr to Anglo–American Bureau of ECCI, 20 June 1932, Comintern records (CI 495/94/94). Higgins's boast is quoted in Ralph Gibson, *The People Stand Up* (Ascot Vale, Vic.: Red Rooster Press, 1983), p. 53.

44 *Argus*, 8 November 1932; Gibson, *The People Stand Up*, pp. 50, 56–7.

45 *Workers' Weekly*, 22 July, 5 August, 21 October, 4, 11 November 1932; minutes and correspondence of Number 4 District, 1932 in file marked 'Melbourne

documents' and additional material in state correspondence and reports 1932–40, CPA records (ML MS 5021 ADD-ON 1936, boxes 4, 5).

46 'Political Statement of No. 4 District to the ECCI and Party Plenum 1932', and minutes of the meeting of the district committee, 8 January 1933, in Melbourne documents and also Comintern records (CI 495/94/109); Waten, *Time of Conflict*, pp. 176–8.

47 Minutes of the Third Plenum, as in note 35; *Workers' Weekly*, 13, 20 January 1933.

48 'Weaknesses and Mistakes of Our Party', *Workers' Weekly*, 1 April 1932.

49 *Workers' Weekly*, 2 December 1932, 14 April, 5 May 1933; minutes of the PB, 14 January 1933, Comintern records (CI 95/94/105); 'Editorial', *Militant*, 1 October 1933; Susannah Short, *Laurie Short: A Political Life* (Sydney: Allen & Unwin, 1992), chs 2–3.

50 *Workers' Weekly*, 6, 13, 20 July 1934 for the expulsions of Tripp and Kavanagh; Kavanagh subsequently joined the Workers' Party. There are frequent reports in the Communist Party press of fights between Melbourne communists and Lovegrove; *Red Star*, 26 August 1932, 13 February 1935 and transcript of interview with Foxley, 28 October 1970, Battye Library (PR 6361/2).

51 *Workers' Weekly*, 18 August, 1 September 1933.

52 A. J. Baker, *Anderson's Social Philosophy: The Social Thought and Political Life of Professor John Anderson* (Sydney: Angus & Robertson, 1979), pp. 79–100; Brian Kennedy, *A Passion to Oppose: John Anderson, Philosopher* (Melbourne: MUP, 1995), ch. 6; *Workers' Weekly*, 6 December 1929.

53 'The Working Class', *Proletariat*, vol. 1, no. 1 (April 1932); 'Freedom and the Class Struggle', *Proletariat*, vol. 1, no. 2 (July 1932); Miles in *Workers' Weekly*, 29 April 1932, and Anderson's reply, 20 May 1932, followed by further criticism in subsequent issues. The suppression of Anderson's third article is related by one of the *Workers' Weekly* editors, Alwyn Lee, in a letter to J. N. Rawling, 1 January 1962, Rawling papers (ANU N57/90) and it appeared as *Censorship in the Working-Class Movement* (Sydney: Sydney University Freethought Society, n.d. [November 1932]). Kavanagh's comment on the typescript is in Rawling papers (ANU N57/206) and the party condemnation in *Workers' Weekly*, 11, 25 November 1932. Baker and Kennedy, ibid., summarise his contributions to the *Militant*.

54 Ralph Gibson discusses the Labour Club in *The People Stand Up*, pp. 45–6; *Workers' Weekly*, 27 May 1932, for Baracchi; Miles in minutes of the Third Plenum, p. 69, as in note 35.

55 *Argus*, 3, 4 May 1932, and *The University Riots* (Melbourne: Workers' Art Club, n.d. [1932]); *Sydney Morning Herald*, 8 November 1932.

56 John Sendy, *Ralph Gibson: An Extraordinary Communist* (Melbourne: Ralph Gibson Biography Committee, 1988), p. 48, and letters from Gibson to his mother during 1931, Gibson papers (NLA MS 7844, box 1, folder 1).

57 O'Day's article, 'Why I Am a Communist', first appeared in *Smith's Weekly*, and was republished in *Workers' Weekly*, 12 February 1932 and then as a pamphlet, *The Dr Who Tells*, Rawling papers (ANU N57/414). His arrest and trial were reported in *Argus*, 8 November, 3 December 1932, the criticism in *Workers' Weekly*, 9 December 1932, and the self-criticism in minutes of the Third Plenum, pp. 171–2, as in note 35.

58 The appraisals of Gibson come from PB minutes, 14 January, 24 February, 13 May 1933.

59 'Statement on the "Lesser Evil Theory" by Paterson, 1932' (AA A8911, item 158), quoted in Ross Fitzgerald, *The People's Champion: Fred Paterson* (St Lucia, Qld: UQP, 1997), pp. 63–71; see also *Fred Paterson: A Personal History* (Brisbane: Labour History Society, 1994).

60 *Workers' Weekly*, 12 August, 2 September 1932, 10 March 1933; letter from DC, District 3 to CC, 13 April 1933; minutes of the Fourth Plenum, [p. 81], as in note 39. Miles gave a lengthy account of his arguments with Paterson to the CC, 22–23 February 1935, [pp. 145–6], CPA records (ML MS 5021 ADD-ON 1936, box 15).

61 Guido Baracchi, interviewed by David Walker in *Overland*, no. 97 (December 1984), p. 20; Jess Grant in Joyce Stevens (ed.), *Taking the Revolution Home: Work Among Women in the Communist Party of Australia 1920–1945* (Fitzroy, Vic.: Sybylla Press, 1987), p. 172; Claude Jones, interviewed by John Sendy, n.d., in possession of John Sendy.

62 Moxon and Lindsay Mountjoy in minutes of the Tenth Congress of the CPA, April 1931, as in note 41; further information from minutes of the closed session of the CC Plenum, 2 January 1932, and interview with Sid Foxley, 28 October 1970, as in note 50.

63 The UWM organiser was Tom Payne, who rejoined the CPA in 1931; in Lowenstein, *Weevils in the Flour*, p. 215.

64 Nelson in minutes of the Tenth Congress of the CPA, April 1931, as in note 41; A. F. Howells, *Against the Stream: The Memories of a Philosophical Anarchist 1927–1939* (Melbourne: Hyland House, 1983), p. 35; Frank Hardy, 'They Eat Their Babies in Russia', in *The Loser Now Will Be Later To Win* (Carlton, Vic.: Pascoe Publishing, 1985), pp. 54–81. Snowy Hall appears in George Bliss's account in Len Fox (ed.), *Depression Down Under*, 2nd edn (Sydney: Hale & Iremonger, 1989), pp. 85–92, as Snowy Paul, though in *Red Leader*, 16 November 1932, he is James Hill.

65 Miles in minutes of the Third Plenum, pp. 18–19, as in note 35; Dixon in minutes of the CC, 22–23 February 1935, [p. 54], CPA records (ML MS 5021 ADD-ON 1936, box 3).

66 Perry Anderson, 'Communist Party History', in Raphael Samuel (ed.), *People's History and Socialist Theory* (London: Routledge & Kegan Paul, 1981), pp. 145–56.

67 Frank Huelin in Lowenstein, *Weevils in the Flour*, p. 385; see also his *Keep Moving: An Odyssey* (Sydney: ABS, 1973).

68 Ferrier (ed.), *Point of Departure*, pp. 129, 174.

Chapter 10   Towards the united front

1 E. H. Carr, *The Twilight of the Comintern, 1930–1935* (London: Macmillan, 1982).

2 Moore in minutes of the Tenth Congress of the CPA, [p. 7], CPA records (ML MS 5021 ADD-ON 1936, box 1); Miles in minutes of the Third Plenum, 25–27 December 1932, pp. 22–3, CPA records (ML MS 5021 ADD-ON 1936, box 3). The main resolution of the plenum was formulated at Anglo–American Bureau meetings in October 1932, Comintern records (CI 495/3/338).

3 'For Unity in Struggle Against Capitalist Offensive and Fascism', *Workers' Weekly*, 21 April 1933.

4 Minutes of the PB, 14 March 1933, Comintern records (CI 95/94/105); 'For the Correct Application of the Line of the Comintern', and 'Some Mistakes Which Must Be Overcome', *Workers' Weekly*, 28 April, 12 May 1933.

5 Carr, *The Twilight of the Comintern*, ch. 6; minutes of the Fourth Plenum, CPA records (ML MS 5021 ADD-ON 1936, box 3) and resolution 'On the Present Situation in Australia and the Tasks of the Party', *Workers' Weekly* 20 April

1934; minutes of the CC, 1 July 1934 [p. 104], CPA records (ML MS 5021 ADD-ON 1936, box 3).

6 Minutes of the CC, 20–23 October 1934, [pp. 5, 49] as in note 5; 'For Unity of Action of the Working Class' and 'Why the United Front With the ALP?', *Workers' Weekly*, 2, 23 November 1934.

7 Letter from State Executive of the Victorian ALP to District Committee CPA, 10 April 1935, Rawling papers (ANU N57/396). Minutes of the CC, 22–23 February 1935, [pp. 8, 131–2, 147], 1–3 June 1935, [p. 151], as in note 5.

8 G. Dimitrov, *The Working Class Against Fascism* (Sydney: Modern Publishers 1935); 'Report of L. Sharkey on 7th World Congress CI', p. 5, in minutes of the Eleventh Congress of the CPA, 27–31 December 1935, CPA records (ML MS 5021 ADD-ON 1936, box 1).

9 Minutes of the CC, 1–3 June, [p. 10], 21–22 September 1935, as in note 5, and minutes of special meeting of the CC, 16 November 1935, (file marked J. Loughran 1935) CPA records (ML MS 5021 ADD-ON 1936, box 28).

10 Miles in minutes of the CC, 22–23 February 1935, [p. 145], as in note 5. Paterson had launched the earlier campaign for a united front at a meeting in the Sydney Domain reported in *Workers' Weekly*, 5 October 1934.

11 Jim Comerford, quoted in Andrew Metcalfe, *For Freedom and Dignity: Historical Agency and Class Structures in the Coalfields of NSW* (Sydney: Allen & Unwin, 1988), p. 111.

12 Minutes of the Anglo–American Bureau, and resolution on 'The Situation and Tasks of the MM in Australia' 15 October 1932, Comintern records (CI 495/72/148); minutes of the PB, 23 September, 5 November 1932.

13 These are among the work bulletins listed in Beverley Symons, *Communism in Australia: A Resource Bibliography* (Canberra: NLA, 1994), part 2. The Noel Butlin Archives of Business and Labour at the ANU holds the fullest collection, but many more are scattered in other repositories. A large sample was sent to Moscow, Comintern records (CI 495/94/61, 75, 100, 108).

14 Brian Costar, 'Two Depression Strikes, 1931', in D. J. Murphy (ed.), *The Big Strikes: Queensland 1889–1965* (St Lucia, Qld: UQP, 1983), pp. 186–201.

15 'For Mass United Struggle Against Capital', *Red Leader*, 19 April 1933.

16 For the mechanism of party control, see J. B. Miles to Number 3 District Committee, 4 October 1933, CPA records (ML MS 5021 ADD-ON 1936, box 5); minutes of the National Congress of the MM, 24 December 1933, CPA records (ML MS 5021 ADD-ON 1936, box 16), and minutes of the Fourth Plenum, pp. 4c, [138], as in note 5. See also the criticism of 'The Plenum of the CC of the Communist Party of Australia', *Inprecorr*, no. 30, 7 July 1933, pp. 670–1.

17 Minutes of the CC, 20–23, October 1934 [pp. 7–8, 22–3]; February 1935 [p. 73]; 30 June–1 July 1934 [p. 168], as in note 5; ECCI to CPA, 23 November 1934, Comintern records (CI 495/3/427).

18 Robin Gollan, *The Coalminers of New South Wales: A History of the Union 1860–1960* (Melbourne: MUP, 1963), ch. 10; Edgar Ross, *A History of the Miners' Federation of Australia* (Sydney: Australasian Coal and Shale Employees' Federation, 1970), ch. 14. Voting figures in *Red Leader*, 3 January 1934.

19 *Red Leader*, 7, 14 February, 21 March, 30 May, 25 July, 1 August 1934; *Workers' Voice*, 22 June, 27 July 1934; see Peter Cochrane, 'The Wonthaggi Coal Strike, 1934', *Labour History*, no. 27 (November 1974), pp. 12–30, and Andrew Reeves, Industrial Men: Miners and Politics in Wonthaggi, 1909–68, MA thesis, La Trobe University, 1977, ch. 2. The union election results are reported in *Red Leader*, 11 July 1934, and the MM membership figures are in minutes of the Fourth Plenum of the CC, 1–2 April 1934, [p. 118], and minutes of the CC, 30 June–1 July 1934 [pp. 25, 70], as in note 5.

20 *Workers' Weekly*, 6 September 1935; Ross quoted in Mark Hearn, *Working Lives: A History of the Australian Railways Union (NSW Branch)* (Sydney: Hale & Iremonger, 1990), p. 52; see also Stephen Holt, *A Veritable Dynamo: Lloyd Ross and Australian Labour 1901–1987* (St Lucia, Qld: UQP, 1996), chs 3–5.

21 Evidence of inability to make progress in the maritime and pastoral industries was presented, for example, in the minutes of the Fourth Plenum [pp. 33, 76–7, 88, 140], as in note 5; see also Rupert Lockwood, *Ship to Shore: A History of Melbourne's Waterfront and its Union Struggles* (Sydney: Hale & Iremonger, 1990), part 6; Brian Fitzpatrick and Rowan Cahill, *The Seamen's Union of Australia 1872–1972: A History* (Sydney: SUA, 1981), chs 10–11; L. J. Louis, 'Recovery from the Depression and the Seamen's Strike of 1935–6', *Labour History*, no. 41 (November 1981), pp. 74–86, and A. E. Davies, *The Meat Workers Unite* (Melbourne: AMIEU (Victorian branch), 1974), pp. 78–115.

22 J. A. Merritt, ''The Federated Ironworkers' Association in the Depression', *Labour History*, no. 21 (November 1971), pp. 48–61; the member is quoted in Robert Murray and Kate White, *The Ironworkers: A History of the Federated Ironworkers' Association of Australia* (Sydney: Hale & Iremonger, 1982), p. 70.

23 Dixon in *Workers' Weekly*, 23 February 1934, and 'Problems of Militant Trade Unionism', *Communist Review*, vol. 1, no. 5 (August 1934), p. 16; Orr in minutes of the CC, 30 June–1 July 1934, p. 28; Miles and Dixon in minutes of the CC, 22–23 February 1935 [pp. 6–9, 37], as in note 5.

24 ibid. [pp. 53, 83, 95] and minutes of the Eleventh Congress of the CPA [p. 175], as in note 8.

25 Nina Fishman, *The British Communist Party and the Trade Unions, 1933–45* (Aldershot: Scolar Press, 1996).

26 *Red Leader*, 14, 21 March, 18 April, 29 August, 5 September 1934; *Workers' Weekly*, 6 April, 2, 30 November 1934, and Dixon in minutes of the CC, 22–23 February 1935 [p. 35], as in note 5. See Diane Menghetti, *The Red North: The Popular Front in North Queensland* (Townsville: History Department, James Cook University of North Queensland, 1981), chs 2–3; 'The Weil's Disease Strike 1935', in Murphy (ed.), *The Big Strikes*, pp. 202–16, and Beris Penrose, The Communist Party and Trade Union Work in Queensland in the Third Period: 1928–35, PhD thesis, University of Queensland, 1993, ch. 7.

27 *Red Leader* and *Workers' Weekly*, June–December 1935 *passim*; Jean Devanny, *Sugar Heaven* (Sydney: Modern Publishers, 1936) and a new edition with an introduction by Carole Ferrier (Flemington, Vic.: Redback Press, 1982).

28 Henry in minutes of the Eleventh Congress of the CPA [p. 237], as in note 8; King in Mona Frame (ed.), *Wherever the Struggle: The Story of Carl King* (Campbelltown, NSW: Sydney Branch of the ASSLH, 1991), p. 19; CC resolution 'on tasks of the party in the sugar industry', 14 January 1936, state correspondence and reports, CPA records (ML MS 5021 ADD-ON 1936, box 5).

29 The approach of the PWIU is reported in minutes of the Eleventh Congress [p. 210], as in note 8.

30 See, for example, Alastair Davidson, *The Communist Party: A Short History* (Stanford, California: Hoover Institution Press, 1969), ch. 3; Robin Gollan, *Revolutionaries and Reformists: Communism and the Australian Labour Movement 1920–1950*, new edn (Sydney: Allen & Unwin, 1985), ch. 2.

31 Miles in minutes of the Eleventh Congress [p. 181], as in note 8; R. Cram, 'The Increased Vote in Hartley', *Communist Review*, vol. 2, no. 6 (June 1935), pp. 51–5; Hills quoted by Les Barnes, recorded April–May 1991, and see Wendy Lowenstein and Tom Hills, *Under the Hook: Melbourne Waterside Workers Remember Working Lives and Class War 1900–1980* (Prahran, Vic.: Melbourne Bookworkers, 1982), pp. 67–82.

32 Eleanor Dark, *Waterway* (Sydney: F. H. Johnston, 1938).

33 *Women in Australia: From Factory, Farm* (Sydney: Central Committee Women's Department, n.d. [1932]); *Working Woman*, January 1932; Kollontai's work had been published in 1920 by Andrade's Bookshop.

34 For the organisation of the Women's Department, see the report to the Women's Department of ECCI, 15 July 1931, Comintern records (CI 495/94/72); and for a frank appraisal of its record, Hetty Weitzel in minutes of the CC, 1–3 June 1935 [p. 143], as in note 5. See Joyce Stevens (ed.), *Taking the Revolution Home: Work Among Women in the Communist Party of Australia 1920–1945* (Fitzroy, Vic.: Sybylla Press, 1987), ch. 1.

35 Thompson in minutes of the Fourth Plenum, 1–2 April 1934 [pp. 160–6], as in note 5; *Red Leader*, 14 February 1934; *Working Woman*, September 1932; Raelene Frances, *The Politics of Work: Gender and Labour in Victoria, 1880–1939* (Melbourne: CUP, 1993), pp. 144–6 discusses a similar dispute of women garment workers in 1935.

36 'The Communist in the Home', *Workers' Voice*, 23 November 1934.

37 Clara Zetkin, 'Lenin on the Woman Question', *Communist Review*, vol. 2, no. 3 (March 1935), pp. 14–24; CC to All Districts, 27 March 1935, CC circulars and statements 1933–41, CPA records (ML MS 5021 ADD-ON 1936, box 5); Miles in minutes of the Eleventh Congress [p. 182], as in note 8; Ryan in Stevens (ed.), *Taking the Revolution Home*, pp. 124–6; Carole Ferrier (ed.), *Point of Departure: The Autobiography of Jean Devanny* (St Lucia, Qld: UQP, 1986), pp. 153–4, 157–8, 169–71.

38 Ray Sutton, Labour Movement Youth Organisation and Policy in Eastern Australia, c.1918–c.1939, PhD thesis, ANU, 1990, esp. chs 3–5.

39 Letter from L. Aarons and Beryl Glendinning to 'Cde Newman', 5 June 1931 (AA A467, bundle 94, SF 42/64); 'Baden-Powell', *Workers' Weekly*, 23 January 1931; 'Build the Young Communist League', *Workers' Weekly*, 9 March 1934; Audrey Blake, *A Proletarian Life* (Malmsbury, Vic.: Kibble Books, 1984), pp. 91–2. Reports to the Youth Department of the ECCI are in Comintern records (CI 533/10/1).

40 Miles in minutes of the CC, 22–24 February 1935 [p, 14], as in note 5, and reports by representatives of the YCL to plenums; Sharkey in *Workers' Weekly*, 6 December 1935; Harry Torr, A Better League of Youth', *Communist Review*, vol. 3, no. 3 (March 1936), pp. 43–8.

41 *Workers' Weekly*, 25 September 1931.

42 See especially Moxon, 'Hands off the Aborigines', *Red Leader* 25 September 1931, various articles by Jeffery in the *Workers' Weekly* earlier in 1931, and a letter from Sawtell to *Workers' Weekly*, supporting Moxon, as well as his encomium to anthropology in *Red Leader*, 20 June 1934. Wright's involvement is described by Mary Wright in Audrey Johnson, *Bread and Roses: A Personal History of Three Militant Women and Their Friends 1902–1988* (Sutherland, NSW: Left Book Club, 1990), pp. 130–1. I have also drawn on an unpublished paper by Bob Boughton and on information about Sawtell provided by Verity Burgmann.

43 The Aboriginal politics are discussed in Heather Goodall, *Invasion to Embassy: Land in Aboriginal Politics in New South Wales, 1770–1972* (Sydney: Allen & Unwin, 1996), and Wright's influence is noted in Raymond Markey, *In Case of Oppression: The Life and Times of the Labor Council of New South Wales* (Sydney: Pluto Press, 1994), pp. 264–5; report of the Western Australian organiser in minutes of the Fourth Plenum [p. 172], as in note 5; *Workers' Weekly*, 4 May, 8, 15 June 3 August 1934; *Red Leader*, 20 June, 4 July, 15 August 1934. See Andrew Markus, 'Talka Longa Mouth', in Ann Curthoys and Andrew Markus

(eds), *Who Are Our Enemies? Racism and the Australian Working Class* (Sydney: Hale & Iremonger, 1978), pp. 138–57.

44 Jack Blake, interviewed by Laurie Aarons, August 1979, and information given to me, July 1997; Gianfranco Cresciani, *Fascism, Anti-Fascism and Italians in Australia, 1922–1945* (Canberra: ANUP, 1980), chs 5–6; Stelios Kourbetis, Ethnicity Versus Class? A Study of Greek Radicals in Australia 1920–89, MA thesis, La Trobe University, 1990, ch. 3; David Rechter, Beyond the Pale: Jewish Communism in Melbourne, MA thesis, University of Melbourne, 1986, ch. 3.

45 The memoirs are in the possession of Amirah Inglis, who kindly allowed me to read them.

46 Justina Williams, *The First Furrow* (Willagee, WA: Lone Hand Press, 1976), pp. 143–7; Ted Docker and Rolf Gerritsen, 'The 1934 Kalgoorlie Riots', *Labour History*, no. 31 (November 1976), pp. 79–82.

47 Chapman in report of the congress, *Workers' Weekly*, 6 October 1933, *Red Leader*, 4, 11 October 1933.

48 Eric Marshall, *It Pays to Be White* (Sydney: Alpha Books, 1973), p. 65; J. N. Rawling, Communism Comes to Australia, pp. 425–8, Rawling papers (ANU N57/1). Rawling was national secretary of the MAWF and his papers contain a substantial documentary record.

49 Burgmann to Rawling, 13 September 1934, Rawling papers (ANU N57/225); Rawling criticised Burgmann in *War! What For?*, vol. 1, no. 10 (January 1935), p. 168.

50 *Workers' Weekly*, 19 October 1934–1 March 1935; *Workers' Voice*, 5 October 1934. L. J. Louis, 'Victorian Council Against War and Fascism: A Rejoinder', *Labour History*, no. 44 (May 1983), pp. 39–54 is the fullest account and employs the Investigation Branch records; see also Egon Kisch, *Australian Landfall* (London: Secker & Waburg, 1937), and Julian Smith [T. M. Fitzgerald], *On the Pacific Front: The Adventures of Egon Kisch in Australia* (Sydney: Australian Book Services, 1936).

51 *Workers' Voice*, 16, 23 November 1934; A. F. Howells, *Against the Stream: The Memories of a Philosophical Anarchist 1927–1939* (Melbourne: Hyland House, 1983), p. 76 and chs 6–8 *passim*. See also Carolyn Rasmussen, *The Lesser Evil? Opposition to Fascism and War in Australia 1920–1941* (Melbourne: History Department, University of Melbourne, 1992), chs 3–5. There is a large file of protests against the government's treatment of Kisch (AA A981, file COM 37).

52 Ralph Gibson, *One Woman's Life: A Memoir of Dorothy Gibson* (Sydney: Hale & Iremonger, 1980), p. 41, quotes Alexander on this challenge, and Len Fox, *Broad Left, Narrow Left* (Chippendale: APCOL, 1982), p. 20 also discusses it.

53 Minutes of the CC, 21–22 September, [pp. 4, 60], as in note 5, for Rawling. The allegations about CC preference for compromise were published subsequently, *Militant*, n.s. vol. 1, nos 1–2 (September, October 1938), and disputed at the time by Miles in a circular, 4 March 1935 (CC circulars and statements 1933–41), as in note 37, and minutes of the CC, 1–3 June 1935 [p. 4]. The extent of party control of the MAWF is argued in Ken Slater, 'Egon Kisch: A Biographical Outline', *Labour History*, no. 36 (May 1979), pp. 94–103; David Rose, 'The Movement Against War and Fascism', *Labour History*, no. 38 (May 1980), pp. 76–90; Len Fox, 'The Movement Against War and Fascism: A View from Inside', *Labour History*, no. 39 (November 1980), pp. 78–82; and Louis, 'The Victorian Council Against War and Fascism: A Rejoinder'. See also Alastair Davidson, The Communist Party of Australia 1920–35: Policy and Organisation, PhD thesis, ANU, 1966, pp. 393–425.

54 Major-General J. H. Bruche to minister for defence, 19 November 1934 (AA A467, SF7/2); Civil Security Intelligence, no. 68 (31 May 1935), 84 (31 October

1936) (AA A8911, file 159). It is clear that the leaders of the CPGB, for example, were kept ignorant of members' espionage activities; Christopher Andrew and Oleg Gordievsky, *KGB: The Inside Story of its Foreign Operations from Lenin to Gorbachev* (London: Hodder & Stoughton, 1990); Francis Beckett, *Enemy Within: The Rise and Fall of the British Communist Party* (London: John Murray, 1995), ch. 5.

55 *Strife*, vol. 1, no. 1 (13 October 1930), quoted in Charles Merewether, 'Social Realism: The Formative Years', *Arena*, no. 46 (1977), pp. 65–80. See also David Carter, Realism as a Contemporary Response to the Modern: Left-Wing Cultural Attitudes and the Concept of Modernity in Australia, 1930–65, MA thesis, University of Melbourne, 1982, ch. 1; Julie Wells, Integrating Literary and Political Activity: Katharine Susannah Prichard, Jean Devanny and Communist Writers During the 1930s, PhD thesis, Monash University, 1994, ch. 2, and Bernard Smith, *Noel Counihan: Artist and Revolutionary* (Melbourne: OUP, 1993), ch. 4. The banners are identified in *Red Leader*, 11 May 1932, and appear on the dustjacket of Judah Waten, *Scenes of Revolutionary Life* (Sydney: Angus & Robertson, 1982).

56 Smith, *Noel Counihan*, p 80; for Finey, *Workers' Weekly*, 11 November 1932, and Ferrier (ed.), *Point of Departure*, pp. 160–4.

57 The argument over workers' theatre ran in *Red Leader* from 12 April to 16 August 1933, and Orr spoke in support of Devanny at the PB, 13 May 1933. Devanny's contribution appeared in *Red Leader* on 24 May 1933, and her unrepentant statement on 14 February 1934.

58 'Notes of the Month', *Strife*, vol. 1, no. 1, p. 7; *Workers' Art*, vol. 1, no. 1 (April 1933), pp. 8, 17.

59 *Workers' Weekly*, 7 September 1934, 19 April 1935; *Red Leader*, 12 December 1934; Len Donald in minutes of the CC, 20–23 October 1934 [p. 30], as in note 5; see Peter Coleman, *Obscenity, Blasphemy, Sedition: Censorship in Australia* (Brisbane: Jacaranda Press, n.d. [1963]), pp. 115–18.

60 M. I. Kalinin, 'On Communist Education', quoted in Ralph Gibson, *The People Stand Up*, p. 56.

61 Statistics from *Workers' Weekly*, 15 June 1934, 5 July 1935; minutes of the CC, 1–3 June 1935, [pp. 110–13], as in note 5; Len Donald, 'Forward to a Mass Bolshevik Party', *Communist Review*, vol. 2, no. 4 (April 1935), pp. 46–51; minutes of the Eleventh Congress [p. 196], as in note 8.

62 Colin A. Hughes and B. D. Graham, *A Handbook of Australian Government and Politics 1890–1964* (Canberra: ANUP, 1968); minutes of the CC, 20–23 October 1934, [p. 12], as in note 5.

63 Minutes of the Fourth Plenum, 1–3 April 1934 [p. 132], as in note 5; minutes of the Eleventh Congress [p. 215], as in note 8.

64 The *Sydney Morning Herald*, 13 February 1934, reported the move of the party headquarters; John Sendy, *Melbourne's Radical Bookshops: History, People, Appreciation* (Melbourne: International Bookshop, 1983), chs 9–11 discusses party shops in that city.

65 Memoirs of Itzhak Gust in possession of Amirah Inglis; John Sendy, *Melbourne's Radical Bookshops*, pp. 102–3.

66 There is a report on the Sydney newspaper press in minutes of the Eleventh Congress [p. 197], as in note 8 and Gil Roper, who worked on it, published allegations of mismanagement in *Militant*, 24 January 1938.

67 *Inprecorr*, no. 30, 7 July 1933, pp. 670–1, discussed in minutes of the PB, 7 September, 6 October 1933, Comintern records (CI 495/94/106), and ECCI to CPA, 23 November 1934, Comintern records (CI 495/3/427); Miles in minutes of the Fourth Plenum [p. 92], and CC, 22–24 February 1935, [p. 11], as in note 5.

68 Blake, interviewed by Laurie Aarons (ML); he changed his name by deed poll to John David Blake in August 1934.

69 ibid.; notebooks from the Lenin School are in the papers of Ted Tripp (UMA) and Richard Dixon (NLA); Alf Watt, *Reminiscences of Sixty Years in the Communist Movement in Australia* (Surry Hills, NSW: SPA, n.d. [1987]), p. 14 describes the Sydney training.

70 Dixon in minutes of the CC, 30 June–1 July 1934 [p. 115], as in note 5; the analogy of the fire brigade was first used by the head of the Comintern Organisation Bureau, Ossip Piatnitsky, and used at the same CC meeting [p. 15]; Gibson, *The People Stand Up*, p. 38 makes the observation about the 'fossilised bureaucrats and chatterers', and the occasion was the Fourth Plenum.

71 Blake, interviewed by Laurie Aarons (ML).

72 Minutes of the CC, 22–23 February 1935 [pp. 16–17], as in note 5.

73 *Workers' Weekly*, 21 November 1931, quoted in L. J. Louis, *Trade Unions and the Depression: A Study of Victoria 1930–1932* (Canberra: ANUP, 1968), p. 35; minutes of the CC, 21–2 September 1935 [p. 107].

74 Agenda and draft resolutions for the Eleventh Congress, Rawling papers (ANU N57/398); minutes of the Eleventh Congress, pp. 3–4, as in note 8.

Chapter 11   Communism by fronts

1 Ralph Gibson, *One Woman's Life: A Memoir of Dorothy Gibson* (Sydney: Hale & Iremonger, 1980), p. 40; Audrey Blake, *A Proletarian Life* (Malmsbury, Vic.: Kibble Books, 1984), p. 104; Len Fox, *Broad Left, Narrow Left* (Chippendale, NSW: APCOL, 1982), pp. 18, 35, chs 7, 16.

2 'The Fascist Offensive and the Tasks of the Communist International', main address to the Seventh Congress, in George Dimitrov, *Against Fascism and War* (New York: International Publishers, 1936), p. 4.

3 'History and Illusion', *New Left Review*, no. 220 (November–December 1996), pp. 117–18.

4 CC to all Districts, 4 October 1935, CC circulars and statements 1933–42, CPA records (ML MS 5021 ADD-ON 1936, box 5); Richard Dixon, *Peace or War?: The Case for Sanctions Explained* (Sydney: CPA, n.d. [October 1935]).

5 ACTU Congress minutes, 1935, in Jim Hagan (ed.), *Australian Trade Unionism in Documents* (Melbourne: Longman Cheshire, 1986), p. 112; see also CC circular, 6 December 1935, as in note 4; E. M. Andrews, *Isolation and Appeasement in Australia: Reactions to the European Crises, 1935–1939* (Canberra: ANUP, 1970), ch. 2; Stephen Holt, *A Veritable Dynamo: Lloyd Ross and Australian Labour 1901–1987* (St Lucia, Qld: UQP, 1996), pp. 48–50.

6 *Workers' Voice*, 22 November 1935, quoted in Susan Blackburn, *Maurice Blackburn and the Australian Labor Party 1934–1943* (Canberra: ASSLH, 1969), p. 15.

7 *Argus*, 3 April 1936. See minutes of the CC, 10–12 April 1936 [pp. 130–3, 149], CPA records (ML MS 5021 ADD-ON 1936, box 4); J. D. Blake, 'The Fight for Unity Against War in Victoria', *Communist Review*, vol. 2, no. 11 (November 1935), pp. 19–26, and L. Donald, 'For the Unity of the Labor Movement in Victoria', *Communist Review*, vol. 3, no. 4 (April 1936), pp. 1–6; Ralph Gibson, *The People Stand Up* (Ascot Vale, Vic.: Red Rooster Press, 1983), pp. 151–3; L. J. Louis, 'Victorian Council Against War and Fascism: A Rejoinder', *Labour History*, no. 44 (May 1983), pp. 39–54.

8 Kate White, *John Cain and Victorian Labor 1917–1957* (Sydney: Hale & Iremonger, 1983), ch. 4; Carolyn Rasmussen, 'Challenging the Centre—the Coburg

ALP Branch in the 1930s', *Labour History*, no. 54 (May 1988), pp. 47–63; minutes of the CC, 10–12 April 1936 [pp. 114–20], as in note 7.

9 Minutes of enlarged PB Meeting, 21 March 1936, CC minutes 1936–40, as in note 7; *Workers' Weekly*, 28 April 1936 et seq. See Murray Goot, 'Radio LANG', in Heather Radi and Peter Spearritt (eds), *Jack Lang* (Sydney: Hale & Iremonger, 1977), pp. 119–37; Bede Nairn, *The 'Big Fella': Jack Lang and the Australian Labor Party 1891–1949* (Melbourne: MUP, 1986), ch. 13; Jim Hagan and Ken Turner, *A History of the Labor Party in New South Wales 1891–1991* (Melbourne: Longman Cheshire, 1991), pp. 88–94.

10 'The United Front in South Australia', *Communist Review*, vol. 3, no. 6 (June 1936), pp. 54–8.

11 IPC records (UMA), and Carolyn Rasmussen, *The Lesser Evil: Opposition to War and Fascism in Australia 1920–1941* (Melbourne: History Department, University of Melbourne, 1992), chs 5–7. Sharkey noted the shift from the MAWAF to the IPC in minutes of the CC, 20–2 November 1936 [p. 108], as in note 7.

12 Quoted in Ralph Gibson, *My Years in the Communist Party* (Melbourne: International Bookshop, 1966), p. 58.

13 Sam Aarons, quoted in Amirah Inglis, *Australians in the Spanish Civil War* (Sydney: Allen & Unwin, 1987), p. 118.

14 The problems of recruitment were discussed in a CC circular, 7 January 1938, as in note 4.

15 Geoffrey Cox, *Defence of Madrid* (London: Victor Gollancz, 1937) on Barry; Jim McNeill, 'Man of Humour and Kindness', in Len Fox (ed.), *Depression Down Under*, 2nd edn (Sydney: Hale & Iremonger, 1989), pp. 68–74 on Dickinson; Walters in *Workers' Weekly*, 8 February 1938; Riley quoted in Inglis, *Australians in the Spanish Civil War*, p 117; Lloyd Edmonds, *Letters from Spain*, ed. Amirah Inglis (Sydney: Allen & Unwin, 1985); for Hurd, Stuart Macintyre, *Militant: The Life and Times of Paddy Troy* (Sydney: Allen & Unwin, 1984); Prichard in *Workers' Weekly*, 28 January 1938 on Stevens. See generally Inglis, *Australians in the Spanish Civil War*, chs 6–7; Nettie Palmer and Len Fox, *Australians in Spain*, 2nd edn (Sydney: Current Book Distributors, 1948).

16 *Workers' Weekly*, 14 May, 6 July 1937; CC to district committees, 20 October 1936, as in note 4; on Hodgson, Judith Keene, *The Last Mile to Huesca: An Australian Nurse in the Spanish Civil War* (Kensington, NSW: NSWUP, 1988); Aileen Palmer quoted in Inglis, *Australians in the Spanish Civil War*, p. 126, and Judith Keene, 'A Spanish Springtime: Aileen Palmer and the Spanish Civil War', *Labour History*, no. 52 (May 1987), p. 85. The detailed dossiers of the Australian volunteers in Comintern records (CI 545/6/67) pay considerable attention to political reliability.

17 Alan Moorehead, *A Late Education: Episodes in a Life* (London: Hamish Hamilton, 1980); Fisher in *ADB*, vol. 14, p. 172; Rowan Cahill, Rupert Lockwood and the Spooks, unpublished paper presented to Espionage and Counter-Espionage conference, University of Western Sydney, 12 October 1996.

18 Keene, 'A Spanish Springtime'; Ken Coldicutt, 'The Party, Films and I', in *Sixty Years of Struggle*, vol. 2 (Sydney: Red Pen Publications, n.d. [1982]), pp. 61–4; Crawford's account of his interest in Spain appears in *Old Bebb's Store and Other Poems*, edited by Stuart Macintyre (Melbourne: History Department, University of Melbourne, 1992), pp. 1–22.

19 Lyons, 151 *CPD*, pp. 56–7 (11 September 1936), quoted in Andrews, *Isolation and Appeasement*, p. 93; *Atheistic Communism: The Encyclical 'Divini Redemptoris'* (Melbourne: Australian Catholic Truth Society, 1937), and Patrick O'Farrell, *The Catholic Church and Community in Australia*, rev. edn (Melbourne: Nelson,

1977), pp. 389–90; Gilroy in *Freeman's Journal*, 9 March 1939, quoted in Keene, *Last Mile to Huesca*, p. 58.

20 The fullest account of the Melbourne debate is in Inglis, *Australians in the Spanish Civil War*, pp. 95–9; for the Adelaide meeting, see the *Adelaide Advertiser*, 6–11 May 1937, *Workers' Weekly*, 11 May 1937.

21 B. A. Santamaria, *Against the Tide* (Melbourne: OUP, 1981), p. 35; see Colin H. Jory, *The Campion Society and Catholic Social Militancy in Australia* (Sydney: Harpham, 1986).

22 Les Barnes, recorded April–May 1991; Thornton in minutes of the CC, 10–12 April 1936; Lithgow report in minutes of CC, 20–22 November 1936, [p. 79], as in note 7.

23 L. Harry Gould, 'Clergymen and Communism', *Communist Review*, vol. 4, no. 6 (June 1937), pp. 51–5; Burgmann reported in *Workers' Weekly*, 2 June 1936, and Peter Hempenstall, *The Meddlesome Priest: A Life of Ernest Burgmann* (Sydney: Allen & Unwin, 1993), pp. 192–6; Farnham Maynard, *Economics and the Kingdom of God* (Melbourne: Student Christian Movement, 1929).

24 Miles in *Workers' Weekly*, 30 June 1936, and also his statements in minutes of the CC, 24–7 July 1936, [p. 138], and 6–7 November 1937 [p. 49], as in note 7; CC to district committees, 19 April 1937, as in note 4; L. L. Sharkey, *An Appeal to Catholics: Democracy, Fascism, Mexico, Spain, Peace, War* (Sydney: Modern Publishers, 1937).

25 O'Day in *Workers' Weekly*, 11 June, 9 July 1937, and quoted in Wendy Lowenstein, *Weevils in the Flour: An Oral Record of the 1930s Depression in Australia*, rev. edn (Newham, Vic.: Scribe, 1989), p. 194, and Alf Watt, *Reminiscences of Sixty Years in the Communist Movement in Australia* (Surry Hills, NSW: SPA, n.d. [1987]), p. 19.

26 *Workers' Weekly*, 27 July 1937; Hagan (ed.), *Trade Unionism in Documents*, p. 113.

27 *Workers' Weekly*, 10 September, 8 October 1937, 28 January, 1 February, 15 April, 10, 27 May 1938; 'A. London' [Jack Blake] to CPA, 25 September 1937, Comintern records (CI 495/14/19), and CC circulars, 5 October 1937, 18 May 1938, as in note 4; Hagan, *History of the ACTU*, pp. 106–7; E. M. Andrews, *Australia and China: The Ambiguous Relationship* (Melbourne: MUP, 1985), ch. 3.

28 Bob Cram in minutes of the CC, 6–7 November 1937 [pp. 44–6], as in note 7; *Workers' Weekly*, 15–26 October 1937, *Sydney Morning Herald*, 15–23 October, 22 November 1937; Vic Bird, SS Silksworth *Dispute of 1937: A Memoir* (Melbourne: May Day Committee, 1991).

29 Roach quoted in Jon White, 'The Port Kembla Pig Dispute of 1938', *Labour History*, no. 37 (November 1979), p. 70. See also *Workers' Weekly*, 18 November 1938–24 January 1939; Len Richardson, 'Dole Queue Patriots: The Port Kembla Pig-Iron Strike of 1938', in John Iremonger, John Merritt and Graeme Osborne (eds), *Strikes: Studies in Twentieth Century Australian History* (Sydney: Angus & Robertson, 1973), pp. 143–58; Rupert Lockwood, *War on the Waterfront: Menzies, Japan and the Pig-iron Dispute* (Sydney: Hale & Iremonger, 1987).

30 Isaacs in *Argus*, 13 January 1939. See also A. W. Martin, *Robert Menzies: A Life. Volume 1, 1894–1943* (Melbourne: MUP, 1993), pp. 251–6; Stan Moran, *Reminiscences of a Rebel* (Chippendale, NSW: APCOL, 1979), pp. 17–18.

31 Cameron Hazlehurst, *Menzies Observed* (Sydney: Allen & Unwin, 1979), pp. 144–5; K. S. Inglis, *This is the ABC: The Australian Broadcasting Commission 1932–1983* (Melbourne: MUP, 1983), pp. 61–2; *Workers' Weekly*, 7, 28 July, 13 October 1936; *Judge Foster's Banned Speech* (Melbourne: Council for Civil Liberties, 1938).

32 *Workers' Weekly*, 8, 22, 25 February 1938, and 2 May, 10 June, 12 July, 17 August, 3 September for protests against von Luckner; *Sydney Morning*

Herald, 16–28 February 1938; L. P. Fox, *Von Luckner—Not Wanted* (Sydney: MAWF, 1938); Gianfranco Cresciani, *Fascism, Anti-Fascism and Italians in Australia 1922–1945* (Canberra: ANUP, 1980), pp. 108–9.

33 CC circular, 17 August 1937, 14 February 1939, as in note 4; L. P. Fox, *Australia and the Jews* (Melbourne: League for Peace and Democracy, 1939); David Rechter, Beyond the Pale: Jewish Communism in Melbourne, MA thesis, University of Melbourne, 1986, ch. 3.

34 Inglis, *Australians in the Spanish Civil War,* pp. 194–9.

35 Statement by Baracchi to CC, 12 February 1940, p. 48, Baracchi file, CPA records (ML MS 5021 ADD-ON 1936, box 25).

36 Minutes of the CC, 5–7 March 1937, as in note 7; Mason's article first appeared in *Inprecorr,* vol. 16, no. 33 (18 July 1936) and then *Communist Review,* vol. 3, no. 9 (September 1936), pp. 25–30, and was followed by 'A Program for Peace for the Australian People', ibid., vol. 4, no. 1 (January 1937). He also wrote several other articles for *Inprecorr* as well as a critical report on the Australian party's implementation of the Seventh Congress decisions, Comintern records (CI 495/20/7). CC circular on the election, 20 September 1937, as in note 4.

37 L. G. Stewart, 'Defeat the Lyons Government But—', *Communist Review,* vol. 4, no. 6 (June 1937), pp. 7–8; Thornton in minutes of the CC, 6–7 November 1937 [p. 24], as in note 7; statement by Baracchi to CC, 12 February 1940, p. 45, as in note 35; Marty in minutes of the Anglo–American Bureau, 27 September 1937, Comintern records (CI 495/14/19).

38 Dixon in *Workers' Weekly,* 11 November 1938; 'People's Front to Advance Australia Fair'; Miles's address to congress, *Workers' Weekly,* 25 November 1938; *Constitution and By-Laws of the Communist Party of Australia* (Sydney: CPA, 1938), p. 4; Blake in *The Way Forward: Decisions of the Twelfth Congress* (Sydney: CPA, 1938), pp. 48–9.

39 Blake in minutes of CC, 24–27 July 1936 [p. 46], as in note 7; J. N. Rawling, *Make the Rich Pay,* Comintern records (CI 495/14/304) and *Who Owns Australia* (Sydney: Modern Publishers, 1937), and CC circular, September 1937 (the pamphlet expanded in three subsequent editions and by 1939 30 000 copies had been sold); see generally Rick Kuhn, Paradise on the Instalment Plan: The Economic Thought of the Australian Labour Movement between the Depression and the Long Boom, PhD thesis, University of Sydney, 1985, ch. 5.

40 Lloyd Ross in minutes of the CC, 17–19 February 1939, as in note 7.

41 Ralph Gibson, *Socialist Melbourne* (Melbourne: State Committee of CPA, n.d. [1939]) in Rawling papers (ANU N57/1128).

42 Browder quoted in Fraser M. Ottanelli, *The Communist Party of the United States from the Depression to World War II* (New Brunswick: Rutgers University Press, 1991), p. 123; Pollitt in Kevin Morgan, *Harry Pollitt* (Manchester: Manchester University Press, 1993), p. 100; PCF in M. Adereth, *The French Communist Party, A Critical History* (Manchester: Manchester University Press, 1984), p. 63.

43 See, for example of communist interest, a commemoration of the seventieth anniversary, Hector Ross, 'Eureka Stockade', *Workers' Weekly,* 5 December 1924.

44 Lloyd Ross, *William Lane and the Australian Labor Movement* (Sydney: self-published, 1937); Brian Fitzpatrick, *British Imperialism and Australia* (London: George Allen & Unwin, 1939).

45 J. N. Rawling, *The Story of the Australian People,* parts 1–6 (Sydney: Modern Publishers, n.d.). See John Pomeroy, 'The Apostasy of James Normington Rawling', *Australian Journal of Politics and History,* vol. 37, no. 1 (1991), pp. 17–38.

46 Holt, *A Veritable Dynamo,* pp. 21–2; Rawling in *Workers' Weekly,* 14 December 1934, *Red Leader,* 12 December 1934; Miles in minutes of CC, 24–27 July 1936

[p. 115], as in note 7; *Workers' Weekly*, 15, 25 September, 30 October 1936; L. P. Fox, *The Truth About Anzac* (Melbourne: VCAWF, n.d. [1936]), pp. 2, 14.

47 Sharkey in minutes of the CC, 20–22 November 1936 [p. 92], as in note 7; Dixon in minutes of the CC, 6–7 November 1937 [pp. 62–3]. See G. Dimitrov, *The Working Class Against Fascism* (Sydney: Modern Books, 1935).

48 Sydney cadres' discussion of sesquicentenary, 28 August 1937, Comintern records (CI 495/14/304); 'The Sesqui-centenary', *Communist Review*, vol. 5, no. 2 (February 1938), pp. 3–4; *Workers' Weekly*, 26 April, 2 May 1938. See Julian Thomas, '1938: Past and Present in an Elaborate Anniversary', in Susan Janson and Stuart Macintyre (eds), *Making the Bicentenary* (Melbourne: Australian Historical Studies, 1988), pp. 77–89.

49 See, for example, Trotsky's 'Against the "People's Front" ' (1935), in David Beetham (ed.), *Marxists in the Face of Fascism: Writings by Marxists on Fascism from the Inter-War Period* (Manchester: Manchester University Press, 1983), pp. 204–7; CC circular, 12 March 1937, as in note 4.

50 Len Fox, *Dream at a Graveside: The History of the Fellowship of Australian Writers 1928–1988* (Marrickville, NSW: Fellowship of Australian Writers, 1989), ch. 12; Angela Hillel, *Against the Stream: Melbourne New Theatre 1936–1986* (Melbourne: New Theatre, 1986), pp. 6–8; Richard Haese, *Rebels and Precursors: The Revolutionary Years of Australian Art* (Ringwood, Vic.: Penguin Books, 1981), chs 2–3.

51 I draw here on Charles Merewether, *Art and Social Commitment: An End to a City of Dreams 1931–1948* (Sydney: Art Gallery of New South Wales, 1984), pp. 9–13, and Andy Croft, 'Authors Take Sides: Writers and the Communist Party 1920–1950', in Geoff Andrews, Nina Fishman and Kevin Morgan (eds), *Opening the Books: Essays on the Social and Cultural History of British Communism* (London: Pluto Press, 1995), pp. 83–101.

52 This version comes from Bernard Smith, *Noel Counihan: Artist and Revolutionary* (Melbourne: OUP, 1993), ch. 7. Judah's version, related to me in the early 1980s, was that he tried to prevent Noel from cruelling their pitch but that his kicks under the table only inflamed a companion who was in his cups.

53 A. A. Zhdanov, *On Literature, Music and Philosophy* (London: Lawence & Wishart, 1950), pp. 9–15; Drusilla Modjeska, *Exiles at Home: Australian Women Writers 1925–1945* (Sydney: Angus & Robertson, 1981), ch. 6; see also Carole Ferrier, 'Jean Devanny, Katharine Susannah Prichard and the "Really Proletarian Novel"', in Carole Ferrier (ed.), *Gender, Politics and Fiction: Twentieth-Century Australian Women's Novels* (St Lucia, Qld: UQP, 1985), pp. 101–17.

54 Jack Beasley, *A Gallop of Fire: Katharine Susannah Prichard On Guard for Humanity* (Earlwood, NSW: Wedgetail Press, 1993), p. 159, asserts that social realism was not advocated in Australia during the 1930s but it is central to A. Lunacharsky, *On Soviet Art* (Sydney: Workers' Art Club, 1933).

55 Julian Smith [Tom Fitzgerald], *Newspaper Reporting and Modern Reportage* (Sydney: Writers' League, 1935), pp. 5, 10, 13; Harcourt quoted in Richard Nile's introduction to a facsimile edition of *Upsurge* (Nedlands, WA: UWAP, 1986), p. xiii; Angela O'Brien's introduction to *Thirteen Dead* (Melbourne: New Theatre Playscripts, 1993), p. 9; David Carter, 'Documenting and Criticising Society', in Laurie Hergenhan (ed.), *The Penguin New Literary History of Australia* (Ringwood, Vic.: Penguin Books, 1988), p. 375.

56 A. F. Howells, *Against the Stream: The Memories of a Philosophical Anarchist, 1927–1939* (Melbourne: Hyland House, 1983), p. 119; Rob Darby, 'Fictions and Histories, in Richard Nile and Barry York (eds), *Workers and Intellectuals* (London: Edward Blackwood, 1992), pp. 84–101.

57 Moorehead, *A Late Education*, p. 30.

58 CC circular, 5 July 1938; Gordon Crane, 'Left Book Club and Labor Movement',

Communist Review, vol. 5, no. 12 (December 1938), pp. 23–6; Robin Gollan, *Revolutionaries and Reformists: Communism and the Australian Labour Movement 1920–1950*, new edn (Sydney: Allen & Unwin, 1985), pp. 66–70.

59 Fitzpatrick to Mollie Bayne, 12 April 1937, quoted in Don Watson, *Brian Fitzpatrick: A Radical Life* (Sydney: Hale & Iremonger, 1978), p. 90.

60 Ross in minutes of the CC, 17–19 February 1939 [pp. 9, 31], as in note 7; Burchett in *Argus*, 18 November 1936, and *At the Barricades* (Melbourne: Macmillan, 1981), p. 48; Evelyn Healy, *Artist of the Left: A Personal Experience 1930s–1980s* (Sydney: Left Book Club, 1993), p. 3.

61 Mary Wright in Audrey Johnson, *Bread and Roses: A Personal History of Three Militant Women and Their Friends 1902–1988* (Sutherland, NSW: Left Book Club, 1990), p. 115; minutes of the Eleventh Congress, p. 94, CPA records (ML MS 5021 ADD-ON 1936, box 1); *Workers' Weekly*, 25 February, 13 March 1936; CC circular, 17 April 1936, as in note 4.

62 Gollan, Grant, Batterham and Davis in Joyce Stevens (ed.), *Taking the Revolution Home: Work Among Women in the Communist Party of Australia, 1920–1945* (Fitzroy, Vic.: Sybylla Press, 1976); Pennefather, Blake and Goodwin in *Red Matildas* (16 mm film, 1984), and Blake, *A Proletarian Life*; Bernice Morris, *Between the Lines* (Collingwood, Vic.: Sybylla Press, 1988); Justina Williams, *Anger & Love* (Fremantle: Fremantle Arts Centre Press, 1993); Betty Roland, *Caviar for Breakfast* (Melbourne: Quartet Books, 1979), and *The Devious Being* (Sydney: Angus & Robertson, 1990); Mona Brand, *Enough Blue Sky* (Potts Point, NSW: Tawny Pipit Press, 1995); Evelyn Healy (Shaw), *Artist of the Left*. The earlier estimate of female membership is from CC circular, 17 April 1936.

63 Daphne Gollan, 'The Memoirs of "Cleopatra Sweatfigure"', in Elizabeth Windschuttle (ed.), *Women, Class and History: Feminist Perspectives on Australia 1788–1978* (Melbourne: Fontana Books, 1980), pp. 313–29.

64 *League Organiser*, December 1935, and reports to YCL in Great Britain, Comintern records (CI 533/10/1); see Ray Sutton, Labour Movement Youth Organisation and Policy in Eastern Australia, c.1918–c.1939, PhD thesis, ANU, 1990, ch. 5.

65 'For a Life with a Purpose', roneoed programme, 1938, Comintern records (CI 495/14/304); *Pix*, 15 July 1939; Audrey Blake, 'The Eureka Youth League: A Participant's Report', *Labour History*, no. 42 (May 1982), pp. 94–105, and 'Notes on the Development of the Eureka Youth League and its Predecessors' (ML). See also Harry Stein, *A Glance Over an Old Left Shoulder* (Sydney: Hale & Iremonger, 1994), chs 6–7.

Chapter 12   Growth pains

1 'Material on Australia' prepared for Anglo–American Bureau, 19 July 1937, Comintern records (CI 495/18/1212); Stanley B. Petzell, The Political and Industrial Role of the Melbourne Trades Hall Council, 1927–1949, PhD thesis, La Trobe University, 1978, ch. 6.

2 Jim Hagan, *The History of the ACTU* (Melbourne: Longman Cheshire, 1981) pp. 105–6

3 Dixon here quoted Stalin; minutes of the Eleventh Congress, 27–31 December 1935 [p. 143], CPA records (ML MS 5021 ADD-ON 1936, box 1).

4 Bruce Mitchell, *Teachers, Education and Politics: A History of the Organization of Public School Teachers* (St Lucia, Qld: UQP, 1975), chs 4–5. A lengthy report

of the Conference on Education appears in the Civil Security Intelligence bulletin, no. 90, 31 May 1937 (AA A8911, item 59).

5 *Workers' Weekly*, 4 February–31 March 1936; J. A. Merritt, A History of the Federated Ironworkers' Association of Australia, 1909–52, PhD thesis, ANU, 1967, ch. 6; Len Richardson, *The Bitter Years: Wollongong during the Great Depression* (Sydney: Hale & Iremonger, 1984), ch. 7; Peter Cochrane, 'Anatomy of a Steelworks: The Australian Iron and Steel Company, Port Kembla, 1935–39', *Labour History*, no. 57 (November 1989), pp. 61–77.

6 Merritt, A History of the Federated Ironworkers' Association, ch. 6; Robert Murray and Kate White, *The Ironworkers: A History of the Federated Ironworkers' Association of Australia* (Sydney: Hale & Iremonger, 1982), ch. 5; and Charlie Morgan, interviewed by Laurie Aarons, n.d. (ML).

7 Thornton quoted in J. A. Merritt, A History of the Federated Ironworkers' Association', p. 296, and *Smith's Weekly*, 23 November 1940; the description of him is given by John Sendy, *Comrades Come Rally! Recollections of an Australian Communist* (Melbourne: Nelson, 1978), ch. 36. The statistics are from Merritt, pp. 223–4, 265–7.

8 *Workers' Weekly*, 9 July–13 August 1937; Robin Gollan, *The Coalminers of New South Wales: A History of the Union 1860–1960* (Melbourne: MUP, 1963), ch. 10; Edgar Ross, *A History of the Miners' Federation of Australia* (Sydney: Australasian Coal and Shale Employees' Federation, 1970), ch. 14.

9 Mark Hearn, *Working Lives: A History of the Australian Railways Union (NSW Branch)* (Sydney: Hale & Iremonger,1990), ch. 3; Stephen Holt, *A Veritable Dynamo: Lloyd Ross and Australian Labour 1901–1987* (St Lucia, Qld: UQP, 1996), ch. 4.

10 Minutes of the Eleventh Congress [p. 177], as in note 3; see L. J. Louis, 'Recovery from the Depression and the Seamen's Strike of 1935–6', *Labour History*, no. 41 (November 1981), pp. 74–86; Brian Fitzpatrick and Rowan Cahill, *The Seamen's Union of Australia 1872–1972: A History* (Sydney: SUA, 1981), part 1, chs 10–11, part 2, ch. 1.

11 Minutes of the CC, 10–12 April 1936 [pp. 30–5, 44, 54]; 24–7 July 1936 [p. 133]; Keenan to Sharkey, 7 September 1936, Melbourne documents 1932–8, CPA records (ML MS 5021 ADD-ON 1936, boxes 4, 5); report by Ron Hurd to ECCI, 18 November 1936, Comintern records (CI 534/7/8).

12 *Workers' Weekly*, 27 October 1936, 12 February–5 March, 26 October 1937; *North Queensland Guardian*, 4 September 1937; Victor Williams, *The Years of Big Jim* (Victoria Park, WA: Lone Hand Press, 1975), chs 5–6.

13 Wendy Lowenstein and Tom Hills, *Under the Hook: Melbourne Waterside Workers Remember Working Lives and Class War 1900–1980* (Prahran, Vic.: Melbourne Bookworkers, 1982), p. 86; Healy in *Workers' Weekly*, 26 October 1938.

14 W. Orr, *Mechanisation: Threatened Catastrophe for Coalfields* (Sydney: Miners' Federation, 1935), p. 13; *Workers' Weekly*, 7 August 1936; see Ross, *History of the Miners' Federation*, pp. 367–8, and *Of Storm and Struggle: Pages from Labour History* (Sydney: APCOL, 1981), p. 61.

15 Rick Kuhn, Paradise on the Instalment Plan: The Economic Thought of the Australian Labour Movement between the Depression and the Long Boom, PhD thesis, University of Sydney, 1985, pp. 35–7.

16 CC circular, 10 January 1936, CPA records (ML MS 5021 ADD-ON 1936, box 5); Orr in minutes of CC, 20–22 November 1936 [pp. 30–3]; R. Cram in minutes of CC, 22 September 1935, as in note 11; minutes of discussion of Sydney cadres, 21 August 1937, Comintern records (CI 495/14/304); minutes of the PB, 21 September 1939, CPA records (ML MS 5021 ADD-ON 1936, box 15).

17 Andrew Reeves, Industrial Men: Miners and Politics in Wonthaggi, 1909–1968,

PhD thesis, La Trobe University, 1977, ch. 3; and *Strikebound*, feature film directed by Richard Lowenstein, 1983; Orr in minutes of the CC, 10–12 April 1936 [pp. 90–1], as in note 11.

18 Thornton in minutes of the Eleventh Congress, [p. 284]; minutes of the CC, 6–7 November 1936, [p. 23]; minutes of the CC, 17 February 1939 [pp. 88–9]; Orr in minutes of CC, 5–7 March 1937, [pp. 54–5].

19 Minutes of the Anglo–American Bureau discussion, 5 July 1937, Comintern records (CI 495/94/19); Orr in minutes of the Eleventh Congress [p. 203], as in note 3; J. B. Miles, 'A Question of Balance', *Communist Review*, vol. 5, no. 11 (November 1938), p. 60; Blake in *The Way Forward: Decisions of the Twelfth National Congress of the Communist Party of Australia* (Sydney: CPA, 1938), pp. 40–1.

20 *The Railroader*, 10 October 1935; see also the minutes of the Education and Organising Committee of his union, 1936–41, Ross papers (NLA MS 3939, box 7).

21 *Newcastle Morning Herald*, 18 October 1937.

22 Comintern records (CI 495/18/212).

23 Bede Nairn, *The 'Big Fella': Jack Lang and the Australian Labor Party 1891–1949* (Melbourne: MUP, 1986), ch. 13; Jim Hagan and Ken Turner, *A History of the Labor Party in New South Wales 1891–1991* (Melbourne: Longman Cheshire, 1991), pp. 88–94.

24 Hughes, interviewed by Laurie Aarons, September 1980 (ML); Gollan, interviewed by Laurie Aarons, n.d (ML); see also David McKnight, 'The Comintern's Seventh Congress and the Australian Labor Party', *Journal of Contemporary History*, vol. 32, no. 3 (July 1997), pp. 395–407.

25 Copy of application in CC circulars and statements, 1933–42, CPA records (ML MS 5021 ADD-ON 1936, box 5); *Workers' Weekly*, 25 February, 27 April 1937; Patrick Weller and Beverley Lloyd (eds), *Federal Executive Minutes 1915–1955* (Melbourne: MUP), pp. 201–3.

26 Minutes of the CC, 20–22 November 1935 [p. 72]; 10–12 April 1936 [p. 181]; 24–27 July 1936 [p. 46], as in note 11.

27 Minutes of the discussion of the Anglo–American Bureau, 5 July 1937, pp. 13–19, Comintern records (CI 495/14/19), and *The Way Forward*, p. 25. Dixon appears in the ECCI minutes as 'Emery'.

28 Miles in minutes of the CC, 5–7 March 1937 [pp. 110–1], as in note 11; Blake, 'Tasks of the Communist Party in the Coming Federal Election', *Workers' Weekly*, 25 May 1937.

29 Letters to the CC from the Cairns and Townsville sections, 27 April, 10 May 1937; report of northern sub-district discussion, 12 May 1937; letters from Jack Henry to CC, 19 May, 3 June 1937, and his article 'Federal Election: Return a Labor Government', *North Queensland Guardian*, 26 June 1937; D. C. Price to *Communist Review*, 15 July 1937; all in state correspondence and reports CPA records (ML MS 5021 ADD-ON 1936, box 4); *Communist Review*, vol. 4, no. 6 (June 1937), pp. 7–15; Miles and Henry in minutes of the CC, 18–20 June 1937 [pp. 27, 71–3], as in note 11.

30 Len Donald in minutes of the CC, 18–20 June 1937 [pp. 44–6]; CC circular, 20 September 1937, and CC to editorial boards, 22 September 1937, CC circulars and statements, 1933–42, as in note 25.

31 Minutes of the discussion of the Anglo–American Bureau. 5 July 1937, p. 9; Colin A. Hughes and B. D. Graham, *A Handbook of Australian Government and Politics.* (Canberra: ANUP, 1968) and *Voting for the Australian House of Representatives 1901–1964* (Canberra: ANUP, 1974), pp. 167, 188, 190.

32 Cram in minutes of the CC, 17–19 February 1939 [pp. 68–70], as in note 11; *North Queensland Guardian*, 1 April 1939.

33 Minutes of the discussion of the Anglo–American Bureau, 23 September 1937, Comintern records (CI 95/14/19).

34 Sharkey in minutes of the CC, 6–7 November 1937 [p. 67], as in note 11; CC circular, 1 July 1939; Orr in minutes of the PB, 21 March 1936, p. 9, as in note 16.

35 Minutes of the CC, 1–12 April 1936 [pp. 165, 245], as in note 11.

36 Sharkey, 'Join the Party', *Workers' Weekly*, 1 September 1936; Miles, 'Go to Masses in Own Name', *Workers' Weekly*, 18 November 1938.

37 Attorney-General's Department special file (AA A467, SF42/89); *Workers' Weekly*, 4, 20 May 1937; Frank Cain, *The Origins of Political Surveillance in Australia* (Sydney: Angus & Robertson, 1983), p. 251.

38 Gibson in minutes of the CC, 17–19 February 1939 [p. 109], as in note 11; Devanny in *Workers' Weekly*, 23 November 1937; Tony Wallis, 'A Guide and Clarion Call', *Workers' Weekly*, 8 November 1938; Mrs Kearney, quoted in Len Fox, *Broad Left, Narrow Left* (Chippendale, NSW: APCOL, 1982), p. 33.

39 *Communist Review*, vol. 2, no. 2 (February 1935), pp. 1–4; E. W. Campbell in *Workers' Weekly*, 2 December 1935; *The Communist Party and its Work: A Course for Party Members* (Sydney: CPA, n.d. [1938]), pp. 3, 4, 16.

40 CC circular, 27 May 1938 and report in *Communist Review*, vol. 6. no. 2 (February 1939), pp. 93–5; Max Thomas, interviewed by Laurie Aarons, 27 March 1980 (ML).

41 E. Fisher, 'More Agitation, More Propaganda', *Communist Review*, vol. 4, no. 10 (October 1937), pp. 40–3; L. Harry Gould, 'Agitation and Propaganda', *Communist Review*, vol. 5, no. 4 (April 1939), pp. 13–16.

42 Kevin Connolly, 'Overhauling Our Language', *Communist Review*, vol. 6, no. 5 (May 1939), pp. 289–95; Rawling, 'Conserving Our Language', vol. 6, no. 8 (August 1939), pp. 497–9; Purdy in vol. 6, no. 6 (June 1939), pp. 370–2; Gould, 'A Grammar of Politics', vol. 6, no. 9 (September 1939), pp. 574–6.

43 Reference to 'diabolical materialism' in Ross Edmonds, *In Storm and Struggle: A History of the Communist Party in Newcastle 1920–1940* (Newcastle: self-published, 1991), p. 29.

44 Minutes of the CC, 10–12 April 1936 [pp. 206–7], 24–7 July 1936 [p. 17], June 1939 [p. 48], as in note 11; Information on Australia for ECCI, 19 July 1937, Comintern records (CI 495/18/212); CC circular, 19 August 1937, as in note 16.

45 Minutes of the CC, 22 February 1935 [p. 42], as in note 11; Len Donald to CC, 11 January 1938, Melbourne documents 1932–38, as in note 11; Jack Blake, interviewed by Laurie Aarons, August 1979 (ML), and Les Barnes, recorded April–May 1991.

46 Minutes of the CC, 17–19 February 1939 [p. 114], as in note 11; Ralph Gibson, *My Years in the Communist Party* (Melbourne: International Bookshop, 1966), pp. 67–8.

47 Gil Burns in minutes of the CC, 10–12 April 1936 [p. 172], as in note 11; Jack Henry in minutes of the PB, 1 June 1939, as in note 16.

48 Miles in minutes of the CC, 24–27 July 1936 [pp. 114–15], as in note 11; Diane Menghetti *The Red North: The Popular Front in North Queensland* (Townsville: History Department, James Cook University of North Queensland, 1981), pp. 169–70; Jim Henderson, interviewed by Ken Mansell, 1983 (ML).

49 Ralph to Dorothy Gibson, 26 May 1937, Gibson papers (NLA MS 7844, box 1, folder 1); see Joanne Scott, 'Don't Cop It Passively': Strikes, Lockouts and Unemployed Protests in Queensland, 1919–1939, BA Hons thesis, University of Queensland, 1990, ch. 3, and *North Queensland Guardian*, 29 January 1938, for Aboriginal protest.

50 Jess Grant in Joyce Stevens (ed.), *Taking the Revolution Home: Work Among Women in the Communist Party of Australia 1920–1945* (Fitzroy, Vic.: Sybylla Press, 1976), p. 171; Ted Bacon, interviewed by Laurie Aarons, n.d (ML); Claude Jones, interviewed by Laurie Aarons, June 1980 (ML).

51 Prichard to Guido Baracchi, 6 November 1938, Baracchi papers (NLA MS 5241, folder 2); see Justina Williams, *The First Furrow* (Willagee, WA: Lone Hand Press, 1976), pp. 152–63; Stuart Macintyre, *Militant: The Life and Times of Paddy Troy* (Sydney: Allen & Unwin, 1984), chs 3–4.

52 *Workers' Weekly*, 7 September 1937; Tony McGillick, *Comrade No More: The Autobiography of a Former Communist Party Leader* (West Perth: self-published, 1980), pp. 78–80; Jim Moss, *Representatives of Discontent: History of the Communist Party in South Australia* (Melbourne: Communist and Labour Movement History Group, 1987), ch. 4.

53 Secretariat to DC, 11 April 1935; DC to Secretariat, 23 June 1935, state correspondence and reports; Higgins to Secretariat, 12 April 1936, Rawling papers (ANU N57/187); Audrey Johnson, *Fly a Rebel Flag: Bill Morrow 1888–1980* (Ringwood, Vic.: Penguin Books, 1986), part 2.

54 CC budget, 1939, in CC circulars and statements, as in note 16; section financial statement in Rawling papers (ANU N57/102).

55 Minutes of the CC, 18–20 June 1937 [p. 71], as in note 11; minutes of special committee to consider case of F. Wiggin, 3, 22 May 1937 and Control Commission to CC, 14 June 1937, Wiggin file, CPA records (ML MS 5021 ADD-ON, box 16); minutes of the PB, 11 July 1939 for Sharkey's sustenance, as in note 16; details of holding companies in Rawling papers (ANU N57/402).

56 For Higgins, Investigation Branch to Attorney-General, 24 August 1928 (AA A4671, SF42/64); for Sharkey and Orr, Orr to Budget Commission of RILU, 3 October 1932 (CI 534/7/8); Ryan to 'Friend' in Berlin, 9 March 1930, Comintern records (CI 534/7/5); for Devanny, Carole Ferrier (ed.), *Point of Departure: The Autobiography of Jean Devanny* (St Lucia, Qld: UQP, 1986), p. 135; Tripp, interviewed by Rawling, 1961, Rawling papers (ANU N57/109).

57 Civil Security Intelligence, no. 90, 31 May 1937 (AA A8911, file 59).

58 Minutes of the PB, 8 May, 1, 24 August 1939, as in note 16.

59 Anglo–American Bureau, 'The Stronger the Party the Stronger the Labour Movement', 22 July 1937, Comintern records (CI 495/18/1212); and Dixon's report to CC, 6–7 November 1937, as in note 11.

60 Minutes of the PB, 3 August 1939, as in note 16; Edmonds, *In Storm and Struggle*, pp. 133–4.

61 Daphne Gollan, 'The Memoirs of "Cleopatra Sweatfigure"', in Elizabeth Windschuttle (ed.), *Women, Class and History: Feminist Perspectives on Australian 1788–1978* (Melbourne: Fontana Books, 1980), p. 317; statement by Baracchi to CC, 12 February 1940, Baracchi file, CPA records (ML MS 5021 ADD-ON 1936, box 25).

62 Jack Kavanagh to Edna Ryan, 5 August 1936, Kavanagh papers (ANU P12/4/38); 'This is J. B. Miles', *Communist Review*, vol. 4, no. 2 (February 1937), pp. 6–10; *Workers' Voice*, 31 August 1938, Jean Devanny in *Workers' Weekly*, 22 March 1938, and Ferrier (ed.), *Point of Departure* pp. 156–8, 168–72.

63 'L. Sharkey, Chairman, C.C., Communist Party of Australia', *Communist Review*, vol. 4, no. 4 (April 1937), pp. 38–9; information from John Sendy; minutes of the PB, 2 February 1939, as in note 16.

Chapter 13   The socialist sixth of the world

1 Robert C. Tucker, *Stalin in Power: The Revolution from Above 1928–1941* (New York: Norton, 1990), p. 356; Alec Nove, 'Stalin and Stalinism—Some Intro-

ductory Thoughts', in Alec Nove (ed.), *The Stalin Phenomenon* (London: Weidenfeld & Nicolson, 1993), p. 13.

2 A fuller account of Australian apprehensions of the Soviet Union is provided by Margaret Lindley Ashworth, A World to Win: Socialist Utopia, the Union of Soviet Socialist Republics and the Communist Party of Australia, PhD thesis, University of Melbourne, 1993.

3 Tom Garland, *Contrasts: A Reply to the 'Progress of Communism' by A. Grenfell Price* (Adelaide: FOSU, 1932), in Rawling papers (ANU P57/1163).

4 See, for example, the diary of Percy Hannett, NSW president of the Electrical Trades Union in 1929 (ANU N62).

5 Memoirs of Itzhak Gust in possession of Amirah Inglis; the report of the Australian delegation for the RILU, dated 22 May 1932, and a minority report of F. Goozeff, are in the papers of Tom Walsh (NLA MS 2123/11/folder 102).

6 For the protracted campaign to reinstate Beatrice Taylor, see Bruce Mitchell, *Teachers, Education and Politics: A History of the Organization of Public School Teachers* (St Lucia, Qld: UQP, 1975), pp. 115–8, and for records of the Beatrice Taylor Defence Committee, the Rawling papers (ANU N57/306); for the sacking of the Victorian delegate, see Alison Churchward, The Australian Railways Union: Railway Management and Railway Work in Victoria, 1920–39, PhD thesis, University of Melbourne, pp. 467–8. *Red Leader*, 8 November 1933, and the *Argus*, 23–4 May 1934 report later dismissals. For official surveillance of the 1934 delegation, see the Investigation Branch file (AA A981, COM11).

7 Ben Scott and J. Healy, *Red Cargo: A Report of the Waterside Workers' Federation . . . Delegates to the Soviet Union, May Day 1934* (Sydney: FOSU, 1934); W. A. Smith, *A Tramwayman Talks on Russia* (Melbourne: Ruskin Press, 1935), reprinting talks broadcast on Radio 3KZ; Alf Northage in *North Queensland Guardian*, 21 August 1937; J. E. Goldsmith in *Workers' Voice*, 3 August 1934.

8 Katharine Susannah Prichard, *The Real Russia* (Sydney: Modern Publishers, n.d. [1934], p. 19; Jack Wall to J. B. Miles, 4 May 1934, CC circulars and statements, CPA records (ML MS 5021 ADD-ON 1936, box 5); Tony McGillick, '21 Years of Revolution', *Communist Review*, vol. 5, no. 11 (November 1938), pp. 37–41; poem dated 7 October 1934, in possession of Laurie Aarons, and Jane Aarons, 'Improvements in Two Years', *Working Woman*, vol. 5, no. 5 (December 1934).

9 The serialisation began in April 1934, and its interruption was noted in *Workers' Voice*, 15 June 1934.

10 Greenwood in *Proletariat*, October 1933, quoted by Ralph Gibson, *The People Stand Up* (Ascot Vale, Vic.: Red Rooster Press, 1983), p. 74; Woodruff in *Workers' Voice*, 1 December 1933. The first usage of the term 'fellow traveller' recorded in the *Oxford English Dictionary* is in 1936.

11 Jessie Street, *Truth or Repose* (Sydney: ABS, 1966), ch. 12.

12 David Caute, *The Fellow-Travellers: Intellectual Friends of Communism*, rev. edn (London: Yale University Press, 1988); Paul Hollander, *Political Pilgrims: Travels of Western Intellectuals to the Soviet Union, China and Cuba* (New York: OUP, 1981); Walter Laqueur, *The Dream that Failed: Reflections on the Soviet Union, 1928–1978* (New York: OUP, 1994), ch. 1.

13 *Workers' Weekly*, 31 December 1935, 17, 24 January 1936.

14 L. Sharkey, 'Stakhanov and the Current Anti-Soviet Misrepresentations', *Communist Review*, vol. 3, no. 5 (May 1936), pp. 1–14; King in *Workers' Weekly*, 27 January, 14, 17 July 1936.

15 Greenwood, loc. cit.; Prichard, *The Real Russia*, p. 193.

16 Robert Conquest, *The Great Terror: A Reassessment* (New York: OUP, 1990), and Dmitri Antonovich Volkogonov, *Stalin, Triumph and Tragedy*, trans. Harold Shukman (London: Weidenfeld & Nicolson, 1991) are cases of such condemnation;

Sheila Fitzpatrick, *The Russian Revolution*, 2nd edn (New York: OUP, 1994), and J. Arch Getty and Roberta Thompson (eds), *Stalinist Terror: New Perspectives* (Cambridge: CUP, 1993) are examples of revisionism.

17 Stan Moran and Ernie Campbell had Sam Aarons buy them a meal in Moscow in 1934, interviewed by Laurie Aarons, 1968 (ML); Betty Roland, *Caviar for Breakfast* (Melbourne: Quartet Books, 1979), pp. 71, 78, 111.

18 Audrey Blake, *A Proletarian Life* (Malmsbury, Vic.: Kibble Books, 1984), pp. 21–35.

19 Jack Blake, interviewed by Laurie Aarons, August 1979 (ML), 'A Free and Happy Life', *Communist Review*, vol. 6. no.1 (January 1939), pp. 8–13, and 'Trotskyites and Labor', vol. 6, no. 7 (July 1939), pp. 439–42; there is an extensive analysis of Stalinism as 'the authoritarian syndrome' in Blake's *Revolution from Within* (Sydney: Outlook, 1971), ch. 2.

20 Gerald Peel, 'Stalin', *Communist Review*, vol. 6, no. 5 (May 1939), 281–2. See the similar fulsome doggerel in *The People's Poetry*, issued by the poetry group of the NSW branch of the Left Book Club, no. 1 (November 1939), pp. 8–9.

21 Frank Hardy, *But the Dead Are Many* (London: Bodley Head, 1975); see also Paul Adams, The Stranger from Melbourne: Crisis and Modernism in the Writings of Frank Hardy, PhD thesis, Monash Uni- versity, 1997, ch. 2.

22 Nettie Palmer quoted by Drusilla Modjeska, *Exiles at Home: Australian Women Writers 1925–1945* (Sydney: Angus & Robertson, 1981), p. 113; Gibson to Baracchi, n.d., Baracchi papers (NLA MS 5241); Gibson, *Freedom in the Soviet Union* (Melbourne: Friends of the Soviet Union, n.d. [1935?]); Baracchi, 'Twenty Years of Karl Radek', *Communist Review*, vol. 4, no. 3 (March 1937), pp. 43–50; statement by Baracchi to CC, 12 February 1940, CPA records (ML MS 5021 ADD-ON 1936, box 25).

23 *Labor Review*, vol. 1, no. 8 (April 1933), p. 17.

24 *Workers' Weekly*, 9 October 1936, 8 February, 4 March 1938.

25 A. London [Blake] in minutes of the Anglo–American Bureau, 23 September 1937, Comintern records (CI 495/14/19); CC circular, 17 June 1937, CC circulars and statements, as in note 8; minutes of the PB, 10 February 1938, Comintern records (CI 495/14/305); Miles in minutes of special committee to consider the case of F. Wiggin, 22 May 1937, p. 1, CPA records (ML MS 5021 ADD-ON 1936, box 16).

26 An English-language edition appeared in Australia in 1939 and it was serialised in the *Communist Review* from June 1939.

27 *History of the Communist Party of the Soviet Union (Bolsheviks)* (Moscow: Foreign Languages Publishing House, 1939), pp. 333–4.

Chapter 14   War

1 Quoted in Cameron Hazlehurst, *Menzies Observed* (Sydney: Allen & Unwin, 1979), p. 138.

2 R. Dixon, *Defend Australia? The Communist Attitude Towards Defence Explained* (Sydney: Modern Press, 1936); Dixon, 'Communist Defence Policy', *Communist Review*, vol. 6, no. 4 (April 1939); CC to state committees, 3 March 1939, CC circulars and statements, CPA records (ML MS 5021 ADD-ON 1936, box 5).

3 Minutes of the PB, 18 May, 29 June, 13, 27, 29 July, 22 August, CPA records (ML MS 5021 ADD-ON 1936, box 15); *Workers' Weekly*, 26 May–1 August 1939; Jim Hagan, *The History of the ACTU* (Melbourne: Longman Cheshire, 1981), p. 175.

4 *Workers' Weekly*, 18 April, 6, 13 June 1939; minutes of the PB, 1 June 1939; see E. M. Andrews, *Isolation and Appeasement in Australia: Reactions to the European Crises 1935–1939* (Canberra: ANUP, 1970), ch. 8.

5 *Workers' Weekly*, 25 August 1939.

6 Minutes of the PB, 24 August 1939; CC circular, 4 September 1939, CC circulars and statements, as in note 2; Diane Menghetti, *The Red North: The Popular Front in North Queensland* (Townsville: History Department, James Cook University of North Queensland, 1981), p. 150. The fullest justification was *Soviet–German Non-Aggression Pact Explained* (Sydney: CC of CPA, n.d.).

7 *Tribune*, 5, 9, 22 September 1939; CC circular, 4 September 1939, as in note 2; party statement in *Sydney Morning Herald*, 15 September 1939.

8 The arguments in the CPGB are examined by Kevin Morgan, *Against Fascism and War: Ruptures and Continuities in British Communist Politics 1935–41* (Manchester: Manchester University Press, 1989).

9 ECCI, 'Regarding the Line of the CPA on the War Question', 4 October 1939, and 'Proposals for the CPA', 3 November 1939, Comintern records (CI 495/14/308); CC circulars, 6 October, 7 November 1939, as in note 2; *Tribune*, 6 October, 7 November 1939; minutes of PB, 14 November 1939, as in note 3; Miles in minutes of the Victorian State Committee, 17 December 1939, state correspondence and reports 1931–40, CPA records (ML MS 5021 ADD-ON 1936, box 4), and letter to *Communist Review*, vol. 6, no. 12 (December 1939), p. 714.

10 Les Barnes, recorded April–May 1991. Ralph Gibson suggests in *The People Stand Up* (Ascot Vale, Vic.: Red Rooster Press, 1983), p. 370 that the declaration of war and the state committee meeting occurred on the Saturday 2 November, and his Sunday address at the party hall followed it, but Paul Hasluck, *The Government and the People 1939–1941* (Canberra: Australian War Memorial, 1952), p. 152 confirms Barnes's chronology, though Menzies's radio announcement occurred at 9.15 p.m. on the Sunday evening.

11 *The Truth About Finland* (Sydney: CPA, n.d.).

12 Minutes of the PB, 15 December 1939, as in note 3 and *Tribune*, 19 December 1939; *J. N. Rawling Breaks With Stalinism* (Sydney: J. McMahon, 17 December 1939); 'An Ex-Member of the Communist Party', *Sydney Morning Herald*, 6 March 1940, and 'Communism in Australia', *Sydney Morning Herald*, 6, 7 March 1940; *Militant*, vol. 3, no. 4 (April 1940). See Rawling's manuscript account of these events (ANU N57/25), and Stephen Holt, 'The Case of James Rawling, Ex-Communist', *Quadrant*, vol. 33, no. 12 (December 1989), pp. 60–4.

13 As related to me by Bob Gollan, a member of the class; there is correspondence with Eric Aarons, another member, in the Baracchi papers (NLAM5 5241) and reference in the minutes of the PB, 17 October 1939, as in note 3. Baracchi and Roland met with Rawling and two other 'dissident communists' in October 1939; notes of the discussion are in the Rawling papers (ANU N57/23).

14 Minutes of special meeting of Central Executive, 18 December 1939, Baracchi file, CPA records (ML MS 5021 ADD-ON 1936, box 25), and subsequent statements by Baracchi in same file; *Tribune*, 23 February 1940; Baracchi, *Who Is the Coward? J. B. Miles' Record and Mine* (Sydney: Communist League (Fourth International), n.d.).

15 Betty Roland to CC, 12 February 1940, in Baracchi file; *Militant*, vol. 3, no. 3 (March 1940), and Roland interviewed by Ken Mansell, 1983 (ML).

16 See, for example, the letter sent by L. Duncan to Miles, October 1940, Melbourne documents 1932–38, CPA records (ML MS 5021 ADD-ON 1936, box 5).

17 *Sydney Morning Herald*, 15 December; *Argus*, 27 January 1940; Les Barnes, recorded April–May 1991 and Ralph Gibson, *My Years in the Communist Party*

(Melbourne: International Bookshop, 1966), p. 82; Jack Williams in Ross Edmonds, *In Storm and Struggle: A History of the Communist Party in Newcastle 1920–1940* (Newcastle: self-published, 1991), p. 94.

18 *Daily Telegraph*, 4, 11, 18 November 1939; Sydney *Sun*, 27, 28 December 1939; *Sydney Morning Herald*, 11, 25, 29 December 1939, 1 January, 8 January 1940; *Tribune*, 1, 5, 9 January 1940; CC circular, 10 January 1940, as in note 2; *Civil Liberty*, vol. 3, no. 3 (February 1940). There is a full police report on the 24 December meeting in AA A467, SF42/43.

19 *Argus*, 12, 16, 19 February; *Tribune*, 20 February 1940; Gibson, *My Years in the Communist Party*, pp. 82–3; reports from Queensland state committee to central committee, 15, 22 February 1940, state correspondence and reports, as in note 9. The pattern of attacks on communist meetings is described by Brian Fitzpatrick, *National Security and Individual Insecurity*, 2nd edn (Melbourne: Left Book Club, April 1940), pp. 43–7.

20 *Sydney Morning Herald*, 4, 8, 15 April, 27 May 1940; *Tribune*, 5, 9, 16 April 1940.

21 Menzies and Chamberlain quoted in Hasluck, *The Government and the People*, pp. 198, 211; letter from Menzies to Bruce, 11 September 1939, in R. G. Neale (ed.), *Documents on Australian Foreign Policy 1937–49*, vol. II (Canberra: AGPS, 1976), p. 256.

22 Robin Gollan, *Revolutionaries and Reformists: Communism and the Australian Labour Movement 1920–1950* (Canberra: ANUP, 1975), pp. 93–4; Warwick Eather, '"Protect the Newcastle Steelworks": BHP, the Trade Unions and National Security', *Labour History*, no. 57 (November 1989), pp. 78–88.

23 As Jack Hughes acknowledged in an interview with Ken Mansell, 7 May 1983 (ML); see *Sydney Morning Herald*, 25 March 1940, and Gollan, *Revolutionaries and Reformists*, pp. 91–3.

24 Military Board memorandum to War Cabinet, 3 January 1940, AA A467, SF42/43; see Frank Cain, *The Origins of Political Surveillance in Australia* (Sydney: Angus & Robertson, 1983), pp. 262–5; David Carment, 'Australian Communism and National Security, September 1939–June 1941', *Journal of the Royal Australian Historical Society*, vol. 65, part 4 (March 1980), pp. 246–56.

25 A copy of the manual, dated 28 November 1939, was obtained and circulated by the party; CPA records (ML MS 5021, box 85).

26 The official war history testifies to the inadequacy of facilities in the camps that were constructed for the trainees; Gavin Long, *To Benghazi* (Canberra: Australian War Memorial, 1952), ch. 3.

27 The *Argus* claimed on 18 January 1940 that the Sydney CIB had discovered an attempt had been made to wreck CSR's caneite plant at Pyrmont, but provided no evidence, and the Investigation Branch observed the same of claims by military intelligence in AA A467, SF 42/43.

28 Les Barnes, recorded April–May 1991; Cecil Sharpley, *The Great Delusion: The Autobiography of an Ex-Communist Leader* (Melbourne: William Heinemann, 1952), p. 27; for agitation in training camps, *Tribune*, 17, 24, 26 November 1939 and after; see also Beverley Symons, All Out for the People's War . . ., BA Hons thesis, University of Wollongong, 1993, ch. 2. The decoded KGB messages are available on the Internet as http://www.nsa.gov/docs/venona/venona.html.

29 *Civil Liberty*, vol. 3, no. 4 (July 1940).

30 *Argus*, 2, 9, 20, 24 April, 6, 22, 25 May 1940; *Communist Review*, vol. 7, no. 5 (May 1940), p. 257, n.s., vol. 1, no, 1 (January 1941), p. 2; 163 *CPD*, p. 1273 (24 May 1940); Carment, 'Australian Communism and National Security'.

31 163 *CPD*, p. 1298 (27 May 1940) and Hasluck, *The Government and the People*, appendix 3; Cain, *Origins of Political Surveillance*, pp. 268–9 notes that a letter from this printing worker, Caldwell, to Sharkey was intercepted by the censor

and concludes that his message did not get through, but several party members state that it did.

32 *Age*, *Argus* and *Courier-Mail*, 17 June 1940. Bill Gollan, interviewed by Ken Mansell, 4 May 1983 (ML) and Marie Gollan in Joyce Stevens (ed.), *Taking the Revolution Home: Work Among Women in the Communist Party of Australia 1920–1945* (Fitzroy, Vic.: Sybylla Press, 1987), pp. 155–6; Ted Bacon, interviewed by Ken Mansell, 21 April 1983 (ML), and by Laurie Aarons n.d. (ML); Laurie Aarons, interviewed by Stewart Harris, 17 December 1991 (NLA); Lila Thornton, interviewed by Ken Mansell, 3 May 1983 (ML).

33 Raid on New Theatre in AA A467, SF42/81; see also Fiona Capp, *Writers Defiled* (Ringwood, Vic.: McPhee Gribble, 1993), p. 160. The CPSU story is related by Ted Bacon, interviewed by Ken Mansell, and Stan Moran in *Reminiscences of a Rebel* (Chippendale, NSW: APCOL, 1979), p. 20. Jess Grant in Stevens (ed.), *Taking the Revolution Home*, pp. 175–6; Betty Roland, interviewed by Ken Mansell, 1983 (ML); Peter Cook, *Red Barrister: A Biography of Ted Laurie* (Bundoora, Vic.: La Trobe University Press, 1994), p. 52; Barbara Boles, interviewed by Ken Mansell, 1 May 1983 (ML).

34 Annie Graham in Stevens (ed.), *Taking the Revolution Home*, p. 166; Eleanor Dark, *The Little Company* (Sydney: Collins, 1945), pp. 102–4; Serg Penna, interviewed by Ken Mansell, 23 April 1983 (ML).

35 Kay Saunders, *War on the Homefront: State Intervention in Queensland 1938–1948* (St Lucia, Qld: UQP, 1993), ch. 5; Les Barnes, 'June 15, 1940', *Recorder*, no. 163 (July 1990), pp. 11–13.

36 *Argus*, 10, 15 June 1940; *Sydney Morning Herald*, 1, 11 June 1940; Justina Williams, *The First Furrow* (Willagee, WA: Lone Hand Press, 1976), pp. 164–72; Stuart Macintyre, *Militant: The Life and Times of Paddy Troy* (Sydney: Allen & Unwin, 1985), pp. 60–2; John A. McKenzie, *Challenging Faith* (Fremantle, WA: Fremantle Arts Centre Press, 1993), pp. 99–104.

37 Eva Bacon, interviewed by Ken Mansell, 21 April 1983 (ML) and by Laurie Aarons, n.d. (ML).

38 Wally Clayton, interviewed by Ken Mansell, 30 April 1983 (ML) and on a video recorded at the Communists and the Labour Movement Conference, Melbourne, 23–24 August 1980 (SLV).

39 There are two substantial files on Clayton, one compiled by ASIO (AA A6119, item 53) and the other by the party's Central Disputes Committee, Hughes papers (ML). The best treatment of the allegations against him is David McKnight, *Australia's Spies and Their Secrets* (Sydney: Allen & Unwin, 1994).

40 A copy of the police report is in AA A6119, item 53.

41 John Sendy, *Ralph Gibson: An Extraordinary Communist* (Melbourne: Ralph Gibson Memorial Committee, 1988), pp. 85–6; Ted Bacon, interviewed by Laurie Aarons, n.d.; Les Barnes, 'June 15, 1940', and recorded April–May 1991; Barbara Boles, interviewed by Ken Mansell; Edgar Ross, *Of Storm and Struggle: Pages from Labour History* (Sydney: APCOL, 1981), ch. 12; *Communist Review*, n.s. vol. 1, no. 1 (January 1941), p. 2.

42 Cain, *The Origins of Political Surveillance*, pp. 270–1; Phyllis Johnson, interviewed by Ken Mansell, 6 May 1983 (ML) on Flo Davis, and in Central Disputes Committee file on the police spy, Rex Cann, Hughes papers (ML); see also *Tribune*, 7 November, 18 December 1940, 24 May 1941, for Johnson's case and AA A467, SF42/6 for Paterson's. A large number of prosecution files are in AA A92, SF42, and Brian Fitzpatrick summarised the use of the national security regulations in *The War and Civil Rights* (Melbourne: ACCL, December 1940).

43 Hobart *Mercury*, 25 February 1941; *The War and Civil Liberties. Second Series* (Melbourne: ACCL, May 1941), pp. 17–18.

44 Margaret Bevege, *Behind Barbed Wire: Internment in Australia during World War II* (St Lucia, Qld: UQP, 1993), pp. 44–5, 121, 123–4; Gianfranco Cresciani, *Fascism, Anti-Fascism and Italians in Australia, 1922–1945* (Canberra: ANUP, 1980), ch. 8; Menghetti, *The Red North*, pp. 161–2; Saunders, *War on the Homefront*, ch. 2.

45 *The Case of Ratliff and Thomas* (Sydney: Australian Civil Rights Defence League, n.d.) and AA A467, SF42, 4–5; *Daily Telegraph*, 21–30 July 1941; Max Thomas, interviewed by Laurie Aarons, 27 March 1980 (ML); Hasluck, *The Government and the People*, appendix 7.

46 Doug Brideson, recorded by Edgar Waters, 7 December 1992 (NLA TRC 2608/29).

47 Lloyd Ross, quoted in Stephen Holt, *A Veritable Dynamo: Lloyd Ross and Australian Labour 1901–1987* (St Lucia, Qld: UQP, 1996), p. 68.

48 L. L. Sharkey, *Congress Report on the Work of the Central Committee from the 12th to the 13th Party Congress* (Sydney: CPA, 1942), p. 6.

49 Quoted in Paul Herlinger, A History of the New Theatre, 1939–1953, MA thesis, University, of Sydney, 1989, vol. 2 pp. 52–3.

50 Gibson, *My Years in the Communist Party*, p. 86; Colin A. Hughes and B. D. Graham, *Voting for the Australian House of Representatives 1901–1964* (Canberra: ANUP, 1975), pp. 199–222.

51 *Tribune*, 4 May 1941.

52 Mason [J. B. Miles] and McShane [Lance Sharkey], *The Coming War in the Pacific* (Sydney: CPA, n.d. [1940]), and *What is This Labor Party?* (Sydney: CPA, n.d. [1941]); *Tribune*, 16 February, 7 April 1941.

53 Paterson reported in AA A467, SF 42, 6.

54 Holt, *A Veritable Dynamo*, pp. 69–75.

55 *Tribune*, 7 April 1941; see Edgar Ross, *A History of the Miners' Federation of Australia* (Sydney: Australasian Coal and Shale Employees' Association, 1970), pp. 386–7, and L. F. Fitzhardinge, *The Little Digger 1914–1952: William Morris Hughes, a Political Biography*, vol. 2 (Sydney: Angus & Robertson, 1979), pp. 652–4.

56 J. A. Merritt, A History of the Federated Ironworkers' Association of Australia, 1909–52, PhD thesis, ANU, 1967, pp. 265–7, 295; AA A467, SF42/120.

57 *Tribune*, 26 April, 22 June 1941.

58 *Tribune*, 27 July 1941.

Conclusion

1 A phrase I owe to Sean Scalmer, The Career of Class: Intellectuals and the Labour Movement in Australia, 1942–1956, PhD thesis, University of Sydney, 1996, p. 69.

Index

Weiner, Bella, 311
Weitzel, Hetty, *see* Ross, Hetty
White, Sam, 324
White Australia policy, 32, 46, 50,
  126–7, 131–2, 148, 265
Wicks, Harry, *see* Moore, Herbert
Wilkinson, Fred, 67, 73
Williams, Idris, 255
Williams, Justina, 326
Willis, Albert, 17, 47, 80, 81, 91–2,
  111
Winter, George, 128
Wobblies, *see* Industrial Workers of
  the World
Wollongong, New South Wales, 225,
  329
Women's Guild of Empire, 303
Women's Peace Army, 18
Wonthaggi, Victoria, 254–5, 257–8,
  337, 344, 369
Wood, Arnold, 316
Woodruff, Harold, 371
Workers' Art Club, **275**, 276–9, 320,
  354
Workers' Defence Corps (WDC),
  181, 210–11, 238
Workers' Educational Association
  (WEA), 122, 255, 355
Workers' International Relief (WIR),
  91, 118, 181, 196, 218, 268, 357
Workers' Party of Australia (Left
  Opposition), 229, 231, 388
  see also Trotskyism
Workers' Sports Federation, 328
World Peace Congress, 296

World War I, 14–15, 29, 38–9, 46,
  48, 204
World War II, 204, 290, 385–411
  passim
Wren, John, 65, 273
Wren, Mary, 273, 324
Wright, Mary, 168, 172, 326
Wright, Tom
  and Aborigines, 266–7
  party organiser, 217, 227, 234, 277
  secretary of Communist Party, 117,
    159
  Sheet Metal Workers' Union, 329
  submission, 171
  and turn to Third Period, 136–8,
    139, 141, 162–3, 168, 170
Writers' Association, 319
Writers' League, 273, 279, 319, 322

Yarra Bank, Melbourne, 200, 205,
  226, 294, 390
Yezhov, N.I., 378
Young Communist Children, *see*
  Communist Party of Australia
Young Communist League, *see*
  Communist Party of Australia
Young Comrades Club, *see*
  Communist Party of Australia
Young Pioneers, *see* Communist Party
  of Australia

Zetkin, Clara, 64, 264
Zhdanov, A.A., 321
Zinoviev, Grigori, 48, 64, 219, 375
Zwolsman, Jack, 270